Dirty Entanglements
Corruption, Crime, and Terrorism

Crime, corruption, and terrorism are increasingly entangled, emerging as ever greater threats. This convergence deserves high-level-policy attention. Using lively case studies from around the world, this book analyzes the transformation of crime and terrorism and the business logic behind illicit networks. Louise I. Shelley concludes that corruption, crime, and terrorism will remain critical security challenges in the twenty-first century as a result of globalization, technological advances, economic and demographic inequalities, ethnic and sectarian violence, climate change, and the failure of nineteenth- and twentieth-century institutions to respond coherently to these challenges when they emerged.

Louise I. Shelley is a University Professor at the School of Public Policy, George Mason University. She founded and directs the Terrorism, Transnational Crime, and Corruption Center (TraCCC). She is the recipient of Guggenheim, National Endowment of the Humanities, IREX, Kennan Institute, and Fulbright fellowships and has received MacArthur grants to establish the Russian Organized Crime Study Center and to study the role of illicit actors in nuclear smuggling. Among her previous books are *Human Trafficking: A Global Perspective* (Cambridge University Press, 2010) and *Policing Soviet Society* (1996). She has written extensively on transnational crime, illicit trade, and money laundering. She has testified before the House Committee on International Relations, the Helsinki Commission, the House Banking Committee, and the Senate Foreign Relations Committee on transnational crime; human trafficking; and the links among transnational crime, financial crime, and terrorism. She serves on the Global Agenda Council on Illicit Trade and Organized Crime for the World Economic Forum and was the first co-chair of its Council on Organized Crime. Professor Shelley presently co-chairs a group on human trafficking within the Global Agenda Councils of the World Economic Forum. She is a life member of the Council on Foreign Relations.

Dirty Entanglements

Corruption, Crime, and Terrorism

LOUISE I. SHELLEY
George Mason University

CAMBRIDGE
UNIVERSITY PRESS

CAMBRIDGE
UNIVERSITY PRESS

32 Avenue of the Americas, New York, NY 10013-2473, USA

Cambridge University Press is part of the University of Cambridge.

It furthers the University's mission by disseminating knowledge in the pursuit of education, learning, and research at the highest international levels of excellence.

www.cambridge.org
Information on this title: www.cambridge.org/9781107689305

© Louise I. Shelley 2014

First published 2014

Printed in the United States of America

A catalog record for this publication is available from the British Library.

Library of Congress Cataloging in Publication Data
Shelley, Louise I.
Dirty entanglements : corruption, crime, and terrorism / Louise I. Shelley.
   pages cm
ISBN 978-1-107-01564-7 (hardback) – ISBN 978-1-107-68930-5 (paperback)
1. Terrorism – History – 21st century.   2. Political corruption – 21st century.
3. Crime – History – 21st century.   4. International relations – 21st century.   I. Title.
HV6431.S46864   2014
363.325 – dc23   2014002080

ISBN 978-1-107-01564-7 Hardback
ISBN 978-1-107-68930-5 Paperback

To Madeleine and Janine and to
all those who helped me get through my long illness

Contents

Figure, Maps, and Tables		*page* ix
Acknowledgments		xi
	Introduction	1

PART I THE LOGIC OF CORRUPTION, CRIME, AND TERRORISM

1	Crime and Corruption behind the Mass Attacks	29
2	Corruption: An Incubator of Organized Crime and Terrorism	64
3	The Evolution of Organized Crime and Terrorism	97
4	Environments, Global Networks, and Pipelines	132

PART II THE DIVERSE BUSINESSES OF TERRORISM

5	The Business of Terrorism and Criminal Financing of Terrorism	173
6	The Drug Trade: The Profit Center of Criminals and Terrorists	218
7	The Less Policed Illicit Trade: Antiquities, Counterfeits, and Diverted Products	259
8	Ultimate Fears: Weapons of Mass Destruction and Crime-Terror Connections	289
	Conclusion	320
Index		353

Figure, Maps, and Tables

Figure

2.1   Illegal economy nexus.   *page 74*

Maps

4.1a   International support network for the Beslan
attacks.   148
4.1b   Triborder area: What would you decapitate to have
any effect on this network?   150
6.1a   Slaves' revenge: European slave trade and Latin
American cocaine trafficking routes.   223
6.1b   Northern and Balkan heroin routes out of
Afghanistan.   224
6.1c   Converging routes: Silk Road and drug trafficking
routes.   226

Tables

3.1a   Transnational Crime and the State   106
3.1b   Terrorists and the State   107

Acknowledgments

The research for this book began in the late 1980s, and in the more than fifteen years that I have been studying dirty entanglements, I have had many help me understand the problem and many different groups and organizations that have funded my travel, which has allowed me to visit regions where these problems are acute. I have worked extensively in the former Soviet states, where many of my colleagues, especially Viktor Luneev, first helped me understand the interactions of crime and terrorism.[1]

In 2003, John Picarelli and I received a grant from the National Institute of Justice to study the links between organized crime and terrorism. This was the last U.S. government grant that I have received to support basic research for the book's overall subject matter.[2]

In January 2013, along with Orde Kittrie, we received a MacArthur grant on "Combating Criminal Involvement in Nuclear Trafficking." With this support, I was able to complete the research for the eighth chapter, on weapons of mass destruction.

George Mason University has been very supportive of my ongoing research during the period this book was in progress. I received a semester off for research in spring 2010, which allowed me to develop the proposal and the outline of the book. My status as University Professor has allowed me more

[1] Viktor Luneev, "Organized Crime and Terrorism," in *High Impact Terrorism: Proceedings of a Russian American Workshop*, ed. Glenn E. Schweitzer (Washington, DC: National Academies Press, 2002), 37–52, who researched this topic in the 1990s.

[2] See Louise I. Shelley, John T. Picarelli, Allison Irby, Douglas M. Hart, Patricia A. Craig-Hart, Phil Williams, Steven Simon, Nabi Abdullaev, Bartosz Stanislawski, and Laura Covill, "Methods and Motives: Exploring Links between Transnational Organized Crime and International Terrorism," National Institute of Justice grant 2003-IJ-CX-1019, http://www.ncjrs.gov/app/publications/abstract.aspx?ID=232473.

time to devote to my writing, and I am grateful to the school, the university, and the state of Virginia for continued support.

In the fifteen years that this book has been researched and developed, I have traveled globally.

I have made numerous trips to the former Soviet Union, where I worked and collaborated with colleagues in Russia, Ukraine, and Georgia on a constant basis during this time period. These collaborations were with Natalia Lopashenko, Vitaly Nomokonov, and Tatiana Pinkevich and the centers they have run in affiliation with the Terrorism, Transnational Crime, and Corruption Center I direct. This collaborative work has given me many insights into the instability of the Caucasus, the role of transnational crime in the post-Soviet transition, and the mass attack in Beslan discussed in the first chapter. My understanding of the problems of nuclear smuggling to and within Georgia has been greatly helped by my long-term collaboration with Drs. Alexander Kukhianidze and Alexander Kupatadze. My collaboration with colleagues in Tajikistan and Kyrgyzstan, especially with Dr. Alexander Zelitchenko, have helped me write the drug chapter.

I have made many trips to Asia, including North, South, Southeast, and Central Asia. In Japan, I appreciate my long-term collaboration with Dr. Shiro Okubo of Ritsumeikan University on transnational crime. These trips have allowed me to meet colleagues working on diverse aspects of transnational crime, corruption, and terrorism. On several U.S. government–sponsored academic visitor programs, I was able to visit the Afghan–Tajik border, the site of sizable drug flows, and to visit the Osh region of Kyrgyzstan after the violent conflict in the region.

I have been hosted in South Africa on a couple of occasions by colleagues at the renowned Institute for Security Studies (ISS) as well as at a regional conference on transnational crime. In North Africa, I was in Morocco, at the Transnational Threats Symposium in Rabat, sponsored by the Ministry of Foreign Affairs, with colleagues from North and West Africa, just as the so-called Arab Spring began and the Tunisian government fell.

My travels to Latin America have taken me to the Southern Cone as well as to the Andes and Central America. Those that have been most relevant to this book have been the Seminário Internacional sobre o Crime Organizado e Democracia (Seminar on Organized Crime and Democracy), on November 26–28, 2007, at the Núcleo de Estudos da Violência, Universidade de São Paolo, which discussed the attack on the city of São Paolo, at the Centro da Violencia in São Paolo. My last trip to Colombia for the fifteenth anniversary of Transparency International in September 2013 was invaluable in helping me complete the book.

As a friend who is a leading expert on the Middle East has said, to understand the region, I just needed to be there and sit in the market and drink tea. My equivalent of this has been my annual trip to Antalya, Turkey, where I have written some of this book and drunk plenty of tea in rug shops and other locales. Antalya receives individuals from all the unstable places in the Middle East region and provides an opportunity for participant observation of the phenomena discussed in this book.

In my travels, I have had the opportunity to confer with colleagues with expertise in the subject matter, such as Professor Xavier Raufer in France; Rohan Gunaratna in Singapore; Turkish colleagues at the Turkish International Academy against Drugs and Organized Crime; and Canadian colleagues at the Canadian Network for Research on Terrorism, Security, and Society. I have received important insights from the Australian filmmaker Wendy Dent on the Bali bombing. My participation in the first meeting of European police chiefs analyzing crime and terrorism gave me access to superior international practitioners.

My participation in Global Agenda Councils of the World Economic Forum on illicit trade and organized crime for the past six years has given me access to the superb global experts from my own council but also to individuals on the terrorism council and many other groups. Many of the works of individual Council members, such as Peter Gastrow and Moisés Naím, and of organizations such as Global Witness and the United Nations Office on Drugs and Crime, are represented in the book. There are high-level practitioners who shared their insights and are cited in this book as well as one who reviewed materials on an investigation he conducted but who chose to stay anonymous.

The book received excellent input from two anonymous reviewers at the initial stage and was read by many insightful readers from around the world in its interim and final stages. I tried to provide a diversity of readers to ensure that the book had the insight of individuals from the practitioner, the business, the nongovernmental, and the academic communities on several different continents. My master's and doctoral students from many diverse cultures and religions have helped ensure my cultural sensitivity.

My many readers to whom I wish to express my gratitude include the following. The whole book has been read by Gretchen Peters, Chris Corpora, and Nazia Hussain. With their enormous knowledge of three elements of the dirty entanglement and their residence among these problems, they provided fine insights on how to improve the manuscript. This enormous and demanding effort is deeply appreciated. My former graduate student Dr. Mahmut Cengiz reviewed materials in reference to Turkey, and my current graduate student Guermante Lailari helped me with materials on terrorism and the Middle East. Roberto Perez-Rocha of Transparency International applied his expertise on Latin America and anticorruption work to his reading of the manuscript. He also obtained additional expertise from colleagues in Latin America, particularly Central America, to improve these analyses. Christian Swan, who works on illicit trade from the corporate perspective and is deeply engaged in these issues in Europe, read Chapter 7 and provided many valuable sources from the corporate world and the European perspective on counterfeiting and diversion. John Schmidt, policy analyst at Fintrac (the financial integrity unit of

Canada) read Chapter 5 on the business of terrorism and provided me with valuable Canadian and financial examples. Orde Kittrie, my collaborator on the MacArthur grant, read Chapter 8 on weapons of mass destruction and shared many insights from his expertise in this area. I am grateful to all for their careful and painstaking work.

I want to thank my editor at Cambridge, Lewis Bateman, who took on this book after my editor, Eric Crahan, left the Press. I want to thank Eric for his initial efforts to provide me superior feedback on my proposal.

I want to thank my partner, Richard Isaacson, for reading and rereading the volume and encouraging me to keep editing to make this the best possible book it could be. His insights were clear, precise, and valuable. I cannot but express my intense gratitude. He supported me in finishing this book when I was so ill in the final months of its completion. I want to thank the many doctors, nurses, and medical professionals who have kept me healthy in my long months of difficult treatment and restored me to undertake future books. My children, Hester and Richard, also helped me throughout the illness, but more important, they provide an important motivation to make the world sustainable for future generations – an important goal of this book.

Introduction

In mid-January 2013, a coalition of diverse jihadi groups[1] seized control of the In Amenas gas field in Eastern Algeria, close to the Libyan border. The field provides 5 percent of the gas produced in Algeria. The attack, blessed by al-Qaeda in the Mahgreb (AQIM), a powerful al-Qaeda affiliate,[2] revealed the power of the radical Islamists to take control of a large and economically important site with more than eight hundred employees. The attack is believed to have been planned by Mokhtar Belmokhtar, who started a splinter group from AQIM not long before the attack.[3]

Operating under a policy that prohibited negotiation with terrorists, the Algerian state launched a military siege against the gas facility that resulted in high numbers of casualties. More than thirty attackers died, and at least three dozen hostages from eight countries also perished.[4] The well-armed assailants had terrorized the hostages before their rescue or death.

These are the simple facts of the case. Yet this single act of terrorism epitomizes the main principles of this book, that the interaction of crime, corruption, and terrorism is having a tremendous impact on both security and the global economy. This attack – designed to command international attention – was characteristic of contemporary security threats, where the challenge comes from nonstate actors rather than governments. This attack was a strike at the core of the Algerian economy yet caused numerous foreign casualties. It reveals the consequences of globalization, where foreign investment and workers from diverse countries are placed in ever more remote locales and unstable regions, especially as the world seeks to tap ever more distant sources of oil and gas. Carried out in a lightly guarded desert locale,[5] it reveals the strategic thinking of the terrorists. They were willing to carry out what was almost certainly a suicide mission to advance their goals by attacking an oil facility employing citizens from many different countries. Yet they did this with advanced weaponry that they had acquired and knew how to deploy.

The January attack of 2013 is reflective of a "new terrorism," discussed more in Chapter 3, that is more spectacular in its operation and its victimization, but also in its global economic effects. The hostages killed came from at least three continents – North America, Europe, and Asia. American, British, French, Japanese, Norwegian, Filipino, and Romanian victims were identified.[6] The attackers reportedly came from at least seven countries, including Algeria, Chad, Egypt, Mali, Mauritania, Niger, and Canada. They entered from Libya, which presently lacks adequate border controls. The presence of two Canadians[7] reveals the capacity of Islamic militant organizations to recruit not only regionally but also globally. The target was even more global than was revealed by the nationalities of the terrorists and their victims. The In Amenas gas field was operated by companies based on four continents, including BP, Statoil of Norway, and Sonatrach (the Algerian national oil company), and was serviced by many international firms. The Japanese engineering firm JGC Corp helped service the field, which explains why the Japanese, despite being far from their home country, suffered the largest number of fatalities.[8]

Globalization has created a world where international businesses from diverse countries, employing citizens from around the globe, can combine in such a remote locale as In Amenas. But globalization has also created a world in which money, arms, and people move readily across borders, making such sites vulnerable.[9] This operation required extensive advanced planning and logistics to move significant numbers of people and arms long distances across borders to this desert site.

Recent decades have seen a decline of borders, as there have been greater efforts to promote trade and move massive amounts of goods.[10] The decline of the border in the In Amenas case was a consequence of the absence of state function in In Amenas after the Arab Spring and the ousting of Qaddafi. In many other cases, the decline of borders is a result of the retreat of the state,[11] in which less control has been exercised over national territory. In the developing world, these borders are often artifacts of colonial rule and other historical legacies rather than defensible geographic divisions of people and cultures.[12] Postcolonial Africa epitomizes this problem, as many of the borders of African states are artificial constructs of the colonial era. With little national desire to police these boundaries, and few financial incentives for law enforcement to perform their jobs effectively, significant corruption prevails at the frontiers. Consequently, without law enforcement capacity to police movements of people, the radical Islamists were able to enter into Algeria, allegedly from Libya, without problems. Many of the arms used came from Qaddafi-era Libya, but they could be moved to diverse locales in Africa, largely unimpeded, because of the absence of effective controls in the chaos that followed the Arab Spring.[13]

Assisting in the movement of people and the smuggling of goods are the Tuaregs, a tribal people who have traditionally moved cargo across the desert. Having fought for Qaddafi, many escaped from Libya. With their displacement after the Arab Spring, they forged an alliance with AQIM that exploited their talents in transporting and smuggling goods, arms, and people across the desert and avoiding border controls. They have helped AQIM take control of northern Mali.[14]

The Tuaregs are just one element of the extensive network that facilitated this attack. Although Belmokhtar claimed credit for the assault on In Amenas, in reality, the group that assaulted the gas field united a heterogeneous group behind a shared objective. Those who participated and facilitated the assault included jihadists, ethnic rebels, and diverse criminal groups. This network construction is representative of the new face of terrorism that combines criminal and terrorist elements with unclear and often hybrid identities in spaces where they can operate together.

The In Amenas attack was justified as a reprisal against the French attacks on AQIM in Mali, but the advanced planning needed for the gas field attack negates this claim. The corruption in Mali has been of concern for years, as its leaders have cut secret deals with AQIM.[15] The significant financial resources of AQIM, derived from its extensive and diversified criminal activity, have allowed the organization, through corruption and force, to create a safe haven for itself in a large part of Mali.[16]

The presence of crime-terror groups in the Sahel is not just a problem of safe havens in weak and loosely governed states. It also reveals the interaction of crime and terrorism with the legitimate economy and the complicity of the corporate world in the financing of terrorism. AQIM, as discussed in reference to the business of terrorism, has profited enormously from kidnapping. The kidnapping of Canadians and Europeans in North and West Africa by insurgent groups, including AQIM, have provided massive funds for these groups, as the payments have totaled approximately $130 million in the last decade, paid by Britain, Germany, Italy, Spain, France, Austria, Sweden, and the Netherlands.[17] This money has been paid both by governments on Continental Europe and by corporations.[18] The money has often come from companies whose workers have been kidnapped, however, insurance firms ultimately are the stakeholders who pay out large ransoms after Western corporations have bought expensive antikidnapping policies. The ransom profits have provided the insurgent and jihadi groups enormous capacity in an environment in which labor and trafficked arms from Libya are cheap.[19]

As is discussed subsequently, some analysts of the crime-terror problem seek to define the problem as one linked to weak and fragile states. But as this Algerian and AQIM example illustrates, without the financial support and complicity of financial institutions in the developed world, insurgent groups would not have the capability to carry out such expensive attacks. Therefore, companies are not only the victims of terrorist attacks, such as in In Amenas, but are also facilitators of this insurgent activity through their large payments to insurgent groups. This illustrates that crime and terrorism intersect with the legitimate economy in diverse ways.

Kidnapping is not the only activity that has supported AQIM, although it may be its largest revenue source. Belmokhtar, the strategist behind the In Amenas attack, has been identified as a "jihadi gangster," a special distinct type associated with AQIM that combines terrorist objectives with significant illicit activity.[20] He has also been referred to as "Mr. Marlboro" for his large role in the lucrative illicit cigarette trade in North Africa, discussed further in Chapter 7.[21] But kidnapping and cigarettes are just part of this criminal panoply that also includes extortion and arms and drugs smuggling, also analyzed in Chapter 6.[22] The diversity of criminal activity that supports this jihadi activity in Africa reveals that drugs are not the central funding source for terrorism, although they receive a disproportionate amount of attention in strategies that seek to address terrorist financing.

All of this illicit cross-border trade can only function because of large and pervasive corruption. Examining the world map of corruption released by Transparency International for 2012 reveals that the Sahel-Sahara region, as well as the adjoining regions of North, West, and central Africa, experience high levels of perceived corruption. Libya, the source of the smuggled arms, is one of the most corrupt countries in the world.[23] With this low level of state capacity, the political will is not present to control crime, terrorism, or the increasingly complex structures built of these ingredients.

The force of the Algerian assault against the militants is a consequence of its past history of conflict with terrorists, the training of its military leadership by the Soviet armed forces, and the strategic importance of the gas fields to Algeria's economy. Its policy of nonnegotiation is a legacy of its conflict with Islamic insurgents in the 1990s, which is estimated to have claimed anywhere from 30 to 150,000 lives.[24] The huge oil and gas industries are pillars of the Algerian economy. They represent 98 percent of its export revenue and 70 percent of its national budget.[25] Therefore, this attack on the energy production of Algeria undermines the economic and political viability of the state. As a major supplier of gas to Europe, the assault on this gas field challenges the security and dependability of gas needed by the European community for its daily life. Therefore, the jihadis are not just striking at individual hostages, as in the past, but are undermining the economic security of Algeria and Europe. The political and economic significance of this attack far surpasses that of previous terrorist acts in Algeria.

Themes of the Book

The central themes of this analysis – the importance of historical legacies, the centrality of state corruption, and networks to the problems of crime and terrorism – are woven throughout the book. The intersection of crime, terrorism, and corruption with the legitimate economy, and the impact that these phenomena have on economic growth, employment, security, development, and the sustainability of the planet, are analyzed in many regions of the world. The increasing challenges to international security from corruption and nonstate actors, which have a complex and interdependent relationship, are presented in different locales throughout the book. Within this analysis, there is a leitmotif that terrorist attacks, but also responses to terrorism, are often accompanied by serious violations of human rights.

Entanglement

This book also introduces the fundamental concept of *entanglement,* a term first used by Erwin Schrödinger in 1935 for a surprising degree of interconnectedness in quantum systems, and in many ways reminiscent of the kinds of important and enduring interactions we are seeing among crime, corruption, and terrorism. According to the concept of entanglement,

> when two systems, of which we know the states by their respective representatives, enter into temporary physical interaction due to known forces between them, and when after a time of mutual influence the systems separate again, then they can no longer be described in the same way as before, viz. by endowing each of them with a representative of its own . . . By the interaction the two representatives [the quantum states] have become entangled.[26]

The concept is "no mere quantum quirk of interest only to physicists, its peculiar possibilities have caught the attention of investment bankers and information entrepreneurs."[27] Yet it is also strikingly parallel to the interactions we are describing and analyzing in the human realm. Once the three phenomena of crime, corruption, and terrorism converge, as we saw In Amenas, they are fundamentally transformed as they evolve into the future. As with the quantum systems, the interacting human components can be separated in the physical world, even by significant distances, but a change in one element is rapidly reflected in the others. This is the enormous challenge the international community faces in addressing the problems epitomized by In Amenas. Once the entanglement occurs, the elements continue to influence each other even when they are apart – hence we have enduring *"dirty entanglements."*

The Developing World

The In Amenas attack illustrates another concept that will recur throughout the book – deadly interactions of crime, terrorism, and corruption may occur most frequently in the developing world.[28] But in the contemporary globalized world, these interactions do not exist in isolation. Rather, it is not only that many of the victims of In Amenas came from the developed world but that the financial support provided by the ransom payments gave the terrorists the working capital for their activity. African governments were dismayed at these payments in the past but were powerless to stop them. American officials had also tried to dissuade the Europeans from making these payments.[29]

An international coalition, including the United States and NATO, ousted Colonel Qaddafi from Libya. Yet in an all-too-familiar pattern, military action was not followed by a program for governance. After years of authoritarian rule, there was no group or party to fill the power vacuum, and nonstate actors came to the fore. The rise of criminals, terrorists, jihadi gangsters, and other complex structures resulted in unsecured borders and a vigorous trade in the vast armaments of what was once the Libyan government. As in Afghanistan, discussed subsequently, where control does not extend beyond Kabul, in Libya, state control is exercised over only certain key institutions in Tripoli and the oil fields. This chaos facilitates terrorist attacks.

International Complicity

The events in a remote part of Algeria are not just Algeria's problem. Nor are they problems just caused by actors in North Africa. The funding for terrorism, as well as the emphasis of outsiders on military solutions rather than state building, contribute to the terrorism that occurred at In Amenas. Therefore, there is a shared complicity. Weak and corrupt states are powerless to stop the enrichment and support structures for the terrorist groups from abroad, especially when they are supported by foreign governments and corporations. Nor can they make the transition from authoritarianism to good governance on their own. The confluence of crime, corruption, and terrorism is an outgrowth of policy failures in the political and economic arenas.

The book will show that once a situation reaches such an acute interaction of crime, corruption, and terrorism, it is very difficult to reverse the outcome. The dirty entanglements perpetuate the change. These problems are self-reinforcing, as change in one triggers a reaction in the others. From a policy perspective, the component elements of this deadly triad must be addressed before they reach such an acute and intractable level.

Methods of Research

The analysis of the political, social, and economic environment surrounding the In Amenas attack is based on many and diverse sources compiled and analyzed since I began the study of crime, terror, and corruption interactions more than fifteen years ago, well before September 11.[30] Many years of studying the dynamics of crime and violence, both within and outside of wars, have contributed to this understanding. For example, my introduction to the Civil War in Algeria came through a more than year-long collaborative project sponsored by the World Bank that tested the concept of whether greed or grievance contributes to the perpetuation of conflict.[31] One of the case studies focused on was Algeria and its long and bloody Civil War.[32]

More recently, I have had the opportunity to understand developments in Africa more closely. I was in Rabat, Morocco, the week the Arab Spring began, speaking at a conference titled "Prospects for Regional Collaboration to Meet

Transnational Threats," hosted by the Moroccan government and attended by representatives of twelve countries.[33] At this conference, which ended the day before Ben Ali was ousted in Tunisia, no one believed that any Arab governments might fall in the face of public protests. But many in the audience understood the power of AQIM, the importance of crime-terror interactions in corrupt environments, and the role of smuggling in the financial capacity of terrorist groups. The weakness of the states in the face of this challenge was apparent to many African specialists, government officials, and leaders of multilateral African organizations with whom I conversed. I also was able to discuss the observed phenomena with French and French-trained specialists who had particular insights into the region following years of colonial rule. Their insights also directed me to some of the most valuable literature to read on the topic to understand developments in Africa.[34]

As a follow-up to this conference, I was invited in spring 2011 to United States Africa Command to discuss human trafficking, the subject of my last book, and the linkages between this phenomenon and other forms of illicit activity in Africa. While visiting at the Africa Command, I was able to meet with Commander Carter Ham and many analysts to understand the growing relationship among illicit networks, crime, and terrorism.

Yet my understanding of the phenomenon in Africa is shaped by much more than official American sources and government officials of different African countries. I have also been able to discuss the illicit networks in Africa and the political environment with corporate security specialists and political analysts for the cigarette industry, pharmaceutical, and energy sectors. The people engaged in this work, while focusing on brand integrity, security, and investment risks for the companies that employ them, have a much broader understanding of the political and criminal environments in which they work. They have contributed much to my understanding of where the illicit world intersects with the legitimate.

The methods used to analyze the situation in North Africa and the Sahel have been applied to the research done for the rest of the book. As in North Africa, where I have relied on my French, I have used my knowledge of Russian, Spanish, and Italian as well, and I have made use of my extensive experience in other regions of the world to help my analysis. I have gone beyond the traditional literature on terrorism or crime-terror relationships to examine historical, political scientific, international relations, economic, and sociological literature. This work is not embedded in one discipline or theoretical perspective. Only a multidisciplinary and comparative perspective can help the reader comprehend the increasingly interconnected relationship of crime, corruption, and terrorism, in different regions of the world.

Many writing on terrorism have had security clearances and access to classified literature on the subject. But I have never had a security clearance in my life, and therefore my knowledge of the subject has come from a reliance on open sources. This has been supplemented by interviews with individuals who have conducted detailed investigations of crime and terrorism or held high-level policy positions in their countries or in multinational organizations. One high-level retired American intelligence official commented after a lecture I gave discussing this book, "Many foreigners have trusted you deeply to provide you such information." This insight was very apt, as I have had access to many individuals with enormous insights that are not often shared with American academics.

Illustrative of this is the Colombian specialist who gave me one of the few copies of his journal with his analyses of the financial records that had been seized from Revolutionary Armed Forces of Colombia (Fuerzas Armadas Revolucionarias de Colombia; FARC) members. Furthermore, he referred me to a book in French with even more details, as much sensitive material was provided to the book's author.[35] Reading this book gave me many insights into the business of terrorism.

In the years it has taken to gain the knowledge to write this book, I have traveled to many parts of the globe. I have been on every continent, except Australia and Antarctica. I have been in such remote places as the Tajik–Afghan border, through which drugs are smuggled, and the North and South Caucasus, which has been a key locale for terrorism and nuclear smuggling. I was invited to São Paulo, Brazil, the year after a criminal gang, the Primeiro Comando da Capital, launched a multiday attack on the city that will be discussed more in Chapter 1. I have made repeated trips to Turkey and the Gulf Region, which have provided me insight into the phenomena I am studying. The last trip for the book was to Colombia in fall 2013 to celebrate the fifteenth anniversary of Transparency International–Colombia, the organization that has played a key role in civil society opposition to corruption, crime, and terrorism that has wracked the country.[36]

The book also includes research conducted in different countries and regions, sponsored by or in affiliation with Terrorism, Transnational Crime, and Corruption Center (TraCCC), a research center I founded and direct. This research has particularly contributed to understanding the interaction of crime, corruption, and terrorism in the vast territory of the former USSR, but it is not confined to this region. In addition, I have benefited from my colleagues at TraCCC who follow the literature and analyze sources in such diverse languages as Arabic, Urdu, Tajik, Turkish, Georgian, and Kurdish.

Often I have been the guest of research centers or have spoken at conferences hosted by foreign institutions, helping me to broaden my perspective beyond the United States. Through my work for the last five years with the Global Agenda Councils of the World Economic Forum (WEF), first working on illicit trade and then on organized crime, I have been able to meet and converse with the current and past top-level officials of countries deeply affected by terrorism, such as Iraq, Afghanistan, and Pakistan, and with experts from Europe and other parts of Asia, Latin America, and Australia.

At these meetings, I have also met some of the top researchers from around the world on the topics of crime, corruption, terrorism, and weak and fragile states. Also, I have met leading human rights activists who have examined the abuses that lead to crime and terrorist recruitment and committed in the name of fighting crime, corruption, and terrorism. Through my participation at the WEF, I was also invited to attend the first meeting of the European Police Chiefs at Europol, where the focus of the meeting was organized crime and terrorism.

I have had broad access to diverse law enforcement officials from around the world, but I also have met with experts on counterfeiting, corporate security specialists working for companies concerned with illicit trade in oil and gas, specialists in art crime, and even an occasional smuggler or facilitator.[37] In addition, the section on cigarette smuggling has benefited from exchanges with investigative journalists conducting in-depth analyses of the problem.[38]

The most valuable part of these interviews, apart from their personal insights, is help in knowing the most relevant literature to read. To understand the large terror attacks discussed in the next chapter, it was necessary to read the voluminous documents of the 9/11 Commission and the significant investigations that were conducted in Russia, Spain, Brazil, and India after their mass attacks. Other records of limited availability, of prosecutions of criminals and terrorists, and financial records obtained from terrorists have been used to understand the interactions of criminals and terrorists, the expenditures on corruption, and the forms of illicit activity that fund and facilitate terrorism. Apart from these fundamental sources, I have used part of the significant literature on terrorism that has emerged worldwide since September 11.

Interviews with key individuals from all inhabited continents have helped me greatly in my analysis. These interviews have pointed me in the right direction and have allowed me to test ideas as they have developed. Often those interviewed have asked not to be cited, but have indicated where I can find significant supporting information in public sources. They have helped me think outside of the American context and to understand how the phenomena I have studied are perceived in other contexts that have a different view of terrorism. This view may be shaped by years of confronting terrorist attacks, as in Turkey, or by a perception of some insurgents as "freedom fighters." Outside the United States, there is more readiness to accept a relationship among crime, corruption, and terrorism. In the United States, Americans have stovepiped the issues of crime and terrorism and have long treated them as separate phenomena. This position officially changed only in 2011, with the adoption of a Transnational Crime Strategy.[39] This strategy has remained seriously underresourced, without the human and financial support to make it effective, and without a vigorous independent basic research component to give it direction.

Goals of the Analysis

When I first studied criminology in the 1970s, there was no instruction on terrorism or corruption. Terrorism was a separate phenomenon, addressed in political science and international relations but distinct from the discipline of criminology. This was not illogical. There have always been some connections between terrorism and crime, but they were much more limited than they are today. Crime, at the time of my graduate studies, was a much more local phenomenon. Corruption was not taught at this time in university curricula, as it was not viewed as a valid field of study. It was thought merely to grease the wheels in societies with rigid bureaucracies.[40]

Globalization

Yet, as this book addresses, globalization has brought profound changes to all three phenomena.[41] Transnational crime is much more complex than cross-border smuggling,[42] and many terrorist acts are supported by global networks. Corruption is now a truly global phenomenon, not only because international companies pay bribes to obtain contracts overseas but because the global nature of financial markets means that dictators can strip the assets of their countries and transmit them to foreign bank accounts.

Illicit Networks

Illicit networks have emerged in which both licit and illicit actors (i.e., crime groups; terrorist, militant, and insurgent groups; and guerillas) collaborate in ways that are often hard to untangle. Some prefer to refer to these as *hybrid threats,* where it is hard to discern the character and the motives of the actors.[43] Hybrids are defined as the offspring of two animals or plants, where the problem defined here is more complex, consisting of at least three elements – crime, corruption, terrorism, or possibly insurgency. Therefore, I prefer to think and analyze them as dirty entanglements – having serious and multiple consequences.

The large number of drug trafficking–related deaths in Mexico and Central America is evidence of the enormous violence and instability that can result from the combination of crime, transnational crime, and corruption.[44] Yet there is a tendency now to group crime and corruption with terrorism when all three elements may not be present. As one American military officer serving in Honduras commented, "We also are disrupting and deterring the potential nexus between transnational organized criminals and terrorists who would do harm to our country."[45] Terrorism need not be added to the mix to obtain great political instability or loss of life.

The addition of terrorism to the already destabilizing phenomena of crime and corruption can have often unforeseen and chaotic consequences for the dynamics of the problem that can multiply the impact of each element in unpredictable ways. This is analogous to what is known in physics as the *gravitational three-body problem*: "While the two-body problem is integrable and its solutions completely understood ... solutions of the three-body problem may be of an arbitrary complexity and are very far from being completely understood."[46] Yet, for our problem, the interactions of the three components are occurring with greater frequency in many regions of the world.

Defining the Problem

The destruction of In Amenas is a result of the combination of crime, corruption, and terrorism. It was committed by an amalgam of terrorist and crime groups and involved severe acts of violence against unarmed civilians. The most known group to have participated in this assault was AQIM, designated a terrorist organization by the U.S. State Department in 2002, but many of the other groups behind this terrorist attack are not among the terrorist groups designated by the Untied States.[47] This highlights the problem of definition.

Terrorism

There is no standard definition of terrorism nor common designation of terrorist organizations. In fact, specialists have identified more than one hundred definitions of terrorism.[48] The U.S. government defines terrorism as "the unlawful use of force and violence against persons or property to intimidate or coerce a government, the civilian population, or any segment thereof, in furtherance of political or social objectives."[49] But this definition is too narrow, as it does not focus on religious or ideological objectives or the threat of force. Yet limitations can be found for any definition, because there is no consensus as to when there is a legitimate use of force. In fact, Walter Laqueur, one of the éminences grises of terrorism analysis, wrote in the 1990s, "Perhaps the only characteristic generally agreed upon is that terrorism always involved violence or threats of violence."[50]

Without a consensus on terrorism, this book focuses primarily on the acts of terrorists and the financing of organizations, rather than focusing on terrorists as "something that one 'is.'"[51] Today, there are so many diverse forms and motivations that lie behind terrorist acts, and politically and religiously motivated violence.[52] The book also refers to insurgents and other violent actors who have been motivated by politics, religion, or other objectives to cause physical harm. Often in cases where they have less capacity than those they attack, the concept has been defined as an asymmetric threat.[53]

Terrorism is the most visible phenomenon discussed in this book, but it is not the most pervasive. Terrorism is consistently linked to crime and corruption, but not all transnational crime is linked to terrorism. Transnational crime is now a pervasive problem. There is not one region of the world or country without crime, or transnational crime.[54] Furthermore, corruption is widespread and endemic in many countries, particularly in some of the most populated regions of the world.

Criminal Acts

The activities that support terrorist groups are both local and transnational crime. Most of the crime committed falls under generally universally recognized definitions of crime – robbery, smuggling, or extortion, for example. When this crime crosses borders, it becomes transnational crime. Transnational crime is much easier to define than corruption and terrorism, as the United Nations has developed a Convention against Transnational Organized Crime to which the preponderance of countries in the world are signatories. According to this definition,

> "organized criminal group" shall mean a structured group of three or more persons, existing for a period of time and acting in concert with the aim of committing one or more serious crimes or offences established in accordance with this Convention, in order to obtain, directly or indirectly, a financial or other material benefit. "Serious crime" shall mean conduct constituting an offence punishable by a maximum deprivation of liberty of at least four years or a more serious penalty. "Structured group" shall mean a group that is not randomly formed for the immediate commission of an offence and that does not need to have formally defined roles for its members, continuity of its membership or a developed structure . . . An offence is transnational in nature if: (a) It is committed in more than one state; (b) It is committed in one state but a substantial part of its preparation, planning, direction or control takes place in another state; (c) It is committed in one state but involves an organized criminal group that engages in criminal activities in more than one state; or (d) It is committed in one state but has substantial effects in another state.[55]

Corruption

There is much less agreement as to the definition of corruption. Transparency International has defined the phenomenon as "the abuse of entrusted power for private gain." The gain can be financial as well as nonmonetary.[56] The United Nations, in its Global Compact against Corruption, has not chosen to develop its own definition. Yet there are limitations on this widely used definition. As this book shows, corruption often involves more than public officials but includes private actors who behave in corrupt ways. Moreover, limiting corruption exclusively to the state sector is difficult in most developing and communist and former communist countries, as there is an absence of clear boundaries between state officeholders and private business.[57]

Much of the definitional work and analyses of corruption are supported by development organizations such as the Organisation for Economic Co-operation and Development, the World Bank, and Transparency International. Therefore, the focus is on economic growth rather than on many other salient and damaging effects of corruption such as governance, rule of law, and problems of access to justice.[58]

The lack of agreed-on definitions (required for international treaties and legal agreements) is not an impediment to analyzing clearly bad behaviors that undermine societies, global sustainability, and results in often senseless and brutal deaths. Increasingly, there are not clear-cut divisions between criminal and terrorist groups but individuals and networks with blended identities.

The definitions in the book are more than academic. The presence or absence of definitions guides the policies of multinational institutions. If a phenomenon is defined, it can be addressed. If not, it is hard for many institutions to develop policies or allocate resources to focus on the problem. The diverse entanglements of crime, corruption, and terrorism discussed in this book cannot easily be subsumed under a simple definition. Therefore, many multinational and state-based institutions refrain from addressing these phenomena, preferring to concentrate their efforts on easier-to-define and more tractable problems.

Understanding the Context

A large literature now exists on each of the component phenomena discussed in this book – transnational crime, corruption, and terrorism. The book is distinct from these significant literatures, as its integrated approach differentiates it from the security literature that characterizes much of terrorism studies, or the economic and financial literature that addresses the funding of terrorism,[59] or the activities of transnational crime. It overlaps with these literatures, as well as literatures of the growing analyses on nonstate actors, illicit networks, weak states and conflicts, and the role and character of the criminal economy.[60] Because the book simultaneously addresses the worlds of corrupt officials and nonstate actors (criminals, terrorists, insurgents), it examines the blending and interactions of the licit and the illicit worlds.

The book very much belongs to the literature that examines the declining role of the state and impact of globalization.[61] Terrorism, transnational crime, and corruption are all major beneficiaries of globalization. Moreover, the globalization of corruption has allowed these nonstate actors to function internationally.[62] Crime and terror groups have exploited the enormous decline in regulation, lessened border controls, and greater freedom to expand their activities across borders and to new regions of the world.[63] Their organizations have globalized, often facilitated by cellular communications, the Internet, and their mastery of cutting-edge modern technology.[64] Whereas the growth of legal commerce is hindered by border controls, customs officials, and bureaucratic controls, transnational crime groups and terrorists exploit the loopholes of state-based legal systems to extend their reach.[65] Criminals and terrorists travel to regions where they cannot be extradited, base their operations in countries with ineffective or corrupted law enforcement, and launder their money in countries with bank secrecy or few effective controls. Often they use systems of underground banking or trade-based money laundering to hide their activities.[66] By segmenting their operations, they benefit from globalization, while simultaneously reducing the risks of detection, prosecution, and asset forfeiture.[67]

Criminal-Terrorism Literature

Analysis of the relationship between crime and terrorism has not been an integral part of the terrorism literature. But important scholarly works on terrorism such as those by Hoffman and Laqueur discuss the phenomenon.[68] Bruce Hoffman analyzes the crime-terror relationship almost exclusively in terms of narco-terrorism. Walter Laqueur devotes a chapter to the subject, particularly in reference to the former Soviet Union. He shows that the crime-terror relationship is not new but has become more acute with the "new terrorism."[69]

Some collections produced by government-supported think tanks have chapters devoted to one aspect of the crime-terror problem, such as the drug trade or the criminal networks that interact with terrorists.[70] More specific terrorist studies focus on a subset of the problem, such as on the counterfeiting of films and DVDs and the financing of terrorism.[71]

Other authors focus on the crime-terror relationship in only one country or region, such as Iraq, Afghanistan, or Colombia.[72] Certain analysts prefer to focus on particular terrorist organizations and their criminal connections.[73] Other studies focus on a particular topic area, such as is discussed in Chapters 6 through 8 for example, the problem of drugs, the problem of weapons of mass destruction (WMD), or art smuggling.[74] There is also a more general literature on terrorist financing that focuses exclusively on the criminal activity that supports terrorism.[75] This literature is quite different from this book, which, for the first time, explores the business logic of terrorists and their reliance on crime.

Much of the literature that connects transnational crime with terrorism focuses on the political-criminal nexus.[76] The focus of this research is both on the high-level and also the more routine corruption that facilitates the commission of criminal acts and allows for the infiltration of criminals into the political process. This latter concept is an important, but not an exclusive, focus of this book's corruption analysis.

Little academic literature connects the problem of corruption and terrorism. Two edited collections address this phenomenon in individual chapters.[77] This is the largest lacuna in the literature, and the most important, as corruption is central for the survival and operations of both terrorism and transnational crime, as Chapter 2 shows.

Researchers on transnational crime rarely discuss the interactions of criminals with terrorists in book-length research.[78] A significant literature has developed to understand the interaction of these phenomena.[79] John Picarelli has grouped this work into the following subheadings: actors and activities, formation of hybrid organizations, blending of criminal and terrorist activities, and the milieu of convergence and transformation.[80]

By writing this book-length manuscript rather than an article, it is possible to develop and analyze more subtle relationships among crime and terrorism, and especially their complex interactions and entanglement with corruption, a discussion that is almost entirely absent from other analyses that have been published.

An Overview of the Book

The book focuses on the relationship of crime, corruption, and terrorism globally, a crucial contemporary and future challenge to human and global security. Although numerous analyses have been done of the individual components of the dirty entanglement, no book-length work has examined the significance of the interaction of the three elements.

By using illustrations from all over the world, the book shows that the entanglements are not confined to jihadi terrorists. Dirty interactions occur in megacities and other locales, among diverse terrorist, insurgent, and politicized crime groups, with deep-seated grievances. And they have effects that are felt much more broadly than in the place where the violence occurs.

The book provides the basic conceptual tools necessary to understand the nature of the problem, which may help to formulate more effective policies in combating this hydra. Such an integrated analysis is, unfortunately, all too frequently absent in conceptualizing ongoing policies, thereby causing them to regularly fail.

There is so much available information on crime and terrorism that not every transnational crime group nor terrorist organization is covered comprehensively. Furthermore, there is a conscious effort to focus less on Colombia, Afghanistan, and Iraq, as well as Israel and its neighboring states. These have already been written about extensively, and so it is more stimulating to provide important illustrative material from a broader range of countries and regions. The selected examples highlight processes and forms of interaction in different regions of the world, within a historical, societal, political, and economic context.

The book's analysis of the entanglement of crime, corruption, and terrorism reveals their far-reaching consequences: undermining global health, attacking the sustainability of the planet, and perpetuating conflict. The counterfeit pharmaceutical trade that funds crime and terrorism results in premature deaths and defeats the eradication of disease. The illicit wildlife trade may lead to extinction of species, undermine ecosystems, and spread disease.[81] Illicit trade in natural resources and drugs helps perpetuate conflict. Illegal forestry, committed by criminals and such terrorist groups as the FARC and Taliban, and facilitated by corrupt officials, undermines global sustainability. Corruption contributes to endemic poverty and great income inequality in much of the developing world.[82] These consequences are in addition to the already significant harm of economic, political, and social instability resulting from the dirty entanglements.

Part I

Part I of the book provides the framework to understand the logic of the crime-corruption-terrorism relationship. As a scholar of piracy has commented, "crime corrupts, terrorism subverts and when they merge they do both."[83] But this does not capture all the complexity, as corruption itself is a key ingredient in understanding the interactions of transnational crime and terrorism. Part II provides three in-depth case studies – drugs and terrorism; underpoliced forms of crime; and, the ultimate fear, WMD – that illustrate the interactions among the three components introduced in Part I.

Chapter 1 analyzes the crime and corruption that facilitated the six most deadly terrorist acts of the 2000s, all of which occurred in the most economically developed or G-20 countries. Starting with 9/11, it examines these geographically diverse attacks in the United States, Brazil, India, Indonesia, Russia, and Spain. Furthermore, crime and corruption supported not only jihadi terrorist attacks, such as those executed by al-Qaeda on 9/11 and in Bali, but other major acts of terrorism, *motivated by different ideologies and rationales,* that had highly lethal consequences. These attacks with the largest numbers of victims were not anomalous. Crime and corruption also lay behind many deadly terrorist crimes with fewer victims.

Chapter 2 shows that corruption contributes to the emergence and sustenance of both organized crime and terrorism. This chapter also addresses state policies that facilitate corruption, thereby creating an enabling environment for illicit state actors. Regions with high levels of corruption provide environments conducive to terrorism recruitment and operations. Terrorist and transnational groups that offer services to citizens in many regions of the world can make major inroads with populations.

In states with high levels of corruption and theft of state assets, many young men are left with diminished opportunities, ripe for exploitation by both terrorists and criminals.

Chapter 3 dismisses the commonly held idea that terrorists are exclusively driven by ideology and criminals are motivated solely by profit. This distinction, if once valid, is often no longer applicable. The relationship between crime and terrorism now exists on a significant scale, because terrorists have incorporated criminals into their ranks, and many terrorists commit crimes to survive. Some terrorists become greed driven over time, engaging ever more in criminal activity. Others, like Dawood Ibrahim, are criminals who become engaged in politics and see instability as good for business.

The new terrorists, seeking to have the maximum destructive impact, will acquire the skills that they need, often using criminals to carry out tasks for their organizations. In recent decades, many newly formed organized crime groups have strong political interests: paramount among them is the destabilization of existing states.

Chapter 4 shows that criminal support for terrorism occurs in a broad range of locales, including diaspora communities in affluent Western societies, ports, and multiborder areas. Numerous crime-terror interactions also occur in Western societies. The support networks for terrorism often link these different environments. The pipeline for a large-scale terrorist attack may find support in a combination of different milieux across the world.

Part II

Part II examines the businesses of terrorism. After laying out the framework for the business of terrorism, a phenomenon profoundly different from terrorism financing, the following three chapters examine three areas of terrorist business – the most lucrative, the drug trade; the least policed activities; and the WMD trade. Part II examines the important interactions of crime, corruption, and terrorism with both the legitimate and the illegitimate economies. This section concludes that a financial and economic approach to dirty entanglements is a particularly promising, less costly, and less intrusive way to address the pernicious consequences of the vicious triad.

Chapter 5 shows that crime has become a vehicle of choice because it provides a steady stream of funding that is essential for the maintenance of the "terrorist business." This chapter focuses on the business strategies of terrorists. It analyzes their approaches to product mix, professional services, cost-benefit analyses, tax strategies, supply chains, market dominance, competitive advantage, profit centers, targets of opportunity, strategic alliances, and innovation and use of technology. It examines the ways they obtain access to the best human capital through their global networks. It also examines how criminals launder money into easily moved commodities, such as gold, that have high net worth but limited weight to facilitate transport, showing the rationality of their thinking.

Chapter 6, on the drug trade, is the first case study of Part II. Drugs represent the most lucrative funding source for terrorism, and the most studied. The term *narco-terrorism* was developed in the early 1980s in regard to the Sendero Luminoso terrorist group in Peru, which supported its activities by the drug trade. More than half the named terrorist organizations identified by the U.S. government traffic in drugs. Many terrorist organizations function simultaneously in the political arena and as drug traffickers. This chapter surveys the crucial role of drugs in terrorist funding and focuses in greater depth on the three regions of the world where the crime-terror relationship is most pronounced – Colombia and its northern neighbors in Latin America, North and West Africa and the Sahel, and Afghanistan-Pakistan and Central Asia.

Chapter 7 examines the criminal activities that deliver significant profits for terrorists internationally but have a low risk of detection, prosecution, and investigation. These crimes are examined in terms of the business model of terrorism developed in Chapter 5. Such criminal activities favored by terrorists include cigarette and art smuggling and trade in counterfeits, including DVDs, pharmaceuticals, and consumer items. These crimes command little of the manpower and funding resources of intelligence agencies or law enforcement.

Chapter 8 discusses the most feared outcome of the crime-terror relationship – that terrorists will acquire WMD – through facilitators: criminals, as well as businessmen, who knowingly and unknowingly break the law. The chapter focuses primarily on the area of nuclear terrorism, although sectarian and nationalist groups are discussed as well, as they have engaged in, or sought to engage in, bioterrorist or chemical attacks. It examines the illicit trade that supports terrorism, particularly in the area of nuclear smuggling.[84] Investigated cases reveal that criminals of many different nationalities are involved in WMD parts and component smuggling. Some are highly educated individuals, with the contacts and the resources to corrupt officials facilitating the acquisition and transport of the materials. Evidence suggests that the most serious trafficking is rarely detected. It is run by professionals with well-established smuggling networks. The A. Q. Khan network in Pakistan showed that such trade is facilitated by corruption and corporate complicity.

The end of the book places the previous analyses in the context of current security analyses,[85] the nature and role of business and commerce in the globalized world, the retreat of the state, and the rising importance of non-state actors. It examines future trends in the global order, the governance of the urban environment, the consequences of increasing economic inequality, demographic shifts, the relationship between the developed and the developing worlds, and the profound impacts of climate change.

Apart from its contribution to academic arguments, the conclusion addresses concrete choices for policy makers. It notes the need for policy makers to end their myopic focus on the narcotics trade and on criminal kingpins. Although drugs play an important role in terrorist funding, many other forms of illicit trade must also be addressed. The business of terrorism must command more attention than the individual crimes that fund terrorist activity.

Corruption is central to the dirty entanglement with crime and terrorism, yet it commands too little attention in efforts to address terrorism. Corruption is crucial to the perpetuation of crime that funds and facilitates terrorism. Hostility to ongoing corruption has proved an important recruitment tool, especially among Islamic terrorist groups. Yet few strategies to address the crime-terror nexus include anticorruption programs as integral components.

There is widespread bureaucratic stovepiping within individual governments, and multilateral organizations, such as the United Nations and the Organization for Security and Cooperation in Europe. Regrettably, crime, terrorism, and anticorruption programs remain separated from each other. This has allowed criminals and terrorists to exploit the gaps in the present response.

A much more comprehensive approach is needed, one that recognizes the significant links between these phenomena.

The book concludes that there are important trends in the world – political, demographic, economic, climate related, and technological – that will have the greatest impact on dirty entanglements. The ability to influence the outcome of these forces will be limited. But to achieve any success, there will need to be a whole-of-society approach that includes not only governmental action but also strategic partnerships with business, civil society, the research community, and universities and with independent and active investigative journalism.

Notes

1. This use of the term *jihad* is different from the historical meanings. See Michael Bonner, *Jihad in Islamic History: Doctrines and Practices* (Princeton, NJ: Princeton University Press, 2006); Richard Bonney, *Jihād: from Quroān to Bin Laden* (New York: Palgrave Macmillan, 2004); Bernard Lewis, *The Crisis of Islam: Holy War and Unholy Terror* (New York: Random House, 2003).
2. "Algérie: Nous, Al-Qaida, annonçons cette opération bénie," *Le Monde,* January 20, 2013.
3. Mouna Sadek, "Algeria Hostage Crisis Over," January 20, 2013, http://www .magharebia.com/cocoon/awi/xhtml1/en_GB/features/awi/features/2013/01/20/ feature-01.
4. "Q & A: Hostage Crisis in Algeria," January 21, 2013, http://www.bbc.co.uk/ news/world-africa-21056884.
5. Clifford Krauss and Nicholas Kulish, "Algerian Facility Lacked Armed Guards," January 23, 2013, http://www.nytimes.com/2013/01/24/world/africa/algerian-gas-facility-did-not-have-armed-guards.html?_r=1&.
6. "Q & A: Hostage Crisis in Algeria."
7. Lamine Chikhi, "Two Canadians among Dead Islamist Militants at Algeria Gas Plant: Report," *Toronto Star,* January 21, 2013, http://www.thestar.com/news/ world/article/1317736–algeria-finds-dead-canadian-islamist-militants-as-gas-plant-siege-toll-rises.
8. "Q & A: Hostage Crisis in Algeria."
9. Fathali M. Moghadda, *How Globalization Spurs Terrorism: The Lopsided Benefits of "One World" and Why That Fuels Violence* (Westport, CT: Praeger Security International, 2008).
10. Willem van Schendel and Itty Abraham, *Illicit Flows and Criminal Things: States, Border, and the Other Side of Globalization* (Bloomington: Indiana University Press, 2005).
11. Susan Strange, *Retreat of the State: The Diffusion of Power in the World Economy* (New York: Cambridge University Press, 1996).
12. Carolynn Nordstrom, *Global Outlaws: Crime, Money, and Power in the Contemporary World* (Berkeley: University of California Press, 2007).
13. Lee Ferran, "Algeria Hostage Crisis: The Libya Connection," January 22, 2013, http://abcnews.go.com/blogs/headlines/2013/01/algeria-hostage-crisis-the-libya-connection.

14. Craig Whitlock, "Algerian Stance Spoils U.S. Regional Strategy," *Washington Post*, January 19, 2013, A9.

15. Ibid.

16. Wolfram Lacher, "Organized Crime and Conflict in Conflict in the Sahel-Sahara Region," September 13, 2012, http://carnegieendowment.org/2012/09/13/organi zed-crime-and-conflict-in-sahel-sahara-region/dtjm.

17. Nasser Weddady, "How Europe Bankrolls Terror," *New York Times*, February 16, 2013, http://www.nytimes.com/2013/02/17/opinion/sunday/how-european-ran soms-bankroll-islamist-terrorists.html?ref=global-home&_r=0.

18. Conversation with high-level U.S. Treasury official, February 20, 2013, Washington, DC.

19. Ibid.

20. Jean-Pierre Filiu, presentation at African Center for Strategic Studies, January 2011, http://africacenter.org/about/acss-news/acss-news-archives/january-2011/.

21. Jamie Doward. "How Cigarette Smuggling Fuels Islamist Violence," *Guardian*, January 26, 2013, http://www.guardian.co.uk/world/2013/jan/27/cigarette-smuggl ing-mokhtar-belmokhtar-terrorism.

22. See Lacher, "Organized Crime," Chapter 6; see also note to cocaine study in UNODC, *The Transatlantic Cocaine Market: A Research Paper*, April 2011, 37, http://www.unodc.org%2Fdocuments%2Fdata-and-analysis%2FStudies%2F Transatlantic_cocaine_market.pdf.

23. Corruption Perceptions Index 2012, http://cpi.transparency.org/cpi2012/results/.

24. Martha Crenshaw, "The Effectiveness of Terrorism in the Algerian War," in *Terrorism in Context* (University Park: Pennsylvania State University, 1995), 484.

25. Ruadhán Mac Cormaic, "Algeria's Oil and Gas Industry: Pillars of Its Economy," *Irish Times*, January 19, 2013, http://www.irishtimes.com/newspaper/world/2013/ 0119/1224329048619.html.

26. "Quantum Entanglement and Information," *Stanford Encyclopedia of Philosophy*, 2010, http://plato.stanford.edu/entries/qt-entangle/.

27. Laura Sanders, "Everyday Entanglement: Physicists Take Quantum Weirdness Out of the Lab," *Science News* 178, no. 11 (2010): 22, http://www.sciencenews.org/ view/feature/id/65060/description/Everyday_Entanglement; Paul Comstock, "The Strange World of Quantum Entanglement," March 30, 2007, http://calitreview .com/51/the-strange-world-of-quantum-entanglement/.

28. Alan B. Krueger and David Laitin, "*Kto Kogo?* A Cross-Country Study of the Origins and Targets of Terrorism," in *Terrorism and Economic Development, and Political Development*, ed. Philip Keefer and Norman Loayza (New York: Cambridge University Press, 2008), 148–73.

29. Weddady, "How Europe Bankrolls Terror."

30. I worked with Russian colleagues, such as Viktor Luneev, "Organized Crime and Terrorism," in *High Impact Terrorism: Proceedings of a Russian American Workshop*, ed. Glenn E. Schwitzer (Washington, DC: National Academies Press, 2002), 37–52, who was doing research on this topic in the 1990s. I also received a research grant from the National Institute of Justice with John Picarelli in 2003 to study the links between organized crime and terrorism based on earlier research we had done on the subject.

31. Paul Collier and Anke Hoeffler, "Greed and Grievance in Civil War," World Bank Policy Research Working Paper 2355, May 2000, http://elibrary.worldbank.org/

content/workingpaper/10.1596/1813–9450–2355; also see Mats Berdal and David M. Malone, *Greed and Grievance: Economic Agendas in Civil Wars* (Boulder, CO: Lynne Rienner, 2000).

32. Miriam R. Levi, "Algeria, 1991–2002: Anatomy of a Civil War," in *Understanding Civil War: Evidence and Analysis*, ed. Paul Collier and Nicholas Sambanis (Washington, DC: World Bank, 2005), 221–46.

33. African Center for Strategic Studies, http://africacenter.org/about/acss-news/acss-news-archives/january-2011/.

34. For example, the writing of Jean-Pierre Filiu, "Could Al-Qaeda Turn African in the Sahel?," June 2010, Carnegie Middle East Center, http://carnegie-mec.org/publications/?fa=40975.

35. Daniel Pécaut, *Les Farc, une guérilla sans fin?* (Paris: Lignes de Repères, 2008).

36. Elizabeth Ungar, "La Lucha por la transparencia," *El Expectador*, September 5, 2013, 6.

37. Many of the companies do extensive business in the Middle East. Because of the sensitivity over the terrorism issue, they did not want to publicly discuss the involvement of terrorist groups in the counterfeiting of their products. But when asked about this directly, they would answer affirmatively and sometimes provide concrete details.

38. See, e.g., the in-depth investigation of the Public Integrity Project "Tobacco Underground," http://www.publicintegrity.org/health/public-health/tobacco/tobacco-underground.

39. "Strategy to Combat Transnational Organized Crime," July 25, 2011, http://www.whitehouse.gov/administration/eop/nsc/transnational-crime/strategy.

40. Susan Rose-Ackerman published her seminal work on corruption titled *Corruption: A Study of Political Economy* (New York: Academic Press, 1978), and, as she explained to the author, she was denied tenure at Yale University because it was thought not to be an appropriate field of study.

41. Peter Andreas, "Transnational Crime and Economic Globalization," in *Transnational Organized Crime and International Security*, ed. M. Berdal and M. Serrano (Boulder, CO: Lynne Rienner, 2002), 37–52; James Mittelman and Robert Johnston, "The Globalization of Organized Crime, the Courtesan State, and the Corruption of Civil Society," *Global Governance* 5, no. 2 (1999): 103–26.

42. For a discussion of this, see Peter Andreas, *Smuggler Nation: How Illicit Trade Made America* (Oxford: Oxford University Press, 2013), 330–52.

43. Xavier Raufer, "New World Disorder, New Terrorisms: New Threats for Europe and the Western World," *Terrorism and Political Violence* 11, no. 4 (1999): 35.

44. UNODC, *2011 Global Study on Homicide*, http://www.unodc.org/unodc/en/data-and-analysis/statistics/crime/global-study-on-homicide-2011.html.

45. Thom Shanker, "Lessons of Iraq Help the US Fight a Drug War in Honduras," *New York Times*, May 5, 2012, http://www.nytimes.com/2012/05/06/world/americas/us-turns-its-focus-on-drug-smuggling-in-honduras.html?pagewanted=all.

46. Alain Chenciner, "Three Body Problem," *Scholarpedia*, http://www.scholarpedia.org/article/Three_body_problem#References.

47. U.S. State Department, "Foreign Terrorist Organizations," http://www.state.gov/j/ct/rls/other/des/123085.htm.

48. Walter Laqueur, *The New Terrorism: Fanaticism and the Arms of Mass Destruction* (Oxford: Oxford University Press, 1999).

49. FBI, http://www.fbi.gov/stats-services/publications/terrorism-2002–2005.
50. Laqueur, *New Terrorism,* 7.
51. John Horgan, *The Psychology of Terrorism* (London: Routledge, 2005), 19.
52. Laqueur, *New Terrorism,* 7.
53. Ivan Arreguin-Toft, *How the Weak Win Wars: A Theory of Asymmetric Conflict* (Cambridge: Cambridge University Press, 2005).
54. UNODC, *A Transnational Organized Crime Threat Assessment,* 2010, https://www.unodc.org/unodc/en/data-and-analysis/tocta-2010.html.
55. United Nations General Assembly, "Convention against Transnational Organized Crime," http://www.unodc.org/unodc/treaties/CTOC/index.html.
56. http://www.unglobalcompact.org/aboutthegc/thetenprinciples/principle10.html.
57. Janine R. Wedel, *Collision and Collusion: The Strange Case of Western Aid to Eastern Europe, 1989–1998* (New York: St. Martin's Press, 1998). The health official responsible for ensuring the health of his population may also have a pharmaceutical business to supply the state hospitals under his control.
58. Barry Hindess, "Introduction: How Should We Think about Corruption?," in *Corruption: Expanding the Focus,* ed. Manuhuia Barcham, Barry Hindess, and Peter Larmour (Canberra: Australian National University, 2012), 1.
59. Thomas J. Biersteker and Sue E. Eckert, eds., *Countering the Financing of Terrorism* (London: Routledge, 2008); Jeanne K. Giraldo and Harold A. Trinkunas, eds., *Terrorism Financing and State Responses: A Comparative Perspective* (Stanford, CA: Stanford University Press, 2007); and more popular works, such as Rachel Ehrenfeld, *Funding Evil, Updated: How Terrorism Is Financed and How to Stop It* (Chicago: Bonus Books, 2005), and Loretta Napoleoni, *Terror Incorporated: Tracing the Dollars behind the Terror Network* (New York: Seven Stories Press, 2005).
60. Stewart Patrick, *Weak States: Fragile States, Global Threats, and International Security* (Oxford: Oxford University Press, 2011); Mary Kaldor, *New and Old Wars: Organized Violence in a Global Era* (Palo Alto, CA: Stanford University Press, 2007); Moisés Naím, *Illicit: How Smugglers, Traffickers and Copycats Are Hijacking the Global Economy* (New York: Doubleday, 2005); Cláudia Costa Storti and Paul de Grauwe, *Illicit Trade and the Global Economy* (Cambridge, MA: MIT Press, 2012); Alain Bauer and Xavier Raufer, *The Dark Side of Globalization* (Paris: CNRS, 2009); David Bayley and Robert Perito, *The Police in War: Fighting Insurgency, Terrorism, and Violent Crime* (Boulder, CO: Lynne Rienner, 2010).
61. Joseph E. Stiglitz, *Globalization and Its Discontents* (New York: W. W. Norton, 2002); Strange, *Retreat of the State.*
62. Frank Vogl, *Waging War on Corruption: Inside the Movement Fighting the Abuse of Power* (Lanham, MD: Rowman and Littlefield, 2012); Laurence Cockcroft, *Global Corruption: Money, Power and Ethics in the Modern World* (Philadelphia: University of Pennsylvania Press, 2012).
63. Van Schendel and Abraham, *Illicit Flows and Criminal Things;* Nordstrom, *Global Outlaws;* R. Richard Friman and Peter Andreas, eds., *The Illicit Global Economy and State Power* (Lanham, MD: Rowman and Littlefield, 1999).
64. Peter Grabosky and Michael Stohl, *Crime and Terrorism (Compact Criminology)* (London: Sage, 2010).
65. Van Schendel and Abraham, *Illicit Flows and Criminal Things.*

66. Edwina A. Thompson, *Trust Is the Coin of the Realm Lessons from the Money Men in Afghanistan* (Karachi: Oxford University Press, 2011); R.T. Naylor, *Wages of Crime: Black Markets, Illegal Finance, and the Underworld Economy* (Ithaca, NY: Cornell University Press, 2002); Friman and Andreas, *Illicit Global Economy and State Power.*

67. Phil Williams and Roy Godson, "Anticipating Organized and Transnational Crime," *Crime, Law, and Social Change* 37 (2002): 311–55.

68. See such works as Bruce Hoffman's *Inside Terrorism,* rev ed. (New York: Columbia University Press, 2006); Laqueur, *New Terrorism*; and John Horgan, *Walking Away from Terrorism: Accounts of Disengagement from Radical and Extremist Movements* (London: Routledge 2009).

69. Laqueur, *New Terrorism,* 210–25; Leslie Holmes, ed., *Terrorism, Organised Crime and Corruption: Networks and Linkages* (Cheltenham, UK: Edward Edgar, 2007).

70. Representative examples of this include such collections as those of John Arquilla and David Ronfeldt, *Networks and Netwars: The Future of Terror, Crime and Militancy* (Santa Monica, CA: RAND, 2001), and James J. F. Forest, *The Making of a Terrorist Recruitment, Training and Root Causes,* 3 vols. (Westport, CT: Praeger Security International, 2006).

71. Gregory F. Treverton, Carl F. Matthies, Karla J. Cunningham, Jeremiah Goulka, Greg Ridgeway, and Anny Wong, *Film Piracy, Organized Crime and Terrorism* (Santa Monica, CA: RAND, 2009).

72. Phil Williams, *Criminals, Militia and Insurgences: Organized Crime in Iraq* (Carlisle, PA: Strategic Studies Institution, 2009); Gretchen Peters, *Seeds of Terror: How Drugs, Thugs, and Crime Are Reshaping the Afghan War* (New York: St. Martin's Press, 2009); Vanda Felbab-Brown, *Aspiration and Ambivalence: Strategies and Realities of Counterinsurgency and State-Building in Afghanistan* (Washington, DC: Brookings Institution Press, 2012); JuanCarlos Garzón, *Mafia & Co.: The Criminal Networks in Mexico, Brazil, and Colombia* (Bogotá: Editorial Planeta Colombiana, 2008).

73. For example, Matthew Levitt, *Hamas: Politics, Charity, and Terrorism in the Service of Jihad* (New Haven, CT: Yale University Press, 2006). On FARC, see Pécaut, *Les Farc*; Rohan Gunaratna, *Inside Al Qaeda* (New York: Columbia University Press, 2002); John Horgan and Max Taylor, "Playing the Green Card: Financing the Provisional IRA, Part 1," *Terrorism and Political Violence* 11, no. 2 (1999): 4–5.

74. Vanda Felbab-Brown, *Shooting Up Counterinsurgency and the War on Drugs* (Washington, DC: Brookings Institution Press, 2009); Rensselaer W. Lee III, *Smuggling Armageddon: The Nuclear Black Market in the Former Soviet Union and Europe* (New York: St. Martin's Press, 1998); and Kathryn Walker Tubb, ed., *Illicit Antiquities: The Theft of Culture and the Extinction of Archaeology* (New York: Routledge, 2002), are illustrative of this.

75. Thomas J. Biersteker and Sue E. Eckert, *Countering the Financing of Terrorism* (London: Routledge, 2008); Jeanne K. Giraldo and Harold A. Trinkunas, *Terrorism Financing and State Responses: A Comparative Perspective* (Stanford, CA: Stanford University Press, 2007).

76. Roy Godson, ed., *Menace to Society: Political Criminal Collaboration around the World* (New Brunswick, NJ: Transaction, 2003); Anthony Harriot, *Organized*

Crime and Politics in Jamaica: Breaking the Nexus (Kingston: Canoe Press, 2008).

77. Robert Rotberg, *Corruption, Global Security and World Order* (Washington, DC: Brookings Institution Press, 2009); Holmes, *Terrorism, Organised Crime and Corruption*.

78. H. Richard Friman, ed., *Crime and the Global Economy* (Boulder, CO: Lynne Rienner, 2009); Misha Glenny, *McMafia* (New York: Alfred A. Knopf, 2008); Jay Albanese, *Transnational Crime and the 21st Century* (New York: Oxford University Press, 2011); Jean-François Gayraud, *Le Monde des mafias Géopolitique du crime organisé* (Paris: Odile Jacob, 2008). For a general review of the literature, see Felia Allum and Stan Gilmour, eds., *Routledge Handbook of Transnational Organized Crime* (London: Routledge, 2012).

79. Tamara Makarenko, "The Crime-Terror Continuum: Tracing the Interplay between Transnational Organised Crime and Terrorism," *Global Crime* 6, no. 1 (2004): 129–45, and those of Alex Schmid, such as "The Links between Transnational Organized Crime and Terrorist Crimes," *Transnational Organized Crime* 2, no. 4 (1996): 40–48; John Rollins and Liana Wyler, *International Terrorism and Transnational Crime: Security Threats, U.S. Policy and Considerations for Congress* (Washington, DC: Library of Congress, 2010); Steven Hutchinson and Pat O'Malley, "A Crime-Terror Nexus? Thinking on Some of the Links between Terrorism and Criminality," *Studies in Conflict and Terrorism* 30, no. 12 (2007): 1095–107; Chris Dishman, "The Leaderless Nexus: When Crime and Terror Converge," *Studies in Conflict and Terrorism* 28, no. 3 (2008): 237–52; Ryan Clarke and Stuart Lee, "The PIRA, D-Company, and the Crime-Terror Nexus," *Terrorism and Political Violence* 20, no. 2 (2008): 376–39; Luciana Fernandez, "Organized Crime and Terrorism: From the Cells towards Political Communication, a Case Study," *Terrorism and Political Violence* 21, no. 4 (2008): 595–616; Max Manwaring, *Insurgency, Terrorism, and Crime: Shadows from the Past and Portents for the Future* (Norman: University of Oklahoma Press, 2008); Michael Kenney, *From Pablo to Osama: Trafficking and Terrorist Networks, Government Bureaucracies, and Competitive Adaptation* (University Park: Pennsylvania State University Press, 2007); Gary Scanlan, "The Enterprise of Crime and Terrorists – The Implication for Good Business," *Journal of Financial Crime* 13, no. 2 (2006): 164–76. See the special issue of *Terrorism and Political Violence* 24, no. 2 (2012), devoted to the intersections of crime and terror.

80. John Picarelli, "Osama bin Corleone? Vito the Jackal? Framing Threat Convergence through an Examination of Transnational Organized Crime and International Terrorism," *Terrorism and Political Violence* 24, no. 2 (2012): 180–98.

81. K.M. Smith, S.J. Anthony, W.M. Switzer, J.H. Epstein, T. Seimon, et al., "Zoonotic Viruses Associated with Illegally Imported Wildlife Products," *PLoS ONE* 7, no. 1 (2012): e29505. doi:10.1371/journal.pone.0029505.

82. Laurence Cockcroft, *Global Corruption: Money, Power and Ethics in the Modern World* (Philadelphia: University of Pennsylvania Press, 2012), 2.

83. Martin N. Murphy, *Boats, Weak States, Dirty Money: The Challenge of Piracy* (New York: Columbia University Press, 2008), 5.

84. Asif Efrat, *Governing Guns, Preventing Plunder: International Cooperation against Illicit Trade* (New York: Oxford University Press, 2012), 265; Project on U.S.

Middle East Nonproliferation Strategy, *US Non-proliferation Strategy for the Changing Middle East*, 2013, http://isis-online.org/uploads/isis-reports/documents/US_Nonproliferation_Strategy_for_the_Changing_Middle_East.pdf; Brian Michael Jenkins, *Will Terrorists Go Nuclear?* (New York: Prometheus Books, 2008); Matthew Bunn, "Securing the Bomb 2010: Securing All Nuclear Materials in Four Years," http://www.nti.org/analysis/reports/securing-bomb-2010.

85. See, e.g., John T. Picarelli, "The Turbulent Nexus of Transnational Organised Crime and Terrorism: A Theory of Malevolent International Relations," *Global Crime* 7, no. 1 (2006): 1–24.

PART I

THE LOGIC OF CORRUPTION, CRIME, AND TERRORISM

Crime and Corruption behind the Mass Attacks

Terrorist attacks over the last two decades have been characterized by increasing violence, with ever larger numbers of victims and less specific human targets. Some of these attacks were directed and funded from overseas as the terrorists exploited the globalized world. This has been called the "new terrorism."[1] Since the turn of the millennium, the most fatal attacks have been distributed across the globe. Many, but not all, have links to jihadi movements. September 11 was the most dramatic and the most fatal, but unfortunately, it was only one of a group of increasingly lethal attacks.[2] These most deadly acts of terrorism have certain important shared characteristics – *all were facilitated and/or financed by crime and corruption.*[3] All the attacks, except the urban violence in São Paulo, Brazil, have international components, including money, personnel, or inspiration. The lethality of some of these attacks is explained, as in Brazil and Russia, by the deadly response of state security officials.

This chapter shows how crime and corruption played a critical role in every major terror attack of the last decade. From drug trafficking to credit card fraud, terror groups have exploited black markets to advance their causes, blurring the line between criminal and political activity. They chose their points of attack to maximize economic harm and have greater political resonance.

It is hardly surprising that the most deadly attacks of the 2000s occurred in countries that now belong to the G-20. Three of the six attacks discussed in this chapter occurred in the so-called BRIC (Brazil, Russia, India, and China) countries, the fastest-growing economies.[4] Four of the six attacks occurred in major urban and economic centers, such as New York, Madrid, São Paulo, and Mumbai, indicating that cities may face the brunt of large-scale terrorism.[5] In other words, terrorists chose to attack global economic centers, seeking to harm the global economy as much as they sought to kill, maim, and cause destruction.

The presence of these particularly lethal attacks in the largest economies belies the centrality of weak states to mass terrorism.[6] Moreover, terrorist attacks occurring in these rapidly changing economies, with increasing economic polarization, suggests that crime and terrorism may be symptomatic of painful transitions and larger systemic problems.

This chapter examines chronologically the crime and corruption that facilitated the 9/11 attacks in New York and Washington, DC, Bali (Indonesia), Madrid (Spain), Beslan (Russia), São Paulo (Brazil), and the Mumbai train (India) in 2006 and Mumbai in 2008.[7] All of these attacks, except the attack in Brazil, are clearly classified as acts of terrorism. Brazil represents a new entanglement of crime, corruption, and terrorism; however, all of the three elements played a significant role in the deadly event. In São Paulo, unprecedented levels of coordinated urban violence by a crime group closed down a megacity and struck terror among the urban population.

The mass terrorist attacks committed between 2001 and 2008 were facilitated or inspired by corruption. The problems of corruption were not confined to developing or emerging economies. Domestic corruption in the United States and Spain also contributed to the mass attacks that occurred on their soil.

September 11, 2001, New York and Washington, DC

The attacks of September 11 on the World Trade Center and the Pentagon, like the attacks in Beslan and Madrid, have been extensively documented by the media and by governmental commissions. The adage that the world has changed since September 11 certainly holds true, as everywhere people know of the attacks on these symbols of American military and commercial power – the Pentagon just outside the U.S. capital of Washington, DC, and the World Trade Center in downtown Manhattan, New York, the commercial center of the United States and the nation's most populous city. These attacks, combined with the downing of another aircraft before it reached its target in Washington, DC, resulted in the greatest number of deaths of any terrorist attack. All told, 3,031 people died,[8] either in the airplane crashes or by being burned alive, being buried in the collapsed Trade Center towers, or jumping to their deaths. With such extensive postmortem accounts of 9/11 worldwide, it would seem that there is not much new that this chapter could add to the analysis. Yet, curiously, almost nowhere is there a discussion of the crime and corruption that facilitated the terrorist attack by the nineteen hijackers.[9]

The 9/11 Commission hardly mentions the problem of crime or criminals in reference to the attack. The problem of crime only emerges in the discussion of the criminal activities of Ahmed Ressam, the man who planned to bomb the Los Angeles airport on New Year's Eve of 2000.[10] Ressam's planned attack was seen as an antecedent to 9/11; his activities were supported by a very extensive crime-terrorist network traced back to terrorist training camps in Pakistan.[11] The 9/11 Commission discusses Ressam as a precursor threat rather than applying the analysis of his criminal support structure to the 9/11 attackers.

Ressam belonged to the Roubaix group in France, near the city of Lille, that supported itself through a range of petty crimes. Ressam, according to the 9/11 Commission, moved to Canada in 1994 using a photo-substituted passport under a false name. He continued to survive through criminal activity, such as credit card theft and petty crime, for more than two years and was not deported despite four arrests.[12] Identified by an imam of the mosque in Montreal as a possible candidate for global *jihad*, he trained in Afghanistan. Ressam also fought in Bosnia in a Mujahedin brigade and received a fake Bosnian passport from an expert forger with whom he had fought in the Balkans.[13] The warning signs concerning Ressam were present for years before the millennium. The Canadian authorities did not intervene, despite warnings from a noted French counterterrorism investigator.[14] The French also directly warned the Clinton administration of the threat Ressam posed but were ignored, and only an astute custom official prevented his entry into the United States.[15]

Despite such indicators of a link between crime and terrorism, there is no mention by the 9/11 Commission of any crimes having been committed by the 9/11 hijackers. The hijackers, as analyses have shown, came from a very different social background than did Ressam. Most of the hijackers were highly educated, and many came from elite families.[16] Therefore, unless they contracted with petty criminals, they would not be linked with small-scale crime. But Mohammed Atta, the mastermind of the 9/11 attacks, has been linked to crimes that are more consistent with his high social status.

In 1999, Mohammed Atta attempted to raise money by selling stolen antiquities from Afghanistan. This is an example of an illicit trade that continues today and is discussed more in Chapter 7. The German secret services learned of this attempt from a German professor whom Atta approached about the antiquities sale. The professor at the University of Gottingen, who declined the offer, asked Atta what he planned to do with the money obtained from the sale. He reported that he needed the money to pay for flying lessons in the United States.[17]

There are also indications that several of the 9/11 hijackers went to casinos in Las Vegas in the months preceding the attack. Mohammed Atta visited on June 28, one of two trips to the U.S. gambling mecca, two months before the attack. Subsequently, on August 10, just three weeks before the attack, Hani Hanjour and Nawaf Alhazmi, two of the hijackers, flew on first-class tickets from Washington to Los Angeles and then on to Las Vegas.[18] Analyses of al-Qaeda funding have shown that operatives are careful about their expenditures and do not spend needlessly to achieve their objectives.[19] Therefore it is highly unlikely that several of the hijackers would pass through Las Vegas at great expense at a critical period before the attack simply to amuse themselves. The hijackers' presence in Las Vegas was investigated by the FBI, but their activities and the reasons for their visit were never clearly defined. However, casinos are used both to launder money and to dispose of counterfeit notes, another staple of al-Qaeda financing.[20] In the following year, an al-Qaeda cell detected in upstate New York had used casinos to launder its money.[21]

The 9/11 hijackers were aided by criminal facilitators. A phony language school in Los Angeles provided false documents to the perpetrators of the September 11 attacks as well as to a human-trafficking ring of high-end prostitutes from the former Soviet Union. Police detectives from the Los Angeles vice squad investigating a significant human-trafficking case that they titled the "White Lace Case" soon found themselves working closely with federal agents. The head of the trafficking ring that brought women to the United States, ostensibly as part of either sporting or religious delegations, needed visas to prolong the women's stay in the United States.[22] She turned to a language school that provided visas for payment of "tuition" without requiring that the women attend class. This same language school turned out to be a visa mill that had also served the hijackers, providing two of them with the visas they needed to stay in the United States.[23]

Investigators in the counterterrorism branch of the Los Angeles Police Department (LAPD) suspect that the visas were not the only form of criminal facilitation provided to the 9/11 hijackers in their community. Some investigators found indications that the hijackers used some of the same channels to move their money as the Latin American drug traffickers they watched. Yet this was never followed up in investigations of 9/11 because the criminal facilitators of terrorist funding were not a priority of the 9/11 Commission.[24]

The criminal traces of the 9/11 hijackers were also present on the East Coast. Two of the hijackers obtained the driver's licenses that they used to board the aircraft through a crime ring that served illegal immigrants in northern Virginia.[25] This crime ring, operating through a corrupt branch of Virginia's Division of Motor Vehicles (DMV), was already known to the Immigration and Naturalization Service (INS) investigators in the late 1990s, when vans of illegal immigrants pulled up at the DMV and, following the payment of bribes by their smugglers, unlawfully obtained driver's licenses that they could use as identity cards. But nothing was done to stem this document fraud by the overburdened INS because it was a low-priority crime. One of the INS investigators explained to the author before 9/11, "We cannot touch this document fraud as we do not have enough personnel to deal with the illegal immigrants exiting prison with convictions for homicide."[26] Yet it was through this corruption that the hijackers were able to carry out their attacks.

This example is illustrative of other points made in this book. First, corruption is a central component of the *deadly triad* of crime, corruption, and terrorism. Second, suppressing seemingly petty crime is crucial to the prevention of both crime and terror, a point that was often made by former mayor Rudolph Giuliani in New York.[27]

The attacks of 9/11 were facilitated by crime. But there is no indication that the criminal facilitators or the corrupt individuals in the DMV knew that they were cooperating with terrorists. Terrorists exploit existing illicit networks. This is different from the Indian case, discussed subsequently, where there was deliberate collaboration of criminals and terrorists.

But what of the financing behind 9/11? Was it funded by illicit activity? According to Rohan Gunaratna, "Al Qaeda has built the most complex, robust and resilient money-generating money-moving network yet seen."[28] Much funding came from donations and legitimate business investments made by al-Qaeda and its supporters.[29] "The Dubai-based Indian criminal Aftab Ansari is believed to have used ransom money he earned from kidnappings to help fund the Sept 11, 2001, terrorist attacks."[30] As Chapter 5 discusses, money that the Saudi royal family thought they were donating to charity through a Riggs Bank account in the United States was siphoned off and used to support the 9/11 hijackers.[31] Yet did money come from crime to fund the acts?

The 9/11 Commission on terrorist financing examined the role that diamonds played in funding al-Qaeda but accepted the view of the Central Intelligence Agency (CIA) and the FBI that al-Qaeda did not rely on illicit or "blood" diamonds for their support. The Commission report suggests that some al-Qaeda operatives may have benefited from this trade, but as Doug Farah, who covered West Africa for the *Washington Post* and had extensive contacts within the Arab community, wrote, "while the monograph is an important document, it is far from a complete map of terrorist financial structures and methods. Its primary methodology, borne out by the footnotes in the document, was to ask the intelligence community to provide any information it had on a specific topic."[32] But as Farah explains, these agencies' analyses of terrorist funding were limited, and particularly so in Africa. Prior to 9/11, they had no agents on the ground in Sierra Leone or Liberia, the epicenter of the illicit diamond trade. Moreover, the CIA's ALEC station, which tracked Osama Bin Laden, followed everything but his finances. Farah concludes that the 9/11 Commission reached an incomplete analysis as a result of an overreliance on classified information.[33]

A Rand study that sent an analyst to Africa concluded that diamonds assumed a more important role than acknowledged by the 9/11 Commission. Al-Qaeda did not use diamonds to generate revenue but instead as a means of transferring and laundering funds.[34] But Global Witness, a highly respected nongovernmental organization that had people on the ground in West Africa in this period, concluded that part of the al-Qaeda network had an important role in the diamond trade,[35] a network that was also linked to the Bali bombings.

October 2002, Bali

In October 2002, three coordinated bomb attacks were executed in Bali. The most fatal was at the resort of Kuta; the attackers were less successful in causing damage at the U.S. Consulate in Denpasar.[36] The American target was part of a strategy to show the anti-Western objectives of the terrorists.[37] Ten months in the planning, the resort attack killed 88 Australians, 38 Indonesians, and 7 Americans among the 202 victims. The victims died in two attacks. The first deadly attack was by a suicide bomber who blew himself up on the floor of a tourist bar dance floor. Before the victims could run away, a second, more powerful bomb went off as a Mitsubishi van filled with explosives was detonated nearby, turning the area into a massive conflagration in which many were trapped. The attackers were part of the Southeast Asian network of Jemaah Islamiah (JI), a radical terrorist organization that has as its goal the creation of an Islamic state in Southeast Asia. But JI had a direct relationship with Osama Bin Laden, and this attack represented "solidarity with al-Qaeda's cause."[38] There was evidence of contact between al-Qaeda's leader and the mastermind of the Bali attack. The Bali attack, like 9/11, and unlike subsequent attacks discussed in this chapter, received direct support from the headquarters of al-Qaeda. Its mastermind, Hambali, arrested in Thailand in 2003, was allegedly the Southeast Asian contact for Osama Bin Laden.[39]

The locale chosen for the attack was significant. Indonesia, a densely populated country, is home to the largest Moslem population in the world. Yet there are Christian and Hindu minorities in the diverse regions of Indonesia. Therefore, the attackers chose to target Bali, where the vast majority of Indonesia's small Hindu population lives and which is viewed as a playground for Western decadence. Contributing to the locale selection was a decision made not to cause personal or financial harm to fellow Moslems. Yet the costs to Bali were so severe that this target backfired on the perpetrators.[40]

The terrorist perpetrators sought criminals to help facilitate the financing of the Bali attack. According to specialists, there is a long tradition that predates JI of "Fa'I," or using money from crime to support religious causes.[41] Therefore, it is not unusual that criminals and crime provided some of the money needed for the 2002 Bali attack. Mukhlas, who headed one of the units of JI and was tried and convicted for organizing the Bali bombing, wrote that joining the *jihad* "was always seen as a good way for sinners to repent, and thus criminals were actively courted."[42]

The attack on the resort was part of an overall strategy to move away from hard targets, such as embassies, and focus on soft targets, such as bars and nightclubs. It also aligned with a strategy of Islamic terrorists to strike at or exploit symbols of Western decadence. Terrorists decided to hit Paddy's Bar, where people would be drinking and dancing. Drinking and immodest dress are both *haram* (forbidden) under Islamic law and are repugnant to many Moslems. The rationale for the attack, according to ringleader Samudra's confession was that "Muslims understand that . . . whether they agree or not . . . there are a handful of [us] who feel called to revenge the barbarity of the Coalition Army of the Cross and its allies,"[43] meaning the United States, Australia, and other Western countries. On a more immediate level, the attack reflected the hostility the attackers felt toward the white tourists and pub owners who posted restrictive signs at their clubs. For example, the Sari Club, a target of the

2002 attack, had posted at its front door "Indonesians not allowed." The only Indonesians allowed into these clubs along with the tourists were the gigolos, who exploited Australian and other Western women.[44]

The attack was originally planned for September 11, but the bombs were not ready, and the attack had to occur in the subsequent month. The terrorists assembled the funds and the bombs and drove the explosives to the site. At least one was on a suicide mission, as he came to the attack site with a bomb attached to his vest.

The selection of the targeted bars was not random but was motivated by the financial logic of terrorism. Paddy's Bar and the Sari Club were not affiliated with Javanese organized crime. The gigolos in the other nightclubs in the Kuta region were Javanese, as was the JI group responsible for the attack. Javanese gangs operating in the bars not only sell sexual services but rob customers, generating significant revenue for the criminal groups.[45] Therefore, the terrorists, who themselves used crime to survive, struck only at the bars that were financial competitors of the Javanese crime groups. The logic of crime and terrorism, however, helped unmask the perpetrators.[46]

The investigations revealed that many more people were behind the attack on Paddy's Bar than the limited number who handled the explosives. The Indonesians, with investigative assistance from the Australians and the Americans, arrested eighty members of JI, and thirty-three were convicted.[47] Forensic examination of the terrorists' computers by the international investigation provided much insight into the perpetrators' international ties and their funding mechanisms.

The devastating attack had far-reaching economic effects, as it crippled the Indonesian tourism industry. The estimated cost of the attack was thirty-five thousand dollars, but the consequences were disproportionate. Most of the funding for the attack appears to have been supplied by the al-Qaeda network, yet crime also played its role. JI, the group behind the attack, also funded itself through petty crime and trade in natural resources such as gems and gold.[48] This illustrates the role of transnational illicit and licit trade in terrorist financing.[49]

Samudra, one of the key figures in the attack, robbed the Elita Gold store in Bali, obtaining about $2,000 that was used to fund the travel, vehicles, chemicals, and explosives used in the attack.[50] The money was deposited, along with the al-Qaeda-supplied funds, into the account of a teacher with modest earnings, a clear case of money laundering. Samudra wanted to fund the attack through credit card fraud, but it was not determined whether this more advanced form of funding was used in the Bali attack.[51]

Whether or not Samudra used credit card fraud for the first attack, he raised money for a subsequent terrorist attack via computer from his prison cell while awaiting execution by firing squad. Because of lax conditions and corruption in Indonesian prisons, he was able to use the Internet to reach out to terrorist supporters, advising them on how to raise funds for their activities. Samudra obtained the laptop for his nefarious activities after it was smuggled in by Mr. Setyadii, an information technology lecturer. Corruption facilitated this Internet activity. Therefore, the deadly trio of crime, terrorism, and corruption is evident in Indonesian terrorism.[52]

Yet Samudra went beyond teaching his fellow extremists the art of credit card fraud through chat rooms on the Internet.[53] After his arrest, he wrote his memoirs in his cell. One chapter, titled "Hacking Why Not?," justified cyber-attacks on U.S. computers in the name of holy war. Through his writings, he taught aspiring hackers how to enter American computer networks to commit credit card fraud and money laundering.[54] Although Samudra was at the fore-front of instruction in this area, others were involved in fund-raising through the Internet. One member of JI, Ba'asyir, was repeatedly asked whether it was immoral to engage in computer hacking. Justifying online fraud, Ba'asyir replied, "You can take their blood, then why not take their property."[55] This is an example of the dual-use crime that is discussed more in Chapter 5.

March 11, 2004, Madrid

The coordinated attacks of ten bombs set off on the Madrid subway during morning rush hour on March 11, 2004, exactly two and a half years after the 9/11 attacks in the United States, reflected a highly symbolic selection of date as well as one that could have massive internal political impact because of imminent national elections in Spain. This was the largest terrorist attack by an Islamic group in Western Europe and left 191 dead and more than 1,500 injured, many very seriously. The terrorists maximized victimization by timing the attack for rush hour on commuter trains. Those killed were of diverse nationalities, just as in 9/11, reflecting contemporary life in a cosmopolitan city.

Just as September 11 was segmented among New York, Pennsylvania, and Washington, DC, the Spanish terrorism was not intended to be an isolated attack. On April 2, additional bombs were found on train tracks, 70 kilometers south of Madrid. A police raid followed, leading to the home of one of the suspected terrorists. Those in the apartment blew themselves up during the raid, thereby destroying key evidence of the attack.[56]

The March 11 attack, although shocking to the ill-prepared Spaniards, was not without warning. After Spanish entry into the war in Iraq, al-Qaeda warned of an attack on Spain, a warning that was reiterated in February 2003. More-over, a suicide bombing in Casablanca, Morocco, in 2003 left forty-five vic-tims dead, including four Spaniards. This attack revealed the potency of North African–based Islamic terrorism and the threat it posed to Spanish lives. Despite this, as the Spanish government investigation revealed, a mere sixty people were assigned to counter nondomestic terrorism, particularly terrorism associ-ated with al-Qaeda and its associates. The national counterterrorism priority remained the Basque Homeland and Freedom group (Euskadi Ta Askatasuna, or ETA), comprising Basque terrorists.[57]

The North African men recruited for the completed and the planned attack shared many of the characteristics of those disillusioned and frustrated men who are affiliated with crime and terrorism in many regions around the world.[58] They are particularly symptomatic of the problems of the North African region, as discussed more fully later, where frustrated young men living in highly corrupt societies are denied legitimate opportunities for employment and advancement. They are vulnerable to recruitment by criminals and terrorists. In the Madrid bombing, the participants were recruited for both forms of illicit behavior.

The suicide of key perpetrators prevented the full revelation of the criminal-terrorist network. But a sophisticated international investigation revealed much of the lives of the personnel and the facilitating crimes that preceded the attack.[59] The attackers acted without personnel directly linked to al-Qaeda's base in Pakistan and Afghanistan. The Spanish cell was, however, inspired by the warnings of al-Qaeda to the Spanish government. This is indicative of the capacity of al-Qaeda to inspire terrorism in Europe, as was seen again in 2012 with the terrorist Mohammed Merah in Toulouse.[60]

Most of the perpetrators were Moroccan. The attacks on Spain can also be seen as part of a long struggle to regain the former Moslem lands of al-Andalus, southern Spain, from which the Moslems were driven by King Ferdinand and Queen Isabella I in 1492.[61] The historical antecedents to contemporary terrorism are crucial, particularly in the ideology of AQIM.[62]

The Spanish commission that investigated the Madrid bombings, like the 9/11 Commission, found many previous missteps by the government. As in the United States, an absence of coordination by diverse government bodies and the failure to share intelligence collected from informants ensured that the terrorist act was not prevented. As in the Ressam case, there were also warnings from the French authorities that were ignored. French security had been following part of the network.[63]

Both the Spanish and American national commissions reveal serious failures in government intelligence sharing and coordination that might have prevented the attacks. But unlike the 9/11 Commission report, the Spanish report contains ample discussion of the crimes that funded and facilitated the attack. The reason is clear: crime and criminals were central to the Madrid attack.

Those behind the Madrid subway bombing had to generate their own funds. The Madrid cell received initial funding from al-Qaeda, but this provided only start-up costs and was not sufficient to fund an attack.[64] Instead, it had to develop its own criminal capabilities by using the drug profits of the ringleader, Jamal Ahmidan.[65]

The attack is estimated to have cost between €41,000 and €50,000.[66] Two weeks before the Madrid bombings, on February 29, Ahmidan, a key figure in the attack, and two of his fellow terrorists went to Seville to secure explosives. They used a stolen Toyota for the pickup. When they were stopped for speeding, Ahmidan could provide neither the car's documents nor the insurance papers and presented his false passport. Despite the irregularities, the police officer let him go with a €300 fine. This event, less than two weeks before the attack, reveals multiple forms of criminal activity: false documents, illicit trade in explosives, and a stolen vehicle. The failure of Spanish law enforcement to police petty crime facilitated the subsequent terrorist act.

The Madrid terrorists tried previously to purchase illicit explosives. According to information in the Spanish system, one of the plotters, while serving as an informant for the Civil Guard,[67] had provided information the previous year to this agency that two men had tried to secure Goma explosives (a powerful explosive used in Spanish mines). The explosives were not cheap – the cost at that time of two and a half kilos was 1 million pesetas – and the intended purchasers, according to the informant, were significant drug dealers and preferred to exchange cocaine for the explosives rather than paying cash. The intended purchasers were introducing fifty to one hundred kilos of hashish into the province of Asturias every ten days and had a distribution network of youths established to move the drugs.[68]

Despite the information provided to the Guardia Civil by the informant, no official had focused on the illicit trade in explosives. Moreover, in the year preceding the attack, eight hundred kilos of explosives had disappeared from the stock of the Conchita Mine, the alleged source of the two hundred kilos used in the Madrid attacks.

Rafa Zouhier, who became a central node in the attack, entered prison in September 2001, where he made the acquaintance of Antonio Toro Castro, who was a friend of Emilio Trashorras. Trashorras and Toro Castro had been detained in June 2001 for drug trafficking in Operación Pipol. The relationship of the three was strengthened when Zouhier was released from prison.[69] Zouhier was an informant for the Guardia Civil. He even gave information on the activities of Toro and Trashorras but ceased to give information in March 2003, a year before the attack. Zouhier became the middleman between the Madrid cell and Trashorras, a former miner and the supplier of the dynamite. Prisons, as discussed more in Chapter 4, play a crucial role in the crime-terror connection.

Prison also played a key role in the radicalization of Ahmidan, the mastermind of the Madrid attacks. Prior to his incarceration in a Spanish prison in 1998, he had been a significant drug dealer selling hashish and ecstasy throughout Western Europe in the 1990s. "He first showed interest in extremist Islamic ideology while in Spanish prison and was completely radicalized while incarcerated in his native country of Morocco from 2000 to 2003."[70] Yet his drug activities continued despite his religious conversion. A raid on a safe house netted thousands of ecstasy tablets, one of the largest drug seizures in Spain until then.[71] Ahmidan is representative of a criminal metamorphosing into a terrorist but keeping his criminal past. His links and experience proved invaluable in acquiring the resources needed to execute a terrorist attack.

The sale or exchange of drugs paid for apartments, phones, transport, and the false documents that were an integral component of the plot. Individuals with criminal expertise were important facilitators, as indicated by Ahmidan's fraudulent passport, unrecognized by law enforcement, even a few weeks before the attack:

> The Madrid case demonstrates how the capabilities of potential terrorists can be greatly amplified when they are able to recruit criminals who possess technical expertise and connections to illicit material. The Madrid case also highlights the increased threat that decentralized cells may pose when cell members harness their criminal resources and capabilities. Moreover, the Madrid bombers' criminal activities may have helped them evade detection. Their established involvement in the drug trade possibly obscured their terrorist motivations and potentially prevented authorities from further investigating their ultimate aims.[72]

September 2004, Beslan

On the first day of school in September 2004, when parents accompany their children, Chechen-based terrorists attacked a primary school in the neighboring region of North Ossetia in the volatile North Caucasus. The school in Beslan, a locale once used as a base for attacks by the Soviet armed forces on the breakaway region of Chechnya, was chosen as an important symbolic target by the terrorists.

That morning of September 1, more than fifteen hundred people gathered for the first day of school. Even though the assembled group of parents and students far outnumbered the attackers, the terrorists were able to force more than eleven hundred of the assembled into the gymnasium because of the shock and the aggressiveness of their methods. The victims were subjected to physical and psychological abuse. There they were forced to sit, each occupying no more than thirty square centimeters. In this stuffy space, in the hot days of early September, the hostages were allowed no water and no food and were not allowed to go to the bathroom. As some commented, "If there is a hell, that was it." Most lived like this until explosives were detonated on the third day, after fifty-two hours of captivity.[73] According to official reports, there were 777 child hostages and approximately 250 adults held by at least 32 terrorists.[74] At the end of the bloody siege, one of the deadliest attacks on record, at least 331 hostages died, including 186 children, and almost 800 were injured.[75] Many of the hundreds of injured lost limbs or eyes and suffered gunshot wounds.

The man behind the attack was the Chechen leader Shamil Basayev. He assumed leadership and an increasingly active role in Chechen resistance to Russian rule as more moderate Chechen leaders were killed by Russian authorities. Basayev was himself killed by governmental forces in 2006.[76]

The attackers, heavily armed men and women, arrived with explosive belts. Victims were also shot with automatic rifles brought to the site by the terrorists. The Chechen terrorists placed mines in the gym and the rest of the school and deployed improvised explosive devices. Yet unlike the sudden deaths at the hands of terrorists in Bali and Madrid, the terrorist attack endured several days. The terrorists repeatedly took drugs to increase their endurance and to stay alert for the days of the attack.

The attacks were so lethal not only because the terrorists were heavily armed but also because the special forces deployed by the state lacked an effective counterterrorism strategy. They applied brute force rather than negotiating with the terrorists because of President Putin's policy on nonnegotiation with terrorists. Therefore, there were few released children or parents. The traumatized children suffered enormously until their deaths. Damage to the school and the facilities also resulted from the use of heavy equipment, including tanks, rockets, and numerous weapons, by the Russian security forces. Therefore, the deaths, unlike in the previous cases, were not solely a result of terrorist action but resulted from an overwhelming show of force by ill-prepared Russian security personnel.

The attackers were mostly from the Moslem regions in the North Caucasus, in close proximity to Chechnya.[77] The attackers were predominantly male, but there were a few female participants. This stands in sharp contrast to the other terrorist cases discussed here but is not inconsistent with the history of suicide bombers in Chechnya. Chechen suicide bombers are often widows or family members of killed militants, who, in the Chechen tradition, seek revenge for their loved ones.[78] Several of the terrorists were non-Chechens, reflecting the Moslem radicalization of sectors of the North Caucasian population by the protracted war, the brutality of the Russian army in the Chechen conflict, and the difficult situation of native populations of the North Caucasus.[79] Although foreign jihadists had previously come to support the Chechens, none were apparently present in the attack.

The Chechen conflict can be characterized as more nationalistic rather than jihadist. In the years leading up to the attack, Islamic fighters from the Middle East trained and spent time in Chechnya. In turn, Chechens traveled to the Balkans, Pakistan, and Afghanistan to train and to fight because of their links with global *jihad*.[80] The background of the attackers in Beslan will never be fully known because the Russian investigators could never determine the total number of attackers and their facilitators, but experienced terrorists were present in the North Caucasus.

The rationale for the attacks was the desire by Chechen rebels to have Russian authorities acknowledge the Chechen Republic of Ikeria. Chechens had a long history of grievances against Russian rule in the tsarist period and suffered even more devastating treatment in the Soviet period under Stalin. Chechens were deported en masse by Stalin from their traditional homelands to Central Asia in the 1930s. Many died en route to their places of exile. Returning to their traditional homelands in the 1950s only after Stalin's death, they were provided no compensation for their losses and no support for their resettlement.[81] Many Chechens, unable to reestablish themselves in their home communities, turned to criminal activity even in the Soviet era. Crime became a vehicle of choice to amass capital. In the Soviet period, especially the last years, when controls were lax, Chechens controlled hotels in Moscow, smuggled oil, stole cars, traded in contraband, and kidnapped people.[82]

Russian criminals were among the major beneficiaries of the globalized economy and moved rapidly and aggressively to expand their operations internationally. The Chechen criminals who were closely associated with Russian organized crime also expanded their operations globally.[83] They benefited from the two-hundred-thousand-person diaspora in Western Europe and elsewhere, as many members of their community received political asylum.[84]

With the breakup of the Soviet Union, Chechens sought autonomy from Russia. Their ability to buy weaponry was facilitated by their heavy involvement in crime during the final years of the Soviet period and the post-Soviet transition.[85] The first war for independence began in December 1994, and Russian leaders justified their violent assault against Chechnya because of their high level of criminality. One of the Russian generals who led the assault on Chechnya was General Anatoly Kulikov, who subsequently acknowledged this as a mistake.[86] After an uneasy peace, a second protracted Chechen war began in 1999, of which Beslan was among its most tragic auxiliary attacks.

Support for training, arms, and sustenance for the Chechens and their family members did not come cheaply. Donations from mosques in England and from Arab states provided money to sustain the Chechen cause.[87] In the late 1990s, Gulf banks provided funds to finance operations in Chechnya. But after it was discovered that the Chechen leadership was using significant amounts of these funds to maintain a lavish personal lifestyle, Osama Bin Laden himself ordered an investigation and dramatically reduced support.[88] Consequently, after reduced funding from the al-Qaeda network, Chechens increasingly relied on organized crime to fund their activities – drug trade, human trafficking, and extortion.[89]

From the mid-1990s, Basayev employed a global network to generate funds through illicit activity, setting up funding cells in Western Europe and in Los Angeles in the United States. This long-term and strategic planning by Basayev allowed him to sustain his movement and fund such actions as the Beslan attack. A 2006 Los Angeles–based cell, discussed in Chapter 5, generated significant revenues by combining the crime capabilities of Armenian criminals with the ambitions of Basayev's emissary.[90]

The Russian investigation of the Beslan attack was limited in its scope and was not as independent an inquiry as the 9/11 Commission or the Spanish investigations after March 11. The role of crime and corruption was given short shrift in the Russian parliamentary investigation as well as in Western reportage. The reasons for this are several – the crime-terror nexus was not much studied at that time. Crime and corruption in Russia only occur with the complicity of Russian officials, a harsh reality that many chose not to recognize. Third, terrorist funding is international, but Russian investigators of Beslan did not look abroad, nor did they seek the assistance of foreign colleagues.[91] Without a global perspective, the Russian investigators could not comprehend the support mechanisms for terrorism. Criminality was as central to this attack as it was to the attack in Madrid, but this has been much less acknowledged.

Corruption also played a key role in enabling this attack. Unlike many cases discussed in this chapter, where corruption enabled attack planning and facilitation, the Chechen situation reveals a more complex relationship with corruption. The transport of the equipment to the Beslan site was facilitated by corruption of Russian authorities, but the corruption of the Chechen leadership, as previously mentioned, had proven an impediment to external funding for their cause.

The Beslan attackers arrived in a police van and military trucks. They may have hijacked the vehicles or they may have had military or police collabora- tors. The Russian prosecutor general acknowledged after the attack that secu- rity officials colluded with criminal gangs. The attackers had traveled some distance to launch the attack, having traversed numerous checkpoints. Russian investigations revealed that police at some checkpoints had been bribed. The fatal consequences of the endemic corruption have made Russian authorities unwilling to conduct full investigations of the attacks or to acknowledge the complicity of state officials in the deaths of Russian citizens.

Citizens also believed in the large role of corruption in the insurgency.[92] Fifty percent of Russian citizens surveyed by one of Russia's most respected polling firms in the month of September 2004 indicated that they thought that the terrorists were able to function largely because of corrupt officials. Black arms markets in the region are stocked, in part, by weapons acquired from corrupt officials. Aid destined to relieve the suffering of Chechens displaced by years of war never reached them, as government officials in Moscow and in the Caucasus, according to President Putin's advisor on Chechnya, siphoned off 80 percent of the aid from the central government.[93]

May 11–14, 2006, São Paulo

Brazil, with its long history of military and authoritarian rule, has had a tra- dition of abuse of rights, not just of political opponents but also of the urban poor. In the 1980s, human rights activists documented the significant killings and disappearances of slum dwellers attributed to police and military officials.[94] In response to abuse by the state, prisoners formed the Primeiro Comando da Capital (First Command of the Capital), or PCC, an antiestablishment Brazil- ian prison gang and criminal organization that has committed many crimes and terrorist acts since established by inmates in a prison in 1993.[95] It vio- lently controls its territory and has many criminal sources of income beyond the drug trade, including kidnapping, extortion, human trafficking, and the arms trade. This organization is not just a criminal gang but has an explicit political agenda. Its membership, estimated at 65,000 to 125,000 full and part time,[96] have learned the organizing methods of the left-wing revolutionaries with whom they were incarcerated during the years of military rule.[97] Since its founding, its professed goal has been to fight oppression within the São Paulo penitentiary system and to use its attacks to demoralize the government.

The urban poor provide a constant supply of inmates for Brazil's penal institutions, where they are guarded by low-paid jailors who can easily be corrupted. The prison staff survives on money obtained from the criminal gangs they "guard."

Despite being the economic powerhouse of South America, Brazil is a highly socially stratified society with enormous inequality. Millions of its poor live in shantytowns, or *favelas,* without the benefit of social services. Levels of urban violence are very high in its two major urban areas, particularly Rio de Janeiro and São Paulo.[98] Its abandoned street children, immortalized in such movies as *Pixote,* live in the slums of major cities, where they are often exploited by the criminal gangs. Prior to the government of President Lula, these children were often shot by the police. This brutal existence is the breeding ground of the criminal groups that are an alternative political power in the *favelas* in the absence of the state.[99]

This culture produced the head of the PCC, Marcos Willians Herbas Camacho, known by his nickname "Marcola." The PCC is responsible for the terrorist attack on the city of São Paulo in May 2006 that shut down the financial center of Brazil for three days.[100]

Marcola's testimony to the Parliamentary Inquiry Commission (CPI) of the House of Representatives, June 8, 2006, shortly after the attack, reveals an awful youth:

> He simplifies everything when he sums up – *"I came from misery."* He's been an orphan since he was nine years old and was raised at Praça da Sé, in São Paulo. When he was a child, he took his bath and slept leaning in one of the Cathedral's walls. His mother drowned to death. He can't remember his father. He has two sisters and his brother was killed. His daughter is just over seven years old. His wife was murdered, but he charges no one for that crime. His body has stabbing scars...He's convinced that those who are tied to violence tend to be killed by it.[101]

As discussed in Chapter 5, his criminal acts were the ones traditionally associated with the funding of terrorism – bank robberies and kidnapping. He had grown from a petty criminal into a major bank robber.[102] Imprisoned since 1999, he educated himself in prison reading Nietzsche, Victor Hugo, Saint Augustine, Voltaire, and the Bible.[103]

Prior to the attack on São Paulo, there was a significant worsening in the mechanisms of social control applied to the poor and the imprisoned. In the early 2000s, there was a rise of police killings of the poor and a 45 percent increase in the prison population in the already crowded prisons between 2003 and 2006.[104] Yet the immediate trigger for the attacks was a planned transfer of 765 gang members to maximum-security prisons.[105] The planned governmental transfer, including that of "Marcola" Willians Herbas Cama-cho, was intended to sever prisoners' ties to gang members outside prison. The date of the attack was moved up as PCC officials bribed a government official to obtain transcripts of the planned transfer.[106] Marcola launched the May attacks from prison, as intercepts on telephones on May 11 revealed. His orders were executed by members of the PCC at liberty. The financing for the attacks that started on May 12 came from the criminals' contribution to the PCC.

Other explanations for the attack are given as well. Just as the Madrid bombings occurred on the eve of crucial elections in Spain, the terrorist attack on the city of São Paulo also occurred within a highly politicized environment, five months before a crucial national election in which the popular President Lula, who enjoyed the sympathy of the people of the *favelas*, the poor urban slum dwellers who comprised the PCC, was up for reelection. President Lula was a break from the past of Brazilian politics whose previous leaders were from the elite. Born into an impoverished family in the north, Lula was raised by a poor mother in São Paulo. A former union activist, he did not forget his roots and developed programs to aid the poor and free enslaved workers.[107] Once Lula's challenger, Geraldo Alckmin, the governor of São Paulo, announced his campaign platform of law and order, citing his record of controlling crime and disorder, some experienced analysts of Brazilian politics anticipated violence, and they did not have long to wait.[108]

The politically sophisticated Marcola and the leadership of the PCC under-stood what the defeat of Lula would mean for the urban poor of such major cities as São Paulo and Rio de Janeiro. The discreditation of Alckmin was crucial. Therefore, this terrorist act could be understood, in part, as an effort by the criminal gangs to derail the political campaign of the opposition.[109] In those terms, it proved successful.

For other analysts, there were other political motivations: "The primary intent was to announce to the state and federal governments that the PCC and its allies in the *favelas* are strong enough to compel the negotiation of terms of state sovereignty vis-à-vis that organization."[110] This attack made Brazilian officials and the citizenry aware of the severe violence that can result from the failure to devote sufficient attention to the urban poor and the violent consequences of state repression.[111]

The PCC attacks, according to another analyst, represent an important turn-ing point in the relations of power-violence and criminality in Brazil. Behind its actions, the PCC has at least two typically terrorist objectives: strengthening the organization through intimidation and public awareness and demoralizing and debilitating the government.[112]

A five-year investigation following the attack reveals that corruption was a major motivation. According to this careful study, "official corruption, trag-ically, was a driving force behind the May attacks. PCC leaders coordinated their assault in large part as a response to a series of organized shakedowns by the police. The evidence indicates that a year prior to the attacks, police were using wiretaps, kidnapping, and other abuse of family members of gang leaders to extract bribes. The PCC decided to retaliate brutally and brought the city to a halt."[113]

Disorder was evident in São Paulo from May 12 to 14, 2006, as approximately 299 sites were attacked throughout the city, including approximately forty police stations, the city's transportation system, and law enforcement institutions. Related uprisings occurred at seventy-four penitentiaries and centers of detention.[114] The participation in the prisons was not limited to the city but extended across the state of São Paulo. A majority of the facilities in each region rebelled, and at least 439 individuals were taken hostage over the three-day revolt.[115]

The terrorist attack left 261 people dead between May 12 and 20, according to one careful study,[116] although the account will never be certain, as the morgue could not differentiate between those who were killed in the attacks and those who died in the ubiquitous violence among the urban poor.[117] Those who died included members of the military and civilian police, prison guards, prisoners, suspected criminals, and a few ordinary citizens.

The terrorist attack in São Paulo in 2006 is different from all the other attacks with mass fatalities discussed in this chapter. São Paulo was a terrorist attack committed and funded by crime and facilitated and motivated by corruption. First, those who orchestrated this attack were all criminals. Second, the attack did not occur in a confined period of time like the 9/11, Bali, and Madrid attacks. Its duration has some parallels with Beslan, where the siege lasted several days and those who died were both those who launched the attack but also significant numbers of security forces. Like in Beslan, the large number of fatalities was a result of the brutality of the security force.[118] The scene of the terror was not confined to a single space, such as a school, the World Trade Center, the Pentagon, or a bar in Bali. Rather, the terror was dispersed throughout this massive city. In that it foreshadows the attacks on Mumbai in 2008, in which numerous targets were scattered throughout the city. Like the Indian attack, the PCC's goal was to terrorize an entire large metropolitan area.

The São Paulo attacks have important points in common with other attacks. Like the Madrid attack, prison played a key role in the preparation for the attack. But the prison's role was even more central in Brazil than in Spain. The mistreatment of the prisoners was a major catalyst for the attack on the city and its institutions, as prisoners and their families were sick of being extorted. Cell phones in prison are an indication of the corruption that facilitated the attack. Cell phones are forbidden in prisons, just as was the computer used by the Bali bomber. But these prisoners had advanced technology because poorly paid prison guards can easily be bribed, facilitating acts of terrorism.

The Brazilian investigation, like those in the United States, Spain, and Russia, showed a lack of coordination of officials, and a lack of preparedness for the attack, despite precedent terrorist attacks. The World Trade Center had been bombed before; North African terrorists had killed Spanish citizens in Casablanca. "In 2003, after Brazilian authorities arrested the leader of the Commando Vermelho (CV) prison gang, the group blew up more than a dozen cars and busses in Rio de Janeiro"[119] and attacked businesses and homes. Therefore, those capable of committing deadly acts of terrorism existed for many years in these diverse societies, but none had taken measures necessary to prevent a grave attack.

July 2006 and November 2008, Mumbai

The roots of India's terrorism lie in British colonial rule and the brutal conflicts between India and Pakistan that followed independence from Great Britain in 1948. The enmity between these two countries is extreme, and the rise of Islamic extremism in the region since the late 1980s has only fueled and deepened the suspicion and hostility between the two countries. Although many think of al-Qaeda and its base of operations as Afghanistan, there have been deep connections between al-Qaeda and the Pakistani intelligence service, and many al-Qaeda sympathizers operate in Waziristan, a tribal area that is part of Pakistan.[120] Al-Qaeda is not alone; other important Islamic terrorist organizations operate in the region.[121] Contributions from the faithful have helped fund these terrorist bodies; crime, criminal organizations, and the drug trade have also become crucially important to the maintenance and operation of these terrorist groups.[122]

In South Asia, the relationships among organized crime, corruption, and terrorism are among the most complicated in the world. In contrast to many regions of the world, some powerful organized crime groups work intentionally with terrorists. The Inter-Services Intelligence (ISI), the state security apparatus in Pakistan, supports both criminal and terrorist organizations as it uses them to promote its political agenda in relation to Kashmir.[123] Corruption is rampant, facilitating the activities of both criminals and terrorists. In India, members of the customs service knowingly allowed explosive materials to enter the country and helped facilitate their delivery for the attack on their country.[124] The main ports of India (Mumbai) and Pakistan (Karachi) are dominated by criminal organizations facilitating the illicit movement of people, arms, and explosives.[125] The 2008 terrorist attack was facilitated by an American-Pakistani, David C. Headley, with a criminal past who served as a Drug Enforcement Agency informant. He raised money and was trained by a Pakistani terrorist organization, Lashkar-e-Taiba, that was responsible for the assault on Mumbai.[126]

The distinctions between crime and terrorism are increasingly blurred in the Indian subcontinent. The 1993 attack in Mumbai was launched by a criminal group (D-Company) functioning as terrorists, whereas the 2008 attack in the same city was perpetrated by terrorists linked to the ISI and aided by a former criminal-turned-terrorist and possibly also by D-Company.[127] The Pakistani

ISI, as in state-sponsored terrorism discussed further in Chapter 3, is complicit in terrorist activity against India.[128]

D-Company, a radicalized organized crime group, has much to offer in terms of support to terrorists.[129] It has grown since its inception in the 1970s from a group of small-time organized criminals to one of the largest crime groups operating in India, with a significant presence in Pakistan and in more than two dozen countries.[130] Its reach extends from Pakistan into many counties in Asia, the United Arab Emirates, and also possibly Indian communities in East Africa.[131] Its membership is estimated at four thousand to five thousand men. Although little in the West is written about Indian organized crime, it has grown enormously along with the Indian economy. It profits from its illicit activities, its influence over *hawalas* (underground banking that is ubiquitous in the region),[132] and its sizable investments in the rapidly growing legitimate economy. Profiting from extortion against Bollywood, the massive movie industry based in Mumbai, D-Company also makes profits from distributing pirated films.[133] Its significant profits from the drug trade led the Bush administration in 2006 to designate Dawood Ibrahim, and his D-Company organization, as a Significant Foreign Narcotics Trafficker under the Foreign Narcotics Kingpin Designation Act (hereinafter "Kingpin Act").[134] D-Company has established key links along the drug routes flowing out of Afghanistan into Pakistan and Central Asia.[135] It also traffics arms for both criminals and terrorists and smuggles computer parts and other substances along its routes, well greased by corruption. D-Company's sizable investments in the legitimate economy include a shopping center, a major hotel in Mumbai, a travel agency, and a major financial stake in an airline, bringing significant annual revenues to the organization.[136]

In 1993, the evolution from criminals to terrorists was completed as Dawood and his organization decided to revenge the 1992 destruction of the Mosque in Uttar Pradesh, India, and the subsequent rioting in Mumbai and other major Indian cities that resulted in the deaths of hundreds of Moslems killed by Hindus.[137] The apparent indifference of the Indian government to the death of the Moslem citizens also contributed to the important transformation of D-Company.[138]

The first major attack on Mumbai was in 1993, when D-Company launched a series of bombing attacks in the city on March 12, killing 257 people, injuring many more, and costing millions of rupees in damages.[139] The 1993 Mumbai attack was allegedly aided by the Pakistani government's ISI, which helped ensure the planning and successful execution of the assault on India's financial capital.[140] Yet, as previously mentioned, the devastating 1993 Mumbai attack could have not succeeded without the participation of D-Company and the corruption of Indian officials. Therefore, crime, corruption, and terrorism were entangled.

For nearly two hours that day, from the initial bomb blast that shattered the walls of the Bombay Stock Exchange, the attackers continued to leave corpses and shattered glass behind. "Next to be hit was the main office of the national airline, Air India, followed by the Central Bazaar and major hotels. At the international airport, hand grenades were thrown at jets parked on the tarmac."[141] The attacks were facilitated by an enormous arsenal that included nearly "4 tons of explosives, 1,100 detonators, nearly 500 grenades, 63 assault rifles, and thousands of rounds of ammunition."[142] Much of this was smuggled into the country via the port of Mumbai and the areas south of it that were controlled by the crime group, D-company.[143] This act reflects the intense corruption of the Indian state apparatus and the capacity of D-Company to neutralize police, immigration authorities, and personnel monitoring checkpoints.[144] The smuggling of the RDX explosives was facilitated by government officials in Raigard, a port to the south of Mumbai. According to Indian courts,

> Customs Inspector Jayvant Gurav and Customs Superintendent S S Talawadekar, who were posted in Srivardhan taluka of Raigad in January 1993, were found guilty of helping Dawood Ibrahim and other prime conspirators in allowing arms and RDX to land in Raigad despite having specific knowledge that such contraband was being smuggled by terrorists.
>
> Gurav was also found guilty of piloting a customs jeep along with a van filled with RDX and arms, to facilitate passage of contraband from Raigad to Mumbai.[145]

Extensive hearings by the Indian government held after these 1993 attacks assessed the organization, financing, and motivation of the attacks. Dawood Ibrahim and his large Mumbai-based criminal organization as well as key crime associates were held responsible.[146]

After the 1993 attack, Dawood Ibrahim no longer lived in India but divided his time between Pakistan and Dubai in the United Arab Emirates.[147] Dawood became more radicalized and formed links with Islamic terrorist groups such as Lashkar-e-Taiba (LeT).[148] Lashkar has been linked to al-Qaeda since its founding in 1993 and has close links with elements of Pakistan's intelligence organization, the ISI.[149]

In the intervening years between the 1993 and 2008 attacks, Mumbai had witnessed other deadly acts of terrorism, but none were as lethal and as encompassing as those that swept the city in 2008. In July 2006, there were multiple attacks on the Mumbai trains, in which more than two hundred were killed and many more were injured. LeT and the Student Islamic Movement of India were held responsible for the attack.[150]

The 2008 Mumbai attacks, also the work of LeT, were devastating in their scale, their lethality, and their psychological and financial impact, even though fewer died than in the train attacks. Over the course of four days, ten separate sites in Mumbai were attacked in a coordinated assault on key central targets and different regions of the immense city. The places attacked included the usual range of strategically significant targets identified so far in this chapter. The railway station and the port were hit by the terrorists. Yet this attack by an Islamist group had an additional target an Orthodox Jewish center, whose Jewish American director and his wife were killed.[151] As always, the places attacked also had symbolic importance – including two of Mumbai's legendary hotels, such as the Taj Mahal Palace Hotel, where many of India's elite dine, along with affluent Western tourists.[152] The attacks were perpetrated with automatic weapons, bombs, and grenades. The 2008 attacks left 175 dead and 308 wounded, and during the siege, 100 were held hostage. Those who died included many prominent individuals from the world of media, business, and the security services. As in Madrid, Bali, and New York, those killed came from many different countries. By attacking deluxe hotels of this international commercial center, the terrorists killed twenty-eight foreign nationals from ten different countries.

Most of the attackers were killed. Only Ajmal Kasab survived and was sentenced to death on May 6, 2010, by the Indian courts and executed in November 2012.[153] Under pressure from India, Pakistan arrested six people, including the alleged mastermind of the attack. A key figure to survive the attack was one of its organizers, David Headley, a son of a Pakistani broadcaster and an American socialite. Despite warnings to U.S. embassies and officials on four occasions since 2001 concerning his involvement with terrorists (by wives and former girlfriends), there was no follow-up. In 2006, Headley, a former drug trafficker, "began using his cover as a businessman to scout targets in Mumbai under the direction of terrorist handlers and a Pakistani intelligence officer, according to investigators and court documents."[154]

While the Pakistan-based LeT has been held responsible for the attack, the ten terrorists could not have achieved such a lethal effect without support on the ground, such as that provided by the criminal Headley. But there were more criminal and corrupt facilitators. The attackers arrived by boat. Yet the port of Mumbai is controlled by organized crime, as are major ports in many locales worldwide.[155] Therefore, D-Company, along with other crime organizations controlling the port, facilitated the entry of the terrorists into the city. Some press accounts have suggested that criminals provided the boat to the attackers.[156] The links may be deeper, as there are indications that D-Company "began to finance LeT's activities, use its companies to lure recruits to LeT training camps, and give LeT operatives use of its smuggling routes and contacts."[157]

As in the São Paulo case discussed previously, Indian law enforcement and security authorities knew that they had a crime group operating in the major financial center of the country, Mumbai, that was capable and motivated to attack or to facilitate an attack on the city. But the coordination and the mechanisms were not put in place to stop such an attack. In Mumbai, as in Brazil, the attack lasted for several days, terrorizing the entire city until Indian government security forces could reassert control and kill or capture the mere ten terrorists who perpetrated the attack. Once again, this case illustrates the potency of the crime-terror relationship facilitated by corruption and the intensified insecurity in a megacity.

Conclusion

The six terrorist attacks discussed in this chapter, committed between 2001 and 2008, each had hundreds of victims; 9/11 had thousands. The analysis of the six attacks shows that these attacks were not pure terrorism but represented a dirty entanglement. All of the attacks combined crime and corruption with the act of terror. They represented more of a hybrid threat than has been realized by most who discuss and analyze these tragic events. Several were made more deadly by the brutal response of the governments.

Governmental commissions studied many of these attacks in detail in sub-sequent years. Yet crime and corruption received short shrift in many of the investigations, starting with 9/11.[158] As was shown, none of these attacks could have been as successful without crime and corruption. Unfortunately, these six attacks are not anomalous. In the previous decade, crime helped facilitate large-scale terrorist attacks. The largest terrorist act in the United States prior to 9/11 was the Oklahoma City bombing. One of the lead perpetrators of Oklahoma City used a falsified driver's license to commit his act.[159] The 1993 terrorist attacks in Mumbai, as previously mentioned, were executed by an organized crime group. Crime and corruption also contribute to many smaller deadly attacks that occur in many regions of the world.[160]

The Brazilian attack foreshadows the urban attack in London in August 2011, in which criminals assumed a major role in destructive and politi-cized violence. In London, one in four rioters had already committed at least ten offenses.[161] This case shows the urban destruction and terror that can come from hardened and previously incarcerated criminals.[162] Conversely, they reveal that brutal repression of slum dwellers such as occurs in Brazil can result in violent outcomes for the society. Urban violence on a massive scale in cities may be more common in the future, as citizens respond to state repression.[163]

The entangled phenomena of crime, corruption, and terrorism is interna-tional. The attacks discussed were committed on four continents – North and South America, Europe, and Asia. But their reach was farther, as perpetrators of the Madrid attack came from North Africa and the preponderance of victims of the Bali attack were Australian. Citizens of almost eighty different countries died on September 11 as a result of al-Qaeda's attack. The terrorists behind Beslan received financial support from the United States, and support from the Middle East provided initial working capital for the Bali attack. Therefore, there is hardly a part of the world that was not involved as attacker, source of funds, or victim in these mass attacks.

Many now associate terrorism with radical Islam or jihadis, but not all these highly lethal attacks fit into this category. The attack in São Paulo, Brazil, was committed by a politicized crime group, and Chechen terrorism is at its core a nationalist movement that has ties to Islamic groups but whose primary motivation is not Islamic.

The deadliness of these attacks is explained not only by the brutality of the terrorists. State security apparati in Brazil and Russia contributed to the deadliness of the attacks. As many of the national commissions that followed these attacks have shown, governments failed to mobilize or improve intra-agency coordination in advance of these attacks, even though almost all had precedents.

The World Trade Center and Mumbai had been previously assaulted by terrorists from related organizations. Russia experienced a deadly attack from Chechen terrorists in a Moscow theater, and Spaniards had been killed in North Africa by groups linked to the Madrid bombers. Indonesia had long-standing connections with Osama bin Laden and militant Islam.[164] In Brazil, *favelas* have long been the locales of deadly violence, with residents suffering abuse at the hands of military and law enforcement.[165] Members of a prison gang in Rio in 2003 had blown up cars and busses after the arrest of a leader.[166]

Ringleaders or key figures who ordered the attack were identified in most of the six attacks. What was their relation to the crime behind the attacks? Mohammed Atta of 9/11 was not accused of any crimes, but German intelligence knew of his interest in antiquities smuggling as a fund-raising tool. Shamil Basayev, who ordered the Beslan attack, was directly involved in the establishment of a phony foundation in Hollywood to generate funds. Jamal Ahmidan, a key figure in the Madrid bombings, was a large drug dealer. Samudra, a central figure of the Bali bombings, robbed a jewelry store and taught his fellow Islamic radicals how to use the Internet to raise funds through credit card fraud. Marcola, who launched the attacks in São Paulo, had a criminal history dating to his youth and was in prison for multiple armed robberies. In the first Mumbai attack, the crime links were more apparent than in the second. But even in the second attack, the crucial figure of David Headley had connections to both the worlds of crime and terrorism. Headley was a figure who linked the United States with Pakistan, his criminal experience never receding far into the background. He is illustrative of increasing terrorist involvement with criminality.[167]

The six attacks have been facilitated by advanced communications and the Internet. Mohammed Atta learned of the date of the attack through an encoded message. Illegal cell phones in prison permitted the planning of the São Paulo attacks. Samudra of the Bali attack used computers to fund terrorism. The use of advanced technology in these deadly attacks provides an important precedent for the future.

Crime both facilitated and funded these terrorist acts. False documents, including driver's licenses and passports, were obtained through corruption and sophisticated forgers; illegal movement of operatives across borders allowed the attackers to gain entry to countries, to drive cars and board airplanes. Diverse sources of legitimate and criminal funding, apart from drugs, provided the operating capital for these mass attacks. Both domestic and transnational crimes, such as extortion, robbery, Internet and credit card fraud, insurance fraud, illicit trade, arms smuggling, and the provision of money laundering services, were key in financing these attacks.

With the transnational nature of contemporary crime, much of the funds were generated far from the locale where the attack took place. Money for September 11 was transferred from the Gulf region: funding for Beslan was raised, in part, in Los Angeles; and the funding for the Bali bombing came from gold trade in the region and possibly from worldwide Internet fraud.

Prisons have assumed a key role in the planning and recruitment for several of these attacks, as is discussed further in Chapter 4. The significance of the prisons is multiple – they are facilities that house the disenfranchised of the society. They are also breeding grounds of resentment and activism against the ruling elite of the society, often a result of the abuse suffered in prison. This is seen more acutely in the São Paulo case,[168] but it is symptomatic of a larger problem. Prisons are far from the Foucaultian model of discipline and punish that this great social scientist suggested epitomized modern industrialized society.[169] Prisons no longer are institutions of reform but serve as warehouses and vocational training centers for crime for individuals excluded from any access to the power structures of society.

Corruption is also a key facilitator as well as a cause of terrorism. Corrupt American officials issued driver's licenses to the 9/11 hijackers in violation of the law, and corrupt prison officials in Brazil allowed inmates to have cell phones and, in Bali, access to computers and the Internet. Beslan attackers crossed internal checkpoints as a result of bribes to officials. The corruption that facilitates the international drug trade provided the financing for some of these attacks. Corrupt Russian customs officials facilitated the transport of arms and explosives, even going so far as to accompany the deadly materials in a customs van. Indian officials facilitated the entry of explosives in the earlier Mumbai attack.

Ever more groups are using terrorism than in the past. Despite extensive inquiries and hearings following these lethal attacks, the countries that were victimized have not addressed the core conditions, such as income disparity, absence of employment, corruption, exclusion from power, and ethnic hatreds, that contributed to this violence. This negligence ensures that these mass casualty attacks will not be the last of their kind, particularly in the emerging economic powers of the G-20 or in conflict regions. They also herald the rise of a new kind of entangled threat (crime, corruption, and terrorism) that threatens global security, particularly that in the increasingly large urban areas.

Notes

1. Bruce Hoffman, *Inside Terrorism* (New York: Columbia University Press, 1998); Walter Laqueur, *The New Terrorism: Fanaticism and the Arms of Mass Destruction* (Oxford: Oxford University Press, 2005).

2. Adrian Guelke, *The New Age of Terrorism and the International Political System* (London: I. B. Taurus, 2009), table on p. viii of major attacks with loss of life. Only the Brazilian attack is not included in this list, as it does not fall under many traditional definitions of terrorism.

3. As Assistant Secretary of State, U.S. Department of State, David Johnson, director of the Bureau of International Narcotics and Law Enforcement Affairs, stated on January 19, 2010, at the Washington Institute for Near East Policy, Washington, D.C., "a convergence of crime and corruption can . . . pave the road for terrorist organizations to finance their terror, as was the case in Bali, Madrid and Mumbai." http://www.state.gov/j/inl/rls/rm/135404.htm. But the pattern is much broader than these attacks.

4. Only China among the BRIC countries has been spared a mass attack. Conversations with top security officials in Beijing in October 2011 revealed an enormous concern for the potential combined impact of crime and terrorism on Chinese society, which is already experiencing mass protests in many urban areas and serious unrest operating in peripheral regions of China.

5. Kees Kooning and Dirk Kruijt, *Megacities: The Politics of Urban Exclusion and Violence in the Global South* (New York: Zed Books, 2009); Enrique Desmond Arias and Daniel M. Goldstein, eds., *Violent Democracies in Latin America* (Durham, NC: Duke University Press, 2010), 55.

6. Stewart Patrick, *Weak Links: Fragile States, Global Threats, and International Security* (New York: Oxford University Press, 2011), 61–104, questions whether weak states are sanctuaries for terrorism.

7. There have been multiple attacks in Mumbai; the train bombing attack in 2006 was the most deadly of these, with 209 killed. Guelke, *New Age of Terrorism,* viii. The section on Mumbai puts this train bombing in context.

8. http://www.cnn.com/SPECIALS/2001/memorial/lists/by-name/.

9. See Louise Shelley, "Countering Terrorism in the US: The Fallacy of Ignoring the Crime-Terror Nexus," in *National Counter-Terrorism Strategies*, ed. R. W. Orttung and A. Makarychev (Amsterdam: IOS Press, 2006), 203–12. Angel Rabasa, Peter Chalk, Kim Cragin, Sara A. Daly, Heather S. Gregg, Theodore W. Karasik, Kevin A. O'Brien, and William Rosenau, *Beyond al-Qaeda, Part 2: The Outer Rings of the Terrorist Universe* (Santa Monica, CA: Rand, 2006), 139–40; see the same discussion in Doug Farah, "Al Qaeda and the Gemstone Trade," in *Countering the Financing of Terrorism*, ed. Thomas J. Biersteker and Sue E. Eckert (New York: Routledge, 2008), 199–200.

10. National Commission on Terrorist Attacks upon the United States, *The 9/11 Report* (New York: St. Martin's Press, 2004), 255–57.

11. See United States of America v. Ahmed Ressam, March 12, 2012, http://www.ca9 .uscourts.gov/datastore/opinions/2012/05/04/09-30000.pdf.

12. See Rohan Gunaratna, *Inside Al Qaeda* (New York: Columbia University Press, 2002), 64; Hal Bernton, Mike Carter, David Heath, and James Neff, "It Takes a Thief," *Seattle Times*, June 23–July 7, 2002, http://seattletimes.nwsource.com/ news/nation-world/terroristwithin/chapter6.html; National Commission on Terrorist Attacks upon the United States, *The 9/11 Report*, 257.

13. Shaul Shay, *Islamic Terror and the Balkans* (New Brunswick, NJ: Transaction, 2007), 148–55.

14. Louise I. Shelley, John T. Picarelli, Allison Irby, Douglas M. Hart, Patricia A. Craig-Hart, Phil Williams, Steven Simon, Nabi Abdullaev, Bartosz Stanislawski, and Laura Covill, "Methods and Motives: Exploring Links between Transnational Organized Crime and International Terrorism," September 2005, 10, 40, http://www.ncjrs.gov/pdffiles1/nij/grants/211207.pdf; "Trail of a Terrorist," *Frontline,* http://www.pbs.org/wgbh/pages/frontline/shows/trail/; National Commission upon Terrorist Attacks on the United States, *The 9/11 Report,* 257.

15. Discussion with Judge de la Brugière on this case in Doha, May 30–31, 2010. Bernton et al., "It Takes a Thief," http://seattletimes.nwsource.com/news/nation-world/terroristwithin/chapter5.

16. Marc Sageman, *Understanding Terror Networks* (Philadelphia: University of Pennsylvania Press, 2004).

17. Christina Ruiz, "9/11 Hijacker Attempted to Sell Afghan Loot," http://www.theartnewspaper.com/articles/9–11-hijacker.../20188; see also the documentary *Blood Antiques,* which mentions this, at http://www.journeyman.tv/?lid=59906.

18. The terrorists had no apparent reason to visit Las Vegas. See John L. Smith, "Terrorist at Casinos," *Las Vegas Review Journal,* November 4, 2001, http://casinowatch.org/terrorists/terrorists_at_casinos.html.

19. Gunaratna, *Inside Al Qaeda,* 64–65.

20. Interview with a retired congressional investigator, March 2012, who analyzed the Las Vegas trips and who expressed concern that the hijackers' trips there were not fully investigated.

21. Joan Walter, "Terror Suspect $100,000 in Casinos Scam," *Toronto Star,* September 20, 2002, http://casinowatch.org/terrorists/terrorists_at_casinos.html.

22. Some of the women were also smuggled across the U.S.–Mexican border. Author's interview with the investigators of the "White Lace Case" in Los Angeles, December 2005. Also see Louise I. Shelley, *Human Trafficking: A Global Perspective* (Cambridge: Cambridge University Press, 2010), 120, 244.

23. Author's interview with the investigators of the "White Lace Case" in Los Angeles, December 2005.

24. Interviews with the counterterrorism unit of the LAPD, December 2005. This unit is unique in pursuing terrorism through its criminal footprint. See Judith Miller, "On the Front Line in the War on Terrorism," http://www.city-journal.org/html/17_3_preventing_terrorism.html. The companion volume on terrorist financing avoided questions of criminal activity. John Roth, Douglas Greenburg, and Serena Wille, *National Commission on Terrorist Attacks upon the United States, Monograph on Terrorist Financing,* http://govinfo.library.unt.edu%2F911%2Fstaff_statements%2F911_TerrFin_Monograph.pdf

25. For a mention of the problem of these illegally obtained driver's licenses, see testimony of Hon. James P. Moran, Virginia, September 29, 2004, *Congressional Record* 150, no. 121 (Thursday, September 30, 2004), http://www.gpo.gov/fdsys/pkg/CREC-2004-09-30/html/CREC-2004-09-30-pt1-PgE1759-3.htm. The author knew of this corruption of the DMV from an INS investigator in northern Virginia in the late 1990s, who reported on this corruption as a low-level priority for his agency, which had more serious crime to investigate.

26. Robert Trent of the INS, interview in the late 1990s, Washington, DC.

27. For a discussion of Giuliani and his use of the broken windows idea, see http://en .wikipedia.org/wiki/Broken_windows_theory; Steven D. Levitt and Stephen J. Dubner, *Freakonomics: A Rogue Economist Explores the Hidden Side of Everything* (New York: HarperCollins, 2005).
28. Gunaratna, *Inside Al-Qaeda,* 61.
29. Thomas R. Eldridge, Susan Ginsburg, Walter T. Hempel II, et al., *9/11 and Terrorist Travel,* http://govinfo.library.unt.edu/911/staff_statements/911_TerrTrav_ Monograph.pdf.
30. Rollie Lal, "Terrorists and Organized Crime Join Forces," *New York Times,* May 24, 2005, http://www.nytimes.com/2005/05/23/opinion/23iht-edlal.html?_r=1.
31. Nimrod Raphaeli, "Financing of Terrorism: Sources, Methods and Channels," *Terrorism and Political Violence* 15, no. 4 (2003): 72.
32. Farah, "Al Qaeda and the Gemstone Trade." Also conversations with Doug Farah.
33. Ibid., 200.
34. Rabasa et al., *Beyond al-Qaeda, Part 2,* 139–43.
35. See Global Witness, "Faced with a Gun, What Can You Do? War and Militarisation of Mining in Eastern Congo," http:// www.globalwitness.org/sites/default/ files/pdfs/report_en_final_0.pdf, on the diamond trade. The role of al-Qaeda in the diamond trade is questioned by Nikos Passas, "Terrorism Financing Mechanisms and Policy Dilemmas," in *Terrorism Financing and State Responses: A Comparative Perspective,* ed. Jeanne K. Giraldo and Harold A. Trinkunas (Stanford, CA: Stanford University Press, 2007), 27–28.
36. Rohan Gunaratna, "Terrorism in Southeast Asia: Threat and Response," http:// www.hudson.org/files/pdf_upload/terrorismPDF.pdf, as well as discussions of the case with one of the lead investigators.
37. Written exchange with a very senior investigator associated with the investigation.
38. Anthony L. Smith, "Terrorism and the Political Landscape in Indonesia: The Fragile Post-Bali Consensus," in *Terrorism and Violence in Southeast Asia: Transnational Challenges to States and Regional Stability,* ed. Paul J. Smith (Armonk, NY: M. E. Sharpe, 2005), 112.
39. Angel Rabasa, Peter Chalk, Kim Cragin, Sara A. Daly, Heather S. Gregg, Theodore W. Karasik, Kevin A. O'Brien, and William Rosenau, *Beyond al-Qaeda, Part 1. The Global Jihadist Movement* (Santa Monica, CA: Rand, 2006), 30–31.
40. Ibid. Interview with one of the major investigators of the case, who came from outside Indonesia, Dubai, November 2010.
41. Zachary Abuza, "The Social Organization of Terror in Southwest Asia: The Case of Jemaah Islamiya," in Biersteker and Eckert, *Countering the Financing of Terrorism,* 82.
42. Ibid., 83.
43. Tracy Dahlby, *Allah's Torch: A Report from Behind the Scenes in Asia's War on Terror* (New York: William Morrow, 2005), 200.
44. The film *Kissed by a Crocodile,* by filmmaker Wendy Dent, addressed the gigolo culture and operations in the Kuta district, where the Bali bombings occurred. http://www.wendydent.com/Kissed_By_A_Crocodile. Interview with the filmmaker, 2013.
45. Dahlby, *Allah's Torch,* 199, refers to the sex for sale as well as interviews.
46. Interviews with individuals who contributed to the investigations.

47. "Bali Bombing Plot," BBC News Service, March 10, 2010, http://news.bbc.co.uk/2/hi/asia-pacific/3157478.stm.
48. Abuza, "Social Organization of Terror in Southwest Asia," 82–83. The court testimony revealed the funding provided by petty crime. The role of natural resources in funding terrorism was discussed in relation to 9/11 and is discussed subsequently in Chapter 5. The previously discussed diamond trade linked to al-Qaeda connected East Africans with South Asians who had close familial ties to JI.
49. It also illustrates the following principle: "Occasionally, a larger hierarchical organization may distribute seed funding and logistical support to a cell to help initiate terrorist plots." Quoted in John Rollins, Liana S. Wyler, and Seth Rosen, *International Terrorism and Transnational Crime: Security Threats, U.S. Policy, and Considerations for Congress* (Washington, DC: Congressional Research Service, 2010), http://www.fas.org/sgp/crs/terror/R41004.pdf, 93, 19.
50. "Jewelry Store Robbers in Indonesia Sentenced for Financing Bali Terrorist Attack," http://www.professionaljeweler.com/archives/news/2003/090803story.html. As discussed more in Chapter 5, robberies remain an important funding tool for terrorists in Indonesia. See V. Arianti, "Indonesian Terrorism Financing: Resorting to Robberies," *RSIS Commentaries*, no. 142 (July 29, 2013), http://www.rsis.edu.sg/publications/commentaries.html.
51. Celina Realuyo and Scott Stapleton, "After Bali Bombing, Donor's Response Viewed as International Success Story," 16–19, http://www.usembassy-mexico.gov/bbf/ej/0904_GlobalWar.pdf.
52. Richard Lloyd Parry, "Death Row Bomber Plotted New Attack on Smuggled Laptop," http://www.timesonline.co.uk/tol/news/world/asia/article617892.ece.
53. David Talbott, "Terror's Server – How Radical Islamists Use Internet Fraud to Finance Terrorism and Exploit the Internet for *Jihad* Propaganda and Recruitment: Law Enforcement Considers Ways of Combating Cyber Terrorists with Computer Engineering Degrees," *Technology Review*, January 27, 2005, reprinted in http://www.militantislammonitor.org/article/id/404.
54. Dennis Lormel, "Terrorists and Credit Card Fraud . . . a Quiet Epidemic," February 28, 2008, http://counterterrorismblog.org/2008/02/terrorists_and_credit_card_fra.php.
55. Zachary Abuza, 82; David E. Kaplan, "Paying for Terror: How Jihadist Groups Are Using Organized-Crime Tactics – and Profits – to Finance Attacks on Targets around the Globe," November 27, 2005, http://www.usnews.com/usnews/news/articles/051205/5terror_2.htm.
56. Rollins et al., *International Terrorism and Transnational Crime*, 93.
57. Comisión de Investigación del 11-M dictamen de conclusiones y recomendaciones, June 8, 2005, 6–8, http://www.elpais.com/elpaismedia/ultimahora/media/200506/09/espana/20050609elpepunac_4_P_PDF.pdf.
58. National Commission on Terrorist Attacks upon the United States, *The 9/11 Report*, 79–80, discusses the social and economic malaise.
59. "Madrid Bombing: Defendants," July 17, 2008, http://news.bbc.co.uk/2/hi/europe/4899544.stm.
60. "Toulouse Hostage Gunmen Arrested," June 20, 2102, http://www.bbc.co.uk/news/world-europe-18516934.
61. Paul Hamilos, "Worst Islamist Attack in European History," *Guardian,* October 31, 2007, http://www.guardian.co.uk/world/2007/oct/31/spain.

62. In his September 19, 2007, video titled *The Power of Truth*, al-Zawahiri explicitly linked Spain and the mission of AQIM: "Restoring al-Andalus is a trust on the shoulders of the nation in general and on your shoulders in particular, and you will not be able to do that without first cleansing the Muslim Maghreb of the children of France and Spain, who have come back again after your fathers and grandfathers sacrificed their blood cheaply in the path of God to expel them." Cited by J. Peter Pham, "Al-Qaeda in the Islamic Maghreb: An Evolving Challenge in the War on Terror," *World Defense Review,* May 8, 2008, http://worlddefensereview.com/pham050808.shtml.

63. Interview with top French terrorism expert, March 2011.

64. Javier Jordán, "The Madrid Attacks: Results of Investigations Two Years Later," *Terrorism Monitor* 4, no. 5 (March 9, 2006), http://www.jamestown.org/pro-grams/gta/single/?tx_ttnews[tt_news]=696&tx_ttnews[backPid]=181&no_cache=1.

65. Elaine Sciolino, "Complex Web of Madrid Plot Still Entangled," *New York Times*, April 12, 2004.

66. Jordan, "Madrid Attacks."

67. Informe de Conclusiones definitivas del Mº Fiscal (Dª Olga Sánchez, Fiscal), http://www.datadiar.tv/juicio11m/bd/intervencion.asp?idIntervencion=690&Idioma=es.

68. Comisión de Investigación del 11-M dictamen de conclusiones y recomendaciones, June 8, 2005, 9, http://3diasdemarzo.blogspot.com/ . . . /ndice-comisin-de-investi gacin-del-11-m.html.

69. Informe de Conclusiones definitivas del Mº Fiscal (Dª Olga Sánchez, Fiscal), http://www.datadiar.tv/juicio11m/bd/intervencion.asp?idIntervencion=690&Idioma=es; translation by the author.

70. Rollins et al., *International Terrorism and Transnational Crime*, 19; Andrea Elliott, "Where Boys Grow Up to Be Jihadis," *New York Times*, November 25, 2007, http://www.nytimes.com/2007/11/25/magazine/25tetouan-t.html?scp=1& sq=where%20boys%20grow%20up%20to%20be%20jihadis&st=cse.

71. Kaplan, "Paying for Terror."

72. Rollins et al., *International Terrorism and Transnational Crime*, 20.

73. Twenty-six people, such as nursing mothers, were released after thirty-two hours. This is how Ms. Aneta Godieva survived. She presented her impressions and the results of her group's investigation at a session in Paris. She lost her older daughter in the attack and serves as vice president of the Mothers of Beslan. "Le terrorisme en Fédération de Russie: le rôle des victimes" (Terrorism in Russia: The Role of the Victims), September 19, 2011, Cape (Centre d'Accueil de Presse etrangère), Grand Palais, http://www.capefrance.com/fr/conferences/2011/9/le-terrorisme-en-federation-de-russie–le-role-des-victimes.html. For an account of the attack, see C. J. Chivers, "The School," *Esquire*, March 14, 2007, http://www.esquire.com/features/ESQ0606BESLAN_140.

74. The number of terrorists who participated is in dispute; officially, one survived and thirty-two died. But Godieva and other witnesses believe that there could have been many more. See the website of the victims, http://www.pravdabeslana.ru/.

75. "August 31, 2006: Beslan – Two Years On," http://web.archive.org/web/2009 0404112922/http://www.unicef.org/russia/media_4875.html.

76. For more discussion on Basayev, see Rabasa et al., *Beyond al-Qaeda. Part 1*, 105–10.

77. For the parliamentary hearings, see доклад парламентской комиссии по расследованию причин и обстоятельств совершения террористического акта в городе Беслане Республики Северная Осетия – Алания 1–3 сентября 2004 года Москва 2006 (Report of the Parliamentary Commission on the Investigation of the Causes and Circumstances of the Terrorist Act in Beslan in the Republic of the North Osetia – Alania, 1–3 September 2004, Moscow). The report states that Russian officials saved 811 hostages, including 547 children. Available on the website along with extensive materials on the trials and investigations at http://www.pravdabeslana.ru/.

78. Diego Gambetta, "Can We Make Sense of Suicide Missions," in *Making Sense of Suicide Missions*, ed. Diego Gambetta (Oxford: Oxford University Press, 2005), 272; Nabi Abdullaev, "Unraveling Chechen Black Widows," http://studies.agentura.ru/english/library/suicide/; "Женщины-шахидки" в Беслане: кто они на самом деле? (Women-shahidy in Beslan: Who Are They?), http://www.pravdabeslana.ru/nagaevaitaburova.htm.

79. Mark Kramer, "Guerilla Warfare, Counterinsurgency and Terrorism in the North Caucasus: The Military Dimension of the Russian-Chechen Conflict," *Europe-Asia Studies* 57, no. 2 (2005): 209–90.

80. Rabasa et al., *Beyond al-Qaeda. Part 1*, 107–9.

81. See the video "Greetings from Grozny: Explore Chechnya's Turbulent Past: 1944: Deportation," http://www.pbs.org/wnet/wideangle/episodes/greetings-from-grozny/explore-chechnyas-turbulent-past/1944-deportation/3314/; James S. Robbins, "Insurgent Seizure of an Urban Area: Grozny, 1996," in *Countering Terrorism and Insurgency in the Twenty First Century: International Perspectives*, ed. James J. F. Forest (Westport, CT: Praeger Security International, 2007), 89, points out that General Dudayev, one of the leaders of Chechen independence, was born in exile.

82. Stephen Handelman, *Comrade Criminal: Russia's New Mafiya* (New Haven, CT: Yale University Press, 1995), 49–52.

83. Mark Galeotti, "'Brotherhoods' and 'Associates': Chechen Networks of Crime and Resistance," *Low Intensity Conflict and Law Enforcement* 11, nos. 2/3 (2002): 340–52.

84. "Chechen Diaspora Upstages Kadyrov," September 6, 2012, http://www.rferl.org/content/Chechen_Diaspora_Upstages_Kadyrov/2149762.html.

85. Handelman, *Comrade Criminal*, 207–24.

86. See the reports on this forum. *Vsemiryniy Antikriminal'nyi i Antiterrosticheskii Forum, Mirovoe soobshchestvo globalizatsii prestupnost i terrorizma (2-aia mezhdunarodnaia konferentsiia)* (Moscow: Ekonomika, 2004). This forum is run by Gen. Anatoly Kulikov, and the author heard the general discuss the mistake at the Third International Forum called World Community against Globalization of Crime and Terrorism, opened at the State Duma, September 27, 2006, http://www.eng.mvdinform.ru/news/2766/, for a public discussion of the event. General Kulikov discussed with the author the mistake made in using such force in Chechnya.

87. Conversation with a European Russian specialist who went to the mosques in London and solicited funds, Vaduz, Liechtenstein, March 2002.

88. Gunaratna, *Inside Al Qaeda*, 64.
89. Galeotti, "'Brotherhoods' and 'Associates.'"
90. Robert Block, "A L.A. Bust Shows Tactics for Fighting Terror," December 29, 2006, http://online.wsj.com/article/SB116736247579862262.html?mod=todays_us_page_one; Kevin Roderick, "LAPD and the Chechen Terrorists," December 29, 2006, http://www.laobserved.com/archive/2006/12/lapd_and_the_chechen_terr.php. The perpetrators functioned for years before the case was discovered. The case was investigated for more than a year and led to the arrest of eight people for fraud in February 2006 and to arrest warrants for eleven others.
91. "Doklad parlamentskoi komissii po rassledovanuiu prichin i obstiatel'stv soversheniia terroristicheskogo akta v gorode Beslane Republiki Severnaia Osetia-Alania 1–3 sentiabria 2004 goda," http://www.pravdabeslana.ru/dokladtorshina221206.pdf.
92. Kramer, "Guerilla Warfare, Counterinsurgency and Terrorism in the North Caucasus," 221.
93. Leslie Holmes, ed., introduction to *Terrorism, Organised Crime and Corruption: Networks and Linkages* (Cheltenham, UK: Edward Elgar, 2007), 3.
94. David Cayley, *The Expanding Prison: The Crisis in Crime and Punishment and the Search for Alternatives* (Cleveland, OH: Pilgrim Press, 1998), 332–34, discusses the work of Raul Zaffaroni, a leading Argentine judge and analyst of human rights abuses in Latin America; Paul Chevigny, *Edge of the Knife: Police Violence in the Americas* (New York: New Press, 1995).
95. For a fuller discussion of PCC, see Juan Carlos Garzón, *Mafia & co. La red criminal en México, Brasil y Colombia* (Bogatá: Planeta, 2008), 94–106.
96. Max G. Manwaring, *A Contemporary Challenge to State Sovereignty: Gangs and Other Illicit Transnational Criminal Organizations in Central America, El Salvador, Mexico, Jamaica and Brazil 2007*, 41, http://www.strategicstudiesinstitute.army.mil/pdffiles/pub837.pdf; also see Max C. Manwaring, "Three Lessons from Contemporary Challenges to Security," *Prism* 2, no. 3 (2011): 106.
97. "Brazil's Mighty Prison Gangs," May 15, 2006, http://news.bbc.co.uk/2/hi/americas/4770097.stm.
98. Michel Misse, "La acumulación social de la violencia en Río de Janeiro y en Brasil: algunas reflexiones," *Revista Co-herencia* 7, no. 13 (2010): 19–40; Enrique Desmond Arias, *Drugs and Democracy in Rio de Janeiro* (Chapel Hill: University of North Carolina Press, 2006).
99. Desmond Arias, *Drugs and Democracy in Rio de Janeiro.*
100. The author attended the conference Seminário Internacional sobre o Crime Organizado e Democracia, November, 26–28, 2007, http://www.nevusp.org/portugues/index.php?option=com_content&task=view&id=1587&Itemid=161, at the Núcleo de Estudos da Violência, Universidade de São Paulo, to examine organized crime in the aftermath of this unprecedented attack on one of the world's largest cities. The PCC has been engaged in renewed violence. See Simon Romero, "Alarm Grows in São Paulo as More Police Officers Are Murdered," *New York Times,* October 2, 2010, http://www.nytimes.com/2012/10/03/world/americas/spike-in-police-officer-deaths-alarms-sao-paulo.html?_r=0.
101. Marco Antônio Coelho, "From Pickpocket to Bank Robber," *Estudos Avançados* 21 (2007), 61, http://www.scielo.br/scielo.php?pid=S0103-40142007000300005&script=sci_arttext&tlng=en.

102. Ibid., 71–72.

103. Ibid., 72.

104. John Bailey and Matthew M. Taylor, "Evade, Corrupt, or Confront? Organized Crime and the State in Brazil and Mexico," *Journal of Politics in Latin America* 1, no. 2 (2009): 14.

105. Ibid., 15–16.

106. Ibid.

107. Shelley, *Human Trafficking*, 284; Jens Glüsing, "Brazil's President Lula: 'Father of the Poor' Has Triggered Economic Miracle," November 24, 2009, http://www .spiegel.de/international/world/0,1518,662917,00.html.

108. The importance of order to Alckmin's campaign is also discussed in Bailey and Taylor, "Evade, Corrupt, or Confront?," 15n15.

109. As a former very high World Bank official at the time in Brazil reported in an interview with the author in 2009 that as soon as the president's opponent announced his campaign platform as his success in controlling urban violence while governor of São Paulo, political analysts with the bank anticipated some kind of political violence from the powerful criminal gangs.

110. Manwaring, *A Contemporary Challenge to State Sovereignty*, 42.

111. This was discussed at Seminário Internacional sobre o Crime Organizado e Democracia, November 26–28, 2007, at the Núcleo de Estudos da Violência, Universidade de São Paolo.

112. Luciana Fernandez, "Organized Crime and Terrorism: From the Cells towards Political Communication, a Case Study," *Terrorism and Political Violence* 21, no. 4 (2009): 608.

113. "Five Years after Deadly May 2006 São Paulo Attacks, Report Documents Role of State Violence and Corruption in Organized Crime," International Human Rights Clinic, Harvard Law School, May 2011, http://harvardhumanrights.word press.com/2011/05/09/five-years-after-deadly-may-2006-sao-paulo-attacks-report-documents-role-of-state-violence-and-corruption-in-organized-crime/.

114. Fernandez, "Organized Crime and Terrorism," 603.

115. Fernando Delgado, Raquel Elias Ferreira Dodge, and Sandra Carvalhor, eds., "São Paulo Sob Achaque: Corrupção, Crime Organizado e Violência Institucional em Maio de 2006," International Human Rights Clinic, Harvard Law School, May 2011, http://harvardhumanrights.wordpress.com/2011/05/09/five-years-after-deadly-may-2006-sao-paulo-attacks-report-documents-role-of-state-violence-and-corruption-in-organized-crime/.

116. Ibid. The five-year study was done by Brazilians in conjunction with Harvard's International Law Clinic.

117. Lívia Marra and Gabriela Manzini, "CRM finaliza relatório sobre suspeitos mortos em ações do PCC," *Folha Online*, May 23, 2006, http://www1.folha.uol.com .br/folha/cotidiano/ult95u121899.shtml.

118. Delgado et al., "São Paulo Sob Achaque."

119. Rollins et al., *International Terrorism and Transnational Crime*, 32.

120. Syed Saleem Shahzad, *Inside Al-Qaeda and the Taliban: Beyond Bin Laden and 9/11* (London: Pluto Press, 2011), wrote on the relationships with al-Qaeda and the government and was murdered almost immediately after the publication of the book. His murder has been thought to have been committed by government security forces.

121. Gretchen Peters, *Haqqani Network Financing: The Evolution of an Industry,* Combating Terrorism Center, West Point, July 2012, http://www.ctc.usma.edu/ posts/haqqani-network-financing.

122. Ryan Clarke, *Crime-Terror Nexus in South Asia: States Security and Non-state Actors* (London: Routledge, 2011).

123. Ibid., 33; Jayshree Bajoria and Eben Kaplan, "The ISI and Terrorism: Behind the Accusations," Council on Foreign Relations, May 4, 2011, https://secure.www .cfr.org/pakistan/isi-terrorism-behind-accusations/p11644.

124. "'93 Blasts: Two Customs Officials Held," *Times of India,* November 2, 2006, http://articles.timesofindia.indiatimes.com/2006-11-02/india/27797664_1_ blasts-shekhadi-coast-aide-of-prime-conspirator. Interview with high-level Indian customs official in Washington, DC, April 2011.

125. Clarke, *Crime-Terror Nexus,* 1.

126. "David C. Headley," May 24, 2011, http://topics.nytimes.com/top/reference/ timestopics/people/h/david_c_headley/index.html?inline=nyt-per; Sebastian Rotella, "Newly Discovered Warnings about Headley Reveal a Troubling Timeline in Mumbai Case," November 5, 2010, http://www.propublica.org/article/newly-dis covered-warnings-about-headley-reveal-a-troubling-timeline-in-mumb; Stephen Tankel, *Storming the World Stage: The Story of Lashkar-e-Taiba* (New York: Columbia University Press, 2011), 221–29. One of Headley's collaborators, Tahawwur Rana, was sentenced by American court in early 2013 and revealed the collaboration of the ISI in the attack. Sebastian Rotella, "Support for Mumbai Terror Group Lands Chicagoan 14-Year Prison Term," *Pro Publica,* January 17, 2013, http://www.propublica.org/article/accomplice-in-mumbai-massacre-faces- sentencing-judge-in-chicago.

127. Tankel, *Storming the World Stage,* 144–47.

128. Pakistan, as an American ally in the war on terrorism, is not listed by the U.S. State Department as a supporter of terrorism.

129. This explains why the U.S. Department of the Treasury designated Ibrahim as a Specially Designated Global Terrorist (SDGT) under Executive Order 13224 in October 2003. See Rollins et al., *International Terrorism and Transnational Crime,* 15.

130. Sumita Sarkar and Arvind Tiwar, "Combating Organised Crime: A Case Study of Mumbai City," http://www.satp.org/satporgtp/publication/faultlines/volume12/ Article5.htm; Clarke, *Crime-Terror Nexus*; Peters, *Haqqani Network Financing.*

131. Clarke, *Crime-Terror Nexus,* 1; interview in April 2011 with former member of the Crown Prosecution Service who had worked in East Africa, who pointed out that the presence of Bollywood DVDs, an industry controlled by D-Company, in East Africa is evidence of the reach of the organization.

132. For a discussion of *hawalas,* see Patrick Jost and Harjit Singh Sandhu, "The Hawala Alternative Remittance System and Its Role in Money Launder- ing," http://www.interpol.int/Public/FinancialCrime/MoneyLaundering/hawala/ default.asp 16/08/2005; see also Edwina A. Thompson, *Trust Is the Coin of the Realm: Lessons from the Money Men in Afghanistan* (New York: Oxford University Press, 2011).

133. Gregory F. Treverton, Carl Matthies, Karla J. Cunningham, Jeremiah Goulka, Greg Ridgeway, and Anny Wong, *Film Piracy, Organized Crime, and Terrorism* (Santa Monica, CA: RAND, 2009), 128–35.

134. U.S. Department of the Treasury, Office of Foreign Assets Control (OFAC), "An Overview of the Foreign Narcotics Kingpin Designation Act and Executive Order 12978 of October 21, 1995"; the latest list is available at http://www.ustreas .gov/offices/enforcement/ofac/sdn/t11sdn.pdf; see also Rollins et al., *International Terrorism and Transnational Crime*, 15.

135. Before the uprising in Kyrgyzstan, there were links between the son of President Bakiyev and representatives of D-Company.

136. Sarkar and Tiwari, "Combating Organised Crime."

137. This violence is featured at the start of the famous movie *Slumdog Millionaire,* which depicts the criminal underworld of Mumbai. Ryan Clarke and Stuart Lee, "The PIRA, D-Company, and the Crime-Terror Nexus," *Terrorism and Political Violence* 20, no. 3 (2008): 390; Tankel, *Storming the World Stage*, 141.

138. Rollins et al., *International Terrorism and Transnational Crime*, 14–16.

139. Clarke and Lee, "PIRA, D-Company, and the Crime-Terror Nexus," 390; Misha Glenny, *McMafia: A Journey through the Criminal Underworld* (New York: Alfred A. Knopf, 2008), 136–37, 140–42.

140. Clarke, *Crime-Terror Nexus*, 2; see also Guelke, *New Age of Terrorism*, viii.

141. Kaplan, "Paying for Terror."

142. Ibid.

143. Clarke, *Crime-Terror Nexus*, 59.

144. Ibid. Clarke also points out that they were able to pay shopkeepers and taxi drivers to conduct surveillance.

145. "'93 Blasts."

146. S. Hussain Zaidi, *Black Friday: The True Story of the Bombay Bomb Blasts* (New Delhi: Penguin, 2002).

147. Douglas Farah, "Who Is Dawood Ibrahim?," http://counterterrorismblog.org/mt/ pings.cgi/2902.

148. Clarke, *Crime-Terror Nexus*, 59. The LeT, the banned military wing of the Islamic organization Markaz-ud-Dawa-al Irshad, is headquartered near Lahore and was named as a terrorist organization by the United States in 2001.

149. Clarke and Lee, "PIRA, D-Company, and the Crime-Terror Nexus," 386.

150. CNN World, "India Police: Pakistan Spy Agency behind Mumbai Bombings," http://articles.cnn.com/2006-09-30/world/india.bombs_1_students-islamic-move ment-pakistan-spy-agency-indian-police?_s=PM:WORLD.

151. Rhys Blakeley, "Foreigners Targeted in Co-ordinated Bombay Attacks," *Sunday Times,* November 27, 2008, http://www.timesonline.co.uk/tol/news/world/asia/ article5240126.ece.

152. *Times Online,* November 27, 2008, http://www.timesonline.co.uk/tol/news/ world/asia/article5241795.ece.

153. Gardiner Harris, "India Executes Pakistani Gunman Involved in 2008 Attacks on Mumbai," *New York Times,* November 21, 2012, http://www.nytimes.com/ 2012/11/22/world/asia/india-hangs-only-surviving-mumbai-attacker.html?ref= ajmalkasab&_r=0.

154. *Pro Publica,* January 24, 2013, http://www.propublica.org/article/david-headley-homegrown-terrorist.

155. Organized crime can extort money in time-sensitive industries. Hence their involve-ment in ports, where they control the loading and unloading of perishable cargo.

156. Rollins et al., *International Terrorism and Transnational Crime*, 15–16.

157. Ibid., 15.

158. Shelley, "Countering Terrorism in the US"; Farah, "Al Qaeda and the Gemstone Trade," 199–200.

159. Peter Israel and Stephen Jones, *Others Unknown: Timothy McVeigh and the Oklahoma City Bombing Conspiracy* (New York: Public Affairs, 2001), 17.

160. Discussion by the author with international counterterrorism professionals at the National Defense University, Washington, DC, February 2010. The failure to find criminal activity by investigators does not always indicate its absence. Moreover, even though the British claimed that they did not find any criminal links to the bombings of their subways, Belgian authorities informed them that they had found a model of what resembled a London tube station in a home searched in connection with a terrorist investigation around the time of the attacks. See Jana Arsovska and Stef Janssens, "Turkish Crime Networks in Europe," *Jane's Intelligence Digest,* February 15, 2008; conversations with Janssens in Vienna, March 2, 2010, and with Arsovska on May 3, 2010, in Washington, DC.

161. Diane Rickman, "UK Riots: One in Four Charged Rioters Had Committed Over Ten Previous Offences," *Huffington Post,* September 15, 2011, http://www.huffingtonpost.co.uk/2011/09/15/uk-riots-25-per-cent-of-c_n_963567.html?view=print.

162. Ibid., Rickman quoting a British law enforcement officer who wrote that the rioters "thought through some of the tactics" for dealing with police "very carefully" and used methods such as burning trash bins so police vans could not pass through burned plastic on the road.

163. Eduardo Moncada, "The Politics of Urban Violence: Challenges for Development in the Global South," *Studies in Comparative International Development* 48 (2013): 217–39.

164. Dahlby, *Allah's Torch,* 6.

165. Martha Knisely Huggins, *From Slavery to Vagrancy in Brazil: Crime and Social Control in the Third World* (New Brunswick, NJ: Rutgers University Press, 1985); Martha K. Huggins, ed., *Vigilantism and the State in Modern Latin America: Essays in Extralegal Violence* (Westport, CT: Praeger, 1991), has written much on the abuse of the poor and urban poor in Brazil; Arias, *Drugs and Democracy in Rio de Janeiro.*

166. John Rollins, Liana Sun Wyler, and Seth Rosen, "International Terrorism and Transnational Crime: Security Threats, U.S. Policy, and Considerations for Congress," Congressional Research Service, January 5, 2010, 32, http://www.fas.org/sgp/crs/terror/R41004.pdf.

167. See discussion of PIRA and D-Company in Clarke and Lee, "PIRA, D-Company, and the Crime-Terror Nexus," 392–93, in relation to two organizations engaged in both crime and terrorism.

168. "Five Years after Deadly May 2006 São Paulo Attacks."

169. The concept of prisons as institutions that discipline and punish has received a broad understanding after Michel Foucault's work in *Discipline and Punish: The Birth of the Prison* (New York: Vintage Books, 1995).

2

Corruption

An Incubator of Organized Crime and Terrorism

Turkey is at the crossroads between Asia and Europe. During the Ottoman period, there was a large and highly trained, but also corrupt, bureaucracy. Modern Turkey shares this attribute. Even though Turkey is one of the world's rising economies and a member of the G-20, its governance is undermined, particularly by corruption in its border regions, but also by the massive corruption in neighboring states.[1]

Turkey's border area with Iran and the Caucasus is impoverished and inhabited by Turkey's minority Kurdish community, who share kinship relations with Kurds in four neighboring Middle East countries. Familial and clan groups have been involved in trade, much of it outside the control of the state, for centuries.[2] The regional instability and the lack of education and employment for youthful males or capital for development result in a great reliance on cross-border smuggling for contemporary survival.[3] People, arms, antiquities, counterfeits, and cigarettes can move easily across borders with Iran, Iraq, and Syria.

A well-meaning senior police officer in the community, in fall 2011, mounted an operation against a particular van, based on intelligence linking this vehicle entering Turkey to a terrorist threat. Unlike in the Ressam case mentioned in Chapter 1, this police stop of the truck was not random. With advanced information, the officer was able to detain the suspicious truck, which contained seventeen young Pakistani men being smuggled on fake Iranian passports and with other falsified documents. Before the police officer could mount a full investigation, the truck driver managed to escape from custody, facilitated by corrupt officials from the community. Without the truck driver's insights and with only a group of youthful males, representing a single node of this larger human smuggling operation, the police officer could not address a criminal operation that spanned several countries.

This relatively routine case illustrates the larger themes discussed in this chapter on corruption. First, in states with high levels of corruption and theft of state assets, such as Pakistan, many young males are left with diminished opportunities and limited chances for survival within the legitimate economy. This problem is compounded by the youth bulge in south Asia, Iran, and the Middle East. These youths, therefore, become ripe for exploitation by both terrorists and criminals. Often, it is the revulsion that they feel with the ever-present corruption that provides an intense motivation to be involved with nonstate actors, who undermine the state's survival and its economic and political order.[4] Great economic inequality fuels both crime and terrorism and contributes to political instability. The movement of the young men in the preceding Turkish example thousands of miles from Pakistan to the eastern border of Turkey was facilitated by corruption at every stage of the process – including the crossing of borders and the issuance of false documents and passports. The passports and other documents were undoubtedly issued in Iran. These documents may have been produced by criminal groups but more likely were supplied by state-sanctioned, corrupt actors, motivated to cause harm to other countries through their facilitation of crime and terrorism.[5] This is the ultimate corruption of the state, exemplified by the problem of state-supported terrorism.

The truck driver did not merely walk away from a Turkish police operation; a facilitator, within law enforcement or within the community, enabled his escape. This illustrates another important point: that regions with high levels of corruption provide environments conducive to the operations of criminals and terrorists. But this corruption, in turn, undermines the capacity of the state to guarantee its security, and that of its citizens. Because the individuals huddled in the truck were beholden to those who moved them, they could be forced to commit criminal or terrorist acts to pay for their transport.

Corruption rates along the route between Pakistan and Turkey may be among the highest in the world, but the problems in this region are far from unique. The centrality of corruption to the growth of crime and terrorism worldwide is apparent in Latin America, Africa, the former USSR, and many parts of Asia. It is also present, to a lesser degree, in the developed world. Although Chapter 1 focused on corruption as a facilitator of terrorist acts, this chapter analyzes corruption as central to the rise, growth, and institutionalization of both crime and terrorism, and to the rise of illicit trade.

How are Corruption, Crime, and Terrorism Linked?

Corruption is a complex phenomenon operating at the local, national, and global levels.[6] Its impact is different in each arena, but in every environment in which corruption operates, it is central to the rise and the perpetuation of crime, terrorism, and other social ills. Corruption can be considered an incubator for the growth of organized crime, violence,[7] and terrorism. The reverse is also true. Crime incubates corruption, as does instability. All of this is self-reinforcing and complex to combat.

Diverse and complex relationships characterize the interaction of crime, terrorism, and corruption. These relationships have allowed illicit trade and transnational crime to assume an ever-larger share of the world's global economy and to become a major political force in many countries and regions. Terrorists could not recruit collaborators, develop their organizations, or maintain a broad support network if it were not for the pervasive corruption that undermines quality of life and is repellent to many innocent civilians. As one analyst of Middle Eastern terrorism wrote, "government corruption also played an important role in the emerging of grassroots movements like Hezbollah and its secular Shiite rival, Amal."[8]

The widely used World Bank definition of corruption as "the abuse of public office for private gain"[9] is not sufficient to describe the diverse phenomena encountered in reality. Corruption, in this work's analysis, involves more than public officials. It also includes private actors who behave in corrupt ways, which accords with the definition of the Asian Development Bank.[10] Moreover, limiting corruption exclusively to the state sector is difficult in most developing and post-Communist countries, as there is an absence of clear boundaries between state office and private business.[11] Combating corruption is even more complex when corruption is associated with international agencies, like the United Nations with its "oil for food" program.

Corruption has been part of human society for millennia.[12] A rich corruption literature exists that examines petty and grand corruption, the symptoms of corruption, and the types of corruption that exist in different political systems.[13] According to these analyses, clan-based corruption is different from oligarchical corruption,[14] which in turn differs from that which thrives in one-party states. Although some analysts once suggested that corruption greases the wheels in overregulated and nonfunctional bureaucracies,[15] the costs of corruption have become so great in the global economy that this analytical perspective is now largely discredited.

Apart from these academic perspectives on the topic, there is a reality that the citizens of much of the world, especially in the developing and transitional countries, experience on a daily basis – that corruption is destroying their society, denying their children and their youth a future. In Africa, where the costs of corruption are among the greatest in the world, corruption results in delayed development and increased inequalities.[16] Compounding the problem is that needed foreign aid is diverted and often goes directly into the pockets of corrupt officials.[17]

In recent decades, globalization has catalyzed a sea change in the level of corruption. Money can easily be moved internationally, to major banking centers and offshore locales, via wire transfers. With the rise of the global financial institutions in the post–World War II period, there is more to steal. Money appropriated for dams and construction projects can be transferred to the pockets of dictators and their cronies and moved overseas with enormous rapidity. This has been a particular problem with the siphoning off of foreign aid that should be used for this infrastructure development. Corruption is the Achilles' heel of the global economy.[18] Citizens feel powerless against corruption that reaches to the highest levels of power and that they cannot counter. The corruption that unleashed the forces of the Arab Spring is symptomatic of the problem, as discussed more fully later.

There is no absolute measure of corruption. This is why Transparency International calls its survey of corruption a Perception Index.[19] According to the survey results, the problem of corruption is most pronounced in the developing world. Yet in many Moslem countries that have strong fundamentalist movements, the problems of corruption are, for them, encountered not only at home, but also evident in the West. Consequently, targets selected by terrorists are frequently symbols of Western corruption. As was seen in two cases discussed in Chapter 1, terrorists chose foreign targets for symbolic value. For this reason, the World Trade Center, a symbol of Western domination over the global financial system, and the Pentagon, seen as a symbol of U.S. military power, were chosen by al-Qaeda as targets of attack. On its website and in chat rooms and communications, al-Qaeda glorified 9/11 as striking at the degenerate and corrupt West. Basayev, the Chechen terrorist behind the Beslan attack, as discussed in Chapter 5, sent his operative to California to raise money for his organization by preying off the wealth of decadent Hollywood.

In contrast, the West presumes that corruption is the norm in the developing world. Far too often, Westerners do not understand how corruption operates outside their context, the key role it assumes in all aspects of developing and transitional societies, or how citizens who live consistently with high levels of corruption perceive and respond to the problem.

The failure of U.S. intelligence analysts to understand the centrality of corruption to Saddam Hussein's rule in Iraq contributed significantly to the faulty conclusion that Hussein had obtained weapons of mass destruction (WMD). In the analysis that followed this intelligence failure, a detailed study was made of how Americans had reached incorrect conclusions. A key piece of evidence used to support the presence of WMD was that Iraqi personnel in the nuclear industry had set up phony front companies. From an American analyst's point of view, this was a clear case of subterfuge. Scientists, it was assumed, set up these accounts to cover up the purchase of WMD and related technology. But if these analysts had realized how corruption operated in every aspect of life in Saddam-era Iraq, they would have reached an entirely different conclusion. These phony accounts were not set up for subterfuge but for the Iraqi scientists to siphon off large amounts of the budget from the WMD procurement program into their own bank accounts. The analysts reached a catastrophically wrong conclusion on weapons proliferation because they misunderstand and underestimated the force of corruption.[20]

The misunderstanding of corruption has similarly impeded the success of the multilateral intervention in Afghanistan. The United States and much of the Western alliance, for many years after the initial intervention in October 2001, believed that Afghan citizens accepted corruption. The coalition ignored and tolerated the growing corruption of the Karzai leadership they supported because they believed that corruption was acceptable to the citizenry. But the Pakistani commentator, Ikhram Sehgal, wrote on Afghanistan,

> How can the honesty and integrity that the Obama Administration stands for tolerate corrupt elements to become the arbiters of a country's destiny under the garb of democracy? Public perception will never tolerate dual standards, the US is at a crossroads with respect to its image in the world, it must practice abroad what it preaches at home. With corruption rife in the upper echelons of the Afghan hierarchy, their version of democracy is counter-productive to the war effort against the perceived "purist" Taliban.[21]

But the Taliban, coming from Afghan society, knew that an intolerable level of corruption had been reached. They capitalized on this revulsion against corruption to reestablish themselves in Afghan society. As discussed more fully later, they, like many other major terrorist organizations in the developing world, have made their anticorruption stance a key recruiting tool. They understand that antipathy toward corruption can be a force for citizen mobilization.

Elsewhere, Hamas, Hezbollah, and Liberation Tigee of Tamil Eelam (LTTE, of Sri Lanka) have broadened their base and strengthened their influence using anticorruption planks.[22] In 2010, the FARC kidnapped a regional governor with the intention of putting him on trial for corruption.[23]

The failure to address corruption, and the resultant costs, can embed terrorists within a society. In Afghanistan and Yemen, citizen repudiation of corrupt leaders can result in challenges to governmental authority. Moreover, corruption used as an operational tool by invading military powers, such as Western forces in Afghanistan that have bribed local officials and warlords extensively to secure supply lines, has undermined their mission and their moral authority, further destabilizing the environment.[24]

As is discussed further, terrorist groups are not the only nonstate actors to deliver social services. Transnational crime groups in corrupt environments also substitute for the state. The Colombian drug cartels, the Mafia in Sicily, and Russian crime groups have all delivered direct services, such as schools and medical facilities, or have provided mediation in the absence of functioning legal institutions.[25] In Pakistan, a terrorist-related group provided flood relief aid, and the *yakuza*, Japanese organized crime, provided assistance following the Kobe earthquake.

Living in a highly corrupt state is not desirable for anyone. There is a great difference between living in a society based on exchange relations, where individuals owe each other favors[26] and corrupt relations exist, and the current environment of global corruption. In the new globalized economic order, worldwide corruption undermines states and permits the siphoning off of large amounts of national revenue with dizzying speed, thanks to rapid electronic movements of money. In these kleptocracies,[27] grand corruption results in the transfer of whole national treasuries abroad. Illustrative of this was the discovery of most of the liquid assets of Equatorial Guinea in Riggs Bank in the United States, those of Turkmenistan in Deutsche Bank in Germany, and the transfer of the assets of the Afghan Central Bank to the largely unregulated financial haven of Dubai. The funds of Equatorial Guinea[28] and Turkmenistan derived from the sale of natural resources, whereas in Afghanistan, the stolen funds came from foreign assistance, national revenues, and a domestic Ponzi scheme.[29] But in these cases, enumerated by Global Witness, the banks were facilitators of kleptocratic corruption.

In many countries, corrupt officials siphon off loans made by multinational organizations for structural adjustment and economic development. The failure of the IMF, the World Bank, and regional international banks in ensuring accountability has allowed billions in development assistance to be misappropriated and sent overseas. Although staffs have been added to the banks to enhance accountability, these investigative departments are severely understaffed relative to the size of the banks' loans and have failed to implement substantial improvement.[30] Citizens at home, who must pay the state debts and the cost of servicing these loans, receive diminished living standards and quality of life as the interest for these stolen loans comes due. These debts incurred by corrupt officials, therefore, deprive countries of the capital needed for economic development, education, social services, and medical care.[31]

The revelations of the financial abuse of national leaders accompanying the Arab Spring served as a rallying cry for those seeking change. One Arab commentator, writing on the impoverished states of Tunisia, Algeria, Jordan, and Egypt in January 2011, shortly after the initial protests in Tunisia, stated that the real terror is marginalization:

> Within its bosom are bred greed, land grab, corruption, monopoly and the new entrepreneurial classes who exchange loyalty and patronage with the political masters as well as the banknotes and concessions with which both fund flashy lifestyles. Thus the map of distribution was gerrymandered at the expense of the have-nots who are placated with insufficient micro credits or ill-managed national development funds. The crumbs – whatever subsidies are allowed by the new economic order built on the pillars of privatisation, the absence of social safety nets and economic protectionism – delay disaffection but never eliminate it.[32]

The abuses of privatization, land grabs, and insider monopolies are not confined to the Arab world. Unfortunately, these are more universal problems of corrupt economic elites. In the 1990s, there was a wave of privatizations worldwide, conducted in the name of increasing economic efficiency and promoting growth. But in highly corrupt states, they were conducted without transparency. Instead of fostering the intended growth, these privatizations increased economic disparity by transferring state resources to corrupt elites. As Latin American analysts wrote, these economic policies "resulted in state corruption, and a precipitous weakening of institutions and their legitimacy in the public mind. Welfare safety nets were removed, exposing millions to the shock of economic failure."[33] The privatization of public services and state resources contributed to greater public insecurity and corruption of law enforcement.[34] In Colombia, Enilse Lopez was convicted in 2011 and sentenced to nine years in prison for her role in the privatization of state lottery companies. She used her role in regional lottery companies to amass a personal fortune that benefitted politicians, and she served as an intermediary for the violent paramilitary groups.[35]

Privatizations benefitted elites and criminals in other Latin American countries, such as Mexico and Argentina, but also in the post-Soviet states. Russia, Ukraine, and Kazakhstan, with the most valuable assets, were most affected, and oligarchs were created overnight, often with the assistance of organized crime. This massive transfer of wealth, and the resulting acute economic differentiation, have helped embed organized crime in the state in both Latin America and the post-Soviet states.[36]

Exposure of these phenomena is much easier than rectifying the abuse, as privatizations are not reversible and money, once stolen, is often hard to locate and even harder to recover. The secrecy of much of the international banking system and the proliferation of offshore banking centers makes the embezzlement of government funds and grand corruption ever easier. Both Nigeria and the Philippines, even after lengthy investigations, were able to repatriate only a small fraction of the billions stolen by their former leaders.[37] Under these circumstances, with serious grounds for discontent, it is hardly surprising that Nigeria and the Philippines remain key nodes for terrorist organizations. Moreover, Nigeria remains among the most important sources of transnational crime, and there are increasing problems of recruitment of youth into terrorism both there and in neighboring states.[38] Both Nigeria and the Philippines are major sources of human trafficking victims transported worldwide.[39] Criminal and corrupt groups in these countries are at the heart of this trade.

Corruption by high officials, such as presidents and prime ministers, undermines delivery of social services to citizens. Money needed for education is diverted, reducing the quality and availability of education.[40] Honduras, with its extremely high rate of homicides, epitomized the problem. For example, in Honduras, "the average number of school days from 2000–2010 was just 125, instead of the 200 required by law. This problem is already producing frightening results: Honduras spends the highest percentage of its GDP on education in the region, but has the second lowest test scores."[41] Corruption and negligence are at the heart of this problem.[42]

The requirement that bribes be paid for entrance into schools, and to pass exams, deprives many of the education they need to obtain legitimate employment. Therefore, millions of youths are left unprepared. In an increasingly competitive global environment, knowledge is the key to jobs and financial security. The large poorly or undereducated youthful populations, deprived of the possibility of education because of corruption, often lack alternatives to employment in transnational crime and terrorist activities. This could be a driver that might lead them into the illicit economy or militant activity. Illustrative of this is a case of a Guatemalan politician who, in the 1980s, had a choice of work on the farms of Colombian drug traffickers or to go into the mountains with the guerillas. He did neither but instead entered politics, where, as a corrupt politician, he traded favors with the criminal organizations.[43]

The relationship between the absence of education and the availability of personnel for criminal organizations is well understood by the illicit nonstate actors. A Colombian reformer attempting to provide access to education for the rural poor found strong opposition from the crime groups, as they feared the loss of available recruits for the future.[44] Medresehs, Moslem religious schools established in Afghanistan, Pakistan, the West Bank, and North Africa, which are not corrupt[45] and provide education to the poor, have been fruitful recruiting grounds for terrorist organizations. The crucial role that terrorist groups have in exploiting the failure of the state to deliver on key social services, and communicating this message to citizens, is discussed subsequently in greater depth.

But lower-level corruption also is key to the growth and vitality of transnational crime and terrorism. Petty corruption is what most citizens experience on a daily basis – the frequent harassment by the police to extract petty bribes, the payments demanded by the inspector to avoid a fine, or the speed payment to a low-level bureaucrat to obtain a needed permit. These are the daily irritants that erode trust in government.[46] With routine abuse, citizens become complicit in violations of the law. Having lost faith in the existing political system, they may bribe officials to cross the border with contraband at the behest of an organized crime group. Or subject to the constant harassment of the authorities, they may be driven to dire action or even terrorism. As Sarah Chayes has pointed out in her work on Afghanistan, frustration with corruption drives young men into the hands of the Taliban. This problem is not confined to Afghanistan but is associated with religious extremism in different parts of the world.[47]

The spark that ignited the Arab Spring was the self-immolation of an Algerian fruit vendor, Mohamed Bouazizi, a man who could no longer tolerate the pervasive corruption.[48] Unable to obtain a job, because most employment is awarded based on connections or payments, he took a last act to support himself. Bouazizi acquired a cart to sell goods in the market. But through this act, he had joined the second or underground economy, because he lacked the requisite permit to be a vendor. On the fateful day that led to his suicide, he was approached by a woman police officer demanding a payment because he lacked the required permit, and his cart was confiscated.

This demand for a bribe humiliated him, and the loss of his livelihood compounded his desperation. The callousness, cruelty, and self-interest of the police officer was more than he could take. He set himself on fire. This self-destructive act mirrors the self-destruction of many terrorists who serve as suicide bombers. In this case, Mohamed Bouazizi chose self-destruction rather than an outwardly directed violence. But in North Africa, terrorist groups look for the disaffected to recruit. In their environment, Bouazizi's revulsion at the corruption of the petty official might instead have been channeled into sacrificing himself as a suicide bomber.

Following his death, other young men took to the streets, and, despite brutal crackdowns, continued to protest against the corrupt elderly leader of their country. President Ben Ali had ruled for twenty-three years, grabbing massive amounts of wealth and property for himself and his family. The rallying cry of the youths was the Arabic word for "humiliation." Facebook, and other communications that fed the protests, contrasted the corruption and glaring ostentation of the ruling family with the frustrating and impoverished lives of the Tunisian youth. The president appropriated the properties of his business partners, his billionaire son-in-law controlled car dealerships, and the president and his wife, while fleeing, ordered the country's gold reserves loaded onto his departing airplane.[49]

Yet, as the citizens of North Africa (Egypt, Libya, Tunisia) and the Middle East protested against the corrupt and authoritarian leaderships that had stolen their nations' resources and their futures, they were creating political chaos. There was no orderly transition of power because there was no opposition waiting in the wings. All opponents had been suppressed. With no authority figure in place, the institutions of social control ceased to function, particularly in the remote parts of the North African states. Nonstate actors exploited the breakdown of social and political control, enhancing the discontent and the growth of terrorism and transnational crime.[50] Human traffickers, preying off the human misery of the conflict, received payments from thousands of desperate people seeking to move from North Africa to Europe. Migrants were exploited by the human smugglers and traffickers, who lacked boats capable of transporting them. Many of these, fleeing corruption and seeking a better future, lost their lives when the flimsy boats improvised to carry them to Europe capsized.[51]

Away from the Mediterranean, in the Arab peninsula, similar patterns were observed. Decades of high unemployment, limited opportunities for the grow-ing youthful population, few public services, and endemic corruption created massive public discontent. In Yemen, youths, communicating by electronic media, protested in the streets. But the breakdown of the old system, while creating hopes for democratization, also created a situation ripe for exploita-tion by terrorists and criminals.[52] AQAP (al-Qaeda of the Arab peninsula) has exploited the chaos to solidify its base. Smuggling activities remain vigorous in the region.[53] Terrorists have been able to operate from Yemen without fear of government intervention.

Ironically, many of the citizens participating in the Arab Spring strove for less corrupt and more accountable government, yet the political disorder accompanying the transition may be facilitating the activities and the provisioning of criminal and terrorist groups.

The previous examples, although drawn mostly from the Islamic world, do not represent a problem confined exclusively to that region. Corruption, as discussed, because of its destabilizing influence, can be a catalyst for crime and terrorism in Latin America, Africa, and non-Moslem parts of Asia. Maoist terrorist groups in such diverse countries as Peru, Nepal, India, and the Philippines[54] "thrive in countries where there is corruption, lawlessness, transnational crime, and the discontent produced by broken political systems."[55]

The Risk of Corruption

The events in Tunisia were unprecedented and unexpected by foreign powers and specialists on North Africa and the Arab world. For too long, many governments believed that these corrupt and authoritarian governments were stable because they observed the repressive apparati of these states maintain order. If the widespread corruption was considered, it was seen as a regrettable but normal part of the culture. Almost no one in the international community fully appreciated the long-term destabilizing impact of corruption and the forces it could unleash.

Yet a few days before the Tunisian government crumbled, the World Economic Forum (WEF) released its annual *Global Risks Report* for 2011. For the first time, the report devoted a full section to the illegal economy nexus, identifying this as a major global risk. The report was released in the midst of the mass rioting in Tunisia, the first domino of the Arab Spring. As the WEF officials responsible for the *Global Risks Report* stated on BBC television at the time of its release, the report indicates that the world has never been so unstable, and the likelihood of a major challenge to global stability is imminent.[56] The report anticipated some intense instability but did not identify where in the world this breakdown in order would occur.

The *Global Risks Report*, based on a well-developed methodology of the WEF, received input from business leaders, policy makers, many members of its Global Agenda Councils, leading academics, heads of important nongovernmental organizations, and multinational officials. They were surveyed as to the greatest global threats, the likelihood of these risks over the next ten years, and the risks that were most closely connected with these phenomena.[57] Hundreds of individuals living and working in many parts of the world identified corruption as a core risk that was closely linked with the illegal economy, fragile states, and organized crime. These core risks were, in turn, associated with global governance failure, terrorism, economic inequality, and geopolitical conflict.

The links of all these forces have been illustrated in the previous discussion. Illicit trade, organized crime, and corruption are highly interlinked. Illicit trade includes the trade not only in drugs, humans, and arms but also in other

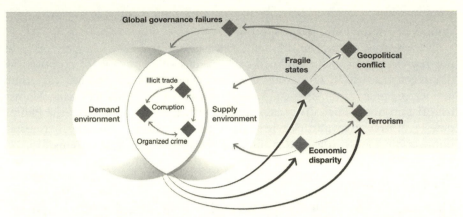

FIGURE 2.1. Illegal economy nexus. *Source*: *Global Risks Report*, World Economic Forum, 2011, 23.

less discussed commodities such as counterfeit pharmaceuticals, electronics, software piracy, counterfeit and diverted cigarettes, environmentally protected species, and natural resources. All these trades, which are discussed more fully later in this book, flourish when there is pervasive corruption in law enforcement, customs, border patrol, and state regulatory agencies. Many engaged in this trade are transnational organized crime groups who must constantly link with politicians and government officials at all levels of government – local, regional, and national – if they are to survive. The links between terrorists and politicians are much less frequent; often they depend on the corrupt links of the criminals.

Yet, as Figure 2.1 reveals, the illicit networks are connected to other systemic risks. In the North African region, where the Arab Spring began, illicit networks are a major part of the economic and political system.[58] Because of the very visible economic inequality and the absence of a future for the bulging youth population, it is an area where the terrorist organization AQIM, discussed in the introduction, has flourished and has linked with criminals in the region.[59]

The events of the Arab Spring revealed a global governance failure in a large swath of the world from North Africa through the Middle East, in which hundreds of millions reside. The extreme violence in Libya that resulted in foreign intervention revealed the escalation of violence when corruption, crime, and terrorism combine. Just as was discussed in the introduction in regard to Syria, this dirty entanglement leads to unprecedented and often uncontrollable outcomes.

The unanticipated fall of many Arab governments within the first months of 2011 suggests that these autocracies were more fragile than anyone imagined. But the international community, accustomed to viewing strength in terms of "strong leaders" and military might, failed to understand the fragility of states where illicit networks and corruption flourish.

The failure to anticipate the overthrow of a national leadership was not confined to North Africa. In advance of the Arab Spring, no one anticipated that citizens would revolt against a corrupt leader in Kyrgyzstan in 2010. In June 2010, the Central Asian country of Kyrgyzstan had its second uprising against a corrupt leader, President Bakiyev.[60] Five years earlier, the country had risen up to oust the highly corrupt President Akayev. President Bakiyev and his family sucked hundreds of millions of dollars out of this small country. The money was stolen via a combination of sweetheart deals in telecommunications, national revenues, and foreign aid. But even a small landlocked country can have critical importance in illicit trade. In Kyrgyzstan, a key node on the drug route out of Afghanistan, many illicit networks flourished. In the prisons of the country, criminals and terrorists confined together contributed to the same general inmate fund (*obshchak*) that was used to corrupt officials and support the inmates' activities. But now, it is the terrorists who have achieved dominance in the prisons:

> HT (Hizb ut-Tahrir) and other groups like Tablighi Jamaat have exploited the weakness of underfunded, demoralised and corrupt prison systems to extend their own networks and recruit within the prison population. They are helped by a program of prison mosque building, allegedly funded in part by a major organised crime figure, where their own imams usually preach their brand of radical Islam. Prison directors, meanwhile, are often reduced to mere observers of the power struggle taking place within their own establishments.[61]

Terrorist and criminal groups in the region both benefit from the drug trade.[62] The *Global Risks Report* explained,

> It should be noted that even when flows of illicit goods and criminal activity are small relative to global markets, they can have an outsized effect on fragile states, as the real value of such activity can dwarf national salaries and government budgets.
>
> The potential for this nexus of risks to cause contagion has arguably been demonstrated recently in Kyrgyzstan . . . The undermining of state leadership and economic growth, by corrupt officials and organized crime, contributed significantly to social tensions which erupted in violent conflict in June 2010, causing widespread destruction, hundreds of civilian deaths and the displacement of 400,000 ethnic Uzbeks.[63]

After the conflict, the president's son, Maksim Bakiyev, moved to England, where he had millions of dollars stashed in British banks. The Kyrgyz anger at his avarice and his ability to lodge his corrupt millions in a financial haven has resulted in concerted efforts by the new government of Kyrgyzstan to have him deported from the United Kingdom and his ill-gotten gains confiscated, so far without success. Once again, this case shows that the problems of fragile states are aggravated by Western support structures for corrupt autocrats.

Violent conflict that results in large-scale social and economic destruction leaves citizens without a viable means for survival. Therefore, citizen recruitment into illicit networks may be an unintended consequence of this disorder.

Corruption and Kleptocracies: A Fertile Ground for Recruitment of Criminals and Terrorists

The preponderance of criminals and terrorists worldwide are youthful males. Women in most societies are underrepresented in ordinary and transnational crime as well as in terrorism. There are noted exceptions: women drug couriers, Chechen female suicide bombers, and female relatives of Mexican cartel leaders who serve as large-scale money launderers. Human smuggling and trafficking is the only area of criminality in which women are significantly represented as both victims and perpetrators.[64]

Terrorists and criminals are often young.[65] Research conducted more than two decades ago reviewing reports of terrorists in Latin America, Asia, the Middle East, and Europe found that the average urban terrorist was between twenty-two and twenty-five years of age, based on analyses of 350 terrorists of different organizations.[66] This pattern has been consistent and continues today. Traditionally, criminals in most societies are youthful males; only the leadership of larger criminal organizations is older.

The problem of pervasive corruption contributes in several ways to the recruitment for illicit networks. (1) Corruption inhibits growth and distorts economic policies. These policies benefit the elites and limit economic development and job creation,[67] denying the youthful population possibilities for legitimate employment, even with education. The large youth population bulge in the developing world has no future because of the pervasive corruption, providing human fodder for crime and terrorist organizations.[68] (2) Revulsion at corruption may provide an incentive to join a terrorist organization. Citizens exposed to daily humiliation are vulnerable to the recruiters of terrorist organizations. (3) The financially successful in many societies have often made their wealth through corruption. When such success is rewarded, it legitimates involvement in criminal networks. (4) The corruption so corrodes society that it becomes ungovernable, allowing for all forms of illicit networks to thrive.

Pervasive corruption in states makes individuals lose trust in government, making some of the citizens ready to destroy it. Regions with high levels of corruption provide environments conducive to terrorism recruitment and operations, particularly for youths.

With limits on international migration,[69] the young are vulnerable to recruitment by drug traffickers as couriers and by terrorists who exploit their vulnerability and disillusionment. In Central America, absence of growth, few governmental services, and enormous economic disparities make employment in a drug organization a viable means of survival.[70] Research revealed that unemployment motivated a number of Gulf states detainees, particularly young unskilled and semiskilled laborers, to join the *jihad*. For them, going on *jihad* was alternative employment.[71]

The same phenomenon is at work in other parts of the world. In Nigeria, it is not only the well-born underwear bomber who was recruited for terrorism but also youths who have no future and who do not consider the violence to themselves or to others through their suicide bombs.[72] Likewise, in the impoverished North Caucasus near to Chechnya, as discussed in Chapter 1, similar forces result in youth recruitment for terrorism.

One Dagestani official explained,

> Ninety percent of the young people in Dagestan have nothing to do. Vocational schools have long since closed due to understaffing. No one trains lathe operators, metal workers or tractor drivers anymore, and few can afford to go to college. When they see nothing good coming from the government, many choose the path of banditry, paid for by the foreign supporters of terrorism.[73]

The desperation of the youths at the absence of opportunities, and the huge inequality created by corruption, drives some to terrorism. An interviewed terrorist explained,

> It was my elder brother Khadzhi-Magomed who assisted in my conversion . . . We talked and he always made an emphasis of the crying injustice every Dagestani encounters every day of his life (let's face it). Hands have to be greased for every minor document. A lot of my friends and acquaintances are unemployed. They would do anything to earn at least some money. On the other hand, there are the fat cats rolling in dough.[74]

Profiles of terrorists recruited in highly corrupt countries reveal that some come from more educated and privileged strata. Analysis of members of the terrorist group Lashkar-e-Taiba (LeT) reveals that they had higher than average educations than Pakistani males and were drawn from the lower middle class.[75] Perceived injustice can also motivate the more privileged. The Peruvian university students who joined the terrorist organization Sendero Luminoso reflect a Latin American tradition of the middle class and elites joining terrorist movements. In the 1970s, members of the Argentine-based terrorist organization Montoneros were often educated and came from the middle class, mobilized by the corruption and social inequality they observed.[76]

A similar phenomenon was identified in Marc Sageman's analysis of the court documents of four hundred terrorists. The members of al-Qaeda "join the jihad at the average age of 26. Three-quarters were professionals or semi-professionals. They are engineers, architects, and civil engineers, mostly scientists."[77]

Revulsion at Corruption

The main plotter of the 9/11 attack was Mohammad Atta, who reached university age in Egypt in the mid-1980s, a time of "obvious corruption and

ostentation on the part of the elite and government officials" and a period
characterized by a dramatic increase in the percentage of citizens living below
the poverty level.[78] His transformation into a terrorist followed a similar path
to that taken by Osama bin Laden, who was born into a wealthy family in
Saudi Arabia but revolted by the corruption he saw around him. In Osama bin
Laden's 1996 fatwa titled "Declaration of War against the Americans Occupying the Land of the Two Holy Places," he wrote,

> Numerous princes share with the people their feelings, privately expressing their
> concerns and objecting to the corruption, repression and the intimidation taking
> place in the country. But the competition between influential princes for personal
> gains and interest had destroyed the country. Through its course of actions the
> regime has torn off its legitimacy.[79]

The level of corruption was formidable. As one powerful Saudi prince explained
following the death of the ruling prince, "with up to $400 billion the kingdom
has spent on development, maybe $50 billion was taken in corruption."[80] The
money siphoned off helped support the maintenance of a 450-foot yacht with a
100-person crew for the ruling prince,[81] just one manifestation of the enormous
ostentation of the ruling family.

The analysis of Afghanistan, conducted at the behest of General Stanley
McCrystal, pointed out that the revulsion against corruption helped foster
sympathy for the Taliban, who market themselves as pure and able to control
the crime and corruption.[82] But this situation is not restricted to Afghanistan.
High levels of corruption are pervasive in the recruiting grounds of Islamic
terrorism – Central Asia, the Caucasus in Russia, the Middle East and North
Africa, Pakistan – all of which score miserably on the Transparency Corruption Perception Index.[83] The development assistance that comes from Wahabi
groups is delivered to the citizenry with limited payoffs to corrupt leaders,
thereby spreading the ideological base for terrorism through schools, mosques,
charities, and other institutions.[84]

The Fish Rots from the Head

A Russian expression, "the fish rots from the head," is well suited to the reality
of Kenya, Russia,[85] and the many other developing and transitional countries.
Criminalization thrives at the bottom of society because the top offers the worst
of examples of entrenched crime and corruption.

Illustrative of this problem is the situation in Kenya:[86]

> Ongoing allegations of the involvement in drug trafficking of politicians, police
> officers, and other government officials, without any of them being successfully
> investigated or prosecuted, have contributed significantly to low levels of public
> trust in politicians and government institutions. In a July 2009 national survey,
> only 7 percent expressed trust in Parliament, 8 percent in the judiciary, and
> 8 percent in the Kenya Police Service.[87]

One former assistant minister and current member of parliament has been named a drug kingpin by the United States, a rare distinction.[88] Only the press is respected by the overwhelming majority of the population. With such deep-seated criminalization of the society at the top, there can be no hope for resistance at the bottom.

Corruption Corrodes Society

Extreme corruption and the loss of the state monopoly of violence create fragile states and lawless areas in which Hobbesian ungovernability may prevail.[89] Examples of this are numerous.[90] In Brazil, there are the numerous *favelas,* places where the Brazilian state is hardly present, that give rise to the politicized urban violence and crime discussed in Chapter 1.[91] Corruption in Latin America "coats almost every level of bureaucracy, from the highest authorities, who require large sums of money to manipulate the political-administrative machine, to the small fry: customs officers, border police, and provincial and municipal officials."[92] In Colombia, the central hub of a criminal network can be an elected mayor, which reveals that the electoral process has been manipulated to ensure that administrative decisions benefit criminals rather than citizens.[93]

Corruption, rather than problems of state creation,[94] is at the core of the reason that criminal and terrorist actors thrive. Ungoverned and poorly governed spaces provide safe havens for criminals, terrorists, and all forms of hybrid networks.[95]

Criminal and Terrorist Groups as Service Providers: Supplanting the Corrupt State

There has been a long history of criminal groups providing services to marginalized groups in places where state authority was absent. Communities have tolerated the violence of organized crime groups because they have maintained order, regulated disputes, enforced contracts, collected rents, and provided services in the absence of the state. They were not just criminals, as the British historian Hobsbawm put it, but "primitive rebels," or in other words, a shadow force providing state services.[96] The Mafia arose on the estates of the rural landowners of Sicily, where there was an absence of governance by the state.[97] Japanese organized crime originated at the end of the Samurai period, when the traditional order had broken down.[98] Both Japanese organized crime and the Mafia helped enforce contracts, collected payment for their services, and meted out justice.[99]

In many developing countries, there is an absence of state capacity as revenues are not collected, or there is little to fund the state. In many parts of the developing world, corruption is so entrenched and pervasive that the state has no capacity to deliver services to its citizens. Moreover, in many countries, particularly in the developing and transitional economies, state officials are so venal that they appropriate for themselves most of the resources intended for their citizens. Therefore, there can be no possibility of viable schools, medical care, or public welfare.

In the absence of the state, nonstate actors step in. These nonstate actors can be nongovernmental and multinational organizations that provide needed services, such as vaccinations for children, emergency medical care, and establishing and equipping schools, or they can be illicit nonstate actors, terrorists, and transnational groups that offer services to citizens to advance *their objectives,* which are not just the welfare of the citizens. Therefore, by supplanting the absent state, the illicit actors make major inroads with populations who otherwise might be repelled by their violence.[100]

The ballads about the drug traffickers of Colombia extol the good they did for the community. These folk songs, known as *narcocorridos,* are sung by each cartel's modern-day troubadours.[101] Even after the death of the notorious drug leader Pablo Escobar, citizens would lay flowers at his grave because they remembered his social welfare activities,[102] his support for sports teams, his payments for medical care for the poor, and other philanthropic activities.

In Japan after the terrible Kobe earthquake of 1995, the *yakuza* of this port city came to the aid of their fellow citizens when the state was slow to respond.[103] Likewise, organized crime delivered services to citizens after the tsunami and earthquake that devastated Japan in 2011.[104]

In the poor Sohrab Goth and Lyari areas of Karachi, the state is effectively banned. Police and security forces cannot enter. Terrorist and criminal groups are part of shadow governance. The gangs of Lyari have alliances with elements of the Taliban and maintain their wealth by kidnapping people and trading in stolen NATO weapons. The resident power brokers resolve municipal problems.[105] In Sorab Gorth, a Pashtun community, the Taliban are extorting money on the grounds of providing protection.[106]

Crime groups' provision of services ensures that they remain embedded in their communities. Citizens will not cooperate with law enforcement to rid their communities of the criminal organizations because they are indebted to them for vital services.

When governments do not deliver on basic social services, extremist and terrorist groups can gain much support from the populace through their publicized anticorruption campaigns. Illustrative of this is the Taliban in Afghanistan. The "Taliban/insurgents derive both financial and political capital from the opium economy."[107] In Yemen, corruption and its affiliated problems results in an absence of public services, the appropriation of natural resource wealth by a few, and the failure to deliver disaster relief. These are prime elements of the recruiting message of AQAP. As one commentator reported, "to date, AQAP continues to display an impressive talent for assimilating broadly popular grievances into a single narrative in which jihad remains the only solution to the country's multiple crises."[108] Similarly, Hamas, Hezbollah, the Abu Sayyaf Group (ASG), and Gamaa Islamiya advance their political agendas by exploiting citizen repulsion at pervasive corruption and focusing on service delivery to people, in the form of schools, public transport, garbage collection, medical care, and/or construction of mosques.[109]

Terrorists provide benefits for different reasons than criminals. Social service delivery not only curries favor in the communities where they operate but also helps inculcate the ideology that is at the basis of the terrorist group. In Basque Spain, the ETA developed and sustained support structures among youth, women, and trade unions.[110] The LTTE in Sri Lanka invested in nongovernmental organization activities.[111] AQAP prioritizes charity work to recruit supporters.[112]

The FARC in Colombia, at its height, became a major provider of public services, including vocational schools, health clinics, and public works, and provided for infrastructure through road paving. Fifteen hundred Colombians surveyed in the late 1990s reported a high usage rate of FARC services. Sixty-eight percent used public health services, and many used mediation services,[113] a function often associated with the Mafia.[114] A clear relationship with state corruption is indicated, as 91 percent of the citizens surveyed viewed the government as corrupt.[115]

Social service delivery by Islamic terrorist groups is particularly pervasive, for several reasons.[116] First, it is a principle of Islam that Moslems donate a percentage of their income to charity (the *zakat*). Second, the need is particularly acute because the terrorist groups are based in highly corrupt environments in which there is little service delivery from the state. Third, many terrorist groups control territory, as do traditional organized crime groups. Therefore, they are able to run institutions and command resources, ensuring the delivery of services. Fourth, these terrorist groups have significant funding streams from private donations, states, and illicit activity that allow them to spend the large amounts of money needed to fund these services. These functioning charities that serve citizens may also be fronts for recruitment. Yet they do provide tangible benefits and must be distinguished from charities that are merely fronts for money laundering.[117]

In Pakistan, the political wing of the LeT, the Markaz Dawa Irshad, "runs about 200 mainstream Dawa schools, 11 madrassas, two science colleges, mobile clinics, blood banks and an ambulance service – services which even the Pakistani government has not been able to provide effectively to the rural populace in Pakistan."[118] In 2010, the humanitarian wing of the Pakistan-based LeT militant group, known as Jamaat-ud-Dawa, provided assistance to those hit by Pakistan's floods.[119]

A 2009 cable from the U.S. embassy in Islamabad, Pakistan, revealed by WikiLeaks explains further how terrorist groups provide services:

> Although Pakistani senior officials have publicly disavowed support for these groups, some officials from the Pakistan's Inter-Services Intelligence Directorate (ISI) continue to maintain ties with a wide array of extremist organizations, in particular the Taliban, LeT and other extremist organizations. These extremist organizations continue to find refuge in Pakistan and exploit Pakistan's

extensive network of charities, NGOs, and madrassas. This network of social
service institutions readily provides extremist organizations with recruits, funding and infrastructure for planning new attacks.[120]

These well-supported groups, according to Gretchen Peters, had better equipment to aid the Pakistani flood victims in 2010 than the U.S. MASH units
that were on the scene to help. The terrorist group could not only buy the
latest medical equipment but could deploy it to locales where the need was
acute.[121]

"In the Philippines, the Raja Sulayman Movement facilitated the construction of mosques and schools under the supervision of Mohammad Shugair,
a Saudi national linked by Philippine authorities to terrorist financing."[122]
In Southeast Asia, Jemaah Islamiya offers free or discounted religious
education.[123] In Egypt, Gamaa Islamiya provides medical care, education,
transport, and other services.[124] After an earthquake in 1989, groups affiliated with the Algerian Islamic Salvation Front provided assistance that was
not forthcoming from the state.[125] This recalls the Japanese experience in Kobe
with organized crime groups.

An even more dramatic example is the terrorist organization[126] Hamas,
which provides a very large range of public services, including operating
schools, scholarship funds, and hospitals; rebuilding roads and businesses; han-
dling garbage collection; and carrying out rural development projects in southern Lebanon, in territory under its control. It is estimated that Hamas, in the
early 2000s, spent 95 percent of its resources on its social welfare programs.[127]
It has become an accepted political force, winning seats in parliament, because
it has supplanted the functions of the state. But what distinguishes Hamas from
a governing political power is that it still engages in criminal acts to support
terrorism, such as credit card and food stamp fraud, as well as distributing and
selling counterfeit goods.[128]

Illustrative of its charity functions is al-Salah, one of three charity arms
of Hamas. According to the Treasury Department, "the al-Salah Society supported Hamas-affiliated combatants during the first intifada and recruited and
indoctrinated youth to support Hamas's activities. It also financed commercial
stores, kindergartens, and the purchase of land for Hamas."[129] This is just
part of the recruitment techniques of al-Salah, "which uses its charity commit-
tees, mosque classes, student unions, sports clubs, and other organizations as
places for Hamas recruiters to spot susceptible youth."[130] Individuals recruited
through the charity and sports organizations of Hamas were employed in terrorist attacks in 2003.[131]

The delivery of public services by terrorist and criminal groups in corrupt
environments is a viable tool for survival, as it gives the groups legitimacy and
allows them to mobilize for their organization. If these groups provide enough
services and eschew excessive force in the communities where they operate,
citizens may overcome their antipathy to the violence that is an integral part of

these groups' identity. This was seen among some sectors of Colombian society or in areas controlled by Hamas. But groups who become too predatory and venal, such as the Tehrik-i-Taliban Pakistan (TTP), lose their legitimacy with the community.[132] As Gretchen Peters observed in Afghanistan and Pakistan, "coupled with increased levels of violence, militant ties to crime have prompted growing numbers of local civilians to question the stated religious, political and ideological motives of the insurgents."[133]

Corruption as an Enabling Environment

The centrality of corruption to the perpetration of organized crime is recognized in the American statute to address the problem, the Racketeer Influenced and Corrupt Organizations Act (RICO). The title of a law to combat organized crime indicates that corruption is at its core. But this relationship between organized crime and corruption is not unique to the United States and Italy, where the Mafia originated. It is repeated in locales throughout the world with different types of organized crime.

Chapter 1 showed that corruption not only helps facilitate mass attacks but also, in certain cases, is indispensable to their commission. Corruption played a much more central role in the attacks that occurred in the developing world – Beslan, Mumbai, São Paulo, and Bali – than in the New York and Madrid cases. In the Beslan, Mumbai, and São Paulo cases, state security personnel assumed important roles in allowing entry of arms, movement of people, or access to wiretaps of state officials. The corruption of the state apparatus was key to the loss of lives and the mass destruction of property.

The mass attacks are not anomalous, they are merely more successful from the new terrorists' point of view, as they cause more deaths and greater economic costs and terrorize the larger community. The following chapters provide numerous examples of corruption enabling illicit trade; the cross-border movement of people, arms, and money; and the existence of safe havens for criminals and terrorists.[134] Without this corruption, neither criminals nor terrorists could sustain their group or perpetrate their acts.

In some societies, victims of terrorist and criminal violence do not receive needed support from the state. The absence of resources explains this in conflict regions and in poverty-stricken countries. But in some cases, pervasive corruption is at the heart of inattention to the victim. Probing the true circumstance of the victimization would reveal the extent of state complicity in the corruption that facilitated many terrorist and large-scale criminal attacks. In Russia, major loss of life from terrorism can be directly traceable to the corruption of officials. As Chapter 1 discussed, suicide bombings of aircraft were facilitated by bribes. Beslan could not have been perpetrated without endemic corruption of civilian and military law enforcement in the North Caucasus. In another deadly attack in southern Russia, for a bribe, a police officer even escorted the terrorist and his deadly explosives to the scene in a police van.[135] But even though probes of these attacks have been conducted and victim's societies have been formed to defend their interests, acknowledgment of the extent of state corruption that provided the enabling environment has been absent. Victims, who remind the state of its failings, have been left to fend for themselves with inconsequential compensation and without needed medical care.[136]

The enabling environment of corruption is discussed in many of the following chapters – in relation to the illicit global networks, the business of terrorism, and associated forms of criminal activity. Furthermore, a history of corruption is one of the preconditions for a terrorist safe haven.[137] Yet a few illustrative examples are provided here to introduce the concept and show its relevance. Of particular concern to many observers is how corruption facilitates the drug trade worldwide:

> Corruption is not the only fuel of international drug trafficking. It is the combination of endemic corruption, weak governments and a weak economic system in conjunction with unsupervised borders that is largely beneficial to drug trafficking activities. Where violence, corruption, organized crime, weapons smuggling, and other illicit activities converge, safe havens for terrorists is merely the next step.[138]

Cultivation of drugs occurs at the lowest level of the drug trade. The real profits are made with the precursor chemicals and the refinement of the product. Colombia receives precursors via Venezuela and Ecuador. "Only corruption at a local level explains how these chemicals continue to flow freely to armed groups and cartels that process coca leaf into cocaine."[139]

Corruption on the Mexican–U.S. border explains the large drug flows across the borders. The return of billions of dollars annually to Mexico provides the capital to pay the bribes.[140]

The enabling environment of corruption for crime and terrorism can be found in many other regions – Asia, especially Central Asia and Afghanistan – Pakistan, and Africa. In the Philippines, high-level official involvement in the drug trade was revealed in an investigation when a former narcotics agent testified to the corruption of a senator who facilitated drug trafficking with the Hong Kong Triads. This corruption enabled not only drug trade but also arms trafficking by the Triads to the terrorist organization ASG.[141]

The nexus of crime and terrorism facilitated by endemic corruption is also apparent in Central Asia. The initial success of the Islamic Movement of Uzbekistan derived from its role in the Tajik Civil War, which gave it contacts at the highest levels of the Tajik government, who facilitated the passage of narcotics along the valuable route out of Afghanistan.[142] But as the president of Tajikistan consolidated his power, he killed off his opposition, labeling some of them terrorists. Thereby, the leadership achieved control of the valuable drug trade.[143]

Pervasive corruption in Tajik law enforcement agencies and penitentiary facilities promotes the distribution of drugs:

Law enforcement officials provide (confiscated) heroin to favored dealers, arrest or harass competing dealers and exploit drug users in various ways for the sake of information, money or sexual favors. Drug users are also routinely arrested, often by planting evidence on them, to meet arbitrary quotas, which all but ensures that the activities of larger criminal and drug trafficking organizations will go unimpeded.[144]

In Afghanistan, the endemic corruption undermines the achievement of military intervention. It is possible to trace the corruption from the diversion of U.S. aid to the bullets that are purchased that kill American soldiers.[145]

Conclusion

This chapter has shown that corruption is key in the emergence, development, and institutionalization of the illicit phenomena of crime and terrorism. This impact may be most pronounced in the developing world, with the highest rates of corruption, but it is not confined to conflict regions or the least developed countries. Corruption provides an incubator for organized crime and terrorism in diverse milieux, as it is at the core of the absence of economic development, widening economic disparity, and political injustice.

In the developing world, particularly in the societies with the greatest population growth, corruption drains the resources needed to develop and provide meaningful employment for youths. Even in wealthy societies, such as Saudi Arabia, where something remains after massive corruption, its scale and the disparities it creates can be alienating. As previously mentioned, Saudi Arabia, because of its perceived corruption, has been a target of al-Qaeda since its inception.[146]

Many in the West look at the countries of the developing world and believe that corruption is the norm. They do not understand that there are levels of corruption that are not only dysfunctional but alienating. Military strategies have been developed in Iraq and Afghanistan presuming that citizens can be mobilized for the defense of their society. But the corruption often accompanying massive illicit trade is a central element of daily life. Its influence is so great that inhabitants do not identify with the state. Therefore, governments cannot expect the citizens of Iraq and particularly Afghanistan to die to defend the corrupt Karzai government. Rather, they may instead support the Taliban, with its message of purity, even though the message may be more rhetoric than reality.

Because some terrorists exploit the message of purity in the face of corruption, some anticorruption activists are labeled terrorists to justify state repression against social activists. Therefore, there is a problem of stigmatizing individuals as terrorists or extremists who are merely opposing corrupt leadership. President Qaddafi in Libya epitomized this problem during the Arab Spring, but unfortunately, it is far from unique and has been seen in Central Asia as well.[147]

Terrorist and criminal organizations, in the absence of a responsive state, may provide services for citizens, thereby currying favor with their communities. This is not the "retreat of the state"[148] but the impotence of the state resulting from corruption. The funding for these services rendered may derive, in part or completely, from criminal activity. For terrorist organizations, the funds obtained from illicit trade, overt criminal activity, and contributions may be combined to provide these services, whereas criminals rely solely on their criminal acts to furnish these revenues. The pervasive corruption allows criminals and terrorists to embed themselves in their base communities.

Criminals and terrorists, having neutralized the corrupt state, can operate with impunity. In this way, corruption is not only a facilitator for both kinds of illicit nonstate actors but provides an enabling environment.[149] Terrorists, like organized criminals, having purchased the cooperation of law enforcement officials, border guards, or other officials and so are able to accomplish operational goals. Moreover, in accordance with the "Robin Hood curse," the bands, like the merry men of Sherwood Forest, do not want conflict to end, as this will deprive them of wealth and power.[150]

The rest of the book provides numerous examples that illustrate this principle. The following chapters also show that the presence of corruption, along with organized crime and terrorism, compounds existing problems, fueling unexpected and uncontrollable outcomes, as in the three-body problem in physics. The interplay of these forces amplifies problems for the state, region, or community, making them even more intractable.

Notes

1. European Foundation for the Improvement of Living and Working Conditions, *First European Quality of Life Survey: Quality of Life in Turkey Summary* (Dublin, Ireland, 2007), 6, http://www.eurofound.europa.eu/publications/htmlfiles/ef0733.htm. This is based on major research done by Richard Rose and Yusuf Ziya Ozcan; see scores of neighboring countries in Transparency Corruption Perceptions Index, http://cpi.transparency.org/cpi2012/.
2. Discussions with Xavier Raufer. See also Xavier Raufer, "Une maffya symbiotique: traditions et évolutions du crime organisé en Turquie," *Sécurité Globale* (Hiver, 2009–10), 91–119; Frank Bovenkerk and Yücel Yesilgöz, "The Turkish Mafia and the State," in *Organised Crime in Europe*, ed. Cyrille Fijnaut and Letizia Paoli (Dordrecht, Netherlands: Springer, 2004), 585–601.
3. Charles Strozier and James Frank, eds., *The PKK: Financial Sources, Social and Political Dimensions* (Saarbrücken, Germany: VDM, 2011). Frank Bovenkerk and Yücel Yesilgöz, "Urban Knights and Rebels in the Ottoman State," in Fijnaut and Paoli, *Organised Crime in Europe*, 203–24.
4. Marc Sageman, *Understanding Terror Networks* (Philadelphia: University of Pennsylvania Press, 2004), 147, wrote that "corruption, lack of meaningful employment and disillusionment with secular socialist nationalism led them to militant Salafi Islam."

5. Matthew Levitt, "Hezbollah Finances: Funding the Party of God," in *Terrorism Financing and State Responses: A Comparative Perspective*, ed. Jeanne K. Giraldo and Harold A. Trinkunas (Stanford, CA: Stanford University Press, 2007), 134–51; Michael Braun, David Asher, and Matthew Levitt, *Party of Fraud: Hizballah's Criminal Enterprises*, Policy Watch 1911 (Washington, DC: Washington Institute, March 22, 2012), http://www.washingtoninstitute.org/templateC05.php?CID=3461.

6. Robert Klitgaard, *Controlling Corruption* (Berkeley: University of California Press, 1988).

7. Martha Elena Badel Rueda, *Costos de la corrupción en Colombia*, República de Colombia Departamento Nacional de Planeación Unidad de Análisis Macroeconómico, Documento 111 (May 24, 1999), 62.

8. Judith Palmer Harik, *Hezbollah: The Changing Face of Terrorism* (London: I. B. Tauris, 2004), 21. She also wrote that "particular incidents or patterns of misrule and corruption in some countries stimulated Muslim discontent to a heightened degree" (20). This was written well before the so-called Arab Spring.

9. For a discussion of this World Bank definition, see Raymond Baker, John Christensen, and Nicholas Shaxson, "Catching Up with Corruption," *The American Interest* (September/October 2008), http://www.the-american-interest.com/article-bd.cfm?piece=466.

10. Asian Development Bank, *Anticorruption: Our Framework and Strategies*, 1998, http://www.adb.org/documents/anticorruption-policy.

11. See, e.g., Janine Wedel, *Collision and Collusion: The Strange Case of Western Aid to Eastern Europe*, 2nd ed. (New York: Palgrave, 2001); Rasma Karklins, *The System Made Me Do It: Corruption in Post-Communist Societies* (Armonk, NY: M. E. Sharpe, 2005). This phenomenon is also observable in China, where the Communist Party still maintains control but private enterprise is extensive.

12. Ramsay Macmullen, *Corruption and the Decline of Rome* (New Haven, CT: Yale University Press, 1990).

13. See some of the work by Susan Rose-Ackerman, *Corruption and Government: Causes, Consequences, and Reform* (Cambridge: Cambridge University Press, 1999); *International Handbook on the Economics of Corruption* (Northampton, MA: Edward Elgar, 2006); Susan Rose-Ackerman, "The Political Economy of Corruption," in *Corruption and the Global Economy*, ed. Kimberly Ann Elliott (Washington, DC: Institute for International Economics, 1997), 31–34; Klitgaard, *Controlling Corruption*; Michael Johnston, ed., *Public Sector Corruption*, 4 vols. (London: Sage, 2010).

14. Michael Johnston, *Syndromes of Corruption: Wealth, Power, and Democracy* (Cambridge: Cambridge University Press, 2005).

15. See this older research on the utility of corruption in Joseph S. Nye, "Corruption and Political Development: A Cost-Benefit Analysis," in *Political Corruption: Concepts and Contexts*, 3rd ed., ed. Arnold Heidenheimer and Michael Johnston (New Brunswick, NJ: Transaction, 2002), 281–300; Nathaniel H. Leff, "Economic Development through Bureaucratic Corruption," in ibid., 307–20.

16. "Africa: Scale of Corruption and Impact on Poor," http://www.u4.no/publications/africa-scale-of-corruption-and-impact-on-poor/.

17. Wolfgang Kasper, *Make Poverty History: Tackle Corruption* (Washington, DC: International Policy Network, 2011), http://policynetwork.net/print/1268.

18. See Raymond W. Baker, *Capitalism's Achilles Heel: Dirty Money and How to Renew the Free-Market System* (Hoboken, NJ: John Wiley, 2005).

19. "What Is the Corruption Perceptions Index," http://cpi.transparency.org/cpi2011/in_detail/.

20. Robert Jervis, *Why Intelligence Fails: Lessons from the Iranian Revolution and the Iraq War*, Cornell Studies in Security Affairs (Ithaca, NY: Cornell University Press, 2010), 123–55; Robert Jervis lectured on this at the Canadian Association for Security and Intelligence Studies (CASIS), Ottawa, October 14–15, 2010.

21. Ikhram Sehgal, "Countering Terrorism at Ground Zero," *International News*, February 12, 2009, http://www.thenews.com.pk/TodaysPrintDetail.aspx?ID=162092&Cat=9&dt=2/12/2009.

22. Daniel Byman, Peter Chalk, Bruce Hoffman, William Rosenau, and David Brannan, *Trends in Outside Support for Insurgent Movements* (Santa Monica, CA: RAND, 2001), http://www.rand.org/pubs/monograph_reports/MR1405.html; Matthew Levitt, *Hamas: Politics, Charity, and Terrorism in the Service of Jihad* (New Haven, CT: Yale University Press, 2006); Justin Magouirk, "The Nefarious Helping Hand: Anti-corruption Campaigns, Social Service Provision, and Terrorism," *Terrorism and Political Violence* 20 (2008): 358.

23. The governor was subsequently killed by the FARC. See Hugh Bronstein, "Colombian Rebels Say Killed Governor, Blame Uribe," Reuters, January 5, 2010, http://www.reuters.com/article/2010/01/06/idUSN05122506.

24. See *Warlord, Inc. Extortion and Corruption along the U.S. Supply Chain in Afghanistan*, Report of the Majority Staff, Rep. John F. Tierney, Chair Committee on Oversight and Government Reform, U.S. House of Representatives, June 1, 2010, http://www.cbsnews.com/htdocs/pdf/HNT_Report.pdf.

25. See Diego Gambetta, *The Sicilian Mafia: The Business of Private Protection* (Cambridge, MA: Harvard University Press, 1996); Frederico Varese, *The Russian Mafia: Private Protection in a New Market Economy* (New York: Oxford University Press, 2005); see also *The Godfather of Cocaine*, documentary, http://www.pbs.org/wgbh/pages/frontline/programs/info/1309.html.

26. Donatella della Porta and Alberto Vannucci, *Corrupt Exchanges: Actors, Resources, and Mechanisms of Political Corruption* (New York: Aldine de Gruyter, 1999); János Kornai, Bo Rothstein, and Susan Rose-Ackerman, eds., *Creating Social Trust in Post-socialist Transition* (Gordonsville, VA: Palgrave Macmillan, 2004); Alena V. Ledeneva, *Russia's Economy of Favours: Blat, Networking and Informal Exchange* (Cambridge: Cambridge University Press, 1998).

27. See Susan Rose-Ackerman, *Corruption and Government: Causes, Consequences and Reform* (Cambridge: Cambridge University Press, 1999), 114–21, on kleptocracies.

28. For a discussion of Equatorial Guinea, see Global Witness, "Undue Diligence: How Banks do Business with Corrupt Regimes," March 11, 2009, http://www.global witness.org/library/undue-diligence-how-banks-do-business-corrupt-regimes.

29. Dexter Filkins, "The Afghan Bank Heist," *New Yorker*, February 14, 2011, http://www.newyorker.com/reporting/2011/02/14/110214fa_fact_filkins; Matthew Rosenberg, "Audit Says Kabul Bank Began as 'Ponzi Scheme,'" *New York Times*, November 26, 2012, http://www.nytimes.com/2012/11/27/world/asia/kabul-bank-audit-details-extent-of-fraud.html.

30. Government Accountability Project, "Review of the Department of Institutional Integrity," Washington, DC, 2007, http://www.whistleblower.org/storage/documents/ReviewoftheINT.pdf.

31. Michael Johnston, "Public Officials, Private Interests and Sustainable Democracy: When Politics and Corruption Meet," in Elliott, *Corruption and the Global Economy*, 61–82.

32. Larbi Sadiki, "From Tunisia and Algeria in the Maghreb to Jordan and Egypt in the Arab East, the Real Terror Is Marginalization," http://english.aljazeera.net/indepth/opinion/2011/01/201111413424337867.html.

33. Julio Cirino, Silvana L. Elizondo, and Geoffrey Wawro, "Latin America's Lawless Areas and Failed States: An Analysis of the 'New Threats,'" in *A Collaborative Inquiry from North and South*, ed. Paul D. Taylor, Naval War College Newport Papers 21 (Newport, RI: Naval War College, 2004), 16.

34. Diane E. Davis, "The Political and Economic Origins of Violence and Insecurity in Contemporary Latin America: Past Trajectories and Future Prospects," in *Violent Democracies in Latin America*, ed. Enrique Desmond Arias and Daniel M. Goldstein (Durham, NC: Duke University Press, 2010), 55.

35. Through deals between private owners and corrupt politicians, the privatized lottery companies have became hubs of money laundering, and new resources for these lotteries are also used to launder money and provide resources for corrupt politicians. "Enilce López Had Powerful Friends," n.d., http://www.laht.com/article.asp?CategoryId=12393&ArticleId=229403; Hannah Aronowitz, "Colombian Businesswoman Convicted of Paramilitary Ties," February 1, 2011, http://colombiareports.co/colombian-businesswoman-convicted-of-paramilitary-ties/.

36. Moisés Naím, "Mafia States Organized Crime Takes Office," *Foreign Affairs*, May/June 2012, 100–11.

37. Transparency International, "Recovering Stolen Assets: A Problem of Scope and Dimension," No. 02/2011, http://www.transparency.org/whatwedo/pub/working_paper_02_2011_recovering_stolen_assets_a_problem_of_scope_and_dimen.

38. Joe Bavier, "Nigeria: Why Boko Haram Terrorists Bombed Churches on Christmas," January 2, 2012, http://pulitzercenter.org/reporting/nigeria-boko-haram-terrorism-violence-islam-christianity-army-government-poverty-youth; "Drivers of Youth Radicalization in East Africa," http://www.currentanalyst.com/index.php/conflictsregional/165-drivers-of-youth-radicalization-in-east-africa.

39. Louise Shelley, *Human Trafficking: A Global Perspective* (New York: Cambridge University Press, 2010), 128–31, 158–61.

40. Susan Rose-Ackerman, "Trust, Honesty and Corruption: Reflections on the State Building Process," *Archives of European Sociology* 42, no. 3 (2001): 526–70.

41. Elise Ditta, "Improving Education in Honduras: Empowering Parents," August 20, 2013, http://blog.transparency.org/2013/08/20/improving-education-in-honduras-empowering-parents/.

42. Ibid.

43. Luis Angel Sas, "El rey Tesucún," June 7, 2011, http://www.d7.plazapublica.com.gt/content/el-rey-tesucun.

44. Conversation with Vicky Colbert, founder of the Escuela Nueva Foundation, Colombia, World Economic Forum, Dubai, 2009.

45. Magouirk, "Nefarious Helping Hand," 356–75.
46. UNODC, *Addiction, Crime and Insurgency: The Transnational Threat of Afghan Opium* (Vienna: UNODC, 2009), 141. In Colombia, citizens are disturbed by both petty and grand corruption; see U4 Expert Answer, "Colombia: Overview of Corruption and Anti-corruption," March 15, 2013, 3, http://www.transparency.org/whatwedo/answer/colombia_overview_of_corruption_and_anti_corruption.
47. Sarah Chayes, *The Punishment of Virtue: Inside Afghanistan after the Taliban* (New York: Penguin Books, 2006); Sarah Chayes, "Government by Crime Syndicate," September 25, 2011, http://articles.latimes.com/2011/sep/25/opinion/la-oe-chayes-corruption-20110925.
48. Robin Wright, *Rock the Casbah: Rage and Rebellion across the Islamic World* (New York: Simon and Schuster, 2011).
49. David Williams, "Wife of Tunisian President Fled Riot-Torn Country with 1.5 Tonnes of Gold (That Should Help Feed the Son-in-Law's Pet Tiger)," *Daily Mail*, January 17, 2011, http://www.dailymail.co.uk/news/article-1347938/Tunisian-presidents-wife-Leila-Trabelsi-fled-riots-35m-gold-bars.html.
50. Yonah Alexander, "Special Update, Terrorism in North, West and Central Africa: From 9/11 to the Arab Spring," Potomac Institute for Policy Studies, January 2012; Alexander, "2011 Report Update: The Consequences of Terrorism – An Update on al-Qaeda and Other Terrorist Threats in the Sahel & Maghreb," http://www.terrorismelectronicjournal.org/knowledge-base/special-report/; Anouar Boukhars, "Simmering Discontent in the Western Sahara," The Carnegie Papers, March 2012, http://carnegieendowment.org/2012/03/12/simmering-discontent-in-western-sahara/a2ah.
51. AFP, "Arab Spring Prompts Surge of Illegal Immigrants to EU," *Times of Malta*, November 16, 2011, http://www.timesofmalta.com/articles/view/20111116/local/arab-spring-prompts-surge-of-illegal-immigrants-to-eu.394158; John Hooper, "300 Migrants Feared Dead after Boat Capsizes off Sicily," *Guardian*, April 6, 2011, http://www.guardian.co.uk/world/2011/apr/06/300-migrants-feared-dead-sicily. The same processes are at work in Central America; see Alejandra Gutiérrez Valdizán, "De esclavas y de siervas," October 28, 2012, http://www.plazapublica.com.gt/content/la-escurridiza-red-de-los-cuerpos-ocupados.
52. Gabriel Koehler-Derrick, ed., *A False Foundation? AQAP, Tribes and Ungoverned Spaces in Yemen* (West Point, NY: Combating Terrorism Center at West Point, September 2011), http://www.ctc.usma.edu/posts/a-false-foundation-aqap-tribes-and-ungoverned-spaces-in-yemen.
53. Ibid., 103–4.
54. Angel Rabasa, Peter Chalk, Kim Cragin, Sara A. Daly, Heather S. Gregg, Theodore W. Karasik, Kevin A. O'Brien, and William Rosenau, *Beyond al Qaeda: The Outer Rings of the Terrorist Universe, Part II* (Santa Monica, CA: RAND, 2006), 65.
55. Ibid., 67.
56. The author watched this BBC broadcast in Morocco. For a link to this report, see http://news.bbc.co.uk/2/hi/8459431.stm.
57. For a discussion of the global risk report methodology, see *Global Risks 2011*, 6th ed., 43, http://reports.weforum.org/global-risks-2011/Global Risks.
58. The author was attending a conference in Rabat, Morocco, in January 2011 on illicit networks on the three days before Ben Ali's fall. The meeting, attended by North Africans, West Africans, Europeans, and Americans, explored all the

relationships identified earlier, with clear examples. The Moroccan government had initiated this conference more than six months previously because they were concerned by the instability related to high levels of corruption and illicit networks. Yet even at the farewell dinner the night before Ben Ali's ouster, not one of the North Africans nor the Arab specialists anticipated his fall or the domino effect.

59. Jean-Pierre Filiu, "Could Al-Qaeda Turn African in the Sahel?," Carnegie Papers 112, June 2010, 1, http://carnegieendowment.org/files/al_qaeda_sahel.pdf.

60. Corruption is also associated with violent conflicts, as Johnston noted in *Syndromes of Corruption*. In the absence of trust and rule of law, competitors often resort to violence to acquire state assets.

61. The quote is from "Central Asia: Islamists in Prison," International Crisis Group, no. 97, 1, http://www.crisisgroup.org/en/regions/asia/central-asia/B097-central-asia-islamists-in-prison.aspx, also discussed by Alexander Kupatadze in his talk titled "Geopolitics, States, and Networks in Central Eurasia," Woodrow Wilson Center, May 9, 2012, based on his recent three months of research in Kyrgyz prison, http://www.wilsoncenter.org/event/geopolitics-states-and-networks-central-eurasia.

62. Alexander Kupatadze, *Organized Crime, Political Transitions and State Formation in Post-Soviet Eurasia* (Houndsmill, UK: Macmillan, 2012).

63. *Global Risk Report, 2011,* 23. The author wrote the part on Kyrgyzstan and visited the country in September 2009, where she observed that the antipathy against the corrupt leader was so great that another revolution against the national leadership was possible. In another visit in September 2010, she observed the devastation to communities resulting from this violent conflict in southern Kyrgyzstan. In one ruined home, all that remained was a traditional Uzbek plate exposed because all the walls of the home had been destroyed.

64. Shelley, *Human Trafficking,* 87–91.

65. See Louise Shelley, "Youth, Crime and Terrorism," in *Political Violence, Organized Crimes, Terrorism and Youth,* ed. M. Demet Ulusoy (Amsterdam: IOS Press, 2008), 133–40.

66. Alan B. Krueger and Jitka Maleckova, "Education, Poverty and Terrorism: Is There a Causal Connection?," *Journal of Economic Perspectives* 17, no. 4 (2003): 133.

67. Johnston, *Syndromes of Corruption,* 10, 38.

68. Richard Cincotta, "Youth Bulge, Underemployment Raise Risks of Civil Conflict," State of the World 2005 Global Security Brief 2, March 1, 2005, http://www.worldwatch.org/node/76.

69. Khalid Koser, *International Migration* (Oxford: Oxford University Press, 2007).

70. Ralph Espach, Javier Melendez, Daniel Haering, and Miguel Castillo, "Criminal Organizations and Illicit Trafficking in Guatemala's Border Communities," December 1, 2011, http://www.cna.org/research/2011/criminal-organizations-illicit-trafficking.

71. Cheryl Bernard, "A Future for the Young Options for Helping Middle East Youth Escape the Trap of Radicalization," Report WR-354 (Santa Monica, CA: RAND, September 2005), 53, http://www.rand.org/pubs/working_papers/2006/RAND_WR354.pdf.

72. Joe Bavier, "Suicide Bomber Kills 7 in Nigerian Church," October 29, 2012, http://www.cnn.com/2012/10/28/world/africa/nigeria-church-bombing/index.html.

73. Musa Musayev, "Massive Military Operation in the Mountain Ends with No Proof of Any Militants Killed or Captured," Caucasus Reporting Service 322, January 11, 2006, http://iwpr.net/report-news/dagestan-assault-fails-deliver. The work of the Terrorism Transnational Crime and Corruption Center's Stavropol Center provides evidence in its reporting and its conferences as to the continued lack of effectiveness of law enforcement in the North Caucasus. See http://cspkitraccc .skforussia.ru.

74. C. W. Blandy, *Dagestan: Birth of Presidential Republic* (Camberley: Defence Academy of the United Kingdom, 2006), 14.

75. Don Rassler, C. Christine Fair, Anirban Ghosh, Arif Jamal, and Nadia Shoeb, "The Fighters of Lashkar-e-Taiba: Recruitment, Training, Deployment and Death," April 2013, 16–24, http://www.ctc.usma.edu/posts/the-fighters-of-lashkar-e-taiba-recruitment-training-deployment-and-death.

76. Richard Gillespie, "Political Violence in Argentina: Guerillas, Terrorists, and *Carapintadas*," in *Terrorism in Context*, ed. Martha Crenshaw (University Park: Pennsylvania State University Press, 1995), 217–25.

77. Marc Sageman, *Understanding Terror Networks* (Philadelphia: University of Pennsylvania Press, 2004); e-notes Marc Sageman, "Understanding Terror Networks," November 1, 2004, http://www.fpri.org/enotes/20041101.middleeast .sageman.understandingterrornetworks.html.

78. Jason Burke, *Al-Qaeda Casting a Shadow of Terror* (London: I. B. Taurus, 2003), 138, 146–47.

79. "Bin Laden's Fatwa," http://www.pbs.org/newshour/terrorism/international/fatwa_ 1996.html.

80. Neal MacFarquhar, "Prince Sultan bin Abdel Aziz of Saudi Arabia Dies," *New York Times,* October 23, 2011, http://www.nytimes.com/2011/10/23/world/ middleeast/prince-sultan-bin-abdel-aziz-of-saudi-arabia-dies.html?_r=1&ref= nayef. His son, Prince Bandar, is cited in the obituary as saying that they were not so bad as people think concerning the level of corruption in the Saudi royal family.

81. Ibid.

82. See the so-called McCrystal Report, "Comisaf's *Initial Assessment*," August 30, 2009, http://media.washingtonpost.com/wpost/Assessment_Redacted_ 092109.pdf.

83. In the 2012 Corruption Perception Index, Morocco has the best ratings and was at 88. All the rest were well below this, and many were ranked among the most corrupt countries in the world. http://cpi.transparency.org/cpi2012/results/.

84. Mai Yamani, "Bin Laden's Ghost," May 3, 2011, http://www.project-syndicate .org/commentary/bin-laden-s-ghost, states that the Saudis spent $75 billion funding schools, mosques, and charities in the 1980s that continue to be supported. She is the daughter of Saudi Arabia's former oil minister.

85. See Karen Dawisha, "Is Russia's Foreign Policy That of a Corporatist-Kleptocratic Regime?," *Post-Soviet Affairs* 27, no. 4 (October–December 2011): 331–65; see the blog of the famous blogger Alex Navalny that reveals corruption in Russia, http://rospil.info/.

86. See Peter Gastrow, "Termites at Work: Transnational Organized Crime and State Erosion in Kenya," summary report (New York: International Peace

Institute, September 2011), 3, http://www.ipinst.org/news/general-announcement/270-ipi-launches-report-on-transnational-organized-crime-in-kenya.html.

87. Ibid.

88. "US Names Kenyan Politician Drug 'Kingpin'," June 2, 2011, http://www.voanews.com/content/kenyan-politician-named-drug-kingpin-by-us-123093448/158227.html.

89. Cirino et al., "Latin America's Lawless Areas and Failed States," 16.

90. See Parts I, II, and III of Anne L. Clunan and Harold A. Trinkunas, *Ungoverned Spaces: Alternatives to State Authority in an Era of Softened Sovereignty* (Stanford: Stanford University Press, 2010), 17–172.

91. Enrique Desmond Arias, *Drugs and Democracy in Rio de Janeiro* (Chapel Hill: University of North Carolina Press, 2006).

92. Ibid., 17.

93. Luis Jorge Garay-Salamanca, Eduardo Salcedo-Albarán, and Isaac De Leon-Beltrán, *Illicit Networks Reconfiguring States: Social Network Analysis of Colombian and Mexican Cases* (Bogotá: Metodo Foundation, 2010), 72–86.

94. See Robert I. Rotberg, "The Horn of Africa and Yemen: Diminishing the Threat of Terrorism," in *Battling Terrorism in the Horn of Africa*, ed. Robert I. Rotberg (Cambridge, MA: World Peace Foundation and Brookings Institution Press, 2005), 5, 8; Leslie Holmes, ed., introduction to *Terrorism, Organised Crime and Corruption: Networks and Linkages* (Cheltenham, UK: Edward Elgar, 2007), 3–4.

95. As Stewart Patrick states in *Weak Links, Fragile States, Global Threats and International Security* (Oxford: Oxford University Press, 2011), 93–94, the state havens are not most likely in the failed states.

96. See E. J. Hobsbawm, *Primitive Rebels: Studies in Archaic Forms of Social Movement in the 19th and 20th Centuries* (New York: W. W. Norton, 1965).

97. Raimondo Catanzaro, *Men of Respect: A Social History of the Sicilian Mafia*, trans. Raymond Rosenthal (New York: Free Press, 1992); Pino Arlacchi, *Mafia Business: The Mafia Ethic and the Spirit of Capitalism*, trans. Martin Ryle (London: Verso, 1986).

98. Peter B. E. Hill, *The Japanese Mafia: Yakuza, Law and the State* (Oxford: Oxford University Press, 2003), and David E. Kaplan and Alec Dubro, *Yakuza: Japan's Criminal Underworld* (Berkeley: University of California Press, 2003).

99. Hill, *Japanese Mafia*; Kaplan and Dubro, *Yakuza*; Catanzaro, *Men of Respect*; Arlacchi, *Mafia Business*.

100. Magouirk, "Nefarious Helping Hand."

101. The idea of the *narcocorridos* harking back to medieval troubadours is an insight gained from Vanessa Neumann.

102. *Godfather of Cocaine*.

103. Howard Abadinsky, *Organized Crime*, 7th ed. (Belmont, CA: Wadsworth, 2003), 172, 209.

104. See the discussion of this by the noted writer on Japanese organized crime Jake Adelstein, "Mobsters on a Mission: How Japan's Infamous Mafia Launched an Aid Effort," *The Independent*, April 9, 2011, http://www.independent.co.uk/news/world/asia/mobsters-on-a-mission-how-japans-mafia-launched-an-aid-effort-2264031.html.

105. Sobia Ahmad Kaker, "Towards an Urban Geopolitical Analysis of Violence in Lyari," Center for Research and Security Studies, July 12, 2013, http://crss.pk/story/4549/towards-an-urban-geopolitical-analysis-of-violence-in-lyari; Zia-ur-Rehman, "The Pakistani Taliban's Karachi Network," Combating Terrorism Center at West Point, May 23, 2013, http://www.ctc.usma.edu/posts/the-pakistani-talibans-karachi-network.

106. Maqbool Ahmed and Mansoor Khan, "Karachi's Pakhtun Areas under Taliban Control," *Sunday Guardian*, January 5, 2013, http://www.sunday-guardian.com/investigation/karachis-pakhtun-areas-under-taliban-control.

107. UNODC, *Addiction, Crime and Insurgency*, 141; see *Warlord, Inc.*

108. Gabriel Koehler-Derrick, ed., *A False Foundation? AQAP, Tribes and Ungoverned Spaces in Yemen* (West Point, NY: Combating Terrorism Center at West Point, September 2011), 41, http://www.ctc.usma.edu/posts/a-false-foundation-aqap-tribes-and-ungoverned-spaces-in-yemen.

109. Erica Chenoweth and Jessica C. Teets, "To Bribe or to Bomb: Do Corruption and Terrorism Go Together?," in *Corruption, Global Security, and World Order*, ed. Robert I. Rotberg (Washington, DC: Brookings Institution Press, 2009), 171.

110. B. Tejerina, "Protest Cycle, Political Violence and Social Movements in the Basque Country," *Nations and Nationalism* 7, no. 1 (2001): 51–52.

111. Pierre Emmanuel Ly, "The Charitable Activities of Terrorist Groups," *Public Choice* 131 (2007): 181.

112. Peter Knoope, "AQAP: A Local Problem, a Global Concern," August 20, 2013, http://icct.nl/publications/icct-commentaries/aqap-a-local-problem-a-global-concern?dm_i=1ADT,1SH80,8J4SN9,6E9R2,1.

113. Vanda Felbab-Brown, *Shooting Up Counterinsurgency and the War on Drugs* (Washington, DC: Brookings Institution Press, 2009), 84.

114. Diego Gambetta, *The Sicilian Mafia: The Business of Private Protection* (Cambridge, MA: Harvard University Press, 1993), 159–94.

115. Felbab-Brown, *Shooting Up Counterinsurgency*, 84.

116. For a general discussion of the role of social support in political communities, see Gilles Kepel, *Jihad: The Trail of Political Islam* (Cambridge, MA: Belknap Press, 2002).

117. Matthew Levitt and Michael Jacobsen, *The Money Trail: Finding, Following and Freezing Terrorist Finances*, Policy Focus 89 (Washington, DC: Washington Institute for Near East Policy, 2008), 48, 54–55, 61–63; see Ly, "Charitable Activities of Terrorist Groups," chart on 187.

118. Arabinda Acharya, "Terrorist Attacks in Mumbai: Picking Up the Pieces," a report by the International Centre for Political Violence and Terrorism Research, S. Rajaratnam School for International Studies, Nanyang Technological University, Singapore, provided by the lead author, 28.

119. "Factbox – Lashkar-e-Taiba Charity Wing in Flood Relief Work," Reuters, August 25, 2010, http://in.reuters.com/article/2010/08/25/idINIndia-51061420100825; Adam B. Ellick and Pir Zubair Shah, "Hard-Line Islam Fills Void in Flooded Pakistan," *New York Times*, August 6, 2010, http://www.nytimes.com/2010/08/07/world/asia/07pstan.html?pagewanted=all.

120. Rob Crilly, "WikiLeaks: Pakistani Intelligence 'Continues to Offer Support to Terrorist Groups,'" *The Telegraph*, May 31, 2011, http://www.telegraph.co.uk/

news/worldnews/asia/pakistan/8547841/WikiLeaks-Pakistani-intelligence-continues-to-offer-support-to-terrorist-groups.html.

121. Gretchen Peters discussed her recently released study *Haqqani Network Financing: The Evolution of an Industry* (West Point, NY: Combating Terrorism Center at West Point, 2012), on September 12, 2012, at TraCCC, George Mason University, http://traccc.gmu.edu/events/previously-hosted-events/.

122. Levitt and Jacobsen, *Money Trail*, 11.

123. Magouirk, "Nefarious Helping Hand," 358.

124. Ibid.

125. Ly, "Charitable Activities of Terrorist Groups," 177.

126. Hamas is listed as a terrorist organization by the U.S. Bureau of Counterterrorism, January 27, 2012, http://www.state.gov/j/ct/rls/other/des/123085.htm. For a discussion of the European Union position, see Levitt and Jacobson, *Money Trail*, 33–34.

127. Ly, "Charitable Activities of Terrorist Groups," 178.

128. Levitt, *Hamas*, 71.

129. Levitt and Jacobson, *Money Trail,* 62.

130. Ibid.

131. Ibid.

132. Ahmed and Khan, "Karachi's Pakhtun Areas under Taliban Control."

133. Gretchen Peters, *Crime and Insurgency in the Tribal Areas of Afghanistan and Pakistan* (West Point, NY: Combating Terrorism Center at West Point, 2010), ii, http://www.ctc.usma.edu/posts/crime-and-insurgency-in-the-tribal-areas-of-afghanistan-and-pakistan.

134. See Thomas M. Sanderson, "Transnational Terror and Organized Crime: Blurring the Lines," *SAIS Review* 24, no. 1 (2004): 49–61.

135. "Terrorism in Russia: The Role of Victims," Paris, September 19, 2011, http://www.capefrance.com/en/conferences/2011/9/terrorism-in-the-russian-federation-the-role-of-victims.html.

136. At the Cape conference, one victim reported receiving about $4 compensation. Others have been left without the family's chief breadwinner.

137. Cristiana C. Brafman Kittner, "The Role of Safe Havens in Islamist Terrorism," *Terrorism and Political Violence* 19 (2007): 307.

138. Ibid., 312.

139. International Crisis Group, *War and Drugs in Colombia Latin America,* Report 11, January 27, 2005, 25, http://www.crisisgroup.org/en/regions/latin-america-caribbean/andes/colombia/011-war-and-drugs-in-colombia.aspx.

140. June S. Beittel, *Mexico's Drug Trafficking Organizations: Source and Scope of the Rising Violence,* Congressional Reference Service, September 7, 2011, 4, http://www.fas.org/sgp/crs/row/R41576.pdf.

141. LaVerle Berry, Glenn E. Curtis, Rex A. Hudson, and Nina A. Kollars, "A Global Overview of Narcotics-Funded Terrorist and Other Extremist Groups," May 2002, Library of Congress Reference Service, 105, http://www.loc.gov/rr/frd/pdf-files/NarcsFundedTerrs_Extrems.pdf. The high-level corruption facilitating the drug trade was discussed by a former Korean ambassador to the Philippines at a TraCCC (Terrorism, Transnational Crime, and Corruption) conference, "Asian Perspectives on Transnational Crime and Human Trafficking," April 19, 2011, http://traccc.gmu.edu/events/previously-hosted-events/.

142. Svante E. Cornell and Regine A. Spector, "Central Asia: More Than Islamic Extremists," *Washington Quarterly* 25, no. 1 (2002): 193–206.

143. International Crisis Group, *Tajikistan: The Changing Insurgent Threats,* Asia Report 205, May 24, 2011, discusses the complexity of the insurgent threat; http://www.crisisgroup.org/en/regions/asia/central-asia/tajikistan/205-tajikistan-the-changing-insurgent-threats.aspx; also interviews in Central Asia and with Central Asians between 2007 and 2012.

144. Alisher Latypov, "Drug Dealers, Drug Lords and Drug Warriors-cum-Traffickers: Drug Crime and the Narcotics Market in Tajikistan," in *Drug Trafficking, Drug Abuse, Money Laundering, Judicial Corruption in Central Asia: Collection of Brief Summaries* (Bishkek: CADPC, 2012), 24.

145. Unnamed high-level official working in U.S. embassy in Afghanistan, 2011.

146. Jason Burke, *Al-Qaeda Casting a Shadow of Terror* (London: I. B. Taurus, 2003), 146–47.

147. BBC News, "Gaddafi Blames Osama Ben Laden for Protests," September 24, 2011, http://www.bbc.co.uk/news/world-africa-12570279; International Crisis Group, "Central Asia: Islamists in Prison," Asia Briefing 97, December 2009, http://www.crisisgroup.org/en/regions/asia/central-asia/B097-central-asia-islamists-in-prison.aspx; Helsinki Commission Briefing on Political Prisoners in Central Asia, Washington, DC, written statement on religious prisoners by Catherine Cosman, Senior Policy Adviser, U.S. Commission on International Religious Freedom (printed copy), May 15, 2012.

148. Susan Strange, *Retreat of the State: The Diffusion of Power in the World Economy* (New York: Cambridge University Press, 1996).

149. The discussion of the enabling environment of Colombia has broader applicability. Richard Clutterbuck, "Cocaine, Terrorism and Corruption," *International Relations* 21 (1995): 77–92.

150. William Zartman, *Rethinking the Economics of War: The Intersection of Need, Creed, and Greed* (Washington, DC: Woodrow Wilson Center Press, 2005), 269, on the *curse,* and Peters, *Haqqani Network Financing,* 8, applies this to the situation in Afghanistan-Pakistan.

3

The Evolution of Organized Crime and Terrorism

A controversy arose at the sentencing of Jose Padilla, who was convicted in 2007 of diverse offenses, including conspiracy to murder, kidnap, and maim and providing material support for terrorism. Arrested in 2002, after landing in Chicago on a flight from Pakistan, he was first accused of being a suicide bomber. He spent three years in detention as an enemy combatant and eventually came to trial, five years after his original arrest. Padilla was accused of being trained by al-Qaeda after arriving in Pakistan in 1998.[1]

But his sentence of seventeen years was challenged, and in 2011 a federal judge handed down a decision, saying that this sentence was too mild because it did not take adequate account of his criminal background, nor of his extensive terrorist training. Mr. Padilla started out on a criminal path early in his adolescence. Even though juvenile criminal records are sealed, the following has been determined about his criminal past, according to the presentence report prepared before his initial sentencing. The judge explained, "The government stated that Padilla was a career offender based on over 17 arrests, his participation in a murder while he was a juvenile, his offense for battery on law enforcement, and his weapons possession offense."[2] Subsequently, the judge explicitly referred to his murder conviction.[3]

Padilla's conversion to Islam and the commencement of his terrorism career followed his release from prison. But Jose Padilla had a long and violent history in ordinary crime before he turned his criminal expertise to the service of terrorists. The same can be said for the recent French terrorist Mohamed Merah, who murdered military and civilian personnel, including children, at a Jewish Day School in Toulouse in southern France in 2012.[4] This trajectory from criminal to terrorist has become increasingly frequent as Islamic terrorists recruit experienced criminals into their ranks. In some cases, criminals are cloaking their terrorist acts in jihadi rhetoric. But as this chapter shows, the increasing links between crime and terrorism are not confined to Islamic terrorism but exist among many different types of terrorist organizations and in many geographic contexts.

Increasing Links between Criminals and Terrorists

Terrorists in the past used crime to support their activities, and criminals, on occasion, resorted to terrorist techniques; but until recent decades, crime and terrorism could be analyzed as distinct phenomena. The growing links between crime and terrorism observed in the past four decades are not merely a result of globalization or the need to assure a more diversified revenue flow. Rather, this change represents a profound evolution in organized crime and terrorism as well as in their relationship to the state. Threats are no longer compartmentalized but are entangled. Crime and terrorism have increasing associations and thrive in an environment in which corruption is pervasive.

The emergence of linked illicit phenomena, often facilitated by corrupt and collusive government officials, presents a serious challenge to local, regional, and international security. In the absence of effective states that serve their citizens, pernicious nonstate actors become important providers of employment and services, particularly in the developing world.[5]

Retreat of the State

Transnational crime groups and terrorists have been major beneficiaries of the new political order, where there has been the "retreat of the state" and the diffusion of economic and political power in the world.[6] They are part of new forms of governance and sometimes substitute for the state, as discussed in Chapter 2. They ascended in power since the nation-state declined and multinational nonstate actors, such as corporations and multinational organizations, rose in power and influence. Criminals and terrorists are just one manifestation of this larger phenomenon of the declining importance of the state. Other manifestations of declining state capacity have already been examined. As Chapters 1 and 4 show, prisons are no longer necessarily institutions of control[7] but can sometimes be centers for spreading and facilitating crime and violence. Corruption can undermine the state's capacity to control its borders and maintain its monopoly on violence. Therefore, the state is faced with challenges from both within and without.

Transformations of Criminals and Terrorists

Terrorists once acted against the state, often supported in these efforts by other states.[8] Organized crime once made its greatest profits by being a parasite on the state. Such clearly defined relationships between the state, terrorists, and crime are no longer valid. Recent decades have seen the rise of al-Qaeda and other terrorist groups whose ideological objectives are not state based. Some seek the establishment of a global Islamic state.[9] Transnational criminals have exploited the movements of people, goods, and new forms of communication, while evading state-based controls. Therefore, some contemporary organized crime is transnational, just as is some modern-day terrorism. The most effective organized criminals and terrorists transcend the state in their modus operandi and their worldview.

Contemporary transnational crime and terrorism are not merely globalized versions of their predecessors. Functioning on a global scale, they are fundamentally different. Some have referred to a *new terrorism* that is more lethal and less predictable.[10] These new terrorists are "prepared to break new ground, to ruthlessly innovate in the name of their cause."[11] They differ from many of the older terrorists who belonged to secular terrorist organizations with specific state-based, political agendas.[12]

But there is also a *new transnational crime*, whose scale is much larger and whose corruption of officials exceeds anything previously seen. Its political impact is disproportionate to its membership, as it is most often based in weak states that have little capacity or political will to stem its growth.[13] These new criminals exist in such war-torn places as Somalia, West Africa, the Balkans, the Caucasus, Central Asia,[14] and Pakistan. They thrive in the chaos of the new world disorder. Their perspectives, operations, and financial objectives are very different from those of their predecessors. The crimes of transnational criminals, such as in Mexico and Russia, can be on the scale of billions of dollars, involving global financial institutions and high-level facilitators.[15] Their criminality is not just a traditional form of crime on a global scale but a quantitatively and qualitatively different phenomenon that has the possibility of distorting global financial markets in commodities and destabilizing states.[16]

New criminals and new terrorists mirror the contemporary organizational structures of the licit world. They use *networks* and outsourcing, and individual cells have limited connections to the leadership.[17] In this they recall the innovative structures of rapidly growing IT companies rather than the top-down hierarchies of old-fashioned corporations such as General Motors. As in the legitimate world, this organizational structure provides operational flexibility and allows for rapid introduction of innovation and quick response to emergent obstacles. This network structure has additional benefits in the illicit world. It frustrates law enforcement and intelligence and makes it more difficult to identify the group's leadership.[18]

The *new transnational crime* and the *new terrorism* fundamentally differ from their antecedents in another important way. They both have a very different relationship to the state and to the citizens of the communities in which they operate.[19]

New and Old Criminals and Terrorists and Their Relationship to the State

Traditional Organized Crime

Historically, established crime groups have developed in Asia, Latin America, Africa, Europe, and the United States; no region of the world, nor any political system, has prevented the emergence of these powerful crime groups.[20] They have developed and thrived in monarchies, one-party states, and democracies. In all these political systems, crime groups have consciously chosen not to associate with terrorists. They have corrupted but never sought to destroy the existing political order as they benefited from the state's survival. Therefore, organized crime groups have endured despite the repressive governments of fascist Italy, the Soviet and Chinese Communist systems, and the targeted antiorganized crime operations of the FBI in the United States.

The older crime groups developed along with the states in which they were based. This symbiotic relationship proved valuable to the rise of traditional crime groups. For example, Japanese and Italian crime groups grew in size and income in the post–World War II recovery period.[21] The criminals grew wealthy as they gained a percentage of construction contracts for schools, roads, and national infrastructure projects. Likewise, the Mafia in the United States became richer as their home bases in New York, Chicago, and Las Vegas grew as business and financial centers.[22] Their growth coincided with the rise of the legitimate economy, as they were dependent on state contracts and planned for growth by extracting their "share" of an expanding economy.

The older transnational crime groups survived because they took a long-term perspective on profits and sought to ensure their long-term sustainability. Even when trading in drugs, which has given them enormous profits, these groups diversified their investments. For example, the Italian Mafia became enormously wealthy as a result of the global drug trade in the 1980s but invested those profits in tourism and in commercial and agricultural real estate.[23] Similarly, Colombian crime groups, having made their profits in drugs, have invested in cattle ranches, businesses that serve the consumer market by selling appliances and pharmaceuticals, and commercial real estate in Bogotá. They have combined investments in the illegitimate with the legitimate economy to ensure diversification and long-term stability.[24] Older organized crime groups, even though they now operate globally, often repatriate significant parts of their profits to their home countries as they associate their future with the state that is their base of operations.[25]

The economic development of the state is, therefore, of paramount importance to "old criminals" because they are parasites on the state's economy and financial institutions. These crime groups also depend on their country and its existing institutional and financial structures to move their products and provide stable investments for large profits. Like legitimate investors, they are dependent on national stability and rational markets to preserve capital and grow their assets. Because of this, like legitimate businessmen, their interests are not in line with those of terrorists, who seek to destabilize the state. Their nationalism as well as their financial interests are strong deterrents against violence. They require the preservation of state structures.[26]

Many analysts of traditional organized crime groups defined these groups solely in terms of the profit motive.[27] This represents an oversimplification. There has always been an important political component to sizeable and sustained organized crime groups.

Old criminals used corruption to achieve political influence, to undermine criminal investigations, to influence the development of legislation, and to obtain lucrative public contracts. To survive, old organized crime has often provided services for the state. In Italy, the Mafia was always in exchange relationships with the state – doing favors and receiving protection in return.[28] The *yakuza* in Japan served the emperor prior to World War II by putting down political opponents.[29] After World War II, they shared the extreme nationalism of the police and were therefore often tolerated by law enforcement.[30] Also during World War II, elements of the Mafia in the United States guarded the waterfront where they controlled the longshoremen's union to prevent German sabotage. Similar strategic service was provided to the U.S. army in World War II, when the Mafia in the United States used its profound knowledge of the island to assist in the invasion of Sicily in 1941. In these historical cases, the crime groups shared the state's objectives.[31]

Political-Criminal Nexus

Also key to criminal groups' survival has been the "political-criminal nexus," defined as "the concentration and fusion of political and criminal power."[32] Crime groups engage in politics by contributing to political campaigns, bribing officials, running candidates for office, or voting as a bloc to influence the electoral process, as has happened in Italy and cities in the United States in the early twentieth century. Studies of organized crime in large American cities reveal that the crime groups were deeply involved in ward politics and got out the vote among immigrants in big cities, helping ensure the political monopoly of the dominant urban political machine.[33] In Italy, the postwar Mafia in Sicily consistently delivered votes to the Christian Democrats, ensuring their long-term domination of national politics. This political alliance gave the Mafia political power and ensured it maintained its economic power.[34]

The criminal-political nexus is evident in an increasing number of countries and at the highest levels of governments of many states.[35] Crime groups expend significant amounts of human and financial capital to influence the state. By corrupting and sometimes penetrating government structures, they have created a secure environment in which to operate. In Colombia, the late noted drug trafficker Pablo Escobar ran for parliament and developed a political party.[36] Escobar was even made an alternative representative to the national legislature. Leaders of financial havens in the Caribbean are routinely bought off by drug lords who offer them *plata o plomo* (silver or lead), or in other words, a payment to cooperate, a bullet if they don't.[37] A powerful political-criminal nexus exists in many other locales such as, but not limited to, the Soviet successor states, Nigeria, Taiwan, Colombia, Turkey, and Mexico.[38]

Traditional criminals supported the state, not only for their own economic good but because they identified with its interests. They did not engage with terrorists, as this would enhance scrutiny by law enforcement. According to Sicilian prosecutors, the Mafia, around the millennium (2000), broke off ties with a particular Albanian crime group when informed by law enforcement that their business associates were terrorists rather than criminals.[39] This was a rational response to their environment – it lowered their risk and represented the Mafia's interests in state stability.

Traditional Crime Groups and the State

Old crime groups rarely strike at the state because their need for it is too great. But they will use extraordinary violence, particularly aimed at symbolic targets, when they are threatened. Illustrative of this were the colossal bombings in Sicily in 1992 that killed Judge Giovanni Falcone and his wife, through a bomb so powerful that it destroyed the bridge they were crossing. Falcone's fellow investigator, Judge Paolo Borsellino, was also killed by a Mafia bomb placed in front of his apartment house. The destruction was so complete that the apartment building resembled a shell in Baghdad after a suicide bomber. Other terrorist attacks included the bombing of religious and cultural symbols in 1994, with the great Ufizzi Museum in Florence and the second greatest church in Rome, the Lateran Church, being the targets.[40] Similar patterns of violence against the state were initiated by Colombian crime groups following crackdowns and the signing of an extradition treaty with the United States. In Bogotá, Colombia, in 1985, the Supreme Court was attacked by members of a terrorist organization, and many judges were killed. This is seen by many as part of a larger culture of violence in Colombia.[41] In Mexico, "in December 2009, the entire police department of Tancitaro, Michoacan resigned, along with the mayor and town council, due to threats from organized criminal groups. Similar mass resignations have been seen in Nuevo León and Chihuahua."[42] More recently in Mexico, a twenty-man police force of a northern Mexican town resigned after a series of attacks by a crime group killed three officers.[43] These are examples of criminal groups engaging in terrorism rather than allying with terrorists.

New Transnational Crime

New Transnational Crime, the State, and the Use of Corruption

Crime groups with loyalty to the state are no longer ascendant. New transnational crime groups have proliferated in number and membership within the last twenty years as a consequence of the end of the Cold War and the rise of globalization.[44] The new criminals, many based in conflict regions and transitional states, have exploited the decline of borders and increased mobility, diverse new forms of communication, and greater ease of international transport. They thrive in the shadow economy, the absence of an effective state, and endemic corruption.[45] As one scholar explained, "terrorist networks, like Mafias, appear to flourish where states are governed badly rather than not at all."[46]

Many new criminals have no interest in the endurance of the state; rather, their profits are made by destabilizing the state and its structures. These groups thrive in the chaos of war, frozen and enduring conflicts, where governments cannot curb their illicit activity and corruption is the norm.[47] They also thrive in the transitional states of the postsocialist world, where old norms were destroyed and new ones have not taken root. Powerful organized crime groups based in the former Yugoslavia, parts of West Africa, the Soviet successor states, or Afghanistan are now global actors, even though they were nearly unknown before the 1990s. Gangs with transnational connections thrive in urban areas such as the United States and Central America.[48] The BACRIM (*bandas criminales*), the emergent criminal bands in Colombia that have filled the void left by the demobilized paramilitaries, are engaged not only in the drug trade but also in the lucrative extractive industry sector, using corruption to obtain access to this sector.[49] In Mexico and Central America, drug cartels hire the gangs, such as the Mara Salvatrucha, to do their dirtiest and most violent work,[50] certainly a dirty entanglement. Corruption is also a central part of this equation.[51] Gangs and organized crime groups operate transnationally, selling drugs, arms, people, natural resources, and contraband. In their illicit activities, they differ little from the more established crime groups. But it is their perspective toward the state that clearly differentiates them from their predecessors.

Competitive Advantage of New Crime Groups

The new transnational groups can grow rapidly because they are based in countries in the developing world where individuals have few options. High birthrates, regions marginalized by globalization,[52] and others destroyed by years of war and conflict have left many desperate individuals with impoverished or nonexistent families. Many new crime groups function in highly stratified societies with few opportunities for those at the lower social strata.

Political transitions from a one-party state have led to major societal dislocations. Conflicts have displaced people and destroyed community values. In these regions with desperate individuals, and the absence of an effective state in control of all its territory, foot soldiers and couriers for the operations of criminal groups are readily available because individuals have no viable alternatives. It is estimated that 450,000 people in Mexico are presently reliant on drug trafficking for a significant proportion of their income.[53] Those who resist cooperation with the criminals face death, as has been seen repeatedly in Mexico.[54]

The new transnational groups can link with members of diaspora communities in developed countries. Members of diaspora communities are often marginalized in their new countries of residence and face high rates of unemployment. Their dissatisfaction and lack of opportunities make some of them ready to cooperate with these illicit networks. Therefore, it may be shocking but not surprising that, as mentioned in Chapter 1, one-quarter of the arrested participants in the British riots in London during August 2011 had more than ten criminal arrests.[55]

New transnational crime groups have different time horizons than their predecessors. Older groups, which were parasites on business and the state, planned for long-term development.[56] But newer crime groups, many based in conflict regions, do not plan for long-term survival or viability. Rather, they have shorter-term horizons, often using the profits of their illicit trade for immediate military objectives. One observes evidence of this trend in contemporary Iraq, in Afghanistan, or among many groups in Africa, such as the Somali pirates.[57]

New transnational crime often has a more fluid, networked, and less hierarchical structure than traditional organized crime such as the Mafia and *yakuza*. It draws on diverse elements of society that contribute in different ways to the perpetuation of the crime activity. Within a single criminal organization, there may be past or present officials from law enforcement, security, and military, along with typical gangsters. This is evidence of the previously mentioned element of the dirty entanglement. High-level officials or family members may be closely associated with the crime group.[58] This pattern has been observed in Mexico, the Balkans, and the Caucasus, as well as in Afghanistan.[59]

Profits not used for immediate military objectives are more likely to be deposited by Middle Eastern and African groups in offshore locales, such as the United Arab Emirates, rather than invested in their home economies, as was the case with old criminal groups like the Italian, Japanese, and American mafias.[60] Newer transnational criminals, such as Mexicans, who make billions annually and reside in a country with a viable, legitimate economy, often keep huge quantities in cash rather than investing with the intention of capital preservation or long-term growth.[61]

New Crime Groups and Corruption
New crime groups do not use corruption to procure government contracts or influence legislation, as they are not businessmen in the construction sector, like traditional organized crime in Japan, Sicily, or New York City.[62] Rather, they contribute to the endemic corruption of their communities and states.

New crime groups need not worry about the passage of specific laws in their chaotic and lawless environment, as there is little chance that any laws will be enforced. They thrive in environments where there are the trappings of a state – police, border guards, customs officials. New criminals must pay these personnel to ensure that they are not obstacles to their illicit trade.[63] These payoffs to officials for safe passage of their smuggled goods, or tolerance of the brothels under their command, are major expenses for the crime group. In Mexico, drug cartels pay millions monthly to ensure that needed officials are on their payroll. The chief of the Mexican drug agency was ousted for being on the payroll of the traffickers.[64]

To ensure compliance, the criminal organization may introduce its own personnel into the law enforcement structures. For example, in Mexico, already in the early 1990s, the crime groups were paying large bribes to ensure that their personnel entered the federal police force, the *policia judicial*.[65] In Russia, interviews with law enforcement personnel in Kazan revealed that many police, instead of being bribed by members of the criminal organizations, were themselves members.[66] This is not the penetration of the state by the crime group, as was the case with the "old crime" groups, but the capture of the state by the criminals.[67] But unlike in the historic past when a king was captured by the enemy, there is little chance of ransoming the captive – the state – from its modern-day captors, organized crime.

New Crime Groups and the Use of Violence

The new crime groups use violence on a mass scale. Illustrative examples coming from Africa, Latin America, Eastern Europe, and the former USSR reveal that this is a shared attribute across regions. Vadim Volkov described post-Soviet organized crime groups as violent entrepreneurs, because violence is at the core of their business activity.[68] Unlike the criminals of the past, they have incorporated much muscle into their organizations so that the sale of protection is one of their primary commodities.[69] The Balkan crime groups have broken into European prostitution markets because of their extraordinary violence.[70] Thousands died in Mexico in 2009–11, victims of the brutal killings of the Mexican drug organizations. Yet one of the most prominent and brutal Mexican drug organizations, the Zetas, also functions on a violent business model. As one analyst commented, "the Zetas are designed more like a modern corporation than a classic Mafia, bound by neither blood nor geography. With a reach deep into Central America and an ample portfolio of revenue sources, the Zetas operate more like 'a meritocracy.'"[71]

At the epicenter of the killing epidemic is Ciudad Juarez, with more than ten killings daily, making it one of the homicide capitals of the world, along with key urban areas of Central America. These homicides are a consequence of the internecine battles over turf by crime groups seeking to control access to the U.S.–Mexican border.[72] Central America, a transit route for drugs, has even

TABLE 3.1A. *Transnational Crime and the State*

	Traditional Organized Crime	New Transnational Crime
Attitude to the state	Often nationalistic	Interests do not coincide with the state
Relationship to the nation-state	Grows with the state; parasitic on nation-state Substitutes for the state Depends on state for contracts and services Rarely violently attacks state authority; uses violence symbolically	Thrives on the absence of effective governance; grows with the weakened state Substitutes for the state Routine use of violence to destabilize state
Relation to corruption	Tool used to influence state officials – operative tool	Depends on high levels of systemic and institutionalized corruption
Relation to terrorism	Usually rejects association with terrorists	May sell services to terrorists or contract terrorists/ insurgents for services

newer crime groups and reaches among the highest homicide rates in the world. Honduras had the highest rates, with 82.1 homicides per 100,000 persons in 2010.[73] The Mexican and Central American instability is discussed in greater detail in Chapter 6.

New Criminals and Terrorists and Relation to the State

New and old transnational criminals differ in their willingness to cooperate with terrorists. The newer crime groups may not share the ideological motivations of the terrorists, but they too do not want a secure state. In fact, the crime groups may promote grievances, because it is through the prolongation of conflict that they enhance their profits.[74] Therefore, as is discussed subsequently, some new groups cooperate with terrorists.

Table 3.1a summarizes the fundamental differences that exist in the relationship of old and new transnational crime. They reveal profound transformations in the relationship of the state to those who would be considered deviant.

New and Old Terrorism

New and Old Terrorism and Their Relation to the State

Old and new terrorism have very different relations to the state. The old terrorism, receiving state support, or in some locales working in tandem with the state, had limited need to corrupt state institutions. In the days before the ascent of transnational organized crime, the crimes of terrorist groups were local in focus, simpler, and not necessarily linked to professional crime groups.

TABLE 3.1B. *Terrorists and the State*

	Old Terrorism	New Terrorism
Attitude to the state	Often supported as proxies by states, which provided training, transport and documents, and other support	Interests often opposed to any state Increasingly lethal More global objectives than state-based
Relationship to the nation-state	Thrive on the existence of support from distinct nation-state	Thrives on the absence of effective governance May substitute for the state, providing social services Grows with the weakened state Many new groups use terrorism as a weapon against the state
Relation to corruption	Tool used to influence state officials – operative tool	Tool used to influence state officials – operative tool Pervasive corruption used as recruitment tool
Funding sources	State funding, bank robberies, extortion, kidnapping	Decline of state sponsorship Great variety of crimes
Relation to organized crime	Limited contact with organized crime	Often seeks criminals to assist; may seek links and more long-term relations with transnational crime Criminal interests may predominate

All of this changed, as discussed with the end of the Cold War, with the demise of much state-sponsored terrorism and the globalization of crime (see Table 3.1b).

The older terrorism of the Irish Republican Army (IRA), Italy in the 1970s,[75] the Basque ETA, the Red Army Faction (RAF) in Germany, the Kurdistan Workers' Party (PKK) in Turkey, or the LTTE movement of the Tamil Tigers in Sri Lanka had more narrow objectives than the many and diverse insurgent and jihadi groups that have arisen in the late twentieth and beginning of the twenty-first centuries.[76] These older terrorist groups wanted political change, often on behalf of minority groups, in their countries or regions, but did not seek to promote change on a more global scale through their acts. They differed from what might be considered intermediary groups in the transformation process – the FARC and Hezbollah – which operate financially on a more global scale. Hezbollah also differs in that it receives so much support from the Iranian state.[77] Hezbollah differed from the older groups in that it planned and committed terrorist acts far from its home base, such as the bombings of the Jewish Community Center in Buenos Aires in 1994 that will be discussed more in Chapter 4.[78]

According to Brian Jenkins, the old "terrorists want a lot of people watching and a lot of people listening and not a lot of people dead."[79] This underestimates the lethality of old terrorist groups like the PKK, whose violent attacks have resulted in the killing of tens of thousands in Turkey since the 1960s.[80] But these people were killed over an extended period of time, rather than in spectacular attacks with simultaneous mass casualties, which have been the hallmark of successful terrorist attacks since the early 1990s in the United States, Russia, India, Spain, and Indonesia, as was discussed in Chapter 1.[81]

Many of these older terrorist groups survived because of state financing or what is most commonly known as "state-sponsored" terrorism. In the 1970s and 1980s, "state sponsors utilized intelligence services, embassies, state airlines and provided training and equipment that resulted in focused lethality attack."[82] The PKK received support from the Soviet state, and its leader, Ocalan, received sanctuary in Moscow.[83] Many other terrorist organizations and guerrilla groups during the extended Cold War period received direct support from the former USSR or its surrogates and allies, such as East Germany, Cuba, Syria, and Libya. Funding flowed to groups such as the Basque ETA from Cuba and Libya,[84] and ETA members have allegedly received training in Algeria, Lebanon, and Nicaragua.[85] The Provisional IRA received heavy machine guns from Libya.[86] Yet it was not only foreign support that allowed some groups to prosper. Some terror groups received tactical assistance from members of their national state security apparati. For example, in Italy, the right-wing terrorists received support from members of the Italian intelligence services.[87]

As Donatella della Porta explains,

> by their very nature, the secret services, are, among the state, apparata, the most exposed to infiltration by groups with such "objective" interests in the survival of terrorist organizations. In this case, the secret services will protect terrorist organizations instead of fighting them ... Moreover, protection of terrorist organizations by the internal security services is much more likely to happen in periods of social and political changes, when the élites are divided about the strategies to be implemented in order to control these changes.[88]

A similar phenomenon existed in Turkey, where members of the security apparatus were part of a "deep state" that consisted of shadowy networks that colluded with organized crime and terrorists. As in the Italian experience, the rise of the state security services was part of the Cold War effort of NATO to prevent the growth of Communism. The rise of the PKK and other Communist and left-wing terrorist groups in Turkey prompted a reaction similar to that observed in Italy. There is "considerable evidence of close ties between state authorities and criminal gangs, including the use of the Grey Wolves to carry out illegal activities."[89] The Grey Wolves is one of several right-wing terrorist organizations in Turkey thought to have received support from the state security services.

Corruption and Old Terrorism

Corruption for the old terrorists was an operative tool. Terrorists relied on their ability to neutralize law enforcement and achieve safe passage across borders. As was cited earlier, the corruption most often was related to the security services and was associated with right-wing terrorism. But there have been examples of corruption associated with[90] left-wing terrorism. For example, the leftist PKK relied heavily on corruption in border areas to smuggle goods and drugs that fund its terrorist cause.[91] But the main areas of criminal activity of the older terrorists did not require much corruption of state institutions as they participated in kidnappings, bank robberies, and murder.[92]

Groups such as the IRA, the ETA, and the Red Brigade made less use of corruption than their successors. In contrast, the newer terrorist groups that rely heavily on cross-border illicit trade, especially large-scale drug trafficking, to fund their activities have much more need to corrupt members of state apparati and thrive where state apparati are corrupt.[93]

Older Terrorism and Crime

Older terrorist groups, as will be discussed in Chapter 5, relied heavily on more traditional forms of criminality to finance their activities as well as the funds provided by the state sponsors of terrorism. As Naylor points out, in "the early stages of an insurgency, a guerilla group may cooperate with domestic and local criminal organizations on the basis of their shared status as social outcasts and their shared immediate objectives."[94] The main activities of the Provisional IRA included kidnapping for ransom, extortion, armed robbery, and, subsequently, the drug trade.[95] The ETA was first reported as involved with the drug trade only in 1984, twenty-five years after its founding in 1959.[96] The PKK are key actors today in the contemporary drug trade, but in its earlier years, funding, like that of the Tamil Tigers, came from extortion against their compatriots residing in Western Europe, the United Kingdom, and Canada.[97] The German RAF had a spree of bank robberies in 1971, and the Weather Underground, in the United States in 1981, attacked a Brinks armored car.[98] The Montoneros in Argentina kidnapped business executives in the 1970s, especially of multinational corporations. The largest payment in Latin America in this period occurred in 1974, when more than $14 million was paid by Exxon to recover one of its executives.[99]

A transition phase occurred in the 1980s with instances of direct cooperation of crime and terror groups. The Red Brigades and the Napolitan-based

Camorra split the ransom for an Italian politician. The Camorra also executed people on behalf of the Red Brigades.[100] This presaged the greater involvement of the Camorra with different terrorist groups, as will be discussed in Chapter 4. Once this cooperation was purely on the national level, but in subsequent decades, the Camorra was serving transnational actors.

The Transformation of Terrorism

The new terrorism is not only more lethal and a greater threat to global security; it is also more criminal and thus more likely to engage in corruption. As Table 3.1b shows, because it less frequently receives support from states, and often seeks to undermine the existing political and religious order, its lethality is not kept in check by any state sponsor. Its goals are more apocalyptic and its violence is less focused. Its membership, as seen in many al-Qaeda affiliates, is recruited from different countries, and its funding is global. The new terrorists, like the new organized crime, exploit the new world order to their advantage.

Environment of New Crime Groups

New terrorists have communications, funding, and personnel who are often hard to trace, and their network structures enhance the difficulty of detection.[101] As is discussed in Chapter 4, they often operate in conflict zones, disputed territories, free-trade zones, and multiborder areas – all regions difficult to control by traditional states. They exploit the post-Westphalian order that has proliferated with the end of the Cold War.

Once the superpower conflict ended with the conclusion of the Cold War, many terrorists and insurgent movements in Africa, Central and South America, and the Middle East lost their state support. State-supported terrorists often lacked autonomy because they were financially dependent on their sponsors.[102] These state sponsors of terrorism were often far from the locale of the terrorist, guerilla, or insurgent organizations.[103] This was the dominant model of the Cold War era. "The end of the Cold War brought an effective end to external support for these groups. The Soviet Union disappeared, and the United States simply lost interest in many of its former clients"[104] such as the Mujaheddin in Afghanistan. According to the U.S. Country Reports on Terrorism for 2011, there are only four remaining state supporters of terrorism – Cuba, Iran, Syria, and Sudan.[105] Without state support, many groups simply dried up, while others had to find other means to fund their existence. Crime became an important funding source,[106] as discussed more in Chapter 5.

New Terrorism and Corruption

The presence of widespread corruption in Africa, Russia, Afghanistan, and the Middle East, as discussed in Chapter 2, has been an important recruiting tool for terrorists, who justify their organizations as purer than the state, and they sell or ingratiate themselves as service providers. But corruption is also a tool used to facilitate the movement of the illicit commodities on which they depend for their survival.

The new terrorists, no longer dependent on countries' funding for their survival, are even more brutal toward states, their institutions, and their symbols of economic and political power. Hence the bombing of the World Trade Center in the United States, core institutions of the police and security apparatus in Pakistan, and numerous ministries in Iraq reflect this new hostility to the state and to its citizens. Moreover, unlike their predecessors, the religious terrorists who predominated in the post–Cold War era "declare war on entire societies and cultures and political status-quo, not just on individual governments as is the case with secular terrorist groups."[107]

The new terrorist organizations operate globally, often existing outside of state structures and legitimate financial institutions. The fact that much terrorist finance exists outside of banks, stock exchanges, and other components of the licit economy is not a matter of choice for terrorists.[108] As a result of the adoption of the Patriot Act in the United States, and efforts by the international community to deny terrorists access to the legitimate economy, terrorism has become increasingly criminalized.[109] Trade-based money laundering, couriers, and underground banking became vehicles of choice to transfer funds in the presence of financial curbs imposed by states.[110] Fortunately for the terrorists, the last two of these means to transfer funds have deep historical roots in many Moslem societies. The movement of the terrorist economy outside state-based financial institutions further reduces the need for terrorists to rely on or co-opt the state.

Crime-Terror Relationship

Since the end of the Cold War and the decline of much state support for terrorism, criminal activity has become the lifeblood for terrorists. The new terrorist needs to cooperate with new crime groups. They can find common financial ground, as both share short-term financial horizons, are networked, and are global in scope. Whereas organized crime in the past was closely linked to the financial health of the legitimate economy through its investments in real estate, stock markets, and even banks, the new organized crime does not care about financial fluctuations in licit markets. Whereas traditional crime groups suffer when real estate markets collapse or stock markets dive, many new crime groups do not share these concerns. Therefore, they will not worry that a spectacular terrorist attack may undercut their investments, such as the stock market tumble that followed September 11.

The existence of a hybrid threat (crime, terrorism, and insurgency) to national and international security was recognized in a new national transnational crime strategy issued by the White House in July 2011 and at the first meeting of European Police Chiefs held at Europol a few weeks earlier.[111] It has also been recognized by Arab law enforcement examining the violence that has followed the Arab uprisings.[112] This recognition on both sides of the Atlantic reflects a new reality of more intense interactions between two formerly quite different types of nonstate actors. As Kim Thachuk has written on this transformation, "organized crime groups rarely cooperated with terrorist groups, or engaged in their activities as their goals were most often at odds . . . yet many of today's terrorist groups have not only lost most of their more comprehensible ideals, but are increasingly turning to smuggling and other criminal activities to fund their operations."[113]

Historical Precedents

The intersection of crime and terrorism is not an entirely new phenomenon. Historians documented similar interactions at the onset of modern terrorism a century and a half ago. The historical works of Walter Laqueur on terrorism of the mid-nineteenth century pointed out that the Russian anarchists engaged in crimes.[114] Russian terrorists engaged in a bank robbery in Russia in 1879, and the practice became widespread in the first Russian Revolution of 1905–6.[115] Their successors, the Bolsheviks, had such notable members as Stalin and Ordzhonokidze, who participated in both terrorist and criminal activity in the prerevolutionary period. Stalin was a noted bank robber, and some of his associates had colorful criminal pasts.[116] Other terrorist groups, such as Indians under British colonial rule, engaged in counterfeiting, and the Croatian Utashe in the 1920s forged bank notes.[117]

Many subsequent traditional terrorist groups had more limited relationships with transnational crime groups. Leftist terrorist groups in Italy, and terrorists in Ireland and Spain, rarely hired professional criminals, because members of the terrorist group would often commit criminal activity on behalf of the organization. Criminal-terrorist relationships, if they existed, were often of a strategic alliance rather than long-term relationships.[118] An exception, as previously mentioned, existed in Italy, where the right-wing groups had links with organized crime.[119] The general absence of profound relationships with organized crime sets the old terrorism apart from the new.

The Emergence of the Concept of Narco-terrorism

Yet the analytical division between crime and terrorism ended with the minting of the term *narco-terrorism* in the 1980s. First applied in Peru, where the Sendero Luminoso terrorist organization supported itself by the drug trade, it rapidly found applicability in other contexts. The terrorist group FARC was identified as engaging in narco-terrorism. Presently, the Drug Enforcement Agency states that more than half of the terrorist groups named by the United States engage in the drug trade and have been defined as narco-terrorists.[120]

The adoption of the concept of narco-terrorism reflected a new reality. The illicit drug trade had become global. Moreover, it was a major part of the world's economy, corrupting officials and tainting and distorting entire economies.[121] The extraordinary profits of this trade[122] added to the potency of terrorist groups who traded in narcotics or extorted money from the drug trafficking organizations "they protected."[123]

The term *narco-terrorism* did not reveal a deeper understanding of the increasing "dirty togetherness" of criminals and terrorists.[124] Rather, the term merely helped people understand that the large ill-gotten gains generated by the drug trade allowed terrorists in Latin America to sustain their violence and their organizations. This insight was not initially extended to the IRA, which was increasingly maintaining its organization through drug trafficking,[125] nor to the PKK, which was enhancing its organizational capacity by shipping increasing amounts of heroin through Turkey to Western European markets.[126]

Eventually, there was greater awareness that narco-terrorism was not exclusively a Latin American phenomenon but was global in scope. But the broader applicability of this concept to other regions of the world and diverse terrorist groups did not lead to an intellectual breakthrough and a paradigm shift – one that would link the actions of the most important group of nonstate actors, terrorists and criminals, as combined threats to global insecurity.

False Dichotomies

Many failed to see this increasing relationship because they were constrained by their false dichotomy of criminals being driven by profit and terrorists by political motivations. Yet something more important was also behind this failure to recognize the increasing linkages. Even before 9/11, terrorism specialists were recognizing that there was a new terrorism that was more global, more lethal, and a greater security challenge.[127] Yet in their analyses of the new terrorism, most terrorist specialists did not focus on the crime that became a crucial source of support for the new terrorism. With their political perspective, they largely overlooked the economics of terrorism.[128]

Pernicious Entanglements

In the last two decades, "there has been a fascinating blurring . . . of the differences between profit-oriented organized crime groups on the one hand and ideologically motivated rebel and terrorist groups on the other."[129] New criminals and new terrorists differ in their time horizons and in their relationship to the state. These criminals and terrorists, operating in the increasingly numerous post–Cold War conflict regions, lack long-term political or financial objectives. They thrive on chaos and seek to perpetuate conflict because it suits their financial and ideological interests and ensures that there is no effective state apparatus to control them.[130] In fact, they often promote grievances because it is through the prolongation of conflict that they enhance their profits.[131]

Illustrative of the pernicious entanglement is the situation in the Balkans in the 1990s, where crime bosses who were also political leaders deliberately engaged with terrorists, thereby frustrating peacekeeping efforts. It was in their financial interest to perpetuate the conflict. Željko Ražnatović, also known as Arkan, a Serbian career criminal and a paramilitary leader, was supported in his activities by high-level members of the Serbian security and military. His repeated serious criminality in Sweden and the Netherlands before his return to Serbia earned him a place in the Top Ten on the Interpol watch list. Arkan's paramilitary group committed atrocities in Bosnia for which he was subsequently indicted by the International Criminal Tribunal for the Former Yugoslavia.[132]

The illicit networks that destabilize conflict regions have been observed in many other locales than the Balkans.[133] The entanglements of transnational crime, terrorism, and corruption may be most evident in the terrorism in Afghanistan; Pakistan; North, West, and East Africa; and Yemen, but they are not exclusive to jihadist groups.[134] They also exist in other conflict regions, such as Sri Lanka, Russia's North Caucasus, the South Caucasus, Central Asia, Northern Ireland, and many parts of Africa that have had their own long-term conflicts.[135]

Environments Conducive to Dirty Entanglements

Moreover, in these unstable regions, where long-term conflicts have eroded traditional norms and values, there are not constraints on community members who can readily be recruited for illicit activity. Poverty and instability also facilitate recruitment. This has been particularly advantageous for AQIM, founded in 2007 and now operating throughout North Africa. In Morocco, where more than 49 percent of the population over age fifteen is illiterate, there is an absence of hope among many in the population who have crowded into recently urbanized cities. Over half the youths desire to emigrate. Organizations with a potential to radicalize Moslem youths are active in the slums, and they offer recruits who will engage in terrorism the possibility of a future in paradise. The relationships between these desperate conditions and acts of terrorism are credible. Explaining the recruits for a 2003 terrorist act in Morocco, experts noted, "By way of example, most members of the cell that carried out the Casablanca terrorist bombings had left school at a very early age and lived in extremely poor conditions. Some of them relied on very unstable jobs and others had no job at all."[136]

Yet the environment in Morocco is better than in other countries to its south. As Jean-Pierre Filiu explains,

> AQIM's criminal dimension hurts it in winning political support, particularly with religiously inclined groups, but it is important to the organization's operations. The Sahel countries are among the poorest on the planet. Annual GDP per capita is $1,042 in Mauritania, $657 in Mali, and $390 in Niger, which ranks last among the 182 states in the United Nations Development Programme's classification of human development. (Neither Mauritania nor Mali fare dramatically better; Mauritania ranks 154th and Mali 178th.) AQIM can afford low-intensity guerrilla activity in such an environment only because the partnership in crime provides a steady flow of recruits, no matter how low their jihadi commitment.[137]

Global Reach

Criminals, terrorists, and their hybrid structures are also major beneficiaries of globalization. Operating regionally or globally, as will be discussed in Chapter 4, they exploit porous borders and dysfunctional state institutions compromised by corruption. They exploit territory outside the control of a particular state, such as multiborder areas, regions of frozen conflict, and fragile states. They capitalize on the fact that legal controls are state based by exploiting differences in legal norms and procedures among jurisdictions.

In this new reality, transnational organized crime and its enabler, corruption, help perpetuate the global reach and operations of terrorist groups. Furthermore, many criminal groups are able to capitalize on a new clientele – terrorists who seek to have the maximum destructive impact by using the best expertise they can buy. They will hire criminal forgers to manufacture false documents and will retain the services of human traffickers. Terrorists will take advantage of the criminals' specialization in logistics to move people, arms, and money. The most advanced and well-financed terrorist groups will also hire computer-savvy professionals to facilitate their communications and to provide training for members. To ensure steady income flows, terrorists' daily lives are increasingly determined by their participation in crime and their interactions with criminals.

As was discussed in Chapter 1, the Madrid bombers had false documents provided by criminals. Turkish human traffickers move terrorists from the Middle East and North Africa to Europe via their territory.[138] Terrorists in Kashmir use criminalized specialists from the high-tech computer industry of India to promote their objectives.[139]

The entanglement of transnational crime, terrorism, and corruption that develops in these unstable environments is extremely threatening to the international order. The inability of both domestic and international militaries, as well as law enforcement agencies, to control these new relationships makes them a growing danger. The failure of the international community to recognize the centrality of these dirty entanglements to international instability has allowed this nexus to flourish in the 1990s and the beginning of the twenty-first century.[140]

Varieties of Crime-Terror Interactions

Flexians

Chris Dishman outlined a process of transformation by which terror groups morph into entities that are "political by day but criminal by night."[141] The criminal-terrorist duality described recalls the *flexians,* high-level political figures who switch identities. Janine Wedel, in her recent book *The Shadow Elite,* focuses on flexians, who float in and out of different identities as the circumstances demand. They can be state officials one day and leading members of think tanks the next. Their ability to span identities is crucial to their success.[142] Illustrative of the way that the illegitimate world mirrors the licit, terrorists often prove to be the ultimate flexians. They may be ordinary criminals one day, terrorists the next. As has been observed in European prisons, they may even themselves be confused as to their actual identities.[143]

Disposable People

Some Islamic terrorist groups are no longer ideologically pure. They exploit criminals in their organizations as they are seen as "disposable people" having already sinned. Saudi Arabia has identified 25 percent of all al-Qaeda members in their rehabilitation programs as former criminals,[144] and the nation's experience is not unique. Furthermore, the Taliban in present-day Afghanistan comprises both the ideologically committed but also others who are nothing but criminal thugs.[145] The relationship is also particularly strong in neighboring Pakistan, where some crime groups deliberately collaborate on a continuing basis with terrorist organizations.[146]

Terrorists Lose Ideological Purity

Many terrorists in Latin America, Asia, Africa, and Europe depend on crime for the survival of their organizations. This dependence may become so strong that the organization decays into a primarily criminal organization.[147] This has been seen in the Philippines, where ASG started out as an al-Qaeda affiliate but now is engaged more in economically motivated kidnapping for large ransoms and in piracy rather than terrorism.[148] Members of the IRA became so deeply involved in crime that they committed a $50 million bank robbery.[149] The same is true of the FARC, for which ever larger percentages of its funding comes from crime.[150]

Incentives for Cooperation

The absence of disincentives in diverse regions allows this cooperation and collaboration to flourish. Criminals and terrorists cooperate in moving large quantities of drugs along the Balkan route because there is little effective enforcement that precludes this collaboration.[151] The same was true in the Philippines, where the amorphous character of ASG has blurred enforcement authority between the police and the military.[152] Africa, with its many fragile and failed states, has become a virtual laboratory of the diverse and complex forms of collaboration between crime and terrorism, because there has been little effort or capacity in many countries to discourage or curtail the entangled networks.

The current state of deadly hybrid networks in Africa is complex and is shaped by diverse historical forces, geography, and the illicit economies of diverse regions on the continent.[153] North Africa is characterized by a terrorism that is closely associated with diverse forms of criminal activity.[154] In East and West Africa, the nature of the vicious triad is different from North Africa. In East Africa, organized crime groups from Latin America interact with criminal groups and terrorist groups such as AQIM and Hezbollah, with corrupt officials being central to these operations.[155] As previously mentioned, AQIM has taken over Mali, driving hundreds of thousands into exile. Boko Haram is increasingly destabilizing Nigeria as it combines terrorist activity with criminal activity, particularly kidnapping.[156] West Africa, as shown in Chapters 4 and 6, has illicit networks that presently connect Latin America, Africa, and Europe. The key criminal and terrorist actors in this equation are now Latin American drug organizations and Hezbollah. Earlier, al-Qaeda assumed a key role in the diamond and arms trade in this region.[157] The area encompassing West and East Africa is creating what Judge de la Bruguière refers to as an arc of instability.[158]

Al Shabaab controls territory along the Horn of Africa just as the Mafia controls territory in Sicily. The East African crime-terror relationship represents the obverse of most known interactions. Generally, it is the criminals who extort their victims, but in East Africa, the terrorists demand tribute from the criminals. Al Shabaab extracts tribute from the pirates, or transnational criminal actors, who are operating in their home territory with limited and highly corrupted governance.[159]

The diversity visible with Africa also exists within other parts of the world. Crime and terrorist interactions are much more complex than models of divergence and convergence that were once posited. Endemic corruption facilitates these interactions without impediment.

Conclusion

Recent decades have seen a major evolution in both terrorism and transnational crime. Diverse scholars have addressed the more global, increasingly lethal, and less frequently state supported new terrorism. Yet few discuss a new transnational crime, even though similarly dramatic changes have occurred in the nature of organized crime. No longer is organized crime necessarily limited to its territorial base, ethnically distinctive, or hierarchically structured. Like many groups of contemporary terrorists, it is ethnically diverse, fluid, and highly mobile and flexible.[160]

Both new criminals and new terrorists exploit and depend on the latest forms of communication and the Internet. They depend on these channels for rapid coordination to ensure secrecy and evade detection. They communicate across vast distances and diverse time zones to achieve success in their operations.

The new terrorists and new criminals are no longer polar opposites. Transnational criminals may be strongly political, whereas terrorists are increasingly concerned by their finances. They coexist in environments in which they can learn and cooperate without interference by state authorities. They share an ecosystem. Terrorists always were disloyal to the state, but many organized criminals benefited from their own loyalty and service to the state. Yet among most new criminals, there is little or no loyalty to the state, and new criminals, like terrorists, benefit from disorder and from hollowing out of state institutions. In the days of the "retreat of the state,"[161] both types of nonstate actors are major beneficiaries of diminished governance, most visible in weak states and conflict regions but by no means confined to just these environments.

Both groups have benefited from the rise of instability in the post–Cold War era, when regional conflicts have become all too common around the world. Therefore, individuals whose lives, families, and communities have been destroyed are vulnerable to recruitment by both terrorists and criminals. Moreover, the increasing international economic disparity that leaves a bulging population of youthful males without the possibilities for decent employment and a future has provided many more individuals ready to be employed by such nonstate actors as criminals, terrorists, insurgents, and warlords.

Criminal and terrorist interactions are increasingly diverse, as the regional case studies from Africa reveal. Unlike in earlier analyses, when scholars discussed symbiosis and convergence, we have seen a variety of patterns shaped by history, culture, ethnicity, and the presence and influence of transnational crime groups from other regions. West Africa is influenced by crime groups from Latin America and the former Soviet Union, and East Africa has been shaped by the presence of Italian organized crime groups and the arrival of terrorists from Yemen and elsewhere. Major nonstate actors in North Africa have been identified as jihadi guerillas,[162] in West Africa we have seen numerous terrorist organizations operating, including Hamas, Hezbollah, al-Qaeda, and others combined with organized crime. In East Africa, pirates and Al Shaabab operate on the same territory. There are diverse forms of interaction that can only be understood by old and new trade routes, patterns of patronage in the Cold War era, legacies of colonialism, and the constant need of powerful organized crime routes to find new routes to markets and to dispose of the detritus of the developed world.

Facilitating the growth of new criminals and new terrorists is the pervasive corruption that exists in much of the developing world and in conflict regions. It is corruption at every level of governance that allows criminals, terrorists, and other lethal nonstate actors to work together. Corruption has been essential in providing a facilitating environment not only for the criminal-terrorist interactions but in facilitating the illicit activities that they need for their financial survival. Yet this corruption exists on every level, from the border guard who allows criminals and terrorists to traverse borders to leading government officials who accept bribes to destroy their countries' land and seas or exploit their natural resources.

The new criminals and the terrorists in many regions of the world are potent actors who have the capacity to undermine governance. In many regions, they thrive in the chaos they help create and perpetuate. The role of these new entanglements in shaping the political economy of the future international community should not be underestimated. The impact of transnational criminals and the new global illicit networks is more destructive than the impact of terrorists alone. An entirely new set of dangerous phenomena arise from the combination of these pernicious components.

Notes

1. BBC News, "Profile: Jose Padilla," August 16, 2007, http://news.bbc.co.uk/2/hi/ 2037444.stm; Lizette Alvarez, "Sentence for Terrorist Is Too Short, Court Rules," *New York Times,* December 15, 2012, http://www.nytimes.com/2011/09/20/us/ jose-padillas-prison-sentence-too-short-appeals-court-says.html?_r=1&hpw.

2. U.S. Court of Appeals, Eleventh Circuit, No. 08-10494, United States of America v. Kifah Wael Jayyousi, aka Abu Mohamed, Adham Amin Hassoun, and Jose Padilla, aka Ibrahim, aka Abu Abdullah Al Mujahir, aka Abu Abu Abdullah the Puerto Rican, September 19, 2011, 65, judges' statement accessed through http://blogs.wsj.com/law/2011/09/19/appellate-court-rules-jose-padillas-terrorist-sentence-too-lenient/.

3. Ibid., 68.

4. "Merah: From Petty Criminal to Killer," March 22, 2012. The French interior minister said he had been arrested at least eighteen times for petty crimes. http:// www.aljazeera.com/indepth/features/2012/03/201232211333224295.html.

5. Anne L. Clunan and Harold A. Trinkunas, "Conceptualizing Ungoverned Spaces: Territorial Statehood, Contested Authority and Softened Sovereignty," in *Ungoverned Spaces: Alternatives to State Authority in an Era of Softened Sovereignty,* ed. Anne L. Clunan and Harold A. Trinkunas (Stanford, CA: Stanford University Press, 2010), 17–33, and Vanda Felbab-Brown, "Rules and Regulations in Ungoverned Spaces: Illicit Economies, Criminals and Belligerents," in ibid., 175–92.

6. See the work of Susan Strange, *The Retreat of the State: The Diffusion of Power in the World Economy* (New York: Cambridge University Press, 1996), who discusses the rise of diverse transnational actors, including transnational criminals. The central chapter on this topic was coauthored with Letizia Paoli.

7. Phil Williams, "Here Be Dragons: Dangerous Spaces and International Security," in Clunan and Trinkunas, *Ungoverned Spaces,* 45–46.

8. Daniel Byman, *Deadly Connections: States That Sponsor Terrorism* (Cambridge: Cambridge University Press, 2005).

9. Ahmed Rashid, *Descent into Chaos: The U.S. and the Disaster in Pakistan, Afghanistan, and Central Asia* (New York: Penguin Books, 2009); Ahmed Rashid, *Jihad: The Rise of Militant Islam in Central Asia* (New Haven, CT: Yale University Press, 2002); Syed Saleem Shahzad, *Inside Al-Qaeda and the Taliban: Beyond Bin Laden and 9/11* (London: Pluto Press, 2011).

10. Walter Laqueur, *The New Terrorism: Fanaticism and the Arms of Mass Destruction* (New York: Oxford University Press, 1999); Ian O. Lesser and Bruce Hoffman et al., *Countering the New Terrorism* (Santa Monica, CA: RAND, 1999); Isabelle Duyvesteyn, "How New Is the New Terrorism?," *Studies in Conflict and Terrorism* 27, no. 5 (2004): 439–55; Paul Wilkinson, "Why Modern Terrorism? Differentiating Types and Distinguishing Ideological Motivations," in *The New Global Terrorism: Characteristics, Causes, Control,* ed. Charles W. Kegley Jr. (New York: Prentice Hall, 2003), 106–38; David Tucker, "What Is New about

the New Terrorism and How Dangerous Is It?," *Terrorism and Political Violence* 13, no. 3 (2001): 1–14; National Commission on Terrorist Attacks upon the United States, *9/11 Report* (New York: St. Martin's Press, 2004), 71–103; Xavier Raufer, "New World Disorder, New Terrorisms: New Threats for Europe and the Western World," in *The Future of Terrorism*, ed. Max Taylor and John Horgan (London: Frank Cass, 2000), 30–51.

11. David Claridge, "Exploding the Myths of Superterrorism," in *The Future of Terrorism*, ed. Maxwell Taylor and John Horgan (London: Frank Cass, 2000), 133.

12. See Yonah Alexander, "Superterrorism: A Global Threat," *World and I* 86, no. 3 (1993): 86–92, and Walter Laqueur, "Postmodern Terrorism," *Foreign Affairs* 75, no. 5 (1996): 24–36.

13. Stewart Patrick, *Weak Links: Fragile States, Global Threats and International Security* (Oxford: Oxford University Press, 2011), 141–42.

14. Peter Andreas, *Blue Helmets and Black Markets: The Business of Survival in the Siege of Sarajevo* (Ithaca, NY: Cornell University Press, 2008). In Central Asia, they exist in Tajikistan and Kyrgyzstan, which have been racked by violence. See Alexander Kupatadze, *Organized Crime, Political Transitions and State Formation in Post-Soviet Eurasia* (Basingstoke, UK: Palgrave Macmillan, 2012). For a discussion of West Africa, see Ashley Neese Bybee, "Narco State or Failed State? Narcotics and Politics in Guinea-Bissau," PhD diss., School of Public Policy, George Mason University, September 2011, and Bybee, "The Twenty-First Century Expansion of the Transnational Drug Trade in Africa," *Journal of International Affairs* 66, no. 1 (2012): 65–80.

15. Douglas Farah, "Fixers, Super Fixers, and Shadow Facilitators: How Networks Connect," in *Convergence: Illicit Networks and National Security in the Age of Globalization*, ed. Michael Miklaucic and Jacqueline Brewer (Washington, DC: National Defense University Press, 2013), 75–95.

16. The role of transnational crime in commodities markets has been seen in the diamond trade and the aluminum industry. On the Russian aluminum wars, see Andrew E. Kramer, "Out of Siberia: A Russian Way to Wealth," *New York Times*, August 20, 2006, http://www.nytimes.com/2006/08/20/business/yourmoney/20oligarch.html?pagewanted=1; Greg Campbell, *Blood Diamonds: Tracing the Deadly Path of the World's Most Precious Stones* (Boulder, CO: Westview Press, 2002). On the profits of the Mexican drug trade, see the two noted specialists Luis Astorga and David A. Shirk, *Drug Trafficking Organizations and Counter-Drug Strategies in the U.S.*-27, http://usmex5.ucsd.edu/assets/024/11632.pdf.

17. Phil Williams, "The Nature of Drug Trafficking Networks," *Current History* 97 (1998): 154–59; Michael Kenney, *From Pablo to Osama: Trafficking and Terrorist Networks, Government Bureaucracies, and Competitive Adaptation* (University Park: Pennsylvania State University Press, 2007).

18. Williams, "Nature of Drug Trafficking Networks," 54.

19. The need to discuss the state and the evasion of state law is discussed in Josiah M. Heyman and Alan Smart, "States and Illegal Practices: An Overview," in *States and Illegal Practices*, ed. Josiah M. Heyman (Oxford: Berg, 1999), 1–24. See also Robert Mandel, *Dark Logic: Transnational Criminal Tactics and Global Security* (Stanford, CA: Stanford University Press, 2011), 145–61.

20. See Manuel Castells on the global criminal economy in *The End of Millennium*, 2nd ed. (Oxford: Blackwell, 2000), 169–211; for an expanded discussion of this,

see Louise I. Shelley, "Transnational Organized Crime: An Imminent Threat to the Nation-State?," *Journal of International Affairs* 48, no. 2 (1995): 463–89.

21. Castells, *End of Millennium*; Pino Arlacchi, *Mafia Business: The Mafia Ethic and the Spirit of Capitalism* (London: Verso, 1986); Peter B. E. Hill, *The Japanese Mafia: Yakuza, Law and the State* (Oxford: Oxford University Press, 2003), 45–64; David E. Kaplan and Alec Dubro, *Yakuza: Japan's Criminal Underworld* (Berkeley: University of California Press, 2003).

22. Howard Abadinsky, *Organized Crime*, 7th ed. (Belmont, CA: Wadsworth/Thomson, 2003), 75–103, 258.

23. Ernesto Savona, "Exploring OC Portfolio Investments for Rethinking Confiscation Policies," presentation at Pan-European High Level Conference on Asset Recovery Offices, Budapest, Hungary, March 7–8, 2011.

24. Rensselaer W. Lee III, *The White Labyrinth: Cocaine and Political Power* (New Brunswick, NJ: Transaction, 1990), 40; see Francisco E. Thoumi, *Illegal Drugs, Economy and Society in the Andes* (Washington, DC: Woodrow Wilson Press, 2002); Menno Vellinga, ed., *The Political Economy of the Drug Industry: Latin America and the International System* (Gainesville: University of Florida Press, 2004). For a discussion of the interaction of the legitimate and illegitimate worlds, see Nikos Passas, "Cross-Border Crime and the Interface between Legal and Illegal Actors," in *Upperworld and Underworld in Cross-Border Crime*, ed. Petrus C. van Duyne, Klaus von Lampe, and Nikos Passas (Nijmegen: Wolf, 2002), 11–41.

25. Thoumi, *Illegal Drugs, Economy and Society in the Andes*, 160, 237–38.

26. This is true of the Mafia and the *yakuza*. Interview with Mafia prosecutors in Sicily, October 2000, who indicated that the Mafia broke off contact with a terrorist group from the former Yugoslavia because they did not want to be associated with them. An exception for the *yakuza* is their association with the cult of Aum Shinrikyu; see David Kaplan and Andrew Marshall, *The Cult at the End of the World: The Terrifying Story of the Aum Doomsday Cult, from the Subways of Tokyo to the Nuclear Arsenals of Russia* (New York: Crown, 1996).

27. R. T. Naylor, *Wages of Crime: Black Markets, Illegal Finance, and the Underworld Economy*, rev. ed. (Ithaca, NY: Cornell University Press, 2004), 45; see Louise Shelley and John Picarelli, "Methods and Motives: Exploring Links between Transnational Organized Crime and International Terrorism," *Trends in Organized Crime* 9, no. 2 (2005): 52–56.

28. Paolo Pezzino, *Una Certa reciprocità di favori: Mafia e modernizzazione violenta nella Sicilia postunitaria* (Milan: Franco Angeli, 1990).

29. Hill, *Japanese Mafia*, 41–42.

30. Ibid., 56–64.

31. Tim Newark, *Mafia Allies: The True Story of America's Secret Alliance with the Mob in World War II* (Minneapolis, MN: Zenith, 2007). This topic has also been much addressed at conferences in Italy I have attended with specialists on the Mafia.

32. Roy Godson, ed., *Menace to Society: Political-Criminal Collaboration around the World* (New Brunswick, NJ: Transaction, 2003). See also, for a discussion of organized crime and politics, Jean-Louis Briquet and Gilles Favarel-Garriques, "Introduction: Violence, Crime and Political Power," in *Organized Crime and States: The Hidden Face of Politics*, ed. Jean-Louis Briquet and Gilles Favarel-Garriques (New York: Palgrave Macmillan, 2010), 1–13.

33. Abadinsky, *Organized Crime*, 7th ed. (Belmont, CA: Wadsworth/Thomson Learning, 2003), 57.
34. Alexander Stille, *Excellent Cadavers: The Mafia and the Death of the First Italian Republic* (New York: Pantheon Books, 1995); Alison Jamieson, *The Anti-Mafia: Italy's Fight against Organized Crime* (London: Macmillan 2000); Umberto Santino, *Storia del movimento antimafia Dalla lotta di classe all'impegno civile* (Rome: Riuniti, 2000); Peter T. Schneider and Jane C. Schneider, *Reversible Destiny: Mafia, Antimafia, and the Struggle for Palermo* (Berkeley: University of California Press, 1993).
35. Godson, *Menace to Society*.
36. Howard Abadinsky, *Organized Crime*, 6th ed. (Belmont, CA: Wadsworth, 2000), 246–47.
37. See the work of Ivelaw Griffith, *Drugs and Security in the Caribbean: Sovereignty under Siege* (College Park: Penn State University Press), 1997; Enrique Desmond Arias, *Drugs and Democracy in Rio de Janeiro* (Chapel Hill: University of North Carolina Press, 2006), 178–79.
38. Andres Oppenheimer, *Bordering on Chaos: Guerrillas, Stockbrokers, Politicians, and Mexico's Road to Prosperity* (Boston: Little, Brown, 1996); Xavier Raufer, "Une maffya symbiotique: tradition et évolutions du crime organisé en Turquie," *Sécurité Globale* (Hiver, 2009–10), 91–119; Lee, *White Labyrinth*; Erica Marat, "Impact of Drug Trade and Organized Crime on State Functioning in Kyrgyzstan and Tajikistan," *China and Eurasia Forum Quarterly* 4, no. 1 (2006): 93–111.
39. Interview by the author with Sicilian prosecutors in Palermo, fall 2002.
40. Stille, *Excellent Cadavers*.
41. Lee, *White Labyrinth*; Peter Waldmann, "Is There a Culture of Violence in Colombia," *International Journal of Conflict and Violence* 1, no. 1 (2007): 61–75.
42. Claire O'Neill McCleskey, "Entire Police Force of Mexican Town Resigns," January 3, 2013, http://www.insightcrime.org/news-briefs/entire-police-force-michoacan-town-resigns.
43. Associated Press, "Mexico: Police Force Quits after Officers Are Killed," *New York Times,* August 4, 2011, http://www.nytimes.com/2011/08/05/world/americas/05briefs-Mexico.html?_r=0.
44. Saskia Sassen, *Globalization and Its Discontents* (New York: New Press, 1998); James Mittelman, *The Globalization Syndrome: Transformation and Resistance* (Princeton, NJ: Princeton University Press, 2000); Moisés Naím, "Five Wars of Globalization," *Foreign Policy*, January 1, 2003; see http://www.foreignpolicy.com/articles/2003/01/01/five_wars_of_globalization.
45. Note that these are poorly governed states, but not the weakest states, as the weakest states are not hospitable for crime groups. See Stewart Patrick, *Weak Links: Fragile States, Global Threats and International Security* (Oxford: Oxford University Press, 2011), 3–4.
46. Kenneth J. Menkhaus, "Somalia and Somaliland: Terrorism, Political Islam and State Collapse," in *Battling Terrorism in the Horn of Africa*, ed. Robert I. Rotberg (Washington, DC: Brookings Institution Press, 2005), 45.
47. Ivan Briscoe and Elisa Dari, *Crime and Error: Why We Urgently Need a New Approach to Illicit Trafficking in Fragile States*, Clingendael Conflict Research Unit CRU Policy Brief 23, May 2012, 3, http://www.clingendael.nl/publications/recent/.

48. National Gang Intelligence Center, *2011 National Gang Threat Assessment – Emerging Trends,* http://www.fbi.gov/stats-services/publications/2011-national-gang-threat-assessment; Douglas Farah, "Central American Gangs: Changing Nature and New Partners," *Journal of International Affairs* 66, no. 1 (2012): 53–67.

49. Frédéric Massé and Johanna Camargo, "Actores Armados Ilegales y Sector Extractivo en Colombia," V informe del Centro Internacional de Toledo para la Paz (CITpax) Observatorio Internacional, 2012, http://www.toledopax.org%2Fuploads%2FActores_armados_ilegales_sector_extractivo.pdf.

50. Steven S. Dudley, "Central America Besieged: Cartels and Maras Country Threat Analysis," *Small Wars and Insurgencies* 22, no. 5 (2011): 890–913.

51. Massé and Camargo, "Actores Armados Ilegales y Sector Extractivo en Colombia," 41.

52. Paul Collier, *The Bottom Billion: Why the Poorest Countries Are Failing and What Can Be Done about It* (Oxford: Oxford University Press, 2007); Joseph Stiglitz, *Globalization and Its Discontents* (New York: W. W. Norton, 2002). Those with a precarious existence are more likely to engage in illicit activities to survive. With the collapse of prices for raw commodities in the globalized economy, many farmers, mentored by drug traffickers, have turned to drug cultivation to survive economically. Others leave their communities, moving vast distances to distant cities or more affluent countries in search of employment to support their families. See Kevin Bales, *Disposable People: New Slavery in the Global Economy* (Berkeley: University of California Press, 2000).

53. David A. Shirk, *Drug War in Mexico: Confronting a Shared Threat,* Council on Foreign Relations, March 2011, 7, http://www.cfr.org/content/publications/attachments/Mexico_CSR60.pdf. Mexico falls into the category of a transitional state, as it has been in transition from long-term one-party rule.

54. Maureen Meyer, *A Dangerous Journey through Mexico: Human Rights Violations against Migrants in Transit* (Washington, DC: WOLA, December, 2010), 1, discusses the murder of seventy-two migrants killed in transit and the abuse of many more. See also Steven Dudley, *Transnational Crime in Mexico and Central America: Its Evolution and Role in International Migration* (Washington, DC: Woodrow Wilson International Center for Scholars and Migration Policy Institute, November 2012).

55. Dina Rickman, "UK Riots: One in Four Charged Rioters Had Committed over Ten Previous Offences," *Huffington Post UK,* September 15, 2011, http://www.huffingtonpost.co.uk/2011/09/15/uk-riots-25-per-cent-of-c_n_963567.html?view=print.

56. Arlacchi, *Mafia Business*; Kaplan and Dubro, *Yakuza*; Hill, *Japanese Mafia*.

57. Phil Williams, *Criminals, Militias, and Insurgents: Organized Crime in Iraq* (Carlisle, PA: Strategic Studies Institute, U.S. Army War College, 2009); Gretchen Peters, *Seeds of Terror: How Heroin Is Bankrolling the Taliban and al Qaeda* (New York: Picador, 2010); Martin N. Murphy, *Small Boats, Weak States, Dirty Money : The Challenge of Piracy* (New York: Columbia University Press, 2008), 101–10.

58. Moisés Naím, "Mafia States," *Foreign Affairs,* May/June 2012, 100–11.

59. Alexander Kukhianidze, Alexander Kupatadze, and Roman Gotsiridze, "Smuggling in Abkhazia and Tskhinvali Region in 2003–2004," in *Organized Crime*

and Corruption in Georgia, ed. Louise Shelley, Erik R. Scott and Anthony Latta (London: Routledge, 2007), 78–83; James A. Piazza, "The Opium Trade and Patterns of Terrorism in the Provinces of Afghanistan: An Empirical Analysis, 2012," *Terrorism and Political Violence* 24, no. 2 (2012): 213–34; Jana Arsovska, "Albanian Crime Laid Bare: The Development of Albanian Organised Crime Groups in the Balkans," *Jane's Intelligence Review* 19, no. 2 (2007): 36–40. For discussion of the protection of the zetas, see Geoffrey Ramsey, "Zetas Corruption Case Could Reflect Changing Tactics," March 15, 2012, http://www.insightcrime.org/news-analysis/zetas-corruption-case-could-reflect-changing-tactics.

60. Arlacchi, *Mafia Business*; Abadinsky, *Organized Crime*, 7th ed.; Hill, *Japanese Mafia*; Kaplan and Dubro, *Yakuza*.

61. Illustrative of this is the house found in Mexico with \$205 million in cash. Hector Tobar and Carlos Martinez, "Mexico Meth Raid Yields \$205 Million in U.S. Cash, Authorities Say It's the Largest Drug Money Haul in History and Reflects a Vast Global Trade. Gang Said to Supply U.S.," *Los Angeles Times*, March 17, 2007, http://www.latimes.com/la-fg-meth17mar17,0,709967.story.

62. Donatella della Porta, *Lo Scambio Occulto Casi di corruzione politica in Italia* (Bologna, Italy: Il Mulino, 1992), 312–28; Ron Goldstock, Martin Marcus, Thomas D. Thacher II, and James B. Jacobs, *Corruption and Racketeering in the New York City Construction Industry: Final Report to Governor Mario M. Cuomo of the New York State Organized Crime Task Force* (New York: New York University Press, 1990); see Hill, *Yakuza*, on Japan.

63. Phil Williams, "Transnational Organized Crime and the State," in *The Emergence of Private Global Authority in Global Governance*, ed. Rodney Bruce Hall and Thomas J. Biersteker (Cambridge: Cambridge University Press, 2002), 166, for a fuller discussion of the crime organizations and their impact on the state.

64. CNN World, "Former Head of Mexican Drug Czar Arrested on Corruption Charges," January 26, 2009, http://articles.cnn.com/2009-01-26/world/mexico .drug.czar_1_drug-czar-drug-cartel-noe-ramirez-mandujano?_s=PM:WORLD.

65. The author in 1993 had a Fulbright in Mexico. She taught at the Instituto de Ciencias Penales, which at that time shared a courtyard with the training school of the policia judicial. She learned about the entrants from the administrative staff as well as some interactions with individuals who were in the academy of the policia judicial.

66. Alexander Salagaev, Alexander Shashkin, and Alexey Konnov, "One Hand Washes the Other: Informal Ties among Organized Crime Groups and Law-Enforcement Agencies in Russia," in *Russia's Battle with Crime, Corruption and Terrorism*, ed. Robert Orttung and Anthony Latta (Abingdon, UK: Routledge, 2008), 76–102.

67. There is now an extensive literature on state capture. See, e.g., the initial writing on the subject by Joel S. Hellman, Geraint Jones, Daniel Kaufmann, and Mark Schankerman, *Measuring Governance, Corruption, and State Capture – How Firms and Bureaucrats Shape the Business Environment in Transition Economies*, Policy Working Paper Series 2312 (Washington, DC: World Bank, 2000), http://econpapers.repec.org/RePEc:wpa:wuwpdc:0308004; Luis Jorge Garay Salamanca, Eduardo Salcedo-Albarán, Isaac de León-Beltrán, and Bernardo Guerrero, *La Captura y Reconfiguración Cooptada del Estado en Colombia* (Bogotá: Fundación Método, Fundación Avina y Transparencia por Colombia, 2008).

68. Vadim Volkov, *Violent Entrepreneurs: The Use of Force in the Making of Russian Capitalism* (Ithaca, NY: Cornell University Press, 2002).

69. Frederico Varese, *The Russian Mafia: Private Protection in a New Market Economy* (Oxford: Oxford University Press, 2001), for a discussion on Russia. On Colombia, see Massé and Camargo, "Actores Armados Ilegales y Sector Extractivo en Colombia," 17–19.

70. Johan Leman and Stef Janssens, "The Albanian and Post-Soviet Business of Trafficking Women for Prostitution: Structural Developments and Financial Modus Operandi," *European Journal of Criminology* 5, no. 4 (2008): 445; see also Jana Arsovska and Stef Janssens, "Policing and Human Trafficking: Good and Bad Practices," in *Strategies against Human Trafficking: The Role of the Security Sector*, ed. Cornelius Friesendorf (Vienna: National Defence Academy and Austrian Ministry of Defence and Sport, 2009); Louise Shelley, *Human Trafficking: A Global Perspective* (Cambridge: Cambridge University Press, 2010), 121–23.

71. Nick Miroff, "Cartel Boss Falls, but Zeta Brand Is Strong," *Washington Post*, July 19, 2013, http://www.washingtonpost.com/world/the_americas/cartel-boss-falls-but-zetas-brand-strong/2013/07/19/.

72. John Paul Rathbone and Adam Thomson, "A Toxic Trade," Financial Times, August 24, 2011, 11; Cory Molzahn, Viridiana Ríos, and David A. Shirk, *Drug Violence in Mexico, Data and Analysis through 2011* (San Diego, CA: Trans-Border Institute, University of San Diego, March 2012); David A. Shirk, *Drug War in Mexico: Confronting a Shared Threat*, Council on Foreign Relations, March 2011, http://www.cfr.org/content/publications/attachments/Mexico_CSR60.pdf; Astorga and Shirk, *Drug Trafficking Organizations*; Juan Carlos Garzón Vergara, *The Rebellion of Criminal Networks: Organized Crime in Latin America and the Dynamics of Change*, Woodrow Wilson Center Update on Latin America, March 2012, http://www.wilsoncenter.org/rebellion.

73. Michael Shifter, *Countering Criminal Violence in Central America* (Washington, DC: Council on Foreign Relations, 2012), 10; see also Cynthia J. Arnson and Eric L. Olson, eds., *Organized Crime in Central America: The Northern Triangle*, Report 29 (Washington, DC: Wilson Center, November 2011), http://www.wilsoncenter.org/node/19779.

74. Mats Berdal and David M. Malone, *Greed and Grievance: Economic Agendas in Civil Wars* (Boulder, CO: Lynne Rienner, 2000).

75. Donatella della Porta, "Institutional Responses to Terrorism: The Italian Case," in *Western Responses to Terrorism*, ed. Roland L. Crelinsten and Alex P. Schmid (London: Frank Cass, 1993), 150–70.

76. Bruce Hoffman, *Inside Terrorism* (New York: Columbia University Press, 2006).

77. Matthew Levitt, *Hezbollah: The Global Footprint of Lebanon's Party of God* (Washington, DC: Georgetown University Press, 2013); Kaveh the Hammersmith, *Global Hezbollah – The Iranian National-Islamist Nebula: Secret Networks and Worldwide Strategy* (Saarbrücken, Germany: Lambert, 2011).

78. Matthew Levitt, "Hezbollah Finances: Funding the Party of God," in *Terrorism Finance and State Responses*, ed. Jeanne Giraldo and Harold Trinkunas (Stanford, CA: Stanford University Press, 2007), 134–51.

79. Brian Michael Jenkins, *Will Terrorists Go Nuclear?* (Amherst, NY: Prometheus Books, 2008).

80. Lyubov Mincheva and Ted Robert Gurr, "Unholy Alliances III: Communal Militants and Criminal Networks in the Middle East, with a Case Study of the Kurdistan Workers Party (PKK)," paper presented at the annual meeting of the International Studies Association, 2008, http://www.humansecuritygateway.info/documents/ISA_unholyalliancesIII.pdf.
81. Adrian Guelke, *The New Age of Terrorism and the International Political System* (London: I. B. Taurus, 2009).
82. David Veness, "Low Intensity and High Impact Conflict," *Terrorism and Political Violence* 11, no. 4 (1999): 9.
83. Micheva and Gurr, "Unholy Alliances III," 12.
84. Angel Rabasa, Peter Chalk, Kim Cragin, Sara A. Daly, Heather S. Gregg, Theodore W. Karasik, Kevin A. O'Brien, and William Rosenau, *Beyond al-Qaeda, Part II: The Outer Rings of the Terrorist Universe* (Santa Monica, CA: RAND, 2006), 78.
85. Ibid., 79.
86. John Horgan and Max Taylor, "Playing the 'Green Card': Financing the Provisional IRA, Part 1," *Terrorism and Political Violence* 11, no. 2 (1999): 4–5.
87. Della Porta, "Institutional Responses to Terrorism," 152.
88. Ibid., 168.
89. Bill Park, "Turkey's Deep State: Ergenekon and the Threat to Democratisation in the Republic," *RUSI Journal: Royal United Services Institute for Defence Studies* 153, no. 5 (2008): 54, http://www.rusi.org/publications/journal/ref:A4901D0D3BF0BA/.
90. Jessica C. Teets and Erica Chenoweth, "To Bribe or to Bomb: Do Corruption and Terrorism Go Together?," in *Corruption, Security and the Global World Order*, ed. Robert I. Rotberg (Cambridge, MA: World Peace Foundation, Harvard Kennedy School Program on Intrastate Conflict, American Academy of Arts and Sciences, 2009), 175.
91. Michael R. Roth and Murat Server, "The Kurdish Workers Party (PKK): Funding Terrorism through Organized Crime, a Case Study," *Studies in Conflict and Terrorism*, October 2007, 903.
92. Jerrold M. Post, *The Mind of the Terrorist* (New York: Palgrave Macmillan, 2007), 130, comments that members of the German terrorist organization RAF liked the solidarity of the organization but found it came at a high cost, as they had to participate in bank robberies, kidnappings, bombings, and murder.
93. Garzón Vergara, *Rebellion of Criminal Networks*, 1–4.
94. R. T. Naylor, *Wages of Crime: Black Markets, Illegal Finance, and the Underworld Economy*, rev. ed. (Ithaca, NY: Cornell University Press, 2004), 56.
95. Horgan and Taylor, "Playing the 'Green Card,'" 1.
96. Glenn E. Curtis and Tara Karacan, *The Nexus among Terrorists, Narcotics Traffickers, Weapons Proliferators and Organized Crime Networks in Western Europe* (Washington, DC: Library of Congress, Federal Research Division, 2002), 5, 9.
97. T. Roule, "The Terrorist Financial Network of the PKK," *Jane's Terrorism and Security Monitor* 17 (June 2002); Raufer, "Une maffya symbiotique," 91–119; Vera Eccarius-Kelly, "Surreptitious Lifelines: A Structural Analysis of the FARC and the PKK," *Terrorism and Political Violence* 24, no. 2 (2012): 235–58; Human Rights Watch, *Funding the "Final War": LTTE Intimidation and Extortion in the*

Tamil Diaspora, 18, no. 1(c), March 16, 2006, http://www.hrw.org/en/reports/2006/03/14/funding-final-war-2.

98. Jodi Vittori, *Terrorist Financing and Resourcing* (New York: Palgrave Macmillan, 2011), 55–56.

99. Jonathan Kandell, "Financier in Argentina Seized Again, Paid $1-Million Ransom First Time," *New York Times,* August 1, 1975, http://select.nytimes.com/gst/abstract.html?res=F00A1FFB3A5E157493C3A91783D85F418785F9.

100. Vittori, *Terrorist Financing and Resourcing,* 56.

101. Joan Arquilla and David Ronfeldt, *Networks and Netwars: The Future of Crime Terror, Crime and Militancy* (Santa Monica, CA: RAND, 2001); see Jennifer L. Hesterman, *The Terrorist-Criminal Nexus: An Alliance of International Drug Cartels, Organized Crime, and Terror Groups* (Boca Raton: CRC Press, 2013), 41–91, for a discussion of new terrorist groups.

102. Daniel Bynum, *Deadly Connections: States That Sponsor Terrorism* (New York: Cambridge University Press, 2005), 15.

103. Audrey Cronin, *How Terrorism Ends: Understanding the Decline and Demise of Terrorist Campaigns* (Princeton, NJ: Princeton University Press, 2009); Martha Crenshaw, ed., *The Consequences of Counterterrorism* (New York: Russell Sage Foundation, 2010).

104. Rabasa et al., *Beyond al-Qaeda,* Part II, xxiii.

105. U.S. State Department, Office of the Coordinator for Counterterrorism, *Country Reports on Terrorism, 2011,* July 31, 2012, Chapter 3, http://www.state.gov/j/ct/rls/crt/2012/. Cuba is cited for its support of the FARC, Syria for its support of Hezbollah, Hamas, and other Palestinian-related terrorist organizations. Sudan was cited for its support of al-Qaeda. Iran is labeled as a growing state supporter of terrorism and uses "the Islamic Revolutionary Guard Corps-Qods Force (IRGC-QF) and terrorist insurgent groups to implement its foreign policy."

106. See Raufer, "New World Disorder, New Terrorisms," 35, for a discussion of the changes post–Cold War and the rise of hybrid threats.

107. James A. Piazza, "Is Islamist Terrorism More Dangerous? An Empirical Study of Group Ideology, Organization, and Goal Structure," *Terrorism and Political Violence* 21 (2009): 64.

108. Financial Action Task Force, *Report on Terrorist Financing,* February 29, 2008, http://www.ctif-cfi.be/website/index.php?option=com_content&view=article&id=83&Itemid=109&lang=en.

109. Louise Shelley and John T. Picarelli, "Organized Crime and Terrorism," in Giraldo and Trinkunas, *Terrorism Financing and State Responses,* 39–55.

110. FATF, *Report on Terrorist Financing.*

111. Strategy to Combat Transnational Organized Crime, July 25, 2011, http://www.whitehouse.gov/administration/eop/nsc/transnational-crime; European Police Chiefs Convention, June 29 to July 1, 2011, https://www.europol.europa.eu/sites/default/.../epcc2011report_0.pdf. The author attended this meeting.

112. Nazim Fethi, "Arab Police Chiefs Meet in Algiers," December 11, 2012, http://www.magharebia.com/cocoon/awi/xhtml1/en_GB/features/awi/features/2012/12/11/feature-01.

113. Kimberly L. Thachuk, "Transnational Threats: Falling through the Cracks?," *Low Intensity Conflict and Law Enforcement* 10, no. 1 (2001): 47–67.

114. Laqueur, *New Terrorism,* 210–25.

115. Walter Laqueur, *The Age of Terrorism* (Boston: Little, Brown, 1987), 112.

116. Bolsheviks who knew of this criminal past, such as Ordzhonokidze, were killed. See Robert Conquest, *The Great Terror: A Reassessment* (Oxford: Oxford University Press, 1990), 167–71; Louise Shelley, "Georgian Organized Crime," in *Organized Crime and Corruption in Georgia*, ed. Louise Shelley, Erik R. Scott, and Anthony Latta (London: Routledge, 2007), 51.

117. Vittori, *Terrorist Financing and Resourcing*, 53.

118. Sam Mullins, "Parallels between Crime and Terrorism: A Social Psychological Perspective," *Studies in Conflict and Terrorism* 32, no. 9 (2009): 311–30; Tamara Makarenko, "Terrorism and Transnational Organized Crime: Tracing the Crime-Terror Nexus in South East Asia," in *Terrorism and Violence in South East Asia: Transnational Challenges to States and regional Stability*, ed. Paul Smith (New York: M. E. Sharpe, 2005), 169–87.

119. Della Porta, "Institutional Responses to Terrorism," 152, in discussing right-wing terrorist groups in the 1970s and 1980s.

120. Michael A. Braun, "Regarding the Growing Confluence of Drugs and Terror and the Face of 21st Century Global Organized Crime," October 12, 2011, testimony before the Subcommittee on Terrorism, Nonproliferation, and Trade, Committee on Foreign Affairs, U.S. House of Representatives, Washington, DC, http://foreignaffairs.house.gov/112/bra101211.pdf.

121. Francisco Thoumi, *Political Economy and Illegal Drugs in Colombia* (Boulder, CO: Lynne Rienner, 1995); Lee, *White Labyrinth*.

122. Letizia Paoli, Victoria A. Greenfield, and Peter Reuter, *The World Heroin Market: Can Supply Be Cut?* (Oxford: Oxford University Press, 2009); UNODC, *World Drug Report 2012*, http://www.unodc.org/unodc/en/data-and-analysis/WDR-2012.htm.

123. For a discussion of extortion from drug organizations, see Alex P. Schmid, "The Links between Transnational Organized Crime and Terrorist Crimes," *Transnational Organized Crime* 2, no. 4 (1996): 40–82; Gretchen Peters, "How Opium Profits the Taliban," U.S. Institute of Peace, http://www.usip.org/files/resources/taliban_opium_1.pdf.

124. Maria Łoś and Andrzej Zybertowicz, *Privatizing the Police State: The Case of Poland* (New York: St. Martin's Press, 2000), 16, discuss Adam Podgorecki's idea of dirty togetherness.

125. Horgan and Taylor, "Playing the 'Green Card.'"

126. Raufer, "Une maffya symbiotique," 92–119.

127. See Bruce Hoffman, *Inside Terrorism* (New York: Columbia University Press, 1998); Ian O. Lesser, Bruce Hoffman, John Arquilla, David Ronfeldt, and Michele Zanini, *Countering the New Terrorism* (Santa Monica, CA: RAND, 1999); Walter Laqueur, *New Terrorism*; Steven Simon and Daniel Benjamin, "America and the New Terrorism," *Survival* 42 (Spring 2000): 59–75; Olivier Roy, Bruce Hoffman, Reuven Paz, Steven Simon, and Daniel Benjamin, "America and the New Terrorism: An Exchange," *Survival* 42 (Summer 2000): 156–72; David Tucker, "What's New about the New Terrorism and How Dangerous Is It?," *Terrorism and Political Violence* 13 (Autumn 2001): 1–14.

128. Only now is some research beginning to discuss this. See Aaron Zelinsky and Martin Shubik, "Research Note: Terrorist Groups as Business Firms: A New Typological Framework," *Terrorism and Political Violence* 21, no. 2 (2009): 327–36;

Alan B. Krueger, *What Makes a Terrorist? Economics and the Roots of Terrorism: Lionel Robbins Lectures* (Princeton, NJ: Princeton University Press, 2007); Eli Berman, *Radical, Religious and Violent: The New Economics of Terrorism* (Cambridge, MA: MIT Press, 2009).

129. Christine Jojarth, *Crime, War and Global Trafficking: Designing International Cooperation* (Cambridge: Cambridge University Press, 2009), 2.

130. For a discussion of these conflicts, see Mary Kaldor, *New and Old Wars: Organized Violence in a Global Era* (Stanford, CA: Stanford University Press, 1999); Braun, "Regarding the Growing Confluence of Drugs and Terror," 12.

131. Mats Berdal and David M. Malone, *Greed and Grievance: Economic Agendas in Civil Wars* (Boulder, CO: Lynne Rienner, 2000).

132. Lenard J. Cohen, "Political Violence and Organized Crime in Serbia," in *Democratic Development and Political Terrorism: The Global Perspective*, ed. William J. Crotty (Boston: Northeastern University Press, 2005), 401.

133. Andreas, *Blue Helmets and Black Markets*; Michael Dziedzic, Laura Rozen, and Phil Williams, *Lawless Rule versus Rule of Law in the Balkans*, Special Report of the U.S. Institute of Peace, December 2002, http://www.usip.org/publications/lawless-rule-versus-rule-law-balkans; Alexandre Kukhianidze, Alexander Kupatadze, and Roman Gotsiridze, *Smuggling through Abkhazia and Tskinvali Region of Georgia* (Tbilsi: Polygraph, 2004), 5; Svante Cornell, "The Narcotics Threat in Greater Central Asia: From Crime-Terror Nexus to State Infiltration?," *China and Eurasia Forum Quarterly* 4, no. 1 (2006): 37–67; CSIS Conference Report, "The Dynamics of North African Terrorism," March 2010, http://csis.org/files/attachments/100216_NorthAfricaConferenceReport.pdf; see travel advisory by the U.K. Foreign and Commonwealth Office that warns against travel in Yemen because of the possibility of kidnapping by terrorists and criminals, http://www.fco.gov.uk/en/travel-and-living-abroad/travel-advice-by-country/middle-east-north-africa/yemen.

134. David T. Johnson, "The Escalating Ties between Middle East Terrorist Groups and Criminal Activity," January 19, 2010, http://www.state.gov/p/inl/rls/rm/135404.htm; Louise Shelley and Nazia Hussain, "Narco-Trafficking in Pakistan-Afghanistan Border Areas and Implications for Security," in *Narco-Jihad: Drug Trafficking and Security in Afghanistan-Pakistan*, NBR Special Report 20 (December 2009), 23–41.

135. Section on Chechnya by Nabi Abdullaev in Shelley and Picarelli et al., "Methods and Motives"; John Richardson, *Paradise Poisoned: Learning about Conflict, Terrorism and Development from Sri Lanka's Civil Wars* (Colombo: International Centre for Ethnic Studies, 2005); Horgan and Taylor, "Playing the 'Green Card'"; E. A. Stepanova, *Rol narkobiznesa v politekonomii konfliktov i terrorizma* (The Role of the Illicit Drug Business in the Political Economy of Conflicts and Terrorism) (Moscow: Ves' Mir, 2005); CSIS Conference Report; Peter Gastrow, *Termites at Work: A Report on Transnational Organized Crime and State Erosion in Kenya* (New York: International Peace Institute, 2011).

136. Rogelio Alonso and Marcos Garcia Rey, "The Evolution of Jihadist Terrorism in Morocco," *Political Violence and Terrorism* 19 (2007): 575.

137. Jean-Pierre Filiu, "Could Al-Qaeda Turn African in the Sahel?," Carnegie Middle East Program, Paper 112, June 2010.

138. Frank Bovenkerk and Yucel Yesilgöz, "The Turkish Mafia and the State," in *Organised Crime in Europe: Patterns and Policies in the European Union and Beyond*, ed. Cyrille Fijnaut and Letizia Paoli (Dordrecht, Netherlands: Springer, 2004), 598–99; Charles Strozier and James Frank, *The PKK: Financial Sources, Social and Political Dimension* (Saarbrücken: VDM, 2011).

139. Transnational Crime, Corruption, and Information Technology, 2000 annual conference of Transnational Crime and Corruption Center, American University, http://traccc.gmu.edu/topics/corruption/traccc-corruption-publications/.

140. Louise Shelley, "The Unholy Trinity: Transnational Crime, Corruption, and Terrorism," *Brown Journal of World Affairs* 11, no. 2 (2005): 101–11.

141. Chris Dishman, "Terrorism, Crime and Transformation," *Studies in Conflict and Terrorism* 24, no. 1 (2001): 43–58.

142. Janine Wedel, *Shadow Elites: How the World's New Power Brokers Undermine Democracy, Government, and the Free Market* (New York: Free Press, 2009).

143. Ian Cuthbertson, "Prison and the Education of Terrorists," *World Policy Journal* 21 (2004): 15–22.

144. Jessica Stern, "5 Myths about Who Becomes a Terrorist," *Washington Post*, January 10, 2010, B4; Stern, "How to Deradicalize Terrorists," *Foreign Affairs*, January/February 2010, 95–108.

145. Documented in literature, such as Khaled Hosseini, *A Thousand Splendid Suns* (London: Bloomsbury, 2007), but also seen in scholarly literature.

146. Ryan Clarke, *Crime-Terror Nexus in South Asia: States, Security and Non-state Actors* (Abingdon, UK: Routledge, 2011); Ikhram Sehgal, "A Deadly Symbiosis," *News International*, December 23, 2010, http://www.thenews.com.pk/TodaysPrintDetail.aspx?ID=21656&Cat=9.

147. Tamara Makarenko, "The Crime-Terror Continuum: Tracing the Interplay between Transnational Organized Crime and Terrorism," *Global Crime* 6, no. 1 (2004): 129–45.

148. Audrey Kurth Cronin, *How Terrorism Ends: Understanding the Demise and Decline of Terrorist Campaigns* (Princeton, NJ: Princeton University Press, 2009), 149, 153.

149. Glen Frankel, "Police Pin Bank Heist on IRA," *Washington Post*, January 8, 2005, A1; see Horgan and Taylor, "Playing the 'Green Card,'" to understand their entry into crime.

150. "Fondeo del terrorismo," *Infolaft* 1, no. 4 (2009): 10–15.

151. Jana Arsovska and Stefen Janssens, "Turkish Delight: Turkish Drug Traffickers Branch Out," *Jane's Intelligence Review* 20, no. 10 (2008): 43–48; Jana Arsovska, "Code of Conduct: Understanding Albanian Organised Crime," *Jane's Intelligence Review* 19, no. 8 (2007): 46–49.

152. Alfredo Filler, "The Abu Sayyaf Group: A Growing Menace to Civil Society," *Terrorism and Political Violence* 14, no. 4 (2002): 141.

153. African terrorism has deep roots in the continent. The anticolonial struggles, particularly that of Algeria, have left a legacy of deep-seated violence within many societies. Many leftists from Africa were trained by the Soviet Union and by its Eastern European vassal states. In Algeria, they were trained for the Front de Libération Nationale, and in other parts of Africa, support was provided for other organizations. In reaction to this, militants from Algeria volunteered in

the 1980s for anti-Soviet jihad in Afghanistan and trained in camps in Pakistan. See Jean-Pierre Filiu, "Al-Qaeda in the Islamic Maghreb: Algerian Challenge or Global Threat?," Carnegie Middle East Program, Paper 104, October 2009, 2. Against this complex patchwork of external state-supported terrorism, the leader of the Islamic government of Sudan provided a safe haven to al-Qaeda and Osama bin Laden in the 1990s. The U.S. Embassy bombings in Tanzania and Kenya in 1998 are reflective of the violent reality of al-Qaeda in Africa before 9/11. Susan F. Hirsch, *In the Moment of Greatest Calamity: Terrorism, Grief, and a Victim's Quest for Justice* (Princeton, NJ: Princeton University Press, 2007); Rohan Gunaratna, *Inside Al Qaeda: Global Network of Terror* (New York: Columbia University Press, 2002).

154. Filiu, "Al-Qaeda in the Islamic Maghreb," 1.
155. Bybee, "Twenty-First Century Expansion of the Transnational Drug Trade in Africa."
156. John Campbell and Asch Harwood, "Boko Haram and Nigeria's Pervasive Violence," December 26, 2012, http://www.cfr.org/nigeria/boko-haram-nigerias-pervasive-violence/p29706. The kidnapping of the mother of Nigeria's famed finance minister, Ngozi Okonjo-Iweala, is described by the authors as a protest against Nigeria's financial policies. This is another example of the dual harms of terrorist groups that are discussed more in Chapter 5.
157. Greg Campbell, *Blood Diamonds: Tracing the Deadly Path of the World's Most Precious Stone* (Boulder, CO: Westview Press, 2002), 186–88.
158. "Un 'arc islamiste radical' menace la France, selon Bruguière," March 14, 2007, http://lci.tf1.fr/france/faits-divers/2007-03/arc-islamiste-radical-menace-france-selon-bruguiere-4861519.html, and discussions with Judge de la Bruguière at annual meetings of the World Economic Forum's Global Agenda Councils.
159. Jonathan Masters, "Al-Shabab," June 23, 2013, http://www.cfr.org/somalia/al-shabab/p18650.
160. Europol, "EU Organised Crime Threat Assessment," April 28, 2011, https://www.europol.europa.eu/latest_publications/3; Nimrod Raphaeli, "Financing of Terrorism: Sources, Methods and Channels," *Terrorism and Political Violence* 15, no. 4 (2003): 59–82; Thomas M. Sanderson, "Transnational Terror and Organized Crime: Blurring the Lines," *SAIS Review* 24, no. 1 (2004): 49–61.
161. Strange, *Retreat of the State*.
162. Filiu, "Could al Qaeda Turn African in the Sahel?," 4.

4

Environments, Global Networks, and Pipelines

A diaspora cell of Bosnian refugees residing in Raleigh, North Carolina, whose members knew each other through the mosque and the local Moslem community were charged in 2009 with conspiring to provide material support to terrorists and to murder, kidnap, maim, and injure persons abroad.[1] They were aided by an American convert to Islam, Daniel Boyd, and his two sons. Boyd had a criminal record: he was arrested for bank robbery in Pakistan in 1991. The Raleigh-based cell was working with a Bosnian in Kosovo, Barjam Asliani, who once lived in the Raleigh area. Asliani sought the cell's help in raising money to establish a base in Kosovo to wage *jihad*. The FBI agent in charge stated, "This case began in Raleigh, N.C. and now stretches across the globe, a circumstance no one would have thought possible less than 10 years ago."[2]

This case illustrates a central theme of this chapter – networks are truly global, and criminal activity and planned terrorist acts are often entangled. This case fused components in the United States, Europe, and Asia. But, as we see in this chapter, networks may combine many more and even more diverse regions than the Raleigh example.

Locating Crime-Terror Interactions

In October 2012, the American and British governments held a high-level conference in London to examine a new policy that focused on crime-terror interactions.[3] This meeting was intended to address a new reality in which transnational criminals and terrorists no longer inhabit separate environments. The program, however, focused only on crime-terror relationships and their remedies in fragile states, without considering that many supporting environments exist far from weak and conflict states.

As this chapter shows, interactions of criminals and terrorists occur in different environments, both in developed and developing countries as well as in fragile states. Some illicit groups are geographically distributed; they diversify along a transnational sphere, conducting some activities in fragile or failing states, while maintaining bases and safe havens in more developed territories, and while maintaining their financial holdings in yet other places. These various conducive environments are shaped by history, demographics, the local culture, and existing political and social conditions. For example, a bank registered in Canada may fund Hezbollah in the Middle East by combining banking activity with shipment of used cars through a West African port.[4] The Taliban generates revenues from extortion of the heroin headed for sale in Russia and Western Europe, and the profits of this trade are laundered through Dubai.[5]

Globally Linked Networks

Crime-terror relationships in weak and conflict regions are often supported by networks located in the most developed societies, which provide funding and logistical support, as the case in Raleigh, North Carolina, exemplified. International support networks for organized crime and terrorism are not new. The IRA, from its earliest days, received significant financial support from sympathizers both in Ireland and the Irish diaspora community in the United States.[6] The Russian anarchists received assistance from their compatriots in Western Europe. During the Cold War era, state-supported terrorism financed, trained, and equipped terrorists, guerillas, and insurgents on different continents. Likewise, organized crime has a long history of international support networks. The Godfather movies vividly illustrated a long-existing reality: the ranks of the Mafia in the United States were replenished by new immigrants from Italy, and Sicily provided a safe haven for American mafiosi in danger. The triads in southern China had long established ties with the communities of Chinese that they had shipped to the United States.[7] In contrast, the contemporary supporting networks for organized crime and terrorism are increasingly complex, encompassing more geographical locales in very different environments.

Prime Locales for Interactions

Interactions of criminals, corrupt officials, and terrorists have been identified in diverse environments globally, but some locales are more conducive to these relationships. These locales recur repeatedly in this book's analyses of the planning and implementation of terrorist attacks as well as in discussions of the business of terrorism. This chapter focuses on the particular locales where these interactions are more likely to occur: diaspora communities, prisons, megacities, ports, multiborder regions, free-trade zones, and conflict zones. The centrality of these environments is explained by the mobility or impersonality associated with a particular locale, the complexity of some borders, or the enhanced likelihood of the presence of criminals, terrorists, and corrupt officials in one location, such as in prisons or at ports.

A successful terrorist or criminal organization will rely on subnetworks located in diverse environments. In environments such as megacities, with intense concentrations of people, and multiborder areas, with extensive movement of goods and people, combating their operations will tax the capacity of even a well-functioning state. It is in these environments, as well as conflict zones, where the crime-corruption interactions are most concentrated.

Networks for Crime and Terrorism

Today the international support networks for crime and terrorism are no longer necessarily distinct.[8] A pipeline of support, as discussed in reference to funding the attack in Beslan, will demonstrate that crime groups may be present in one locale, corrupt officials at another, and criminals and terrorists may cooperate at a third node. All three of the elements of crime, corruption, and terrorism need not be present at every stage of the pipeline.

A support network of criminals and terrorists may connect nodes in the most diverse environments of the contemporary world – the largest and wealthiest cities, conflict regions, and ports – thereby combining nodes in the developed and developing world.[9] By operating in multiple jurisdictions, with diverse legal systems and distinct law enforcement capacity, they reduce risk. A successful terrorist support cell may get support from a diaspora community on the West Coast of the United States, through a port in Europe, to a conflict zone in the Caucasus. A prison may provide the command center for an attack on a megacity. A dispersed network may also provide needed equipment for a developing nuclear state, as discussed more in Chapter 8.[10]

These illustrations affirm that crime-terror interactions are not confined to conflict regions, the developing world, or even the most corrupt countries. Rather, by linking diverse environments with highly differentiated levels of wealth and political development, the criminals and terrorists are exploiting the vacuums of enforcement, thereby minimizing the risk of detection and disruption of their support networks.

The marriage of convenience of criminals and terrorists, according to Gretchen Peters,

> produced another disturbing trend: Around the globe, criminal and terrorist groups have formed once-improbable relationships, and they are finding new, often frightening ways to collaborate with each other – sometimes for a one-time transaction, but often for enduring partnerships. Criminal and terror groups are learning from each other, adapting to each other's successes and failures and, in many cases, morphing into hybrid entities that are neither strictly criminal, nor strictly political in nature.[11]

Diaspora Communities

Beslan Attack

The Beslan attack, analyzed in Chapter 1, exemplifies the support that is provided by diaspora communities for terrorism, often in locales far from the home base of the terrorist group. Although the tragedy occurred in Russia, essential support for the organization came from a funding cell established by the Chechen terrorist leader Basayev in Los Angeles, California, as early as 1995, many years before the deadly attack. The California cell was just one of several overseas cells established within diaspora communities that provided sustained funding, allowing Basayev's terrorist organization to survive. As discussed subsequently, the funding for Beslan is characteristic of a larger pattern where terrorist groups derive essential financial and logistical support from immigrant communities, often, but not exclusively, in developed countries. This case exemplifies the fact that crime and terrorism links are not confined to fragile regions such as the North Caucasus, where the Beslan attack occurred, but are supported by international networks that can exist in the financial centers of the developed world.

Diaspora funding for the Chechen cause began in the first half of the 1990s as the operationally savvy Shamil Basayev, the ringleader behind the Beslan attack, sent his people to different locales in Western Europe and the United States to raise funds.[12] A lone Chechen arrived in Hollywood. Basayev chose Hollywood because it symbolized Western degeneracy and capitalism.[13] Moreover, it was part of the Los Angeles area, which had a large and diverse diaspora community from the former USSR. The Los Angeles community also had its share of émigré criminals, a legacy of Soviet policies. The Soviet government, like the Cubans, restricted emigration but were happy to let their criminals emigrate. Hollywood already had a significant Armenian community. Many sophisticated swindlers and organized criminals went to Hollywood, a fact frequently regretted in the local Armenian newspapers already in the 1970s. The links between criminals in Armenia and Los Angeles have endured.[14]

Armenians come from the South Caucasus, a region a few hundred miles from Chechnya. Orthodox Christian Armenians and Moslem Chechens have extremely limited associations with each other back home, but in the Los Angeles diaspora communities of émigrés from the former USSR, they interacted. In Hollywood, a group of Armenians had established an organization called Global Humanitarian Services (GHS), allegedly a humanitarian assistance organization providing aid to Russia, Armenia, Georgia, and Jordan. But as many post-9/11 investigations have revealed, some charities are not legitimate or have been exploited for criminal and terrorist purposes.[15] This was true in this case, as the lead Los Angeles police investigator explained: "GHS's license had been revoked by the state of California in February 2004 for failure to file a 2003 income-tax return. Moreover, it turned out that GHS was incorporated in November 1999 as a regular business and wasn't registered as a nonprofit charity."[16] This so-called Armenian charity was a criminal front and ripe for exploitation by the Chechens seeking to raise money for Basayev.

Basayev's envoy, upon arrival in Los Angeles, looked for ways to operate before he teamed up with the Armenian criminals. He also registered his own Foundation, named Ikeria (the traditional name of Chechnya, evoked by the Beslan attackers). This effort to raise funds for the Chechen insurgency was a source of pride – confiscated in a court-sanctioned search by the Los Angeles Police Department of the Chechen's home was a photo of him with Shamil Basayev, the two smiling and holding the registration certificate for the foundation that would support the Chechen cause through criminal means. It is yet another example of the exploitation of foundations for illicit goals.[17]

But the Chechen envoy eventually found a way to cooperate with the Armenians' foundation that also operated as a criminal front. The resulting Chechen-Armenian scheme was as follows. At the point of origin, a criminal-terrorist relationship operated. Armenian criminals bought expensive Land Rovers and sport utility vehicles. They shipped them out of the country through the port of Houston, after having declared them stolen to the insurance company and collecting the proceeds. The vehicles traveled to Naples, a Mediterranean port city dominated by the criminal organization the Camorra.[18] Before the Los Angeles Police Department caught up with them in 2006, shortly before Basayev's killing by Russian security forces, more than three hundred luxury vehicles had been exported in two hundred such shipments to Georgia. The shipments were worth more than $5 million, not including the losses that the insurance companies suffered as a result of the fraudulent claims of theft.[19] In Georgia, Chechens close to the banned rebel groups would sell the cars at several times their U.S. value.[20]

In the last shipment followed by the Los Angeles police, several of the expensive vehicles were shipped to Poti, a Black Sea Port in Georgia, a country at that time with a very high level of corruption, particularly elevated in law enforcement. There, senior police officials, after declaring their willingness to cooperate in the international investigation, called several subordinates to move the cars from the port to Tbilisi, where they were easily disposed of, thereby destroying the evidence and the case itself.[21] The proceeds would be carried in cash across the border into Chechnya.[22] Others in Georgia familiar with the case suggested that the expensive vehicles were also transferred to other regions of the Caucasus and beyond. Still others were used as potent bribes. The proceeds would be divided among the corrupt officials, criminals, and terrorists.[23]

Along the eight thousand mile route that the vehicles traveled from their point of origin in Los Angeles to their destination in the Caucasus, there emerged different elements of the crime, terror, and corruption relationship. At the point of origin, there was a crime-terror relationship. In Naples, the shipping manifest was successfully altered, probably a result of a successful collaboration of corrupt port officials and criminals employed at the ports. In Georgia, corrupt officials allowed entry of the vehicles, criminal-terrorist networks disposed of the vehicles, and funding was delivered to the terrorist organization. Diverse and complex crime-terror-corruption interactions were distributed along the pipeline.

The Beslan case is just one example of a more pervasive phenomenon, whereby diaspora communities are key supporters of terrorist organizations.[24] The following chapter on the business of terrorism examines the mechanisms by which this funding is obtained from diaspora communities, often by means of extortion. In contrast, this section focuses on the immigrant and overseas communities that are a basis of the financial and logistical support for terrorist groups. It examines diverse types of terrorist organizations, including jihadi, nationalist, and separatist groups, that are supported by émigré communities. This support need not only be financial but can include the purchase of needed military equipment, dual-use technology, the provision of false documents, and the facilitation of terrorist movement.[25] Diaspora communities can also help in target reconnaissance and identification.

Diaspora Communities: Willing or Unwilling Supporters?
Sometimes the overseas communities are willing supporters of the terrorist organization, as has been seen with Irish American support for the IRA or Tamil support for the Tamil Tigers in Sri Lanka.[26] The Somali diaspora community has sent funds to invest in piracy,[27] but in other cases, members of diaspora communities are extorted to contribute to the terrorist cause. In some communities, there is a mix of voluntary or coerced support.

The coercion is often undetected as it proceeds in immigrant communities, where the local law enforcement lacks the language, culture or capacity to police. The PKK forces Turks of Kurdish origin residing in Belgium, the Netherlands, Germany, the United Kingdom, and other Western European countries to contribute to their cause or face great physical harm. Investigations in Germany and Belgium reveal ongoing extortion of enormous sums from Kurdish businesspeople in legitimate businesses, such as restaurants, as well as in the drug trade. Turkish organized crime groups and militants using these extortion schemes net tens, if not hundreds, of millions of dollars annually.[28] According to one comprehensive study, the PKK extorted £2.5 million from Kurdish immigrants and businessmen within Great Britain in 1993 alone.[29]

Diaspora communities in North America continue to be victims of extortion by terrorist groups. Arabs who reside in and around Detroit in the United States and in the Toronto area in Canada have been forced to make payments that are transferred to Hezbollah.[30] The Canadian government has initiated cases against members of the Tamil Tigers for extorting from members of the Tamil business community residing in Toronto, who were forced to provide approximately $1 million monthly to the Tamil Tigers.[31] The Canadian example is not unique, as the Tamil Tigers had agents in fifty-four countries who sought funding from members of expatriate communities.

Canadian authorities differentiate between two types of diaspora funding. The large-scale funding supports insurgencies in the country of origin. For example, Tamil and Sikh communities in Canada have often been compelled to give money to support the Tamil Tigers and the Sikh Khalistan movement (responsible for the 1985 bombing of the Air India flight that had departed Canada). The Tamil and Khalistan insurgencies require significant money to maintain armies, and the commission of terrorist acts is a consequence of this fund-raising. In contrast, much smaller sums are collected from Canadian diaspora communities for terrorist organizations not linked to insurgencies.[32]

Diaspora support communities can also be found in the developing world. Hezbollah exploits Middle East expatriate businesspeople, often those of Lebanese origin, in West Africa and also in Latin America. An epicenter of this is the triborder area (TBA) of Argentina, Brazil, and Paraguay, with Hezbollah collecting up to 20 percent of the income of Lebanese store owners.[33] The extensive presence of Hezbollah there has made some suggest that it is a safe haven for terrorism, and its presence there is discussed in greater depth later in the chapter.[34] The following chapter addresses the investigation of the Lebanese Canadian Bank that uncovered the Hezbollah-controlled money laundering channels in West Africa that funneled money back to Lebanon.[35] There has been a decades-long tradition of Hezbollah obtaining funding from diaspora communities, both in West Africa and the Congo region.[36]

Support from diaspora communities can include material support for terrorism, not just donations. This support can include development and dissemination of propaganda, training, weapons, and on-the-ground intelligence. In 2010, two Canadians of Tamil origin were sentenced to lengthy periods in prison by American courts for attempting to buy military equipment in the United States for the Tamil Tigers. A call monitored by the FBI to LTTE in Sri Lanka revealed that, in 2006, the Tamil representatives in Canada had attempted to purchase ten heat-seeking antiaircraft missiles and launchers, five hundred AK-47 assault rifles, and other military equipment. The sentenced Tamil émigrés were longtime Canadian residents, who were educated and otherwise law abiding. Those trying to make the illegal military purchases were sympathizers of LTTE for many years before it was entered on the list of identified terrorist organizations. This case reflects the fact that those behind the crime-terror interactions in developed countries can be "good citizens" who are generally outside the range of law enforcement.[37]

Services Provided by Diaspora Communities

Diaspora cells can also provide false documents and facilitate the illicit movement of people. European cases illustrate these forms of support. Electronic surveillance in Milan of Rabei Osman Sayed Ahmed, part of an al-Qaeda support cell linked to the Madrid bombings, revealed that he was a specialist in furnishing false documents to terrorists.[38]

Smuggling networks operating in Belgium and the United Kingdom both generated funds for terrorism and moved potential terrorists. In two linked cases in 2002 and 2005, a British citizen of Turkish origin was investigated and convicted of human trafficking. Set up to move immigrants seeking work in Europe, these networks were also exploited by the PKK. The trafficker and three of his associates "were found with €39,750 and £9,700 and written documents on which the PKK and different amounts of money were mentioned. UK intelligence indicated that the money was probably collected for financing of the PKK."[39] Further evidence of the possible multiple functions of the smuggling networks was that in one authorized search of an apartment linked to a Belgian-U.K. smuggling ring, a model of a London tube station was found at the time of the 2005 London bombings.[40]

Diaspora communities far from the locale of a terrorist attack may provide essential and varied support for terrorist organizations. The Beslan case provides the most well-documented example relevant to the mass attacks analyzed in Chapter 1, but it is merely illustrative of a much larger phenomenon. In a globalized world, with large-scale immigration, support networks for terrorism may be distributed across the globe, in locales such as Hollywood, California; Raleigh, North Carolina; and Toronto, Canada, that few would suspect.

The Prison

Prisons play a key role in bringing criminals and terrorists together. They conform to the central attributes of a safe haven for terrorism – they are often locales with weak governance, traditions of corruption and violence, and individuals raised in poverty. Although safe havens are thought to be particular locales, such as the TBA of Latin America, the prison environment shares these attributes precisely.[41]

Prisons and the Mass Attacks

The analyses of the mass attacks in Chapter 1 revealed that prisons played a key role in half of the most devastating attacks. In Madrid in Spain, São Paulo in Brazil, and Bali in Indonesia, prisons influenced the attacks in diverse ways. Prisons were a source of recruitment for the Madrid bombers, where North African terrorists recruited criminals. Samudra, the kingpin of the Bali attack, remained active from the prison after his arrest, using the Internet and the virtual world to recruit and finance the perpetuation of his organization. The Brazilian criminal gang, the PCC, disturbed by members' treatment in prison, planned and launched a coordinated attack from multiple prisons within the São Paulo region against the larger community.

Explaining the Centrality of the Prison

The centrality of the prison to terrorism on three very different continents suggests that the prison, possibly even more than diaspora communities, is a central facilitating environment for crime-terrorism interactions. As the great American criminologist Edwin Sutherland explained in his theory of "differential association," the extent of involvement in crime is explained by the intensity and duration of the relationship.[42] Prison, by its very nature and its cell structure, facilitates intense interactions.

The Polish sociologist Adam Podgorecki coined the concept of *dirty togetherness* during the Communist era. This concept can be adapted to the interaction of criminals and terrorists in prison. He developed this term to describe the cliquishness and "close-knit networks in the context of scarcity and distrust of the state,"[43] a situation that existed under the Communist system but certainly characterizes the common attitude toward the state of many criminals and terrorists incarcerated together for extended periods.

Prisons and False Identities

In prisons, especially the moderate regimes that exist in many Western European prisons, interaction occurs among criminals and terrorists in various cell blocks. In the Netherlands, a report on jihadis found that those in prison "also approached criminal fellow detainees to secure weapons and explosives in the future."[44] The Spanish authorities, in the aftermath of the March 11 bombing, developed recommendations to identify and limit the possibilities of terrorist recruitment among prisoners.[45] But in many European countries, incarcerated criminals, both knowingly and unknowingly, engage with terrorists. Terrorists often operate under false identities, therefore their true identities are not known to their fellow prisoners or prison authorities.[46] Moreover, terrorists have often been arrested for criminal acts such as document fraud, illegal cross-border transport of people, and money laundering.[47] Therefore, they are not tagged as terrorists and subject to specific surveillance.

Prisons in Europe

The problem of prison interactions of criminals and terrorists is particularly acute in Europe, where, in many countries, the two types of criminals are not separated, as terrorists are not viewed as a separate type of offender but merely as criminals who have broken the law. Terrorists, under European and international human rights conventions, cannot be permanently isolated.[48] In European prisons, the preponderance of prisoners are foreigners in the countries in which they are confined.[49] Isolated, vulnerable, and removed from their social support networks of friends and family, they are vulnerable to recruitment. European analysts in the years after the Madrid bombing suggested that "the prime training ground for Europe's jihadist criminals may well be prison."[50] Prisons may politicize inmates even if falling short of turning them into terrorists.

Corruption and Prisons

Corruption of prison officials is key to the crime-terror interactions in penal institutions in many regions of the world, even in developed countries, where levels of corruption are generally lower. Guards in most countries have low salaries and morale, making them likely to take bribes. They allow inmates to obtain and use computers and cell phones. They can also provide access to prisoners that terrorists deem ready for recruitment. Such interactions have been identified in the United States as well as such diverse countries of Western Europe as Great Britain, France, Italy, Austria, Switzerland, and Israel.[51]

Hamas prisoners in Israeli jails use cell phones to communicate in a locale where cell phones are forbidden.[52] Prisoners in the United States have unlawfully obtained PDAs and smartphones with Internet access.[53] Terrorists can corrupt more than prison officials. In 2006, the American defense lawyer of Sheik Omar Abdel Rahman was sentenced to prison for illegally passing messages from the imprisoned sheik to his followers in Egypt.[54]

Prison Recruitment and Radicalization

Prison recruitment has also resulted in terrorist threats in the United States, but, as a top FBI official explained, "the majority of cases involving prison radicalization and recruitment have not manifested themselves as a threat to national security. There have been, however, instances where charismatic elements within prison have used the call of Global Jihad as a source of inspiration to recruit others for the purpose of conducting terrorist attacks in the United States."[55] There have also been cases of gang members adopting radical views in prison.[56] In the United States, members of black organized crime groups and the Black Muslims interacted in penal institutions, laying the groundwork for a politicized underworld outside the prison.[57]

The following American case provides an excellent example of the prison radicalization process, the nexus between street-level crimes and terrorism. It reveals how homegrown terrorists are often inspired by ideology and events overseas but have no affiliation with a larger terrorist organization. It also illustrates how local police are key to identifying terrorism suspects who would not be on the federal law enforcement radar otherwise.

Kevin Lamar James, incarcerated in California, was a former Hoover Street Crip gang member. While in prison, he founded a group called Jamiat al-Islam al-Saheeh (Authentic Assembly of Islam, or JIS). While serving a ten-year sentence for robbery and possession of a weapon in prison, James converted a fellow inmate who, once released in 2004, was instructed to recruit others for terrorist operations against the United States and Israel and to provide logistical support. Mr. James and his initial convert developed a four-person cell that, in 2005, actively started researching targets such as military installations, offices of organizations affiliated with Israel, and synagogues. They funded their operations through a series of gas station robberies – all orchestrated by James from behind prison walls. It was a robbery of a Torrance, California, gas station that led to the cell's discovery and capture by local police in summer 2005. The search warrant resulting from the robbery led to the discovery of jihadi propaganda and disclosed the conspiracy. The four men involved were indicted on October 2006. Three of the four, including James, pled guilty.[58]

In 2011, a prison convert to Islam, Michael Finton, pled guilty and was sentenced to twenty-eight years in prison for planning to bomb the Paul Findley Federal Building and the adjacent offices of a congressman in downtown Springfield, Illinois.[59] Imprisoned between 2001 and 2006 in Illinois for aggravated robbery and aggravated battery, he came to the attention of federal authorities upon his release when a letter professing his desire to be a martyr was found in a search of his car. A subsequent 2009 sting operation led to his arrest when he attempted to bomb these Illinois federal facilities using a car that he thought carried a ton of explosives.[60]

Prisons in the Middle East and Former USSR

The problem of crime-terror interactions is even more intense in prisons in countries with greater proximity to terrorism. In prisons in Turkey,[61] Russia,[62] and Kyrgyzstan in Central Asia,[63] intense crime-terror interactions are of concern to officials. In Afghanistan, terrorists and criminals mix freely, facilitating both Taliban and al-Qaeda attacks.[64] Hamas has recruited members from within jails in Israel. This is an increasingly common phenomenon in the Middle East. In analyzing an attack, Matthew Levitt writes,

> Members of the network included more than twenty criminals recruited by jailed Hamas operatives in Israel's Ketziot Prison. Most of them were near the end of their terms at the time of recruitment and were soon released, whereupon they focused their efforts on recruiting more members and plotting kidnapping operations aimed at securing the release of Hamas leaders in Israeli prisons.[65]

In Turkey, a usual relationship exists between the PKK and its members who are incarcerated. The PKK is present in some municipal governments in the eastern part of Turkey. In these communities, PKK contractors, similar to their Mafia counterparts in Sicily, receive government contracts.[66] PKK members released from prison receive employment in these PKK-controlled firms, thereby creating an economic dependence on the organization. This contrasts with the Italian experience, where released inmates are dependent on the criminal organization for their support. But this pattern of support of released recruits for terrorist groups is also observed in Central Asia, as the following discussion indicates.

The crime-terror interaction has unique characteristics in the prisons in Kyrgyzstan in Central Asia, a country close to the intense conflicts in Afghanistan and Pakistan and a key point on the trajectory of drugs out of Afghanistan to Russian and Western markets.[67] Corruption has been rampant in post-Soviet prisons, and criminals have been able to operate with impunity because of bribes to penitentiary officials. What is new is that the funds raised by the inmates in prison, the *obshchak* traditionally controlled by the criminal world, are now coming increasingly under the control of imprisoned Islamists.[68] This means that the criminals are losing control over the prisons to the incarcerated Islamist groups, a trend that has accelerated in recent years.[69]

Recruitment occurs through prison mosques in Kyrgyzstan, facilitated by the great social inequality and social injustice both within and outside the prison.[70] These prisons are providing terrorists and terrorist sympathizers "the opportunity to extend their influence among convicts, at first inside prison and then on their release."[71] With no postrelease financial or support services, and in a country with endemic unemployment, terrorists direct released criminals to mosques where supporters supervise their activities.

In summer 2013, more than a thousand suspected terrorists escaped from prisons in Iraq, Pakistan, and Libya. The escape of these inmates from such geographically separated Moslem countries within a short period of time points to the coordination behind these prison breaks as well as the likely complicity and corruption of prison officials in diverse environments. It is believed that al-Qaeda's affiliates were behind two attacks on Iraqi prisons that freed hundreds of inmates.[72] The links established in prison, and the massive release of identified terrorists by their supporters, suggests that these prison networks will be an important force in ongoing terrorism in North Africa, the Middle East, and South Asia.

Contemporary Prisons: A Challenge to Foucault

The fact that prisons are no longer merely schools of crime[73] but major loci for crime-terror interactions negates the core idea of the prison as an institution of state control. The famous French sociologist Foucault, in his classic work on the development of the prison within Western society, *Discipline and Punish,* notes that the model of control in the prison represents the broader controls that developed in industrialized society.[74] The prison characterized society during and after the Industrial Revolution. Yet at the present time, we are observing the converse of Foucault, where the prison is punishing society, instead of the state disciplining and punishing its inmates. Rather, the state's effort to control has been sabotaged by the interactions that occur in the prison. The harm to the state comes from within its prisons – Bali, Madrid, and São Paolo. The prison becomes the instrument of the state's destruction rather than the state's instrument of control.

Megacities

Four of the six most deadly attacks discussed in Chapter 1 occurred in megacities, cities of more than 10 million population in the city and its surrounding communities: Jakarta, Mumbai, São Paulo, and New York.[75] Three out of four of these were in the developing world, where megacities are most pervasive.

Growth of Megacities: Quality of Life

The growth of these cities has occurred primarily in the second half of the twentieth century.[76] In megacities, particularly in the developing world, there is an enormous contrast between the minority of the affluent and the majority of the population, who live a precarious existence. For many of the poorest, life represents a Hobbesian order, where it is brutal and short. Corruption, as discussed in Chapter 2, is rampant, exacerbating the growing social and economic inequalities. Opportunities for youthful men are limited, and participation in crime, gangs, and drug trafficking organizations is often the only viable option. Law enforcement in these communities is often absent because the police collude with the criminal gangs or do not dare enter the poorest communities.[77] The following description of Karachi is applicable to many other megacities. "Informal processes then take over, promoting anarchy, administrative helplessness, and corruption."[78] The collaboration of the corrupt and the criminal undermines the control of the state in these massive urban centers.

Megacities and the Deadly Attacks

The locales chosen by the terrorists behind the most deadly attacks were locations of maximum impact – New York, Jakarta, Mumbai – rather than operational centers for the terrorist and criminal groups. Only the São Paolo attack, which does not conform to the usual concept of a terrorist act, was perpetrated by urban criminals from the *favelas* of that city. Another megacity was, however, instrumental in the preparation of the Mumbai attacks. The two attacks on India's financial center were planned and launched from the city of Karachi, where criminal groups often freely collaborate with terrorist groups.[79] Karachi, as an environment favorable to these criminal-terrorist interactions, is discussed more fully in the following section on ports.

Ports

Cargo shipped annually by liners totaled $4 trillion, and 580 million TEUs (twenty foot equivalent units) of containers were moved in 2011. The vast volume and value of goods transiting ports are desirable prey for criminal groups.[80]

Organized Crime and Corruption in Ports

Organized crime operates in major ports in all regions of the world.[81] It is a visible presence in such disparate locales as Colombia, Japan, the Russian Far

East, the United States, the Mediterranean, Somalia, Karachi, and Mumbai in South Asia. Criminal organizations can be most successful at extorting funds when they are dealing in time-sensitive industries. As ports often transport perishable goods and products that are needed by retailers and producers, transporters are vulnerable to pressure by criminal groups, which can refuse or delay in delivering cargo.

Corruption is also very present in many ports around the world. In many countries with sea ports, large amounts of imports enter by ships. The customs office that oversees the importation of goods is a highly corrupt agency in many countries.[82] Customs officials are often among the most corrupt of government employees because they can demand certain sums to allow entry of legitimate goods and can also command money to look the other way in regard to illicit imports and exports.

Terrorists' Use of Ports

Ports are also critical to terrorists. Terrorists need ports to generate revenues, to obtain weapons and other needed supplies, and to launch operations. Prior discussions have shown that Basayev's funding cell could not have succeeded unless passage of the expensive vehicles was facilitated through the port of Naples and delivered through the port of Poti in Georgia. As Chapter 1 discusses, corrupt Indian customs officials in Mumbai permitted the entry of RDX explosives belonging to D-Company through the port of Mumbai, even though they knew that the smugglers were terrorists. The explosives were subsequently used in the violent attack against the city in 1993.[83]

Naples and Karachi

The following discussion of Naples and Karachi shows the centrality of ports to the crime-terror-corruption relationship. Naples is a central node in the funding scheme of the Chechen terrorists, but this is not the only time in which this corrupt port in the Camorra-dominated city has been used to facilitate terrorism. As was explained in Chapter 3, the Camorra has less loyalty to the Italian state than the more established and known Mafia based in Sicily. After the collapse of the Soviet Union, criminals based in Naples became key intermediaries in the supply of weapons to terrorist groups in Latin America, the Balkans, and Africa.[84] For example, the ETA contracted with the factions of the Camorra, specifically the Genovese clan of Avellino, in 2001 to secure missile launchers and ammunition in return for payments of narcotics.[85]

Karachi is a port city that represents an even more complex example of the convergence of crime-terrorism and corruption. Groups based in Karachi played a key role in the terrorist attacks on Mumbai in 1993 and again in 2008, as Chapter 1 showed. Yet the interactions of the three entangled elements have not diminished since then. Rather, 2013 was inaugurated by major attacks by the Pakistani Taliban on the criminalized and corrupt Muttahida Qaumi Movement (MQM) party that dominates Karachi politics.[86]

Karachi is the major port of Pakistan as well as its financial center. Housing approximately 18 million people, it is characterized by very high rates of violence that are explained by the presence of many diverse terrorist organizations, including the TTP, the Pakistani wing of the Taliban movement, the Lashkar-e-Jhangvi movement (a very violent Sunni Moslem group),[87] and al-Qaeda, as well as criminal-terrorist hybrids such as D-Company, discussed previously in Chapter 1.[88] The more than eighteen hundred people who died in 2012 included "Shia religious scholars, political activists belonging to one or other of the city's warring political parties, shopkeepers who failed to pay bribes to land mafias, and of course the random people caught in the cruel crossfire."[89] This homicide rate of approximately one hundred per one hundred thousand makes Karachi's homicide rate one of the highest in the world and a truly anomalous figure for Asia.[90] Only five cities in Central America and Mexico had higher rates of homicide.[91]

Violence is great, as the criminalized political parties enjoy both significant political and economic influence. The dominant political forces are the MQM[92] and its rival, the ethnic Pashtun-based Awami National Party (ANP), each of which is deeply involved in the targeted killings that characterize life in contemporary Karachi. The hybrid of crime and terrorism within this port city facilitates terrorism abroad, both in Afghanistan and India, but also contributes to the large-scale urban violence that was previously discussed in the context of São Paulo.

The crime-terror groups survive not only because of the nature of the local government but because the national government has used the crime and terror groups to advance its political agenda in Kashmir and elsewhere. Through the Inter-Services Intelligence under the Pakistani military,[93] support has been provided to LeT, a terrorist organization discussed in reference to the Mumbai attacks. Integral to LeT's operations is its cooperative relationship with D-Company, based in Karachi.

The terror groups exploit the strategic location of Karachi to engage in the international drug trade. This trade is used to help finance attacks. For instance, during a 2009 raid in Karachi, police arrested members of the banned Lashkar-e-Jhangvi movement (with heroin stashes, suicide vests, and explosives) who were planning attacks on government officials, police, and intelligence agencies in the city.[94] According to police investigations, the gang shipped heroin to China, Malaysia, Singapore, and the United Arab Emirates, transferring profits to a Taliban commander in Chaman, an area on Pakistan's southwestern border with Afghanistan.[95]

Centrality of Ports

Ports are so central to the operations of criminal and terrorist groups because they facilitate the movement of goods and people. Moreover, time-sensitive businesses like shipping are ripe for exploitation by criminalized actors who can extort money to prevent delays. The presence of significant corruption in so many locales and the inability of officials to examine only a small percentage of freight that transits through ports make these key support nodes for insurgents, terrorists, and those engaged in armed conflict. As Map 4.1a shows in reference to the Beslan case, ports figure prominently in the supply chain for terrorist organizations.

Multiborder Areas

Ports are locales where cargo ships of many different countries intersect without much regulation. The land equivalent of this unregulated space are multiborder areas in which the borders of several countries intersect. As in ports, where the vessels of numerous countries interact, the absence of clear lines of authority and adequate supervision of government officials facilitates bribery.

Characteristics of Multiborder Areas

There are also important characteristics of multiborder areas that make them conducive to the interactions of crime, corruption, and terrorism. The countries bordering each other may have very different histories, cultures, traditions, institutions, and even languages. Often the boundaries dividing these countries are a result of decisions made by colonial powers or conflicts, rather than a logical geographical divide. The legal system of bordering countries often reflects these cultural and historical differences, and their laws and legal systems may be distinct. All of these combine to make very different environments in which cooperation is difficult. Moreover, the strong antagonisms that characterize some border areas may result in ongoing conflicts and large-scale unregulated trade. In these conditions, the illicit may easily be hidden within the licit.

Multiborder areas can house multiple jurisdictions in close proximity, or they can be countries sharing a common body of water, such as the Mediterranean Sea, the Black Sea, or the Arabian Sea. In these environments, people and goods can often pass with limited oversight, because they are often lightly policed, poorly guarded, or locales where corruption of police, border guards, customs officials, and other government officials is rampant.[96] In some border areas, there are artificial divisions of communities, separating families and clans from each other. This is discussed more in reference to the drug trade between Afghanistan-Pakistan and Central Asia and the smuggling in the Kurdish regions of eastern Turkey. These cross-border networks and relationships may be stronger than the legal divide. With centuries of collaboration across these borders, unregulated trade, sometimes referred to as smuggling, continues despite the state's desire to regulate and stem this activity.

Several of these multiborder regions have already figured prominently in this book's analyses – the North and South Caucasus were discussed in reference to the Beslan attack. In the mountainous border areas of the Caucasus, significant smuggling occurs across borders between the North and South Caucasus and

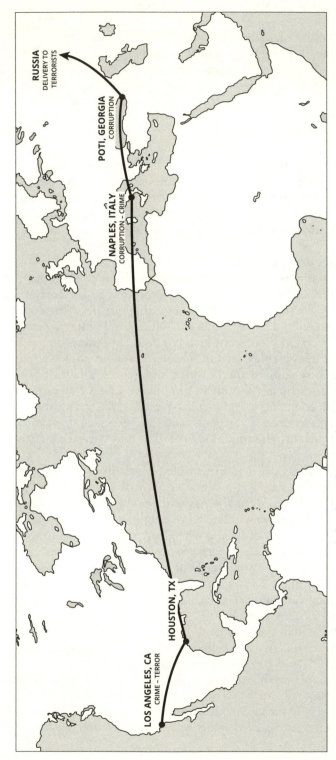

MAP 4.1A. International support network for the Beslan attacks.

the separatist areas in the region.[97] Other multiborder areas, such as eastern Turkey, West Africa, the Arabian Gulf, and the Horn of Africa, are discussed in greater depth in subsequent chapters. In these regions, crime-terror interactions contribute to deadly attacks, locally as well as on a global scale.

The Triborder Area of Paraguay, Brazil, and Argentina

A locale that has epitomized the problem of multiborder jurisdictions is the TBA in South America. For many years, the TBA was one of the larger foreign support centers for Middle Eastern terrorism. Furthermore, the TBA has been linked to major terrorist attacks against the Argentine Jewish community in Buenos Aires in the 1990s. The problem of multiborder jurisdiction is enhanced in the TBA as this region also houses a free-trade zone – minimizing regulation and compounding the possibilities for illicit trade.

The TBA, located where Argentina juts into Brazil and Paraguay, including the three cities close to the beautiful Iguaçu Falls (Puerto Iguaçu, Foz de Iguacçu, and Ciudad del Este [CDE]), has served as a virtual laboratory of all the phenomena discussed in this book.[98] As Map 4.1b shows, the terrorist and crime groups operating there are connected to many regions in the world far from this remote locale. The map reveals the home bases of these diverse organizations, but their links are global. Hezbollah, Hamas, al-Qaeda, and the FARC have all been identified as operating here, as have major organized crime groups such as the Chinese triads and the Japanese *yakuza* as well as more locally based drug organizations.[99] American investigations of Hezbollah have found links between groups operating here and in the United States.[100] Terrorist training camps have been found in the dense jungle area near the TBA.

The TBA's facilitating role has been explained "more by laxity and corruption than by overt challenges to state authority."[101] International pressure, applied after September 11, has resulted in the arrest of key actors in the TBA of Argentina, Paraguay, and Brazil.[102] Law enforcement efforts have lessened the impact but have not eliminated this key node where criminals, corrupt officials, terrorists and facilitators converge.

At its peak, Hezbollah fund-raising from Paraguay in the TBA was estimated by Latin American specialists at $10 million a year, or one-tenth of its total fund-raising.[103]

How did the TBA, such a remote locale, far removed from the Middle East, become such an important center for terrorist financing, facilitation, and planning? The answer lies in its history. Latin America has seen much immigration from the Middle East for more than a century, and many prominent families in Argentina, Brazil, Mexico, and elsewhere are of Arab origin. But the significant Middle Eastern migration to the TBA is of more recent origin. In the last fifty years, approximately twenty-five thousand Syrians, Lebanese, and displaced Palestinians moved to this region as a result of the numerous Arab-Israeli conflicts and the wars in Lebanon.[104] The immigrants settled primarily

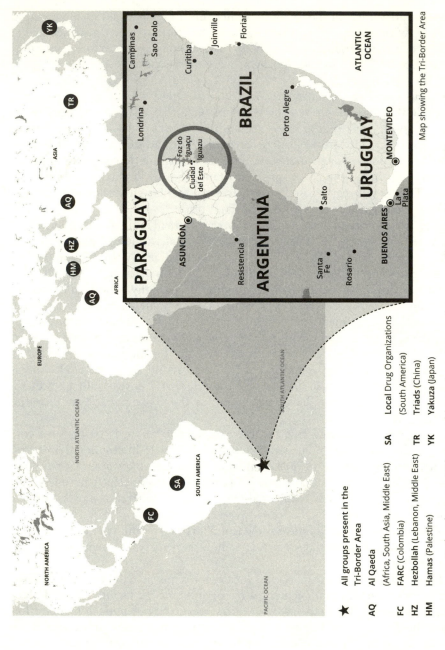

MAP 4.1B. Triborder area: What would you decapitate to have any effect on this network?

★ All groups present in the
    Tri-Border Area

AQ Al Qaeda
    (Africa, South Asia, Middle East)

FC FARC (Colombia)

HZ Hezbollah (Lebanon, Middle East)

HM Hamas (Palestine)

SA Local Drug Organizations
    (South America)

TR Triads (China)

YK Yakuza (Japan)

Map showing the Tri-Border Area

in CDE, a border city in Paraguay. They arrived during Stroessner's long-term dictatorship, when Paraguay was one of the most corrupt countries of the world. It was then a paradise for fugitives on the run, including the notorious Nazi war criminal Josef Mengele.[105] With such tolerance for gross illegality, the city and its surrounding border region became a haven for extremists.

Middle Eastern businessmen who do not choose to support this extremism are subjected to extortion by means of violence. Their relatives in Lebanon can also be threatened for their failure to make payments.[106] Murder is easy, as hitmen can be hired for as little as $1,000. One notable victim was Ussein Mohamed Taiyen, president of the CDE Chamber of Commerce, who was murdered in 2002 because he refused to make payments.[107] This illustrates the coercion of members of diaspora communities, discussed earlier in the chapter, and the business of terrorism that is analyzed in Chapter 5.

The TBA was not on the world's radar screen until two devastating terrorist attacks in the 1990s against the Argentine Jewish community were launched from this locale.[108] These attacks, linked to Hezbollah and the Iranian government, revealed the long reach of crime-terror networks. On March 17, 1992, a bomb exploded outside the Israeli Embassy in Buenos Aires, killing 29 and injuring 250. Two years later, in Buenos Aires, a car bomb outside the Jewish community center, the Argentina-Israel Mutual Association, destroyed the building, killing eighty-seven people and injuring more than two hundred. Security guards for the buildings were inexplicably absent before the attacks. Argentine investigations implicated an Iranian embassy official as having a key role in the bombings, a cultural attaché who in reality worked for the Iranian secret service. As always, corruption played a key role in the attack. Not only had security personnel been bribed to stay away but corruption in Argentina reached to a very high level. Credible allegations emerged that former president Carlos Saul Menem accepted a $10 million bribe from the Iranian government to purposely foil the investigations. Additionally, several state police officers were charged as accomplices in the bombing for allegedly handling the vehicle that was used in the bombing.[109]

Until Memem's departure from office in 1999, little progress was made on investigating the perpetrators of the crime. In November 2006, more than a decade after the attacks, an Argentine judge issued arrest warrants in connection with the 1994 bombings. Those sought included an internationally wanted Hezbollah militant from Lebanon, Imad Mughniyah, and eight Iranian government officials, including former Iranian president Hashemi Rafsanjani.[110] This judicial action was a first step, but the perpetrators have evaded justice, and the region remains an area of intense concern for its facilitating role in crime and terrorism.

What crime groups and criminal activity in the TBA help support different forms of terrorism? Apart from South American drug organizations, Chinese, *yakuza,* and Central American groups are present. The previously mentioned extortion is accompanied by smuggling, illicit arms trade, trade in cocaine, and a large trade in stolen cars, which helped finance terrorist activity. Significant counterfeiting activity in the region is discussed more in Chapter 7. Unusual crime-terror interactions have been observed in this poorly controlled territory. "At least two Chinese criminal families based in the TBA had been reportedly engaging in illegal business ventures with the operatives of Egyptian Gamaa Islamiya. One of these, the Sung-I family, is known to have sold munitions to that group in December 2000. The shipment, marked as medical equipment and sent to Egypt, was intercepted in Limassol, Cyprus."[111]

The sale of stolen cars from Latin America, Europe, and the United States is another important fund-raiser, recalling the Basayev financial cell. Paraguayan police estimated in the early 2000s that about 70 percent of the six hundred thousand cars in their country were purchased on the black market, with at least a portion of the profits likely going to terrorist groups. Even Paraguay's president drove a stolen car.[112] Paraguay and the TBA were also exploited as important transit zones for cocaine. Often cocaine was traded for arms.[113]

Free-Trade Zones

With the heightened scrutiny of the TBA, other multiborder jurisdictions and free-trade zones in Latin America have been identified as key crime-terrorism nodes, including the borders of Argentina, Brazil, and Uruguay and the triple border area in Colombia, Peru, and Brazil.[114] Other free-trade zones in South America with "large Middle Eastern populations also allow Islamic terrorist groups, organized crime mafias, and corrupt officials to thrive in a mutually beneficial, symbiotic relationship."[115] These areas include Colombia's Maicao, Venezuela's Margarita Island, and Chile's Iquique.[116] Yet the TBA still remains a concern for those watching the convergence of diverse threats.

Conflict Regions

The introduction of the book began with descriptions of some of the contemporary world's most destructive conflicts – those in Mali and Syria – where crime, corruption, and terrorism all operate together. These ongoing conflicts in Africa and the Middle East have contributed to the death and displacement of hundreds of thousands. One of the six major attacks discussed in Chapter 1, Beslan, occurred in a conflict region – the North Caucasus.

Unfortunately, conflict regions are the environments in which smaller terrorist attacks also occur on a regular basis.[117] In regions as diverse as the Balkans, Colombia, the Middle East, South Asia, and West Africa, frequent crime-terror-corruption interactions have maintained and intensified conflict.[118] The dirty entanglements in many of these conflict regions – Afghanistan; Colombia; eastern Turkey; and East, West, and North Africa – are discussed more in Chapter 6 and in other chapters addressing the business of terrorism. Therefore, the examples given in the following illustrate the deadly illicit networks that converge in conflict regions – the Balkans, Iraq, and the Gaza Strip – that are less discussed in this book.

Proliferation of Conflict Regions

Ethnic and separatist conflict proliferated at the end of the Cold War.[119] Crime-terror interactions thrive in these locales, because there is no effective legal system or a state capable of enforcing the law. Multinational bodies, interventions by foreign powers, and international civil society have done little to curb the violence, crime, and illicit trade that perpetuate these conflicts.

Why Are Conflict Regions So Critical?

Many of the most serious conflicts of the 1990s and the early part of the 2000s were supported by illicit trade in drugs and such natural resources as diamonds and oil.[120] Greed, rather than grievance, far too often perpetuates these conflicts.[121] Local leaders profit, and the absence of any effective justice system ensures that crime pays.[122]

The number of refugees and displaced people has stayed at record levels because conflicts remain in the poorest countries and persist for years.[123] There is no legitimate employment because the conflict destroys the economy and deters investment. Desperate individuals will do anything to support themselves and their families. They are susceptible to recruitment by criminal gangs and criminal warlords, as well as terrorist groups such as the FARC, Hamas, Hezbollah, and the Taliban, who can offer members a living by participating in diverse forms of illicit trade, such as drugs, people, and arms trafficking, as well as diamond smuggling.[124]

The Balkans

Crime, terror, and corruption interactions proliferated during the Balkan wars. Well-intentioned measures taken by President Tito in the late 1980s, before the breakup of Yugoslavia, contributed to the subsequent growth of terrorism. The decision by Tito to allow the building of mosques in Bosnia-Hercegovina had unanticipated consequences. The mosques served as a base for recruitment for Islamist organizations and sent 250 students annually from Bosnia to attend seminaries in Iran.[125]

With the outbreak of the war, a large illicit economy developed, run by political leaders, members of the police and armed forces, and preexisting criminal groups and paramilitary units.[126] The criminal-corruption links were strong, but these illicit networks also intersected with the Kosovo Liberation Army (KLA), a terrorist organization that benefited from diaspora funding, heroin smuggling,[127] and significant cigarette smuggling.[128]

The crime-terror connections were international as well as domestic. Members of the KLA, posing as ordinary criminals, engaged in business operations with the Sicilian Cosa Nostra.

In the early 2000s, a major Balkan crime faction led by a Tunisian named Mohamad bin Saleh bin Hmeidi specialized in smuggling migrants, narcotics, and arms. His clients were not just in the Balkans, as he was sought in several countries for supplying arms to the "IRA, the ETA, Islamic organizations, and Italian organized crime groups."[129]

Deeply rooted crime groups, high-level corruption, and ongoing links with terrorist groups continue in the region, especially in Bosnia.[130] The porous borders, established criminal networks, and corrupt officials have allowed some of these networks to persist. Evidence of this is the July 2012 bombing in Burgas, Bulgaria, that killed five Israelis. The attack was allegedly facilitated by Hezbollah on behalf of Iran. Phone calls prior to the attack indicated links between Bulgaria and Iran.[131]

Iraq

Corruption was at the core of the crime-terror relationship in Iraq. As a Library of Congress study explained, the corruption contributed "to a sense of impunity among criminal and terrorist elements such as Al Qaeda in Iraq, exacerbating violence, and rendering major Iraqi government agencies ineffectual."[132] The chief agency in charge of combating corruption in Iraq, the Commission on Public Integrity, lost more than forty employees and their families to assassinations.[133] Judge Radhi Hamza al-Radhi, who headed the Commission, was forced to seek asylum in the United States in 2007. Investigators who disclosed the theft and diversion of large quantities of oil that went into the pockets of officials, often members of the Oil Ministry and members of the insurgency, were murdered.[134] Billions were thus lost through corruption in the years after the invasion. The corruption was not novel, as the Chapter 2 discussion on the Iraqi weapons of mass destruction (WMD) program mentions, but it was vastly amplified in the conflict years that followed the ouster of Saddam Hussein.

Without an effective government, crime, terrorists, and insurgents thrived in the conflict environment of Iraq. Criminal groups were often established by former members of Saddam Hussein's government, especially former members of its intelligence service, which had long had a predatory attitude toward the Iraqi population.[135] Tribal smuggling groups contributed to the criminal mix.[136] Insurgents from within Iraq were supplemented by foreign jihadis who were often smuggled into Iraq after having completed training.[137] Al-Qaeda of Iraq was the most significant of the terrorist organizations, but it represented just one of the organizations operating within Iraq, including also Shiite militias[138] and the PKK, which operated in northern Iraq, close to the Turkish border.[139]

The terrorists were deeply engaged in such diverse forms of criminal activity as kidnapping, extortion, smuggling, and drug trafficking.[140] Their involvement in crime was often hard to distinguish from that of the criminal population. As Phil Williams explains, "clear distinctions between criminals on the one side, and terrorists, insurgents, and militia members on the other, are not always compelling. There are several reasons for the fuzziness. First is that individuals often have roles which are multiple, overlapping, and compatible rather than single, distinct, and mutually exclusive."[141]

The conflict in Iraq also provided a ready source of arms that was exploited by criminal and terrorist groups, both within the country and in neighboring countries. By 2006, an estimated 14,000 weapons, of the 370,000 the United States had provided in the previous few years, were unaccounted for.[142] Weapons provided to Iraqi police recruits were often put into the market as the newly enlisted law enforcement personnel left the service and sold their guns. Other police sold their weapons to compensate for pay delays owing to political infighting or the corruption of Iraqi government officials. Weapons were also stolen from U.S. military warehouses, and there are indications that some of these thefts were facilitated by corrupt American military personnel.[143] These weapons traded in Iraq at low prices.

Significant quantities of guns were trafficked to Turkey by crime and terrorist groups. Many of the most serious acts of terrorism in Turkey in recent years, such as the killing of a priest in Trabzon in 2006 near the Georgian border, were committed with arms stolen from Iraq.[144]

Israeli-Palestinian Conflict

The conflict between Palestinians and Israelis in the Gaza Strip resulted in one of the largest continuous smuggling operations in the world, as cash, consumer goods, materials for public works projects, and guns and advanced weaponry were smuggled through many large underground tunnels between Egypt and Gaza that functioned until summer 2013, when Morsi was ousted by the Egyptian military. The conflict that followed the Arab Spring made more weapons available for smuggling. In May 2012, three Egyptian Bedouin smugglers were arrested near the Libyan border transporting "40 surface-to-surface missiles, 17 rocket-propelled grenade launchers, mortar rounds, automatic rifles, and around 10,000 artillery shells."[145] This illustrates how conflict in one region fuels conflict and illicit trade in another. It also reveals how the weapons were available for the In Amenas attack that opened the book.

The smuggling in Gaza transpires under the rule of Hamas, a Sunni Moslem Palestinian party that has governed the Gaza Strip since 2007, after Hamas, an outgrowth of the Muslim Brotherhood, took control of this "territory from its rival Fatah, which governs the West Bank."[146] Hamas has been designated by the U.S. government as a terrorist organization since 1997.[147]

In 2006, Hamas managed to gain a majority in the parliament of the Palestinian Authority because it was widely seen as less corrupt.[148] Hamas, as discussed in Chapter 5, also provides significant services for Palestinians.

The Al Rafah smuggling tunnels have long historical precedents as the "region of Gaza has been fought over – and burrowed under – since long before Israel assumed control of it from Egypt in 1967."[149] The conqueror Alexander the Great lay siege to Gaza City by digging beneath its walls.[150]

The massive, lighted tunnels of today can accommodate rails and trucks. The hundreds of tunnels have individual owners or are owned by groups of individuals who have pooled their resources to construct and man these tunnels. Individuals work twelve-hour shifts, six days a week, moving commodities through the tunnels, performing this dangerous work as alternative employment is absent.[151] Hamas profits off this smuggling in diverse ways: through taxation, rentals, receipt of cash,[152] and protection of tunnel operators from prosecution when tunnel workers die. In late 2011, smugglers were told to get licenses for an essentially illegal activity. The rationale for this was perceived to be a revenue shortfall that may be explained by the transfer of funds from Islamists to groups in Egypt and elsewhere.[153] This is the logic of the business of terrorism, which is discussed more in Chapter 5.

Hamas shuts down tunnel operators who fail to pay them. Consequently, corruption and bribery are believed to be rampant.[154] "Tunnel revenue was estimated to provide Hamas with as much as $750 million a year but has diminished significantly with the crackdown on the tunnels after the ouster of Morsi's government.[155] Hamas has also smuggled in cash from exiled leaders and patrons in Syria, Iran, and Qatar that helps keep it afloat."[156]

The conflict between Israel and Gaza that ended in November 2012 concerned the deployment of rockets supplied by Iran that were smuggled through the Gaza tunnels and then fired at Israel. Before the conflict, Hamas was assessed to have amassed approximately ten thousand to twenty thousand Iranian rockets, of which approximately fifteen hundred were fired during the conflict.[157] In retaliation, Israel bombed Gaza and destroyed some of the smuggling tunnels.[158] In early 2013, in the Sinai, Egyptian authorities seized six antiaircraft and antitank rockets of unknown origin, which they believe were headed for the smuggling tunnels.[159]

The source of the smuggled weapons has primarily been Iran, named by the U.S. government as a state supporter of terrorism.[160] But weapons also come from other conflict regions, such as Libya. Therefore, the conflict region of Gaza has diverse sources of arms, whose entry into Gaza is facilitated through crime and corruption. The combination of these with terrorism creates a high and unpredictable level of violence, as discussed in the introduction.

Conclusion

There is a widely held perception and a significant literature that support the idea that the interactions of criminals and terrorists are most pronounced in fragile state and conflict regions.[161] As the previous section pointed out, the consequences of the interactions in conflict regions are especially devastating to life and security. But as this chapter reveals, the environments that facilitate crime and terrorism interactions are much more diverse and distributed internationally.

Terrorist groups and new transnational criminal organizations may often be based in weak states or poor and lawless areas of stronger states. Yet they will also operate, or have outposts in, the developed world or at major transport hubs. These international support networks are crucial because failed states lack communications, infrastructure for travel, and an environment in which criminals and terrorists can coordinate their activities transnationally and keep their supply chains functioning.

Acts of terrorism occur more often in poorly governed, rather than failed, states – which are inhospitable to terrorists and transnational criminals. As one analyst discussing the absence, until recently, of a significant crime-terror presence in the Horn of Africa explains,

> in general, terrorist networks have instead found safety in weak, corrupted states – Pakistan, Yemen, Kenya, the Philippines, Guinea and Indonesia. Terrorist networks, like mafias, appear to flourish where states are governed badly rather than not at all.[162]

Certainly crime and terrorism have flourished in these locales, but as the discussions in this book indicate, these locales are linked to more global support networks. D-Company, which is based in Pakistan, has a network that extends from Africa to Indonesia, with an important hub in the United Arab Emirates. The AQAP, which is based in Yemen, has recruited potential terrorists globally. Its firebrand leader, Anwar al Awlaki, killed in 2011 by an American drone attack, was using the Internet to recruit American jihadists, one of whom was stopped just before boarding a plane to Somalia.[163] Samudra, the mastermind of the Bali bombing, also used the Internet while in prison to obtain support and to communicate with a larger community of jihadists.

The effort to compartmentalize crime and terror interactions in the globalized world is unrealistic. Networks are truly global in reach. As Map 4.1b, on the TBA, reveals, the links from this remote region in South America extended from the Far East through South America to Africa and the Middle East. All three elements of crime, corruption, and terrorism were present at the core of this larger network, but not necessarily at all its nodes.

This chapter identified six environments that are disproportionately associated with the interactions of crime, terrorism, and corruption: diaspora communities, prisons, megacities, ports, multiborder regions, and conflict regions.

Of the approximately 44 million displaced people in the world, more than 15 million are considered refugees.[164] In addition to those who have been forced to leave their homes, millions more have emigrated looking for greater opportunity. The forces of migration and displacement have created significant diaspora communities in many regions of the world. These communities are composed of both legal and illegal immigrants and are often not well integrated into larger society, as they often differ in religion, ethnicity, and language from the citizens of the country where they reside. Diaspora communities, both willingly and unwillingly, provide logistical and financial support for terrorist and insurgent activities in the communities they left behind. Often members of diaspora communities, even in states with well-established legal systems, cannot expect protection from extortion and other pressures because their culturally and linguistically distinct communities are not assisted by local law enforcement.

Globalization has contributed to the retreat of the state and the rise of potent nonstate actors.[165] Once powerful state institutions of control, prisons, no longer epitomize the order and discipline of the state.[166] But now the prison, run by corrupt and corruptible officials, is often the corporate headquarters for crime-terror interactions that undermine the viability of the state. Modern-day communications capabilities, through cell phones and the Internet, allow crime-terrorist interactions to flourish even within the prison. Therefore, the crisis and limitations of the contemporary state are epitomized by the state's inability to control the interactions of criminals and terrorists within prisons.

One commentator on Latin America has stated that "the outright elimination of empty spaces, lawless areas, and collapsed states would not necessarily end the terrorist and criminal threats. Almost all of the activities related to terrorism and organized crime take place, to varying degrees, in large urban centers."[167] The urban centers maintain key links with the lawless areas.[168] This conclusion may exaggerate the role of cities and megacities, but even outside Latin America, the explosion of cities has provided environments conducive to terrorist attacks and the support structures for criminals and terrorists. The precarious existence of many in the contemporary city and the enormous contrasts in wealth[169] are both criminogenic and increase the likelihood of recruitment into terrorism.

The centrality of the port to the crime and terror interaction is explained both by the long historical involvement of organized crime with ports but also by the logistical needs of terrorist groups. Criminals and terrorists exploit the corrupt environment of ports to facilitate the movement of arms and, sometimes, personnel. It is also a supporting environment in which the commercial world can be deeply implicated in enabling crime and terrorism. Shippers pay off criminals to prevent delays in the loading and downloading of freight. Moreover, international insurance companies will insure the vessels of shippers to ensure that they avoid the risks of piracy when setting out from port into dangerous waters.

Multiborder areas often exist because of the historical legacy of conquest, the convergence of diverse civilizations, or the arbitrary decisions of authoritarian leaders. Different ethnic groups often meet at these borders having limited common culture, language, or legal attitudes. In other circumstances, families and clans may be artificially divided by arbitrary borders. Clan connections may prove more powerful than national boundaries. Both these circumstances have been analyzed in this chapter. The Kurdish clans that engage in smuggling transcend Turkey's borders with Iraq and Syria. These clans are a consequence of the division among the Kurdish population among different countries. The artificial borders of the Caucasus are a consequence of Stalin's jiggering of national frontiers, and those of Africa result from the arbitrary decisions of colonists who ruled by the philosophy of divide and conquer. But the consequences of these decisions from the past are environments that are presently conducive to both crime and terrorism.

Successful transnational criminal and terrorist organizations now have their operations and support structures distributed across diverse enabling environments. By linking these multiple locales, they exploit the vulnerabilities of the global political economy and the absence of harmonized laws and enforcement. As many examples in this chapter have shown, networks link these diverse environments from the developing and developed world into one pipeline, to ensure that the illicit organizations survive and perpetrate their destructive activities. These diverse environments are complemented by financial mechanisms and locales, discussed in Chapter 5, that provide the monetary lifeblood to criminals and terrorists.

Notes

1. Carrie Johnson and Spencer S. Hsu, "Terror Suspect Boyd Daniel Seemed to Have Typical Suburban Life," *Washington Post,* July 29, 2009, http://www.washingtonpost.com/wp-dyn/content/article/2009/07/28/AR2009072803193.html; U.S. Department of Justice, "Seven Charged with Terrorism Violations in North Carolina," press release, Attorney's Office, Eastern District of North Carolina, July 27, 2009, http://www.justice.gov/opa/pr/2009/July/09-nsd-725.html.

2. Yonat Shimron and Mandy Locke, "N.C. Terror Case Widens," June 18, 2010, http://www.newsobserver.com/2010/06/18/539100/nc-terror-case-widens.html.

3. Home Office Conference, Organised Crime and Terrorism Conference, London, October 22–23, 2012. The author spoke at the conference.

4. Abha Shankar, "Lebanese Canadian Bank to Pay $102 Million in Hizballah Laundering Case," June 27, 2013, http://www.investigativeproject.org/4061/lebanese-canadian-bank-to-pay-102-million-in.

5. "US Embassy Cables: Afghan Taliban and Haqqani Network Using United Arab Emirates as Funding Base," January 7, 2010, http://www.guardian.co.uk/world/us-embassy-cables-documents/242756.

6. John Horgan and Max Taylor, "Playing the 'Green Card': Financing the Provisional IRA: Part 1," *Terrorism and Political Violence* 11, no. 2 (1999): 1–38.

7. Sterling Seagrave, *Lords of the Rim: The Invisible Empire of the Overseas Chinese* (New York: G. P. Putnam's Sons, 1995); FBI, "Mafia Takedown Sixty-Two Indicted in New York," press release, February 7, 2008, http://www.fbi.gov/news/stories/2008/february/mafia_takedown_020708. This case examined the links between Italy and the United States that went back several decades.

8. Patrick Radden Keefe, "The Geography of Badness: Mapping the Hubs of the Illicit Global Economy," in *Convergence: Illicit Networks and National Security in the Age of Globalization*, ed. Michael Miklaucic and Jacqueline Brewer (Washington, DC: National Defense University Press, 2013), 97–109, focuses on the importance of hubs.

9. This observation was also identified in Julio A. Cirnio, Silvana L. Elizondo, and Geoffrey Wawro, "Latin American Security Challenges: A Collaborative Inquiry from North and South," in *Latin America's Lawless Areas and Failed States: An Analysis of the New Threats*, ed. Paul D. Taylor (Newport, RI: Naval War College Press, 2004), 9–10. This work explained that there is usually a well-oiled relationship between the operatives in urban centers and those settled in lawless areas, so that an active fight against criminal activities and terrorists at a specific geographical point can momentarily break the circuit but not end the problem.

10. David Albright, Andrea Stricker, and Houston Wood, "Future World of Illicit Nuclear Trade: Mitigating the Threat" (Washington, DC: Institute for Science and International Security, 2013), iii–iv.

11. Gretchen Peters, unpublished paper provided to the author.

12. Reports from informed U.S. government personnel indicate that a second funding cell, apart from the Hollywood cell, was found in Florida.

13. Interviews with personnel of the Los Angeles Police Department (LAPD). A planning meeting of participants in the Basayev funding case was photographed in Disneyland. As is shown throughout this book, crimes and locales are chosen not just to raise money but to cause harm. Hollywood and Disneyland, symbols of capitalism, were exploited by Chechens for their cause.

14. "From Glendale to Yerevan: The Law Will Hunt You Down," *Armenian Weekly*, September 6, 2011, http://www.armenianweekly.com/2011/09/06/from-glendale-to-yerevan-the-law-will-hunt-you-down/. This cites from Wikileaks cables on the transnational crime connections.

15. Illustrative of this is the Holy Land Foundation case, where senior leaders of the Foundation in 2009 received lengthy prison sentences for their support for Hamas. "Federal Judge Hands Down Sentences in Holy Land Foundation Case; Holy Land Foundation and Leaders Convicted on Providing Material Support to Hamas Terrorist Organization," March 27, 2009, http://www.fbi.gov/dallas/press-releases/2009/dl052709.htm.

16. "An L.A. Police Bust," December 29, 2006, originally published on p. 1 of the *Wall Street Journal*, http://lapdblog.typepad.com/lapd_blog/2006/12/an_la_police_bu.html.

17. Ibid., as well as discussions with the LAPD.

18. For a discussion of the Camorra, see Roberto Saviano, *Gomorrah: A Personal Journey into the Violent International Empire of Naples' Organized Crime System*, trans. from the Italian by Virginia Jewiss (New York, NY: Picador/Farrar, Straus, and Giroux, 2008); Tom Behan, *The Camorra* (London: Routledge, 1996); Xavier Raufer, *La Camorra, una mafia urbaine* (Paris: La Table Ronde, 2005). The Camorra was singled out in the government targeting order of the U.S. Treasury on July 25, 2011, http://www.treasury.gov/press-center/press-releases/Pages/tg1255.aspx.

19. Ibid.

20. Ibid.

21. Author's interview in 2006 with one of the Georgian police officers who was asked to move a car by his law enforcement superiors.

22. Interview with a member of the Russian presidential administration responsible for terrorism, in Beijing, in November 2011. He said that in one case, the border patrol officer who tried to counter the smuggling of the money was killed and was honored posthumously.

23. Author's interviews in Georgia in 2007.

24. Olivier Roy, *Globalized Islam: The Search for a New Ummah* (New York: Columbia University Press, 2004), discusses diasporas as a future source of terrorists.

25. Elaine Sciolino and Jason Horowitz, "The Talkative Terrorist on Tape: The Madrid Plot 'Was My Project,'" July 12, 2004, http://www.nytimes.com/2004/07/12/world/the-talkative-terrorist-on-tape-the-madrid-plot-was-my-project.html?pagewanted=all&src=pm; Ersel Aydinli, "From Finances to Transnational Mobility: Searching for the Global Jihadists' Achilles Heel," *Terrorism and Political Violence* 18 (2006): 301–13, focuses on the facilitation of transnational mobility as a key element of network support for terrorism.

26. See Kevin Cullen of *Frontline* for a fuller discussion of support for the IRA in North America. Cullen suggests that the financial and weapons support was never as great as was reported by the U.S. and U.K. governments. "The IRA and the Sinn Fein: America and the Conflict," http://www.pbs.org/wgbh/pages/frontline/shows/ira/reports/america.htm. Much support for the Tamil Tigers came from professional Tamils in the United States, Canada, Australia, and Western Europe. The convicted billionaire hedge fund owner, Raj Rajaratnam, was a Tamil who donated to the Tamil Tigers. See David Rose, "Crouching Tiger, Hidden Raj," *Vanity Fair*, October 1, 2011, http://www.vanityfair.com/politics/features/2011/09/tamil-and-raj-201109.

27. Diaspora communities can also invest in criminal activity that can support terrorism. Somalian diaspora communities are sending money to participate in auctions that will fund piracy. "Somali Sea Gangs Lure Investors at Pirate Lair," December 1, 2009, http://www.reuters.com/article/2009/12/01/us-somalia-piracy-investors-idUSTRE5B01Z920091201.

28. Mitchel P. Roth and Murat Sever, "The Kurdish Workers Party (PKK) as Criminal Syndicate: Funding Terrorism through Organized Crime, a Case Study," *Studies in Conflict and Terrorism* 30, no. 10 (2007): 901–20; Cyrille Fijnaut and Letizia Paoli, eds., *Organised Crime in Europe: Patterns and Policies in the European Union and Beyond* (Dordrecht, Netherlands: Springer, 2004). According to Peter Knoope, director of the Netherlands-based International Center for Counterterrorism at the Fourth International Symposium on Terrorism and Transnational Crime, December 7–9, 2012, Antalya, Turkey, the Dutch police do not have the capacity or the awareness to stop the extortion by PKK associates of Kurdish Turks residing in the Netherlands.

29. Roth and Sever, "Kurdish Workers Party (PKK) as Criminal Syndicate," 910.

30. Stewart Bell, "Ontario Extortion Racket Has Ties to Hezbollah," *National Post*, July 11, 2011, http://news.nationalpost.com/2011/07/21/ontario-extortion-racket-has-ties-to-hezbollah/.

31. Pat O'Malley and Steven Hutchinson, "Actual and Potential Links between Terrorism and Criminality," *ITAC-CIEM* 5 (2006), 4, www3.carleton.ca/cciss/res_docs/itac/omalley_e.pdf; "Tamil Tigers Are Extorting from Canadian Families:

Report," March 15, 2006, http://209.157.64.201/focus/f-news/1597290/posts?
page=1. Émigré Tamils in Western Europe were also subject to the same pressure;
see the Human Rights Watch Report "Funding the 'Final War': LTTE Intimidation
and Extortion in the Tamil Diaspora," March 15, 2006, http://www.hrw.org/en/
reports/2006/03/14/funding-final-war-2.

32. Insights gained at the conference Turning a New Leaf: Developments in
    Research and Policy on Terrorism and Counter-terrorism, Ottawa, Canada,
    May 2–3, 2013, Canadian Network for Terrorism, Society, and Se-
    curity.

33. Bartosz Stanislawski wrote the part on the triborder area in Louise Shelley and John
    Picarelli et al., "Methods Not Motives: Exploring Links between Transnational
    Organized Crime and International Terrorism," June 2005, 59–64, http://www
    .ncjrs.gov/pdffiles1/nij/grants/211207.pdf.

34. Cristiana C. Brafman Kittner, "The Role of Safe Havens in Islamist Terrorism,"
    Terrorism and Political Violence 19 (2007), 307–29.

35. "US Seizes $150m 'Linked to Hezbollah Money-Laundering,'" August 20, 2012,
    http://www.bbc.co.uk/news/world-middle-east-19327919.

36. Carl Wege, "Hizbollah in Africa," *Perspectives on Terrorism* 6, no. 3 (2012),
    http://www.terrorismanalysts.com/pt/index.php/pot/article/view/wege-hizballah-
    in-africa/html.

37. QMI Agency, "Two Canadians Jailed for Aiding Tamil Tigers," January 22, 2010,
    http://cnews.canoe.ca/CNEWS/Canada/2010/01/22/12580766-qmi.html.

38. Sciolino and Horowitz, "Talkative Terrorist on Tape."

39. Stef Janssens and Jana Arsovska, "People Carriers: Human Trafficking Networks
    Thrive in Turkey," *Jane's Intelligence Review*, December 2008, 46.

40. This lead was reported to the British police, but the Belgian authorities do not
    think it was pursued. Conversation with Stef Janssens, March 3, 2011, in Vienna.

41. Kittner, "Role of Safe Havens in Islamist Terrorism," 307.

42. http://criminology.fsu.edu/crimtheory/sutherland.html.

43. Janine R. Wedel, "Corruption and Organized Crime in Post-Communist States:
    New Ways of Manifesting Old Patterns," *Trends in Organized Crime* 7, no. 1
    (2001): 10.

44. C. J. de Poot and A. Sonnenschein, *Jihadi Terrorism in the Netherlands* (The
    Hague: WODC, 2011), 125.

45. "Conclusiones de la Comision," 248–50, http://www.elmundo.es/documentos/
    2004/03/espana/atentados11m/documentos.html.

46. Ian M. Cuthbertson, "Prisons and the Education of Terrorists," *World Policy
    Journal* 21, no. 3 (2004): 15–22. For an indication of this problem, see the Swiss
    acknowledgment of their confinement of a major terrorist, but his short term in
    prison indicates that he was confined as an ordinary criminal. Craig Whitlock,
    "In Neutral Switzerland, a Rising Radicalism," *Washington Post*, June 20, 2006,
    A14–A15.

47. Walter Laqueur, *The New Terrorism: Fanaticism and the Arms of Mass Destruc-
    tion* (Oxford: Oxford University Press, 1999), 210–25.

48. International Center for the Study of Radicalisation, *Prisons and Terrorism:
    Radicalisation and De-radicalisation in 15 Countries*, August 2010, 17–20,
    http://icsr.info/2010/08/prisons-and-terrorism-radicalisation-and-de-radicalisation
    -in-15-countries/.

49. Cuthbertson, "Prisons and the Education of Terrorists"; International Center for the Study of Radicalisation, *Prisons and Terrorism*, 28.

50. David E. Kaplan, "Paying for Terror: How Jihadist Groups Are Using Organized Crime Tactics – and Profits – to Finance Attacks on Targets around the Globe," *US News and World Report,* November 27, 2005, http://www.usnews.com/usnews/news/articles/051205/5terror.htm.

51. Discussions with an Italian judge who had a case of an Italian prisoner recruited by terrorists within the Italian prison system. Discussion in Georgia, September 2007; Cuthbertson, "Prisons and the Education of Terrorists." The article of the late Ian Cuthbertson is based on the experiences of someone who lived undercover in Swiss and Austrian prisons. The author interviewed the source for this article. Throughout Europe, the majority of those incarcerated are foreigners, or the children of migrants, often coming from North Africa or the Middle East. The vulnerability of the illegal immigrants makes them susceptible to the ploys of the terrorists, who know how to play on their fellow inmates' insecurity. See *EU Foreign Prisoners Project, Foreigners in European Prisons, 2006,* http://www.foreignersinprison.eu/pages/page.asp?page_id=1190, which discusses the large numbers of foreigners in European prisons and their exclusion from the language and culture.

52. Liad Porat, "Tighten Supervision over Hamas Prisoners," July 4, 2011, http://www.israelhayom.com/site/newsletter_opinion.php?id=135.

53. Patrick Dunleavy, testimony before the House Committee on Homeland Security, "The Threat of Muslim American Radicalization in U.S. Prisons," June 15, 2011, http://homeland.house.gov/hearing/threat-muslim-american-radicalization-us-prisons; National Gang Intelligence Center, "National Gang Threat Assessment, 2011, Emerging Trends," 31–32, http://www.fbi.gov/stats-services/publications/2011-nation al-gang-threat-assessment.

54. Julia Preston, "Lawyer, Facing 30 Years, Gets 28 Months, to Dismay of U.S.," October 17, 2006, http://www.nytimes.com/2006/10/17/nyregion/17stewart.html?ref=omarabdelrahman.

55. Donald Van Duyn, Deputy Assistant Director, Counterterrorism Division, FBI, "Prison Radicalization: The Environment, the Threat, and the Response," statement to Senate Homeland Security and Governmental Affairs, September 19, 2006, http://www.fbi.gov/news/testimony/islamic-radicalization.

56. National Gang Intelligence Center, "National Gang Threat Assessment, 2011, Emerging Trends," 32–33.

57. Sean Patrick Griffin, *Black Brothers Inc.: The Violent Rise and Fall of Philadelphia's Black Mafia* (Wrea Green, UK: Milo Books, 2005), 47–48.

58. Kevin Smith, testimony before the House Committee on Homeland Security, "The Threat of Muslim American Radicalization in U.S. Prisons," June 15, 2011, http://homeland.house.gov/hearing/threat-muslim-american-radicalization-us-prisons.

59. Michael Downing, testimony before the House Committee on Homeland Security, "The Threat of Muslim American Radicalization in U.S. Prisons," June 15, 2011, http://homeland.house.gov/hearing/threat-muslim-american-radicalization-us-prisons; Indictment U.S. Government v. Michael C. Finton, October 7, 2009, available at http://www.investigativeproject.org/case/347.

60. Dirk Johnson, "Suspect in Illinois Bomb Plot 'Didn't Like America Very Much,'" *New York Times,* September 27, 2009, http://www.nytimes.com/2009/09/28/us/28springfield.html?pagewanted=all.

61. Interviews in Ankara with Turkish police researchers on terrorism, June 10–11, 2010.

62. For Russian discussion of the rise of Islam in prison, see "Islam na zone, Beseda s aktivistom dav'ata v mestakh zakliucheniia," http://www.islam.ru/pressclub/gost/zona/.

63. International Crisis Group, "Central Asia: Islamists in Prison," Update Briefing, Asia Briefing 97, Bishkek, Brussels, December 15, 2009, http://www.crisisgroup .org/en/publication-type/media-releases/2009/asia/central-asia-islamists-in-prison .aspx.

64. Ibid., 29.

65. Matthew Levitt, "Hamas Shifts to an Outside-In Operational Strategy," Policy Watch 1848, Washington Institute, September 26, 2011, http://www .washingtoninstitute.org/templateCo5.php?CID=3398.

66. See Pino Arlacchi, *Mafia Business: The Mafia Ethic and the Spirit of Capitalism*, trans. Martin Ryle (London: Verso, 1986); Raimondo Catanzaro, *Men of Respect: A Social History of the Sicilian Mafia*, trans. Raymond Rosenthal (New York: Free Press, 1992); *Terörün Ekonomisi: Sınır Illerinde Kaçakçilik ve Terörün Finansmanı* (Ankara: Police Academy, 2009), 6.

67. "Central Asia's 'Drug Capital' Fights to Stem Tide of Narcotics," January 4, 2013, http://www.rferl.org/content/osh-is-awash-in-drugs/24815565.html.

68. "Central Asia: Islamists in Prison," Report Summary http://www.crisisgroup.org/ en/regions/asia/central-asia/B097-central-asia-islamists-in-prison.aspx.

69. Alexander Kupatadze, "Geopolitics, States, and Networks in Central Eurasia," May 9, 2012, Wilson Center, Washington, DC, http://www.wilsoncenter.org/ event/geopolitics-states-and-networks-central-eurasia, discussed this problem at his talk.

70. International Crisis Group, "Central Asia: Islamists in Prison," 1–13.

71. Ibid., 1.

72. Mark Mazzetti, "Interpol Asks Nations to Help Track Terror Suspects Freed in Prison Breaks," *New York Times*, August 3, 2013, http://www.nytimes.com/2013/ 08/04/world/interpol-issues-alert-on-prison-breaks-in-9-nations.html?_r=0.

73. This draws on previous research of the author published on nuclear smuggling, "Trafficking in Nuclear Materials: Criminals and Terrorists," *Global Crime* 7, nos. 3–4 (2006): 549–50.

74. Michel Foucault, *Discipline and Punish: The Birth of the Prison* (New York: Vintage Books, 1995); see the author's review of *Discipline and Punish* in *American Journal of Sociology* 84 (1979): 1508–10.

75. http://www.megacitiesproject.org/.

76. M. Davis, *Planet of Slums* (New York: Verso, 2006); the author first wrote about the emergence of this problem; see Louise Shelley, *Crime and Modernization: The Impact of Industrialization and Urbanization on Crime* (Carbondale: Southern Illinois University Press, 1981).

77. Enrique Desmond Arias, *Drugs and Democracy in Rio De Janeiro* (Chapel Hill: University of North Carolina Press, 2006); see also the monograph of Phil Williams, in which he discusses the rise of cities and of alternatively governed spaces, "From the New Middle Ages to a New Dark Age: The Decline of the State and U.S. Strategy," Strategic Studies Institute, June 2008, 21–27, http://www.StrategicStudiesInstitute.army.mil/. Williams draws his title from John Rapley, "The New Middle Ages," *Foreign Affairs,* May–June 2006, 93–103, who

discusses how law enforcement colludes with the drug traffickers in the slums of the third world.

78. Arif Hasan, *The Unplanned Revolution: Observations on the Processes of Socio-economic Change in Pakistan* (Karachi: Oxford University Press, 2009), 207.

79. See the works of Ikhram Sehgal on the crime-terror relationship as well as discussions with the author on this relationship, in Pakistan, 2011. For example, Ikram Sehgal, "Nexus between Organised Crime and Terrorism," *Daily Star,* November 1, 2007, http://www.thedailystar.net/newDesign/news-details.php? nid=9715.

80. Liners represent 60 percent of sea trade. See World Shipping Council, http://www .worldshipping.org/about-the-industry/global-trade.

81. "Piracy, Ports and Failed States, Crime's Frontlines?," http://www.nato.int/docu/ review/2009/organized_crime/Terrorism_Relation_OrganizedCrime/EN/index. htm.

82. Bryane Michael and Nigel Moore, "What Do We Know about Corruption (and Anti-corruption) in Customs?," *World Customs Journal* 4, no. 1 (2010): 1–12, http://works.bepress.com/bryane_michael/54.

83. "'93 Blasts: Two Customs Officials Held," *Times of India,* November 2, 2006, http://articles.timesofindia.indiatimes.com/2006-11-02/india/27797664 _1_blasts-shekhadi-coast-aide-of-prime-conspirator.

84. Saviano, *Gomorrah.*

85. Ibid.; Martin Arostegui, "ETA Has Drugs for Weapons Deal with Mafia," *United Press International,* October 3, 2002, http://www.upi.com/Business_News/ Security-Industry/2002/10/03/ETA-has-drugs-for-weapons-deal-with-Mafia/UPI-80091033676439/.

86. "TTP Targets MQM Supporters in Karachi, Kills Four," January 1, 2013, http:// tribune.com.pk/story/487465/explosion-heard-in-karachi-express-news/.

87. Asif Farooqi, "Profile: Lashkar-e-Jhangvi," January 11, 2013, http://www.bbc.co .uk/news/world-asia-20982987.

88. D. Ryan Clarke, *Crime-Terror Nexus in South Asia: States, Security and Non-state Actors* (New York: Routledge, 2011). According to this analysis, D-Company is also deeply involved in the ports of the United Arab Emirates and the economy of Dubai. Discussions with Clarke, Ikhram Sehgal, assistance from Nazia Hussain, in 2011–12.

89. Rafia Zakaria, "Fighting Is Forbidden," *Guernica,* November 16, 2012, http:// www.guernicamag.com/daily/rafia-zakaria-fighting-is-forbidden/. Eighteen thousand were killed by mid-November 2012. On an annualized basis, this would be close to twenty thousand.

90. The average global homicide rate is 6.9 per 100,000. See UNODC, *Global Study on Homicide 2011* (Vienna: UNODC, 2011), 19–23, http://www.unodc. org/documents/data-and-analysis/statistics/Homicide/Globa_study_on_homicide_ 2011_web.pdf.

91. Seguridad, Justicia y Paz, "San Pedro Sula, la ciudad más violenta del mundo; Juárez, la segunda," January 11, 2012, http://www.seguridadjusticiaypaz.org.mx/ sala-de-prensa/541-san-pedro-sula-la-ciudad-mas-violenta-del-mundo-juarez-la-segunda.

92. The dominant MQM represents the Mohajirs, descendents of Urdu speakers who migrated from India after the creation of Pakistan in 1947.

93. For a discussion of the ISI's relationship to terrorist groups, see Syed Saleem Shahzad, *Inside Al-Qaeda and the Taliban: Beyond Bin Laden and 9/11* (London: Pluto Press, 2011). The author suggested that there was also a relationship between al-Qaeda and the Pakistani government. Syed was murdered just after the release of the book, and some point to the ISI as being linked to the killing.
94. Associated Press, "Series of Raids by Pakistan Police Foils Attacks," *New York Times*, August 24, 2009.
95. Ibid.
96. Willem V. Schendel, "Spaces of Engagement: How Borderlands, Illicit Flows, and Territorial States Interlock," in *Illicit Flows and Criminal Things*, ed. Willem van Schendel and Itty Abraham (Bloomington: Indiana University Press, 2005), 38–68; Carolyn Nordstrom, *Global Outlaws* (Berkeley: University of California Press, 2007).
97. The separatist regions of Abkhazia and Ossetia are discussed further in Chapter 8, on WMD. For a discussion of the conflict regions in and around Georgia, see Timothy Wittig, *Understanding Terrorist Finance* (Houndsmill, UK: Palgrave Macmillan, 2011), 5–15.
98. Rensselaer Lee, "The Triborder-Terrorism Nexus," *Global Crime* 9, no. 4 (2008): 332–47; Rex Hudson, "Terrorist and Organized Crime Groups in the Tri-Border Area," revised 2010, 4, http://www.loc.gov/rr/frd/pdf-files/TerrOrgCrime_TBA .pdf.
99. Shelley and Picarelli et al., "Methods and Motives," 3.
100. Matthew Levitt, *Hezbollah: The Global Footprint of Lebanon's Party of God* (Washington, DC: Georgetown University Press, 2013), 84.
101. Cirnio et al., "Latin American Security Challenges," 23.
102. U.S. Department of State, *Patterns of Global Terrorism 2002 – Triborder Area (Argentina, Brazil, and Paraguay)*, April 30, 2003, http://www.unhcr.org/ refworld/docid/468107b423.html; Angel Rabasa, Peter Chalk, Kim Cragin, Sara A. Daly, Heather S. Gregg, Theodore W. Karasik, Kevin A. O'Brien, and William Rosenau, *Beyond al-Qaeda, Part II: The Outer Rings of the Terrorist Universe* (Santa Monica, CA: RAND, 2006), 153–60.
103. Matthew Levitt and Michael Jacobsen, *The Money Trail: Finding, Following and Freezing Terrorist Finances*, Policy Focus 89 (Washington, DC: Washington Institute, November 2008), 57–58, http://www.washingtoninstitute.org/policy- analysis/view/the-money-trail-finding-following-and-freezing-terrorist-finances; see Cirnio et al., "Latin American Security Challenges," 24n6.
104. Rabasa et al., *Beyond al-Qaeda*, Part II, 153.
105. Shelley and Picarelli et al., "Methods and Motives," 59.
106. Levitt and Jacobsen, *Money Trail*, 57–58, quoting the U.S. Treasury.
107. Shelley and Picarelli et al., "Methods and Motives," 63; Kittner, "Role of Safe Havens in Islamist Terrorism," 322.
108. There is a direct link between the phenomena. One of the bombers associated with the 1994 attack, Mugniyeh, masterminded the attack on French paratrooper headquarters in 1983. Rabasa et al., *Beyond al-Qaeda*, Part II, 157.
109. Kittner, "Role of Safe Havens in Islamist Terrorism," 317.
110. Mark P. Sullivan, "Latin American: Terrorism Issues," September 9, 2009, Library of Congress, http://4fpc.state.gov/documents/organization/128377.pdf.

Imad Mughniyah was also identified as the mastermind of the October 23, 1983 simultaneous truck bombings against French paratroopers and the U.S. Marine barracks attacks in Lebanon, which killed 58 French soldiers and 241 U.S. Marines. On September 20, 1984, Mughinyah is alleged to have attacked the U.S. Embassy annex building.

111. Ibid., 60.

112. Rabasa et al., *Beyond al-Qaeda, Part II*, 157–58.

113. Frank Shanty and Patit Paban Mihra, *Organized Crime: From Trafficking to Terrorism* (Santa Barbara, CA: ABC-Clio, 2008), 304.

114. Cirnio et al., "Latin American Security Challenges," 18–19. For a further discussion of the general problem of free-trade zones, see ICC (BASCAP), "Controlling the Zone: Balancing Facilitation and Control to Combat Illicit Trade in the World's Free Trade Zones," May 2013, http://www.iccwbo.org/Advocacy-Codes-and-Rules/BASCAP/International-engagement-and-Advocacy/Free-Trade-Zones/.

115. Hudson, "Terrorist and Organized Crime Groups in the Tri-Border Area," 4.

116. Ibid.

117. Angel Rabasa, Steven Boraz, Peter Chalk, Kim Cragin, Theodore W. Karasik, Jennifer D. P. Moroney, Kevin A. O'Brien, and John E. Peters, *Ungoverned Territories: Understanding and Reducing Terrorism Risks* (Santa Monica, CA: RAND, 2007), discusses Afghanistan-Pakistan, East Africa, the North Caucasus, and West Africa as well as others.

118. Edward Newman, "Weak States, State Failure and Terrorism," *Terrorism and Political Violence* 19, no. 4 (2007): 467. Newman suggests that interactions also occur outside of weak states. But the interaction is observed in such large-scale conflicts as Iraq, Afghanistan, and parts of Pakistan and in the numerous regional conflicts that have emerged globally since the end of the Cold War, such as the Balkans, Kyrgyzstan, the Caucasus, and Somalia. See also Martin Kalulambi Pongo and Tristan Landry, *Terrorisme international et marchés de violence* (Saint Nicolas, Canada: Les Presses de l'Université Laval, 2005), 93–99, to discuss conflict situations.

119. Center for Systemic Peace, *Global Conflict Trends*, October 31, 2012, Figure 10, http://www.systemicpeace.org/conflict.htm.

120. Ibid.; Bilal Wahab, "How Iraqi Oil Smuggling Greases Violence," *Middle East Quarterly* 13, no. 4 (2006): 53–59.

121. See Paul Collier and Anke Hoeffler, "On Economic Causes of Civil War," *Oxford Economic Papers* 50, no. 4 (1998): 563–73; Karen Ballentine and Jake Sherman, *The Political Economy of Armed Conflict: Beyond Greed and Grievance* (Boulder, CO: Lynne Rienner, 2003).

122. Kittner, "Role of Safe Havens in Islamist Terrorism," 314; R. T. Naylor, *Wages of Crime: Black Markets, Illegal Finance, and the Underworld Economy* (Ithaca, NY: Cornell University Press, 2005); Philippe Le Billon, "Overcoming Corruption in the Wake of Conflict," Global Corruption Report 2005, Transparency International, 73, http://www.transparency.org/content/download/4270/26215/file/corruption_ post_conflict_%20rec.pdf.

123. Center for Systemic Peace, *Global Conflict Trends*, Figure 7.

124. Greg Campbell, *Blood Diamonds: Tracing the Deadly Path of the World's Most Precious Stones* (Boulder, CO: Westview Press, 2002).

125. Shaul Shay, *Islamic Terror and the Balkans* (New Brunswick, NJ: Transaction, 2007), 123–27.

126. Vera Stojarova, "Organized Crime in the Western Balkans," *Humsec Journal* 1 (2007): 91–114.

127. Peter Andreas, "The Clandestine Political Economy of War and Peace in Bosnia," *International Studies Quarterly* 48 (2004): 47.

128. Jana Arsovska, "Networking Sites – Criminal Group Expands across the Balkans," *Jane's Intelligence Review* 21, no. 12 (2009): 43–47.

129. Glenn Curtis, *The Nexus among Terrorists, Narcotics Traffickers, Weapons Proliferators and Organized Crime Networks in Western Europe*, U.S. Library of Congress Federal Research Division, December 2002, 11, http://www.loc.gov/rr/frd/pdf-files/WestEurope_NEXUS.pdf.

130. For much reporting on the region, see the Organized Crime and Corruption Reporting Project based in the Balkans, https://reportingproject.net/occrp/. Bosnia has been identified as a source for recruiting "so-called 'white al Qaeda' – Muslims with Western features who could easily blend into European or U.S. cities and carry out attacks." "Embassy Shooting in Bosnia Called Terror Attack," October 28, 2011, http://www.cbsnews.com/8301-202_162-20127120/embassy-shooting-in-bosnia-called-terror-attack/.

131. For a discussion of the bombing, see Nicholas Kulish and Jodi Rudoren, "Plots Are Tied to the Shadow War of Israel and Iran," *New York Times*, August 8, 2012, http://www.nytimes.com/2012/08/09/world/middleeast/murky-plots-and-attacks-tied-to-shadow-war-of-iran-and-israel.html?pagewanted=all&_r=0.

132. John Rollins and Liana Sun Wyler, "International Terrorism and Transnational Crime: Security Threats, U.S. Policy, and Considerations for Congress," 13, http://www.fas.org/sgp/crs/terror/R41004.pdf.

133. Ibid.

134. Interviews with Judge Rahdi in Washington in 2007.

135. Phil Williams, *Criminals, Militias, and Insurgents: Organized Crime in Iraq* (Carlisle, PA: Strategic Studies Institute, U.S. Army War College, 2009), 225–26.

136. Ibid., 227–29.

137. Michael Bronner, "Al-Qaeda's Migrant Martyrs," *Vanity Fair*, December 16, 2009, http://www.vanityfair.com/politics/features/2009/12/iraqi-terrorists-200912.

138. Williams, *Criminals, Militias, and Insurgents*, 234.

139. Kamil Yilmaz, Disengaging from Terrorism: Lessons from the Turkish Penitents (London and New York: Routledge, 2014).

140. Rollins and Wyler, "International Terrorism and Transnational Crime," 28.

141. Williams, *Criminals, Militias, and Insurgents*, 222.

142. Ibid., 183.

143. Interviews with U.S. personnel deployed in Iraq.

144. Interviews with U.S. personnel deployed in Iraq and discussions with terrorist specialists in Turkey, 2007–10.

145. Associated Press, "Arms Smugglers Detained Near Libyan Border," *Boston Globe*, May 11, 2012, http://www.bostonglobe.com/news/world/2012/05/10/egypt-seizes-heavy-weapons-from-arms-smugglers/svvWYlkSgo3aSFYlS3vcIK/story.html.

146. Johnathan Masters, "Hamas," November 27, 2012, http://www.cfr.org/israel/hamas/p8968.

147. Ibid.

148. Ibid.

149. James Verini, "Gaza Tunnels," *National Geographic,* December 2012, http://ngm
.nationalgeographic.com/2012/12/gaza-tunnels/verini-text.

150. Ibid.

151. "The Tunnels of Gaza," http://ngm.nationalgeographic.com/2012/12/gaza-tunnels
/pellegrin-photography#/02-gazan-student-tunnel-worker-670.jpg.

152. Levitt and Jacobsen, *Money Trail,* 67.

153. Hugh Naylor, "Anger in Gaza over New Fees and Taxes," *The National* 4, no.
176 (October 9, 2011): 1.

154. Verini, "Gaza Tunnels."

155. Isabel Kershner, "As Gaza Tunnels Closed, Hamas Lost Cash, Israeli Official
Says," January 30, 2014, http://www.nytimes.com/2014/01/31/world/middleeast/
hamas-cash-flow.html.

156. Ibid.

157. David Sanger and Thom Shanker, "For Israel, Gaza Conflict Is Test for an Iran
Confrontation," *New York Times,* November 22, 2012, http://www.nytimes
.com/2012/11/23/world/middleeast/for-israel-gaza-conflict-a-practice-run-for-a-
possible-iran-confrontation.html?_r=0.

158. Isabel Kershner and Rick Gladstone, "Israel Destroys Hamas Prime Minister's
Office," *New York Times,* November 16, 2012, http://www.nytimes.com/2012/
11/17/world/middleeast/israel-gaza-assault.html?pagewanted=all.

159. Yousri Mohamed and Dan Williams, "Egypt Seizes Anti-tank, Anti-aircraft
Rockets in Sinai," January 4, 2013, http://www.reuters.com/article/2013/01/04/
us-egypt-sinai-weapons-idUSBRE9030HU20130104.

160. U.S. State Department, "State Sponsors of Terrorism," http://www.state.gov/j/ct/
list/c14151.htm.

161. Robert I. Rotberg, *Corruption, Global Security and World Order* (Washington, DC: Brookings Institution Press, 2009); Rotberg, *When States Fail: Causes
and Consequences* (Princeton, NJ: Princeton University Press, 2003); Michael
Ignatieff, "State Failure and Nation-Building," in *Humanitarian Intervention,* ed.
J. L. Holzgrefe and Robert O. Keohane (Cambridge: Cambridge University Press,
2003), 299–321; Tatah Mentan, *Dilemmas of Weak States: Africa and Transnational Terrorism in the Twenty-First Century* (Aldershot, UK: Ashgate, 2004).
Stewart M. Patrick challenges this concept of the centrality of weak states in his
work *Weak Links: Fragile States, Global Threats, and International Security* (New
York: Oxford University Press, 2011).

162. Kenneth J. Menkhaus, "Somalia and Somaliland," in *Battling Terrorism in the
Horn of Africa,* ed. Robert I. Rotberg (Cambridge, MA: World Peace Foundation,
2005), 45.

163. Warren Richey, "Zachary Chesser and Paul Rockwood: Latest US Citizens Linked
to al-Awlaki," July 22, 2010, http://www.csmonitor.com/USA/Justice/2010/0722/
Zachary-Chesser-and-Paul-Rockwood-latest-US-citizens-linked-to-al-Awlaki.

164. "Mapping   Displaced   People   around   the   World,"   http://education
.nationalgeographic.com/education/media/mapping-displaced-people-around-
the-world/?ar_a=1.

165. Susan Strange, *The Retreat of the State: The Diffusion of Power in the World
Economy* (Cambridge: Cambridge University Press, 1996).

166. Foucault, *Discipline and Punish*.
167. Cirnio et al., "Latin American Security Challenges," 25.
168. Ibid.
169. See Kees Koonings and Dirk Kruijt, *Megacities: The Politics of Urban Exclusion and Violence in the Global South* (London: Zed Books, 2009).

PART II

THE DIVERSE BUSINESSES OF TERRORISM

5

The Business of Terrorism and Criminal Financing of Terrorism

Osama bin Laden's confiscated documents revealed that he was considering an increased use of kidnapping to generate money to fund his organization. With a decline in donor contributions amid efforts by Western powers to stop funds from ideological supporters reaching al-Qaeda, Bin Laden needed to generate more cash. As is increasingly common, he turned to traditional crime to fund terrorism – kidnapping. The reason that Osama favored this form of crime was not only its feasibility but its low risk and long-term use by terrorists as a funding source. Osama analyzed the success of al-Qaeda affiliates in North Africa (AQIM), Yemen (AQAP), and Iraq, who actively used kidnapping as a revenue generator. Some individual ransoms in North Africa have been as large as $2 million, and, since 2008, according to French experts, AQIM has gained $80 million through its kidnapping rackets.[1] Government and multinational employees have sometimes been ransomed, but really significant profits were achieved by kidnapping individuals working for corporations, where the ransoms received were frequently greater. Kidnapping is now believed to be AQIM's largest revenue source and enhances its ability to conduct operations.[2]

It is hardly surprising that bin Laden reasoned like a businessman. His family owned one of the largest businesses of the Middle East. He grew up in a family of businesspeople, not a hereditary elite. His mother was the daughter of a Syrian trader.[3]

Terrorism as Business

The business analysis of Osama bin Laden resembles that of a legitimate business executive analyzing his global operations. It reveals that major terrorist groups now mirror the legitimate world by analyzing diverse revenue streams, new profit lines, and successes from one region that can be replicated in others.

The major difference is that the new product line – kidnapping – was being promulgated by violent nonstate actors, who chose to enhance their funding through violent criminal means. It also is an especially effective fund-raising source in a traditional society, where family ties are particularly close.

There is, increasingly, a business component of terrorism that is supported by crime[4] and is facilitated by corruption. This business extends beyond terrorist groups supporting franchises and brands and providing venture capital.[5] Terrorism's reliance on the two Cs (corruption and crime) further decimates countries already wracked by terrorism. Adding these two dimensions to the destructive model of terrorism is key. As one captured Taliban underscored, "Whether if it is by opium or by shooting, this is our common goal [to harm all infidels as part of jihad]."[6] This concept of harm causation through criminal activity has been seen not only among Islamic terrorist groups but was given as a justification for the drug trade in Peru decades ago. Selling drugs is part of a strategy to do harm as well as to garner large profits for the organization. This crime, like kidnapping, has a dual utility. Kidnapping by removing a loved one also reduces resistance to terrorists in a community consumed with the loss of a member. This secondary function sets apart terrorist participation in crime from that initiated by ordinary criminals.

Terrorism and Corruption

The need for terrorist groups to regularly use corruption recalls the latter's centrality to organized crime. Both are often operating in the illicit economy, requiring the collusion and cooptation of government officials generally and law enforcement in particular. But the consequences of this corruption are grave, for society but also for the terrorist group. Many terrorist groups seek to overthrow unjust societies or create a purer religious order, but their corruption of existing societies violates their core mission. The business of terrorism has consequences that transcend the mere generation of operational funds.

Despite the attention given to terrorist financing, too little attention has been paid to the business of terrorism.[7] Even though organized crime has been addressed as a "continuing criminal enterprise" that depends on corruption to survive,[8] this same approach has not often been applied to politicized nonstate actors. In contrast to studies of the business services and logic of organized crime,[9] very few analyses have been done of the business side of terrorist organizations. Terrorist analyses have generally focused on individual actors, group dynamics, or the general issue of terrorist financing of a specific group rather than understanding that terrorists in different contexts can function like businessmen. The seizures of files and computer discs from the FARC, Turkish Hezbollah and PKK, the IRA, the Haqqani Network, and al-Qaeda in Afghanistan have given a window into the financial operations of these terrorist groups – their organizations' revenues and expenditures.[10] But these are the exceptions rather than the rule. Without such focus on the business of terrorism, it is hard to understand the modus operandi of these groups or to develop strategies to counter their support activities.

Business Strategies of Terrorists

Because the primary concern of terrorist groups is political rather than criminal, they often approach criminal activity and corruption rationally. This chapter, instead of providing a shopping list of crimes in which terrorists participate, focuses on their business strategies. It dissects their approach to product mix, professional services, cost-benefit analyses, tax strategies, supply chains, market dominance, strategic alliances, competitive advantage, targets of opportunity, and innovation and use of technology. It examines the ways they obtain access to the best human capital through their global networks. The following two chapters examine more specifically the particular funding sources of terrorists and hybrid organizations, such as the narcotics trade, and underpoliced areas of criminal activity, where terrorists have flocked because of the low risks. Chapter 8 examines the business of the weapons of mass destruction trade and its distinct financial features.

Terrorists, Crime, and Corruption

Motivations for Terrorist Involvement in Crime

Terrorists engage in crime for several reasons. Their purposes are quite different from those of criminals. For organized criminals, the main focus is making money through illicit activity. In contrast, for terrorists, these acts are a means of achieving their political objectives as well. But terrorists can also degenerate into primarily criminal actors, as they become accustomed to committing crime and engaging in corrupt activities, as has become the case with the IRA, ASG, and, increasingly, the FARC.[11]

Terrorists are often rational criminals. Like legitimate businesspeople, they choose activities that can ensure continued funding and in which they have the potential of success.[12] Illustrative of this is the following example drawn from the IRA. Robberies committed in Ireland, Northern Ireland, and other parts of Great Britain have long been used by the IRA to sustain their organization, as the money was often stored locally and used for regional operations.[13] This was the major funding source of the Provisional IRA until they acquired financial analysts and money laundering specialists.[14] They understood that bank robberies were not the most successful fund-raising vehicle, as there were collateral costs. Specialists helped them understand that a bank robbery that netted £92,000 might not be as profitable as it seemed, because the risks of capture were great and the subsequent costs for the group were significant. For example, family members of individuals captured in botched robberies had to be supported for extended periods, which could undermine the profitability of this criminal act. Instead, a pub purchased for £7,000 was worth £200,000 a few years later and delivered a steady income not only through the sale of alcohol but through the placement of slot machines on its premises.[15] Therefore, the terrorists had learned the lesson of many real estate investors in Ireland before the crash: that real estate was the place to be for appreciation and income.

Wiretaps on the PKK by European law enforcement provide evidence of additional rational thinking. When Western European governments crack down on PKK criminal activity, wiretaps on members of this terrorist organization reveal their need to increase extortion from the diaspora business community to compensate for the revenue losses resulting from the crackdowns.[16]

A similar example of strategic thinking is evident from Dawood Ibrahim, the crime boss behind the 1993 Mumbai attacks. In 1992, India's trade liberalization policies changed the economics of the gold and silver market and made smuggling less lucrative.[17] To make up for the losses, Ibrahim sought to diversify his business lines, first taking on narcotics and arms trafficking, then moving his racketeering into the entertainment business. This afforded Ibrahim the double benefit of raising his social status and also enabling him to serve as a loan shark for dozens of producers who desperately needed his funds. Furthermore, his gang D-Company's power increased dramatically as it began to control more facets of the film production process, culminating with film piracy.[18]

Economic analyses of terrorists have drawn strong parallels with the legitimate business world, describing terrorist organizations as hierarchies, franchises, brand strategists, and venture capitalists.[19] This book concurs with Zelinsky's and Shubik's conclusion[20] that terrorists follow these business models but chooses to classify or organize terrorist business in a different fashion. The following analysis will focus instead on the way terrorists *maximize their advantages in different environments,* to sustain their business.

Terrorists Maximizing Business Advantage

Different terrorist groups have distinct funding strategies, often reflecting the culture, traditions, and geographical location of the group and the capacity of the members. Their choice of crime is determined not only by its profitability and ease of entry but also by the extent of competition in this sphere of criminal activity and the costs of corruption.[21] Yet determinations of risk of detection and asset loss are also associated with the calculations of the more sophisticated criminal terrorists. Terrorists exploit their strategic advantages, just as do legitimate people. Understanding the position of a terrorist group within this financing framework is key to determining their sustainability and deriving strategies to deprive them of revenues.

Terrorists use crime as a means to generate needed revenues, to obtain logistical support, and use criminal channels to transfer funds. Criminals provide operational tools, such as falsified documents, new identities, and transit across borders.[22] They can pay off officials, thereby providing terrorists and their commodities safe passage across borders. The criminal support structures can include either petty criminals or developed crime groups, such as the Camorra in Naples,[23] complemented by the services of facilitators from the legitimate world, such as bankers, lawyers, and corporations that intentionally or inadvertently assist in the perpetration of terrorism.[24] Corrupt military personnel can serve as suppliers of weapons to criminal and terrorist groups.[25] There are also facilitators that serve the criminal world, especially drug traffickers and those moving dual-use materials, as discussed more in Chapters 6 and 8.[26] Terrorists also recruit criminals into their organizations to take advantage of their criminal skills.[27]

Terrorists increasingly use crime to fund their activities, having lost much of the state-sponsored funding of the past. In addition, recent crackdowns on distributions from charities and on bank transfers to terrorist organizations have forced terrorists to change and diversify their financing, such as was the Osama Bin Laden experience. Crime has become a vehicle of choice, because if properly managed, it provides a steady stream of funding that is essential for the maintenance of the "terrorist business" and ensures that terrorists stay engaged.[28] It may also allow expansion into new territory needed by the terrorists.[29] Some criminal activity of terrorists exists solely in the criminal arena, but many forms of illicit activity prey off or interact with the legitimate economy.[30]

The Costs of Terrorism

Although many studies claim that terrorist attacks cost relatively little money, the ongoing costs of maintaining and supplying an organization are much greater than these attack figures suggest. Funds can sometimes not be sufficient for desired objectives. As Ramzi ben Yousef explained to an FBI agent after the first World Trade Center attack on why the building still stood, "They wouldn't be if I had enough money and explosives."[31]

Osama Bin Laden became strapped for funds, not only because of a decline in support from donors, but because his costs were high. The development of terrorists ready to engage in an attack is a long process, from recruitment through training, and often including payments to family members for those killed in a suicide attack.[32] Feeding, arming, and providing the high level technical capacity to run a terrorist organization is not cheap. Paying off officials can prove expensive. An analysis of counterterrorist threat finance points out these other costs of maintaining a terrorist organization: travel, communications, purchase of weapons and material, maintenance of safe houses and safe havens, payment of bribes, transport and purchase of vehicles, purchasing forged identification and travel documents, intelligence gathering, and media time and advertising are significant.[33]

For example, the report on terrorist financing of the U.S. 9/11 Commission reported that al-Qaeda spent approximately $30 million annually prior to the attack on "funding operations, maintaining its training and military apparatus, contributing to the Taliban and their high-level officials, and sporadically contributing to related terrorist organizations."[34] The operations of Hamas were estimated to cost $30 million to $90 million annually.[35]

Terrorists' Criminal Businesses: Resembling the Legitimate Business Economy

Older terrorist groups, and those with less educated membership, have a different criminal profile from those of the Islamic and jihad groups who are at the forefront of technology. The IRA was on the verge of becoming more technical just before its extinction, as Ireland became more prosperous.[36] Ireland became a technology center, but its criminal group did not make that transition. But throughout its existence, its support came primarily from traditional crimes.

The PKK, like legitimate Turkish businessmen, take advantage of their strategic geographic location along trade routes. The PKK, unlike legitimate commerce, facilitates illicit trade from East to West, primarily drugs, arms, and people, and capitalizes on its location on a transit route to extract revenues from smugglers by neutralizing any official border controls through corruption.[37] It relies on diaspora communities to facilitate its criminal business and product delivery in Western Europe.[38] Therefore, PKK financing mirrors the strength of the legitimate Turkish economy as a trade hub linking East and West.[39] As this shows, terrorist groups' business practices often resemble the trade and business patterns of their host countries.

Terrorists and Their Need for Capital

Obtaining, maintaining, and expanding access to funding, therefore, are some of the core concerns for terrorist groups. Just like any business, without the capital needed to operate, they cannot continue to maintain and train personnel, obtain weapons, and launch attacks. Hezbollah is an example of a terrorist organization that has successfully diversified. It generates revenue from school fees, stationery shops and bookstores, farms, fisheries, and bakeries. It has also profited extensively through its investment in Lebanese real estate markets. It shows an entrepreneurial spirit as "Hezbollah will advertise certain projects and call on interested parties to join them in a financial partnership. These deals usually work on a percentage basis: the partner receives a share of the profits while Hezbollah reinvests its own percentage into the project or into another charitable service."[40]

Terrorist groups may also depend on funds to enjoy safe havens. This is true in tribal societies, where the willingness to shelter terrorists depended on payments to the chief. "In Yemen, Sheik Faisal Aburas of the northern governorate of al-Jawf claims to know of several occasions where terrorists paid tribal leaders to ensure their protection: 'If a terrorist comes to my area, the thing that binds me to him is not ideology. It's [financial] need.'"[41]

As the cost of operations has also increased for terrorists, as for other businesses, in the last two decades, they have required greater financial savvy to survive. Terror groups that have failed "to cross the economic divide between hand-to-mouth existence and sound economic planning" have not survived. "In contrast, the groups that have survived have diversified their income sources and learned the trick of money laundering."[42]

Product Mix

Almost every known form of criminal activity has been used to fund terrorism. The choice of criminal activity reflects the geographic location of the group, its human capacity, and the profitability of the crime. Crimes are selected based on the ability to evade detection, access corrupt officials, and obtain profits.

Terrorists and other political nonstate actors, such as insurgents, finance their activity through criminal activity in both the licit and illicit economies. They prey on ordinary citizens as well as smaller and larger businesses through extortion and kidnapping. They commit fraud against legitimate financial institutions through credit card abuse and other financial manipulation of markets.[43] They also engage in specifically illicit activity as people smuggling, drugs and arms trafficking, and illicit trade in natural resources, types of criminal activity characterized by skyrocketing growth and significant demand.

Therefore, terrorists and insurgents have exploited their dirty entanglements with criminals to benefit from what the United Nations has defined as the three most lucrative forms of transnational crime.[44] Drug, arms, and human trafficking have growth rates that far exceed those of even the most highly profitable legitimate corporations. In the late 1990s, the United Nations World Drug Report estimated that the international drug business represented 7 percent of world trade, equal to the trade in steel and textiles.[45] But the contribution of the narcotics trade to the illicit economy is now even greater.[46] Many terrorist groups benefit from this trade, as discussed more in Chapter 6.

Human Smuggling and Trafficking

Human smuggling and trafficking has also grown exponentially, and modest estimates place its earnings at $7 billion to $34 billion annually.[47] Even though terrorism generates a much smaller percentage of profit from trade in people than in narcotics, it is part of the funding mix for diverse terrorist groups and the highly violent crime groups of Mexico and Central America.[48]

Pakistani terrorists buy children to serve as suicide bombers,[49] and Maoist insurgents in Nepal have exploited the long-standing trade of young girls taken from their country to the brothels of India to finance their activities.[50] Rebels in Africa trade in children to fund their conflicts and obtain child soldiers.[51] Evidence suggests that the LTTE smuggled Sri Lankans to finance their activities.[52] Cells of the Ulster Volunteer Force of Northern Ireland received narcotics as payment from Snakeheads in support of their smuggling networks.[53] German authorities in 2006 arrested an Iraqi and a Syrian who smuggled individuals from their home and were suspected of having links with the Ansar al-Islam terrorist network.[54]

Arms Trade

With the end of the Cold War and the rise of regional conflicts worldwide, there has also been a great demand for arms.[55] Criminals and military personnel from the former USSR, sometimes defined as "war criminals," such as Victor Bout, met the demands of guerillas, insurgents, and terrorists for arms, often supplied by the arsenals of the former Soviet Union.[56] Terrorist groups from the Middle East, Latin America, and Africa have purchased weapons that they acquired from the collapsing socialist states of Eastern Europe and the former Soviet Union.[57]

The post–Cold War era has also turned the corrupt Cambodian military into a major source of weapons that were acquired during its long-term conflict. The problem is not so much of small-scale theft by Cambodian military personnel as "the well-organized diversion of large numbers of military weapons to arms dealers and brokers. These transactions required the complicity of senior Cambodian government officials and military officers, and in some cases brokers have been able to deal directly with government ministries."[58] The buyers include the LTTE, Burmese ethnic militias, and armed groups from northeast India and Indonesia. The groups identified in the movement of these arms out of Cambodia through Thailand include corrupt officials, including persons from the military, police, and other branches of government; arms brokers; terrorism operatives; and criminal gangs.[59]

Elsewhere in Asia, ASG in the Philippines has developed an active trade in weapons at affordable prices in the southern region of Mindanao. It acts

> as an intermediary for the regional trafficking of Philippine-source weaponry. An established maritime tradition, combined with the lack of active coastal surveillance around Mindanao . . . has ensured that Abu Sayyaf smugglers can move arms caches quickly with relatively little risk of interdiction.[60]

Other Crimes

Apart from these high-profit and large-scale sources of criminal activity, terrorists and insurgents participate in a diverse range of criminal actions, from those used by earlier generations of terrorists and guerillas, such as kidnapping, extortion, and bank robbery,[61] also ranging up to those at the forefront of technology, such as credit crime and Internet fraud. Trade in materials, such as coltran, needed by computer and cell phone technology also figures significantly in the mix.[62] The traditional crimes have the greatest range of participation by diverse terrorist groups.

There are many other forms of illicit activity, discussed in greater depth in other chapters, that have become the lifeblood for terrorism, including art smuggling, cross-border smuggling of goods, trade in counterfeit and diverted goods, and piracy on the seas off the coast of Somalia and in Southeast Asia.[63] Illicit trade in natural resources, oil, gold, and other commodities also provides funding.[64] Commodities such as gold and diamonds are particularly sought because they have great inherent value and limited weight. Some activities, such as people smuggling and trafficking, are "dual use": they both generate money and provide terrorist groups the ability to move operatives. Piracy can generate money through extortion but can yield needed weapons and equipment if the proper transport ships are targeted. With such diversity, terrorists have developed a full product line that ranges from the most basic to the most sophisticated crimes.

Skills and Crime Selection

Many of the criminal activities conducted by terrorists, like those of traditional organized crime, require little or no expertise. For example, kidnapping, extortion, armed robbery, and the commission of petty crimes such as pickpocketing and purse snatching are often the entry-level crimes of organized crime because they may require force but limited skill.[65] Terrorists, like criminals, take time to train their members to become good pickpockets, to plan a bank robbery, or to determine levels of payments to be extorted from businesses. But these skill sets are less than those needed by terrorist groups at the forefront of Internet crime or cybercrime.

Exploiting Comparative Advantage

Terrorist exploitation of natural resources is illustrative of the real estate principle of "location, location, location." They take advantage of their critical location next to a valuable commodity, which provides them targets of opportunity. Al-Qaeda, as previously discussed in Chapter 1, was involved in the diamond trade, particularly in Sierra Leone, Liberia, and Tanzania.[66] The FARC and the Ejército de Liberación Nacional (National Liberation Army, or ELN) use their territorial control in different regions of Colombia to extort money and to lead attacks against energy infrastructure,[67] such as was seen for Algeria in the book's introduction. This has been a problem for more than a decade, because seized FARC records of the early 2000s have calculated that 1 percent of FARC funding came from the theft of hydrocarbons.[68]

Terrorist and insurgent groups are also contributing to the decimation of some of the largest and most sought after animals in the world – elephants and rhinoceroses. The involvement of these violent groups in illicit trade differs from smuggling in the past, as they are leading to irreversible damage in ecosystems. As an in-depth *New York Times* investigation of poaching in Africa revealed, blood diamonds and valuable minerals are being replaced by the ivory trade as a revenue generator. Rhinoceros horns are also part of this illicit market.[69] The tragedy of this is that this trade requires the death of these rare animals, rather than just the mining of an inanimate object:

Some of Africa's most notorious armed groups, including the Lord's Resistance Army, the Shabab and Darfur's janjaweed, are hunting down elephants and using the tusks to buy weapons and sustain their mayhem. Organized crime syndicates are linking up with them to move the ivory around the world, exploiting turbulent states, porous borders and corrupt officials from sub-Saharan Africa to China, law enforcement officials say.[70]

Facilitating this trade are African armies in the Congo, Uganda, and southern Sudan. Some of these armies receive American training assistance.[71] As has been shown throughout the book, the illicit trade in fragile states does not exist in isolation but is supported by links to the developed world.

Yet Africa is not the only continent in which natural resources fund terrorism. In Afghanistan, illicit and large-scale deforestation helps fund the Taliban.[72] This diversification indicates that they do not lose any funding opportunity.

Revenue Generation and the Licit Economy

Yet not all revenue generation is tied to the illicit economy. Trade of legitimate goods can be exploited in illegitimate ways. Trade-based money laundering allows transfer of funds for terrorist organizations through over- and under-invoicing of goods.[73] For example, Hamas moved large amounts of textiles through Panama, more than needed for the domestic Panamanian market, to transfer resources for its activities in Central America.[74] Lebanese Hezbollah used cars as "stored value" objects to move money across continents,[75] often from the United States to Africa.

Terrorists adapt their targets to their environment to avoid detection and ensure success. Natural resources are exploited in the absence of other revenue generators. In the target-rich environments of urban areas, terrorists operate differently. They use petty crime to fund their activities in countries where law enforcement does not prioritize low-level crime. They target immigrant communities in the developed world, where local police without language capacity cannot penetrate. They operate like businesspeople, analyzing their strategic advantages and choosing the crimes with which they can enhance profit and reduce risk.

Bread-and-Butter Crimes

The traditional criminal activity of terrorist groups still provides core funding. As is seen in the following analysis, even terrorists who use scams and the Internet to finance their organizations do not appear to abandon the traditional criminal ways of raising money – robbery, extortion, and kidnapping.[76] Groups such as the FARC and the Taliban, infamous for their role in the drug trade, rely heavily on these traditional forms of crime to maintain their organizations. According to confiscated records, FARC extortion yields almost as much revenue as the drug trade.[77] As discussed subsequently, extortion can be an extremely powerful tool when the terrorist group controls territory.

In Afghanistan, terrorist groups received large flows of money through their extortion of American contractors. The extortion money paid to the Taliban, the Haqqani network, and local warlords (to allow the transit of American and allied equipment and to fund development projects) had the obverse of the desired effect.[78] Instead of preventing the reemergence of the Taliban and al-Qaeda, these large payments to "grease the wheels" and respond to extortionate demands strengthened the hand of these groups, which were initially the target of the allied intervention. Moreover, these payments boosted the newer Haqqani, which combined criminal and terrorist activity within a single network. It is also created a moral hazard, as the extortion of assistance for road construction funded terrorism.[79]

Robberies

Terrorists have used robberies for well over a century to fund their cause. Stalin engaged in bank robbery in the prerevolutionary period. Jewish terrorist groups, before the establishment of the state of Israel, robbed banks to fund their movement.[80] The utility of robberies has not diminished for many contemporary terrorist groups. They have supported the ETA, the IRA, the PKK, Moroccan terrorist groups, and even jihadist groups operating within the United States. In Turkey, robberies helped fund the Turkish People's Liberation Front.[81]

Within Europe, the ETA in northern Spain generated significant revenues through robberies. From 1967 to 1977, the ETA raised $1 million from bank robberies alone. In 1978, the ETA perpetrated about fifty bank robberies, netting the terrorist organization approximately $4 million.[82] Al-Qaeda-inspired cells also use robberies in Europe. "One cell in France netted about €1 million when a member whose job was to restock ATMs enacted robberies on several."[83]

Robberies are used in North Africa to generate funds for terrorism. A 2005 report by the Moroccan Direction Générale de Surveillance du Territoire (General Directorate of Territorial Surveillance) revealed that bank robberies were carried out to finance terrorist operations.[84]

International success in cutting off donations to terrorists in Indonesia has resulted in an increase in bank robberies since 2010. The leading Indonesian terrorist organization Mujahidin Indonesia Timur (Mujahidin of Eastern Indonesia) has robbed banks, "gold shops, mobile phone shops, post offices, money changers, internet cafes, grocery stores, and construction material shops."[85] In the first six months of 2013, $180,000 was raised from bank robbery.[86] The role of gold shop robberies in financing the Bali bombing was discussed in Chapter 1. This criminal activity can, however, undermine support for the terrorist group and disrupt its efforts to expand its base.[87]

In the United States, this traditional form of terrorist financing coexists with the most advanced forms of technology. On the West Coast of the United States in the early 2000s, "four men allegedly plotted to wage a jihad against some 20 targets in Southern California, including National Guard facilities, the Israeli Consulate, and several synagogues."[88] One of the perpetrators, an American prison recruit for *jihad*, explained that the cell had robbed gas stations because oil is a political symbol.[89] Therefore, even terrorist criminal activity such as low-level robbery can have political as well as financial utility. This is a different view than that of a professional criminal, Willy Sutton, who is alleged to have said that he robbed banks because that was where the money was. This is another illustration of the dual uses of criminal activity perpetrated by terrorists.

Robberies are also used by right-wing groups in the United States to fund their terrorist acts. Two domestic terrorist organizations, the Aryan Republic Army and the Phineas Priests, committed the largest number of terrorist-related robberies in the United States. On the basis of data from criminal prosecutions, they were together responsible for thirteen robberies.[90]

Kidnapping

Kidnapping for ransom knows no geographical limitations. Terrorist groups have kidnapped people in Europe, Latin America, Africa, Southeast Asia, the Middle East, and the former Soviet Union.[91] Through this criminal act, terrorists extort money from states, rich individuals, and corporations, who seek to have family members and employees returned. The Financial Action Task Force suggests that kidnapping by terrorists differs from that undertaken by criminals. Terrorists often espouse a political position before focusing on the financial benefits. On the basis of financial success, terrorist groups may choose to target particular nations.[92]

Kidnapping spreads fear within communities. It also undermines the societies' social solidarity, as members focus on protecting their own immediate relatives. They often then lack the capacity to mobilize to address larger issues.

Historically, kidnapping was used to great advantage by the now extinct group the Red Brigade in Italy, where family ties are extremely strong. The frequency of these kidnappings was so great in the 1970s and 1980s that members of the Italian financial elite sent family members into residence abroad to ensure their safety. Yet the Red Brigade's kidnapping extended to the political elite, as such prominent figures as Aldo Moro, the president of the Christian Democratic Party, the leading political party at the time, was kidnapped in 1978. Prior to this act, there were no laws against kidnapping for terrorist purposes.[93]

At the same time, kidnapping was used elsewhere in Europe to generate revenues. The IRA, before its transition to fraud and other offenses as major funding sources, relied heavily on kidnapping.[94] The Spanish ETA, a group with a traditional fund-raising profile, also used kidnapping to generate revenues.[95]

The Turkish terrorist group PKK, an early user of kidnapping, employed this crime as a revenue source but also as a tactical tool to intimidate opponents.[96]

Kidnapping has also been used in Latin America. The Frente Farabundo Martí para la Liberación Nacional (FMLN) in El Salvador in the 1970s built up a multi-million-dollar treasury through bank robberies and "kidnapping local oligarchs, diplomats and foreign executives for ransom."[97] Kidnapping was also frequent in Colombia. Between 1981 and 2003, the guerilla and terrorist groups FARC, ELN, and smaller groups kidnapped more than thirty-one thousand people. Between 1996 and 2002, there were an average of 2,704 cases annually, with one region averaging more than fifty kidnappings per one hundred thousand annually. The FARC and the ELN, the two major terrorist groups, together represented 47 percent of the kidnappings, with the FARC responsible for slightly more than the ELN.[98] In 1998 alone, the FARC was estimated to have derived 265.5 billion pesos, or $236 million, from kidnappings.[99] As in Italy, Colombian families of the commercial elite were particularly targeted. There was hardly a wealthy industrial family in this period that escaped the fate of a member being kidnapped, with one industrialist family having seven members taken hostage.

Kidnapping declined as a tool of revenue raising in the mid-1990s but reemerged as a major revenue source again later in the decade.[100] Between 1996 and 2007, in Columbia, there were around 24,000 victims of kidnapping, and 1,269 were killed, approximately 5 percent of the total. In this period, the FARC was responsible for 6,772, or 28 percent, of the kidnappings; the ELN for 5,389, or 22 percent; and common criminals for approximately 14 percent, whereas over one-fifth of kidnappings were committed by unidentified individuals. Therefore, terrorists were identified as the perpetrators in over half the cases. Kidnapping reached its zenith in 2000, with 3,211 cases. As the state began to reassert its authority, the number of kidnappings dropped to 1,652 in 2006 and to fewer than 1,000 in 2007.[101]

The FARC did not hesitate to kidnap individuals associated with the government, such as diverse members of the family of the minister of education, and technical employees of public enterprises. One of the most well-known victims was Ingrid Betancourt, a courageous member of parliament who denounced terrorism in Colombia and was kidnapped.[102] She was held for six and a half years by the FARC, in a region under their control, until she was liberated in a Colombian governmental raid in 2008. Once married into a prominent French family, her photo hung over the front of the Paris City Hall for many years, until her liberation.

Betancourt's period of confinement was especially long, but lengthy confinements that often exceeded a year enhanced the ability of terrorists to extract payments. By atomizing victimized families, they could prevent a negotiating bloc of victims against the terrorists. By this profit-maximizing strategy, approximately 30 percent of the ransoms paid exceeded a billion pesos, or approximately $500,000. Some multinational companies paid sums in excess of $2 million for return of their employees.[103] Killing of the hostage did not eliminate the possibility of securing funds. Family members, once notified of a loved one's death, might be extorted for a supplementary sum for the return of the body.

Other conflict regions have provided fertile ground for terrorist kidnappers. In Iraq and Afghanistan, many employees of multinational corporations have been kidnapped by terrorists and insurgents.[104] In Iraq, in 2005, kidnapping for ransom had "ballooned into a major industry, with up to 10 abductions a day. Among those targeted: politicians, professors, foreigners, and housewives. Those with political value may find they've been sold to militants."[105]

The ASG in the conflict region of the southern Philippines have also long used kidnapping to raise "funds for operational and logistical purposes."[106] "Since 1998, however, abductions have increasingly been aimed at generating money for its own sake. The practice has been encouraged by the general willingness of the victims' families to pay ransoms, as well as their reticence to involve the authorities or seek judicial redress, even in the event that the hostage takers are subsequently apprehended."[107] The ASG have repeatedly kidnapped foreign tourists and aid workers.[108] The ASG in 2000 abducted fifty schoolchildren and teachers as well as a Roman Catholic priest, who was subsequently killed. This was the largest-scale abduction and turned the ASG into a "kidnap-for-ransom business."[109] The next month, the ASG operated outside its base in the southern Philippines, kidnapping twenty-one people, including ten foreign tourists from the Malaysian island of Sipadan. They eventually released the hostages, but only after a ransom estimated at between $16 million and $25 million was paid.[110] The money from the Sipadan operation allowed the ASG to buy the loyalty of poor villagers and acquire weapons and logistical support. "More to the point, it proved that 'crime paid' both monetarily and in terms of institutional bargaining power, and ensured that kidnapping would remain the ASG's favored means of financial procurement."[111]

The ASG is not the only group in a conflict region in southern Asia to rely on kidnapping to support its activities. The Tamil Tigers in South Asia have also used kidnapping to realize their financial objectives, but they have not done this on the scale of the ASG in the Philippines.[112]

Kidnapping is also used to generate funds in Russia and Africa. In Russia, the Chechens have used kidnapping as both a revenue source and a means of retaliating and intimidating the enemy. This is not a new criminal activity for the Chechens, as already in the nineteenth century they had kidnapped a leading member of Georgia's nobility and his family and held them for ransom.[113] The more recent victims of these kidnappings have been Russian soldiers as well as members of rival groups within Chechnya. The problem was so common that Russian legislation on human trafficking was considered by the National Security Committee of the Duma. Human trafficking in kidnapping victims in the North Caucasus was seen as a national security threat.[114]

Kidnapping is used by terrorist groups in both North and East Africa, either on its own or in conjunction with piracy. The Salafist Group for Prayer and Combat in Algeria tried to collect $2.2 million from the Algerian government to release some dozen Western tourists that they had kidnapped in 2003.[115] Furthermore, the al-Qaeda affiliate known as AQIM[116] is reported to have derived up to 80 percent of its revenues from kidnapping and ransom.[117] AQIM kidnaps

> foreign tourists and workers in the Sahel, in what resembles a very efficient "supply chain," whereby local criminals extract profits by kidnapping foreigners and selling them to the terrorists. Indeed, AQIM's activities in the Sahel are best described as a loose network of Islamist terrorists and local criminals, who profit from the smuggling and kidnapping trade.[118]

Extortion

The crime of extortion is a financial staple of terrorist groups throughout the world, but it is very different from the previously discussed offenses – robbery and kidnapping. Those crimes are exceptional events with high-value targets, whereas the value of extortion is the regularity and frequency of payment. This technique of terrorist fund-raising recalls that of organized crime in Sicily, which is able to extort local businesses in communities under its control to fund its criminal organizations.[119] Therefore, it is a form of revenue generation based on control of territory, a basic principle of classic organized crime. It also recalls the principles of legitimate business, which seeks to achieve territorial or market dominance in a particular sector. Unfortunately, for the victims of extortion, this dominance is achieved through violence or threats of violence.

Yet, as was discussed in the previous chapter, diaspora communities of Irish, Turks, Lebanese, Sri Lankans, and many others have been extorted by terrorist organizations of their home communities. This phenomenon existed before globalization, as discussed in reference to the Irish, but with the globalization of business, the exploitation of diaspora communities by terrorist groups has proliferated. Terrorists have become "violent entrepreneurs"[120] on a global scale because they can enforce retaliation overseas and against relatives at home.

Middle Eastern businessmen made payments to al-Qaeda to avoid attacks on their interests, and the ASG in the Philippines collects taxes from Filipino residents and businesses.[121] Yet these levels of extortion pale in comparison to the documented sums collected by Colombian terrorist organizations.

Within Latin America, it is the FARC that benefits most from extortion. In 1998, Colombian authorities estimated that the various illegal organizations of different political persuasions derived 620 billion pesos ($551 million) from the drug trade and 350 billion pesos ($311 million) from extortion.[122] At this time, extortion represented less than one-quarter of the FARC's total revenues, as many other crimes, such as kidnapping, contributed critical components of their working capital. But data seized from the FARC in 2003 by the Colombian military indicated that extortion had become a much more important component of FARC income. At that time, the FARC derived 45 percent of their income from the drug trade and 42 percent from extortion, and only 7 percent from kidnapping. Their extortion money came from large-scale cattle ranchers and from businesses that operated in territories under FARC control.[123] This shows how the business of extortion is most successful when it is tied to the control of territory, and businesses in an organization's region become targets of opportunity.

The previous data reveal that the concept of the narco-terrorist, that is, defining terrorist groups as drug traffickers, is too narrowly focused. This is further explored in Chapter 6, devoted to the drug trade. Instead, terrorist drug organizations run diversified criminal businesses, shifting their revenue base and their product line to their advantage.

The PKK relies much more on extortion than it does on kidnapping. It profits through this activity both in Western Europe and in Turkey. It smuggles people to Europe and then extorts money from those for whom they have found jobs. They then charge a compulsory "membership fee."[124] Extortion PKK-style is referred to in less sinister terms as a "revolutionary tax" or "voluntary contribution." In any case, by most accounts, the majority of extortion victims avoid making formal complaints because of the obvious consequences.

Terrorist groups in regions through which drugs transit can make extensive profits by extorting fees for safe passage of their commodity. These fees are collected by the PKK, the Taliban, and AQIM in North Africa, as Chapter 6 discusses.

Innovation and Use of Information Technology

The previous staples of terrorist funding target particular victims, whereas the more recent crimes of terrorist groups have less personal victimization. Relying heavily on the new technology, real individuals suffer through credit card fraud, identity theft, and financial fraud committed through the Internet. But in this new criminality, the terrorists do not have direct contact with their victims. Rarely are the victims or victimized corporations aware that their victimizers are terrorists rather than transnational criminals.

Crimes of the new high-tech economy are an important and evolving part of the product mix of terrorists, as seen in Chapter 1's discussion of the Bali bombing. Terrorists' ability to innovate in fund-raising, logistics, and communications has explained part of the success of the new terrorism.

Terrorists can function well in crimes related to the latest technology because new terrorist groups are structured like modern high-tech businesses. They are networked, flat rather than hierarchical, and flexible.[125] Therefore, they reflect the models of legitimate business most suited for innovation and growth. Yet, their goals are not to profit through innovation but to exploit new technology to cause maximum harm to a broad range of individuals who participate in the global economy.

Many terrorists are now committing crimes that are at the forefront of the illicit political economy. Increasingly, the new financier of terrorism does not use violence to raise funds. As one observer commented two decades ago in reference to the IRA, "the terrorist is now much more likely to conform to the image of middle-ranking clerk than to a gun-toting hoodlum."[126] This trend has amplified as jihadi terrorist groups, having many highly trained engineers and computer professionals within their ranks or at their disposal, are using high-tech crime to commit global fraud and other offenses.[127]

Fraud

Fraud has been an increasingly important source of terrorist funding in the last two decades, aided by the speed and anonymity of the Internet. At first, terrorist frauds were simple, as exemplified by the crime of one of the 1993 World Trade Center bombers. That attack was supported by a retail coupon scam, carried out in a series of stores owned by a Middle Eastern man. Yet the scale of fraud has gotten larger. An enterprising pair of jihadists in Germany hoped to fund a suicide mission to Iraq by taking out nearly $1 million in life insurance and staging the death of one in a faked traffic accident.[128] It is estimated that Middle East terrorist groups net $20 million to $30 million annually through a variety of such scams.[129]

Yet moving into the digital world has allowed innovative terrorists to procure funds globally without detection and to move funds with ease. Facilitating this global movement are cell phones, e-gold, and cashU, which are increasingly used by terrorists. Easily accessible, they facilitate transfers that are hard to trace. These transfers, enabled by the new technology, are crucial to organizations such as Hezbollah, Hamas, PKK, and the Palestinian Islamic Jihad, which need to maintain international networks.[130]

Credit Cards

Credit cards are extremely vulnerable to fraud, and there has been a proliferation of hacking and theft of credit card information by both criminals and terrorists. Terrorists steal credit card information through hacking, phishing, and other means. For example, "in the United States, an al-Qaeda member convinced a Moroccan waiter to steal customers' credit card information via a scanner that could be worn on a belt." The al-Qaeda cell was able to create copies of the credit cards and exploit the numbers.[131] Instruction in the needed skill sets for credit card fraud has been provided online. In October 2005, a man described as "a suspected Palestinian supporter of Middle Eastern terrorist groups posted credit card numbers online with instructions on how to steal active credit card numbers from American businesses' databases."[132]

Terrorists use the stolen cards both for their groups' financial advantage, to transmit funds, or may sell the numbers for a profit, often by means of the Internet. Identity theft is often combined with credit card theft.[133] Therefore, in many instances, when terrorist operatives are apprehended, they have multiple identifications and credit cards in a variety of names in their possession.

Within Western Europe, Algerians associated with al-Qaeda raise an estimated $1 million monthly from credit card fraud. These networks span Belgium, France, Spain, and the Netherlands.[134] The profits from these cards serve two purposes – fund-raising and operations. This money supports communications, propaganda, and recruitment as well as the purchase of equipment needed for terrorist acts. The 2005 London subway bombing was funded, in part, by credit card fraud.[135] As Chapter 1 mentioned, the Madrid bombers financed their activities through credit card fraud,[136] as did Ressam, who planned to bomb the Los Angeles airport at the millennium.[137]

Illustrating the extent of credit card theft and the large sums involved is the 2005 case of a young terrorist:

> Younes Tsouli, aka Terrorist 007, and his two associates, Waseem Mughal and Tariq al-Daour, investigators in the United States (U.S.) and U.K. determined the trio used computer viruses and stolen credit card accounts to set up a network of communication forums and web sites that hosted everything from tutorials on computer hacking and bomb making to videos of beheadings and suicide bombing attacks in Iraq.[138]

The extent of the loss racked up by these three was significant. Stolen credit cards registered "more than 180 web site domains at 95 different web hosting companies in the U.S. and Europe."[139] On one of al-Dour's computers, there were thirty-seven thousand stolen credit card numbers along with full information on the credit card holder such as the address, date of birth, and credit balance and limits. These cards were used to make $3.5 million in fraudulent charges. These cards also aided their operations as 110 different credit cards had been used at 46 airlines and travel agencies to buy 250 tickets used by terrorist operatives.

The extent to which credit card fraud is used to fund terrorism is not a result of individual cells communicating knowledge to others. Rather, as Rohan Gunaratna explains, terrorists in training camps in Afghanistan study the art of credit card fraud. "They were instructed to read and write credit cards by accessing and copying the information from a magnetic strip. At the request of Al Qaeda Afghanistan, the European network bought equipment for encoding and decoding credit cards from unsuspecting legitimate companies."[140] This is illustrative of al-Qaeda's business model placing itself at the forefront of the new technology.

The purchase of this equipment is just one more illustration of how terrorists intersect with the legitimate world. In this case, the suppliers of the decoding equipment were unsuspecting collaborators. But all too often, credit card companies and banks write off these credit card losses as just a cost of doing business rather than investigating the terrorists and criminals who commit these crimes.[141] In this way, they allow this terrorist business model to succeed.

Cybercrime and Cyberterrorism

Cybercrime and cyberterrorism are also new tools of terrorists, although they are also used to great advantage by technologically advanced criminals and governments.[142] Older organized crime groups recognized the potential of cybercrime. "The Irish Republican Army had computer-oriented cells, and was very close to engaging in cyberterrorism before they made peace."[143]

But these techniques have become more widespread, destructive, and sophisticated since the days of the IRA. These computer-related crimes consist of the destruction of files; hacking; information attacks, including defacing of websites; denial of service; service overloading; message flooding; and spreading malware, viruses, worms, Trojans, and software bombs. Also included in this broad range of crimes possible through computers are infrastructure attacks and disabling vital services. This crime is facilitated by secret communications as a result of advanced cryptography, steganography, and encryption.[144] Prepaid phone cards and telephones are also valuable tools for terrorists' secret communications.[145]

Examples of terrorist exploitation of computers for secure communications are numerous. The final message to Mohammed Atta, three weeks before the 9/11 attack, was, "The semester begins in three more weeks. We've obtained nineteen confirmations for studies in the faculty of law, the faculty of urban planning, the faculty of fine arts and the faculty of engineering."[146] The readiness of the nineteen hijackers was disguised in this message.

In 2008, investigators in Great Britain, Spain, and Italy analyzed computers seized from Islamic militants and found significant quantities of child pornography. Although the investigators were not certain, they suspected that the pornographic images were not merely being downloaded for personal use but were being used to convey encoded messages through steganography, a form of secret communications, in which one image can be hidden with another.[147] Already a decade ago, the FARC was relying heavily on encrypted data that even the National Security Agency, with its masses of skilled cryptographers, could not decode.[148] The funds and the resources of terrorists allow them to exploit the Internet for secure communications that cannot be decoded by the best experts and the most sophisticated computers.

Terrorists are able to innovate in their crime commission because they learn through the Internet and through professional education provided in training camps. Many Islamic groups, although seeking to destroy advanced societies, will use the most advanced techniques of communications and commerce to achieve their goal. Yet sometimes, they do not have needed skills internally or cannot or do not choose to develop them. Therefore, like every other business, they must sometimes contract for professional services.

Supply Chains

Supply chains are a major concern of legitimate businesses, as they need to ensure the safe and timely delivery of goods without disruption. Diversion and substitution of commodities are a constant concern for suppliers as goods travel great distances to reach their destination.

Supply chains are also a great concern to terrorists, as they need to move the money, goods, and people that support their operations. These can be illicit goods, such as narcotic drugs, counterfeit pharmaceuticals, and cigarettes, which are shown in Chapter 7 to be the lifeblood of terrorist organizations, or high-value diverted goods such as oil. These three are all desirable products, because they all have high profit margins.

Terrorists make money by controlling supply chains for delivery of their products, such as drugs, as well as by taxing the smuggling of others that pass through borders or territory that they control. The ability to tax the transit of commodities is key to their financing. Organized crime groups' extortion of trade has been known for a significant period, which is why they are so deeply involved in ports and the trucking industry. Yet terrorist groups on many different continents also profit from taxing trade. Therefore, criminals and terrorists prey off of both trade and supply chains.

Reliable supply chains are required to move money and its substitutes, such as gold. Gold assumes an important role, particularly in the Middle East, in the funding of terrorism.[149] With restrictions on bank transfers, al-Qaeda shifted significant assets from cash to easy-to-transport gold, a strategy that has been subsequently followed by others. When the price of gold rises (as it did from 2008 to 2012), there are multiple advantages. Smaller quantities now carry greater value, making transport easier. Furthermore, there are ready conversion centers globally, with pervasive gold souks in the Middle East and Asia. With gold's appreciation, all costs of transfer are outweighed.[150] Terrorists, like legitimate businesspeople, can thus use commodity and currency trades to their advantage. But they are also susceptible to fluctuations in gold markets (and the declines since 2012), as are other businesspeople.

Control of Territory

Terrorists benefit from the control of territory, which can be land in strategic border areas or crucial sea passages used for the shipment of goods. Illustrating this are the following examples of exploitation of land borders. In Afghanistan, large-scale illegal logging has destroyed the livelihoods of many. However, it has benefited the Taliban, as they have taxed timber exiting from Afghanstan.[151] In the Middle East, oil smuggling has been a major source of funding for the insurgency and for terrorist attacks within Iraq.[152] Massive oil smuggling out of Iraq and Iran into neighboring Turkey benefits the PKK, as they tax this valuable commodity as it traverses the territory in which they operate.[153] It has also provided funding for terrorist attacks within Iraq.[154] Yet despite the extensive profits made from taxing oil shipments, the PKK does not ignore even low-value cross-border shipments that can make them money. Therefore, they also tax cigarettes that cross on mules from Iran and Iraq to Turkey, charging as little as 5 lira or $3.50 for every mule crossing PKK-controlled territory, as discussed more in Chapter 7.

Other Middle East terrorist groups benefit from taxing the illicit oil trade. In July 2008, "Egyptian authorities discovered some twenty underground tunnels, arrested several smugglers, and seized thousands of gallons of fuel being smuggled through tunnels into Gaza. The smugglers were reportedly in the process of laying an eight-hundred-meter underground pipeline to facilitate further illegal fuel shipments into Gaza."[155]

Piracy

The rise of piracy, discussed in reference to Somalia, is a broader problem. As Martin Murphy points out, piracy is an organized criminal activity that has always had an important political dimension.[156] Piracy is the result of several factors identified by Murphy: legal and jurisdictional opportunities; favorable geography; conflict and disorder; underfunded law enforcement; inadequate security; permissive political environments; cultural acceptability; and long-standing maritime tradition and reward.[157] It permits disruption by terrorists of large-scale shipments and the supply chains for valuable legitimate commodities. Sea routes controlled by terrorists can be exploited to great advantage. Maritime piracy of large vessels also represents another area of dual-use criminality, where terrorists can not only command lucrative cargoes but can also "commandeer lethal cargoes such as chemicals, gas, arms."[158] The same principle applies not only in the Horn of Africa but also in the Straits of Malacca, close to Malaysia and Indonesia, where terrorists have adopted long traditions of piracy to their utilitarian purposes. In 2008, included in the numerous attacks off the Somalia Coast and the Gulf of Aden was the seizure of a Ukrainian vessel transporting $30 million worth of T-72 Russian tanks and smaller weaponry and ammunition.[159]

Human Trafficking and Illicit Trade

In these cases, terrorists exploited licit and illicit trade to their financial advantage. But supply chains used for the movement of people can also be exploited by terrorists. In the following case, criminals controlled territory and terrorists took advantage of their strategic location. A joint United States, Colombian, and Panamanian investigation brought down a major alien smuggling network linked to terrorism. The case, named Operation Pipeline, was the first case conducted by the U.S. Immigration and Customs Enforcement agency (ICE), in which smugglers provided material support to a terrorist organization, the FARC. The case was initiated in 2004 when Panamanian authorities apprehended three Iranians, transiting to the United States using counterfeit Colombian documents. Twelve "additional Special Interest Aliens (SIA's) were identified as operating in South America that assisted in the smuggling of aliens, arms, narcotics, and money laundering violations . . . the investigation revealed that a vast criminal network comprised of predominantly Special Interest Aliens (SIA's) had operated without detection for three years; the organization was very adept at exploiting weak border and internal immigration controls in Colombia, Venezuela, Panama, and Mexico."[160] Operation Pipeline revealed that criminal organizations located in the northern part of South America had exploited their strategic location in Colombia as a key launching point, seeking to smuggle contraband and aliens to Europe, the United States, and Pacific Rim destinations.[161]

The strategic transit routes of Latin America are also being exploited by some Africans who are believed to have links to terrorist organizations operating in Somalia. South African officials posted in Argentina have discovered suspicious Somalians transiting South Africa on the way to Latin America. They then travel north through Latin America, intending to enter the United States.[162]

Professional Services

Terrorists, when functioning as criminal entrepreneurs, require a variety of services.[163] They need accountants, bankers, and lawyers. But they also need corrupt officials and often witting and unwitting facilitators from the corporate world. Therefore, they have multiple forms of interaction with the legitimate economy. They also require professional services from the criminal world as they retain the services of human smugglers and specialists in "non-traceable communications, forgers, and money launderers."[164] Without hiring this expertise, they cannot make their business function.[165]

Like legitimate businesspeople, they achieve strategic advantage by retaining the best personnel globally. Terrorists will hire criminal forgers to manufacture false documents and will retain the services of human traffickers.[166] Terrorists will take advantage of the criminals' specialization in logistics to move people, arms, and money. The most advanced and well-financed terrorist groups will also hire computer-savvy communications professionals to facilitate their communications and to provide training for members. As discussed in Chapter 1, the Madrid bombers had false documents provided by criminals. Turkish human traffickers move terrorists from the Middle East and North Africa to Europe via their territory.[167] Terrorists in Kashmir use criminalized specialists from the high-tech computer industry of India to promote their objectives.[168]

Lawyers

There are only a limited number of cases of prosecutions of individuals in these service industries because the focus of counterterrorism activity has been on threat finance rather than the support services. But groups such as Europol and the Australian Crime Commission point to the centrality of facilitators' activities.[169] Cases of prosecution of these professionals reveal how they can contribute to a terrorist organization. In cases in both Israel and the United

States, defense lawyers have been accused of being the conduits for messages passed from jailed terrorists to members of their organizations at liberty. The American lawyer, a longtime defender of unpopular clients, was convicted of passing messages from the blind fundamentalist cleric Sheik Omar Abdel Rahman to his Egyptian followers. In these cases, lawyers have taken advantage of the attorney-client privilege and transcended the limits of defense.[170]

The Brazilian PCC, discussed in reference to the São Paolo attacks, is aided by a group of corrupt officials and lawyers who do their bidding.[171] But this politicized Brazilian criminal organization has a more long-term strategy in relation to the legal profession and the state:

> The organization has 18 to 20 lawyers who work full-time. They act as not only advocates for gang members, but also mentors for young gang members. One of the great successes of the PCC has been to infiltrate or "colonize" the governmental organizations that administer the entrance examinations necessary to enter Brazilian public service. The job of the PCC lawyer-mentor is to ensure that young gang members (and children of the convicts) who have the ability and desire to enter public service can and do get the necessary education and pass the appropriate examinations. As a consequence, the PCC is putting its own people into bureaucratic positions that it considers important in the Brazilian system.[172]

Through its preparation of people for public service, the PCC in its third generation has infiltrated the state in ways that transcend the original conceptualization of the criminal-political nexus.[173]

Accountants

Two American cases reveal the contribution accountants may unwittingly provide to the operations of terrorist groups. In the investigation of the Holy Land Foundation case, formerly the largest Islamic charity in the United States, its accountant was summoned to testify as to his knowledge of money movements and tax reporting. He testified that foreign bank accounts controlled by the Holy Land Foundation for Relief and Development (HLF) were never reported to the Internal Revenue Service, or even to the charity's own auditors, but he stated he was unaware that the Foundation was founded by the Muslim Brotherhood to help Hamas.[174]

In a Detroit based-case, an accountant was accused of helping to set up a foundation that would fund terrorist activity in Iraq. This was a homegrown terrorist cell, and the leaders were sentenced to lengthy periods of confinement. The accountant was not American, and he was convicted and deported.[175]

Money Launderers

Money laundering is essential for the funding of terrorist groups, as it allows them to store and use funds acquired from criminal sources and limits the risk that such funds might trigger suspicion from regulators or businesses. Bank officials since 9/11 have been increasingly careful not to be identified as accessories to terrorist funding. The consequences were significant, as a Saudi account at Riggs Bank was used as a conduit to fund the 9/11 hijackers. "In December, 2002, it was revealed that Princess Haifa al-Faisal, the daughter of the late King Faisal and the wife of the Saudi Ambassador to the United States, Prince Bandar bin Sultan, had paid a monthly stipend of $2,000 to the allegedly needy Saudi family of Omar al-Bayyuni between December 1999 and May 2002 through Mrs. Osama Basnan in Santiago, California. Part of this stipend found its way to two of the terrorists who participated in the 9/11 attack on the Twin Towers in New York, Khaled al-Mihdhar and Nawwaf al-Hazemi."[176]

Consequently, terrorists hire specialists – money launderers. This is another example of their use of professionals, such as bankers, accountants, and lawyers. Not all of these money movers are illegal, as they may mix criminal and terrorist funds with legitimate ones. Money has been moved through banks, as recent cases against banks indicate. HSBC paid a record fine in late 2012 of close to $2 billion for knowingly moving large amounts of money for Mexican drug cartels, the Iranian government, and many other dubious clients.[177] A U.S. Senate investigation revealed that between 2001 and 2010, the bank had failed to stop illegal behavior. In one case, according to the investigation, HSBC's American operations supplied at least $1 billion to a Saudi bank, after "an HSBC executive reportedly argued that the bank should resume its relationship with Al Rajhi Bank, a Saudi Arabian bank founded by an early supporter of Al Qaeda."[178]

The Lebanese Canadian Bank was directly implicated in transferring millions of dollars for Hezbollah.[179] Under this scheme, according to the U.S. federal prosecutor's New York office,

> funds were wired from Lebanon to the United States to buy used cars, which were then transported to West Africa. Cash from the sale of the cars, along with proceeds of narcotics trafficking, were then funneled to Lebanon through Hizballah controlled money laundering channels. Substantial portions of the cash were paid to Hizballah, which the U.S. Department of State designated as a Foreign Terrorist Organization in 1997. As alleged in the Complaint, the Hizballah-linked financial institutions involved in the scheme include the Lebanese Canadian Bank ("LCB").[180]

Subsequently, $150 million was seized from the defunct bank by the U.S. government. The bank had a representational office in Montreal, which allowed it to solicit funds for the Beirut-based banks but not to transfer funds through Canada. The bank served a multicontinental funding scheme for Hezbollah.[181]

The money may also be moved through wire transfer businesses, underground banking, and real estate[182] and is sometimes carried by cash couriers. The so-called Hamas Heights case in Oxon Hill, Maryland, was an example of Hamas-related funds laundered into multiple properties in a suburb of Washington, DC. In these transactions, a legitimate investment vehicle was used for illicit means.[183]

The Haqqani network, based in Pakistan, provides financial services for the Taliban, an illustration of a strategic alliance.[184] Records of the Haqqani network, confiscated by the U.S. government, indicate that the Haqqani network uses only specific hawaladars (the dealers for the *hawala*) to conduct their financial transactions. The seized records indicated that they relied on the hawaladars of the crime-terror group D-Company for their financial transactions.[185]

In contrast, cash movement of large undeclared sums is illegal in most countries and is often facilitated by corruption of border officials and members of customs services. It is hard to detect cash couriers, unless law enforcement is tipped off by foreign counterparts to be on the lookout for a particular person.[186]

Underground Banking

The crackdowns on official financial markets have driven terrorists to use traditional systems of underground banking that are not easily traceable. They exploit informal value transfer mechanisms, such as *hawala* or *hundi*, and trade-based money laundering.[187] All forms of underground banking are hard to trace because these transfers are generally done within ethnic communities in which there is limited law enforcement access. For example, members of the Somali diaspora can transfer funds through Kenya intended for al-Shabaab.[188]

Most of these informal transactions are legal and compensate for the absence of banking and the high costs of money transfers internationally.[189] But terrorist funding is comingled with the large amounts of remittances and other financial transactions associated with legitimate sources. Therefore, it is often difficult to establish the illegal funds and to find individuals who knowingly are facilitators of terrorist money movement.

An international investigation in the United States, Canada, Spain, and Belgium of a network of forty-five underground bankers and associates charged in moving drug-related money revealed links to terrorism. Informants in the investigation, named "Cash Out," helped penetrate the normally closed network of money transfer agents, thus revealing that[190] Saifullah Ranjha, who ran a money laundering business in Washington, DC, from October 2003 and 2007, believed he was transferring funds to al-Qaeda. He was sentenced to nine years in 2008 for concealing money laundering of more than $2.2 million of funds that he had transferred and failed to report.[191] In this case, the blending of terrorist and criminal-support services is apparent. Laundering money by terrorists can also help generate money for the cause. In this way, they become professional service providers.

Other Facilitators

Facilitators of terror networks can be drawn from the religious community. This is seen not only in Afghanistan, Pakistan, and the Middle East but also in Europe and Kenya. In the Netherlands, facilitators can identify people as well as ways of moving money.[192] According to research of the International Peace

Institute in Kenya, "a key pillar of this support network is a community of wealthy clerics-cum-businessmen, linked to a small number of religious centres notorious for their links to radicalism . . . in Nairobi."[193]

Corrupt Officials

Important service providers to terrorists are corrupt officials who facilitate their illicit activity. Official corruption is present in all kinds of supporting acts but is most often present in logistics and the most profitable forms of illicit activity, such as drug and arms trafficking and human smuggling and trafficking. Corrupt officials often siphon off or divert weapons and explosives that are then used by terrorists. But as was illustrated earlier in the first chapter, the explosives used by the terrorists in Mumbai entered thanks to the corruption of customs officials at the port. The corruption of border, customs, and other officials is often undertaken by the terrorists or done on their behalf by criminal associates.

Corrupt officials are central to terrorist operations, especially travel. Corrupted officials let terrorists without adequate documentation pass border controls.[194] As the 9/11 Commission report pointed out, bribed border and customs guards can facilitate terrorist travel across borders and security checkpoints,[195] but corrupted officials can also help terrorists procure passports and visas.[196] Human smugglers obtain genuine passports and visas from corrupt government officials through criminal document vendors.

> One smuggler, Salim Boughader-Mucharrafille, smuggled Lebanese nationals sympathetic to Hamas and Hizbollah into the United States and relied on corrupt Mexican officials in Beirut, Mexico City and Tijuana to facilitate their travel. Specifically, Boughader obtained Mexican tourist visas from an official at the Mexican embassy in Beirut to facilitate the travel of humans to Mexico.[197]

The forging of documents is essential to the movement of terrorists, as corrupt officials cannot always meet the full need. Fake visas and passports are supplied by criminals to facilitate terrorists' travel. In Pakistan, a criminal visa mill provided forged degree certificates, fake income tax returns, and bogus pay slips that enabled potential students and terrorists to obtain entry into Great Britain.[198] Another case of forged documents in Spain, linked back to Pakistan, reveals the centrality of the criminal supply services of Thais and Pakistanis in providing essential documents for the perpetration of terrorism.[199] In this case, a criminal ring, based in Barcelona and Thailand, doctored stolen passports and provided them to criminals and terrorists. It is believed they helped facilitate the entry into Spain of some of the Madrid bombers as well as the documents needed by members of the Mumbai attack. It is revealing that this globally linked forgery network could be tied to different and geographically separated attacks discussed in Chapter 4. Criminal facilitators serve a broad range of clients.[200]

Corrupt individuals in the corporate world can also facilitate the mobility of terrorists. In the case of the bombing of Moscow's Domodedovo Airport in August 2004, two Chechen women were able to buy tickets for a sold-out flight and to board without the proper identification. According to the general prosecutor, a ticket speculator was paid 2,000 rubles by one of the suicide bombers, and the other paid 3,000 rubles. The speculator passed a bribe of 1,000 rubles to a Siberian Airlines employee to get one of the women on a plane just before takeoff and the other on a proximate flight. The facilitating function of this airplane employee, after receipt of a bribe, illustrates how corrupt corporate officials can also enable terrorism.[201]

Corporate Facilitators

Links with the corporate world also facilitate the movement of funds for terrorist organization. This is another form of professional facilitation. This can be achieved by the infiltration of a member of the terrorist organization into a wire transfer business. For example,

> in some cases, where the local Western Union agent is a Hizballah member or supporter, experts believe Hizballah gets a cut of the 7 percent service fee to wire money. In other cases, Hizballah simply uses the company to launder and transfer funds. For example, Hizballah funding to Palestinian terrorist groups in the West Bank is almost entirely transferred via Western Union – including some $3 million in 2003–2004 alone.[202]

These illustrations of corruption in the corporate world occurred at low levels. In later chapters, there are further illustrations of individual and small-scale participation by business, wittingly and unwittingly aiding terrorist financing. But there have also been knowing and unknowing facilitators at much higher levels in the corporate world. A major fine at Chiquita Brands International and corporate payments to Somali pirates to release cargoes and personnel reveal how terrorists can interact with and exploit major corporations to their advantage.

In 2003, the banana company Chiquita Brands International informed the U.S. Justice Department that it had been making payments to a designated terrorist organization to protect the lives of its workers in Colombia. After a long Justice Department investigation into the company's payment of $1.7 million between 1997 and 2004 to the right-wing terrorist organization Autodefensas Unidas de Colombia (United Self-Defense Forces of Colombia, or AUC) and to the left-wing organizations ELN and FARC as their areas of banana cultivation shifted, Chiquita agreed to a $25 million fine to the U.S. government. It sold its banana operations in Colombia in 2004.[203] These payments were made with the knowledge of high-ranking corporate officials. Therefore, there are long-term financial costs for corporations that try to ensure the safety of their employees in regions dominated by terrorists. The Chiquita experience has produced a moral dilemma for many corporations, particularly American, that seek to operate in regions where there is a significant likelihood of kidnapping of their employees by terrorists.[204]

Part of the business strategy of terrorists is to target companies that have the possibility of paying significant sums. This has been seen not only in Colombia but in Somalia as well.

The previously discussed Somali piracy also yields significant sums from the corporate world. Hostage taking also occurs in conjunction with piracy of large boats off of the Somalian coast. Ransoms paid ranged from $30 million to $120 million in 2008.[205] The ransoms are paid not only by private citizens but also by corporations from many countries, who are being forced to bear these costs. In two days in 2008, gunmen hijacked a "German cargo ship, an Iranian bulk carrier and a Japanese-operated tanker."[206] This followed the capture of an oil-laden Malaysian tanker the previous day.[207]

Venture Capitalists
The profits have been so significant from the piracy that "venture capital" funds were established so that local Somalians and members of the diaspora community in the United States and Canada could benefit.[208] In contrast to what was discussed in the previous chapter, where diaspora communities are forced to contribute to crime and terrorist groups, in this case, proceeds of criminal acts are shared with members of the diaspora. A stock exchange was set up in Haradheere, once a small fishing village 250 miles from Mogadishu, to share in the proceeds from the attacks on vessels off the Somali coast.[209] One former pirate explained, "Four months ago, during the monsoon rains, we decided to set up this stock exchange. We started with 15 'maritime companies' and now we are hosting 72. Ten of them have so far been successful at hijacking. The shares are open to all and everybody can take part, whether personally at sea or on land by providing cash, weapons or useful materials . . . we've made piracy a community activity."[210] By providing a system of profit sharing from the venture capital, there is support for this illicit activity that likely helps support Al-Shabab, the powerful Islamist terrorist organization in Somalia. This is hardly surprising, as there is a long tradition in the Islamic world of piracy for *jihad* dating back to the seventh century in the Mediterranean.[211]

Insurance Companies
Some insurance companies also profited inadvertently from this piracy, as corporations have bought large insurance policies to cover their risks. From 2006 to 2009, the American insurance company Chubb Group reported a 15 to 20 percent increase in the number of kidnapping and ransom insurance policies.[212] Insurance premiums for a single passage through the Gulf of Aden, where the Somali pirates operate, rose from a low of $500 to as much as $20,000.[213] As the increasing purchase of these policies indicates, insurance and businesses are providing some of the funding for terrorist organizations.

With such concern about the large sums derived from this piracy, serious and successful efforts have been made to limit it.[214]

Conclusion

Terrorist groups that have survived and prospered have had to ensure that they generate and sustain regular levels of funding. With the decline in state support for terrorism, and especially since 9/11, when efforts to curtail money flows to terrorist organizations have had some success, terrorists have increasingly used crime and corruption to remain solvent, although they also rely on charities, state sponsors, and legitimate businesses.[215] As this chapter indicates, terrorists have engaged in crime and corruption as a business. They have diversified their product mix and engaged in crime where they have competitive advantage and where there is possibility for growth because there is no market saturation. They retain diverse professional services, from the illicit and licit spheres, and engage in strategic alliances to make their businesses function effectively.

Terrorist revenue generation from crime differs from that of criminals. Organized criminals' primary focus is making money and ensuring the survival of their criminal organizations. But for terrorists, this criminal activity often has a dual utility. Crimes such as kidnapping reduce social solidarity, making it more difficult for society to mount the political will to oppose these politically motivated organizations. Corruption is not only a facilitator of crime for terrorists but a strategic means to undermine the existing state. Hijacking of a ship with military cargo may yield a ransom but, even more importantly, the equipment needed for an attack. Therefore, engaging in crime is a rational act that has calculated benefits that often transcend the financial.

Terrorists, by participating in crime, spread fear and insecurity. They raise security costs for state actors and spread the perception that the state is weak and ineffective.[216] In this regard, organized crime serves as part of a terror or insurgent group's asymmetrical warfare campaign.

Certain crime, such as kidnapping, bank robbery, and extortion, is engaged in by all groups. Yet, like legitimate businesses, the groups capitalize on targets of opportunity. Therefore, terrorists exploit their geographical advantage to generate revenues through illicit trade. Consequently, terrorists in Africa and Latin America rely on theft of natural resources; for terrorists near the straits of Malacca, piracy becomes an important funding source; and in Iraq, oil smuggling becomes a valuable modality. Competitive and strategic advantage is well understood by terrorist businessmen.

The crimes of competitive advantage often rely on taxing the supply chains that move legitimate and illegitimate products across territory they control. Through corruption of officials and application of violence, terrorist groups undermine the state presence and bolster their own in key border areas, ports, and other transport hubs. Therefore, they have learned from organized crime the importance of controlling territory and have capitalized on the corporate world's need to move commodities long distances in the increasingly globalized economy.

As terrorist entrepreneurs, they are always looking for new product lines and seek to learn from regional successes in one area that can be transferred elsewhere. Therefore, the FARC, known as narco-terrorists, are really a much more diversified business that even generated income from the exploitation of hydrocarbons. Diversification is as much a key to survival as it has been to the legitimate business world.

Terrorist businessmen share a key concern of their legitimate counterparts – the retention of professional services. These service providers allow them to move their money, corrupt needed officials, and obtain falsified documents.

Terrorists also have tax strategies. Theirs differ from legitimate businesses because they survive in the shadow economy. But like organized crime, they may pay some taxes for their front companies to intentionally cover their tracks and not attract the attention of law enforcement. But nonstate actors are more concerned with extracting their own "taxes" through extortion than with minimizing their tax burdens. While many corporations spent significant sums and manpower to minimize taxes, terrorists are engaging in the mirror activity in the illegitimate world. They are maximizing their capacity to levee revenues, and in this respect, they are performing a function normally performed by the state. But the state should provide services in return for taxes. Organized crime, in exchange for extorting community members, sometimes provides dispute resolution.[217] But it is not clear that older-style terrorist groups, such as the ASG, PKK, or IRA, provide any services in exchange for these "taxes" imposed on communities. It is the most abusive form of both "taxation without representation" and also "taxes without services rendered." Therefore, it is terrorism in a broad exploitative form – it deprives large numbers of individuals of their livelihood through terror without any exchange. This terror rarely results in death but, if resisted, can result in very costly losses of property – the business side of terrorism.

In contrast, some of the increasingly powerful newer terrorist organizations, such as the FARC, Hezbollah, Hamas, and the Taliban, that seek to supplant the state provide services in exchange for their extortion, as was discussed in Chapter 2. The new crime and new terrorism diverge significantly in this respect from old terrorist groups. Because they are service providers, they have a much greater base of support than groups that merely tax their communities.

The most successful terrorist entrepreneurs have deployed modern technology to their advantage. Using the Internet, websites, and all forms of advanced communications, they can ensure the security of communications and the continuation of their operations without disruption. Yet, unlike legitimate entrepreneurs, who see technological innovation as an end in itself, for terrorists, this technology has a lethal function – to destroy the existing order. This is not the basis of a science fiction film but of a destructive reality.

Notes

1. "Bin Laden was about to branch out into the kidnapping business to boost cash reserves," *Mail Online*, June 20, 2011, http://www.dailymail.co.uk/news/article-2005715/Osama-Bin-Laden-kidnapping-business-boost-cash-reserves.html #ixzz1XxFcPxvK. There is presently discussion within the IOM and the trafficking community of whether kidnapping and the sale of people represents a form of human trafficking.

2. FATF/OECD, "Organised Maritime Piracy and Related Kidnapping for Ransom," July 2011, 31, http://www.fatf-gafi.org/topics/methodsandtrends/documents/organisedmaritimepiracyandrelatedkidnappingforransom.html; Adam Nossiter, "Millions in Ransoms Fuel Militants' Clout in West Africa," *New York Times*, December 12, 2012, http://www.nytimes.com/2012/12/13/world/africa/kidnappings-fuel-extremists-in-western-africa.html?pagewanted=all. This was discussed in reference to In Amenas in the introduction. Some of this money was shared with Malian officials, which made them unwilling to crack down on the kidnapping. See Adam Nossiter, "For Mali's New President, Corruption Issue Lingers," *New York Times*, August 22, 2013, http://www.nytimes.com/2013/08/22/world/africa/for-malis-new-president-corruption-issue-lingers.html?ref=world.

3. Jason Burke, *Al-Qaeda Casting a Shadow of Terror* (London: I. B. Tauris, 2003), 43–45.

4. Loretta Napoleoni, "The Evolution of Terrorist Financing since 9/11: How the New Generation of Jihadists Fund Themselves," in *Terrornomics*, ed. Sean S. Costigan and David Gold (Aldershot, UK: Ashgate, 2007), 13–24; Rachel Ehrenfeld, "Funding Evil: How Terrorism Is Financed and the Nexus of Terrorist and Criminal Organizations," in ibid., 27–48.

5. Aaron Zelinsky and Martin Shubik, "Research Note: Terrorist Groups as Business Firms: A New Typological Framework," *Terrorism and Political Violence* 21, no. 2 (2009): 327–36.

6. U.S. Department of Justice, "Member of Afghan Taliban Sentenced to Life in Prison in Nation's First Conviction on Narco-terror Charges," December 22, 2008, http://www.justice.gov/opa/pr/2008/December/08-crm-1145.html.

7. There are a few studies, such as Zelinsky and Shubik and Alan B. Krueger, *What Makes a Terrorist? Economics and the Roots of Terrorism*, Lionel Robbins Lectures (Princeton, NJ: Princeton University Press, 2007); Tilman Brück, ed., *The Economic Analysis of Terrorism* (London: Routledge, 2007); and R. T. Naylor, *Satanic Purses: Money Myth and Misinformation in the War on Terror* (Montreal, QC: McGill-Queen's University Press, 2006), but there is not an extensive body of research compared to terrorist financing. See also Jodi Vittori, *Terrorist Financing and Resourcing* (New York: Palgrave Macmillan, 2011), who examined the resourcing menu of terrorists with funding from diasporas and the multinationals of the terrorist world.

8. For a definition of continuing criminal enterprise, part of U.S. Criminal Code, Chapter 13 of Title 21, Subchapter I, Part D, § 848, see the RICO statue on continuous criminal enterprise, http://www.law.cornell.edu/uscode/text/21/848.

9. See Diego Gambetta, *The Sicilian Mafia: The Business of Private Protection* (Cambridge, MA: Harvard University Press, 1996); Gianluca Fiorentini and Sam

Peltzman, eds., *The Economics of Organized Crime* (Cambridge: Cambridge University Press, 1995).

10. Rohan Gunaratna, *Inside Al Qaeda: Global Network of Terror* (New York: Columbia University Press), 62–67, discusses al-Qaeda's financial strategy; John Horgan and Max Taylor, "Playing the 'Green Card': Financing the Provisional IRA: Part 1," *Terrorism and Political Violence* 11, no. 2 (1999): 10, looks at PIRA's annual income. "Fondeo del terrorismo," *Infolaft* 1, no. 4 (2009): 10–15, which analyzes the seizures of financial records of the FARC; Angel Rabasa, Peter Chalk, Kim Cragin, Sara A. Daly, Heather S. Gregg, Theodore W. Karasik, Kevin A. O'Brien, and William Rosenau, *Beyond al-Qaeda, Part I: The Global Jihadist Movement* (Santa Monica, CA: RAND, 2006), 57–61; Charles Strozier and James Frank, *The PKK: Financial Sources, Social and Political Dimensions* (Saarbrücken, Germany: VDM, 2011); Gretchen Peters, *Haqqani Network Financing: The Evolution of an Industry* (West Point, NY: Combating Terrorism Center at West Point, July 2012), http://www.ctc.usma.edu/wp-content/uploads/2012/07/CTC_Haqqani_Network_Financing-Report__Final.pdf. The author has been able to interview analysts of the seized records of the FARC, the PKK, and the Haqqani Network. This information has been published in some publications with very limited circulation, such as *Fondeo del terrorismo* and *Terörün Ekonomisi: Sınır Illerinde Kaçakçilik ve Terörün Finansmanı* (Ankara: Police Academy, 2009).

11. See Horgan and Taylor, "Playing the 'Green Card,'" 1–38; McKenzie O'Brien, "Fluctuations between Crime and Terror: The Case of Abu Sayyaf's Kidnapping Activities," *Terrorism and Political Violence* 24, no. 2 (2012): 320–36; *Fondeo del terrorismo*, 10–15, which analyzes the seizures of financial records of the FARC.

12. As Timothy Wittig points out in *Understanding Terrorist Finance* (Houndsmill, UK: Palgrave Macmillan, 2011), 75–78, terrorists also use the legitimate economy.

13. Horgan and Taylor, "Playing the 'Green Card,'" 9, 16.

14. Ibid., 13.

15. Ibid., 4.

16. "The Crime-Terror Nexus: Perspectives and Lessons Learned from International Researchers and Practitioners," remarks at the Terrorism, Transnational Crime, and Corruption Center, George Mason University, Arlington, VA, May 3, 2010.

17. Sumita Sarkar and Arvind Tiwari, "Combating Organised Crime: A Case Study of Mumbai City," *Faultlines* 12 (2002), http://www.satp.org/satporgtp/publication/faultlines/volume12/Article5.htm.

18. "India's Fugitive Gangster," *BBC News*, September 12, 2006, http://news.bbc.co.uk/2/hi/south_asia/4775531.stm; Gregory F. Treverton, Carl Matthies, Karla J. Cunningham, Jeremiah Goulka, Greg Ridgeway, and Anny Wong, *Film Piracy, Organized Crime and Terrorism* (Santa Monica, CA: RAND, 2009), 93–94.

19. Zelinksky and Shubik identify these recognizable business models among different terrorist organizations. For example, the franchise activities of al-Qaeda have been described in many locales worldwide. Yet other models operate, such as the hierarchy model that has characterized Hezbollah and IRA business, whereas the Earth Liberation Front is a brand organization. The successful al-Qaeda has followed many of these successful business models simultaneously.

20. Ibid.

21. *Fondeo del terrorismo*, 10–15, reveals that FARC's financial records calculated their expenditures for corruption as a cost of business.

22. C. J. de Poot and A. Sonnenschein, *Jihadi Terrorism in the Netherlands* (The Hague: WODC, 2011), 109–10.

23. Roberto Saviano, *Gomorrah*, trans. from the Italian by Virginia Jewiss (New York: Farrar, Straus, and Giroux), 2007, 181–86.

24. Mark Pieth, ed., *Financing of Terrorism* (Dordrecht, Netherlands: Kluwer Academic, 2003); Nikos Passas, "Terrorism Financing Mechanisms and Policy Dilemmas," in *Terrorism Finance and State Responses: A Comparative Perspective*, ed. Jeanne Giraldo and Harold Trinkunas (Stanford, CA: Stanford University Press, 2007), 30, which discusses how the 9/11 hijackers used the established banking system. The nuclear proliferation of the A. Q. Khan network was facilitated by businessmen in Europe. Rebekah K. Dietz, "Illicit Networks: Targeting the Nexus between Terrorists, Proliferators and Narcotraffickers," (Monterey, CA: U.S. Naval Post Graduate School, 2010), http://www.dtic.mil/dtic/tr/fulltext/u2/a536899.pdf; *IISS Nuclear Black Market Dossier: A Net Assessment* (London, 2007), 43–64, http://www.iiss.org/publications/strategic-dossiers/nbm/nuclear-black-market-dossier-a-net-assesment/.

25. Illustrative of this is the Cambodian military. See David Capie, "Trading the Tools of Terror: Armed Groups and Light Weapons Proliferation in Southeast Asia," in *Terrorism and Violence in Southeast Asia: Transnational Challenges to States and Regional Stability*, ed. Paul J. Smith (Armonk, NY: M. E. Sharpe, 2005), 191.

26. See Douglas Farah, "Fixers, Super Fixers, and Shadow Facilitators: How Networks Connect," in *Convergence: Illicit Networks and National Security in the Age of Globalization*, ed. Michael Miklaucic and Jacqueline Brewer (Washington, DC: National Defense University Press, 2013), 75–95; FATF, *Proliferation Financing Report*, June 18, 2008, 9–11, http://www.fatf-gafi.org%2Fmedia%2Ffatf%2Fdocuments%2Freports%2FTypologies%2520Report%2520on%2520Proliferation%2520Financing.pdf; World Economic Forum, Global Agenda Council on Organised Crime, "Organised Crime Enablers," August 3, 2012, http://reports.weforum.org/organized-crime-enablers-2012/. The author was a member of the group that prepared this report.

27. This was discussed earlier in reference to Jose Padilla and the Saudi experience with its incarcerated population. Jessica Stern, "Mind over Martyr: How to Deradicalize Terrorists," *Foreign Affairs*, January–February, 2010, 95–108.

28. Eli Berman, *Radical, Religious and Violent: The New Economics of Terrorism* (Cambridge, MA: MIT Press, 2009).

29. This has been the case for AQAP, which, having expanded "its criminal fundraising efforts (e.g., robberies, protection rackets, blackmail, smuggling)," has been able to push into new territory in Yemen after being pushed back in 2011. See Daniel Green, "Al Qaeda's Resiliency in Yemen," PolicyWatch 2014, August 7, 2013, http://www.washingtoninstitute.org/policy-analysis/view/al-qaedas-resiliency-in-yemen.

30. This has been seen with the al-Qaeda network; see Gunaratna, *Inside Al Qaeda*, 67.

31. Matthew Levitt, "Follow the Money: Leveraging Financial Intelligence to Combat Transnational Threats," *Georgetown Journal of International Affairs*, Winter/Spring 2011, 36.

32. Krueger, *What Makes a Terrorist?*

33. Marilyn B. Peterson, *A Guide to Counter Threat Finance Intelligence*, 2009, unclassified training manual provided to the author. An example of media would be Roj TV in Denmark; see Hasan Cücük, "Danish Bank Freezes Roj TV Accounts over PKK Links," February 2, 2012, http://www.todayszaman.com/newsDetail_getNewsById.action?load=detay&newsId=270329&link=270329.

34. John Roth, Douglas Greenburg, and Serena Wille, *Monograph on Terrorist Financing* (Washington, DC: National Commission on Terrorist Attacks upon the United States, 2004).

35. Matthew Levitt, *Hamas Politics, Charity and Terrorism in the Service of Jihad* (New Haven, CT: Yale University Press, 2006), 54.

36. J. Bowyer Bell, *The IRA 1968–2000: Analysis of a Secret Army* (London: Frank Cass, 2000), 176.

37. Glen E. Curtis and Tara Karacan, *The Nexus among Terrorists, Narcotics Traffickers, Weapons Proliferators and Organized Crime Networks in Western Europe*, December 2002, 18–19, http://www.loc.gov/rr/frd/pdf-files/WestEurope_NEXUS.pdf.

38. See discussion on diaspora communities in Michael Hess, "Substantiating the Nexus between Diaspora Groups and the Financing of Terrorism," in Costigan and Gold, *Terrornomics*, 49–63.

39. Mitchel P. Roth and Murat Sever, "Cutting Off the Hand That Feeds It: Countering Terrorist Financing in the 21st Century," http://www.utsam.org/images/.../4.Cutting-off-the-hand-that-feeds-it.pdf; Mitchel P. Roth and Murat Sever, "The Kurdish Workers Party (PKK): Funding Terrorism through Organized Crime, a Case Study," *Studies in Conflict and Terrorism*, October 2007, 901–20; Strozier and Frank, *The PKK*.

40. Hala Jaber, *Hezbollah Born with a Vengeance* (New York: Columbia University Press, 1997), 152.

41. Cristiana C. Brafman Kittner, "The Role of Safe Havens in Islamist Terrorism," *Terrorism and Political Violence* 19 (2007): 313.

42. David Veness, "Low Intensity and High Impact Conflict," in *The Future of Terrorism*, ed. Maxwell Taylor and Paul Horgan (London: Frank Cass, 2000), 11.

43. Matthew Levitt and Michael Jacobsen, *The Money Trail: Finding, Following and Freezing Terrorist Finances*, Policy Focus 89 (Washington, DC: Washington Institute, November 2008), 50–51, http://www.washingtoninstitute.org/policy-analysis/view/the-money-trail-finding-following-and-freezing-terrorist-finances, and Gunaratna, *Inside Al Qaeda*, 63–65; de Poot and Sonnenschein, *Jihadi Terrorism in the Netherlands*, 111.

44. UN World Drug Report, 2007, 170, http://www.unodc.org/pdf/research/wdr07/WDR_2007.pdf.

45. UN International Drug Control Programme, *World Drug Report* (New York: Oxford University Press, 1997), 124.

46. Moisés Naím, *Illicit: How Smugglers, Traffickers, and Copycats Are Hijacking the Global Economy* (New York: Anchor Books, 2006).

47. Louise I. Shelley, *Human Trafficking: A Global Perspective* (Cambridge: Cambridge University Press, 2010), 7.

48. Ibid., 71. On funding for Tamil Tigers, see Jodi Vittori, *Terrorist Financing and Resourcing* (New York: Palgrave Macmillan, 2011), 31; Jennifer J. Adams and

Jesenia M. Pizarro, "MS13: A Gang Profile," *Journal of Gang Research* 16, no. 4 (2009): 1–14.

49. "Rape for Profit: Trafficking of Nepali Girls and Women to India's Brothels," *Human Rights Watch/Asia* 12, no. 5(A) (1995); Augustine Anthony, "Pakistan Rescues Boys Trained as Suicide Bombers," July 28, 2009, http://www.reuters.com/article/asiaCrisis/idUSISL90520.

50. Interview with Nepalese general, National Defense University, Washington, DC, March 2004.

51. Shelley, *Human Trafficking*, 265–70.

52. Louise Shelley and John T. Picarelli, "Methods Not Motives: Implications of the Convergence of International Organized Crime and Terrorism," *Police Practice and Research* 3, no. 4 (2002): 313; Logan Burruss, "Human Smuggling aboard Seized Ship," August 13, 2010, http://articles.cnn.com/2010-08-13/world/canada.human.smuggling_1_sri-lankan-human-trafficking-toews?_s=PM:WORLD.

53. Shelley and Picarelli, "Methods Not Motives," 312.

54. Phil Williams, *Criminals, Militias, and Insurgents: Organized Crime in Iraq* (Carlisle, PA: Strategic Studies Institute, 2009), 185, http://www.strategicstudiesinstitute.army.mil/pdffiles/pub930.pdf.

55. The United States is exceptional in that most acts of terrorism have been carried out without a significant trade in weapons. This may be explained in part by the ready availability of arms for purchase in the United States. Emblematic of this are the tragic Oklahoma City bombing, where the terrorists used fertilizer to make explosives, and the World Trade Center attack, where they employed airplanes. The international trade in firearms is particularly associated with terrorist acts committed outside the United States; see Mark S. Hamm, "Crimes Committed by Terrorist Groups: Theory, Research and Prevention," NIJ, September 2005, http://www.ncjrs.gov/pdffiles1/nij/grants/211203.pdf.

56. Phil Williams, "Drugs and Guns," *Bulletin of the Atomic Scientists* 55 (January/February 1999): 46–48; Douglas Farah and Stephen Braun, *Merchant of Death: Money, Guns, Planes, and the Man Who Makes War Possible* (Hoboken, NJ: John Wiley, 2007).

57. Curtis and Karacan, *Nexus among Terrorists*.

58. Capie, "Trading the Tools of Terror," 191.

59. Ibid.

60. Angel Rabasa, Peter Chalk, Kim Cragin, Sara A. Daly, Heather S. Gregg, Theodore W. Karasik, Kevin A. O'Brien, and William Rosenau, *Beyond al-Qaeda, Part II: The Outer Rings of the Terrorist Universe* (Santa Monica, CA: RAND, 2006), 111–18.

61. R. T. Naylor, "The Insurgent Economy: Black Market Operations of Guerrilla Organizations," *Crime, Law and Social Change* 20, no. 1 (1993): 13, 20.

62. Patrick Alley, a founder and codirector of Global Witness, "Conflict and Extractive Industries," at Scenarios for Peace: Transparency and Anti-corruption, fifteenth anniversary of Transparency International, September 5, 2013, Bogotá.

63. Tanner Campbell and Rohan Gunaratna, "Maritime Terrorism, Piracy and Crime," in *Terrorism in the Asia-Pacific: Threat and Response*, ed. Rohan Gunaratna (Singapore: Eastern Universities Press, 2003), 75–77; Martin N. Murphy, *Contemporary Piracy and Maritime Terrorism: The Threat to International*

Security (London: IISS, 2007); Martin N. Murphy, *Small Boats, Weak States, Dirty Money: The Challenge of Piracy* (New York: Columbia University Press, 2008).

64. For a discussion of the underworld of gold, see R. T. Naylor, *Wages of Crime: Black Markets, Illegal Finance, and the Underworld Economy*, rev. ed. (Ithaca, NY: Cornell University Press, 2004), 196–246; for extractive industries, such as oil, see Frédéric Massé and Johanna Camargo, "Actores Armados Ilegales y Sector Extractivo en Colombia," V informe del Centro Internacional de Toledo para la Paz (CITpax) Observatorio Internacional, 2012, http://www.toledopax .org%2Fuploads%2FActores_armados_ilegales_sector_extractivo.pdf.

65. Ibid. For a discussion of the funds supporting diverse groups, see 59–63.

66. Global Witness, "For a Few Dollars More: How al Qaeda Moved into the Diamond Trade," April 2003, http://www.globalwitness.org/library/few-dollars-more; Greg Campbell, *Blood Diamonds: Tracing the Deadly Path of the World's Most Precious Stones* (Boulder, CO: Westview Press, 2002); Douglas Farah, *Blood from Stones: The Secret Financial Network of Terror* (New York: Broadway Books, 2004).

67. Massé and Camargo, "Actores Armados Ilegales y Sector Extractivo en Colombia," 49.

68. "Fondeo del terrorismo."

69. Leo R. Douglas and Kelvin Alie, "High-value natural resources: linking wildlife conservation to international conflict, insecurity, and development concerns," *Biological Conservation*, 171 (March 2014), 270–77.

70. Quote is from Jeffrey Gettleman, "Elephants Dying in Epic Frenzy as Ivory Fuels Wars and Profits," *New York Times*, September 3, 2012, http://www.nytimes.com/ 2012/09/04/world/africa/africas-elephants-are-being-slaughtered-in-poaching-frenzy.html?pagewanted=all&_r=0. For more discussion of this problem, see Marina Ratchford, Beth Allgood, and Paul Todd, *Criminal Nature: The Global Security Implications of the Illegal Wildlife Trade* (Washington, DC: IFAW, 2013).

71. Gettleman, "Elephants Dying in Epic Frenzy."

72. Gretchen Peters, *How Opium Profits the Taliban* (Washington, DC: U.S. Institute of Peace, 2009); Peters, *Seeds of Terror: How Drugs, Thugs, and Crime Are Reshaping the Afghan War* (New York: Picador, 2010); Louise Shelley and Nazia Hussain, "Narco-trafficking in Pakistan-Afghanistan Border Areas and Implications for Security in Narco-jihad: Drug Trafficking and Security in Afghanistan and Pakistan," NBR Special Report 20 (December 2009), 30–31, 35, 37, 40.

73. FATF, "Trade Based Money Laundering," August 31, 2012, http://www.fatf-gafi.org/dataoecd/60/25/37038272.pdf; also http://www.fatf-gafi.org/media/fatf/ documents/reports/Trade%20Based%20Money%20Laundering.pdf.

74. Interview with former customs official, September 2011.

75. Joby Warrick, "U.S. Accuses Lebanese Companies of Laundering Money for Hezbollah," *Washington Post*, April 23, 2013, http://articles.washingtonpost .com/2013-04-23/world/38756339_1_hezbollah-ayman-joumaa-lebanese-canadian-bank; Juan C. Zarate, *Treasury's War: The Unleashing of a New Era of Financial Warfare* (New York: Public Affairs, 2013), 359.

76. See discussion of kidnapping in Phil Williams and Vanda Felbab-Brown, *Drug Trafficking, Violence and Instability*, SSI Monograph (Carlisle, PA: Strategic Studies Institute, U.S. Army War College, April 2012), 41.

77. "Fondeo del terrorismo."

78. Peters, *Haqqani Network Financing*, 39–44; see *Warlord, Inc., Extortion and Corruption along the U.S. Supply Chain in Afghanistan*, report of the Majority Staff, Rep. John F. Tierney, Chair Committee on Oversight and Government Reform, U.S. House of Representatives, June 1, 2010, http://www.cbsnews.com/htdocs/pdf/HNT_Report.pdf.

79. Gretchen Peters, *Crime and Insurgency in the Tribal Areas of Afghanistan and Pakistan* (West Point, NY: Combating Terrorism Center at West Point, 2010), 31–32, http://www.ctc.usma.edu/posts/crime-and-insurgency-in-the-tribal-areas-of-afghanistan-and-pakistan.

80. Interview with an Israeli who engaged in bank robbery in the 1940s for his political organization.

81. Turkish People's Liberation Front, http://www.start.umd.edu/start/data_collections/tops/terrorist_organization_profile.asp?id=4294.

82. Horgan and Taylor, "Playing the 'Green Card,'" 13.

83. Levitt and Jacobsen, *Money Trail*.

84. Rogelio Alonso and Marcos Garcia Rey, "The Evolution of Jihadist Terrorism in Morocco," *Terrorism and Political Violence* 19, no. 4 (2007): 576.

85. See V. Arianti, "Indonesian Terrorism Financing: Resorting to Robberies," RSIS Commentaries, No. 142, July 29, 2013, http://www.rsis.edu.sg/publications/commentaries.html.

86. Ibid.

87. Ibid.

88. David E. Kaplan, "Paying for Terror: How Jihadist Groups Are Using Organized-Crime Tactics – and Profits – to Finance Attacks on Targets around the Globe," November 27, 2005, http://www.militantislammonitor.org/article/id/1429.

89. Jeffrey Cozzens and William Rosenau, "The 'Homegrown' Case of Jami`at al-Islam al-Sahih," August 15, 2009, http://www.ctc.usma.edu/posts/training-for-terror-the-%E2%80%9Chomegrown%E2%80%9D-case-of-jamiat-al-islam-al-sahih.

90. Mark Hamm, "Crimes Committed by Terrorist Groups," NIJ, September 2005. The data analyzed dated from 1980 to 2002. http://www.ncjrs.gov/pdffiles1/nij/grants/211203.pdf.

91. The United States is exceptional in escaping kidnapping of Americans at home, although many have been kidnapped overseas because their families and employers can buy generous ransoms.

92. FATF/OECD, "Organised Maritime Piracy," 29.

93. Donatella della Porta, "Left-Wing Terrorism in Italy," in *Terrorism in Context*, ed. Martha Crenshaw (University Park: Pennsylvania State University Press, 1995), 105–59.

94. Horgan and Taylor, "Playing the 'Green Card,'" 9–12.

95. Rabasa et al., *Beyond al-Qaeda*, Part II, 78–80.

96. Roth and Sever, "The Kurdish Workers Party (PKK)," 905; Lyubov Mincheva and Ted Robert Gurr, "Unholy Alliances III: Communal Militants and Criminal Networks in the Middle East, with a Case Study of the Kurdistan Workers Party (PKK)," paper presented at the annual meeting of the International Studies Association, http://www.cidcm.umd.edu/publications/papers/unholy_alliances.pdf.

97. John Lee Anderson, *Guerillas: The Men and Women Fighting Today's Wars* (New York: Random House Times Books, 1992), 107.

98. Dirección de Justicia y Seguridad, "Cifras de Violencia, 1996–2002," 2002, 3–4, copy provided to the author.

99. Rabasa et al., *Beyond al-Qaeda, Part II*, 130–31.

100. Daniel Pécaut, *Les Farc, une guerilla sans fin?* (Paris: Lignes de Repères, 2008), 77. Pécaut's analyses, according to a Colombian official interviewed, are based on data provided to him by Colombian authorities with access to seized materials from the FARC.

101. John Rollins and Liana Wyler, *International Terrorism and Transnational Crime: Security Threats, U.S. Policy, and Considerations for Congress* (Washington, DC: Congressional Research Service, 2010), 18, http://fpc.state.gov/documents/organization/134960.pdf.

102. Ingrid Betancourt, *La Rage au Coeur* (Paris: Pocher, 2001).

103. Pécaut, *Les Farc, une guerilla sans fin?*, 80.

104. Rollins and Wyler, *International Terrorism and Transnational Crime*, 22, 51.

105. The quote is from Kaplan, "Paying for Terror." For further discussion of kidnapping in Iraq, see Chapter 4 of Williams, *Criminals, Militias, and Insurgents*, 105–56.

106. O'Brien, "Fluctuations between Crime and Terror," 320–36.

107. Rabasa et al., *Beyond al-Qaeda, Part II*, 115.

108. Alfredo L. Filler, "The Abu Sayyaf Group: A Growing Menace to Civil Society," *Terrorism and Political Violence* 14, no. 4 (2002): 131–62.

109. Rabasa et al., *Beyond al-Qaeda, Part II*, 115.

110. Filler, "Abu Sayyaf Group"; Rabasa et al., *Beyond al-Qaeda, Part II*, 139.

111. Rabasa et al., *Beyond al-Qaeda, Part II*, 116.

112. Rollins and Wyler, *International Terrorism and Transnational Crime*, 8.

113. This is the case of the David Chavchavadze family captured by Imam Shamil, http://chavchavadze.si.edu/shamil.html.

114. Anna Repetskya, "The Classification of the Criminal Exploitation of People and Problems of Criminal Responsibility for It," in *Torgovliia Liudmi: Sotsiokriminologicheskii Analiz* (Trade in People: Socio-criminological Analysis), ed. E. V. Tiuriukanova and L. D. Erokhina (Moscow: Academia, 2002), 59–88.

115. LaVerle Berry, Glenn E. Curtis, and John N. Gibbs, *Nations Hospitable to Organized Crime and Terrorism* (Washington, DC: Federal Research Division, Library of Congress, 2003), 4–5, http://www.loc.gov/rr/frd/pdf-files/Nats_Hospitable.pdf.

116. Rollins and Wyler, *International Terrorism and Transnational Crime*, 27.

117. John Thorne, "Kidnapping Westerners Is a Lucrative Business in the Sahel," *The National*, December 20, 2009, http://www.thenational.ae/news/world/africa/kidnapping-westerners-is-a-lucrative-business-in-the-sahel.

118. Dario Cristiani and Riccardo Fabiani, "Al Qaeda in the Islamic Maghreb (AQIM): Implications for Algeria's Regional and International Relations," Instituto Affari Internazaionali, April 2011, 7, http://www.isn.ethz.ch/isn/Digital-Library/Publications/Detail/?ots591=0c54e3b3-1e9c-be1e-2c24-a6a8c7060233&lng=en&id=128337.

119. Pino Arlacchi, *Mafia Business: The Mafia Ethic and the Spirit of Capitalism*, trans. Martin Ryle (London: Verso, 1986); Raimondo Catanzaro, *Men of Respect: A Social History of the Sicilian Mafia*, trans. Raymond Rosenthal (New York: Free Press, 1992); Gambetta, *Sicilian Mafia*.

120. Vadim Volkov, *Violent Entrepreneurs: The Use of Force in the Making of Russian Capitalism* (Ithaca, NY: Cornell University Press, 2002), discusses extortion in Russia, but it has broader applicability, as this analysis here suggests.

121. Jonathan Winer, "Origins, Organization and Prevention of Terrorist Finance," testimony before the Senate Committee on Governmental Affairs, July 31, 2003, http://handy.gslsolutions.com/gov/senate/hsgac/public/_archive/073103winer.htm.

122. Rabasa et al., *Beyond al-Qaeda*, Part II, 126.

123. "Fondeo del terrorismo," 10–15, and interview with one of the researchers who did this analysis.

124. Roth and Sever, "Kurdish Workers Party (PKK)," 910.

125. Michele Zanini, "Middle East Terrorism and Netwar," *Studies in Conflict and Terrorism* 22 (1999): 247.

126. Horgan and Taylor, "Playing the 'Green Card,'" 1–2, quoting J. Adams, "The Financing of Terrorism," in *Contemporary Research on Terrorism*, ed. P. Wilkinson and A.M. Stewart (Aberdeen: Aberdeen University Press, 1987), 401.

127. Levitt and Jacobsen, *Money Trail*.

128. Kaplan, "Paying for Terror."

129. Levitt and Jacobsen, *Money Trail*, 56.

130. Ibid., 8.

131. Ibid., 50–51.

132. Ibid., 67.

133. Jeremy M. Simon, "Plastic and Terror: Study Describes How Terrorists Use Credit Cards," October 1, 2008, http://www.creditcards.com/credit-card-news/terrorist-credit-cards-theft-1282.php.

134. Gunaratna, *Inside Al Qaeda*, 65.

135. Levitt and Jacobsen, *Money Trail*, 51.

136. Josh Lefkowitz, "The Crime-Terror Nexus," New York State Office of Homeland Security, March 13, 2006, 5, http://info.publicintelligence.net/NY-CrimeTerrorNexus.pdf.

137. Benjamin Weiser, "A Nation Challenged: An Arrest; Algerian Man Faces Charges in a Millennium Terror Plot," *New York Times*, November 17, 2001, http://www.nytimes.com/2001/11/17/nyregion/nation-challenged-arrest-algerian-man-faces-charges-millennium-terror-plot.html.

138. Dennis Lormel, "Credit Cards and Terrorists." January 16, 2008, http://counterterrorismblog.org/2008/01/credit_cards_and_terrorists.php.

139. Ibid.; Gordon Corera, "The World's Most Wanted Cyber-jihadist," January 16, 2008, http://news.bbc.co.uk/2/hi/americas/7191248.stm.

140. Gunaratna, *Inside Al Qaeda*, 65.

141. Author's interviews with individuals in the credit card industry.

142. For examples, see cyberattack against Estonia and Georgia, attributed to the Russian government, and Chinese attacks against U.S. computer systems, such as the National Defense University, whose network was allegedly brought down by Chinese hackers who could not operate without, at least, the encouragement of the Chinese government.

143. Süleyman Özeren, *Cyberterrorism and Cybercrime: Vulnerabilities and International Cooperation* (Saarbrücken, Germany: VDM, 2009), 17; Roderic Broadhurst and Peter Grabosky, eds., *Cyber-crime: The Challenge in Asia* (Hong Kong: Hong

Kong University Press, 2005); M. Zanini and S. J. A. Edwards, "The Networking of Terror in the Information Age," in *Networks and Netwars*, ed. J. Arquilla and D. Ronfelt (Santa Monica, CA: RAND, 2001), 29–60.

144. D. E. Denning and W. E. Baugh Jr., *Hiding Crimes in Cyberspace: Cybercrime: Law Enforcement, Security and Surveillance in the Information Age* (New York: Routledge, 2000); Özeren, *Cyberterrorism and Cybercrime*, 6–25.

145. Phil Williams, "Warning Indicators, Terrorist Finances, and Terrorist Adaptation," *Strategic Insights* 4, no. 1 (2005), http://www.nps.edu/Academics/centers/ccc/publications/OnlineJournal/2005/Jan/williamsJan05.htm.

146. Özeren, *Cyberterrorism and Cybercrime*, 21.

147. Richard Kerbaj and Dominic Kennedy, "Link between Child Porn and Muslim Terrorists Discovered in Police Raids," October 17, 2008, http://www.technewsreview.com.au/article.php?article=6237.

148. Interview with DEA analyst for Latin America, 2000.

149. John Cassara, *Hide and Seek: Intelligence, Law Enforcement, and the Stalled War on Terrorist Finance* (Washington, DC: Potomac Books, 2006), 150–54, 176–81.

150. See Nimrod Raphaeli, "Financing of Terrorism: Sources, Methods and Channels," *Terrorism and Political Violence* 15, no. 4 (2003): 74–75.

151. Peters, *Seeds of Terror*.

152. Williams, *Criminals, Militias, and Insurgents*, 63–104.

153. Ibid.; Bilal Wahab, "How Iraq Oil Smuggling Greases Violence," *Middle East Quarterly*, Fall 2006, 53–59, http://www.meforum.org/1020/how-iraqi-oil-smuggling-greases-violence; conversations with Turkish National Police, Ankara, June 2010.

154. Williams, *Criminals, Militias, and Insurgents*, 63–104.

155. Levitt and Jacobsen, *Money Trail*, 61.

156. Martin N. Murphy, *Somalia: The New Barbary? Piracy and Islam in the Horn of Africa* (New York: Columbia University Press, 2011); see also Murphy, *Weak States, Dirty Money: Piracy and Maritime Terrorism in the Modern World* (New York: Columbia University Press, 2010), 4.

157. Murphy, *Weak States*, 28.

158. Thomas M. Sanderson, "Transnational Terror and Organized Crime: Blurring the Lines," *SAIS Review* 24, no. 1 (2004): 51–52.

159. Jeffrey Gettleman, "Somali Pirates Capture Tanks and Global Notice," *New York Times*, January 26, 2008, http://www.nytimes.com/2008/09/27/world/africa/27pirates.html?pagewanted=all.

160. Chair's Report of November conference in Hawaii Trans-Pacific Symposium on Dismantling Illicit Networks, Honolulu, November 9–12, 2009, http://www.state.gov/documents/organization/137524.pdf.

161. The author learned this in attendance at the Trans-Pacific symposium.

162. Chair's Report of November conference in Hawaii Trans-Pacific Symposium on Dismantling Illicit Networks, ibid., 20. The author heard more detailed analyses than are presented in the released report.

163. Sherzod Abdukadirov, "Terrorism: The Dark Side of Social Entrepreneurship," *Studies in Conflict and Terrorism* 33, no. 7 (2010): 603–17; Douglas Farah, "Fixers, Super Fixers, and Shadow Facilitators: How Networks Connect."

164. *Organised Crime in Australia Key Trends 2008*, 2, http://www.crimecommission .gov.au/publications/organised-crime-australia/organised-crime-australia-2008-report; Farah, "Fixers, Super Fixers, and Shadow Facilitators."

165. For an analysis of an Auckland, New Zealand, facilitator for organized criminals and terrorists, see "Offshore Registration Business Halts Operations," June 28, 2011, http://www.reportingproject.net/occrp/index.php/en/ccwatch/cc-watch-indepth/930-offshore-registration-business-forced-to-halt-operations.

166. Mark S. Hamm, *Terrorism as Crime: From Oklahoma City to Al-Qaeda and Beyond* (New York: New York University Press, 2007), 16–17, states that terrorists need these services, such as false documents, transportation, and communications, and this is the easiest way to apprehend them.

167. Frank Bovenkerk and Yucel Yesilgöz, "The Turkish Mafia and the State," in *Organised Crime in Europe: Patterns and Policies in the European Union and Beyond*, ed. Cyrille Fijnaut and Letizia Paoli (Dordrecht, Netherlands: Springer, 2004), 598–99; Charles Strozier and James Frank, *The PKK: Financial Sources, Social and Political Dimension* (Saarbrücken, Germany: VDM, 2011).

168. Transnational Crime, Corruption, and Information Technology (TraCCC Annual Conference Report, 2000), November 30 to December 1, 2000, American University, Washington, DC, http://traccc.gmu.edu/topics/corruption/traccc-corruption-publications/.

169. Farah, "Fixers, Super Fixers and Shadow Facilitators"; European Police Chiefs Convention also discussed the role of facilitators at the meeting, attended by the author. For a further discussion of the ideas, see European Police Chiefs Convention, The Hague, Netherlands, June 29 to July 1, 2011, http://www.europol .europa.eu/.../european-police-chiefs-convention-491.

170. Nir Hasson, "Four Arab Lawyers Suspected of Passing Messages for Islamic Jihad. The Four Are Suspected of Passing Information from Islamic Jihad Prisoners in Israel to the Group's Officials in Gaza, in Return for Thousands of Shekels," *Ha'aretz*, April 20, 2011, http://www.haaretz.com/news/national/four-arab-lawyers-suspected-of-passing-messages-for-islamic-jihad-1.356924; Colin Moynihan, "Radical Lawyer Convicting of Aiding Terrorist Is Jailed," *New York Times*, November 20, 2009, http://www.nytimes.com/2009/11/20/nyregion/20stewart .html?scp=3&sq=Lynne+Stewart&st=nyt.

171. See also *Brazil: Primeiro Comando da Capital (PCC)*, January 1, 2008, http:// www.pbs.org/wnet/wideangle/tag/gang/. For a further discussion of their finances, see Juan Carlos Garzón, *Mafia & Co: The Criminal Networks in Mexico, Brazil and Colombia*, translated by Kathy Ogle (Bogotá: Planeta, 2008), 76, http://www .wilsoncenter.org/sites/default/files/mafiaandcompany_reducedsize.pdf.

172. Max C. Manwaring, "Three Lessons from Contemporary Challenges to Security," *Prism* 2, no. 3 (2011): 107.

173. Roy Godson, ed., *Menace to Society: Political-Criminal Collaboration around the World* (New Brunswick, NJ: Transaction, 2003).

174. IPT News, "Bookeeper Defends HLF Accounting," November 6, 2008, http:// www.investigativeproject.org/800/bookkeeper-defends-hlf-accounting; see also *Dallas News* blog on the Holy Land Foundation case, http://crimeblog.dallasnews .com/archives/holy-land-foundation/, where the appeal of the case and its history are discussed.

175. Government's Sentencing Memorandum, in The United States District Court for the Northern District of Ohio Western Division United States of America, Case No. 3:06CR719, Plaintiff, Chief Judge James G. Carr v. Mohammad Zaki Amawi, Marwan Othman El-Hindi, Wassim I. Mazloum, May 10, 2009; see http://www .investigativeproject.org/1483/two-other-toledo-defendants-sentenced.

176. Nimrod Raphaeli, "Financing of Terrorism: Sources, Methods and Channels," *Terrorism and Political Violence* 15, no. 4 (2003): 72.

177. Devlin Barrett and Evan Perez, "HSBC to Pay Record U.S. Penalty U.K.-Based Bank Expected to Admit Money-Laundering Lapses as Part of $1.9 Billion Agreement," *Wall Street Journal,* December 11, 2012, http://online.wsj.com/article/SB 10001424127887324478304578171650887467568.html; Matt Tabibi, "Gangster Bankers: Too Big to Jail How HSBC Hooked Up with Drug Traffickers and Terrorists. And Got Away with It," February 14, 2013, http://www.rollingstone .com/politics/news/gangster-bankers-too-big-to-jail-20130214.

178. Jessica Silver-Greenberg, "Cash Moves by HSBC in Inquiry," *New York Times,* August 24, 2012, http://www.nytimes.com/2012/08/25/business/us-said-to-investigate-money-laundering-at-hsbc.html?pagewanted=all&_r=0.

179. Zarate, *Treasury's War,* 359–61; Matthew Levitt, *Hezbollah: The Global Footprint of Lebanon's Party of God* (Washington, DC: Georgetown University Press, 2013), 259.

180. U.S. Attorney's Office, Southern District of New York, "Manhattan U.S. Attorney Files Civil Money Laundering and Forfeiture Suit Seeking More Than $480 Million Dollars from Entities Including Lebanese Financial Institutions That Facilitated a Hizballah-Related Money Laundering Scheme," press release, December 11, 2011, http://www.investigativeproject.org/case/605; U.S. Senate Permanent Subcommittee on Investigations, "U.S. Vulnerabilities to Money Laundering, Drugs and Terrorist Financing: HSBC Case History," Majority and Minority Staff Report, July 17, 2012.

181. Jessica Hume, "US Seizes $150 Million from Hezbollah-Linked Lebanese Canadian Bank," *Toronto Sun,* August 21, 2012, http://www.torontosun.com/2012/ 08/21/us-seizes-150m-from-hezbollah-linked-lebanese-canadian-bank.

182. Matthew Levitt, *Hamas: Politics, Charity, and Terrorism in the Service of Jihad* (New Haven, CT: Yale University Press, 2006), 165.

183. Ibid. and author's discussion with lead investigator of this case, fall 2010.

184. U.S. Department of the Treasury, "Treasury Imposes Sanctions on Individuals Linked to the Taliban and Haqqani Network," press release, May 17, 2012.

185. Gretchen Peters, "The Haqqani Financing Network: The Evolution of an Industry," talk on her research at the Terrorism, Transnational Crime, and Corruption Center, George Mason University, September 12, 2012, as well as the author's discussions with Gretchen Peters. In her talk, she discussed that the Haqqanis used specific hawaladars identified with D-Company.

186. Discussions with the Financial Intelligence Unit, Ankara, Turkey, June 2010. There is much concern to stop the cash that returns from drug sales in Europe that fund the PKK, but there are few advisories from Western European law enforcement that would allow them to act in real time. The vast movements of people across the border, especially to Turkey, which is a major tourist destination, reduces the likelihood of finding cash transfers without clear intelligence.

187. Nikos Passas, "Informal Value Transfer Systems, Terrorism and Money Laundering," January 2005, http://www.ncjrs.gov/pdffiles1/nij/grants/208301.pdf; for a fuller discussion of *hawala*, see Edwina A. Thompson, *Trust Is the Coin of the Real: Lessons from the Money Men in Afghanistan* (Karachi: Oxford University Press, 2011); see also Zarate, *Treasury's War*, 96–101.

188. Peter Gastrow, *Termites at Work: Transnational Organized Crime and State Erosion in Kenya* (New York: International Peace Institute, 2011), 8.

189. Edwina A. Thompson, "Misplaced Blame: Islam, Terrorism and the Origins of Hawala," Max Planck Volume of United Nations Law, ed. A. von Bogdandy and R. Wolfrum, 2007, 11, 279–305, http://www.mpil.de/shared/data/pdf/pdfmpunyb/08_thompson_11.pdf; Maryam Razavy, "Hawala: An Underground Haven for Terrorists or Social Phenomenon?," *Crime, Law, and Social Change* 44, no. 3 (2005): 277–99.

190. "Operation Cash-Out Charges 45 Defendants in International Money Laundering and Bribery Schemes," September 20, 2007, http://www.justice.gov/usao/md/Public-Affairs/press_releases/press07/OperationCash-outCharges45DefendantsinInternationalMoneyLaunderingandBriberySchemes.html.

191. "FBI's Top Ten News Stories for the Week Ending November 7, 2008," http://www2.fbi.gov/pressrel/pressrel08/topten_110708.htm; see also US v. Ranjha, Saifullah, et al., http://www.investigativeproject.org/case/251.

192. De Poot and Sonnenschein, *Jihadi Terrorism in the Netherlands*, 131–32.

193. Gastrow, *Termites at Work*, 8.

194. 9/11 Commission, *Terrorist Travel*, 59, http://www.9-11commission.gov/staff_statements/911_TerrTrav_Ch3.pdf.

195. Ibid., 61; *Combating Terrorism: Additional Steps Needed to Enhance Foreign Partners' Capacity to Prevent Terrorist Travel*, GAO-11-637 (Washington, DC: U.S. Government Accountability Office, June 2011), 6.

196. Ersel Aydinli, "From Finances to Transnational Mobility: Searching for the Global Jihadists' Achilles Heel," *Terrorism and Political Violence* 18 (2006): 307–9.

198. Emal Khan and Andrew Alderson, "Revealed: Pakistan's 'Cottage Industry' in Forged Documents Sought by Terrorists," *The Telegraph*, April 11, 2009, http://www.telegraph.co.uk/news/uknews/law-and-order/5141619/Revealed-Pakistans-cottage-industry-in-forged-documents-sought-by-terrorists.html.

197. 9/11 Commission, *Terrorist Travel*, footnote 151, 67.

199. "Madrid Bombings Link to Forged Passports Arrests, Suspected Members of an International Ring Providing Forged Passports to Terrorists May Have Links to 2004 Train Bombings," *Guardian*, December 2, 2010, http://www.guardian.co.uk/world/2010/dec/02/madrid-bombings-link-forged-passports-arrests.

200. Farah, "Fixers, Super Fixers, and Shadow Facilitators"; World Economic Forum, "Organised Crime Enablers." Ana Baric, Trafficking and Terrorism: How Organized Crime Thrives on Passport Fraud," March 13, 2014, https://reportingproject.net/occrp/index.php/en/cc-blog/2369-trafficking-and-terrorism-how-organized-crime-thrives-on-passport-fraud-.

201. Aleksandr Zheglov, "Before the Flight Examination: How the Women Bombers Got on the Planes," *Kommersant*, September 16, 2004, http://www.kommersant.com/p505825/Before_the_Flight_Examination/.

202. Levitt and Jacobsen, *Money Trail*, 59.

203. "Chiquita Admits to Paying Colombia Terrorists," March 15, 2007, http://www
.msnbc.msn.com/id/17615143/ns/business-us_business/t/chiquita-admits-paying-
colombia-terrorists/; "Chiquita to Pay $25M in Terrorist Case," March 15, 2007,
http://www.abcmoney.co.uk/news/15200739657.htm.

204. Accusations have been made in U.S. federal court that Del Monte hired a known
family of drug traffickers named Mendoza that provided them with security and
intimidated workers. Therefore, there are also corporate relations with crime
groups. See Plaza Pública, "Del Monte contrató a los Mendoza para intimidar
sindicalistas, según denuncia," August 8, 2011, http://www.plazapublica.com.gt/
content/del-monte-contrato-los-mendoza-para-intimidar-sindicalistas.

205. Blog of Amb. David Shinn, "Rise of Piracy and Other Maritime Insecurity in
Somalia," Somali Piracy Conference, hosted by the National Maritime Intelligence Center and the Office of Naval Intelligence, April 7, 2009, http://davidshinn
.blogspot.com/2009/09/my-remarks-on-rise-of-piracy-in-somalia.html.

206. Daniel Wallis, "Piracy Ransoms Funding Somalia Insurgency," Reuters,
August 24, 2008, http://www.reuters.com/article/2008/08/24/us-somalia-piracy-
interview-idUSLO005723200808224.

207. Ibid.

208. Aaron Zelinsky and Martin Shubik, "Research Note: Terrorist Groups as Business
Firms: A New Typological Framework," *Terrorism and Political Violence* 21,
no. 2 (2009): 327–36, discuss terrorist groups as venture capitalists. I am using
this differently to explain the funding streams related to terrorism.

209. Rear Admiral Chris Parry CBE, "Piracy in the Horn of Africa," World
Check White Paper, March 11, 2010, http://www.country-check.com/WhitePaper/
&name=5; "Somali Sea Gangs Lure Investors at Pirate Lair," Reuters,
December 1, 2009, http://www.reuters.com/article/2009/12/01/us-somalia-piracy-
investors-idUSTRE5B01Z920091201; Avi Jorisch, "Today's Pirates Have Their
Own Stock Exchange: Western Powers Patrol the Seas but Do Little to Stop
Pirate Financing," *Wall Street Journal*, June 16, 2011, http://online.wsj.com/
article/SB10001424052702304520804576341223910765818.html; discussions
at Africom in Stuttgart, Germany, May 2011.

210. "Somali Sea Gangs Lure Investors at Pirate Lair."

211. Raymond Ibrahim, "The Fallacy of Grievance Based Terrorism, from Barbary
Wars to Somaly Pirates, the 'Water Jihad' Has a Long Lineage," http://www
.meforum.org/2126/barbary-wars-somali-piracy-water-jihad.

212. Nicholas Schmidle, "The Hostage Business," *New York Times*, December
6, 2009, http://www.nytimes.com/2009/12/06/magazine/06kidnapping-t.html?
pagewanted=all. Insurance firms have also suffered at the hands of rogue
states, such as North Korea, that have engaged in insurance fraud. See Blaine
Harden, "Global Insurance Fraud by North Korea Outlined," *Washington Post*,
June 18, 2009, http://articles.washingtonpost.com/2009–06–18/world/36841372_
1_insurance-fraud-suspicious-claims-state-insurance.

213. Shinn, "Rise of Piracy and Other Maritime Insecurity in Somalia."

214. David Smith and Clar Ni Chonghaile, "Somali Pirates Hijacking Fewer Merchant Ships: Robust Action by International Navies and Hiring of Armed Security
Guards Drive Piracy to Three-Year Low," *Guardian*, October 23, 2012, http://
www.guardian.co.uk/world/2012/oct/23/somali-piracy-declines.

215. Wittig, *Understanding Terrorist Finance.*
216. Peters, *Crime and Insurgency,* i.
217. Diego Gambetta and Frederico Varese, "Is Sicily the Future of Russia: Private Protection and the Rise of the Russian Mafia," *European Journal of Sociology* 42, no. 1 (2001): 186–220.

6

The Drug Trade

The Profit Center of Criminals and Terrorists

The Drug Trade: A Political Act

A captured Taliban underscored, "Whether it is by opium or by shooting, this is our common goal [to harm all infidels as part of jihad]."[1] This concept of harm causation through criminal activity has not only been seen among jihadi terrorist groups but was given as a justification for the drug trade in Peru decades ago. "Coca cultivation is a political act in a much fuller sense than is conventional criminal behavior. By cultivating coca, one is not only enhancing one's own income, one is also contributing – intentionally or unintentionally, directly or indirectly to Sendero Luminoso's efforts to depose the government."[2] Using the drug trade as part of a terrorist strategy sets terrorists apart from ordinary criminals. They have a political as well as a financial agenda. But terrorists engage in the drug trade, as do a wide variety of actors – criminals, insurgents, and corrupt officials – because it generates large profits relative to investment. In the drug trade we see visible and consistent dirty entanglements that are key to its successful operation. Drug trade is a crime of choice for diverse nonstate actors because risks of confiscation and arrest are relatively small relative to potential gains.

Profits and Consequences for the Perpetrators

The drug trade is one of the most profitable and rapidly growing forms of trade in the world. The United Nations Office on Drugs and Crime's latest estimate is that the profits from heroin trafficking out of Afghanistan total $13 billion annually for the northern route through Central Asia to the Russian Federation. The market value for heroin that heads in a more southerly direction through Turkey and on to the Balkans and Western Europe is $20 billion.[3] Add to this sales for cocaine, synthetic drugs, and marijuana, and there are many more billions in sales. This sum far exceeds the profits from any other area of illicit trade. Drug trafficking has made certain criminal organizations enormously rich and has provided terrorist groups the resources that they need to recruit individuals and sustain their activities. In many regions of the world, it is hard to define purely criminal or purely terrorist organizations that engage in the drug trade. Hybrids of criminal and terrorist organizations presently exist on many continents. Working with corrupt officials, they have been operating drug trafficking networks for several decades.[4] As a result of their years of involvement with the lucrative drug trade, some terrorist groups have devolved into more criminal than terrorist groups. ASG in the Philippines and the FARC in Colombia epitomize this phenomena, as their criminal interests now supersede their political.[5]

The Drug Trade Functions as a Business

The drug trade illustrates many of the principles discussed in the previous chapter on the business of terrorism. Despite its extreme violence, there are many rational aspects of the narcotics trade both for terrorists and transnational criminals. They include the drug traffickers' efforts to ensure production, develop and maintain delivery routes, and expand into new markets. Many drug traffickers try to control all aspects of the supply chain, whereas others outsource to reduce risk and cost, just like in legal businesses. Corruption is an essential element of their operations. Diversification and technology are also key to their operations in many parts of the world. Both criminals and terrorists often use the same routes they develop to move drugs to transport other illicit commodities. With their vast resources, they can hire sophisticated IT professionals who can encrypt their messages and market their produce.[6]

The profitability of the drug trade, both to the traffickers and to the farmers who cultivate many of the raw materials, suggests that this business has an economic utility for diverse participants contributing to its sustainability. Moreover, it brings resources, particularly to the corrupt elites of some of the world's poorest countries. Afghanistan, Guinea-Bissau, Tajikistan, and Kyrgyzstan are extremes, but these countries are just representative of a much more widespread problem.[7]

The wealth of the most successful traffickers allows them to make significant investments in necessary infrastructure, such as developing landing strips, maintaining roads, and building smuggling tunnels.[8] They also invest in personnel by buying officials at all levels and securing the services of high-level facilitators such as lawyers, accountants, and money launderers.[9] The corruption can go up to the level of the head of state. The Colombian–U.S. drug route was facilitated by the collaboration between Colombian drug dealers and the dictatorship of General Manuel Noriega of Panama. He accepted massive bribes to let the drugs flow through this corridor.[10]

The success of drug organizations results not only from their use of advanced technology and high-level personnel. Many survive and prosper because they are rooted in traditional family and kinship structures. These tight-knit networks allow operations to function on the basis of trust and make them difficult to disrupt.

The most successful drug traffickers, as is discussed, ensure that the drug trade takes advantage of the existing social, economic, and political structures of the community in which they operate. This is true both along the trade routes out of Afghanistan and on the ground in South America or North Africa,[11] where peasants are engaged in the cultivation of drugs.

The dirty entanglements operating the drug trade are dealing with a commodity that is of recent demand on a large scale in international markets. Its growth is an important negative consequence of globalization. But the drug trade is not an entirely new phenomenon; it functioned on a mass scale in China and was used as a tool of domination by the British Empire in the nineteenth century.[12]

Terrorists and Drug Organizations

The Concept of Narco-Terrorism

The term *narco-terrorism,* linking terrorist groups with the drug trade, was developed in the early 1980s in regard to the Peruvian Sendero Luminoso.[13] But this term is an oversimplification of the phenomenon, as it fails to recognize that most terrorist groups simultaneously engage in other illicit acts, such as was discussed in Chapter 5, to support their activity. Terrorist groups do not just trade drugs but trade in arms, kidnap people, and extort from businesses in their region. Moreover, the term *narco-terrorism* ignores the high-level corruption of government officials that facilitates this drug trade. For example, in 2012 in Peru, the sentence of President Alberto Fujimori's right hand, Vladimiro Montesinos, for involvement in death squads was reduced by a tribunal of the Peruvian Supreme Court to twenty years.[14] The prison sentence of Montesinos, the former head of the Peruvian intelligence service, was combined with a stiff financial penalty, as he also sold weapons to the Colombian terrorist group FARC while he served as one of the Peruvian government's top officials.[15] His trial revealed the centrality of government officials to the drug trade as well as the centrality of the illicit arms trade to "narco-terrorism."

There were other negative consequences of the minting of the term *narco-terrorism,* as the terrorism specialist Bruce Hoffman explained: "The emphasis on 'narco-terrorism' as the latest manifestation of the communist plot to undermine western society, however, had the unfortunate effect of diverting official attention away from a bona fide emerging trend. To a greater extent than ever in the past, entirely criminal (that is, violent, *economically* motivated) organizations were now forging strategic alliances with terrorist and guerrilla organizations."[16] This trade was not only corrupting officials but tainting and distorting entire economies.[17] The extraordinary profits of this trade[18] added to the potency of terrorist groups, who traded in narcotics or extorted money from the drug trafficking organizations "they protected."[19]

The term *narco-terrorism* was not initially extended beyond Latin America. Analysts overlooked the fact that the IRA was increasingly sustaining its organization through drug trafficking[20] or that the PKK was enhancing its organizational capacity by shipping ever larger amounts of heroin through Turkey to Western European markets.[21] Observers of Lebanon in the 1990s became aware of the deep involvement of Hezbollah in the drug trade.[22] Eventually, there was greater awareness among policy makers that terrorist involvement in the drug trade was not exclusively a Latin American phenomenon but was global in scope.

Terrorist Groups and the Drug Trade

The United Nations Security Council has recognized the relationship of drugs and terrorism.[23] The U.S. Department of State identifies terrorist organizations.[24] In 2008, the chief of operations at the Drug Enforcement Administration (DEA), Michael Braun, indicated that of the then forty-three designated terrorist groups, nineteen were involved in the drug trade.[25] Of the eleven new terrorist organizations added since Braun made his pronouncement, several of them are known to be significantly involved in the drug trade – Jundallah, TTP, and the Haqqani Network.[26] Almost all of these designated terrorist organizations are based in the developing world. Examples of terrorist groups involved in the global drug trade include the FARC, the Taliban, Hezbollah, and Hamas.[27] Many other terrorist groups are active in the drug trade, particularly on the regional level. Illustrative of this is AQAP in Yemen,[28] and most recently, AQIM in North Africa has been particularly involved.[29] The long-term survival of the Tamil Tigers was attributable in part to their stream of funding from narcotics.[30] These groups' involvement in drug trafficking is a consequence of their geographical locale, their proximity to drug cultivation, and their need to generate significant and consistent revenues.

Americans are forbidden to provide material support to these terrorist organizations. Therefore, Americans and business owners can be sanctioned not only for engaging with terrorists but for helping their financial interests. Terrorist organizations and their leaders can be subject to economic sanctions by the United States under the Narcotics Kingpin Designation Act.

The identification of an individual as a drug kingpin places an individual on a special list for financial scrutiny by banks and other financial institutions. Drug kingpins have been identified as members of several of these terrorist organizations, including the PKK and Dawood Ibrahim's crime-terror organization, D-Company. Shakeel, one of the named kingpins, was accused of managing D-Company's associations with organized crime and terror groups.[31]

Yet the involvement of terrorist groups with narcotics is not limited to the developing world. For example, the Aum Shinrikyo cult, responsible for the sarin gas attack on the Tokyo subway in 1995, was also one of the most significant producers and distributors of methamphetamines in Japan, rivaling the well-entrenched *yakuza* organized crime syndicates at the time.[32] Moreover, the IRA profited from the drug trade, as did the ETA in Spain.[33]

Relationships established between the terrorist organizations and the drug traffickers can be based on mutual advantage, but they may also result from coercion by the terrorists. This resembles the roving bandits defined by Mancur Olson, who destroy the incentive to invest and produce.[34] Often the terrorist organizations tax the cargo of the drug traffickers as narcotics transit territory under their control.[35] This is particularly common in Afghanistan, Turkey, and Colombia. This action of terrorist groups recalls that of states that extract revenues from traders who traverse their lands. It also mimics the activities of organized crime groups that, since the rise of the Mafia in nineteenth-century Sicily, have sought to establish dominance over territory to maximize profits.[36]

The Diversity of the Narcotics Trade

Regional Elements
On every continent, there are consumers of narcotic drugs, but consumption markets differ significantly, with some regions consuming more heroin, others consuming greater quantities of cocaine and synthetic drugs.[37] There is a logic to this business, as shown in Chapter 5. The drug trade, like licit commerce, is very much shaped by historical traditions, trade routes, cultures, social relations, and the economy of the region in which it is based.

Present drug traffickers, whether criminals, terrorists, or a hybrid of illicit actors, have exploited traditional trade routes to present-day advantage. They have introduced a new, highly valuable commodity into old routes that once were conduits for commerce in slaves, spices, tea, and many other valuable goods. This chapter focuses most particularly on three regions of the world – Colombia in Latin America, North and West Africa, and Afghanistan-Pakistan in Asia – finding that the routes presently exploited for the illicit drug trade were once used for very different commodities.

The Global South and the Drug Trade
As these geographically separated examples illustrate, the illicit drug trade flourishes in the developing world or in the global south, thriving often in highly corrupt countries whose capacity to govern is further reduced by this narcotics trade. The only type of illicit drugs to be produced on a significant scale in the developed world are synthetic drugs and marijuana, the latter of which is still the most widely produced narcotic.[38] Therefore, the heroin and cocaine trades are the largest multinational businesses based primarily in the developing world that market a high-value commodity to the developed world.[39] Map 6.1a shows the market for cocaine from Latin America, and Map 6.1b shows the markets for heroin from Afghanistan. The profits from

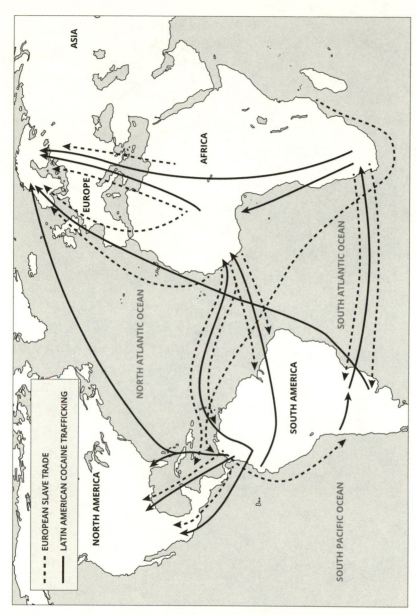

MAP 6.1A. Slaves' revenge: European slave trade and Latin American cocaine trafficking routes.

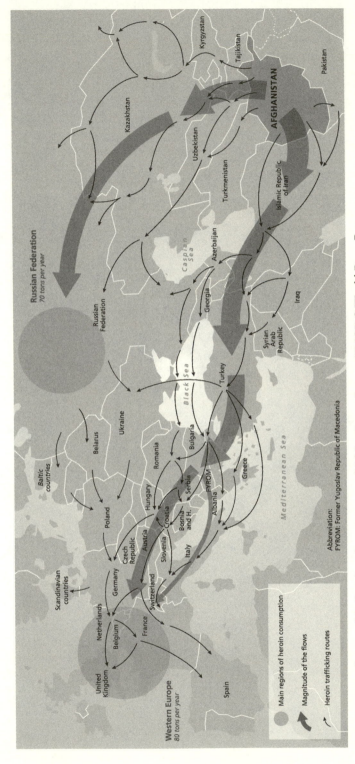

MAP 6.1B. Northern and Balkan heroin routes out of Afghanistan. *Source:* UNODC World Drug Report 2010, 54.

the drug trade increase the farther one gets from the source of production, a phenomenon that has been true for decades.[40] Therefore, the profits of this illicit trade are still earned by transnational crime, terrorist, and insurgent groups and by corrupt officials often far from the points of production.

Yet profits are now increasingly generated from transit and developing countries. Once the major demand for illicit drugs came from the United States, Europe, and Japan. But with the spread of the international drug trade in recent years, increasingly, there are regular users of narcotics in the countries of the developing world.[41] The increasing problems of drug abuse in Russia, China, Central Asia, Brazil, Mexico, and East Africa and South Africa attest to the fact that the market for drugs is no longer confined to the most developed countries in the world but also is plaguing the emerging economies of the G-20 and developing countries with growing, youthful, urban populations.[42]

Opiate drugs traverse the vast routes of the Ottoman Empire, connecting Turkey with the Middle East, the Balkans,[43] and the Caucasus. Drugs leaving Afghanistan follow many of the familiar roads of the ancient Silk Road, across Central Asia to Istanbul and beyond (see Map 6.1c). The important difference between the trade that traversed the Ottoman Empire, the Silk Road, and the historic slave routes and the drug trade is that the former were once legal trades that were often sanctioned or even encouraged by the state.[44] The historic slave road between West Africa and the New World had its greatest numbers of victims flow to South America and the Caribbean. That trade was controlled by Europeans. Today that route is reversed with the drugs flowing from South America through Africa to Europe, but unlike in the past, this current trade is not state sanctioned.

With the expansion of drug trade, many other lesser trade routes have reemerged in impoverished regions. Once valuable trade and religious pilgrimage routes that supported famed centers of wealth and urban development in Mali, Yemen, and Honduras are once again being used by the drug traffickers. Timbuktu in Mali was once a legendary trade center, as was Copan in Honduras and San'aa in Yemen. "Indeed, Mali has become an important node in the drug trade, as Latin American cocaine passes through the Sahara en route to Europe and the Middle East. This lucrative trade has tempted many Malians, including government officials, who have profited handsomely from it"[45] (see Map 6.1a). Yet the reemergence of these trade and pilgrimage routes is not leading to prosperity and growth. Rather, the recent takeover of Timbuktu, Mali, by jihadis; the terrorist attacks in Shibam in Yemen; and the urban violence of criminal gangs that wrack Honduras, presently suffering from the highest homicide rates in the world today, are all evidence that criminals and terrorists engaged in drug trafficking are further destabilizing areas whose citizens were already vulnerable.[46]

Analysis of the historical drug trade should not be ahistorical. There are other legacies of the Ottoman era than the Balkan trade route. The Turkish

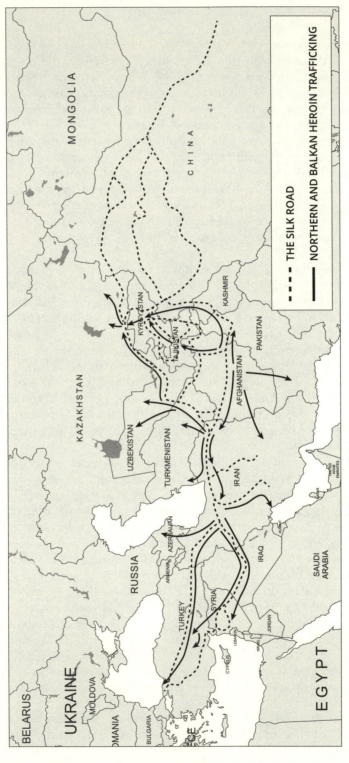

MAP 6.1C. Converging routes: Silk Road and drug trafficking routes.

and Kurdish involvement in the international drug trade dates to the 1960s, but they are inheritors of a centuries-old criminal tradition that goes back to revolts against the authoritarian and bureaucratic structures of the Ottoman Empire.[47] This recalls the "primitive rebels" described in Hobsbawm's seminal work of the same name. According to Hobsbawm's book, the violence of primitive groups, such as the Mafia, often in rural areas, had greater political significance. Therefore, the Ottoman legacy of cyclical revolts by Kurds followed by repression, according to Hobsbawm's analysis, helped translate into the founding of the Marxist PKK and its maintenance through the international drug trade.

Historical legacies also contributed to the Tamils as suppliers of drugs for expanding drug markets of South Asia and Europe. The British colonization of India resulted in the forced displacement of Tamils from Southern India to the island of Ceylon to harvest its famed tea. At the end of colonial rule and the emergence of the independent state of Sri Lanka (formerly Ceylon), Tamils experienced discrimination and were unable to protect their rights in postindependence Sri Lanka. The less moderate activists among the Tamils founded the terrorist group the Tamil Tigers, who survived for decades through illicit activity, including the sale of drugs in Australia, South Asia, and Europe.[48] The route of the drug trade, in part, follows the tea trade that went from Ceylon to Europe.

The previous examples indicate that the drug trade is not sui generis. It is often a regional phenomenon shaped by long-term trade relations and routes with neighboring states, as well as legacies of repression and discrimination. Many drug analyses and counternarcotics policies have focused on drugs in a single country, for example, Colombia or Afghanistan, but as the following analysis reveals, without placing this analysis in a broader regional context, it is not possible to anticipate future developments in the drug trade or to develop effective strategies to counter the narcotics business.

Colombia

Colombia may be the first large-scale success story of the illicit international drug trade. Starting in the 1960s, a group of extraordinary criminal entrepreneurs were able to capitalize on the growth of drugs in neighboring countries in the Andes to develop a refinement, transport, and marketing business that would reach lucrative markets in North America. These "godfathers of cocaine" thought of themselves as the Henry Ford of a new industry.[49] They dominated the cocaine industry, producing 80 percent of the world's cocaine.[50]

Many of the diverse Colombian groups that profited from the multinational drug trade are gone. Only the FARC, identified by the U.S. government as a terrorist organization in 1997, remains a potent force.[51] But it is much diminished from its capacity of a couple decades ago. Many of the successful next-generation drug traffickers are located outside of Colombia. The current leaders of the cocaine trade are not terrorist groups and do not have ideologies that commit them to the destruction of the state. But many successors to the

Colombian giants are as violent and destructive as their terrorist predecessors but have less commitment of service to the community than did the FARC.

The drug and terrorist organizations of Colombia relied on their comparative business advantage; as is said in real estate – "location, location, location." They lay between the coca production fields of the Andes and the lucrative consumption markets for refined coca in the United States. Being the first to recognize their crucial geographic advantage, the godfathers of the cocaine industry made billions of dollars annually through their market innovation and dominance. In the late 1980s, an estimated 70 percent of the manufactured cocaine was in the hands of the Medellín and Cali cartels. An estimated 20 to 30 percent of the trade was divided among small producers and refiners who had links to the FARC. In the mid-1980s, the Medellín and Cali cartels grossed $3 billion to $4 billion annually, and their profit on this was estimated to exceed 70 percent. Three of the drug traffickers, including the notorious Pablo Escobar, were named by Forbes as among the richest men in the world.[52]

Drug traffickers sought not only wealth but political influence. Carlos Lehder, a major drug lord of the Medellín cartel, organized a political party named the Latin Nationalist Movement and, while a fugitive, ran for the Colombian Senate.[53] Pablo Escobar was elected as an alternative deputy to Congress in 1982.[54] Apart from the direct entry of drug traffickers into politics, the organized criminals spent large sums on financing campaigns at the local and national levels. Former president Ernesto Samper's administration was tainted by substantial campaign contributions from the Cali cartel in the mid-1990s.[55] President Samper was denied entry into the United States. The conduit for this money from the traffickers was Samper's campaign manager, Fernando Botero Zea, the son of the legendary painter and sculptor, Fernando Botero. Botero Zea was convicted in 1996 and was released in 1998 after thirty months in prison.[56] His involvement is symptomatic of the corruption that reached to the highest levels of Colombian society and the tragedy of the drug trade immortalized in the works of his father.[57]

The violence and money corrupted the judiciary as well as the political process.[58] Judges were threatened if they convicted drug traffickers and were offered bribes if they did not. The Spanish expression *plomo o plata* (silver or lead) explained this corruption of the judiciary.[59] Principled judges went into exile. The major drug figure Jorge Luis Vásquez Ochoa was released from prison in 1987 after his supporters cowed members of the judiciary.[60] The alternatives to such compliance were patently clear. In November 1985, the M-19, a guerilla group, assaulted the Palace of Justice at the time that the Colombian Supreme Court judges were to rule on the extradition of a group of prominent drug traffickers to the United States. At the end of the twenty-eight-hour attack, one hundred people had died, including nine judges of the Supreme Court.[61] This tragic attack was not an anomaly. At the height of the drug trade, Colombia had among the highest homicide rates in the world. In the mid-1990s, the national homicide rate was eighty per one hundred thousand persons, and the rates were even higher in the locales where the cartels were concentrated.[62]

The Colombian state had long been absent from many rural areas, thereby giving an opening to the drug cartels and rural-based guerilla movements such as the FARC.[63] In these rural areas, the criminals, terrorists, and insurgents provided employment and services, such as discussed in Chapter 2, gaining support from the local populace.

Drug cartels were also proactive in urban areas. Pablo Escobar "underwrote the development of a local welfare system in Envigado, his home town, and also built a housing development in a slum and gave away 1,000 houses to low-income residents."[64] With the absence of the state, many others deployed violence other than the state. The benefits provided to the rural poor and the destruction of the state institutions at the national and regional levels through corruption and violence resulted in the Colombian state losing control over its territory. The legacy of this endures today, even though rates of homicide have declined dramatically.[65] As a United Nations report from 2005 explained,

> the biggest problem is that in parts of Colombia, the State does not have a monopoly on the use of force. Highly organized criminal structures such as drug trafficking mafias and paramilitary groups are well armed and dangerous. There are many private security companies, some of which use illegal weapons. Most Colombians who die from bullets do not die through indiscriminate violence. Rather, firearms are being used in the "professional" exercise of violence.[66]

As the Colombian state undertakes peace talks with the FARC in 2013, one of its greatest challenges is for the state to reassert itself and put an end to the violence and illegality in these regions where the government has long been absent.[67]

The drug trade's impact was not just political. Many of the billions in profit from the drug trade were repatriated to Colombia arriving in cash, through banks or complex money laundering schemes.[68] According to Felbab-Brown, Colombian drug traffickers by the late 1980s had accumulated between $39 billion and $60 billion.[69] The vast income flows from the drug trade also contributed to enormous distortions in the Colombian economy as members of the cartel laundered their money into legitimate businesses, bought valuable commercial real estate[70] in Bogotá, and purchased extensive ranch properties. As one Colombian economist explained, the price of beef was artificially low as drug traffickers purchased cattle ranches that required less daily cultivation than agricultural land-yielding fruits.[71]

Colombia still has significant levels of violence, although there has been a dramatic decline from the highs of the 1980s and 1990s. This is one indicator of the reassertion of control of the Colombian state over its territory. Colombia is a unique example of the recovery of a state from the abyss of drug-based violence. In U.S. governmental circles, Plan Colombia, which helped the Colombians attack the drug cartels, is credited for this improvement.[72] The large cartels of Medellín and Cali have been broken up, and the FARC and the ELN, another terrorist organization, have seen dramatic declines in membership. Critics of Plan Colombia suggest that these improvements have been made at the cost of great human rights violations[73] and ignore the emergence of important new violent groups, like the BACRIM (*bandas emergentes,* "emergent bands"), that also trade in drugs.[74] Yet what is ignored in these polarized discussions is the vital role that civil society has assumed in addressing the state-based corruption and providing services. Transparency International Colombia has addressed the criminal-political nexus,[75] Fundación Escuela Nueva has provided massive elementary education for the rural poor,[76] and church-based groups have worked on the grassroots level in urban slums, preventing recruitment into drug organizations and promoting reintegration.[77]

The decline of the drug threat to the Colombian state and citizenry has unfortunately displaced the problem elsewhere. Venezuela has at times provided a safe haven for members of the FARC, according to records seized from the rebels. But Venezuela's inconsistent support for this terrorist group is more related to territory than finances, as the FARC has significant resources from the drug trade.[78]

As the market for cocaine persists in the United States and Europe, other states have assumed a key role in the cocaine trade. In what may be called the "fudge effect," the devastation of the drug trade has merely been moved northward to central America and Mexico, undermining the quality of life and governance in what were once transit regions for the Colombian drug trade. As is discussed later, the same destabilization is now occurring in West Africa, which serves as the transit route for Latin American cocaine to Europe.

Mexico and some countries in Central America now have the distinction, once held by Colombia, of having among the world's highest rates of violence.[79] The groups behind this drug-related violence are merely criminal; they are not the amalgam of crime, terrorist, and insurgent, as seen in Colombia.[80] But the level of violence of these groups is so great, and their attacks on communities can be so spectacular, that some, including U.S. secretary of state Hilary Clinton, have equated this violence with an insurgency.[81] But these drug traffickers are undermining, rather than trying to deliberately destroy, the state, as characterized by the ideology of the Colombian-based FARC.

Historical Background

Colombia has had a long history of aggression that predates drug-related violence. This violence dates from Colombia's independence from Spanish rule in 1819. In the nineteenth century, there were close to twenty wars of regional or national significance. The final years of the nineteenth century were marked by the war of a thousand days that lasted from 1899 to 1902. This war had more than one hundred thousand victims among a population that then numbered less than 5 million.[82] This aggression has not only been described in the historical and social science literature but has been immortalized in the writings of the Nobel Prize–winning author Gabriel Garcia Marquez.[83]

In 1946, violence resumed and lasted until 1962. This twenty-six-year period, known as *La Violencia,* had high levels of brutality and laid the ground-work for the emergence of the powerful crime, terrorist, and insurgent groups.[84] Some also suggest that the general revolutionary violence also followed from Castro's success in Cuba in 1959.[85] The most notable of the groups to emerge was the FARC, which was officially established in 1964 as the military wing of the Colombian Communist Party. The FARC is the largest guerilla or insurgent organization in Latin America and at its height had a membership of around seventeen thousand.[86] Its antecedents lay in the agrarian conflicts that have transpired in several regions of Colombia since the 1920s and in the establish-ment of the Communist Party in 1961, which advocated all forms of struggle, including armed struggle, to achieve its goals.[87] The mid-1960s also marked the emergence of the smaller ELN. Inspired by the Latin American revolu-tionaries Fidel Castro and Che Guevara, its three thousand to five thousand members carried out high-profile kidnappings and bombings.[88] The ELN had a very different membership as it represented an amalgam of left-wing urban intellectuals with ties to rural farmers, with radicalized members of the oil sec-tor union.[89] FARC involvement in the drug trade was earlier and greater than the ELN's involvement, but neither terrorist group initially was a beneficiary of the drug trade.

The drug industry in Colombia began with marijuana. But the lower profit levels for marijuana, the need for bulk shipment, and the vagaries of the American market made the cocaine market more attractive to entrepreneurial drug dealers.[90] According to Francisco Thoumi, the marijuana business differs in several important ways from the coca trade. The profits of coca are higher, its value is greater both in reference to weight and volume, and it requires production to be a marketable crop.[91] By 1970, Colombia had a lengthy but not extensive experience in coca production. The development of this market required significant entrepreneurship in developing sources of supply and new delivery routes to American markets.

The expansion of this trade was facilitated by two powerful family-based networks that were located in two different cities of Colombia – Medellín and Cali. At the height of their power, all state organizations suffered from the corrupting power of the Medellín and Cali drug organizations.[92] The defining characteristic of the drug organizations was their lack of respect for Colombia's legal system and formal institutions.[93] As new criminal groups, they were not dependent on the state and shared the negative attitude to the state with the terrorist groups, a phenomenon discussed previously in Chapter 3.

The drug organizations drew on criminals with experience in other areas of crime. The founders of the Cali cartel in the late 1970s, Gilberto and Miguel Rodríguez Orejuela, as well as their associate, José Santacruz Londoño, began in the marijuana business but subsequently switched to the more lucrative cocaine markets.[94] The Cali cartel used less violence than the Medellín drug traffickers. The Cali-based criminals relied on bribes and focused on integration into Colombian society.[95]

In contrast, the Medellín cartel, founded in the same period by the Ochoa Vázquez brothers together with Pablo Escobar, was very violent. This violence included the assassination of high-level government officials as well as massacres of peasants who collaborated with guerillas.[96]

The Colombian government began a concerted effort against the power of the drug cartels in the late 1980s. A contentious extradition agreement with the United States was finally put in place in 1987. The Medellín cartel responded violently – assassinating judges, journalists, and five presidential candidates.[97] The level of violence was even greater than the Mafia was to demonstrate against the Italian state following governmental crackdowns in the early 1990s.

Despite this level of violence, the Colombian government extradited more than twenty suspected drug traffickers to the United States and seized substantial drug assets. Pablo Escobar was killed in 1993. President Samper, after his previously mentioned discreditation for receiving contributions from the drug traffickers, continued to pursue them.[98] A later president, Álvaro Uribe, undertook very aggressive efforts against the FARC between 2002 and 2010, often at the cost of serious human rights violation. A peace deal concluded in 2003 authorized tens of thousands of members of the insurgent group to have shorter jail terms and escape extradition to the United States.[99]

Initial attacks on drug traffickers led to the decline of the cartel system and the possibility for new actors to enter into the drug trade. "By the mid-1990s, Colombia was awash in unorganized small- and medium-sized drug producers and traffickers profiting from the expanded production and transport of narcotics."[100]

The FARC and other insurgent groups, such as the ELN and the subsequently formed right-wing paramilitary AUC, became involved with the drug trade. They filled some of the void left by the attacks on the cartels. The AUC, composed of a diverse group of actors – former members of the security apparati of the drug cartels, regional elites of the landholding class, and smaller drug lords[101] – was founded later in 1997, numbering thirty thousand at its height, and used drugs to finance its cause of opposing the state.[102] At its pinnacle of power, the FARC and other insurgent groups controlled more than one-third of the country's municipalities.[103]

The last of the drug organizations to be founded was the BACRIM, which emerged out of the demobilization of the AUC.[104] Since these groups were identified in 2005, there has been much discussion as to where they fall in relation to their violent Colombian predecessors. Analysts have disagreed as to whether they are a new paramilitary, a new type of criminal gang, yet another drug trafficking organization, or a new type of crime-insurgent organization. These distinctions are not just semantic but determine how they will be treated under the peace agreements that have been negotiated in Colombia.[105]

With Colombia's successes against its drug trafficking organizations, there has been the ascendency of Mexican drug groups. Since the late 1980s and early 1990s, smuggling routes into the United States have been increasingly controlled by Mexican drug traffickers. The Mexicans had previously just been service providers to the more powerful Colombian drug cartels.[106]

Relationship among Crime, Insurgent, and Terrorist Groups

The relationship among the crime, terrorist, and insurgent groups in regard to the drug trade is complex and has changed much over time. When Rensselaer Lee III published his book *White Labyrinth: Cocaine and Political Power* in 1990, there was much less of a relationship between the terrorist and crime groups and the drug trade than there was subsequently. At that time, he wrote that the FARC controlled the "dregs of the cocaine trade" and that the most profitable parts of the business were in the hands of the drug syndicates.[107] The insurgents and guerillas profited most by shaking down the drug traffickers and taxing the trade in areas they controlled.[108]

Lee's book was completed just before the fall of the Soviet Union in 1991. This event had a major impact on the nature of transnational crime and terrorism, as discussed in Chapter 3. Michael Braun, former chief of DEA operations, explained the major transformation of the FARC, its relation to drug crime after 1991, and its constant evolution:

> When the Soviet Union fell and the funding stream from Cuba dried up, the FARC executive secretariat, realizing they were perfectly poised at the center of gravity for the global cocaine trade, made a corporate decision after no more then [sic] 10 minutes of debate: they were in. They really had no choice; the FARC would have to become involved in the cocaine trade if they wanted to keep their movement alive. The FARC got its start by taxing poor farmers . . . They then formed alliances with traditional drug traffickers and began providing security at clandestine drug laboratories and cache sites and the FARC also provided critical security at clandestine airstrips and on river transit routes.
>
> They taxed the movement of drugs through their own country, as well as across clandestine smuggling routes with bordering nations. They next became involved in the full-scale production, transportation and distribution of cocaine, and are now recognized as the world's largest manufacturer and distributor of cocaine.[109]

The FARC became so involved in the drug trade that Braun refers to it as a hybrid that is part terrorist organization and part a transnational crime group.[110] But as was earlier discussed, the FARC's involvement in drugs is so great that it may be more a criminal than a terrorist organization at the present time. The FARC did not stand alone in its involvement with the drug trade. According to Vanda Felbab-Brown, by the late 1990s, the ELN could no longer sustain its previous decision to eschew the drug trade as this decision placed it at a comparative disadvantage relative to the FARC. Consequently,

from the point of its decision to the early 2000s, 20 percent of ELN income
was estimated to come from the drug trade.[111]

Regional and Broader Impact

The criminal and terrorist organizations engaged in the drug trade have had
an important regional and global influence. The decline of the drug cartels
in Colombia gave an opening that has been exploited by the Mexican drug
traffickers that now control the delivery of drugs to the United States. The
transit of drugs through Central America has made Honduras and El Salvador,
in particular, important hubs of the transnational drug trade.[112]

Colombian government officials reported in 2008 that Mexican drug organizations are buying the drugs they sell directly from the FARC. Some of the
FARC operations were operated out of neighboring Ecuador.[113] A Colombian intelligence report, obtained by journalists in summer 2012, reported that
there were links between four FARC fronts and the Mexican Beltran Leyva
drug cartel.[114] The Beltran Leyva cartel is one of the most brutal and functions
on the west coast of Mexico.[115]

The political wing of the FARC, the Continental Bolivarian Movement
(Movimento Continental Bolivariano), is involved in many countries in Latin
America, able to finance activities because of its proceeds from drugs. A
2005 internal FARC report identified active groups in Mexico, the Dominican
Republic, Ecuador, Venezuela, and Chile, with some involvement in Europe.[116]
In 2010, the Colombian government accused Venezuela of housing both the
FARC and the ELN and of providing support to both.[117]

The FARC is also believed by the DEA to be involved in the shipment of
drugs to West Africa that are destined for Europe. According to congressional
testimony in 2011, the FARC was operating in the West African nation of
Guinea Bissau, as were other Colombian and Mexican drug organizations.[118]
The involvement of the terrorist group as well as other Latin American drug
traffickers is addressed in the following section on the drug trade in Africa.

Africa: West, North, and the Sahel

West and North Africa are large multinational regions separated by the Sahel
and the Sahara. But as developments from the early 2000s indicate, it is no
longer possible to divide these regions for the purposes of this book's analysis,
because they face common problems of transnational crime, high-level facilitating corruption, and the presence of terrorist groups such as AQIM, among
others.

The North Africa coast has traditionally provided a base for illicit actors
who thrived on the rich trade that linked North Africa and Western Europe
across the Mediterranean. Pirates in the eighteenth century attacked well-
loaded cargo vessels with valuable freight. The piracy that operated from the
Barbary Coast, primarily the ports of Tunis, Tripoli, and Algiers, was a threat

to both European and American commerce. It was a major concern in the first decades of the United States' existence and led to a war to control the pirates, which the United States settled by paying off the pirates, creating a bad precedent.[119] The pirates, like some of today's illicit actors, received support from rulers. Historically, some pirates were equipped and supported by Ottoman rulers. No longer is this illicit activity supported by rulers overtly, but the extensive corruption of state officials in the countries of North Africa and the Sahel make them complicit in new forms of illicit trade discussed subsequently.[120]

There has been a long tradition of the black economy in Algeria and its neighboring states. The illicit trade between North Africa and Europe in tobacco, drugs, human smuggling, fuel, and other commodities has been run for much of the twentieth century, by criminal organizations and networks as well as terrorist organizations. The Armed Islamic group al-Jama'ah al-Islamiyah al-Musallaha, known in French as Groupe Islamique Armé (GIA), always survived by smuggling. AQIM, previously known as the Salafist Group for Preaching and Combat (al-Jamaa'atu l-Salafiyyatu li l-Da'wati wa l-Qitaal, or in French, Groupe Salafiste pour la Prédication et le Combat, GSPC) has acquired many of the networks once controlled by the weakened GIA.[121] AQIM, as discussed in Chapter 5, supported itself by a diversity of criminal activities, including kidnapping.

A key figure in AQIM is Afghan veteran Mokhtar Belmokhtar, a gifted survivor in "the highly volatile world of jihadi guerrillas,"[122] who epitomizes the intersection of crime, corruption, and terror in the vast territory from North Africa to the Sahel. He was identified as the chief strategist of the attack on In Amenas in Algeria discussed in the introduction. Operating from safe havens in Mali and Algeria and eschewing the extortion that characterized the GSPC, Belmokhtar earned the nickname "Mr. Marlboro" for his extensive cigarette smuggling. This was combined with drugs, arms, and people smuggling in a web of criminal partnerships that "grew tighter in the vast area covering eastern Mauritania, northern Mali, and southwestern Algeria."[123]

The West African region has a past that also linked crime and terrorist groups. As mentioned previously in reference to the 9/11 attacks in the United States, a diamond smuggling network linked to Hezbollah and the Lebanese diaspora community in West Africa helped provide funding for al-Qaeda.[124] Transnational crime groups from Russia, South Africa, Israel, and Ukraine were complicit. The corrupt and criminalized government of President Charles Taylor of Liberia encouraged these interactions, which allowed Taylor to stay in power, acquire weapons, and generate significant sums for himself.[125] Victor Bout, a notorious arms trafficker from the former USSR, used the networks, the aircraft, and many of the displaced military of the former Soviet state to arm groups in Liberia. He is an emblematic figure of the new hybrid who works with both criminals, terrorists, and corrupt government officials to provide arms to all who will pay.[126]

AQIM's increased involvement in the drug trade through its taxation of drug traffickers and its movement outside its traditional base in North Africa has brought the crime-corruption-terrorism entanglement to the forefront.[127] The centrality of criminal activity to AQIM makes analysts uncertain as to whether it is a "criminal organization with a veneer of religious ideology," "or a criminal organization with an attachment to al-Qaeda."[128] AQIM and its affiliates, as well as other Islamic groups, such as Boko Haram out of Nigeria, have taken over the legendary city of Timbuktu, displacing hundreds of thousands as they have imposed their own brand of Islamic governance on Mali, complete with sharia justice.[129] Mali represents the meeting place of AQIM, "its offshoot the Movement for Oneness and Jihad in West Africa, and Ansar Dine, a group of Tuareg rebels from the north."[130] The Tuaregs, having lost their historical trading routes, turned to diverse kinds of smuggling and have moved people across the desert,[131] thereby becoming facilitators for AQIM. Movement across the desert is hard to detect, giving the smugglers a comparative advantage over the police.

The movement into Mali is the culmination of an escalation of activity since 2001 by AQIM and other Maghreb- and Sahel-based extremists. Between 2001 and the 2009, attacks increased by almost 560 percent, so that "more than 900 terrorist bombings, murders, kidnappings, and ambushes – against domestic and international targets – have claimed more than 1,500 lives and 6,000 victims in Algeria, Chad, Libya, Mali, Mauritania, Morocco, Niger, and Tunisia."[132]

The Sahel in recent years has experienced increased flows of Latin American drugs destined for Europe that have entered through West Africa and even by plane into Mali (see Map 6.1a). The weak governance, widespread corruption, and porous borders of these parts of Africa have made them a haven for the intersection of different forms of illicit nonstate actors.[133] At present, Latin American drug trafficking and terrorist organizations such as the FARC and other Colombian and Mexican drug organizations exploit the absence of state control and the corruptibility of officials. They pay their local operatives in drugs, thereby increasing the problems of local addiction. "This phenomenon has resulted in the creation of new markets for cocaine and crack cocaine (base) in West Africa, where these homegrown groups can set and control retail market prices with the cocaine they have received as payment for their services, expand into surrounding countries, and further corrupt already weak governments."[134]

The Latin American organizations move massive amounts of drugs through Guinea Bissau and neighboring states[135] to their ultimate destination of Western Europe (see Map 6.1a). Illustrative of this is a seizure of six hundred kilograms of cocaine in Sierra Leone from a Venezuelan aircraft in 2008.[136] The involvement of the Venezuelans is also demonstrated through the discovery in Mali, in November 2009, of a Boeing 727 that might have crashed on a makeshift airstrip.[137] This plane's capacity to hold drugs was truly significant.

With such large sources of supply, it is hardly surprising that a 2007 estimate placed 60 percent of Europe's cocaine transiting through West Africa, a figure that declined to 30 percent by early 2009 because of the greater external attention to this route.[138]

> Most of the cocaine passing through West Africa on its way to Europe first arrives in one of the coastal states – notably Guinea and Guinea-Bissau, as well as Togo, Benin, and Ghana – and is then transported by air or boat. Alternatively, cocaine is sent by air couriers to Europe, including from airports in the West African interior. Bamako, Ouagadougou, and Niamey airports are among the hubs for air couriers, some of whom transit via Algiers airport. These routes remain active, as seizures during 2011 and 2012 at these airports underline.[139]

With greater attention to West Africa, the Latin American traffickers moved their routes to other locales. This displacement resulted in the reporting of more seizures post-2009 in West Africa and South Africa.[140] Yet the West African route, the reverse of the historic slave route, has far from disappeared.

One might say that the present drug route is the historic revenge of the slave trade (see Map 6.1a). It does significant harm to Europe, as the slave trade once did to Africa and to those who were enslaved in Latin America. But the costs are high again for Africa as there is a rise in corruption, addiction, and violence such as has been observed in Timbuktu. Therefore, there are multiple losers today, as diverse crime, terror, and hybrid groups from Latin America and Africa profit from the drug trade through West Africa and the Sahel to Europe.

Afghanistan[141]

Presently 90 percent of the world's opium cultivation occurs in Afghanistan, with dramatic growth since 2005.[142] A culture dependent on illicit trade has developed along with the societal norms supportive of this criminal activity. The drug business is now so deeply embedded in Afghanistan that it requires much more than alternative employment to reduce the drug trade. It has become a key funding source of the Taliban, according to United Nations analyses, generating a significant share of its annual budget.[143]

The drugs grown primarily in southern Afghanistan are trafficked through Pakistan,[144] Central Asia, and Iran, providing an important income source for citizens, terrorist and criminal organizations, and corrupt officials. Although the illicit drug trade assumes a significant portion of Afghanistan's revenues, its impact is far more than economic. As World Bank analysts perspicaciously wrote in 2005 about the drug trade,

> it contributes to a vicious circle whereby the drug industry financially supports warlords and their militias, who in turn undermine the Government – which is also corrupted and captured at different levels by bribes from the drug industry.

As a result the state remains ineffective and security weak, thereby perpetuating an environment in which the drug industry can continue to thrive.[145]

The instability, corruption, terrorism, and insurgency funded by the drug trade compounds and perpetuates the political instability of Afghanistan, which now dates back more than thirty years, since the time of the Soviet invasion. Furthermore, it undermines not only current security but the future development of the state. It also creates economic distortions that make it hard for regular commercial businesses to compete. The consequences are most severe for Afghanistan, but the narcotics trade has a destabilizing influence on the entire region through which the drugs transit.

The instability related to the drug trade is more acute in Afghanistan than in Colombia. The revenues tied to the drug trade in Afghanistan represent a much greater share of national revenue than in Colombia. In 2012, the United Nations Office on Drugs and Crime (UNODC) estimated Afghanistan's opium exports to be $2.4 billion – or 15 percent of gross domestic product in 2011 – and the report released for 2013 by the UNODC revealed that heroin production was at an all-time high with an increase of 36 percent from 2012.[146] This large contribution to the economy existed despite extensive efforts to eradicate poppy fields in Afghanistan.[147] Drugs in Afghanistan contributed 50 percent more to the national economy than they did in Colombia at the height the drug trade, when drug production possibly accounted for a maximum of 10 percent of the economy.[148] Moreover, Afghanistan may be unique in that, according to the former finance minister, Ashraf Ghani, an estimated 60 percent of the country's economy is based on illicit trade.[149] Although the drug trade is the largest of the illicit commodities, it is not the sole one, as Chapter 5 discussed.

The consequences of the drug – and other forms of illicit – trade in Afghanistan are particularly acute. In Afghanistan, in contrast to Pakistan and Colombia, there is no central government that has control over a significant share of national territory. The control of the central government does not extend much beyond Kabul. Throughout the country, local warlords and tribal chiefs control territory at the regional level. Local warlords use their control over rural society to force the cultivation of drugs.[150] Therefore, counterdrug policies established at the national level are very difficult to implement at the local level.

Without containment at the source, drugs from Afghanistan and Pakistan flow from these countries, heading to Russia, Western Europe, and Asia, by traversing Pakistan, Iran, or the Central Asian countries.[151] There are also increasing flows into China, although consumption is presently less than in Russia and Europe.[152] The drugs transiting through the bordering countries increase addiction among the citizens of transit states but also aggravate already elevated and destabilizing levels of corruption and instability, as discussed subsequently.

The Afghanistan–Pakistan border area is a region of particular security concern. Although under separate governments, the populations on both sides of the border share common armed groups with tribal links that transcend national borders. The loyalties of these groups to clan and tribe are greater than to the nation-state. The border regions of both societies have impoverished populations and poor social indicators, rendering their residents susceptible to the pressures of criminal and terrorist groups, through direct or implied threats of violence. The great wealth acquired by these criminal and insurgent groups through the highly profitable drug trade allows them to exercise inordinate influence over the populations of the border regions.

History and Background of Afghanistan's War Economy

To understand the political economy of the contemporary narcotics business in Afghanistan, it is important to understand the history of Afghanistan. For centuries, Afghanistan assumed a key role in the fabled Silk Road that moved valuable commodities from China and other parts of Asia to Constantinople and on to Venice and European markets. This route functioned for centuries as a conduit for silk, spices, and the exchange of food and technology. The decline of the Silk Road led to the decline of Afghanistan, and in the nineteenth century, Afghanistan became part of the so-called Great Game, in which the Russians and British vied for influence in the region. The Durand line that established the boundary between Afghanistan and Pakistan is a consequence of British influence in the region, as the British drew this artificial divide.[153]

After the Anglo-Afghan War in 1919, the Afghan king ruled with a Western focus. Yet the king's efforts were frustrated by more conservative forces. The Soviet state became involved in Afghanistan in the postwar period, as it sought to counter the U.S. influence in the region. When the government of Afghanistan sought to pursue a more independent course, the Soviets launched a brutal invasion in 1979 to prop up the Marxist regime.[154] A significant war economy developed during the Soviet occupation years. The drug trade that began in the 1950s on a small scale was already notable by the time the Soviet soldiers departed Afghanistan.[155] They used and abused drugs, and some returned home addicted, creating the first significant demand in the USSR for drugs.[156]

The Soviet invasion of Afghanistan triggered a large inflow of financial and military assistance to the mujahedin, the religious fundamentalist opposition to the Soviet occupation at the time. Several of the leading mujahedin leaders were early sponsors of the opium economy, and their involvement in it allowed them to rise to leadership positions. A blind eye was turned to the drug involvement of these leaders. One of the most prominent was Gulbuddin Hekmatyar, who also had refineries in Pakistan.[157] Hekmatyar used the funds from *zakat* (required giving expected of Moslems) collected internationally, from the Pakistan Inter-Services Intelligence, and from the opium trade to consolidate his position.[158] Little thought was given at this time to the long-term consequences for the United States of providing arms and provisions to a fundamentalist force. Neither were the long-term political implications, nor the impact on the drug trade, seriously considered.[159]

The devastation brought by the Soviet invasion and occupation, which lasted until 1989, resulted in the emigration of millions of Afghans to neighboring countries, and those who remained could not support themselves through traditional agricultural products. Then, as today, farmers reported that they cultivated opium because it paid so much better than alternatives.[160] Proof of this is a 2012 poll by the UNODC in which 71 percent of Afghan opium growers surveyed cited need as their principal reason for cultivating drugs. The rewards were significant, as in the mid-2000s,

> farmers made *11 times more* in gross income from cultivating poppy than they did from growing wheat. Even day-laborers are financially incentivized to support the trade – the average day wage for lancing and gum collection in Afghanistan in 2011 was the equivalent of $12.60 in U.S. dollars, as opposed to $5.60 for general manual labor and $6.60 for wheat harvesting.[161]

The Drug Trade under and after the Taliban

The war economy laid the basis for the production, processing, and trafficking of opium by warlords, who in turn funded the insurgency and enjoyed untaxed control over resources.[162] According to some analysts, this led to rentier rebels and a rentier state,[163] or one that pitted a "rentier state government economic system against an illicit rentier rural economy."[164] But the consequences of these rentier relationships were all too familiar – an absence of democratization, civil society, or stability.

As the Taliban established their rule over Afghanistan and controlled the means of predation and coercion, they also consolidated their hold over the opium economy.[165] In 1999, the height then of cultivation, the Taliban produced forty-six hundred metric tons of opium.[166] Although Taliban insurgents provided protection for opium farmers, they also taxed their opium yields. In some districts, they allowed local mullahs to collect *ushr*, a 10 percent Islamic agricultural levy.[167] A 20 percent tax was imposed by the Taliban in the south of Afghanistan on the trucks filled with opium leaving farms.[168] This is consistent with the business of terrorism discussed in Chapter 5. The Taliban taxed the territories they controlled. Furthermore, they taxed road exports and "turned the state-run Ariana Airlines into a 'narco-terror' charter service that carried Islamic militants, timber, weapons, cash, and heroin to the United Arab Emirates and Pakistan."[169]

The Taliban, both before and after the invasion, tracked how much farmers and other members of the local community were earning by maintaining informants in each community.[170] Each village-level subcommander paid a percentage of the opium proceeds to the district-level military commander, who in turn paid off the district-level Taliban governor.[171] A portion of these funds, often in the form of raw or partially refined opium, filtered up the Taliban chain of command to the provincial commander and was then given to the

Taliban's central financial committee.[172] It has also been reported that Taliban commanders ran opium refineries in the Pakistan–Iran border regions.[173]

The fall of the Taliban after the U.S.-led invasion in 2001, however, did not result in the dismantling of the coercion networks that had sustained the warlords and made them powerful. Rather, the Taliban diversified the way they profited from the drug trade, permitting their resurgence.[174] The post-Taliban Afghanistan witnessed cooptation of the same warlords and militia leaders into the political milieu, thereby buttressing the same power networks. For instance, according to one verified account, it was common knowledge in Kandahar that the major leaders of the province, who provided militias to help the United States fight the Taliban, split the proceeds from taxing the opium trade.[175] Therefore, the deadly and destabilizing entanglement of corruption, crime, and terrorism prevailed and undermined the capacity of the foreign forces to establish control over the territory controlled by the Taliban.[176] Interdiction and antinarcotics programs have failed to have the desired impact, despite the investment of large sums by the United States and its allies to curtail eradication and trade.[177]

Major drug traffickers pay directly to the Taliban leadership, often millions of dollars, earning them influence among the top decision-making group, the Quetta Shura.[178] Traffickers have paid for fighters' medical expenses, provided Toyota Hilux pickup trucks, and built madrassas in Pakistan.[179]

The drug economy could persist because there was corruption at the top of President Karzai's government in Kabul as well as at the local level. The web of actors, networks, and institutions, like the opium economy, constantly evolved, and the patterns of corruption shifted across ministries, thereby evading regulatory mechanisms.[180] Yet there was also no political will to address the corruption. The chief protector of the drug economy was reputedly the half-brother of President Karzai, Wali Karzai, until his assassination in summer 2011.[181] The Kabul Bank functioned as a Ponzi scheme whereby top officials used the bank's resources as their personal treasury, until it ran out of money and needed to be bailed out by the Afghan government with hundreds of millions of dollars. Much money from the bank flowed to the United Arab Emirates.[182]

The drug economy continued to function on the local level because it used the rural patronage networks that had been in existence for centuries.[183] Loyalties function on a local and a tribal level, and there is an absence of loyalty to the central state. Traditions were more important than the policies of the Afghan government.[184] The opium economy provided local strongmen the focus around which they could compete for political and economic domination; for instance, it was noted that in some districts, farmers were coerced not to cultivate opium poppy or to eradicate their crops completely.[185] In other areas, the local strongmen used their power to protect opium crops in areas from which they draw their political and military support, including control over key positions in local government.[186] The structured loans that local leaders provide to members of rural communities keep members of Afghan communities indebted and in subordinate relationships,[187] an essential element of the financing behind terrorist and insurgent networks.

The high-level power holders not only benefit from drug profits but also garner political influence. They controlled drug production by switching it on or off through coercion, made deals with local power brokers and traders, and promised development assistance.[188] This recalls the service functions of terrorist and crime groups discussed previously. Eradication and interdiction also played into the hands of powerful actors who were able to exercise greater control over the opium economy, possibly through management and control of eradication (providing leverage over production), and harassment of smaller traders and seizure of stock, forcing smaller traders out of the market.[189] Currently local strongmen do not market all the opium that they cultivate – some of it is retained to cover losses from seizures – whereas other supplies are withheld from the market in the hope that prices will rise. This also shows the business side and violent entrepreneurship of the drug trade and of terrorist financing, as discussed in Chapter 5.[190]

The opium economy operates in an environment of insecurity and pervasive risk, yet provides many rural households the means to survive under such abysmal conditions.[191] Research shows that opium poppy cultivation has tended to be at its most concentrated in areas with limited access to irrigated land, with high population densities, with insecurity, and limited opportunities for employment off the farm and few income opportunities not related to agriculture.[192] Inextricable links between corruption, state officials, local power holders, and insurgents exist parallel to the reality that opium provides the only means of survival in extremely volatile conditions of insecurity and weak government control.[193]

In 2004, the opium crop represented 60 percent of legitimate gross domestic product, estimated in 2003 as $4.6 billion. At this time, only an estimated $600 million (farm-gate price) of the $2.8 billion export value of the opium trade stayed with the local-level farmers or within the traditional village structure. Yet this industry employed 350,000 families and generated revenues that were a multiple of what the rural farmers could gain through other crops.[194] Cultivation persists today because no legitimate crop can equal the revenue from opium, and some farmers grow cannabis in addition to their annual opium crop.[195]

Therefore, there is a daily reality that results in participation in the drug trade. There are terrorists and insurgents involved in the drug trade, but, as this section showed, there are many other actors, including warlords; corrupt officials, including military and law enforcement; and crime groups with deep connections to high-level officials. Sébastien Peyrouse explained, "Indeed, in Afghanistan, drug trafficking has become an *official* activity as much – if not more – than it is an *insurgent* one. According to UNODC figures, in 2009 Afghan traffickers made an estimated $2.2 billion in profits, while insurgent groups made only $155 million."[196]

Regional and Broader Impact

The drugs transported through Afghan's neighboring states and through Central Asia have an extremely destabilizing influence.[197] There are increasingly high levels of corruption, with the power of criminal organizations linked to the government, insurgencies, and terrorist groups. The profits of this trade are enjoyed by those along the transit routes, but the United Nations concludes that some of the profits "fund insurgents in Afghanistan."[198]

Those most profiting from this heroin trade are the large-scale crime groups with governmental links, whereas the small-scale traffickers and the Islamist movements profit less.[199] Patterns in some countries in Central Asia resemble those of Afghanistan, where close family members of the leader assume key roles as protectors of the drug trade. For example, Russian officials stated that members of deposed president Kurmanbek Bakiyev's inner circle were trafficking narcotics through southern Kyrgyzstan.[200] The corruption also deeply penetrated the court system, as recalls the Colombian experience.[201] As was previously discussed in Chapter 4, the corruption in prison facilitates the interaction of criminals and terrorists.

The large-scale narcotics trade has further negative consequences beyond corruption and funding insurgencies. It is increasing addiction in transit regions and resulting in economies dependent on the narcotics trade, without needed investment being made in other sectors of the economy.[202]

Ethnic links between Tajik, Uzbek, Pashtun, and Baloch Afghans and their counterparts in Central Asia, Pakistan, and Iran provide a basis for the organization and networking fundamental to delivering Afghan opiates to those who consolidate the shipments on the regional level. The drugs can then be transported farther by transnational drug trafficking organizations along the routes shown in Map 6.1c.[203] The map shows that the routes of the contemporary drug trade have much in common with the ancient routes of the Silk Road. The historical routes have found a new commodity.

Drugs leave Afghanistan through several Central Asian states, including Uzbekistan, Turkmenistan, and Tajikistan. They travel east, as in the past, but also north, as shown in Map 6.1c. Although the Silk Road fostered a commerce that contributed to the regions along the Silk Road, some of these cross-border networks weaken the authority of the state as corruption increases and there is no viable legitimate economy.

Tajikistan suffered a long civil war that was financed by the drug trade in the 1990s. The civil conflict reasserted itself in summer 2012 in the Badakhshan area that borders Afghanistan and has been a key transit zone for drugs exiting Afghanistan.[204] Drugs play a key role in the Tajik economy and in the patronage system that supports the current leadership.[205] Drugs from Tajikistan often traveled through Kyrgyzstan. In Kyrgyzstan, many Uzbeks and Tajiks controlled the drug trade until the pogroms and massive displacement of hundreds of thousands of Uzbeks that accompanied the overthrow of the corrupt President Bakiyev in April 2010.[206] Those participating in the massive destruction of communities included participants in the drug trade, professional criminals, and members of the two ethnic groups – Kyrgyz and Uzbeks.[207] These ethnic conflicts are exacerbated by the desire to control the drug trade.

Neighboring Pakistan has had significant drug trade through the Federally Administered Tribal Areas (FATA) and into the frontier provinces of Baluchistan and Khyber Pakhtunwa.[208] This border area has always been a tribal area over which Pakistan's central government has had limited control. In particular, Waziristan, Khyber Pakhtunwa, and Baluchistan have become increasingly destabilized and fertile territory for drug smuggling. Another group operating between Afghanistan and Pakistan is the Haqqani Network, involved with the drug trade in areas that it controls.[209]

Conclusions

The drug trade reflects the principles discussed in the previous chapter. Drug trafficking is an attractive business, because it ensures sustained funding for criminals, terrorists, insurgents, and corrupt officials, because its addictive nature creates continued demand. Drug trafficking has high growth rates and has expanded into many areas, such as West Africa, in recent years, where the trade was not previously existent.

The illicit drug trade reflects the strategic business thinking of criminals, terrorists, and insurgents. They develop their businesses by compelling production by local farmers, corrupting officials, and exploiting kinship relationships, particularly in critical transit areas.

Drug traffickers have addressed problems of maintaining and accessing funds to sustain their businesses. They have engaged in diversification of markets, routes, suppliers, and drug commodities. They withhold supply to provide replacements and to have stocks if prices escalate. Drug traffickers occupy territory where there has been the retreat of the state or where they have forced out the state. Traffickers such as the Taliban, the PKK, and the FARC, as well as hybrid crime and terror organizations, tax those who seek to transit territory they control. In this respect, they mirror the taxation authority of legitimate governments. In Colombia, crime groups were early users of sophisticated encryption and other advanced forms of technology.

Strategic alliances are formed among diverse actors, just as seen in legitimate markets. In all the case studies examined – West Africa, Latin America, Afghanistan, and Pakistan – working relationships are established between government officials of all ranks and a diverse range of illicit actors.

The drug trade does differ from legitimate commerce, as violence is an integral part of the illicit narcotics trade. It is not just the illegality of the drugs but the corrosive nature of the commodity that provides unique elements of the drug trade – the commodity itself does harm to the individual and, by extension, the community.

The large-scale drug trade is extremely destabilizing, even when the trade is dominated by just one type of illicit actor – corrupt officials, criminals, terrorists, insurgents, or guerrillas. The consequences of the drug trade on a massive scale, such as seen in contemporary Mexico, can resemble terrorism in its large-scale violence and the intense fear that it instills in the population.

The instability that results from the illicit drug trade is not confined to the source countries of the drug trade. Colombia's intense involvement in the drug trade and its resultant political and social instability have not been localized to that country. Rather, over the past two decades, its impact has spread to Central America, Mexico, and West Africa, regions that lie on the transit routes for the narcotics. The drug flows from Afghanistan have destabilized the trade routes in Central Asia, particularly in Kyrgyzstan and Tajikistan, and the consequences for Pakistan are also apparent. The drug trade in North Africa, which has benefited the AQIM and other insurgent groups, provided some of the resources needed to occupy Mali and launch the attack on the Algerian In Amenas facility discussed in the introduction.

The trade routes for the contemporary drug trade were previously used for other high-value commodities. European slave traders moved African slaves to South America. The famed Silk Road was used to move silk and spices from China through Afghanistan, Persia, and Central Asia, on to Istanbul and the markets of Europe. There are enormous historical legacies of these trade routes – migration of peoples and exchanges of culture, religion, art, and music. Yet what will be the consequences of this drug trade that has traversed these different countries and regions? Will it be only enhanced corruption, political instability, and the addiction of youth? If so, the impact of the drug trade contravenes all concepts of global trade as a force for economic development and global integration.

As in the past, the contemporary drug trade united many and diverse countries in its supply chains. As shown in Chapter 4, these supply chains combine many different types of environments from the source of the drugs to their point of distribution. At different points of the drug supply chain, criminals, terrorists, insurgents, and/or corrupt officials, or a combination of these different actors, may move the narcotics toward their intended market.

Many counternarcotics and counterterrorism strategies have focused only on the drug trade, as if this were a distinct form of illicit trade. As this chapter and Chapters 2 and 5 have shown, corruption is absolutely central to the drug trade. The drug cartels in Colombia have entered politics and funded presidential candidates. High-level corruption in West Africa has allowed the entry of Latin American drug traffickers into the region. President Karzai's late brother was a focal point for the drug corruption in Afghanistan, as was the immediate family of former president Bakiyev in Kyrgyzstan. But the corruption is not limited to these level figures. As "the fish rots from the head," the corruption is distributed more broadly in areas of drug cultivation or at key nodes on transit routes. Corruption need not be initiated by the government official. The

Spanish-language expression of "silver or lead" can be applied more broadly to the drug trade in regions outside of Latin America.

The term *narco-terrorism,* as previously discussed, is erroneous. Drugs may be the most dominant of illicit activity in the markets discussed, but they are not the only one. As discussed in Chapter 5, Colombian terrorist groups engage in kidnapping, extortion, and trade in nature to natural resources. Moreover, the impunity of the drug traffickers may lead to the development of this other criminal activity.[210] The same patterns have been observed with the AQIM in Africa and the Taliban and other terrorist groups in the Afghanistan-Pakistan region. These groups are opportunistic in their criminal activity. The myopic focus on the drug trade rather than the range of activities of the illicit economy has contributed to the overall ineffectiveness of antinarcotics policy and often serious violations of human rights.

Notes

1. U.S. Department of Justice, "Member of Afghan Taliban Sentenced to Life in Prison in Nation's First Conviction on Narco-terror Charges," December 22, 2008, http://www.justice.gov/opa/pr/2008/December/08-crm-1145.html; also discussed in Gretchen Peters, *Seeds of Terror: How Heroin Is Bankrolling the Taliban and al Qaeda* (New York: St. Martin's Press, 2009), 68.

2. T. David Mason and Christopher Company, "Guerillas, Drugs and Peasants: The Rational Peasant and the War on Drugs in Peru," *Terrorism and Political Violence* 7, no. 4 (1995): 144.

3. UNODC, "Drug Trafficking," http://www.unodc.org/unodc/en/drug-trafficking/index.html.

4. Xavier Raufer, *Les nouveaux dangers planétaires: Chaos décèlement précoce* (Paris: CNRS, 2009), 217–18; Vanda Felbab-Brown, *Shooting Up Counterinsurgency and the War on Drugs* (Washington, DC: Brookings Institution, 2009); Felbab-Brown, "The Intersection of Terrorism and the Drug Trade," in *The Making of Terrorist Recruitment, Training and Root Causes,* Vol. III: *Root Causes,* ed. James J. F. Forest (Westport, CT: Praeger Security International, 2006), 172–88.

5. Audrey Kurth Cronin, *How Terrorism Ends: Understanding the Decline and Demise of Terrorism Campaigns* (Princeton, NJ: Princeton University Press, 2009), 27–28, on ASG; Daniel Pécaut, *Les Farc, une guerilla sans fins?* (Paris: Lignes de Repères, 2008), 82–88.

6. Nicolas Christin, "Traveling the Silk Road: A Measurement Analysis of a Large Anonymous Online Marketplace," http://arxiv.org/pdf/1207.7139.pdf. The head of the Silk Road was arrested by the FBI in October 2013: "FBI Shuts Down the 'Silk Road' Black Market, Arrests Infamous Owner 'Dread Pirate Roberts,'" *Huffington Post,* October 2, 2013, http://www.huffingtonpost.com/2013/10/02/silk-road-fbi_n_4030750.html.

7. George Kamm, "Tajikistan Led by 'Cronyism and Corruption,'" WikiLeaks, December 13, 2010, http://www.eurasianet.org/node/62564; Matthew Rosenberg and Graham Bowley, "Intractable Afghan Graft Hampering U.S. Strategy," March

7, 2012, *New York Times*, http://www.nytimes.com/2012/03/08/world/asia/corruption-remains-intractable-in-afghanistan-under-karzai-government.html?pagewanted=all; Ariel Cohen, "Kyrgyzstan's Corruption Instigated Revolution," http://www.forbes.com/2010/04/09/kyrgyzstan-revolution-corruption-opinions-contributors-ariel-cohen.html; Ashley Neese Bybee, "Narco State or Failed State? Narcotics and Politics in Guinea-Bissau," PhD diss., School of Public Policy, George Mason University, September 2011.

8. Jamese Verini, "The Tunnels of Gaza," December 2012, http://ngm.nationalgeographic.com/2012/12/gaza-tunnels/verini-texi; Samuel Blackstone, "Why Mexican Drug Cartels Love Building Tunnels," August 3, 2012, http://www.businessinsider.com/mexican-drug-cartelos-use-tunnels-for-drug-transport-2012-8.

9. "Organized Crime Enablers," http://www.weforum.org/reports/organized-crime-enablers.

10. Larry Rohter, "Noriega Is Linked to Drug Flights," *New York Times,* November 17, 1991, http://www.nytimes.com/1991/11/17/us/noriega-is-linked-to-drug-flights.html.

11. North African farmers are engaged in the cultivation of marijuana. See UNODC, *World Drug Report 2012*, 3, http://www.unodc.org/unodc/en/data-and-analysis/WDR-2012.html.

12. Arthur Waley, *The Opium War through Chinese Eyes* (New York: Macmillan, 1958).

13. Loretta Napoleoni, *Terror Incorporated: Tracing the Dollars behind the Terror Networks* (New York: Seven Stories Press, 2005), 65–80.

14. "Humala Says State Attorney to Appeal Supreme Court Ruling That Tightens Sentence of Death Squad and Montesinos," http://www.peruviantimes.com/24/humala-says-state-attorney-to-appeal-supreme-court-ruling-that-lowers-sentence-of-ex-spy-chief-montesinos-and-death-squad/16292/.

15. Coletta Youngers, "Peruvian President Fujimori's Right-Hand Man Was a Gun Runner and Drug Dealer – and Employed by the U.S.," September 3, 2010, http://www.fpif.org/blog/peru_drug_dealer_gun_runner_CIA_Montesinos_Fujimori.

16. Bruce Hoffman, *Inside Terrorism* (New York: Columbia University Press, 1998), 27.

17. Francisco Thoumi, *Political Economy and Illegal Drugs in Colombia* (Boulder, CO: Lynne Rienner, 1995); Rensselaer W. Lee III, *The White Labyrinth: Cocaine and Political Power* (New Brunswick, NJ: Transaction, 1990).

18. UNODC, *World Drug Report, 2012*; Letizia Paoli, Victoria A. Greenfield, and Peter Reuter, *The World Heroin Market: Can Supply Be Cut?* (New York: Oxford University Press, 2009).

19. Gretchen Peters, *How Opium Profits the Taliban* (Washington, DC: U.S. Institute of Peace, 2009), 20, http://www.usip.org/files/resources/taliban_opium_1.pdf.

20. John Horgan and Max Taylor, "Playing the 'Green Card': Financing the Provisional IRA: Part 1," *Terrorism and Political Violence* 11, no. 2 (1999): 1–38.

21. Xavier Raufer, "Une maffya symbiotique: traditions et évolutions du crime organisé en Turquie," *Sécurité Globale* (Hiver 2009–10), 92–119.

22. Johnathan V. Marshall, *The Lebanese Connection: Corruption, Civil War and the International Drug Traffic* (Stanford, CA: Stanford University Press, 2012), 158–52; UNODC, *World Drug Report, 2012*, 85.

23. "Drug Trafficking and the Financing of Terrorism," http://www.unodc.org/unodc/en/frontpage/drug-trafficking-and-the-financing-of-terrorism.html.

24. U.S. State Department, Foreign Terrorist Organizations, September 28, 2012, http://www.state.gov/j/ct/rls/other/des/123085.htm.

25. Michael Braun, "Drug Trafficking and Middle Eastern Terrorist Groups: A Growing Nexus?," July 25, 2008, http://www.washingtoninstitute.org/policy-analysis/view/drug-trafficking-and-middle-eastern-terrorist-groups-a-growing-nexus.

26. Muhammad Sahimi, "Who Supports Jundallah," http://www.pbs.org/wgbh/pages/frontline/tehranbureau/2009/10/jundallah.html; Gretchen Peters, *Haqqani Network Financing: The Evolution of an Industry*, July 31, 2012, http://www.ctc.usma.edu/posts/haqqani-network-financing; Shahan Mufti, "Funding the Pakistan Taliban," *Global Post*, updated May 30, 2010, http://www.globalpost.com/dispatch/taliban/funding-the-pakistani-taliban.

27. Braun, "Drug Trafficking and Middle Eastern Terrorist Groups," 5; Jennifer L. Hesterman, *The Terrorist-Criminal Nexus: An Alliance of International Drug Cartels, Organized Crime, and Terror Groups* (Boca Raton, FL: CRC Press, 2013), 85–86; Peters, *Seeds of Terror*.

28. Gabriel Koehler-Derrick, ed., *A False Foundation? AQAP, Tribes and Ungoverned Spaces in Yemen* (West Point, NY: Combating Terrorism Center at West Point, October 3, 2011), 104, http://www.ctc.usma.edu/posts/a-false-foundation-aqap-tribes-and-ungoverned-spaces-in-yemen.

29. Braun, "Drug Trafficking and Middle Eastern Terrori Groups," 3.

30. Kate Pickert, "A Brief History of the Tamil Tigers," January 4, 2009, http://www.time.com/time/world/article/0,8599,1869501,00.html; UNODC, *World Drug Report, 2012*, 85.

31. Office of Foreign Assets Control, U.S. Department of the Treasury, "Narcotics: What You Need to Know about U.S. Sanctions against Drug Traffickers," http://www.treasury.gov/resource-center/sanctions/Programs/Documents/drugs.txt; "US Sanction Two as Aides to Mumbai Drugs Kingpin," May 16, 2012, http://dawn.com/2012/05/16/us-sanctions-2-as-aides-to-mumbai-drugs-kingpin/.

32. David E. Kaplan and Andrew Marshall, *The Cult at the End of the World: The Terrifying Story of the Aum Doomsday Cult, from the Subways of Tokyo to the Nuclear Arsenals of Russia* (New York: Crown, 1996), 162.

33. Horgan and Taylor, "Playing the 'Green Card'"; G. E. Curtis, "The Nexus among Terrorists, Narcotics Traffickers, Weapons Proliferators and Organized Crime Networks in Western Europe," Library of Congress, December 2002, 9, http://www.loc.gov/rr/frd/pdf-files/WestEurope_NEXUS.pdf.

34. Mancur Olson, "Dictatorship, Democracy, and Development," *American Political Science Review* 87, no. 3 (1993): 567–76.

35. Peters, *How Opium Profits the Taliban*, 1.

36. Salvatore Lupo, *Storia Della Mafia dalle origini ai giorni nostri* (Rome: Donzelli Editore, 1993).

37. UNODC, *The Globalization of Crime: A Transnational Organized Crime Threat Assessment* (Vienna: UNODC, 2010), 95–96, 110–11, http://www.unodc.org/unodc/en/data-and-analysis/tocta-2010.html; UNODC, *World Drug Report, 2012*.

38. UNODC, *World Drug Report, 2012*, 3.

39. Louise Shelley, "The Internationalization of Crime: The Changing Relationship between Crime and Development," in *Essays on Crime and Development*, ed. Ugljesa Zvekic (Rome: United Nations Interregional Crime and Justice Research Institute, 1990), 119–34. See also maps of UNODC, *Globalization of Crime*, 95, 110; UNODC, *World Drug Report, 2012*, 8.

40. UNODC, *World Drug Report, 2012*, 34.

41. Ibid., 5.

42. Ibid. Liana Sun Wyler and Nicolas Cook, "Drug Trade in Africa: Trends and US Policy," Congressional Reference Service, September 30, 2009, http://www.fas .org/sgp/crs/row/R40838.pdf.

43. Ibid., 30.

44. "The Abolition of the Slave Trade: Illegal Slave Trade," http://abolition.nypl.org/ print/illegal_slave_trade/.

45. Benjamin F. Soares, "Mali's Tomb Raiders," *New York Times*, July 9, 2012, A15.

46. Hakim Almasmari, "Yemen Headquarters for Drug Traffickers," *Yemen Post*, April 10, 2010, http://yemenpost.net/Detail123456789.aspx?ID=1&Sub ID=1666; Wolfram Lacher, "Organized Crime and Conflict in Sahel–Sahara Region," September 2012, http://carnegieendowment.org/2012/09/13/organized- crime-and-conflict-in-sahel-sahara-region/dtjm#; Clare Ribando Seelke, "Gangs in Central America," Congressional Research Service, November 26, 2012, http://www.fas.org/sgp/crs/row/RL34112.pdf.

47. Frank Bovenkerk and Yucel Yesilgöz, "Urban Knights and Rebels in the Ottoman Empire," in *Organised Crime in Europe: Patterns and Policies in the European Union and Beyond*, ed. Cyrille Fijnaut and Letizia Paoli (Dordrecht, Netherlands: Springer, 2004), 203. Kurdish groups are also deeply involved in marijuana pro- duction and trade.

48. John Richardson, *Paradise Poisoned: Learning about Conflict, Terrorism and Development from Sri Lanka's Civil Wars* (Kandy, Sri Lanka: International Cen- ter for Ethnic Studies, 2005), 29, on displacement and problems of Tamils; "Sri Lankan Tamil Caught Running a Drug Trafficking Ring in Australia," *Asian Tribune*, April 29, 2005, http://www.asiantribune.com/news/2005/04/29/ sri-lankan-tamil-caught-running-drug-trafficking-ring-australia; Phil Williams, "Terrorist Financing and Organized Crime: Nexus, Appropriation or Transforma- tion?," in *Countering the Financing of Terrorism*, ed. Sue E. Eckert and Thomas J. Biersteker (Abingdon: Routledge, 2008), 139.

49. See film *Godfather of Cocaine*, which first aired on *Frontline*, March 25, 1997, http://www.pbs.org/wgbh/pages/frontline/shows/drugs/archive/godfathercocaine .html.

50. Felbab-Brown, *Shooting Up: Counterinsurgency and the War on Drugs*, 69.

51. U.S. State Department, "Country Reports on Terrorism – 2010," http://www .state.gov/j/ct/rls/crt/2010/index.htm; Connie Veillette, "Colombia: Issues for Congress," Congressional Research Service, January 19, 2005, 3, http://www.ndu .edu/library/docs/crs/crs_rl32250_19jan05.pdf.

52. Lee, *White Labyrinth*, 8–9.

53. Ibid., 136–38.

54. Thoumi, *Political Economy and Illegal Drugs in Colombia*, 141; Felbab-Brown, *Shooting Up: Counterinsurgency and the War on Drugs*, 74.

55. In particular, a named legal investigation, Proceso 8000, identified Samper's campaign manager, Fernando Botero Zea, and multiple congressmen for having financial dealings with the Cali cartel. Botero eventually went to jail for his part in receiving drug money for the campaign. See Horacio Serpa, "Botero se volvió experto en enredar la pita," http://historico.elpais.com.co/paisonline/notas/Febrero152007/serpita.html.

56. "Fernando Botero: Colombian Artist Turns 80 and Has No Plans to Retire," *Huffington Post*, April 19, 2012, http://www.huffingtonpost.com/2012/04/19/fernando-botero-turns-80_n_1435609.html.

57. Juan Forero, "Turning an Eye from Whimsy to War; the Colombian Artist Fernando Botero Captures the Agony and Absurdity of a Drug-Fueled Conflict," *New York Times*, May 3, 2004, http://www.nytimes.com/2004/05/03/arts/turning-eye-whimsy-war-colombian-artist-fernando-botero-captures-agony-absurdity.html.

58. Jorge Orlando Melo, "The Drug Trade, Politics and the Economy: The Colombian Experience," in *Latin America and the Multinational Drug Trade*, ed. Elisabeth Joyce and Carlos Malamud (Houndsmill, UK: Macmillan, 1998), 64.

59. Lee, *White Labyrinth*, 10.

60. He was freed following the appearance of his crime group at the prison, demanding his release.

61. Velbab-Brown, *Shooting Up: Counterinsurgency and the War on Drugs*, 91. The author at the time of the attack was attending a conference in the Andes of Venezuela. Many people in attendance knew Colombian judges who were in self-imposed exile, and others knew some of the slain judges and their families.

62. UNODC, *Violence, Crime and Illegal Arms Trafficking in Colombia*, December 2006, 18, http://www.unodc.org/pdf/Colombia_Dec06_en.pdf; Sandro Calvani headed the United Nations drug office in Colombia when this report was done. See his book *La Coca Passato e Presente Miti e realtà* (Torino: Effata, 2008), 113–42, discussing the contemporary Colombian situation.

63. James Brittain, *Revolutionary Social Change in Colombia: The Origin and Direction of the FARC-EP* (New York: Pluto Press, 2010), 56.

64. Thoumi, *Political Economy and Illegal Drugs in Colombia*, 141.

65. In 2012, there were 17,459 homicides in Colombia, or approximately 37.7 deaths per 100,000 inhabitants. "Colombian Homicides are among the Worst in the Region," September 14, 2012, http://colombiareports.com/colombia-news/news/26024-colombian-homicide-rate-among-the-worst-in-region.html.

66. UNODC, *Violence, Crime and Illegal Arms Trafficking in Colombia*, 6.

67. Adam Isaacson, "Consolidating 'Consolidation': Colombia's Plan to Govern Neglected Territories Stumbles," January 10, 2013, http://www.wola.org/publications/consolidating_consolidation.

68. Peter Reuter and Edwin M. Truman, *Chasing Dirty Money* (Washington, DC: Institute for International Economics, 2004); Oriana Zil and Lowell Bergman, "The Black Peso Money Laundering Scheme," http://www.pbs.org/wgbh/pages/frontline/shows/drugs/special/blackpeso.html, analyzes the black peso system used to launder money back to Colombia. See also discussion of the U.S. federal case against HSBC for laundering drug money in Jessica Silver-Greenberg, "HSBC to Pay Record Fine to Settle Money-Laundering Charges," December 11,

2012, http://dealbook.nytimes.com/2012/12/11/hsbc-to-pay-record-fine-to-settle-money-laundering-charges/?ref=opinion.

69. Felbab-Brown, *Shooting Up: Counterinsurgency and the War on Drugs*, 73.

70. Lee, *White Labyrinth*, 47.

71. Thoumi, *Political Economy and Illegal Drugs in Colombia*; also conversations with Francisco Thoumi.

72. Kevin Young, "Two, Three, Many Colombias," Foreign Policy in Focus, December 29, 2010, http://www.fpif.org/articles/two_three_many_colombias.

73. Isaacson, "Consolidating 'Consolidation.'"

74. Juan Carlos Garzón, *Mafia & Co. La red criminal en México y Colombia* (Bogotá: Planeta, 2008), 66–78.

75. See website of Transparency International in Colombia, http://www.transparencia colombia.org.co/index.php?option=com_content&view=article&id=94&Itemid= 510, as well as discussions with its director, Elisabeth Ungar, at the Transparency International meeting in November 2010, Bangkok, Thailand.

76. http://www.escuelanueva.org/. The author interviewed the founder of Escuela Nueva, Vicky Colbert, at the World Economic Forum in 2009 in Dubai, where she discussed how Colombia, through programs such as hers, had the highest levels of rural education in Latin America, and she discussed the difficulties of working in rural areas, where the drug traffickers recruited their workers. She also worked with children in communities displaced by the conflict.

77. The author interviewed Sicilian church-based groups that were assisting their colleagues in urban areas in Colombia to counter recruitment by organized crime groups, Palermo, Sicily, January 2002.

78. "Colombian Farc Rebels' Links to Venezuela Detailed," May 10, 2011, http://www.bbc.co.uk/news/world-latin-america-13343810.

79. Woodrow Wilson Center, *Organized Crime in Central America: The Northern Triangle*, executive summary, http://www.wilsoncenter.org/sites/default/files/LAP_single_page.pdf.

80. Cory Molzahn, Viridiana Ríos, and David A. Shirk, *Drug Violence in Mexico: Data and Analysis through 2011* (San Diego, CA: Trans-Border Institute, University of San Diego, March 2012), http://www.sandiego.edu/peacestudies/tbi/publications/reports.php.

81. "Clinton Says Mexico Drug Crime Like an Insurgency," September 9, 2010, http://www.bbc.co.uk/news/world-us-canada-11234058.

82. Pécaut, *Les Farc, une guerilla sans fins?*, 11; Michael LaRosa and Germán Mejía, *Colombia: A Concise Contemporary History* (New York: Rowan and Littlefield, 2012), 79.

83. Gabriel García Márquez, *Living to Tell the Tale*, trans. Edith Grossman (London: Penguin, 2003); Pécaut, *Les Farc, une guerilla sans fins?*, 11.

84. Pécaut, *Les Farc, une guerilla sans fins?*

85. Eduardo Pizarro Leongómez, "Las FARC-EP: ¿Repliegue Estratégico, Debilitamiento, o Punto de Inflexión?," in *Nuestra Guerra sin Nombre*, ed. Francisco Gutiérrez (Bogotá: Norma, 2006), 173.

86. William Horno, "Colombians Restart Talks in Hopes of Ending War," *New York Times*, October 17, 2012, http://www.nytimes.com/2012/10/18/world/americas/colombia-tries-again-to-end-drug-fed-war.html.

87. Pécaut, *Les Farc, une guerilla sans fins?*, 18–19.
88. Veillette, "Colombia: Issues for Congress," 4.
89. Start, "Terrorist Organization Profile, ELN (National Liberation Army)," http://www.start.umd.edu/start/data_collections/tops/terrorist_organization_profile.asp?id=218.
90. Thoumi, *Political Economy and Illegal Drugs in Colombia*, 123–30.
91. Ibid., 138.
92. Lee, *White Labyrinth*, 102.
93. Thoumi, *Political Economy and Illegal Drugs in Colombia*, 152.
94. Felbab-Brown, *Shooting Up: Counterinsurgency and the War on Drugs*, 72.
95. Lee, *White Labyrinth*, 102; Thoumi, *Political Economy and Illegal Drugs in Colombia*, 157.
96. Thoumi, *Political Economy and Illegal Drugs in Colombia*, 157.
97. Felbab-Brown, *Shooting Up: Counterinsurgency and the War on Drugs*, 75; William R. Long, "Colombia Confirms Bomb Killed 111 on Plane: Terrorism: Cocaine Traffickers Are Suspected in the Nov. 24 Explosion," *LA Times*, December 6, 1989, http://articles.latimes.com/1989-12-06/news/mn-88_1_bomb-explosion.
98. Felbab-Brown, *Shooting Up: Counterinsurgency and the War on Drugs*, 76.
99. Veillette, "Colombia: Issues for Congress," 4; "Colombia's Alvaro Uribe Investigated for 'Militia Links,'" January 9, 2013, http://www.bbc.co.uk/news/world-latin-america-20956820.
100. Bilal Y. Saab and Alexandra W. Taylor, "Criminality and Armed Groups: A Comparative Study of FARC and Paramilitary Groups in Colombia," *Studies in Conflict and Terrorism* 32 (2009): 461.
101. Ibid.
102. "AUC," http://www.insightcrime.org/groups-colombia/auc; U.S. State Department, "Country Reports for Terrorism 2010: Colombia," http://www.state.gov/j/ct/rls/crt/2010/170259.htm.
103. "FARC," September 29, 2012, http://colombiareports.com/colombia-news/profiles/26260-farc.html; June S. Beittel, "Mexico's Drug Trafficking Organizations: Sources and Scope of Rising Violence," Congressional Reference Service, September 7, 2011, 2, http://www.fas.org/sgp/crs/row/R41576.pdf, makes the same point about Mexico.
104. Garzón, *Mafia & Co.*, 66–78.
105. Mariel Perez-Santiago, "Colombia's BACRIM: Common Criminals or Actors in Armed Conflict?," July 23, 2012, http://www.insightcrime.org/news-analysis/colombias-bacrim-common-criminals-or-actors-in-armed-conflict.
106. Luis Astorga and David A. Shirk, "Drug Trafficking Organizations and CounterDrug Strategies in the U.S.-Mexican Context," 2010, http://usmex.ucsd.edu/assets/024/11632.pdf.
107. Lee, *White Labyrinth*, 13.
108. Ibid.
109. Homeland Security Digital Library, Michael Braun Testimony to Committee on Homeland Security, U.S. House of Representatives, "Iran, Hezbollah and the Threat to the Homeland," March 21, 2012, http://homeland.house.gov/sites/homeland.house.gov/files/Testimony-Braun.pdf.
110. Ibid.

111. Felbab-Brown, *Shooting Up: Counterinsurgency and the War on Drugs,* 93.

112. Douglas Farah, "Central American Gangs: Changing Nature and New Partners," *Journal of International Affairs* 66, no. 1 (2012): 53–67.

113. "Colombia Rebels Linked to Mexico Drug Cartels," *New York Times,* October 7, 2008, http://www.nytimes.com/2008/10/08/world/americas/08mexico.html?_r=0.

114. Olle Ohlsen Pettersson, "Report Claims Links between FARC and Mexican Drug Cartel," July 5, 2012, http://colombiareports.com/colombia-news/news/24945-farc-mexican-drug-cartel-links-highlighted-report.html.

115. "Profile: Mexico's Beltran Leyva Drug-Trafficking Gang," December 17, 2009, http://news.bbc.co.uk/2/hi/americas/8417914.stm.

116. Douglas Farah, *Transnational Organized Crime, Terrorism, and Criminalized States in Latin America: An Emerging Tier-One National Security Priority* (Washington, DC: Strategic Studies Institute, U.S. Army War College, 2012), 50.

117. U.S. State Department, "Country Reports on Terrorism 2010, Colombia," August 18, 2011, http://www.state.gov/j/ct/rls/crt/2010/170259.htm.

118. Michael Braun, Testimony to Committee on Homeland Security, U.S. House of Representatives, "Iran, Hezbollah and the Threat to the Homeland," 2012.

119. Frederick C. Leiner, *The End of Barbary Terror: America's 1815 War against the Pirates of North Africa* (Oxford: Oxford University Press, 2006).

120. Lacher, "Organized Crime and Conflict in the Sahel-Sahara Region."

121. Dario Cristiani and Riccardo Fabiani, "Al Qaeda in the Islamic Maghreb (AQIM): Implications for Algeria's Regional and International Relations," Instituto Affari Internazaionali, April 2011, 7; see also J. L. Marret, "Al-Qaeda in Islamic Maghreb: A 'Global' Organization," *Studies in Conflict and Terrorism* 31, no. 6 (2008): 541–52; Jean-Pierre Filiu, "Al-Qaeda in the Islamic Maghreb: Algerian Challenge or Global Threat?," Carnegie Middle East Program, Paper 104, October 2009, 7.

122. Jean-Pierre Filiu, "Could Al-Qaeda Turn African in the Sahel?," Carnegie Middle East Program, Paper 112, June 2010, 4.

123. Ibid.

124. Doug Farah, "Terrorist-Criminal Pipelines and Criminalized States: Emerging Alliances," *Prism* 2, no. 3 (2011): 22–23.

125. Michael P. Arena, "Hizballah's Global Criminal Operations," *Global Crime,* August 1, 2006; Douglas Farah, "Hezbollah's External Support Network in West Africa and Latin America," International Assessment and Strategy Center, August 4, 2006; Matthew Levitt, "Hezbollah: Financing Terror through Criminal Enterprise," in *Testimony before the Senate Committee on Homeland Security and Governmental Affairs* (Washington, DC, May 25, 2005); "Treasury Targets Hizballah Network in Africa," U.S. Department of the Treasury, Washington, DC, May 27, 2009.

126. Douglas Farah and Stephen Braun, *Merchant of Death: Money, Guns, Planes and the Man Who Makes War Possible* (Hoboken, NJ: John Wiley, 2007).

127. Neil MacFarquhar, "Mali Tackles Al Qaeda and Drug Traffic," *New York Times,* January 1, 2011, http://www.nytimes.com/2011/01/02/world/africa/02mali.html?pagewanted=all&_r=0.

128. CSIS Report of Middle East Program, "The Dynamics of North African Terrorism," March 2010, http://csis.org/files/attachments/100216_NorthAfricaConferenceReport.pdf.

129. Mohammed Adow, "Mali Sharia Amputee and Displaced Speak Out," January 15, 2013, http://blogs.aljazeera.com/blog/africa/mali-sharia-amputees-and-displaced-speak-out.

130. Vicki Huddleton, "Why We Must Help Save Mali," *New York Times,* January 15, 2013, A21.

131. Gregory A. Smith, "Al-Qaeda in the Lands of the Islamic Maghreb," *Journal of Strategic Security* 2, no. 4 (2009): 60–62; "Niger: Desert Smuggling Profits Climb," IRIN, October 15, 2008, http://www.irinnews.org/Report/80929/NIGER-Desert-smuggling-profits-climb.

132. Yonah Alexander, "Maghreb & Sahel Terrorism: Addressing the Rising Threat from al-Qaeda & Other Terrorists in North & West/Central Africa," International Center for Terrorism Studies, Arlington, Virginia, January 2010, 26.

133. Audra K. Grant, "Smuggling and Trafficking in Africa," in *Transnational Threats: Smuggling and Trafficking in Arms, Drugs and Human Life*, ed. Kimberley L. Thachuk (Westport, CT: Praeger Security International, 2007), 113–30.

134. Mike Braun, "The Confluence of Drugs and Terror – 21st Century Organized Crime," October 14, 2011, http://securitydebrief.com/2011/10/14/the-confluence-of-drugs-and-terror-21st-century-organized-crime/.

135. Adam Nossiter, "Leader Ousted, Nation Now a Drug Haven," *New York Times,* November 1, 2012, http://www.nytimes.com/2012/11/02/world/africa/guinea-bissau-after-coup-is-drug-trafficking-haven.html?pagewanted=all&_r=0; Liana Sun Wyler and Nicolas Cook, "Illegal Drug Trade in Africa: Trends and U.S. Policy," Congressional Reference Service, September 30, 2009, 4.

136. Ashley Neese Bybee, "Narco State or Failed State? Narcotics and Politics in Guinea-Bissau," PhD diss., School of Public Policy, George Mason University, September 2011, 10.

137. Ibid., 15.

138. Ashley Neese Bybee, "The Twenty-First Century Expansion of the Transnational Drug Trade in Africa," *Journal of International Affairs* 66, no. 1 (2012): 75.

139. Lacher, "Organized Crime and Conflict in Sahel–Sahara Region."

140. Bybee, "Twenty-First Century Expansion of the Transnational Drug Trade in Africa," 75.

141. This draws on research conducted by the author with Nazia Hussain and published as Louise Shelley and Nazia Hussain, "Narco-Trafficking in Pakistan-Afghanistan Border Areas and Implications for Security," in *Narco-Jihad: Drug Trafficking and Security in Afghanistan-Pakistan*, NBR Special Report 20 (National Bureau of Asian Research, December 2009), 23–41.

142. UNODC, *Globalization of Crime,* 109. Heroin production has risen since its low in 2010; UNODC, *World Drug Report, 2012,* 32.

143. Hakan Demirbüken, who is in charge of the UN Afghan drug survey, spoke on "Heroin Smuggling on a Global Scale" at the Fourth International Symposium on Terrorism and Transnational Crime, UTSAM, December 7–9, 2012, Antalya, Turkey. This share has been estimated in this speech as 20 percent, but it is hard to determine because there are three Taliban factions. According to Gretchen Peters (private communication), narcotics form the majority of what the quetta shura earns, however, it is hard to say how much, since there is overlap among the factions.

144. UNODC and Islamic Republic of Afghanistan Ministry of Narcotics, *Afghan Opium Survey 2012*, 3, http://www.unodc.org%2Fdocuments%2Fcrop-monitoring%2FAfghanistan%2FORAS_report_2012.pdf.

145. World Bank Country Study, *Afghanistan: State Building, Sustaining Growth, and Reducing Poverty* (Washington, DC: World Bank International Bank for Reconstruction and Development, 2005), 119.

146. "Afghanistan's Opium Profits Soared in 2011," January 17, 2012, http://www.pbs.org/wgbh/pages/frontline/afghanistan-pakistan/opium-brides/afghanistans-opium-profits-soared-in-2011/. UNODC and Islamic Republic of Afghanistan Ministry of Narcotics, "Afghan Opium Risk Assessment," http://www.unodc.org/documents/islamicrepublicofiran//ORAS_report_2013_phase12.pdf; Rod Nordland and Azam Ahmed, "Afghan Opium Cultivation and Production Seen Rising," *New York Times*, November 13, 2013, A6.

147. UNODC and Islamic Republic of Afghanistan Ministry of Narcotics, "Afghan Opium Survey 2012," http://www.unodc.org/documents/crop-monitoring/Afghanistan/ORAS_report_2012.pdf.

148. Francisco Thoumi, "Illegal Drugs in Colombia: From Illegal Economic Boom to Social Crisis," *Annals of the American Academy of Political and Social Science* 582, no. 1(2002): 102–16.

149. Conversation with Dr. Ashraf Ghani by the author, Dubai, November 2008.

150. Christopher L. Byrom, "Dismantling the Afghan Opiate Economy: A Cultural and Historical Policy Assessment, with Policy Recommendations," 33, September 2005, http://www.nps.edu/programs/ccs/Docs/Pubs/Byrom_thesis.pdf.

151. UNODC, *Globalization of Crime*, 110. Russia is estimated to present a $13 billion market for Afghanistan's opium and Europe a $20 billion market.

152. Ibid.

153. Peter Hopkirk, *The Great Game: The Struggle for Empire in Central Asia* (New York: Kodansha International, 1992); see also the play *The Great Game: Afghanistan*, which was presented at the Arena Stage, Washington, DC, in February 2011, http://www.shakespearetheatre.org/stc_presents/greatgame.aspx. The author attended the production that brought these slices of Afghan history to the stage.

154. Felbab-Brown, *Shooting Up Counterinsurgency*, 14–115; Thomas H. Johnson, "Financing against Terrorism: Thugs, Drugs, and Creative Movements of Money," in *Terrorism Financing and State Responses: A Comparative Perspective*, ed. Jeanne K. Giraldo and Harold A. Trinkunas (Stanford, CA: Stanford University Press, 2007), 94.

155. UNODC, *The Globalization of Crime*, 109. Drug use in Afghanistan dates to the eighteenth century but only became significant in the 1980s.

156. Svante E. Cornell and Louise I. Shelley, "The Drug Trade in Russia," in *Russian Business Power: The Role of Russian Business in Foreign and Security Relations*, ed. Andreas Wenger, Jeronim Perovic, and Robert W. Orttung (London: Routledge, 2006), 196–216.

157. Vanda Felbab-Brown, "The Drug Economy in Afghanistan and Pakistan, and Military Conflict in the Region," in *Narco-Jihad: Drug Trafficking and Security in Afghanistan-Pakistan*, NBR Special Report 20 (Washington, DC: National Bureau of Asian Research, December 2009), 6–7.

158. Thomas H. Johnson, "Financing Afghan Terrorism: Thugs, Drugs and Creative Movements of Money," in Giraldo and Trinkunas, *Terrorism Financing and State Responses*, 106–9.

159. Lawrence Wright, *Looming Tower: Al-Qaeda and the Road to 9/11* (New York: Knopf, 2006).

160. Felbab-Brown, *Shooting Up: Counterinsurgency and the War on Drugs*, 115; UNODC, *Afghan Opium Survey 2012*, 27.

161. Jennifer Quigley-Jones, "The High Costs of Afghan's Opium Economy," June 8, 2012, http://www.americanprogress.org/issues/security/news/2012/06/08/11715/the-high-costs-of-afghanistans-opium-economy/.

162. Ibid. See also Vanda Felbab-Brown, "Kicking the Opium Habit? Afghanistan's Drug Economy and Politics since the 1980s," *Conflict, Security, and Development* 6, no. 2 (2006): 127–49.

163. Jonathan Goodhand, "Corrupting or Consolidating the Peace? The Drugs Economy and Post-conflict Peacebuilding in Afghanistan," *International Peacekeeping* 15, no. 3 (2008): 405–23.

164. Byrom, "Dismantling the Afghan Opiate Economy," 37.

165. Goodhand, "Corrupting or Consolidating the Peace?"

166. UNODC, *Afghanistan Opium Survey 2004*, 4, http://www.unodc.org/pdf/afg/afghanistan_opium_survey_2004.pdf.

167. Peters, *How Opium Profits the Taliban*, 12.

168. Ibid.

169. Ibid., 13.

170. Ibid., 18.

171. Peters, *Seeds of Terror*, 123–25.

172. Ibid., 125.

173. Peters, *How Opium Profits the Taliban*, 21.

174. Ibid., 5.

175. Barnett R. Rubin, *Road to Ruin: Afghanistan's Booming Opium Industry* (New York: New York Center on International Cooperation, October 2004).

176. James A. Piazza, "The Opium Trade and Patterns of Terrorism in the Provinces of Afghanistan: An Empirical Analysis," *Terrorism and Political Violence* 24 (2012): 213–34.

177. For a fuller discussion of this, see Vanda Felbab-Brown, *Aspiration and Ambivalence: Strategies and Realities of Counterinsurgency and State Building in Afghanistan* (Washington, DC: Brookings Institution Press, 2013), Chapter 9, 161–88.

178. There is scant confirmed information on Quetta Shura. However, the Shura has been described as the grouping of Taliban leadership operating out of the Pakistani city of Quetta and that derives its funding from the narcotics trade and external donors. The Shura is not considered as the major planner that coordinates other militant groups but is deemed as the first-order threat to American interests in General McChrystal's report. See Stanley A. McChrystal, General U.S. Army Commander, U.S. Forces–Afghanistan/International Security Assistance Force, Afghanistan, *Comisaf's Initial Assessment* (Washington, DC: Headquarters International Security Assistance Force Kabul, Afghanistan, 2009). See also Peters, *Seeds of Terror*, 126–28.

179. Peters, *Seeds of Terror*, 124.
180. Doris Buddenberg and William Byrd, "Introduction and Overview," in *Afghanistan's Drug Industry, Structure, Functioning, Dynamics and Implications for Counter-narcotics Policy,* ed. Doris Buddenberg and William Byrd (Kabul: United Nations Office on Drugs and Crime, World Bank, 2006), 189–214.
181. "Afghan President's Brother, Ahmed Wali Karzai, Killed," http://www.bbc.co.uk/news/world-middle-east-14118884July 12, 2011.
182. Matthew Rosenberg, "Audit Says Kabul Bank Began as a 'Ponzi Scheme,'" *New York Times,* November 26, 2012, http://www.nytimes.com/2012/11/27/world/asia/kabul-bank-audit-details-extent-of-fraud.html?ref=hamidkarzai&_r=0.
183. Byrom, "Dismantling the Afghan Opiate Economy," 32.
184. Olivier Roy, *Islam and Resistance,* 2nd ed. (New York: Cambridge University Press, 1990).
185. David Mansfield and Adam Pain, *Evidence from the Field: Understanding Changing Levels of Opium Poppy Cultivation in Afghanistan* (Kabul: Afghanistan Research and Evaluation Unit, November 2007). The author has also presented with David Mansfield at the White House Office of National Drug Policy in 2009 and has had a chance for discussion.
186. Ibid.
187. Byrom, "Dismantling the Afghan Opiate Economy," 33; Quigley-Jones, "High Costs of Afghan's Opium Economy."
188. Mansfield and Pain, *Evidence from the Field.*
189. Adam Pain, *Opium Trading Systems in Helmand and Ghor* (Kabul: Afghanistan Research and Evaluation Unit, January 2006).
190. Demirbüken, "Heroin Smuggling on a Global Scale."
191. Mansfield and Pain, *Evidence from the Field.*
192. Ibid.
193. Edouard Martin and Steven Symansky, "Macroeconomic Impact of the Drug Economy and Counter-narcotics Efforts," in *Afghanistan's Drug Industry: Structure, Functioning, Dynamics, and Implications for Counter-narcotics Policy,* ed. Doris Buddenberg and William A. Byrd (Kabul: World Bank and United Nations Office on Drugs and Crime, 2006); see UNODC and Islamic Republic of Afghanistan Ministry of Narcotics, *Afghan Opium Survey 2012,* which analyzes the extreme insecurity in Afghanistan.
194. UNODC, *Afghanistan Opium Survey 2004.*
195. UNODC and Islamic Republic of Afghanistan Ministry of Narcotics, *Afghan Opium Survey 2012,* 12.
196. Sébastien Peyrouse, "Drug Trafficking in Central Asia: A Poorly Considered Fight?," PONARS Eurasia Policy Memo 218, September 2012, http://www.ponarseurasia.org/policy-memos/2012.
197. Svante E. Cornell and Niklas L. P. Swanström, "The Eurasian Drug Trade: A Challenge to Regional Security," *Problems of Post-Communism* 53, no. 4 (2006): 10–28.
198. UNODC, *Globalization of Crime,* 6–7.
199. Ibid.
200. George Kamm, "Kyrgyzstan: Moscow Slams Bakiyev Officials for Trafficking Drugs," February 22, 2011, http://www.eurasianet.org/node/62931.

201. K. Abdiev, "Analiz korruptsii v sudebnoi organakh Kyrgyzskoi respubliki, napravlennosti povysheniia effektivnosti proivodeistviia" (Analysis of corruption in judicial organs of the Kyrgyz republic and enhancing the effectiveness to counter it), in *Kyrgystan skvoz' prizmu narkonomiki*, ed. Alexander Zelichenko (Bishkek: Tsental'no-Aziastskii tsentr narkopolitiki, 2011), 5–61.

202. UNODC, *World Drug Report 2010* (Vienna: UN Office on Drugs and Crime, 2010), 35, http://www.unodc.org/documents/wdr/WDR_2010/World_Drug_Report_2010_lo-res.pdf; Alisher Latypov, "Otchet po issledovaniiu na temu: Barygi, narkobarony i narkodel'tsy: Narkoprestupnost' i rynki narkotikov v Tadzhikistane" (Report on investigation on drug dealers, narcobarons and narcotics traffickers: Drug crime and the market for drugs in Tajikistan), in *Kyrgystan skvoz' prizmu narkonomiki*, ed. Alexander Zelichenko (Bishkek: Tsental'no-Aziastskii tsentr narkopolitiki, 2011), 271–319.

203. Christopher Blanchard, *Afghanistan: Narcotics and U.S. Policy* (Washington, DC: U.S. Congressional Research Service, Library of Congress, June 2009), 29, http://www.fas.org/sgp/crs/row/RL32686.pdf.

204. Latypov, "Otchet po issledovaniiu na temu"; "Violence in Tajikistan's Badakhshan Province: A Legacy of Civil War," July 26, 2012, http://www.rferl.org/content/explainer-violence-in-tajikistan-badakhshan-province-a-legacy-of-the-civil-war/24657769.html.

205. Latypov, "Otchet po issledovaniiu na temu."

206. Alexander Kupatadze, *Organized Crime, Political Transitions and State Formation in Post-Soviet Eurasia* (Houndsmills, UK: Palgrave Macmillan, 2012).

207. The author was in Kyrgyzstan in September 2009 and in September 2010 after the violent conflicts in the south. She was in the south and observed some of the destroyed communities. For a discussion of this, see International Crisis Group, "Pogroms in Kyrgyzstan," Asia Report 193, August 23, 2010, http://www.crisisgroup.org/en/regions/asia/central-asia/kyrgyzstan/193-the-pogroms-in-kyrgyzstan.aspx.

208. *Securing, Stabilizing and Developing Pakistan's Border Area with Afghanistan: Key Issues for Congressional Oversight*, GAO-09-263SP (Washington, DC: U.S. Government Accountability Office, 2009), 11.

209. Peters, *Haqqani Network Financing*.

210. Mónica Serrano and María Celia Toro, "From Drug Trafficking to Transnational Organized Crime in Latin America," in *Transnational Organized Crime and International Security*, ed. Mats Berdal and Mónica Serrano (Boulder, CO: Lynne Reiner, 2002), 155.

7

The Less Policed Illicit Trade

Antiquities, Counterfeits, and Diverted Products

Blood Antiques, a fascinating documentary produced by specialists on the illicit art trade, commences with an interview of a high-end Brussels art dealer using an undercover camera. The dealer frankly states, "All these pieces were looted in Afghanistan, every object which comes from Afghanistan is by definition stolen, if you have a problem with that... but you cannot buy better."[1] Many wealthy buyers do not care that their purchases fund terrorism; they choose not to investigate too closely the origins of the art they acquire.

Ancient tombs have been looted by the Taliban, and houses are raided by Taliban members looking for antiquities that can be sent abroad to fund their activities. These antiquities arrive in Paris, Brussels, and the United States, having been shipped from Pakistan, after poorly paid Afghan customs officials were bribed to look the other way. Law enforcement in the West does not address the problem effectively. As one officer in the firm called in to inspect a suspicious shipment explains, "I can hardly be expected to know all about the art history of the world." As a result, *Blood Antiques* reveals that Brussels, the site of European Union and NATO headquarters, is packed with Taliban-supplied Afghan contraband.[2] The chance of any of the facilitators of this high-end trade being caught is minimal, as very little attention is allocated by European law enforcement to the policing of art markets.[3] Even if perpetrators are caught, the chance of serious punishment is negligible. Hence the sale of these exquisite antiques is a high-profit, low-risk crime for terrorists and criminals.[4]

The Business Logic of Product Diversification

Blood Antiques illustrates many of the principles that are explored in this chapter on criminal and terrorist diversification into areas of high profit and little risk of detection or confiscation of profits. Terrorists and criminals, as discussed in Chapter 5, are rational and often highly successful businessmen. Understanding markets and competition, they increasingly trade in commodities other than narcotics, where there is less market saturation, less or ineffective regulation, reduced competition, and more limited law enforcement focus. They focus on the least policed forms of transnational crime, which yield billions of profits annually.[5]

One of the most criminalized sectors is the illicit trade in cigarettes. In 2010, the World Customs Organization estimated that governments lost $31 billion due to counterfeit cigarettes every year, a much lower estimate than that provided by other organizations.[6] For example, the Euromonitor placed the losses in the $40 billion to $50 billion range globally in 2012.[7] Of great concern is that this trade has grown significantly in the recent decade, and the revenue losses are a multiple of what they were less than a decade ago.[8]

The illicit trade that benefits criminals and terrorists reaches different sectors of the consumer market. The illicit art market is a high-end "boutique" type of crime. It serves an elite clientele that is willing to pay top dollar for a unique and prestigious item. Therefore, each item can be sold for a significant sum. Antiquities crime is motivated more by greed than by need, in sharp contrast to trade in counterfeit and diverted goods, where items purchased are consumed on a daily basis.

The trade discussed in this chapter differs from the previously discussed drug trade not only in its distribution but also in its production. Whereas heroin and cocaine are often produced outside of factories, often in remote locales, counterfeits are often produced on a mass scale in established factories either after hours in licensed factories[9] or in factories specially designed to produce counterfeits.

This illicit trade, unlike the drug markets, enters both into expensive stores and street markets that are pervasive in the developing world. These products, in contrast with drugs, are often sold overtly. Moreover, they intersect much more directly and visibly with the legitimate economy from the point of production, along transit routes, to the point of sale to consumers. This illicit trade, benefiting a range of actors, including criminals and terrorists, requires the complicity of sellers, middlemen, consumers, and government officials. Most businesspeople are not as clearly complicit as the high-end art dealers of Brussels, who are so concerned with procuring marketable commodities that they are indifferent to provenance and the harm that their participation in this trade may cause. But many consumers willingly buy commodities produced and marketed by malicious nonstate actors. These include counterfeit DVDs, CDs, software, cigarettes, and cosmetics, knowing that these goods are not produced by legitimate producers. Others buy counterfeit commodities such as pesticides, pharmaceuticals, and spare parts, believing that they are authentic and will serve their needs.[10] Still others are deceived.

Many counterfeit purchases pose a threat to human security. With counterfeit and diverted pharmaceuticals, many are unwilling victims. They seek medicines in public markets or legitimate drug stores in the developing world, to cure life-threatening ailments, only to die from the purchase of counterfeit and diverted pharmaceuticals. Purchasers of building or spare parts in both developed and developing societies are injured or die from accidents because of faulty counterfeit components. Therefore, the harms caused by illicit actors are compounded – they generate funds for their group and directly harm others' lives. Yet, unlike in the drug trade, purchasers are not aware that they may be harmed.

Antiquities Smuggling, Sales, and Money Laundering

The problem of antiquities looting and smuggling is a far broader problem than identified by the film *Blood Antiques*.[11] There has been a long tradition of looting of art treasures during war and conquest. The great art museums of the Western world are filled with antiques acquired as war booty, starting with the Crusades and proceeding with Napoleon's conquest of Egypt, which filled the Louvre with priceless antiquities, and continuing with the British, who "bought" and brought the Elgin marbles to London.[12]

To address the looting of national cultural treasures, various international conventions were enacted in the latter half of the twentieth century to protect cultural property.[13] But these conventions function on the state level, and much of the contemporary threat to cultural patrimony comes from nonstate actors, such as criminals and terrorists, although the smuggling is often facilitated by corrupt state officials. With the rise of nonstate actors in recent decades, there is a particular problem in relation to historical artifacts. Antiquities are just one more commodity that can travel the same routes as other illicit commodities. "As a byproduct of continued trafficking in antiquities, the networks that connect collectors to looters accrue political risk and enable clandestine channels through which terrorist groups may conduct operations."[14]

As Neil Brodie, an expert on the illicit art trade, explains, "direct links between drugs trafficking and antiquities smuggling in Central America for instance have been reported on more than one occasion. In Belize and Guatemala jungle airstrips are used by criminals to smuggle out drugs and antiquities while at the receiving end a smuggler's plane arriving in Colorado from Mexico was found to contain 350 lb of marijuana and many thousands of dollars-worth of Pre-Columbian antiquities."[15]

The idea that looted antiques travel the same routes as other illicit commodities can be seen as well in Turkey. In the first decade of the 2000s, antiquities were found accompanying weapons of mass destruction.[16] A similar situation was found in Iraq, as antiquities and guns often exited Iraq together; furthermore, antiquities were never recovered without guns.[17] As the U.S. Central Office of Interpol explains, "the criminal networks that traffic in the illicit sale of Works of Art and Cultural Property are often times the same circles that deal in illegal drugs, arms, and other illegal transactions, illustrating the convergence of illicit activities. It has also been found recently that many insurgent and terrorist groups fund their operations through the sales and trade of stolen Works of Art and Cultural Property."[18]

Looted antiquities are not just a commodity to be sold but serve other functions in narcotics transactions. They can serve "either as initial collateral in drug deals or potentially replacing diamonds and bouillon as payment for narcotics."[19] Because this area of activity is underpoliced, it can provide an important supporting role for other types of illicit transactions.

Convergence of Illicit Actors

The growing dirty togetherness of diverse illicit actors in the antiquities trade has been observed increasingly in recent decades. As discussed in Chapters 3 and 4, both new terrorists and criminals are concentrated in the developing world, wracked by conflict, where there is little effective governance and antiquities can be dug up without disruption. For terrorists, antiquities are not only a relatively accessible source of revenue generation but have symbolic value. Erik Nemeth explains,

> Exploiting the symbolic value, terrorists have also publicized the destruction of religious monuments to garner diplomatic attention. In the secular realm of the burgeoning international art market, insurgents and terrorists can further exploit cultural property by collaborating with organized crime to profit from trafficking in stolen fine art and looted cultural artifacts. As a valuable commodity, antiquities serve not only as a tool in political violence but also as a medium for cooperation between organized crime and terrorist groups.[20]

The sale of antiquities from Afghanistan to fund terrorism has been ongoing since the time of al-Qaeda's entry into the country. As discussed in Chapter 1, Mohammed Atta, the mastermind behind the 9/11 attacks, approached a professor in Germany in 1999 offering to sell Afghan antiquities. German authorities were alerted to this situation; Atta explained that he wanted to buy a plane through their sale.[21]

To obtain antiquities, terrorists rely on organized rings of professional criminals who hire poor rural people to dig for antiquities. This has been seen in both Iraq and Afghanistan. According to a senior American counterterrorism official in Iraq, "objects are funneled out of the country in concealed shipments along smuggling routes that have been plied for centuries, in a system in which artifacts are sold for cash or sometimes for weapons that wind up in the hands of insurgents in Iraq."[22] Some archaeological experts estimate that the illegal antiquities trade may pump tens of millions of dollars into the underground economy in Iraq.

The looting of antiquities and transport to Western markets has occurred on a large scale in both Iraq and Afghanistan.[23] Photographs in archaeological magazines show the massive holes that now pockmark Iraq as diggers have searched for objects and plundered ancient sites. The looting of the National Museum in Baghdad immediately after the invasion revealed that there were many types of individuals ready to engage in looting the patrimony. Subsequent investigations indicated that the looters consisted of diverse groups – corrupt employees of the museum, criminals, and terrorists. The involvement of insurgents and terrorists in this activity was clear in June 2005 when U.S. Marines found underground bunkers in northwestern Iraq where five insurgents were hiding out. Along with automatic weapons, ammunition, black uniforms, ski masks, and night vision goggles were found thirty vases, cylinder seals, and statuettes stolen from the National Museum.[24]

Yet there is an entire business of antiquities theft apart from the looted Baghdad museum. The sale of antiquities, according to experts, has reached unprecedented levels, a fact facilitated by the ease with which these items can be sold through the Internet.

According to estimates published by the Archeological Institute of America (AIA),

> contractors pay looters in Iraq $10 million to $20 million each year for artifacts that fetch upwards of $100 million on the black market... The AIA estimates 100,000 to 150,000 tablets and cylinder seals are looted from Iraq each year. Many of them wind up on Ebay.[25]

This is a further illustration of how the Internet and the web can facilitate illicit trade.

There is limited allocation of resources to police this crime, and limited chance of success in disrupting the supply chain – the FBI only had eight agents dedicated to combating art and antiquities theft.[26] Without adequate databases of recently looted antiquities, theft is hard to prove. But much more could be done on detection by examining suspicious transactions on the Internet.[27]

The profits of this trade, as Phil Williams points out in his book on crime in Iraq, benefit both Sunni insurgents and Shiite militias. Apart from direct participation, they may also be taxing the trade.[28] This link is one that disturbs many in the world.[29]

Corruption and the Antiquities Trade

The illicit antiquities trade is facilitated not only by criminals and insurgents but also by corrupt military personnel. An FBI investigation conducted by a recently established art crime unit discovered that in 2004, stolen antiquities were taken by "Department of Defense contractors traveling through the Babylon region of Iraq." Investigators learned that the contractors collected the items and used them as gifts and bribes or sold them to other contractors, who then smuggled them into the United States. Two of the contractors were sentenced to prison for their roles in the fraud scheme.[30] The involvement of these military personnel shows the links that exist among corruption and illicit transnational networks.

Corruption in the business world is present through the complicity of art dealers and galleries that provide faulty provenance and documentation for these looted antiquities,[31] and by knowledgeable customers. As one of the principals behind *Blood Antiques* explained several years before the production of the film,

> connecting the dots between Taliban-controlled Afghanistan and Hezbollah-controlled Lebanon and stolen antiquities is common knowledge among collectors and dealers. The obvious link is when a hundred thousand people in the United States buy antiquities coming out of the Iraq, Iran, Lebanon and Pakistan... Nine out of 10 artifacts that come out of the Middle East are controlled by Hezbollah and Islamic Jihad.[32]

The problem discussed is not confined to Afghanistan, Iraq, or Pakistan. Illicit trade in antiquities has occurred from other regions such as Latin America, Turkey, and other countries in the Middle East, Southeast Asia, and Nigeria.[33] In Egypt, the power vacuum has contributed to massive looting of archaeological sites and museums.[34] The absence of regulation and law enforcement dedicated to this problem has allowed major markets in Europe to facilitate these illicit sales. Therefore, the corruption of sectors of the corporate world and the demand by an elite market are key to this important funding source for criminals, insurgents, and terrorists. This illicit trade in antiquities integrates actors of both the legitimate and the illegitimate economy along with corrupt officials into a single network that contradicts many visions of terrorist finance as a phenomenon confined to the gray economy. It confirms patterns discussed in Chapters 4 and 5.

Counterfeits

The problem of counterfeits dates back thousands of years, as product seals were counterfeited in the Roman era.[35] The problem is not new, but its scale has increased enormously with globalization, modern manufacturing, the rise of Internet marketing, and the failure to disrupt the sales of counterfeits.

Participation in this illicit trade can be subdivided into two categories: (1) those that merely represent copyright infringement and (2) those that cause harm to life and society. In the first category are such counterfeits as clothing, purses, other consumer goods, and DVDs and other forms of intellectual property. In the second category are counterfeit and diverted pharmaceuticals, food, wine, cigarettes, and spare parts.

The most common counterfeits come from both categories, including clothing and purses, cigarettes, DVDs, spare parts, electronics, software, and pharmaceuticals.[36] A significant problem of counterfeit currency exists, but fake currency is not generally produced in major or emerging economic powers, nor is it an area that is consciously underpoliced.[37] Therefore, it is outside the scope of this chapter.

Present estimates suggest that 2 billion consumers worldwide purchase counterfeits, and many suffer from the inferior quality of these goods.[38] The revenues from this trade are not distributed equally throughout the world. The problem is great in the developed world – Europe and North America – but is much greater in the developing world, where there is less regulation of markets and quality control of product. Yet the European Union has seen an enormous rise in counterfeits entering Europe from Asia, with a tenfold increase recorded between 1999 and 2008, an estimated value of counterfeit trade at $8.2 billion annually.[39]

Why the Rise of Counterfeits and Diverted Goods?

There has been an enormous increase in the number of counterfeit goods in recent decades because of their increased availability, the absence of regulation, the low risk of detection, and their profitability. In the United States, the trade in counterfeit goods has been calculated as even more profitable than trade in narcotics.[40]

Massive amounts of illicit goods enter into diverse trade routes. In 2008, the World Customs Organization detected counterfeits destined for 140 different countries. Asia figured disproportionately as the source of the detected counterfeits,[41] just as European law enforcement found.

Developing countries, especially the BRIC countries (Brazil, Russia, China, and India), are the sources of significant quantities of counterfeit consumer goods.[42] Yet other regions figure as well. The illicit production of cigarettes occurs in illegal factories in many countries, including the Balkans, Iraq, Russia, North Korea, Georgia, and within the European Union.[43] Illicit whites, cigarettes explicitly produced to be sold in markets and evade taxation, are produced in large numbers in Paraguay, United Arab Emirates, Cyprus, and Eastern Europe.[44]

Illicit trade follows the general trade trends of the contemporary world, where developing countries are increasingly significant importers and exporters. The share of world trade of goods produced in the developing world is expected to grow in the coming decades.[45] This will in turn contribute to a rise in counterfeits.

Absence of Regulation

The extensive availability of counterfeit and diverted goods is, in part, a consequence of the global failure to regulate international trade within a harmonized framework.[46] The World Trade Organization has been unable to incorporate a great number of countries into its framework. Despite its decade-long membership, the absence of firm commitment by China, the second largest economy in the world, and a source of much of the world's counterfeit goods, is illustrative of the problem.[47] Furthermore, the growing contribution of developing countries to international trade is creating a sea change, as the developed world can no longer define the rules and parameters of global trade.[48] In the absence of an effective regulatory regime, illicit trade is thriving. It exploits the gaps in the regulatory system, allowing massive movement of counterfeit, diverted, and untaxed goods to be moved.

Global supply chains, combined with the sheer volume of contemporary international commerce, make it difficult to monitor the authenticity and quality of goods at different stages of the transport route. Different types of illicit actors may be associated with this trade, facilitated by corrupt officials at such transport hubs as airports, railroad stations, and ports, as is shown in this chapter. The movement of money through the system of underground banking also makes it harder to monitor the flows. *Hawala* dealers help move the money related to counterfeits, diverted pharmaceuticals, and illicit white cigarettes in Africa and Asia.[49]

Corruption at borders, in customs, and in other governmental agencies further ensures that little attention is paid to the movement of the counterfeit and diverted goods at different points in the supply chain. Free-trade zones are exploited by criminal groups to sanitize shipments and disguise the origins of goods before they reach their final destination.[50]

Many governments are reluctant to crack down seriously on counterfeit production because of the economic dislocations it would cause. Therefore, inadequate regulatory and law enforcement resources are allocated at the source, and the products get harder to trace after they depart from the point of production. These commodities remain underpoliced, particularly in the developing countries, where states do not have the resources to control even the most violent of crimes and cannot monitor the supply chain for commodities.

The Low Risk

The crime of trading in counterfeits is so desirable because it is low risk. It is hard to detect within the massive shipments of legitimate goods.[51] Illustrative of this is the very limited attention to the highly dangerous counterfeit pharmaceutical trade. In 2011, only approximately 1,300 people worldwide were arrested for the counterfeiting, diversion, and theft of pharmaceuticals, with more than half the arrests occurring in Asia.[52] This is in a business, as previously stated, that is worth billions of dollars.

Even in the developed world, only a small share of counterfeits is intercepted. New York City, a major port of entry for the United States, faces significant imports of counterfeits, apart from its local production. Law enforcement in New York estimated that they confiscated only 2.5 million of the 19.5 million illicit sound recordings destined for the streets of New York, or approximately three illegal CDs per capita.[53]

As a member of the Los Angeles County Sheriff's Office for countering intellectual property crime declared in congressional testimony, intellectual property rights "(IPR) crime is attractive to gang members because of the high profit and minimal jail sentences. In the parlance of one suspect, it is better than the dope business, no one is going to prison for DVDs."[54] But it is also attractive to terrorists because there is limited chance of detection, confiscation of assets, or prison sentences for offenders.[55]

Online criminals who market counterfeit goods face even more minimal risks. Many of them are located in countries with limited capability or political will to go after Internet crime. Furthermore, their computer skills often make it hard to detect their exact locale. They work through banks in countries that have little enforcement capacity over their financial institutions.[56]

Who Profits, and by How Much?

Counterfeiting of both money and commodities is a major source of funding for terrorists, criminals, and corrupt officials.[57] North Korea is distinctive in having the sale of counterfeits be a major source of profits for the state.[58] The trade in some counterfeit commodities draws participants from diverse groups of nonstate actors. According to United Nations research, Chinese, South Asian, and European criminal groups are deeply involved in disseminating counterfeit goods.[59] Illustrative of this is the illicit pharmaceutical trade, which involves post-Soviet organized crime, Colombian drug cartels, Chinese triads, Mexican drug gangs; Hezbollah, and al-Qaeda are also believed to be involved.[60] So many diverse groups participate because the counterfeit pharmaceutical market is estimated to range from a low of \$14 billion annually to an estimated figure as high as five times that.[61] Online criminals also benefit, as they assume an important role as facilitators of this trade.[62]

Those profiting from this trade are not just criminals and terrorists; corrupt officials also participate. This is particularly evident with antimalarial drugs in Africa.[63] Officials sell medicines donated by pharmaceutical companies for their personal profit, or they may reward lowly paid officials with donated malarial drugs that can then be sold by the officials to the community to supplement their salaries. Unfortunately, these diverted drugs, which provide an income source for corrupt officials, are no longer fully effective, as they are not kept at the temperatures needed to maintain their potency.[64] This has contributed to the global failure to eliminate malaria. The costs of this illicit trade are also devastating for African development, as the presence of malaria is believed to reduce economic growth in some African countries by 1.3 percent annually; this loss compounded annually reduces development significantly over time.[65]

The corruption that facilitates illicit trade can involve very high-level officials. For example, in Montenegro, the president was indicted in Italy for his role in the cigarette trade, as were several of his close associates.[66]

Terrorist Engagement in Counterfeits

Much more has been written about the involvement of criminals than terrorists in the trade in counterfeits.[67] Yet, according to the Secretary General of

Interpol, Ronald K. Noble, there are diverse ways that terrorists engage in counterfeit trade:

> **Direct involvement** where the relevant terrorist group is implicated in the production, distribution or sale of counterfeit goods and remits a significant proportion of those funds for the activities of the group. Terrorist organizations with direct involvement include groups who resemble or behave more like organized criminal groups than traditional terrorist organizations. This is the case in Northern Ireland where paramilitary groups are engaged in crime activities. These crime activities include IPC. Involvement by these groups ranges from control or investment in manufacturing or fabrication to taxing the market stalls where counterfeit goods are sold. It is possible for illicit profit to be generated for terrorist groups at different points in the process.

> **Indirect involvement** where sympathizers or militants are involved in IPC and remit some of the funds, knowingly to terrorist groups via third parties.[68]

As shown in Chapter 4, the funding generated by these illicit sales in one part of the world may help fund a terrorist organization or attack that is thousands of miles away. For example, money made from selling cigarettes produced in illicit factories in Paraguay can be transferred thousands of miles to Hezbollah or Hamas in the Middle East.[69] As the introduction showed, Belkmokhtar's (aka "Mr. Marlboro") cigarette trade helped fund the In Amenas attack. The profits from counterfeit sales may be transferred across long distances, through underground banking or trade-based money laundering, within closed networks based on trust that are hard for outsiders to penetrate.[70] Therefore, the terrorist activity often occurs far from where the counterfeit sales occur.

Regional Perspectives

The following discussion provides diverse examples from North America, Europe, Africa, Latin America, the Middle East, and parts of Asia, revealing the involvement of criminals and terrorists and corrupt officials in the counterfeit trade and its important regional differences. The discussion shows the diversity of this trade globally and how it is shaped by many factors, including traditional trade routes, the production capacity of the region, demand for the product, and the variety of illicit actors present in the region. The global networks that link production and consumption contribute to a complex picture that reveals the convergence of different forms of illicit trade and the involvement of diverse kinds of actors. Particular emphasis is placed on how terrorist groups are behaving as criminal actors, facilitating this trade.

North America

The illicit counterfeit trade in the United States combines the theft of intellectual property from the United States and the importation of counterfeits produced largely in Asia. Intellectual property stolen in the United States will be counterfeited both in the United States and abroad and will be marketed both domestically and internationally. Despite the regulation and enforcement capacity in the United States, it has proven increasingly difficult to control the trade in counterfeit clothing, pharmaceuticals purchased through the Internet, and the illicit sales of counterfeit DVDs and software in large metropolitan areas. Counterfeit and diverted cigarettes are an additional concern, particularly in states with high tax rates on cigarettes.[71] Illustrative of this is the case of New York, with the highest tax rates per pack, where 60 percent of cigarettes sold are smuggled.[72] Counterfeits have been identified in what should be the most secure of supply chains. The U.S. military has identified eighteen hundred cases of counterfeit parts entering into U.S. military combat hardware.[73]

There are several important locales in the United States where theft of intellectual property is a particular concern. The theft of intellectual property related to software and technology is a particular concern on the West Coast, particularly in the Silicon Valley and Seattle areas. Most of the pirated movies that are disseminated worldwide on DVDs originate from California, as does music from the Latin recording industry, which is disseminated through counterfeit CDs.[74] Key parts of the American recording industry whose artists' recordings are subject to counterfeiting are based in New York City. In Los Angeles, Russian, Eurasian, Asian, Latin American, and Lebanese organized crime groups as well as criminal gangs have been identified as benefiting from intellectual property crimes.[75] The Lebanese crime groups in Los Angeles, according to Los Angeles police investigations, are associated with Hezbollah, as the following congressional testimony from a member of the Los Angeles County Sheriff's Office reveals:[76]

> During the search of a residence pursuant to an IPR related search warrant, I saw small Hezbollah flags displayed in the suspect's bedroom. Next to the flags was a photograph of Hassan Nasrallah whom I recognized as the leader of Hezbollah. The suspect's wife asked me if I knew the subject of the photograph. I identified Nasrallah and the wife said, "We love him because he protects us from the Jews." Also in the home were dozens of audio tapes of Nasrallah's speeches. During the search, one of my detectives also found a locket which contained a picture of the male suspect on one side and Sheik Nasrallah on the other.[77]

In another authorized IPR search warrant of other Los Angeles locales, photo albums were found of an event of the Holy Land Foundation, a charity that was shut down in the United States for its support of Hamas.[78]

Illustrative of the transnational dimensions of the phenomenon, and the high-status nature of some participants, is the case of Chang Shan Liu,[79] who defies the stereotype of criminals. The Lius were a Chinese American couple in their sixties. May Liu was a retired official of the World Bank, and her nephew, who was a part of the network, was also a former employee of the World Bank. Together, they ran a multinational counterfeit operation that involved a billion counterfeit cigarettes and more than $3 million in counterfeit cash, weapons, and Viagra.[80] In this case, the actors were people who had one foot in China and the other in the United States. In China, the Lius bribed customs officials to smuggle counterfeit cigarettes, Viagra, wallets, and cash. Outside of China, they were responsible for selling the counterfeit goods. The Liu case revealed the intersection of the illicit trade in counterfeit drugs and cigarettes.

The Internet can also make a small-scale legitimate entrepreneur a participant in the international counterfeit trade. Illustrative of this is the case of James George, a licensed pharmacist based in Houston, Texas, who willfully ordered counterfeit Viagra and Cialis from China via the Internet and intended to sell the drugs to unsuspecting customers. The Chinese-produced counterfeit drugs were extremely cheap in price, as compared to prices in the United States. The average wholesale price for a normal Viagra tablet was $9.55, and $13.55 per tablet for Cialis. George paid 30 cents per counterfeit tablet of Viagra and 35 cents per tablet for Cialis.[81]

Analysis of terrorists profiting from counterfeit trade reveals a similar phenomenon. In two cases in Detroit, one Hezbollah network trading in diverted cigarettes intersected with another network trading in illegal cigarettes and counterfeit Viagra.[82] The presence of terrorists in counterfeits is reflective of a previously identified principle of terrorist involvement in crime – to do harm not just by making profits but by harming individuals.

In *Illicit,* Moisés Naím explains how counterfeit T-shirts sold on Broadway helped fund the bombing of the World Trade Center in 1993.[83] But this was not the only crime that helped finance this terrorist act. According to the Financial Action Task Force, the prime international body to counter money laundering, "phony cigarette tax stamps were found in apartments used by the perpetrators."[84] These stamps are central to the illicit trade in cigarettes. Counterfeit T-shirts and cigarettes recur in other cases of terrorist financing.

Three years later, "the FBI seized 100,000 counterfeit T-shirts that were to be sold during the summer Olympics in Atlanta; this operation was allegedly masterminded by followers of the Blind Sheikh Omar Abdel Rahman, who is serving a life sentence for plotting to bomb New York City landmarks."[85] This problem did not end in the 1990s in the United States. Investigators in Los Angeles discovered Hezbollah involvement in counterfeit clothing:

> In 2004, detectives served an IPR search warrant at a clothing store in Los Angeles County. During the course of the search, thousands of dollars in counterfeit clothing was recovered as were two unregistered firearms. During the booking process, the suspect was found to have a tattoo of the Hezbollah flag on his arm.[86]

Yet the problems of counterfeits and terrorist financing are not confined to Middle East groups seeking to fund terrorism. Rather, the largest case of cigarette smuggling detected in the United States, in which at least $100 million was identified, provided financial support for the Real IRA. The smuggling operation ended in 2009 after four years of joint European and U.S. investigations. The cigarettes were transported to the most southerly countries in Latin

America, and then they traveled northward. IRA operatives arranged for the transport of cigarettes northward, many transiting Panama before arriving at the Port of Miami, before being shipped to Europe. Crime groups in Spain and Ireland helped distribute the cigarettes that benefited the Irish terrorist organization.[87]

Europe
The highly regulated markets of Europe provide some control over the entry of counterfeits. Europe, however, has a long and vulnerable coastline and historical trade routes that date back to the Ottoman Empire. Furthermore, there are significant problems of corruption in the Eastern part of Europe, especially along the historic Balkan route that links Europe with Turkey.[88] The conflicts in the former Yugoslavia and the extensive problems of organized crime in Italy, where criminal groups such as the Naples-based Camorra have significant control over major ports,[89] contribute greatly to the growth of illicit trade. The sheer volume of trade, such as arrives at the port of Rotterdam in the Netherlands, limits the ability to ensure quality control at the entry points to Europe.[90] Therefore, imports of counterfeits are growing in frequency. In "2008, the European Customs Union detected over 3,200 attempts to import bogus drugs, involving almost 9 million items, over half of which originated in India."[91]

Yet not all the counterfeits are imported into Europe. Counterfeit cigarettes are produced en masse within Europe. The number of known illegal factories has increased rapidly. In 2010, five factories for the production of counterfeit cigarettes were discovered in the European Union, whereas in 2011, member states discovered nine illegal factories estimated to have a combined production capacity of more than 9 million cigarettes per day.[92] With such large production and the import of contraband cigarettes, illicit cigarettes accounted for more than 11 percent of the European market in 2012, the highest recorded percentage since annualized surveys were commissioned. This represented revenue losses to the European Union of 12.5 billion euros annually, or approximately one-quarter of global revenue losses.[93]

The prime criminal actors in the European counterfeit trade are the Camorra, who may earn "more than 10 percent of its roughly $25 billion annual profit through the sale of counterfeit and pirated goods – such as luxury clothing, power tools, CDs, DVDs, and software."[94] They are also active in the trade in counterfeit pharmaceuticals. As a less traditional crime group than the Sicilian-based Mafia, they also cooperate with terrorists. A recent parliamentary investigation in Italy has raised serious concerns as to the extent and diverse costs of their significant role in importing and disseminating counterfeits.[95] Italian governmental corruption is a key component in their ability to operate on such a large scale.[96]

Terrorists also participate in this trade. Danish customs officials in 2002 "seized a container filled with counterfeit shampoos, creams, colognes, and perfumes, along with eight tons of fake Vaseline jelly, sent by a member of Al Qaeda."[97]

Two conflict regions in Europe have been at the center of the trade of counterfeit DVDs – Northern Ireland and Bosnia-Hercegovina.[98] The production and sale of counterfeits benefited both republican and loyalist paramilitary factions during the conflicts in Northern Ireland.

During the Balkan conflicts of the 1990s, the Arizona market in Brcko in Bosnia-Hercegovina was a major provider of counterfeit DVDs and other commodities. Behind this market was a diverse variety of criminals, terrorists, and insurgents benefiting greatly from the sale of these products to the peacekeepers. In this way, those sent to stabilize the situation were providing operating funds to those who were intentionally destabilizing the political environment.[99]

These problems persist. Data on the consumption of counterfeit cigarettes indicate that an estimated 49 percent of cigarettes consumed in Bosnia-Hercegovina are illegal, among the highest recorded level in the world.[100] The war years and massive illicit trade that occurred have established a large and permanent second economy.

The counterfeiting of DVDs, software, and other multimedia is rampant in Russia. This is the type of crime at which post-Soviet organized crime excels, because of the many technically sophisticated criminals within their ranks. But in the North Caucasus, a highly corrupt region where both terrorists and criminals operate, there is the involvement of both groups in the DVD trade. A decade ago, according to Interpol, Russian law enforcement officials disrupted the operation of a Chechen-run counterfeit CD manufacturing plant. The Russian security service estimated that the criminal organization earned $500,000 to $700,000 and sent some of the funds to Chechen rebels.[101] This is an example of the indirect involvement of terrorist groups receiving funds from criminals who are directly engaged in counterfeiting activity.

More recently, Russian researchers in Stavropol in the North Caucasus have observed the continued involvement of both terrorist and criminal groups in counterfeiting in the highly unstable region of the North Caucasus. Analysis of many court cases in the region reveal that illicit trade benefits terrorists, as well as criminal groups, as in the case of the Chechen DVD factory.[102] But the sampling of cases may be skewed, because of the widespread corruption and the complicity of government officials in this trade. They may only be ready to act against counterfeiting when there is a terrorist component.

Africa
Africa receives many types of counterfeits and diverted drugs into its markets. The most dangerous form of counterfeit is, of course, the counterfeit pharmaceuticals, particularly antimalarial drugs, as previously mentioned, which are harmful to individuals but also increase drug resistance by bacteria. A 2011 World Health Organization study of Nigeria, the continent's largest market for drugs, found that 64 percent of antimalarial drugs were fake.[103] A recent study

estimated that 20 percent of the antimalarial drugs sold in Africa are falsified, and an additional 35 percent failed chemical analysis.[104]

But almost every other type of counterfeit enters African markets, including counterfeit cigarettes, textiles, DVDs, and CDs. The Ghanian domestic textile production that employs tens of thousands is being destroyed by the importation of counterfeit textiles, smuggled into the country often with the complicity of corrupt officials. The quantities that are smuggled are large, with four or five twenty-three-ton shipping containers entering Accra markets daily.[105]

The illicit cigarette trade is enormous in Africa. South Africa is a destination for counterfeit cigarettes produced in China.[106] The government has seized nearly 1 billion fraudulent cigarettes.[107] As discussed in the introduction, in North Africa, the smuggling of cigarettes, including counterfeits, has been a major funding source for AQIM.[108] According to Peter Gastrow, "approximately 25 percent of cigarettes smoked in the East African region are smuggled and illicit, causing governments to lose $100 million in taxes."[109]

An in-depth analysis of the counterfeit trade in Kenya reveals a diversity of actors, both in government and in the illicit economy, who make this trade possible. Corruption is key in facilitating this illicit trade:

> Smuggling and trafficking in counterfeit goods is undertaken by networks of small-scale traders as well as by established criminal networks powerful enough to compromise senior figures in government, the police, the judiciary, and customs and administrative officials. The larger and more powerful networks tend to establish and then control their own turf area.[110]

The Kenyan experience is the most dramatic example of the costs to a country of counterfeit trade, as Kenya is the largest recipient of counterfeit goods in East Africa, totaling more than $900 million annually. Originating primarily from India and China, the counterfeits deprive the state of revenues of between $84 million and $490 million. Manufacturers estimate their loss at $368 million.[111]

While the state and businesses lose, illicit actors, including al-Shabaab, an al-Qaeda affiliate operating in the Horn of Africa, win. Consistent with the model articulated by Interpol's secretary general Ronald K. Noble, al-Shabaab profits by "taxing" the illicit trade between northern Kenya and Somalia. The network, according to an authoritative study using extensive field research, includes "some of al-Shabaab's top officials and several Somali powerbrokers, who pay protection fees to authorities."[112] The network leader is al-Turki, listed by the United Nations as an al-Qaeda associate and financier.[113] The mutual interaction of illicit trade, corruption, and terrorism is evident in this example.

Another terrorist group also profits from this trade – D-company. The counterfeit DVDs produced by this crime-terror group are trafficked to East Africa.[114] As is discussed more lately, this is a major revenue source for this crime-terrorist group based in Pakistan.

South America

The sale of counterfeits is pervasive in Latin America, involving all categories of counterfeit goods. The large and famed Tepito market of Mexico City is an epicenter of trade in counterfeits of every type, including DVDs.[115] Counterfeit medicines produced in Central America are sold in the United States.[116] This trade survives because of the presence of transnational and local criminal actors, corrupt officials at all ranks, and small-scale traders, who depend on these illicit products for their survival.

Within this larger world of counterfeit products exists a subregion in Latin America, a highly important node where crime, corruption, and terrorism intersect. The triborder area of Brazil, Argentina, and Paraguay survives because of its significant trade in counterfeit goods: electronics, cigarettes, cell phones, drugs, and DVDs. The triborder area has also emerged as an important external financing center for terrorism in the Middle East, particularly for Hezbollah, which functions as an Iranian proxy in Latin America. The facilitators of this trade include Chinese organized crime, Paraguayan corrupt officials and members of the terrorist organization Hezbollah.[117]

Produced in cooperation with Chinese organized crime operating in the region, pirated CDs generate multi-million-dollar sales.[118] Even though the criminals benefit from the trade, some of the profits return to the Middle East to support Hezbollah. Evidence of this is that at least one transfer of $3.5 million was donated by known DVD pirate Assad Ahmad Barakat, for which he received a thank-you note from the Hezbollah leader.[119] Barakat is believed to provide a significant share of the $20 million that flows annually to Hezbollah, representing about 20 percent of its budget.[120] As a result, Barakat was labeled a "specially designated global terrorist" by the U.S. government in 2004.[121]

The core of this illicit trade is the 165 store, Galeria Plage, in Ciudad del Este, Paraguay, owned by Barakat. Through this center flow not only counterfeit DVDs but many other illicit goods and counterfeits. Another large-scale counterfeiter, Ali Khalil Mehri, also operated out of the same building. "Financial records indicated that Mehri had provided funds to al Moqawamah – the militant branch of Hezbollah with which Barakat is alleged to have worked."[122] The following example of Mehri's operations epitomizes the entanglement of corruption, crime, and terrorism. Mehri

> took advantage of weak evidentiary requirements and widespread corruption in Paraguay's copyright, trademark, and patent office to obtain certificates that purportedly gave him exclusive rights to manufacture the merchandise that he counterfeited...
>
> Pirates and counterfeiters effectively turned Paraguay's intellectual-property system into an extortion mechanism. If merchants tried to sell products that had been "registered," they were subject to extortion, and the police became the ultimate enforcers of this racket.[123]

Middle East, Afghanistan, and Pakistan

The Middle East, according to the Organisation for Economic Co-operation and Development, consumes the highest level of counterfeit automotive parts and large quantities of pirated music, movies, and software. This trade benefits both criminals and terrorists.[124] In 2003, officials in Lebanon intercepted counterfeit shock absorbers worth $1.2 million, whose sale Interpol believes was to profit Hezbollah.[125]

Consumption of counterfeits is high in all the countries of the Middle East.[126] The Gulf Region is a transport hub for counterfeits leaving Asia in transit to other regions of the world.[127] In Sharjah, for example, an enormous shopping center is filled almost entirely with counterfeit goods.[128] High levels of corruption in law enforcement, and an absence of a regulatory framework, permit the dissemination of large quantities of counterfeit pharmaceuticals, spare parts, cigarettes, electronics, and the software and DVDs mentioned earlier.

Many merchants are beneficiaries of this trade, as are international crime groups. Terrorist groups that function as businessmen are integrated into this trade and also profit extensively from the sale of counterfeits. In the Middle East, a diverse range of terrorist groups benefits from the trade in counterfeit, including Hamas, Fatah, Hezbollah, and al-Qaeda,[129] PKK,[130] and insurgent groups. As has just been shown, Hezbollah also benefits from this trade in Latin America. This is a rational business decision, as the profits are high, and the chances of punishment and imprisonment are low for such offenses. According to the model laid out by Ron Noble, members of Hamas, Fatah, and even senior members of the Palestinian Authority are thought to tax the criminals who sell the pirated DVDs and other multimedia products in the West Bank and Gaza.[131]

In Turkey, the PKK benefits from the cross-border trade in counterfeit cigarettes as well as other commodities, such as drugs that move across Turkey's eastern borders with Iran, Iraq, and Syria. PKK members serve as facilitators of this trade or derive revenues through taxation of counterfeit cigarettes that are transported to Turkey from factories in the Middle East.[132] This longstanding trade, as discussed previously, functions because of kinship ties that exist among the Kurds who live on the eastern border and have kinship ties with Kurdish communities in neighboring countries.[133]

Afghanistan and Pakistan

The control of film and musical piracy is concentrated in this region in the hands of one criminal-terrorist group, D-Company.[134] Since the 1980s, Dawood has "been able to vertically integrate D-company throughout the Indian film and pirate industry, forging a clear pirate monopoly over competitors and launching a racket to control the master copies of Pirated Bollywood and Hollywood films."[135]

The failure of the Indian government to recognize the film industry as legitimate until the late 1990s denied legal investors a means to invest in Bollywood, even though it produced large numbers of films and spread Indian popular culture globally. Furthermore, without filmmakers and distributors enjoying access to capital from commercial businesses and private investors, they were subject to the extortionate demands of D-Company to obtain needed working capital.

D-Company, after assuming a key role in the Mumbai terrorist attacks in 1993, as discussed in Chapter 1, was forced to move its home base from Mumbai to Karachi. Its production base for pirated films shifted, but not its close relationship to and domination of the Mumbai-based film industry. In Kararchi, D-Company acquired the SADAF brand, which allowed the crime-terror group to market its pirated Bollywood and Hollywood films globally.[136] These pirated films are sold in India and South Asia, throughout the Middle East, and are even found in East Africa.

In Afghanistan, American and other foreign soldiers buy these counterfeit DVDs at stalls on the bases where they are stationed. Therefore, military personnel are buying commodities that fund terrorism, at the same time that they are risking life and limb to combat terrorism in Afghanistan.[137]

The amount generated from the sale of pirated DVDs is enormous. On one mid-sized base, there are typically nine vendors selling bootleg DVDs. These DVDs sell for $1 apiece on base, relative to their market price in the Kabul market, where they retail for approximately 15 cents. Estimated sales on a mid-sized base total fifteen hundred pirated DVDs daily. This reflects more than a sevenfold markup for U.S. military personnel, or profits on each base of approximately $1,300 daily. Many of these videos are the SADAF brand; therefore, the crime-terror group profits from its initial control over the film industry, but also from the money it is paid by the sellers on the bases. The pirated DVDs thus profit D-Company and other related groups, both at the production stage and at the retail level, where vendors are "taxed" – the business model of counterfeiting Noble identified earlier.

Conclusion

This chapter has focused on two very different forms of crime, where the intersection of crime, terrorism, insurgency, and corruption is apparent – art smuggling and the illicit trade in counterfeit and diverted goods. The antiquities trade is a relatively infrequent crime, whereas counterfeiting is one of the most pervasive forms of transnational crime. Yet these commodities, with very different markets, can benefit diverse types of illicit actors because these crimes do not command the law enforcement and regulatory attention of more notorious crimes.

Such large-scale illicit trade requires significant numbers of participants in production, transport, and distribution of counterfeit goods. There are many types of individuals in the supply chain, from the point of origin to the point of sale. Producing counterfeits provides large-scale employment in

China and India, the focal point of production. Shippers, transporters, and owners of warehouses are major beneficiaries. Moreover, a great variety of actors, including officials, entrepreneurs (both legal and illegal), producers of spam (who market the counterfeits), and transnational criminals (consisting of crime groups, online criminals, and terrorists) enable this trade. The corruption that facilitates this trade is most common among members of border services, customs officials, and members of regulatory agencies.

Counterfeiting is one of the most profitable transnational crimes, with estimated revenues of hundreds of billions of dollars annually. Its profits exceed those of human trafficking and may be exceeded only by the international narcotics and arms trade.[138] Yet it is rarely mentioned among the most threatening of transnational crimes. This underevaluation of the problem may be a consequence of the fact that many view this issue as merely an "infringement of intellectual property," without understanding the broader consequences for trade, state stability, and human security. Corruption and an unregulated Internet contribute to the proliferation of this trade. Consequently, states cannot curb counterfeit trade, thereby losing state revenues and capacity. Under these conditions of high profitability and low risk, it is a highly attractive criminal venture.

Many purchasers of these smuggled goods are not aware that they may be causing harm to themselves and others. Purchasers of smuggled art and antiquities may not be conscious that they are depriving countries of their cultural patrimony. Purchasers of bootlegged cigarettes are indifferent "to the existence of smuggling – an indifference that results in some citizens paying higher taxes than they might otherwise experience or receiving a lower level of services because states and localities are deprived of essential revenue."[139] Another societal effect stemming from the availability, purchase, and consumption of illicit cigarettes and counterfeits is the erosion of the rule of law:

> Where the general public becomes aware that laws are not being complied with and no consequences arise, there is a gradual erosion of respect for legislation and enforcement authorities. If people rarely hear of arrests and successful prosecutions of those involved in illicit trade, then the perception will spread both that enforcement authorities are ineffective and that the law doesn't really matter. People who habitually break the law without suffering any consequences can influence others thus lowering the standards of acceptable law abiding behavior.[140]

Purchasers of counterfeit goods are often not cognizant that there is an absence of quality and health control over the production of these goods, such as cigarettes and pharmaceuticals.[141] Therefore, the demand for counterfeit goods by consumers is great, and the perceptions of costs of purchase are low.

Consequently, citizens do not press for governmental action in these areas of illicit trade, as they do in the narcotics drug arena. The pressures applied by corporations for enforcement of copyright are often seen as self-serving.

Therefore, neither the global community nor individual states demonstrate the political will to counter aggressively the large and growing problem of counterfeits, nor the illicit trade in antiquities.

To address these very damaging forms of transnational crime, there must be a greater awareness that smuggling of art and counterfeits and diverted goods cause a range of harms and undermine human security and patrimony, as well as stifling innovation and undermining the development of needed new technologies. The problem of counterfeiting and diversion transcends the problem of intellectual property rights and should be of concern, not just to corporate interests but to society generally. Without such attention, diverse illicit actors and corrupt officials are considerably rewarded, compounding the inherent harm caused by this illicit trade. Commanding such low-level priority among law enforcement, these crimes are a particular point of convergence of the dirty entanglement – crime, corruption, and terrorism.

Notes

1. *Blood Antiques* website, http://www.journeyman.tv/?lid=59906. The film was produced in 2009.
2. Ibid.
3. Review of the Europol annual report shows that this is not one of the areas in which they are conducting significant operations. See *Europol Review 2011: General Report on Europol Activities,* September 28, 2012, http://www.europol.europa.eu/content/publication/europol-review-2011-1779.
4. Ian Johnston, "New 'Intelligence' Body Set to Fight Illicit Trade in World's Priceless Treasures," November 14, 2012, http://worldnews.nbcnews.com/_news/2012/11/14/14944606-new-intelligence-body-set-to-fight-illicit-trade-in-worlds-priceless-treasures.
5. For discussion on how developing countries decided that the benefits of cracking down on counterfeits were of limited benefit, see Asif Efrat, *Governing Guns, Preventing Plunder: International Cooperation against Illicit Trade* (New York: Oxford University Press, 2012), 265.
6. World Customs Organization, *Customs and Tobacco Report 2009* (Brussels: World Customs Organization, 2010), 1, http://www.wcoomd.org/files/1.%20Public%20files/PDFandDocuments/Enforcement/WCO_Customs_Tobacco_2010_public_en.pdf; Sharon A. Melzer provides higher figures in "Counterfeit and Contraband Cigarette Smuggling: Opportunities, Actors, and Guardianship," PhD diss., American University, 2010.
7. See Elizabeth Allen, *The Illicit Trade in Tobacco Products and How to Tackle It*, 2nd ed. (Washington, DC: ITIC, 2013), 19, http://www.iticnet.org/publications/studies-and-reports.
8. Moisés Naím, *Illicit: How Smugglers, Traffickers, and Copycats Are Hijacking the Global Economy* (New York: Doubleday, 2005), 109–30.
9. Irregularly produced items include a wide range of products. Their production manufacture is not necessarily illegal, but they are outside licensed production. For

example, they may be produced in a factory after hours, without the authorization of the manufacturer, and sometimes without the same content.

10. The counterfeit pesticides are now assuming 25 percent of the European market. Counterfeit toiletries and cosmetics are also increasing problems. See *Europol Review 2011*, 23, 50–53.

11. See, e.g., Christina Alder and Kenneth Polk, "Stopping This Awful Business: The Illicit Traffic in Antiquities Examined as a Criminal Market," *Art Antiquity and Law* 7, no. 1 (2002): 35–53; Kathryn W. Tubb, ed., *Antiquities Trade or Betrayed: Legal, Ethical and Conservation Issues* (London: Archetype, in conjunction with UKIC Archaeology Section, 1995); Neil Brodie and Kathryn Walker Tubb, eds., *Illicit Antiquities: The Theft of Culture and the Extinction of Archaeology* (New York: Routledge, 2002); Kate FitzGibbon, ed., *Who Owns the Past? Cultural Policy, Cultural Property and the Law* (New Brunswick, NJ: Rutgers University Press, 2005).

12. Erik Nemeth, "Cultural Security: The Evolving Role of Art in International Security," *Terrorism and Political Violence* 19, no. 1 (2007): 23.

13. Kate Fitzgibbon website, http://www.fitzgibbonlaw.com/art-and-cultural-property-issues; see UNESCO, "Cultural Property: Its Illicit Trafficking and Restitution," http://portal.unesco.org/culture/en/ev.php-URL_ID=35252&URL_DO=DO_TOPIC&URL_SECTION=201.html.

14. Nemeth, "Cultural Security," 37.

15. Neil Brodie, "The Concept of Due Diligence and the Antiquities Trade," *Culture without Context,* no. 5 (1999): 12–15, http://www.mcdonald.cam.ac.uk/projects/iarc/culturewithoutcontext/issue5/brodie.htm.

16. Mahmut Cengiz, "Analysis of WMD Cases in Turkey: Police Seizure of WMD Materials," paper presented at the Criminal Networks, Smuggling, and WMD Conference, February 25 and 26, 2010, TraCCC (Terrorism, Transnational Crime, and Corruption Center), George Mason University, Arlington, VA, http://traccc.gmu.edu/events/previously-hosted-events/.

17. Matthew Bogdanos and William Patrick, *Thieves of Baghdad: One Marine's Passion for Ancient Civilizations and the Journey to Recover the World's Greatest Stolen Treasures* (New York: Bloomsbury, 2005), 249.

18. "US Justice Department and Central Bureau of Interpol Rate Art Crime Third Highest-Grossing Criminal Trade and Links It to Organized Crime," December 8, 2009, http://art-crime.blogspot.com/2009/12/us-justice-department-central-bureau-of.html.

19. Nemeth, "Cultural Security," 35.

20. Ibid., 22.

21. Laura de la Torre, "Terrorists Raise Cash by Selling Antiquities," *GSN: Government Security News* 4, no. 3 (2006): 10, http://www.savingantiquities.org/wp-content/pdf/GSNarticle.pdf.

22. David Johnson, "Marine's Mementos Turn Out to Be 5,000 Years Old," *New York Times*, June 15, 2005, http://www.nytimes.com/2005/02/14/world/africa/14iht-artifacts.html.

23. Gretchen Peters, "More Than 1,500 Stolen Afghan Artifacts Return to Kabul," *National Geographic Magazine,* March 6, 2009, http://news.nationalgeographic.com/news/2009/03/090306-afghanistan-artifacts-returned-missions.html.

24. Lawrence Rothfield, ed., *Antiquities under Siege: Cultural Heritage Protection after the Iraq War* (Lanham, MD: AltaMira Press, 2008), 60; Rothfield, *The Rape of Mesopotamia: Behind the Looting of the Iraq Museum* (Chicago: University of Chicago Press, 2009).

25. De la Torre, "Terrorists Raise Cash by Selling Antiquities," 10.

26. Ibid., 15.

27. Ibid.

28. Phil Williams, *Criminals, Militias, and Insurgents: Organized Crime in Iraq* (Carlisle, PA: U.S. Army War College, Strategic Studies Institute, 2009), 177.

29. R. T. Naylor, "The Underworld of Art," *Crime, Law, and Social Change* 50, nos. 4–5 (2008): 290.

30. FBI, "Iraqi Antiquities Returned Artifacts Seized during Public Corruption Investigation," July 7, 2011, http://www.fbi.gov/news/stories/2011/july/artifacts_070711/artifacts_070711.

31. A. J. G. Tijhaus, "The Trafficking Problem: A Criminological Perspective," in *Crime in the Art and Antiquities World: Illegal Trafficking in Cultural Property*, ed. S. Manacorda and Duncan Chappell (New York: Springer, 2011), 91–92; Nemeth, "Cultural Security," 19–42.

32. De la Torre, "Terrorists Raise Cash by Selling Antiquities," 10, is quoting Arthur Brand. As De la Torre describes Brand, he has "worked with law enforcement agencies and publishes his findings of allegedly illicit deals on a Website maintained by a colleague, Michel van Rijn. A Dutch art smuggler turned art investigator, van Rijn is known to have outed suspected illicit deals before law enforcement ever entered the picture" (15). After leaving a note on the web page of *Blood Antiques*, the author of this book was contacted by Arthur Brand, who appears in *Blood Antiques* interviewing art dealers involved in the illicit trade. This exchange occurred just prior to the author's planned visit to the major international art fair in Maastricht in March 2010. Mr. Brand informed the author how to identify recently excavated antiquities from Afghanistan. At Maastricht, the author saw Ghandaran treasures from Afghanistan that still had sand from their recent excavation. These treasures were displayed for sale at the fair for very large sums.

33. Folarin Shyllon, "Looting and Illicit Traffic in Antiquities in Africa," in *Crime in the Art and Antiquities World: Illegal Trafficking in Cultural Property*, ed. S. Manacorda and Duncan Chappell (New York: Springer, 2011), 135–42. See also the work of Safe, which is working to save antiquities; its website is http://www.savingantiquities.org/topic/looting-and-the-trade/ and provides examples from different regions. In museums in Turkey, there are signs on archaeological treasures that they have been recovered from art smugglers and international auction houses.

34. Sarah Gauch, "Triage for Treasures after a Museum Blast: Sorting through the Rubble of the Museum of Islamic Art in Cairo," *New York Times*, January 31, 2014, http://www.nytimes.com/2014/02/01/arts/design/sorting-through-the-rubble-of-museum-of-islamic-art-in-cairo.html.

35. Mickael Roudaut, "From Sweatshops to Organized Crime: The New Face of Counterfeiting," in *Criminal Enforcement of Intellectual Property: A Handbook of Contemporary Research*, ed. Christopher Geiger (Northampton, MA: Edward Elgar, 2012); Nicholas Schmidle, "Inside the Knockoff-Tennis-Shoe Factory,"

New York Times, August 19, 2010, http://www.nytimes.com/2010/08/22/magazine/22fake-t.html.

36. UNODC, *Globalization of Crime: Transnational Organized Crime Threat Assessment* (Vienna: UNODC, 2010), 173–74.

37. Paul Kaihla, "Forging Terror: How Rapid Advances in Scanning, Printing, and Other Technologies Have Made Counterfeiting a Potent New Weapon of Holy War," *Business 2.0,* December 1, 2002, http://money.cnn.com/magazines/business2/business2_archive/2002/12/01/333256/index.htm. The location of some counterfeit printing presses in areas controlled by terrorist groups, such as Hezbollah in the Bekaa Valley in Lebanon, have prevented law enforcement from shutting down their operations. For more on North Korea, see Stephen Mihm, "No Ordinary Counterfeit," *New York Times,* July 23, 2006, http://www.nytimes.com/2006/07/23/magazine/23counterfeit.html?pagewanted=all&_r=0.

38. Pierre Delval, *Le Marché Mondial Des Faux Crime et Contrefaçons* (Paris: Ares, 2010), 13. Individuals can die from counterfeit pharmaceuticals, food, and alcohol products; counterfeit parts for cars, trucks, and airplanes cause severe accidents, sometimes resulting in death. See the website of the WAITO Foundation, dedicated to combating harmful counterfeits, http://www.waitofoundation.org/.

39. UNODC, *Globalization of Crime,* 11, Figure 12; *Europol Review 2011,* 8.

40. Gregory Treverton, Carl F. Matthies, Karla J. Cunningham, Jeremiah Goulka, Greg Ridgeway, and Anny Wong, *Film Piracy, Organized Crime, and Terrorism* (Santa Monica, CA: RAND, 2008), 28; Mark S. Hamm, *Terrorism as Crime: From Oklahoma City to Al-Qaeda and Beyond* (New York: New York University Press, 2007), 128, which discusses diverse terrorist involvement with counterfeit goods.

41. UNODC, *Globalization of Crime,* 173.

42. Ruchir Sharma, "Broken BRICs," *Foreign Affairs* 91, no. 6 (2012): 2–7, discusses that the BRICs are the largest economies in their respective regions.

43. Information on the source of the factories comes from published reports. See R. Hudson and Library of Congress, Washington, DC, Federal Research Division, "Terrorist and Organized Crime Groups in the Tri-Border Area (TBA) of South America," 2003 (revised 2010) http://www.loc.gov/rr/frd/pdf-files/TerrOrgCrime_TBA.pdf; A. R. Sverdlick, "Terrorists and Organized Crime Entrepreneurs in the 'Triple Frontier' among Argentina, Brazil, and Paraguay," *Trends in Organized Crime* 9, no. 2 (2005): 84–93. Other sources are interviews with individuals in the cigarette industry following illicit trade and the investigative project of Public Integrity. One of the few times I have been threatened was after I reported on our TraCCC Georgia center's research on illicit cigarette factories in the country tied to Iraqi investment. This was later confirmed through interviews with anti-illicit trade specialists in the cigarette industry. See also Melzer, "Counterfeit and Contraband Cigarette Smuggling."

44. FATF Report, "Illicit Tobacco Trade," June 2012, 11, 44, http://www.fatf-gafi.org/media/fatf/.../Illicit%20Tobacco%20Trade.pdf. The report acknowledges that this illicit trade may be funding terrorism. On illicit whites, see "The Illegal Cigarette Industry in Pakistan Has Grown to Become One of the Largest Tax Evaders in Country, Causing Great Loss to the National Economy," November 24, 2012, http://dawn.com/2012/11/25/illegal-cigarettes-cause-rs40bn-loss/; KPMG,

"Philip Morris International: KPMG Study Shows Illicit Cigarettes in EU Reach Highest Recorded Level in 2011, Fifth Consecutive Yearly Increase," press release, June 20, 2012, http://www.pmi.com/eng/media_center/press_releases/pages/201206200200.aspx. The figures for 2012 are even higher, reaching 11.1 percent of total sales in Europe; see http://www.pmi.com/eng/media_center/media_kit/pages/star_report_2012.aspx. The entire 2012 report is available at http://www.pmi.com/eng/media_center/media_kit/documents/project_star_2012_final_report.pdf. On Paraguay, see Associated Press, "Magnate Becomes Paraguay's President, Wooing Foreign Investment and Denying Past," *Washington Post,* August 15, 2013, http://www.washingtonpost.com/politics/congress/paraguays-new-president-target-of-undercover-us-probe-is-a-millionaire-tobacco-magnate/2013/08/15/c86122f4-057f-11e3-bfc5-406b928603b2_story.html. Illicit whites are cigarettes produced to evade taxation and be sold in the shadow economy. Illicit whites may be produced under license in the country where they are manufactured but then are smuggled to evade collection of taxes by other countries.

45. Shimelse Ali and Bennett Stancil, "Developing Countries Changing the World of Trade," International Economic Bulletin, November 19, 2009, https://www.carnegieendowment.org/ieb/2009/11/19/developing-countries-changing-world-of-trade/uqg.

46. Discussions with Trade Council at the Global Agenda Council of the World Economic Forum, Abu Dhabi, October 10–12, 2011.

47. See James Bacchus, "China Must Recommit to the WTO," December 19, 2011, http://www.chinausfocus.com/slider/china-must-recommit-to-the-wto.

48. Uri Dadush and Moisés Naím, working group discussion of unpublished paper, Global Agenda Council of the World Economic Forum, Abu Dhabi, October 10–12, 2011.

49. Peter Gastrow, *Termites at Work: A Report on Transnational Organized Crime and State Erosion in Kenya* (New York: International Peace Institute, 2011), 45. The author has discussed the study with the author; http://www.treasury.gov/resource-center/terrorist-illicit-finance/Documents/FinCEN-Hawala-rpt.pdf. Discussion with corporate security officials of the international cigarette trade in December 2012.

50. ICC (BASCAP), "Controlling the Zone: Balancing Facilitation and Control to Combat Illicit Trade in the World's Free Trade Zones," May 2013, http://www.iccwbo.org/Advocacy-Codes-and-Rules/BASCAP/International-engagement-and-Advocacy/Free-Trade-Zones/.

51. Naím, *Illicit,* 109–30; Jay Albanese, *Transnational Crime and the 21st Century: Criminal Enterprise, Corruption, and Opportunity* (New York: Oxford University Press, 2011), 38–48.

52. Pharmaceutical Security Institute, "Arrests by Region: CY 2011," 2012, http://www.psi-inc.org/arrestData.cfm.

53. City of New York, Office of the Comptroller, "Bootleg Billions: The Impact of the Counterfeit Goods Trade on New York City," 2004, 12, http://www.comptroller.nyc.gov/bureaus/bud/.../Bootleg-Billions.pdf.

54. U.S. Senate Committee on Homeland and Security and Governmental Affairs, "Counterfeit Goods: Easy Cash for Criminals and Terrorists," testimony by John

C. Stedman, 109th Congress, 1st session, May 28, 2005, http://purl.access.gpo.gov/GPO/LPS66671.

55. Josh Lefkowitz, *The Crime-Terror Nexus* (New York: Homeland Security, New York State Office, March 13, 2006), 3, http://info.publicintelligence.net/NY-CrimeTerrorNexus.pdf.

56. Damon McCoy, Andreas Pitsillidis, Grant Jordan, Nicholas Weaver, Christian Kreibich, Brian Krebs, Geoffrey M. Voelker, Stefan Savage, and Kirill Levchenko, "PharmaLeaks: Understanding the Business of Online Pharmaceutical Affiliate Programs," paper presented at USENIX Security Symposium, Bellevue, WA, August 2012, http://krebsonsecurity.com/2011/07/spam-fake-av-like-ham-eggs/; http://krebsonsecurity.com/2011/02/spamit-glavmed-pharmacy-networks-exposed/.

57. Paul Kaihla, "Forging Terror: How Rapid Advances in Scanning, Printing, and Other Technologies Have Made Counterfeiting a Potent New Weapon of Holy War," *Business 2.0*, December 2002. http://money.cnn.com/magazines/business2/business2_archive/2002/12/01/333256/index.htm; Ryan Clarke, "Lashkar-I-Taiba: The Fallacy of Subservient Proxies and the Future of Islamist Terrorism in India," The Letort Papers, U.S. Army War College, 2010, 20–21, http://www.strategicstudiesinstitute.army.mil/pubs/display.cfm?pubid=973; Matthew Levitt and Michael Jacobsen, *The Money Trail: Finding, Following, and Freezing Terrorist Finances*, Policy Focus 89 (Washington, DC: Washington Institute for Near East Policy, November 2008), 51, http://www.washingtoninstitute.org/policy-analysis/view/the-money-trail-finding-following-and-freezing-terrorist-finances.

58. Stephen Mihm, "No Ordinary Counterfeit," *New York Times*, July 23, 2006, http://www.nytimes.com/2006/07/23/magazine/23counterfeit.html?pagewanted=all; Sheena Chestnut Greitens, "A North Korean Corleone," *New York Times*, March 3, 2012, http://www.nytimes.com/2012/03/04/opinion/sunday/a-north-korean-corleone.html?pagewanted=all.

59. UNODC, *Globalization of Crime*, 175.

60. B. D. Finlay, "Counterfeit Drugs and National Security," 2011, 1, http://www.stimson.org/images/uploads/research-pdfs/Full_-_Counterfeit_Drugs_and_National_Security.pdf; interview with member of corporate security of an international pharmaceutical firm, December 2012.

61. Roger Bate, *Phake: The Deadly World of Falsified and Substandard Medicines* (Washington, DC: AEI Press, 2012), 223.

62. Nicolas Christin, "Traveling the Silk Road: A Measurement Analysis of a Large Anonymous Online Marketplace," Cornell University, 2012, http://arxiv.org/abs/1207.7139; Damon McCoy, in discussion with the author, August 2012.

63. Kathleen E. McLaughlin, "'Malaria Is Not Going Away Because We Are Getting Fake Treatment': China Suspected as Source of Counterfeit Drugs That Are Holding Back Fight against Malaria in Africa," *Guardian*, December 23, 2011, http://www.guardian.co.uk/world/2012/dec/23/malaria-fake-medicines-africa-china; Bate, *Phake*, 45–46, on diversion of antimalarial drugs.

64. Interview with the head of corporate security of a major pharmaceutical company, December 2012.

65. Roll Back Malaria Partnership, http://www.rbm.who.int/cmc_upload/0/000/015/363/RBMInfosheet_10.htm.

66. "Djukanovic Indicted, Avoids Trial," October 9, 2008, https://reportingproject
.net/occrp/index.php/en/ccwatch/cc-watch-briefs/153-djukanovic-indicted-avoids-
trial.

67. Jay Albanese, *Transnational Crime and the 21st Century: Criminal Enterprise,
Corruption, and Opportunity* (New York: Oxford University Press, 2011), 38–
48; Bate, *Phake*; Naím, *Illicit*.

68. IPC is "intellectual property crime." U.S. House Committee on International Relations, "The Links between Intellectual Property Crime and Terrorist Financing,"
testimony by Ron Noble, 108th Congress, 15th session, July 16, 2003, http://
commdocs.house.gov/committees/intlrel/hfa88392.000/hfa88392_of.htm.

69. Marina Walker Guevara, Mabel Rehnfeldt, and Marcelo Soares, "Smuggling
Made Easy: Landlocked Paraguay Emerges as a Top Producer of Contraband
Tobacco," June 28, 2009, updated February 24, 2012, http://www.publicintegrity
.org/2009/06/29/6343/smuggling-made-easy.

70. See John A. Cassara, *Hide and Seek Intelligence, Law Enforcement, and the
Stalled War on Terrorist Finance* (Dulles, VA: Potomac Books, 2006); Nikos Pas-
sas, "Fighting Terror with Error: The Counter-productive Regulation of Informal
Value Transfers," *Crime, Law, and Social Change* 45, nos. 4/5 (2006): 315–36; see
Edwina A. Thompson, *Trust Is the Coin of the Realm: Lessons from the Money
Men of Afghanistan* (Karachi: Oxford University Press, 2011).

71. Diverted cigarettes are untaxed cigarettes that enter into the black market; see U.S.
Department of Justice, *The Bureau of Alcohol, Tobacco, Firearms and Explosives
Efforts to Prevent the Diversion of Tobacco* (Washington, DC: U.S. Department
of Justice, September 2009), 92.

72. Aaron Smith, "60% of Cigarettes Sold in New York Are Smuggled:
Report," January 10, 2013, http://money.cnn.com/2013/01/10/news/companies/
cigarette-tax-new-york/index.html.

73. Merrill Goozner, "U.S. Military Equipment Built with Counterfeit Parts," *Fiscal Times*, May 22, 2012, http://www.thefiscaltimes.com/Articles/2012/05/22/
US-Military-Equipment-Built-with-Counterfeit-Parts.aspx#page1.

74. Testimony by Stedman, "Counterfeit Goods," 7. California Office of the Attorney
General, "Gangs Beyond Borders: California and the Fight Against Transnational
Organized Crime," March 2014, http://oag.ca.gov/sites/all/files/agweb/pdfs/toc/
report_2014.pdf?.

75. Ibid.; National Gang Intelligence Center, "National Gang Threat Assessment:
Emerging Trends," 2011, 43, http://www.fbi.gov/stats-services/publications/
2011-national-gang-threat-assessment.

76. U.S. Senate Committee on Homeland Security and Governmental Affairs, "Counterfeit Goods: Easy Cash for Criminals and Terrorists," testimony by Kris
Buckner, 109th Congress, 1st session, May 28, 2005, http://purl.access.gpo.gov/
GPO/LPS66671; according to Matthew Levitt, *Hezbollah: The Global Footprint
of Lebanon's Party of God* (Washington, DC: Georgetown University Press,
2013), 317–53, Hezbollah functions as a criminal organization in the United
States.

77. Testimony by Stedman, "Counterfeit Goods," 8.

78. Ibid., 9. "DOJ: CAIR's Unindicted Co-Conspirator Status Legit," March 12, 2010,
http://www.investigativeproject.org/1854/doj-cairs-unindicted-co-conspirator-
status-legit.

79. United States of America v. Chang Shan Liu, discussed in Troy Graham, "Smuggler in Global Ring Gets 11 Years; The U.S. called Chang Shan Liu a Leader in the Newark Operation. He Said He Had Done the Bidding of Others," *Philadelphia Inquirer,* August 1, 2007, B01.

80. Jonathan Abel, "Gaithersburg Trio Charged in Smuggling," *Washington Post,* August 29, 2005, http://www.washingtonpost.com/wpdyn/content/article/2005/08/28/AR2005082800898.html.

81. U.S. Department of Justice, "Pharmacist Convicted of Purchasing Chinese Counterfeit Drugs," press release, May 25, 2006, http://www.justice.gov/criminal/cybercrime/press-releases/2006/georgeConvict.htm.

82. Tom Diaz and Barbara Newman, *Lightning Out of Lebanon: Hezbollah Terrorists on American Soil* (San Francisco: Presidio Press, 2005), 84–92; Louise Shelley and Sharon A. Melzer, "The Nexus of Organized Crime and Terrorism: Two Case Studies in Cigarette Smuggling," *International Journal of Comparative and Applied Criminal Justice* 32, no. 1 (2008): 43–63.

83. Naím, *Illicit,* 127.

84. FATF Report, *Illicit Cigarette Trade,* June 2012, 37, http://www.fatf-gafi.org/media/fatf/documents/reports/Illicit%20Tobacco%20Trade.pdf.

85. Lefkowitz, *Crime-Terror Nexus,* 3.

86. Testimony by Stedman, "Counterfeit Goods," 9.

87. Tim Elfrink, "South Florida Cigarette Smuggling Funds Terrorism," July 2, 2009, http://www.browardpalmbeach.com/2009-07-02/news/south-florida-cigarette-smuggling-funds-terrorism/www.wolfgangsvault.com/; see Allen, *Illicit Trade in Tobacco Products,* 25; also author's interview with one of the investigators of the cited case, April 2013, Vilnius, Lithuania.

88. Aida Hozic, "Between the Cracks: Balkan Cigarette Smuggling," *Problems of Post-Communism* 51, no. 3 (2004): 35–44, discussed the corruption that facilitates this trade.

89. Tom Behan, *The Camorra: Political Criminality in Italy* (New York: Routledge, 1996); Roberto Saviano, *Gomorrah* (New York: Farrar, Straus, and Giroux, 2007).

90. UNODC, *Globalization of Crime,* 177, 179; see map of European seizures.

91. Ibid., 184.

92. Communication from the Commission to the Council and the European Parliament, "Stepping Up the Fight against Cigarette Smuggling and Other Forms of Illicit Trade in Tobacco Products – A Comprehensive EU Strategy," June 6, 2013, 8, http://ec.europa.eu/anti_fraud/documents/2013-cigarette-communication/1_en_act_part1_v9_en.pdf.

93. Allen, *Illicit Trade in Tobacco Products,* 8–9.

94. Daniel L. Glaser, *Combating International Organized Crime: Evaluating Current Authorities, Tools, and Resources,* 2011, 3, http://www.treasury.gov/press-center/press-releases/Pages/tg1346.aspx.

95. Discussion at a WAITO board meeting in Geneva, Switzerland, February 2012, with a member of the UNICRI staff who did research on this topic, which was discussed in the Italian parliament. See research of UNICRI, http://counterfeiting.unicri.it/.

96. Donatella della Porta, *Lo Scambio Occulto Casi di corruzione politica in Italia* (Bologna, Italy: Società Editrice Il Mulino, 1992); *Mafia e Potere* (Rome:

l'Unità, 1993) discusses governmental corruption; UNODC, *Globalization of Crime*, 180.

97. Lefkowitz, *Crime-Terror Nexus*, 3.

98. BCC, "Border Raid on Fake CD Plant," BBC News, December 17, 2000, http://news.bbc.co.uk/2/hi/uk_news/northern_ireland/1074672.stm; Susan Watts, "Counterfeit CDs Threaten the Record Industry: Northern Ireland Terror Groups Believed to Be Involved in Importing Discs from China and Eastern Europe," *The Independent*, August 8, 1994, http://www.independent.co.uk/news/uk/counterfeit-cds-threaten-the-record-industry-northern-ireland-terror-groups-believed-to-be-involved-in-importing-discs-from-china-and-eastern-europe-1382140.html; Peter Andreas, "Symbiosis between Police Operations and Illicit Business in Bosnia," *International Peacekeeping* 16, no. 1 (2009): 233–46.

99. Andreas, "Symbiosis between Police Operations and Illicit Business in Bosnia."

100. Melzer, "Counterfeit and Contraband Cigarette Smuggling," 92, provides international data on the percentage consumption of illicit tobacco in many countries based on Euromonitor data. A caveat needs to be applied to these data, as there is no clarity on the methodology used by Euromonitor to assess illicit trade penetration. Recent analyses by the cigarette industry, according to an interview with an industry expert on illicit trade, identify Brunei as presently the largest market for illicit cigarette trade.

101. Testimony by Noble, "The Links between Intellectual Property Crime and Terrorist Financing."

102. Discussions with Tatiana Pinkevich of the Stavropol Center on organized crime; see their website, http://cspkitraccc.skforussia.ru.

103. "Fake Pharmaceuticals, Bad Medicine: The World's Drug Supply Is Global. Governments Have Failed to Keep Up," *The Economist*, October 13, 2012, http://www.economist.com/node/21564546.

104. Gaurvika M. L. Nayyar, Joel G. Bremen, Paul N. Newton, and James Herrington, "Poor-Quality Antimalarial Drugs in Southeast Asia and Sub-Saharan Africa," *The Lancet Infectious Diseases* 12, no. 6 (2012): 488–96.

105. Rose Skelton, "Ghana: Motifs for Survival," January 4, 2012, http://www.theafricareport.com/news-analysis/ghana-motifs-for-survival.html.

106. "Cigarette Smuggling Still Booming," http://www.reportingproject.net/underground/index.php?option=com_content&view=article&id=5&Itemid=1.

107. "Fake Cigarettes Seized near Billion Mark," November 10, 2011, http://www.news24.com/SouthAfrica/News/Fake-cigarettes-seized-near-billion-mark-20111110.

108. Kate Willson, "Terrorism and Tobacco – How Cigarette Smuggling Finances Jihad and Insurgency Worldwide," Center for Public Integrity, June 9, 2009, http://www.thecuttingedgenews.com/index.php?article=11427; Jamie Doward, "How Cigarette Smuggling Fuels Africa's Islamist Violence," *Guardian*, January 26, 2013, http://www.guardian.co.uk/world/2013/jan/27/cigarette-smuggling-mokhtar-belmokhtar-terrorism.

109. Gastrow, *Termites at Work*, 4.

110. Ibid., 44.

111. Ibid., 39.

112. Ibid., 45. The author has discussed the study with Peter Gastrow.

113. Ibid., 44.

114. Discussion with member of the Crown Prosecution Service, Washington, DC, 2011.

115. Treverton et al., *Film Piracy, Organized Crime, and Terrorism,* xiii; "Section III: USTR Announces Results of Special 301 Review of Notorious Markets," December 20, 2011, http://www.ustr.gov/about-us/press-office/press-releases/2011/december/ustr-announces-results-special-301-review-notorio, includes Tepito on the list.

116. Bryan A. Liang, "Fade to Black: Importation and Counterfeit Drugs," *American Journal of Law and Medicine* 32 (2006): 281.

117. Michael Braun, *Drug Trafficking and Middle Eastern Terrorist Groups: A Growing Nexus?* (Washington, DC: Washington Institute for Near East Policy, July 25, 2008), http://www.washingtoninstitute.org/policy-analysis/view/drug-trafficking-and-middle-eastern-terrorist-groups-a-growing-nexus.

118. Treverton et al., *Film Piracy, Organized Crime, and Terrorism,* 77.

119. Ibid., xi.

120. John L. Lombardi and David J. Sanchez, "Terrorist Financing and the Tri-Border Area of South America: The Challenge of Effective Governmental Response in a Permissive Environment," in *Terrorism Financing and State Responses,* ed. Jeanne Giraldo and Harold A. Trinkunas (Stanford, CA: Stanford University Press, 2007), 230–46, for background on Barakat; Treverton et al., *Film Piracy, Organized Crime, and Terrorism,* 77; Rex Hudson, "Terrorist and Organized Crime Groups in the Tri-Border Area (TBA) of South America," 2003, http://www.loc.gov/rr/frd/pdf-files/TerrOrgCrime_TBA.pdf.

121. Treverton et al., *Film Piracy, Organized Crime, and Terrorism,* 77; Michael P. Arena, "Hizballah's Global Crime Operations," *Global Crime* 7, no. 3 (2006): 454–70.

122. Treverton et al., *Film Piracy, Organized Crime, and Terrorism,* 81.

123. Ibid., 82.

124. Interview by the author in Istanbul, Turkey, in 2008 with a representative of a major multinational car part supplier representative for security of supply chains and investigation of crime and terror links in supply chains.

125. Roger Wilkison, "Interpol Warns of New Terrorist Tactics to Finance Terrorism," VOA, Brussels, May 26, 2004, http://www.iwar.org.uk/news-archive/2004/05-26-4.htm.

126. Ibid., 34.

127. UNODC, *Globalization of Crime,* 177, 179, map of European seizures.

128. Afkar Abdullah, "900,000 Fake Items Confiscated in Sharjah," *Khaleej Times,* October 17, 2011, http://www.khaleejtimes.com/displayarticle.asp?xfile=data/theuae/2011/October/theuae_October403.xml&section=theuae&col=.

129. Nimrod Raphaeli, "Financing of Terrorism: Sources, Methods, and Channels," *Terrorism and Political Violence* 15, no. 4 (2003): 75.

130. Interviews with Turkish law enforcement who have investigated these cases; Mahmut Cengiz, Sharon Melzer, and Selcuk Turan, "The PKK and Cigarette Smuggling," in *The PKK: Financial Sources, Social and Political Dimensions,* ed. Charles Strozier and James Frank (Saarbrücken, Germany: VDM, 2011), 166–83.

131. Levitt and Jacobsen, *Money Trail.*

132. Interviews with Turkish National Police, officials of different cigarette companies, and journalists. These diverse sources provide consistent results; see also

Terörün Ekonomisi: Sınır Illerinde Kaçakçilik ve Terörün Finansmanı (Ankara: Police Academy, 2009), 6, and also "New Trends in Smuggling and Combating Strategies," a panel at the Fourth International Symposium on Terrorism and Transnational Crime, December 7–9, 2012, Antalya, Turkey.

133. Cengiz et al., "PKK and Cigarette Smuggling."

134. Treverton et al., *Film Piracy, Organized Crime, and Terrorism*, 91.

135. Ibid.

136. Ibid., 94–95.

137. The author has discussed this problem with her students who served on bases in Afghanistan and also with staff of the Senate Foreign Relations Committee who contacted the author, as the committee was concerned about these DVD sales on bases, which were funding terrorism.

138. For a comparison with the profits of human trafficking, see Louise I. Shelley, *Human Trafficking: A Global Perspective* (Cambridge: Cambridge University Press, 2010), 7–8.

139. Robert E. Merriam, preface to *Cigarette Bootlegging: A State and Federal Responsibility* (Washington, DC: Advisory Commission on Intergovernmental Relations, 1977), iii, http://digital.library.unt.edu/ark:/67531/metadc1354/m1/5/.

140. Allen, *Illicit Trade in Tobacco Products*, 13–14.

141. Center for Regulation Effectiveness, *The Countervailing Effects of Counterfeit Cigarettes* (Washington, DC: Center for Regulation Effectiveness, July 2011), 3–9, http://www.fda.gov/downloads/AdvisoryCommittees/.../UCM263564.pdf.

8

Ultimate Fears

Weapons of Mass Destruction and Crime-Terror Connections

In the 1990s, the Japanese cult Aum Shinrikyu sought nuclear, biological, and chemical weapons, representing a convergent threat that may be replicated in the future. Analyses of this well-known case reveal that the chemical weapons of mass destruction (WMD) program of this sect was ultimately much more successful than its biological efforts.[1] The cult's failure is explained by their inability to recruit Russian scientists in the difficult final years of the Soviet state,[2] making them dependent on Japanese engineers and scientists, who lacked experience in WMD deployment.[3] Having to train its own personnel, Aum's weapons preparation proceeded slowly.

> The first cult laboratory for toxin production was actually in place by 1990 and was subsequently replaced with two new laboratories, one at Kamakuishki and the other in Tokyo. Aum dabbled in many different biological agents. They cultured and experimented with botulin toxin, anthrax, cholera, and Q fever. In 1993, Ashahara led a group of 16 cult doctors and nurses to Zaire, on a supposed medical mission. The actual purpose of the trip to Central Africa was to learn as much as possible about, and, ideally, to bring back samples of, Ebola virus. In early 1994, cult doctors were quoted on Russian radio as discussing the possibility of using Ebola as a biological weapon.[4]

An attempted release by Aum of anthrax from its midrise Tokyo office building and laboratory in June 1993 was unsuccessful, as the group unknowingly used a nonlethal vaccine strain of anthrax.[5]

Finally, the group turned to chemical WMD and unleashed a sarin gas attack in the Tokyo metro in March 1995, in which twelve people died and approximately five thousand more were injured. The high number of casualties is explained by the dissemination of the sarin gas in five separate subway cars on three different lines at times of peak morning travel. This attack followed several attempted attacks, including a successful one in Matsumoto, Japan, the previous year, in which fewer people were killed and injured.[6] The sect was able to proceed to the Tokyo attack as the Japanese police lacked the investigative capacity to identify the perpetrators behind the Matsumoto incident.[7]

What rarely gets discussed about the Aum Shinrikyo attacks is the extent to which organized crime and corruption made them possible. Much of the cult's funding came from legitimate companies it owned as well as members' contributions. But its estimated billion dollars in assets were also generated by the sale of illegal drugs and insurance fraud. Aum manufactured illegal drugs, such as LSD, and even had a marketing agreement with the *yakuza*, Japanese organized crime syndicates.[8] Members of Aum Shinrikyo were implicated in, and convicted of, murder, kidnapping, and assault, among other violent offenses.[9]

Aum's activities were not confined to Japan. Its membership and activities spanned several continents – North America, Asia, Australia, and Europe. Its largest external membership was in Russia.

Engagement in corruption as well as crime was a key to the group's acquisition of technology. Through its tens of thousands of Russian members and its payment of approximately $12 million to Russian officials, it was able to purchase buildings and weapons,[10] including an MI-17 helicopter in 1994.[11] In the chaotic years after the collapse of the Soviet Union, significant payments were made in the early 1990s to the secretary of the Russian Security Council, Oleg Lobov, who even traveled to Japan in 1992 and met the Aum leader, Asahara.[12]

Russia was just one of Aum's source countries for illegal weapons acquisition. Their *yakuza* connections facilitated weapons purchases, and their links with a Chinese gang furnished them with hand grenades.[13] Contacts with professional criminals provided access to arms that would be otherwise unattainable in Japan because of its tight gun control laws. Aum did not need to use its vast wealth to hire the *yakuza,* as a powerful crime boss voluntarily joined the cult. The *yakuza*-Aum relationship contravenes traditional conceptions of the crime-terror relationship, in which terrorists are thought to purchase the services of criminals.[14] In this case, a crime boss found common cause with the terror group.

Aum was able to exploit high-level corruption and the absence of state control over WMD in Russia to pursue its terrorist ambitions. The chaos that once characterized Russia is now present in Syria, possibly providing jihadis access to the massive stockpiles of chemical weapons before they are destroyed.[15] In the event of a breakdown in order in Iran, Pakistan, or North Korea, one might expect that criminals and/or different violent militant groups might seek to acquire WMD. Terrorist groups like the Taliban and the FARC, enriched by their criminal earnings, may have the capacity to buy such weapons or pay off corrupt officials, such as Aum did in Russia.

WMD: An Asymmetric Threat

The most feared outcome of the crime-terror relationship is that criminals will help terrorists acquire WMD – biological, chemical, and nuclear weapons. The WMD trade, which is relatively rare, is very different from the illicit businesses discussed in the previous chapters. Narcotics smuggling and the trade in counterfeit and diverted goods are core elements of the criminal business of terrorists, with known suppliers and purchasers. In contrast, relatively little is known about the criminal logistical operations that move trafficked nuclear materials or how the criminal realm intersects with states that engage in unsanctioned proliferation.[16]

WMD trade operates on a different economic logic – one based not on volume but on scarcity and risk. Furthermore, some of the buyers of dual-use technology[17] and nuclear materials are state actors who have much greater budgets, the capacity to use state institutions to disguise their activity, and the motivation and capacity to engage in the most high-stakes sector of the illicit underworld.

The illicit trade in WMD leads to the ultimate asymmetric threat. A WMD attack of any kind – nuclear, biological, or chemical – could have many serious and long-term consequences. The spread of disease through the dissemination of anthrax or other deadly organisms, or the poisoning of land or water as a result of a biological, chemical, or nuclear attack, or the release of radiological materials would not only generate death and illness but also might have long-term consequences. These could include the sustainability of the planet, human life, and health and the viability of diverse species. Even a lesser attack than a nuclear bomb might require evacuation of citizens and massive and costly cleanup efforts.[18]

This chapter focuses primarily on the movers and facilitators of the illicit trade in WMD materials, examining the role of nonstate actors, corrupt officials, and corporations that unwittingly or consciously move WMD materials.[19] Proliferators of dual-use technology to Iran for nuclear facilities are also discussed.[20]

This following analysis also identifies the broad range of terrorist actors who have sought or deployed WMD, making a distinction between biological and chemical WMD from nuclear weapons. The latter may have a lower chance of deployment but potentially a far graver impact.[21]

The Character of Illicit Trade in WMD

It is helpful to divide the illicit trade in WMD into two segments. The first involves *radiological and dual-use materials,* which are traded more frequently by nonstate actors and corporate entities. The second involves trade of actual *WMD materials,* such as highly enriched uranium (HEU) or biological materials. But trade in the first area has tangible benefits for participants – it generates either outsized profits for those in this niche black market and/or the realization of their objective to acquire needed technology or WMD.[22] Although aspects of this trade are distinctive, it often shares the same routes with other types of illicit flows.[23]

The illicit trade in WMD materials is primarily a post–Cold War concern. Early analyses of the topic have borne such names as *Smuggling Armageddon: The Nuclear Black Market in the Former Soviet Union and Europe* and *The Cult at the End of the World: The Terrifying Story of the Aum Doomsday Cult, from the Subways of Tokyo to the Nuclear Arsenals of Russia.*[24] These titles, while alarmist, reflect the anxiety of the 1990s, when there was great concern about the security of the nuclear arsenal in the Soviet successor states. The current anxiety is that terrorists might smuggle a dirty bomb into the United States and set it off in lower Manhattan or that terrorists might launch multiple chemical attacks in major urban centers around the world. These would cause mass psychological damage and also long-lasting economic impact.

United Nations Response to WMD

The member states of the United Nations (UN) are fully aware of the potential costs of the WMD trade. The focus of the UN resolution on WMD adopted in April 2004 is on peace and security.[25] Through a unanimous decision, the UN Security Council adopted in 2004 Resolution 1540, under Chapter VII of the UN Charter. This resolution affirms that

> proliferation of nuclear, chemical and biological weapons and their means of delivery constitutes a threat to international peace and security. The resolution obliges States, *inter alia*, to refrain from supporting by any means non-State actors from developing, acquiring, manufacturing, possessing, transporting, transferring or using nuclear, chemical or biological weapons and their delivery systems...
>
> Resolution 1540 (2004) imposes binding obligations on all States to adopt legislation to prevent the proliferation of nuclear, chemical and biological weapons, and their means of delivery, and establish appropriate domestic controls over related materials to prevent their illicit trafficking.[26]

Unfortunately, the UN has yet to vigorously implement Resolution 1540. It has not sufficiently elaborated the standards of what is needed to be in compliance, nor has it given itself the authority to invest the budgetary and other resources necessary to encourage and assist with compliance. In the absence of UN implementation, members of the G-8 and other countries have resolved to provide assistance to implement Resolution 1540 and otherwise improve strategic trade controls.[27] Significant international and coordinated efforts to arrest this trade have been implemented.

Biological and Chemical WMD

Diverse jihadi groups, such as the Egyptian Islamic Jihad, Jemaah Islamiya, LeT, and al-Qaeda, "figure most prominently among the groups that have manifested some degree of intent, experimentation, and programmatic efforts to acquire nuclear, biological and chemical weapons."[28] In 1998, Osama made it a religious duty for his followers to pursue the acquisition of WMD.[29]

Yet despite this order, the identified successes of terrorists in this arena have been limited. In 2006 and 2007, at least a dozen mass casualty attacks in Iraq were carried out by al-Qaeda using chlorine gas, an industrial chemical employed as a chemical warfare agent in World War I.[30] The deployment by the Syrian state of chemical weapons against civilians in Damascus in August 2013 galvanized international action to eliminate Syria's WMD capacity.[31] There has been concern that the diverse militants fighting in Syria could gain access to the massive chemical weapon stockpiles of President Bashir al-Assad before they are destroyed.[32] According to the U.S. State Department, Syria has shipped out less than 5 percent of its chemical weapons.[33]

Al-Qaeda historically displayed a strong interest in both chemical and nuclear weapons but did not initially show much interest in biological weapons. It implemented a biological program only in response to Western powers' concern that they might acquire biological weapons. This made them understand the utility of investing in this area. Information found after the invasion of Afghanistan indicated that al-Qaeda was much further along in its biological weapons program than previously believed, having begun in the late 1990s.[34] They had "obtained the materials required to manufacture two biological toxins – botulinum and salmonella – and the chemical poison cyanide."[35] Their plan to develop anthrax as a weapon for a mass attack against the United States was run under the direction of Ayman Zawahiri, Osama's deputy.[36]

One of the best understood cases of the successful involvement of a terrorist group with WMD does not involve an Islamic group but rather the Japan-centered transnational cult Aum Shinrikyu. Yet Aum's biological terrorism is not the only case with no relationship to today's primary security concern – jihadi terrorism. A California case shows the intersection of WMD with other serious criminal and violent acts.

Dr. Larry Ford, a California doctor, may not only have stockpiled pathogens but apparently also tried to develop techniques to deploy these diseases as weapons. Dr. Ford's suicide prevented the full investigation of the source and intended use of a diverse variety of deadly pathogens stored in his home and office in southern California. This case is linked with the state-supported biological and chemical weapons program of apartheid-era South Africa, called Project Coast.[37]

Dr. Ford once served as a scientific researcher at one of the United States' top medical centers, at the University of California, Los Angeles. But Dr. Ford was dismissed from his position as clinical professor after violating university standards for disposal of biohazards and other questionable behavior.[38] Also disturbing were his ties to racist and militia movements in the United States, but these were not known before his suicide. In retrospect, these ties might suggest the intended targets of his bioweapons.[39]

Criminal activity, once again, helped lead to the disclosure of this potential terrorist activity. Dr. Ford and a partner, James Patrick Riley, jointly owned a biotechnology firm. "The case at first unfolded as a classic story of greed and envy, a corporate power struggle between Riley, the voluble CEO and marketing whiz, and his partner, Dr. Larry Creed Ford, the visionary with big ideas and the scientific skills to carry them out."[40] Yet the struggle took a more violent turn in early 2000, as a masked hitman shot James Riley in the head outside the company offices. Dr. Ford initially appeared as the hero as he ran outside and helped stem the blood from Riley's gaping head wound. But a couple of days later, suspicion fell on Dr. Ford, as the hired killer had escaped in a van that belonged to one of Ford's old friends. Dr. Ford was questioned by the police concerning the killing of his partner and shortly thereafter committed suicide at home with guns chosen from his extensive weapons collection.

After Ford's suicide, a trove of potential biological and more conventional weapons was found in his southern California home and office, following tips from informants that poured in after his death. More than one hundred firearms were found buried in the backyard, but even more alarming were the possible bioweapons:[41]

> Buried next to his swimming pool they found canisters containing machine guns and C-4 plastic explosives. In refrigerators at his home and office, next to the salad dressing and employee lunches, were 266 bottles and vials of pathogens – among them salmonella, cholera, botulism and typhoid. The deadly poison ricin was stored, with a blowgun and darts, in a plastic bag in the family room.[42]

Dr. Ford's suicide prevented the investigators from ever determining the intended use of this diverse collection of potential biological weapons. There were hints that some people had previously been subject to Dr. Ford's experimentation, but assistance from the Centers for Disease Control and Prevention did not unravel the problem, as their focus "was limited to whether there was a public health risk, such as the threat of an epidemic,"[43] rather than whether there was potential bioterrorism.

After his death, investigators also learned of Dr. Ford's repeated trips to South Africa during the period of apartheid; his consultations to the South African Project Coast, which developed biological weapons against enemies of apartheid; and his reading of the same literature that allegedly inspired the Oklahoma City bombers. These various clues suggest that he might have been intending to deploy these weapons to advance white supremacism.[44]

This was not the first known case of white supremacists intending to use biological weapons. In 1995, three such cases were detected in the United

States. Two members of a militia group, the Minnesota Patriots Council, were convicted of acquiring enough of the deadly substance ricin to kill 129 people. Two months later, a microbiologist with links to the Aryan Nation ordered bubonic plague through the mail. An inquiry as to the reasons for a delay in delivery brought the FBI to the door of Larry Wayne Harris, who was arrested and subsequently convicted of mail and wire fraud.[45] In December of that year, an Arkansas resident with links to white supremacists tried to import ricin from Canada. Apart from this, he had large caches of weapons and manuals that detailed how to deploy these toxic substances to kill people.[46]

Both the Aum Shinrikyu case and that of Dr. Ford in California reveal the involvement of highly educated individuals with some of the skill sets necessary to develop and deploy WMD. In the Japanese case, investigations after the sarin attack revealed the presence of crime, corruption, and terrorism, whereas in the southern California case, a planned homicide led to an illicit cache of weapons along with the raw materials for many potential biological attacks.

Nuclear WMD

The eminent nuclear terrorism expert Graham Allision explains, "To date, the only confirmed case of attempted nuclear terrorism occurred in Russia on November 23, 1995, when Chechen separatists put a crude bomb containing seventy pounds of a mixture of cesium-137 and dynamite in Moscow's Ismailovsky Park. The rebels decided not to detonate this 'dirty bomb' but instead informed a national television station as to its location."[47] The Chechen leader Dzohkar Dudayev was believed to have begun planning nuclear terrorism in 1992. This advanced planning in this chaotic period in Russia allowed him to secure the material for the deadly dirty bomb.[48]

Safeguards over the former Soviet nuclear arsenal have improved since the early 1990s, but an illicit trade still exists in nuclear weapons material. Terrorist groups from the North Caucasus have repeatedly sought to acquire nuclear weapons and have succeeded in acquiring radioactive materials. A recent joint study by the Belfer Center for Science and International Affairs and the Russian Academy of Sciences concluded that the threat of nuclear terrorism posed by these North Caucasus groups is increased by "widespread crime in the armed forces" and "corrupt bureaucracies and law-enforcement agencies whose personnel allow terrorists to cross from one Russian region to another, carrying illicit cargo."[49]

Illustrative of the most recent trend in this illicit trade is a Moldovan case from 2011, in which a 4.4-gram sample of weapons-grade uranium was seized, allegedly part of a 1-kilogram cache.[50] It was reputedly transported through the conflict region of Transdniester by at least six nonstate actors intending to sell their materials to a buyer in North Africa.[51] Georgia, consistently a transshipment point for illicit nuclear materials, had cases detected as recently as 2012.[52] The Georgian route is analyzed subsequently in this chapter.[53]

The preceding examples of smuggled nuclear materials indicate that criminal involvement with the nuclear trade can be a major security challenge as the transport of these materials occurs in high-risk areas such as Transdniester and the North and South Caucasus. But too little attention has been paid to criminal involvement in this illicit trade.[54] The place where there is greatest concern about terrorists getting their hands on nuclear materials is Pakistan, precisely because there is a known history of proliferation by the state and known state support for Islamic and other terror groups, and because the network that proliferated weapons relied on criminal networks to do so. Leaked documents by Edward Snowden from the intelligence community reveal that fears about the security of Pakistan's "nuclear program are so pervasive that a budget section on containing the spread of illicit weapons divides the world into two categories: Pakistan and everybody else."[55]

The Abdul Qadeer Khan network was based in Pakistan but operated globally from the 1980s. It subcontracted criminal organizations to "transfer black market nuclear technology" and relied on institutions of the Pakistani state to cover up its activities.[56] The proliferation threat remains because the A. Q. Khan network was never fully dismantled, neither in Pakistan nor overseas.[57] Moreover, the Pakistani state has used crime and terrorist groups to advance its interests.[58] Therefore, the powerful South Asian criminal organizations persist,[59] and they and their key facilitators could serve as proliferators, as they did in the past.

A massive international illegal supply network was run by A. Q. Khan, the father of the Pakistani bomb, his actions allegedly unknown to the top authorities of his country.[60] But this has been called into question by the leak of a letter from a North Korean official indicating that the top Pakistani army leadership knew of this trade and received payments from North Korean officials.[61] As the then chair of the International Atomic Energy Agency (IAEA), Mohamed ElBaradei, described the Khan network, "it's mind-boggling. All I know is there's at least more than 30 companies in 30 countries all over the globe involved in this fantastic, sophisticated illicit trafficking network with Mr. A. Q. Khan acting as CEO."[62] The Khan case illustrates the principle that the most serious trafficking may rarely be detected because it is run by professionals whose well-established smuggling networks, facilitated by corruption, have the capacity to move significant quantities of diverse contraband without apprehension.[63]

Yet corruption does not explain all. There are important political reasons for this trade. Khan was seen as providing an enormous service to his country and is still considered a hero by many Pakistanis. He enabled Pakistan to acquire a nuclear weapon in the face of what his government perceived as an existential security threat from India.

The detonation of India's first nuclear device in 1974 was seen as an enormous challenge to Pakistan's security. To Khan, his people had been humiliated by India's nuclear capability. Therefore, from the mid-1970s, the ambitious

A. Q. Khan played the key role in Pakistan's development of its nuclear capability.[64] To that end, he attempted to acquire both expertise and materials, often acquired from the black market, with the complicity or knowledge of top leadership, who provided him significant sums for these acquisitions.[65]

A. Q. Khan also sold uranium enrichment technology and nuclear weapons designs to several countries. As a result of this proliferation, the "United States and other countries, as well as the IAEA, are expending enormous amounts of time and resources to address the threats that resulted from Dr. Khan's engagement with Iran, North Korea, and possibly other states."[66] The scale of this proliferation is significant, as it is estimated, based on statements from his associates, that the Khan network sold information and technology to Libya for between $100 million and $200 million. The costs were so large because "Khan was directly involved in providing Libya with a complete centrifuge plant."[67] Yet this was only a piece of his illicit operations. There is strong evidence that the Khan network transferred to North Korea key centrifuge technology and the know-how in the 1990s.[68] In the early 2000s, North Korea became a full member of this illicit trade network and was ready to supply Libya uranium hexafluoride.[69]

The trade of A. Q. Khan continued undeterred for almost two decades, until U.S. governmental authorities in the early 2000s challenged the Pakistani authorities with intelligence concerning the range and scope of the Khan network.[70] These revelations resulted in the 2004 placement of Khan under house arrest, where he remained until 2009. General Pervez Musharaf used his service as the father of the Pakistani nuclear program in explaining Khan's pardon.[71] The Pakistani government also showed significant leniency with key perpetrators of the network apart from Khan.[72] Therefore, there has been neither certainty nor severity of punishment for Pakistani members of the proliferation network.

As a direct result of Khan's supply network, a group of so-called rogue states have developed or are developing the capacity to make nuclear weapons. Iran and North Korea are the foci of this concern, but earlier countries, such as Iraq, Libya, and Syria, fell into this category. In the post-Khan period, state-sponsored smuggling networks from Iran and North Korea work with both legitimate and illegitimate actors to bypass export regulations and avoid detection.[73] The physical size of the materials for the nuclear fission devices makes it hard to imagine A. Q. Khan and his network could have smuggled the equipment to places like Iran and North Korea without state help.

The materials and WMD from these states will provide an even greater proliferation threat in future decades than the residue of the Soviet weapons program. The Soviet successor states have cooperated in many ways to enhance security to prevent proliferation, a policy not pursued by these "rogue states," who began and maintained their programs outside of the international regulatory framework. Analyses of the current trade in dual-use materials, often destined for these rogue states, reveal a far wider range of illicit actors and a far broader geographic reach than that of the A. Q. Khan network.[74] The globalization of proliferation networks represents a significant security challenge.

The Centrality of Corruption

Corruption is a key element of the WMD materials trade. Acquisition of nuclear material has often been facilitated by corrupt insiders.[75] Without corruption, much of the goods and know-how could not transit states to reach potential proliferators. Yet corruption can also have unexpected consequences. As Chapter 2 pointed out, the pervasive corruption in Iraq also undermined that country's capacity to build nuclear weapons, as officials siphoned off revenues intended for construction of the bomb.

Corruption is key to nuclear trafficking,[76] and two key countries that might be important sources of nuclear material, Pakistan and Russia, have high levels of corruption.[77] At present, the United States and Russia possess 95 percent of the world's nuclear weapons. With much of the world's weapons-usable nuclear material in Russia, corruption remains a significant problem in safeguarding its nuclear facilities.[78]

Corrupt officials were at the top of the nuclear hierarchy in both Pakistan and Russia. In both countries, very senior officials exploited their positions for personal profit. A. Q. Khan's long-term clandestine nuclear trade epitomizes the corruption that existed at the top of the Pakistani nuclear industry. In 2005, Swiss authorities, at the request of the U.S. government, arrested Russia's former atomic energy minister, Yevgeni Adamov, after he was accused by a U.S. court of appropriating $9 million of U.S. assistance funding intended to safeguard Russia's nuclear facilities and instead used the funds for his personal investments. He was extradited to Russia but, like A. Q. Khan, suffered no long-term consequences. In 2008, he was tried in Russia and exited prison with a suspended sentence.[79]

Before the Soviet collapse, nuclear facilities were secure, but afterward, many nuclear facilities and weapons sites lacked adequate protections, a problem exacerbated by the corruption of top officials in the closed nuclear cities where the nuclear materials were produced or stored.[80] In early 2005 in Novosibirsk, the director of the Novosibirsk Chemical Concentrate Plant, Nikolai Zabelin, was removed from his job after criminal cases were filed against him for using plant money for his own private purposes and for paying a consulting firm to provide him sophisticated advice on manipulating plant finances for his benefit.[81]

Corruption such as this facilitated losses. According to Yury Vishnevsky, the former head of the monitoring agency Gozatomnadzor, plants in the Moscow region and the Novosibirsk plant lost "grams of weapons grade or kilograms of low enriched uranium" in 2002.[82]

Nuclear weapons production facilities during the Soviet era were contained within a group of remote closed cities that were heavily regulated by the state security apparatus. Only individuals who had high-level security clearances could live there. The communities were isolated from the rest of society, and even the children who resided there were sent to summer camps designed only for the residents of these closed cities. Only individuals with special permits could enter.

In the post-Soviet period, the system of controls over residence and entry broke down. Moreover, the controls that once ensured law-abiding behavior among residents of these closed cities collapsed. Drug sales thrived, released prison inmates once prohibited residence in these cities lived there, and entry into these once walled-off communities could be gained for the payment of a small bribe to the guards. The following analysis focuses on problems in closed cities in the region of Chelyabinsk, the site of a very large diversion attempt of 18.5 kilograms of HEU.[83]

Ironically, before the drug trade proliferated throughout Russia in the 2000s, in the late 1990s, drug abuse was most pronounced in one of the closed nuclear cities near Chelyabinsk, close to the border of Kazakhstan. For example, in 1999, the closed city of Ozersk had the most drug users per capita in Russia. Drug addicts consumed mainly heroin and marijuana, according to Andrei Glukhov, deputy head of the Ozersk federal antidrug agency.[84] The drug problem spread to workers of the neighboring nuclear facility of Mayak, even though efforts were made to dismiss addicted employees once their habit was discovered. Rates of drug addiction did not decline even after this problem was identified by Russian authorities. Therefore, the threat of drugs in the closed cities was still growing in March 2005, according to the head of the Snezhinsk police force.[85] The growth is explained, in part, by the geography of the closed cities, their proximity to Kazakhstan and the drug route, and the absence of prevention and treatment programs for drug addiction.

Inmates released from labor camps after the collapse of the USSR could not survive in the Russian economy. There were no welfare or unemployment payments and no assistance in finding employment or housing. Therefore, some former inmates came to stay with relatives in the closed cities. Between 2003 and 2005, there was a threefold rise in the number of returning convicts to closed cites.[86] These released inmates had been incarcerated with serious criminals from across Russia and the Soviet successor states, providing them easy access to a transnational network that could be exploited for shipments of drug and possibly WMD materials.

Corruption also facilitated the entry of a significant number of illegal entrants into the closed nuclear cities near Chelyabinsk, further undermining security. According to official statistics, the number of illegal entries into Ozersk rose to 224 in 2003 and 138 for the first five months of 2004, making this problem a major concern.[87] The official estimates of illegal entries probably represent only a small fraction of the total number of people who arrived in closed cities illegally. These trespassers entered closed cities for an extremely small sun, according to some reports, for as little as $5.00[88], revealing that even low-level corruption could undermine security significantly.

Illegal entry was achieved sometimes even without financial payments. Residents of nearby villages developed relationships with individual soldiers and used them as a channel to get in and out of the closed city. One smuggler explained the process in the following way: "I pick one guard and get to know him, giving him cigarettes and candy. After a month of our 'friendship,' I can bring in anyone I want. Of course, I have to agree with the soldier about the exact time of entry and exit."[89] The costs of engaging in this corrupt practice were insignificant. People found guilty of smuggling workers faced meaningless penalties that did not deter them.

Organized crime involvement in the closed cities occurred on a larger scale than just that facilitated by illegal entrants. Firms supplying retail goods to closed cities were owned and infiltrated by organized crime. Mob-controlled construction firms worked in closed nuclear cities. Through these companies, Russian crime groups could gain access to the nuclear facilities.[90]

The criminalization of the closed cities might have permitted the movement of nuclear materials and/or equipment from these supposedly secure locales. The HEU found in recent years could have been moved in this period of heightened insecurity, either by malicious nonstate actors working independently or in conjunction with corrupt state officials.[91] Therefore, the investment made to secure the facilities under the Nunn-Lugar program, also known as the Cooperative Threat Reduction Program,[92] might not have achieved the full desired result of securing all at the source.

If materials or equipment left the nuclear facilities, high levels of corruption in transit states along smuggling routes would allow some of it to reach its target. Examining Turkish data on nuclear materials apprehended since the 1990s reveals that most originated in the former Soviet states and traversed long distances before being detected in Turkey.[93] Moldova and Transdniester, the sites of the 2011 smuggling incident, have high levels of corruption, as does Armenia, through which materials transited in several instances before detection in Georgia.[94] Many of the recorded cases of nuclear trafficking involve the North and South Caucasus, including the separatist regions of Abkhazia and Ossetia, where controls were even more limited, as there was an absence of effective law enforcement.[95]

Often the smuggled nuclear materials were detected in Georgia. Between 2002 and 2009, according to data from the Supreme Court of Georgia, "thirteen criminal cases overall have been brought against smugglers of radioactive materials, with a total of twenty-seven individual purported smugglers involved in the cases. These smugglers were mostly ethnic Georgian (twenty individuals), as well as Armenian (four), Ossetian (one), Turkish (one), and Azerbaijani (one)."[96]

Georgian detection did not necessarily reflect the greater integrity of Georgian border guards. Rather, reporting in the mid-2000s revealed that corruption as well as poor work attitudes facilitated transit. The American government equipped Georgian borders with monitors needing a continuous electrical supply to detect nuclear smuggling. Interviews conducted with border guards revealed that when faced with limited electrical power, the guards preferred to turn off the nuclear detectors rather than stop watching television.[97] This negligent attitude may have contributed to the cross-border movement of nuclear and radiological materials into Georgia, only some of which was subsequently detected through undercover investigations.

In other regions of the world, organized criminals and corruption also facilitate the movement of radiological materials. Italian organized crime groups have been in the waste disposal business for decades and subsequently moved into the disposal of hazardous waste. The contracts to dispose of this waste were obtained because these groups corrupted government officials. Officials of the Italian state energy company were convicted by the Italian courts of collusion with the Sicilian Cosa Nostra and the Calabrian 'ndrangheta in the disposal of nuclear materials in Somalia.[98] This led to the killing of fish, which, by destroying the local economy, contributed to the growth of piracy.

Initially, the toxic waste was disposed of closer to home. In 2009, Italian authorities found a shipwreck with more than 120 barrels of radioactive waste, approximately twenty-eight kilometers off the southern coast of Italy near Calabria. According to an organized crime turncoat, who was behind the explosion that brought down the detected ship, as many as thirty-two ships carrying toxic radioactive waste had been sunk in the Mediterranean since the late 1980s by this crime group hired to dispose of the material.[99]

With the exception of Italy, the previously analyzed corruption occurred primarily in the developing world. But as the nuclear proliferation expert, Matthew Bunn, has written, "weak nonproliferation and anti-corruption cultures in the 1970s and 1980s were a major problem that helped these networks succeed – in Europe, the United States, and elsewhere."[100] Strategies, tactics, and laws for deterring, detecting, and disrupting nuclear trafficking need to target the particular characteristics of corrupt government officials in diverse environments. Measures must also deal with officials at all levels ranging from senior nuclear program managers, like A. Q. Khan and Yevgeni Adamov, to junior border guards and customs officials. We must also understand the "business" behind moving these illicit goods: who are the transport coordinators? How is it financed? How does money move? How do the goods physically move, and are there key nodes in the supply chain?

Trade in Nuclear Weapons, Materials, Know-How, and Components

Threatening elements of nuclear trade range from the most alarming, the illegal trade in complete nuclear weapons, to the least worrisome, the trade in dual-use materials that could be used to construct a bomb. In between these extremes exists the trade in nuclear materials, plans, and expertise. There is

evidence that several of these have occurred repeatedly.[101] Weapons-grade
nuclear materials are still being smuggled, significant shipments of dual-use
materials continue, and the export of know-how of the nuclear bomb industry
remains a reality, even years after the identification of the A. Q. Khan network.
Several Middle Eastern states desire their own WMD capacity. Therefore, a
serious threat remains that some of these states will seek to acquire the know-
how and material to launch a weapons program outside the existing regulatory
framework.[102]

Different actors and routes are represented in distinct components of this
illicit trade. The dual-use trade uses different routes from those used to move
HEU and radiological materials, because it functions on a much larger scale and
is furnishing materials to states that allocate significant resources to developing
nuclear capacity. The illicit trade in nuclear materials, including both weapons-
grade and radiological materials, is much more linked to criminals who engage
in ordinary criminal activity than other categories of WMD activity. Criminals
who capitalize on available opportunities to profit are more often active in
the trade of less valuable radioactive materials that cannot be used for bomb
construction.[103] In contrast, more professional criminals with known criminal
records have been identified in some cases of smuggling of the most valuable
radioactive materials, such as enriched uranium.[104] Those who engage in the
trade of dual-use materials to Iran engage in criminal acts but may never have
been previously identified with criminal activity.

The trajectory for the movement of the nuclear and radiological material has
changed over time. In the early post-Soviet period, much of the material headed
to Western Europe, and German authorities were mounting sting operations
to detect these flows. "These controversial undercover operations, which had
apparently had a local political agenda, were prohibited in 1996 as a result
of the parliamentary investigation into the 1994 seizure of 363 gram of plutonium transported to Munich Airport on an ordinary Lufthansa flight from
Moscow."[105]

WMD materials smuggling subsequently transitioned from heading straight
west from former Soviet territory to moving south, via Turkey, to Iran or Central Europe.[106] Turkish WMD interceptions of the past decade have shown that
WMD materials trafficking has increasingly followed a southern path, traveling
south from Russia to Iran, or alternatively, through the Caucasus, particularly
from Georgia to Turkey.[107] The Balkans continue to play an important role
as a transit point. Furthermore, the importance of the Black Sea as a trade
channel for this material has been shown through actual cases in Ukraine,
Romania, Russia, and Georgia.[108] Preferred routes may be tied to the survival
of crime groups of the Soviet era, where Caucasians were disproportionately
represented among the criminal elite.

Surprisingly, the trade in nuclear materials has also been detected in Africa
and South Asia. "Between 1996 and 2000, 12 cases were recorded on the
African continent and 9 cases in South Asia. Interestingly, all of the incidents

registered in South Asia involved uranium in some form, ranging from depleted and low-enriched to yellowcake."[109]

Key superfacilitators have been critical to the illicit trade in nuclear weapons and dual-use materials, such as the notorious Tinner family, which worked out of Switzerland and knowingly assisted the A. Q. Khan network from the late 1990s to June 2003. The Tinners also helped the Libyan government develop its nuclear weapons program by supplying needed equipment and expertise to members of the A. Q. Khan network in Switzerland, the United Arab Emirates, Turkey, Malaysia, and elsewhere in the world.[110] In rare cases, facilitators like the Tinners turn and become paid informants and subsequently help identify and round up the network.[111] But more often, superfacilitators remain in place for extended periods and are key figures in the proliferation networks.[112]

Another WMD superfacilitator is the notorious export broker Asher Karni, an Israeli living in Cape Town, South Africa. Karni brokered a deal for a Pakistani buyer whereby he bought from a Massachusetts-based company dual-use spark gaps that could detonate a nuclear warhead and disguised the shipment, stating that the spark gaps were intended for medical use in a hospital in Soweto, South Africa. A U.S. Department of Justice investigation revealed the criminal intent as federal prosecutors found "emails between Karni and Pakistani Humayun Khan that discussed how unlicensed shipments violated export laws and how they decided to push forward after acknowledging that it was illegal."[113]

Illicit smuggling networks rely on superfacilitators like the Tinners and Karni to move goods. Often the same superfacilitators are used by multiple networks, which will subcontract their services. These superfacilitators, who make high-level profits, provide key nodes for supply chains of illicit goods, including WMD and dual-use materials. Understanding the role of superfaciliators is, or should be, a key objective for security officials, law enforcement, the intelligence community, and all who seek to disrupt illicit supply networks.

The Smuggling of Weapons-Grade and Radiological Materials

From January 1993 to December 2012, the International Atomic Energy Agency recorded more than two thousand incidents of theft or other unauthorized activity involving nuclear and radioactive materials. "Of the 2,331 confirmed incidents, 419 involved unauthorized possession and related criminal activities. Incidents included in this category involved illegal possession, movement or attempts to illegally trade in or use nuclear material or radioactive sources. Sixteen incidents in this category involved highly enriched uranium (HEU) or plutonium. There were 615 incidents reported that involved the theft or loss of nuclear or other radioactive material."[114] This database provides individual data points but does not shed light on the supply chains or the ultimate purchasers of the nuclear materials.

The Database on Nuclear Smuggling, Theft, and Orphan Radiation Sources (DSTO), operated by the University of Salzburg in Austria, supplements IAEA data with open-source information and presents more illustrative material on the criminals engaged in this smuggling.[115] Yet even this more comprehensive data do not give a full picture of the buyers, the facilitators, and the functioning of the market.

The reported data of the IAEA reveal that in about 10 percent of reported cases, members of organized crime groups are involved in the smuggling.[116] Yet there appears to be a significant number of unreported cases, implying that the IAEA data may understate criminal involvement in proliferation.[117]

Because nuclear trafficking remains such a hidden phenomenon, it is likely that the number of detections represents just a small percentage of the nuclear material actually being smuggled. Supporting this assumption is the fact that there have been relatively few detected smugglers of nuclear and radiological materials relative to the reported number of thefts of materials. The nuclear smuggling situation is thus analogous to the illicit trade in other commodities, where estimates of the amount of illicit commodities detected and intercepted remain consistently less than 20 percent.[118] Compounding the problems of detection is that "smuggling networks are reported to have acquired containers capable of smuggling enriched uranium without detection by even sophisticated monitoring equipment."[119]

The Turkish experience has shown that the smuggling of nuclear materials is not a sui generis phenomenon. Detected cases of nuclear and radiological material in Turkey, an important fulcrum for the trade, have not been found in distinct locales or among distinct criminal or terrorist groups. Despite many Western analysts' hypothesis that the potential value of the WMD materials would ensure it a special trajectory,[120] WMD materials detected in Turkey usually moved through the same routes as the drug trade and may coincide with other forms of smuggling – illicit arms, antiquities, and human trafficking. The observed convergence in Turkey suggests that nuclear and radiological smuggling is an opportunistic crime. Moreover, materials can be more safely moved when they travel along with significant quantities of illicit goods, as bribes have often been paid for officials to look the other way.[121]

This convergence is not confined to Turkey. In Soviet successor states, crime groups detected trafficking in nuclear materials have also have had arms caches and dealt in drugs.[122] They act as facilitators. Cases linking drugs and nuclear trade have also been identified along the ancient Silk Road in Central Asia.[123] A crime group linking Siberia, China, and Mongolia was involved in nuclear trade before the millennium.[124] These diverse examples are consistent with present analyses of illicit networks and their likelihood to converge.[125]

Investigated cases in the Caucasus and Turkey, as well as the databank of the DSTO, reveal that criminals of many different nationalities are involved in smuggling nuclear materials. Identified smugglers were from twenty-five countries in Asia, Africa, and Europe, with the largest numbers coming from the Soviet successor states.[126]

Some who move nuclear materials consciously move the materials, even at risk to themselves, because they are motivated by the immense profits.[127] Fortunately, these opportunists move materials that are often of little potential danger to larger society because of their low levels of radiation content. Of much greater concern is the weapons-grade HEU, which, if properly encased by those transporting it, will often not be detected by radiation monitors presently in place.[128] Individual smugglers may unknowingly carry this dangerous cargo. Mules for the nuclear trade may resemble those in a drug trafficking organizations; the actual transporter of the materials is isolated from the larger organization. Upon arrest, carriers of these materials have little knowledge as to the organization that hired them or the intended destination of the cargo.

Georgian investigations of individuals caught engaging in nuclear smuggling reveal that in a majority of cases, smugglers have ostensibly collaborated only on a particular instance of smuggling. The most studied Georgian case of smuggling is that of the Russian Oleg Khintsagov, caught in 2006 after trying to sell one hundred grams of HEU to an undercover Georgian investigator. The subsequent investigation of Khintsagov's network revealed that his collaborators were connected by blood or close friendship. Mr. Khintsagov's passport, with extensive travels in the Middle East before his arrest in Georgia, as well as his refusal to answer questions, suggests that he had links to the Soviet-era intelligence community.[129]

Investigators often find it difficult to unravel all of the smuggler's connections. Members of illicit networks manage to establish trust across ethnic groups and borders, but the law enforcement and intelligence community that seeks to apprehend them is fragmented. For example, little cooperation exists among the former Soviet states or Turkey and its neighboring Soviet successor states.[130] This imbalance between the trust established among illicit actors and the mistrust that exists among the countries who seek to control them creates ample opportunity for the smuggling networks to continue.

Illicit Networks and Present-Day Smuggling by States

International networks that facilitate smuggling to nations seeking to establish covert nuclear weapons have been in place since the mid-1970s, when A. Q. Khan was caught stealing URENCO technology.[131] Already in the 1980s, a North Korean national sought to procure needed technology in Germany and Switzerland, using a convoluted system to disguise the intended end user with payments routed though a Kuwaiti bank.[132] Now the international networks, serving Iran and others seeking to build nuclear weapons, have expanded, as Asia and the United States are also key sites for acquisition of needed technology. The United States has been a key site for decades dating back to the Cold War era. Shipments and payments can travel through Asia and the Middle East, in particular Dubai, and to a lesser extent through Turkey, to facilitate this trade.[133]

Illustrative of this is a joint German-Turkish investigation in 2013 tracing parts destined for the nuclear facility in Arak, Iran. The parts were obtained in India and Germany and sent via five separate shell companies that Iranian nationals established in Istanbul. This closed illicit network consisted exclusively of Iranians, as well as a Turk of Iranian origin, residing either in Germany or Istanbul. Between 2010 and 2012, the smugglers carried out nine hundred shipments of cooling devices and other apparati; eight hundred shipments originated from India and a further one hundred from Germany. The Istanbul-based front companies misidentified the exported commodities as valves and plumbing fixtures.[134] This large-scale industrial trade, financed by the state of Iran, is distinct from the criminal networks that engage in other forms of illicit trade, such as that of humans and cigarettes.[135]

Further insights into the illicit networks that facilitate smuggling to Iran is provided by successfully prosecuted cases, for export control violations, by the U.S. Department of Justice (DOJ). The four prosecuted cases in 2012 for violations of nuclear controls underestimate the law enforcement response. Many smugglers, possibly associated with this trade, are charged only with smuggling military technology and arms because these charges are easier to prove. There are indications that some of the sixteen DOJ export prosecutions dealing with Iranian networks used to procure military equipment may have had links to the nuclear industry.[136]

Illustrative of one of the four nuclear-related prosecutions of 2012 is the following case, summarized by the DOJ:

> Carbon Fiber and Other Materials to Iran and China – On Dec. 5, 2012, prose-cutors in the Southern District of New York unsealed charges against four individuals for exporting various goods to Iran and to China, including carbon fiber (which has nuclear applications in uranium enrichment as well applications in missiles) and helicopter components. Hamid Reza Hashemi, an Iranian national, and Murat Taskiran, a Turkish citizen, were charged in one indictment with conspiracy to violate and violating the International Emergency Economic Powers Act (IEEPA) by working to arrange the illegal export of carbon fiber from the U.S. to Hashemi's company in Iran via Europe and the United Arab Emirates. Hashemi was arrested upon arrival in New York City on Dec. 1, 2012.[137]

Other DOJ cases reveal themes and variations on the patterns described earlier. Chinese, Taiwanese, and Hong Kong firms have been used as purchasers.[138] In some cases, there is much more direct Iranian involvement in the acquisition of materials. Front companies as well as established legitimate companies are an important part of this trade, just as was seen in the German-Turkish investigation of 2013. State-sponsored trade for nuclear facilities involves millions of dollars in parts and significant shipments of materials; it is understandable that this trade functions well when it is disguised as legitimate trade. Illustrative of this is a 2012 DOJ prosecution case that concerned shipments for Iran. "From Oct. 9, 2007, to June 15, 2011, the defendants obtained or attempted to obtain from companies worldwide over 105,000 parts valued at some $2,630,800 involving more than 1,250 transactions."[139]

Expensive operations like these were feasible for Iran, because despite sanctions, it had access to the international banking system. From 2000 to 2007, HSBC bank was fully cognizant that it was processing dollar-related transfers for Iranian institutions.[140] A financial audit of HSBC business in regard to Iran observed, "The review identified almost 25,000 U.S. dollar transactions involving Iran, involving assets in excess of $19.4 billion."[141] This was part of an overall pattern of noncompliance with anti–money laundering provisions globally, for which the bank eventually settled with the U.S. government for a fine of a little more than $1.9 billion.[142] HSBC was not the only bank to be investigated and charged by the U.S. government for moving money for Iran and other countries such as Sudan, Libya, and Myanmar, for whom financial transactions could not legally be undertaken. Those sanctioned included such major international banks as ING, Barclays, ABN Amro, and Credit Suisse.[143]

These banks were cognizant of the fact that they were moving money for Iran. Moreover, senior officials in HSBC were knowingly and purposely disguising these transactions. But in other cases, the banks might not have been able to recognize the patterns of proliferation finance and might need further training and guidance from investigators and experts in the government tracking of proliferators.[144]

Proliferators and their facilitators can include high-status individuals. They can be not only bankers but also transport and logistics experts. The analysis of their involvement takes years, globally coordinated investigations, and the investment of large amounts of state resources by diverse international actors. By the time that the network has been unraveled, significant shipments and/or movements of money or technology may already have been realized. This corporate involvement represents a very significant part of the proliferation challenge but has not aroused popular concern, as have the shipments of actual nuclear materials, such as uranium-235 and cesium, that have been detected.

Conclusion

Future trade in WMD may be very different from the earlier phases discussed extensively in this chapter. Diverse WMD cases detected in the 1990s, and to a lesser degree in the present, were tied to state weapons programs of the Cold War era. The collapse of the Soviet Union, the decline of nuclear safeguards, and the end of apartheid-era South Africa made available biological pathogens and nuclear materials that could potentially be deployed as weapons of mass destruction. The threats that exist from that era have not disappeared but have only diminished.

The A. Q. Khan proliferation network operated concurrently with the post–Cold War cases. Functioning in thirty countries, it used profit-seeking criminals and legitimate businesses to spread nuclear capability to many countries, including Libya, North Korea, and Iraq. This phenomenon is different from the central theme of the book, as it focuses on state acquisition of nuclear capacity by means of corruption and criminal facilitators. But its legacy is significant. Because A. Q. Khan enjoyed such a hallowed status in Pakistan, he was never severely sanctioned, nor his illicit networks disrupted. Therefore, these networks may continue to play a role in nuclear proliferation today.

New threats may dwarf these others. The strongest emerging trend is a shift from the threat posed by the Cold War–era weapons programs to post–Cold War challenges. This change reflects the transformation from a bipolar world to one with more diverse threats, often emanating from nonstate actors cooperating with state actors.

The current conflict in Syria, with the presence of fighters from many different countries, and the rise of nuclear capacity in Iran and instability in Pakistan point to the possibility of diverse source countries for supply for both nuclear and chemical WMD. Emergent terrorist groups in the Middle East, Africa, and Central and South Asia and the expressed desire of jihadi terrorists to acquire WMD have aroused justifiable concern.[145] Illustrative of this developing threat may be the Moldovan uranium smuggling incident in 2011, which shows the links between traditional sources of supply – Russia – with new areas of intense and diverse terrorist activity, such as North Africa.[146]

The instability following the so-called Arab Spring, and the present disorder in Syria, with its vast stock of chemical weapons, may make the illicit trade in chemical WMD much more important in the future. In May 2013, "the Turkish government uncovered a plan to use Sarin gas as part of a potential bomb attack in southern Turkey. Al Qaeda's branch in Syria, Jabhat al-Nusra (JN), was allegedly behind the plot, and the subsequent arrests highlighted the increasing trouble jihadi radicals could pose for Ankara."[147]

The threats extend beyond Syria's immediate neighbors, both in the Middle East and beyond, as militants who have fought in Syria disperse across a vast region.[148] The precedent for this was a planned radiological attack in Kocaeli, Turkey, in the mid-2000s, conceived by about forty Islamist militants who had settled in the conservative religious city of Konya in central Turkey, most of them after being trained by terrorist groups overseas. The group planned an attack on a factory in Kocaeli, near Istanbul, that produced radiological isotopes used in the medical equipment they manufactured. The police in Konya disrupted this attack in the mid-2000s and also a planned accompanying conventional attack on top government officials in Ankara. This catastrophe was prevented by combining forces of the criminal investigative police with the antiterrorist police force.[149] Such radiological attacks may be a serious concern for the future in other parts of the Middle East as well.[150]

Apart from a heightened threat of chemical WMD, the continued trade in dual-use materials in the nuclear and biological arena, and the possible future misuse of biodefense programs, may present serious security concerns for the future.[151] The charging of the Boston marathon bomber with a WMD offense suggests a widening of the use of the concept of WMD terrorism.[152] But the Tsarnaev brothers' use of an improvised explosive is very different from the WMD problems that were discussed in this chapter.

If present trends continue, nonideological criminals could increasingly serve as a source of supply and assistance to state sponsors of terrorism, terrorist groups, or other proliferators who seek stolen or diverted fissile material. The White House *Strategy to Combat Transnational Organized Crime*,[153] issued in July 2011, states that "terrorists and insurgents increasingly are turning to transnational organized crime to generate funding and acquire logistical support to carry out their violent acts." The report expresses concern that the crime-terror nexus could result in "the successful criminal transfer of WMD material to terrorists,"[154] a problem that has not been definitively seen since the Chechens in Moscow in the mid-1990s.

American extremists discussed in this chapter have attempted to obtain and deploy WMD. This threat has not diminished over time. Rather, in the decade since the September 11 attack in the United States, "right-wing and left-wing extremist groups and individuals have been far more likely to acquire toxins and to assemble the makings of radiological weapons than al-Qaida sympathizers."[155] At least eleven right-wing and left-wing extremist groups have obtained, or attempted to obtain, chemical, radiological, and biological weapons that they planned to utilize in the United States. Therefore, domestic threats in the United States remain very much a contemporary concern.[156]

Containing the threat of WMD terrorism in the future will be much more complex, as it will involve many and varied state and nonstate actors, both the legitimate and illegitimate economy, diverse source countries, and potential proliferators on many different continents. Preventing terrorist acts using WMD will require very different strategies than the post–Cold War era approach of locking up materials at the source. Technology alone will not be sufficient to detect and deter nuclear or biological smuggling but must be combined with action based on careful intelligence and footwork by law enforcement and on findings from independent field research. The understanding of financial flows, the role of facilitators from the legitimate economy, and the centrality of particular routes and nodes are crucial to addressing the problem. By focusing only on the crime and terror components, while ignoring the centrality of corruption, it is not possible to effectively address the threat of WMD proliferation, or the possibility of attack. Analysis of the dirty entanglements will be crucial to preventing future attacks.

Notes

1. Richard Danzig, Marc Sageman, Terrance Leighton, Lloyd Hough, Hidemi Yuki, Rui Kotani, and Zachary M. Hosford, *Aum Shinrikyo: Insights into How Terrorists Develop Biological and Chemical Weapons*, 2nd ed. (Washington, DC: Center for a New American Security, December 2012), 4, http://wwwnc.cdc.gov/eid/article/5/4/99–0409_article.htm; Walter Laqueur, *The New Terrorism: Fanaticism and the Arms of Mass Destruction* (Oxford: Oxford University Press, 1999), 54–55.

2. David E. Kaplan and Andrew Marshall, *The Cult at the End of the World: The Terrifying Story of the Aum Doomsday Cult, from the Subways of Tokyo to the Nuclear Arsenals of Russia* (New York: Crown Books, 1996), 190–98.

3. Ibid., see discussion of biographies of participants.

4. Kyle B. Olson, "Aum Shinrikyo: Once and Future Threat?," *Emerging Infectious Disease* 5, no. 4 (1999), http://wwwnc.cdc.gov/eid/article/5/4/99-0409.htm.

5. "Terrorist Organization Profile: Aum Shinrikyo/Aleph," http://www.start.umd.edu/start/data_collections/tops/terrorist_organization_profile.asp?id=3956.

6. Judith Miller, "Some in Japan Fear Authors of Subway Attack Are Regaining Ground," *New York Times*, October 11, 1998, http://www.nytimes.com/1998/10/11/world/some-in-japan-fear-authors-of-subway-attack-are-regaining-ground.html; Danzig et al., *Aum Shinrikyo*, 20–21.

7. Kaplan and Marshall, *Cult at the End of the World*, 64–65.

8. Olson, "Aum Shinrikyo: Once and Future Threat?"

9. Ibid.; Kaplan and Marshall, *Cult at the End of the World*, 148–49.

10. Olson, "Aum Shinrikyo: Once and Future Threat?"

11. Senate Government Affairs Permanent Subcommittee on Investigations, "Global Proliferation of Weapons of Mass Destruction," staff statement, October 31, 1995, https://www.fas.org/irp/congress/1995_rpt/aum/part06.htm.

12. Ibid., Part VI.

13. Kaplan and Marshall, *Cult at the End of the World*, 169.

14. Ibid., 169–71.

15. Bill Keller, "Playing Chess with Putin," September 10, 2013, http://keller.blogs.nytimes.com/2013/09/10/playing-chess-with-putin/.

16. Lyudmila Zaitseva, "Nuclear Trafficking: 20 Years in Review," Contribution to WFS Meeting, Erice, August 2010, http://www.physics.harvard.edu/~wilson/pmpmta/2010_Zaitseva.doc.

17. Dual-use technology can be used to design, build, and disseminate WMD.

18. David Smigielski, "Addressing the Nuclear Smuggling Threat," in *Transnational Threats Smuggling and Trafficking in Arms, Drugs and Human Life*, ed. Kimberley L. Thachuk (Westport, CT: Praeger Security, 2007), 57.

19. U.S. Department of Justice, "Summary of Major U.S. Export Enforcement, Economic Espionage, Trade Secret and Embargo-Related Criminal Cases," January 2007 to the present, updated February 14, 2013, handout; David Albright, Andrea Stricker, and Houston Wood, *Future World of Illicit Nuclear Trade: Mitigating the Threat* (Washington, DC: Institute for Science and International Security, 2013).

20. See Institute for Science and International Security, illicit trade section of http://isis-online.org/studies/category/illicit-trade/.

21. Richard M. Medina and George F. Hefner, *International Terrorism: An Introduction to Spaces and Places of Violent Non-state Groups* (Boca Raton, FL: CRC Press, 2013), 190.

22. Rick Gladstone, "U.S. Bans 37 Firms in Dispute with Iran," *New York Times*, June 5, 2013, A9.

23. Lyudmila Zaitseva, "Organized Crime, Terrorism and Nuclear Trafficking," *Strategic Insights* VI, no. 5 (2007), http://www.gees.org/documentos/Documen-02583.pdf.

24. Rensselaer W. Lee, *Smuggling Armageddon: The Nuclear Black Market in the Former Soviet Union and Europe* (New York: St. Martin's Press, 1998); Kaplan and Marshall, *Cult at the End of the World*. The concerns of this earlier period have not disappeared. See Daniel Benjamin and Steven Simon, *The Next Attack: The Failure of the War on Terror and a Strategy for Getting It Right* (New York: Times Books, 2005).

25. Chapter VII requires a finding of threat to peace and security before binding action can be taken under it. Article 39 (part of Chapter VII) reads as follows: "The Security Council shall determine the existence of any threat to the peace, breach of the peace, or act of aggression and shall make recommendations, or decide what measures shall be taken in accordance with Articles 41 and 42, to maintain or restore international peace and security."

26. http://www.un.org/en/sc/1540/.

27. Ian Anthony and Vitaly Fedchenko, "International Non-proliferation and Disarmament Assistance," chapter 16, 2005 Yearbook, http://www.sipri.org/research/disarmament/dualuse/researchissues/resultoutput/yearbook.

28. Rolf Mowatt-Larsen, "Al Qaeda Weapons of Mass Destruction Threat: Hype or Reality," Harvard Belfer Center, January 2010, 5, http://belfercenter.ksg.harvard.edu/publication/19852/al_qaeda_weapons_of_mass_destruction_threat.html; David Albright, Mark Dubowitz, Orde Kittrie, Leonard Spector, and Michael Yaffe, *U.S. Nonproliferation Strategy for the Changing Middle East* (Washington, DC: Project on U.S. Middle East Nonproliferation Strategy, 2013), 103.

29. Rahim Kanani, "Al Qaeda's Religious Justification of Nuclear Weapons," *Huffington Post*, November 19, 2010, http://www.huffingtonpost.com/rahim-kanani/al-qaedas-religious-justi_b_786332.html.

30. Albright et al., *U.S. Nonproliferation Strategy for the Changing Middle East*, 104.

31. "Assad and Chemical Weapons: All 'Red Lines' in Syria Have Been Crossed: Turkish FM," August 21, 2013, http://www.hurriyetdailynews.com/all-red-lines-in-syria-have-been-crossed-turkish-fm.aspx?pageID=238&nID=52950&NewsCatID=338.

32. Albright et al., *U.S. Nonproliferation Strategy for the Changing Middle East*, 12 and 104.

33. "'Dragging Their Feet': US Struggling to Make Assad Turn Over Chemical Weapons on Time," January 31, 2014, http://www.foxnews.com/politics/2014/01/31/dragging-their-feet-us-scrambles-to-persuade-syria-to-honor-chemical-weapons/.

34. Mowatt-Larsen, "Al Qaeda Weapons of Mass Destruction Threat."

35. Barton Gellmann, "Al Qaeda Near Biological, Chemical Arms Production," *Washington Post*, March 3, 2003, http://www.washingtonpost.com/wp-dyn/content/article/2006/06/09/AR2006060900918.html.

36. Mowatt-Larsen, "Al Qaeda Weapons of Mass Destruction Threat."

37. The author was able to interview the law enforcement official who was deeply involved in this case in 2009 and on which the story by Edward Humes is based. See Humes, "The Medicine Man – a Story about Larry C. Ford, a Monster," *Los Angeles Magazine*, July 2001, http://www.byhigh.org%2FAlumni_F_to_J%2FFord%2FEdwardHumes-Dr. Jo Thomas, "California Doctor's Suicide Leaves Many Troubling Mysteries Unsolved," November 3, 2002, http://www.nytimes.com/2002/11/03/us/california-doctor-s-suicide-leaves-many-troubling-mysteries-unsolved.html. This case has been analyzed and taught as a case study in the U.S. Naval Academy. On Project Coast, see Joby Warrick, "Biotoxins Fall into Private Hands; Global Risk Seen in S. African Poisons," *Washington Post*, April 21, 2003, A1, http://file:///Files/SORT%20%20backup/To%20transfer/NIJ%20Examples/NIJ%20Documents/Biotoxins%20Fall%20Into%20Private%20Hands.htm, accessed June 1, 2013.

38. Thomas, "California Doctor's Suicide Leaves Many Troubling Mysteries Unsolved."

39. Ibid.

40. Humes, "Medicine Man."

41. Ibid.

42. Thomas, "California Doctor's Suicide Leaves Many Troubling Mysteries Unsolved."

43. Humes, "Medicine Man."

44. Thomas, "California Doctor's Suicide Leaves Many Troubling Mysteries Unsolved," and author's interview with the investigator of the case.

45. Harris was subsequently charged in 1998 with collecting anthrax, a charge which fell apart. "2 Charged with Making Biological Weapons," February 19, 1998, http://www.cnn.com/US/9802/19/fbi.arrest.pm/; "Beyond Anthrax: Extremists and the Bioterrorism Threat: The Harris Hoax," http://archive.adl.org/learn/anthrax/Harris.asp?xpicked=3&item=5.

46. Bruce Hoffman, *Inside Terrorism* (New York: Columbia University Press, 1998), 201–2.

47. Graham Allison, *Nuclear Terrorism: The Ultimate Preventable Catastrophe* (New York: Times Books, 2004), 31. This overlooks the Kocaeli case that will be discussed subsequently in the chapter.

48. Ibid., 31–32. For a further discussion of Chechen involvement in nuclear terrorism, see Simon Saradzhyan, "Russia: Grasping Reality of Nuclear Terror," Discussion Paper 2003-02, International Security Program, Belfer Center for Science and International Affairs, Harvard Kennedy School, March 2003, http://belfercenter.ksg.harvard.edu/publication/2938/russia.html?breadcrumb=%2Fexperts%2F1897%2Fsimon_saradzhyan%3Fgroupby%3D0%26hide%3D1%26id%3D1897%26back_url%3D%2525252Fexperts%2525252F%26%253Bback_text%3DBack%252Bto%252Blist%252Bof%252Bexperts%26filter%3D2003; Charles D. Ferguson and William C. Potter, *The Four Faces of Nuclear Terrorism* (New York: Routledge, 2005). See Alexander Kupatadze, "Organized Crime and the Trafficking of Radiological Materials: The Case of Georgia," *Nonproliferation Review* 17, no. 2 (2010): 226.

49. See *The U.S.-Russia Joint Threat Assessment on Nuclear Terrorism*, Belfer Center for Science and International Affairs and Russian Academy of

Sciences, 2011, http://belfercenter.ksg.harvard.edu/files/Joint-Threat-Assessment%20ENG%2027%20May%202011.pdf.

50. NTI Illicit Trafficking Initiatives, NIS Nuclear Trafficking Initiative, 2, 2011 Illicit Trafficking Incidents Summary Table, http://www.nti.org/analysis/reports/nis-nuclear-trafficking-database/.

51. "Moldova Sentences Would Be Uranium Dealers," May 25, 2012, http://www.nti.org/gsn/article/moldova-sentences-would-be-uranium-dealers/; Desmond Butler, "Moldova, U.S. Pursue HEU Held by Criminal Organization," September 27, 2011, http://www.nti.org/gsn/article/moldova-us-pursue-heu-held-by-criminal-organization/.

52. Global Security Newswire, "Georgia Conducted 15 Nuclear Smuggling Probes since 2005," December 10, 2012, http://www.nti.org/gsn/article/georgian-conducted-15-nuclear-smuggling-probes-2005-report/. Also, a researcher affiliated with the author has had recent cases officially released by the Georgian government for analysis from this period.

53. The author began the study of WMD in Georgia after a retired U.S. ambassador to Georgia suggested that the crime-terror relationship be examined as nuclear smuggling had been detected during his years of service in Georgia in the late 1990s.

54. For example, see *U.S.-Russia Joint Threat Assessment on Nuclear Terrorism*, which devotes less than a page to criminal activity.

55. Greg Miller, Craig Whitlock, and Barton Gellman, "Top-Secret U.S. Intelligence Files Show New Levels of Distrust of Pakistan," *Washington Post,* September 2, 2013, http://articles.washingtonpost.com/2013-09-02/world/41690725_1_intelligence-u-s-spy-agencies-other-adversaries.

56. Ryan Clarke, *Crime-Terror Nexus in South Asia: States, Security and Non-state Actors* (London: Routledge, 2013), 63.

57. Special Report: The Khan Network; Kenley Butler, Sammy Salama, and Leonard S. Spector, "Where Is the Justice?," *Bulletin of the Atomic Scientists,* November–December 2006, 25–34; Mark Hibbs, "The Unmaking of a Nuclear Smuggler," *Bulletin of the Atomic Scientists,* November–December 2006, 35–41.

58. Clarke, *Crime-Terror Nexus,* 63. This analysis is also based on discussions with individuals who closely follow South Asian crime beyond that of D-Company, which is the focus of Clarke's book.

59. Ghulam Hasnain, "The Story of Mumbai's Underworld Don, Dawood Ibrahim, Reads Like a Page from The Godfather," http://www.hindinest.com/srajan/02948.htm. The author was a very courageous investigative journalist who can no longer live in Pakistan.

60. Bruno Tertrais, *Le Marché noir de la bombe Enquête sur la prolifération nucléaire* (Paris: Buchet/Chastel, 2009); Hassan Abbas, "Pakistan: Lessons from AQ Khan Nuclear Proliferation Practices," Criminal Networks, Smuggling, and WMD Conference, February 25–26, 2010, at Terrorism, Transnational Crime, and Corruption Center, George Mason University, Arlington, VA.

61. "Letter to A.Q. Khan," *New York Times,* July 7, 2011, http://www.nytimes.com/interactive/2011/07/08/world/asia/20110708_KHAN_LETTER_DOC.html?_r=0.

62. "Still Time for Diplomacy," interview with ElBaradei, September 30, 2004, http://news.bbc.co.uk/2/hi/programmes/hardtalk/3704816.stm.

63. See Doug Farah, who has written much on facilitators, in particular, his discussion in reference to the A. Q. Khan network in "ARY Gold and Terrorist Finance," December 19, 2006, http://blog.douglasfarah.com/article/50/ary-gold-and-terrorist-finance. See also Christopher O. Clary, "The A. Q. Khan Network: Causes and Implications," Monterey Naval Post-Graduate School, December 2005, http://www.fas.org/irp/eprint/clary.pdf.

64. David Albright, *Peddling Peril: How the Secret Nuclear Trade Arms America's Enemies* (New York: Free Press, 2010), 18–22.

65. Ibid., 30–51.

66. David Albright, "Holding Khan Accountable: An ISIS Statement Accompanying Release of Libya: A Major Sale at Last," December 1, 2010, http://isis-online.org/isis-reports/detail/holding-khan-accountable-an-isis-statement-accompanying-release-of-libya-a-/.

67. Ibid.

68. David Albright and Paul Brannan, "Taking Stock: North Korea's Nuclear Enrichment Program," Institute for Science and International Security, October 8, 2010, 6–10, http://isis-online.org/uploads/isis-reports/documents/ISIS_DPRK_UEP.pdf.

69. Ibid., 9.

70. *Nuclear Black Markets: Pakistan, A.Q. Khan and the Rise of Proliferation Networks* (London: International Institute for Strategic Studies, 2007).

71. "Pakistan Pardons 'Father of Bomb,'" February 5, 2004, http://news.bbc.co.uk/2/hi/south_asia/3460685.stm.

72. Ibid.; *Nuclear Black Markets*.

73. Albright, "Holding Khan Accountable"; Jack Caravelli, *Nuclear Insecurity: Understanding the Threat from Rogue Nations and Terrorists* (Westport, CT: Praeger Security International, 2008).

74. See Institute for Science and International Security, illicit trade section of http://isis-online.org/studies/category/illicit-trade/; U.S. Department of Justice, "Summary of Major U.S. Export Enforcement, Economic Espionage, Trade Secret and Embargo-Related Criminal Cases"; Lyudmila Zaitseva and Kevin Hand, "Nuclear Smuggling Chains Suppliers, Intermediaries, and End Users," *American Behavioral Scientist* 46, no. 6 (2003): 822–44.

75. Zaitseva, "Nuclear Trafficking: 20 Years in Review."

76. Matthew Bunn, "Corruption and Nuclear Proliferation," in *Corruption, Global Security, and World Order*, ed. Robert Rotberg (Washington, DC: Brookings Institution, 2009), 1–48.

77. In 2012, Russia ranked 133 and Pakistan ranked 139 out of 174 countries on the Corruption Perception Index ranking. See http://cpi.transparency.org/cpi2012/results/.

78. Matthew Bunn and Eben Harrell, "A Blueprint for Preventing Nuclear Terrorism," March 30, 2012, http://ideas.time.com/2012/03/30/a-blueprint-for-preventing-nuclear-terrorism/.

79. http://www.bellona.org/english_import_area/international/russia/nuke_industry/co-operation/37946; "Russian Ex-nuclear Minister Adamov Released from Prison," April 17, 2008, http://en.rian.ru/russia/20080417/105342331.html.

80. For an early warning about this, see William C. Potter, "Before the Deluge: The Threat of Nuclear Leakage from the Post-Soviet States," http://www.pbs.org/wgbh/pages/frontline/shows/nukes/readings/potterarticle.html.

81. A. Kuznetsov and I. Zvereva, "Kadrovye resheniya bez rezkikh dvizhenii," *Novaya Sibir*, February 4, 2005; A. Kuznetsov, "Amortizatsiya s ekspropriat-siei," *Novaya Sibir*, October 8, 2004; see also Louise I. Shelley, "Trafficking in Nuclear Materials: Criminals and Terrorists," *Global Crime* 7, nos. 3–4 (2006): 554.

82. Charles Digges, "GAN Says Nuclear Materials Have Been Disappearing from Russian Plants for 10 Years," November 15, 2002, http://www.bellona.org/english_import_area/international/russia/nuke-weapons/nonproliferation/2727Y.

83. Ibid., Table 2. The table indicates that the grade of enrichment was unknown.

84. "Shkval'nyi veter," *Ozerskii vestnik*, March 26, 2005. According to the speech of S. K. Lynov, head of the central medical-sanitary unit, in the city of Ozersk at a meeting with Mayak workers on the results of 1999 and signing a new collective bargaining agreement, February 24, 2000. Research of TraCCC (Terrorism, Transnational Crime, and Corruption Center), American University, 2004–5, in which project the author participated.

85. Research of TraCCC (Terrorism, Transnational Crime and Corruption Center), American University, 2005, project of which the author participated.

86. *Ozerskii vestnik*, July 10, 2004.

87. Ibid.

88. Ibid.

89. "Prizrak Usamy brodit po 'zapretke,'" *Chelyabinskii rabochii*, August 12, 2004; research of TraCCC, American University, 2004–5, in which project the author participated.

90. In one interview conducted in 2005 by the author with an American defense contractor working on a nuclear site in the Russian Far East, the contractor reported that his former Russian construction manager refused to comply with the demands of organized crime. He was murdered. The new Russian manager of this project to secure a high-priority nuclear facility had no such problems. The American manager of the U.S. government contract presumed his Russian project manager had made a deal with organized crime.

91. Zaitseva, "Nuclear Trafficking: 20 Years in Review." Nuclear material retains its properties for a long time.

92. Justin Bresolin, "Fact Sheet: The Nunn-Lugar Cooperative Threat Reduction Program," http://armscontrolcenter.org/publications/factsheets/fact_sheet_the_cooperative_threat_reduction_program/.

93. James Martin Center for Non-proliferation Studies, "Overview of Reported Nuclear Trafficking Incidents Involving Turkey 1993–1999," http://cns.miis.edu/wmdme/flow/turkey/index.htm; Mahmut Cengiz, "Analysis of WMD Cases in Turkey: Police Seizure of WMD Materials," Criminal Networks, Smuggling, and WMD Conference, February 25–26, 2010, at the Terrorism, Transnational Crime, and Corruption Center, George Mason University, Arlington, VA.

94. Georgia presently scores better on Transparency International indices in regard to present-day corruption but had a comparable level of corruption to other successor states at the time that the majority of nuclear smuggling cases were detected. See Kupatadze, "Organized Crime and the Trafficking of Radiological Materials," 219–34. Analysis by Alexander Kupatadze of recent Georgian cases reveals that one case tried in Georgia in 2012 involved Abkhazia. "In case N4 the group of 5 smugglers found an unidentified accomplice in Abkhazia that provided material. At least two of the group were the residents of the regions bordering Abkhazia

(Samtredia and Martvili) and supposedly had the pre-existing networks and trade experience across the ceasefire line."

95. One of the most notorious was the Khintsagov case discussed by Michael Bronner, *100 Grams (and Counting...): Notes from the Nuclear Underworld* (Cambridge, MA: Report for Managing the Atom Project, Harvard University, June 2008); Alexander Kupatadze, "Radiological Smuggling and Uncontrolled Territories: The Case of Georgia," *Global Crime* 8 (February 2007): 40–57. Research done by Alexander Kupatadze in summer 2013 reveals that "previously many of the smuggling cases have been related with the two conflict zones but the smuggling has significantly subsided after the regime change in 2004 and more importantly since the 2008 August war with Russia. However the 2012 case suggests that some of the smuggling networks remain active."

96. Kupatadze, "Organized Crime and the Trafficking of Radiological Materials," 222; Alexander Kupatadze, "Is Radiological Trafficking Organized Crime? The Case of Georgia," paper presented at the Criminal Networks, Smuggling, and WMD Conference, February 25–26, 2010, at Terrorism, Transnational Crime and Corruption Center, George Mason University, Arlington, VA.

97. Michael Bronner, "What Should We Learn from Nuclear Smuggling, between Russia and Georgia?," paper presented at What Is Needed? The Way Ahead for WMD Policy, April 16, 2009, Terrorism, Transnational Crime, and Corruption Center, George Mason University, Arlington, VA.

98. "Mafia Clan Connected with Trafficking Nuclear Waste," *Nuclear Monitor,* no. 661 (October 11, 2007): 1–2, http://www.nirs.org/mononline/nm661.pdf.

99. "Authorities Find Radioactive Waste Ship Sunk by Mafia," December 11, 2009, http://www.france24.com/en/20090917-authorities-find-radioactive-waste-ship-sunk-mafia.

100. Matthew Bunn, "Strengthening Nonproliferation and Anti-corruption Cultures," presented at CNS and Belfer Center meeting, Project on Stopping Black-Market Nuclear Technology Networks, Carnegie Endowment for International Peace, April 10–11, 2013.

101. Smigielski, "Addressing the Nuclear Smuggling Threat," 52–59.

102. Albright et al., *U.S. Nonproliferation Strategy for the Changing Middle East.*

103. Kupatadze, "Organized Crime and the Trafficking of Radiological Materials," 219–220.

104. Lyudmila Zaitseva and Kevin Hand, "Nuclear Smuggling Chains: Suppliers, Intermediaries, and End Users," *American Behavioral Scientist* 46, no. 6 (2003): 822–44; Zaitseva, "Nuclear Trafficking: 20 Years in Review"; Zaitseva, "Organized Crime"; Lee, *Smuggling Armageddon*. Also analysis done by Alexander Kupatadze of cases prosecuted in Georgia of nuclear smuggling post-2009.

105. Zaitseva, "Organized Crime," 2.

106. Mahmut Cengiz, "Analysis of WMD Cases in Turkey: Police Seizure of WMD Materials," paper presented at Criminal Networks, Smuggling, and WMD Conference, February 25–26, 2010, at Terrorism, Transnational Crime, and Corruption Center, George Mason University, Arlington, VA; Mahmut Cengiz, *Turkish Organized Crime: From Local to Global* (Saarbrücken, Germany: VDM, 2011).

107. Cengiz, *Turkish Organized Crime*. Also see *U.S.-Russia Joint Threat Assessment on Nuclear Terrorism.*

108. Zaitseva, "Organized Crime." Also seen in the author's research with Robert Orttung in the mid-2000s.

109. Zaitseva, "Organized Crime," note 10.

110. "Nuclear Case Wrapped Up, Authorities Destroy Copies of Tinner Files," March 26, 2013, http://www.swissinfo.ch/eng/swiss_news/Authorities_destroy_copies_of_Tinner_files.html?cid=35329342.

111. David Albright and Michael Rietz, "Closing the Tinners' Swiss Criminal Case," October 26, 2012, http://isis-online.org/isis-reports/detail/closing-the-tinners-swiss-criminal-case/20.

112. Douglas Farah, "Fixers, Super Fixers and Shadow Facilitators: How Networks Connect," in *Convergence Illicit Networks and National Security in the Age of Globalization*, ed. Michael Miklaucic and Jacqueline Brewer (Washington, DC: NDU Press, 2013), 75–95.

113. Jeffrey Benzing, "As Security Threats Evolve, Justice Department's Pelak Focuses on Illegal Exports," March 18, 2012, http://www.mainjustice.com/justanticorruption/2012/03/18/as-security-threats-evolve-justice-departments-pelak-focuses-on-illegal-export-deals/.

114. IAEA, "Illicit Trafficking Database," http://www-ns.iaea.org/security/itdb.asp.

115. Zaitseva, "Organized Crime."

116. Ibid.

117. The author learned of unreported cases while doing research in Georgia. See also Zaitseva, "Nuclear Trafficking: 20 Years in Review," for discussion of these cases that appear in open sources.

118. Albright et al., *Future World of Illicit Nuclear Trade*, 100.

119. Ibid.

120. This insight was expressed at many conferences the author attended in the mid-2000s on nuclear proliferation and smuggling. See also Michael Levi, *On Nuclear Terrorism* (Cambridge, MA: Harvard University Press, 2007), 88, that says nuclear materials and cocaine would travel separate routes.

121. Cengiz, *Turkish Organized Crime*. Dr. Cengiz worked in the anti–nuclear smuggling division of the Turkish National Police in the mid-2000s.

122. Zaitseva, "Organized Crime."

123. Ibid., 37–38, suggests that there is much movement in this direction; see also ibid. for a discussion of two specific cases.

124. Case discussed by the Russian authorities with one of the Russian organized crime study centers that the author funded through the U.S. State Department since the mid-1990s. Case discussed by the Russian researcher with the author.

125. Mike Miklaucic and Jacqueline Brewer, *Convergence: Illicit Networks and National Security in the Age of Globalization* (Washington, DC: Center for Complex Operations, 2013).

126. Zaitseva, "Organized Crime," Table 1.

127. Based on interviews by the TraCCC team in Georgia concerning individuals who have been caught transporting low-level radiation sources.

128. Rensselaer Lee, "Nuclear Smuggling, Rogue States and Terrorists," *China and Eurasia Forum Quarterly* 4, no. 2 (2006): 30.

129. Bronner, *100 Grams (and Counting...)*. For a fuller discussion, see note 85. Mr. Khintsagov was not forthcoming either with his investigators or with Dr. Kupatadze, who interviewed him in prison.

130. The author's analysis of individual cases as well as interviews with practitioners from Soviet successor states and Georgia.

131. "Chronology: A. Q. Khan," *New York Times,* April 16, 2006. http://www.nytimes.com/2006/04/16/world/asia/16chron-khan.html?pagewanted=all&_r=o.

132. Albright and Brannan, "Taking Stock," 6–10.

133. This is based on an analysis of DOJ prosecutions for violations of import-export controls. Also see the website and cases of ISIS, http://isis-online.org/studies/category/illicit-trade/; see also Albright et al., *Future World of Illicit Nuclear Trade,* 11–12.

134. UPI, "Nuclear Materials Smugglers Arrested," March 11, 2013, http://www.upi.com/Top_News/World-News/2013/03/11/Nuclear-materials-smugglers-arrested/UPI-80861362997303/; Nihat Uludag, "Nuclear Operation: Seven Iranians Captured in Simultaneous Operations in Turkey and Germany," http://www.upi.com/Top_News/World-News/2013/03/11/Nuclear-materials-smugglers-arrested/UPI-80861362997303/, as well as information provided by Leonard Spector.

135. Interview with Turkish official, June 2013.

136. Leonard Spector, "Strengthening the Global Law Enforcement Response," presented at CNS and Belfer Center meeting, Project on Stopping Black-Market Nuclear Technology Networks, Carnegie Endowment for International Peace, April 10–11, 2013.

137. U.S. Department of Justice, "Summary of Major U.S. Export Enforcement, Economic Espionage, Trade Secret and Embargo-Related Criminal Cases."

138. The following cases are illustrative of this. *Military-Sensitive Parts to Iran,* October 24, 2012; *Materials for Gas Centrifuges and Other Nuclear-Related Goods to Iran,* July 12, 2012; *Aerospace-Grade Carbon Fiber to China,* September 26, 2012; *Nuclear-Related Equipment to Iran,* July 29, 2010; cases listed in U.S. Department of Justice, *Summary of Major U.S. Export Enforcement, Economic Espionage, Trade Secret and Embargo-Related Criminal Cases.*

139. *Military-Sensitive Parts to Iran.*

140. U.S. Senate Permanent Subcommittee on Investigations, Committee on Homeland Security and Governmental Affairs, "U.S. Vulnerabilities to Money Laundering, Drugs, and Terrorist Financing: HSBC Case History," July 17, 2012, 118; "Helping Clients Evade US Sanctions," January 3, 2013, http://www.financialtransparency.org –20.

141. Ibid., 120.

142. Heather Lowe, "HSBC Deferred Prosecution Agreement: /2013/01/03/the-hsbc-deferred-prosecution-agreement-helping-clients-evade-u-s-sanctions/.

143. U.S. Senate Permanent Subcommittee on Investigations, "U.S. Vulnerabilities to Money Laundering, Drugs, and Terrorist Financing," 117; Javier Serrat, "Financial Interdictions to Curb Proliferation," July–August 2012, http://www.armscontrol.org/2012_07–08/Financial_Interdictions_To_Curb_Proliferation.

144. Sonia Ben Ouagrham-Gormley, "Banking on Nonproliferation: Improving the Efficiency of Counter-Proliferation Financing Policies," *Nonproliferation Review* 19, no. 2 (2012): 241–65.

145. Mowatt-Larsen, "Al Qaeda Weapons of Mass Destruction Threat"; Brian Michael Jenkins, *Will Terrorists Go Nuclear?* (New York: Prometheus Books, 2008), 84–96.

146. NTI Illicit Trafficking Initiatives, NIS Nuclear Trafficking Initiative, 2, 2011, Illicit Trafficking Incidents Summary Table, http://www.nti.org/analysis/reports/nis-nuclear-trafficking-database/; "Moldova Sentences Would Be Uranium Dealers," May 25, 2012, http://www.nti.org/gsn/article/moldova-sentences-would-be-uranium-dealers/; Butler, "Moldova, U.S. Pursue HEU Held by Criminal Organization."

147. Soner Cagaptay and Aaron Y. Zelin, "Turkey's Jihadi Dilemma," August 5, 2013, http://www.washingtoninstitute.org/policy-analysis/view/turkeys-jihadi-dilemma.

148. Eric Schmidt, "Worries Mount as Syria Lures West's Muslims," *New York Times,* July 27, 2013, http://www.nytimes.com/2013/07/28/world/middleeast/worries-mount-as-syria-lures-wests-muslims.html.

149. This attack was discussed in detail by one of the investigating officers, Anadolou Atayun, "Crime-Terror Nexus: Concrete Examples from the Field," at Criminal Networks, Smuggling, and WMD Conference, February 25–26, 2010, at Terrorism, Transnational Crime, and Corruption Center, George Mason University, Arlington, VA.

150. Nilsu Goren, Aviv Melamud, Ibrahim Said Ibrahim, and Ariane Tabatabai, "Anger Management in the Middle East," August 9, 2013, http://www.middleeast-armscontrol.com/2013/08/09/anger-management-in-the-middle-east/.

151. Weapons of Mass Destruction Commission, *Weapons of Terror: Freeing the World of Nuclear Biological and Chemical Arms* (Stockholm, Sweden: WMD Commission, 2006). Note that rapid advancements in the life sciences have outpaced the regulations associated with them.

152. Associated Press, "Dzhokhar Tsarnaev Indictment Includes WMD Use among 30 Charges," *Clarion Ledger,* June 27, 2013, http://www.clarionledger.com/viewart/20130627/NEWS03/130627018/Dzhokhar-Tsarnaev-indictment-includes-WMD-use-among-30-charges. Tamerlan Tsarnaev may have been involved in criminal activities before his visit to Dagestan, and he may have been involved in a drug-related triple murder in Massachusetts in 2011. This is another illustration of the criminal links to terrorism. See Serge F. Kovaleski and Richard A. Oppel Jr., "In 2011 Murder Inquiry, Hints of Missed Chance to Avert Boston Bombing," *New York Times,* July 10, 2013, http://www.nytimes.com/2013/07/11/us/boston-bombing-suspect-is-said-to-be-linked-to-2011-triple-murder-case.html. The Tsarnaev terrorist act, like the Oklahoma City bombing, caused serious harm, but not by the type of WMD discussed in this chapter.

153. "Strategy to Combat Transnational Organized Crime," July 25, 2011 http://www.whitehouse.gov/administration/eop/nsc/transnational-crime.

154. Ibid.

155. "Data Points to Home-Grown WMD Terror Threats in U.S.: Experts," August 8, 2012, http://www.nti.org/gsn/article/data-points-home-grown-wmd-terror-threats-experts/.

156. Homegrown Terrorism Cases, 2001–2013, http://homegrown.newamerica.net.

Conclusion

From Fiction to Present-Day Reality

Decades before policy makers ever considered the crime-terror phenomenon, Ian Fleming, in his 1961 novel *Thunderball*, dreamed up SPECTRE (Special Executive for Counter-intelligence, Terrorism, Revenge, and Extortion), a supranational profit-making organization. In the James Bond film *Dr. No*, Joseph Wiseman, archly playing the eponymous villain from SPECTRE, explains that his network does not represent the Soviet bloc, then the primary security concern of that period. Rather, the SPECTRE agent explains, they are not confined to a single region but represent the four cornerstones of power run by the world's greatest minds.[1]

Today, there is no actual SPECTRE, a unified organization spanning continents that blends terror and criminal acts. Yet, much as Ian Fleming imagined, the interrelationship of crime and terrorism is a critical global security challenge, commanding attention at the highest levels of national and multinational governance.

The actual problem is even more complex than its fictional precedent. Unlike in the Bond films, it is no longer possible to vanquish a single evil organization like SPECTRE to rid the world of crime and terror. The links between crime and terrorism are global, networked, and interrelated. The problem is like a cancer, constantly mutating and reappearing in new places. It operates not unlike the quantum entanglements of the physical world, where changes in one locale produce profound changes far from the original source.

There is another reason why a fictional movie villain is relevant to the conversation today. SPECTRE was a business, making its money through extortion. In contemporary reality, the crimes associated with terrorism are much more diverse. But from the outset of this book, I have demonstrated that *there is a business logic to terrorism*.

Moreover, the relationship of crime and terrorism transcends the need for financing. The location of the In Amenas attack was chosen because of its critical financial importance to the Algerian economy; the bar attacked in the Bali bombing belonged to a rival criminal group not associated with the JI terrorists; Basayev had established overseas funding cells well in advance of the Beslan attack to ensure a diversified revenue stream.

Although often operating in the shadows, the hybrid of crime and terrorism often intersects with both the legitimate economy and government officials. Beyond the financial challenge, the even more deadly triad of crime, terrorism, and corruption exacerbates political and social security. It thrives on the chaos of conflict regions, poorly governed and ungovernable locales.

Crime and Terrorism: Strategy Concern for the Global Community

The crime-terror challenge of Hollywood entertainment in the 1960s was a threat to Western security, but in contemporary reality, the human, political, and economic security consequences of this entangled relationship may be most devastating to the developing world. Therefore, this issue has become a prime concern at the United Nations, where developing countries represent a majority of its membership.

In January 2013, the United Nations (UN) Security Council initiated a day-long discussion on responding to terrorism with this statement that linked crime and terrorism:

> The Security Council recognizes the need to prevent and suppress the financing of terrorism and terrorist organizations, including from the proceeds of organized crime, inter alia, the illicit production and trafficking of narcotic drugs and their chemical precursors, and the importance of continued international cooperation towards that aim.[2]

Representatives of more than fifty countries spoke. UN delegates from Africa, Latin America, and Asia, Russia, in particular, addressed the links between crime and terrorism, especially in the Sahel region, West Africa, and Afghanistan-Pakistan. Other speakers drew on their specific national experiences to reveal how a range of crimes, not just the drug trade, contributed to terrorism in their country.[3] Among the most articulate was the delegate from the Economic Community of West African States (ECOWAS), who said, the "intent of terrorists in Mali was to turn that vast territory into a safe haven for terrorist groups and organized crime and to use it to recruit, train and launch operations across the world and then withdraw in total impunity." His statement epitomizes the security challenges of the globalized and interconnected contemporary world. Today, a major transnational threat can emanate from one remote region not well integrated into the global economy.

The high-level attention to the relationship of crime and terrorism at the UN marked a dramatic change from fifteen years ago, when I first began to study the relationship between the two phenomena. At that time, many people were skeptical that any such relationship existed. Some still are, especially in North America and Europe, where these links are less close to the surface than in other regions.[4]

Unfortunately, not one person speaking at the Security Council on the crime-terror relationship mentioned corruption, even though indirect mention was made by oblique references to the need for good governance and the rule of law. The international policy community has consistently failed to recognize the centrality of corruption to the perpetration and perpetuation of crime and terrorism. Even the United States, which confronted rampant corruption in Afghanistan and Iraq that undermined its countercrime and counterterrorism efforts, failed to develop a Transnational Crime Strategy that highlights corruption, which should be a central element.[5] Instead, the 2011 White House strategy reduces what should be a triad of crime, corruption, and terrorism into a dyad of crime and terrorism. This simplification of the problem prevents the international community from developing appropriate strategies to successfully address this complex problem. This is because the addition of a third component adds a complexity that far exceeds the challenges posed by the presence of merely two destructive components.

The contemporary failure to acknowledge the centrality of corruption resembles the situation at the World Bank before the mid-1990s. "President Jim Wolfensohn never missed an opportunity to remind audiences around the world how corruption had gone from an unspeakable c-word to top priority since he joined the Bank. The Bank's previous approach to corruption was described by an ex-Bank staffer as the 'three-monkey policy': see nothing, hear nothing, say nothing."[6] The "c-word" is still too often ignored in national and global policy, or is subsumed under discussions of good governance, as in the Security Council meetings, thereby failing to confront the reality of corruption and the exacerbating impact it has on the phenomena of crime and terrorism.

The Growth and Consequences of the Deadly Triad

The entangled threat of crime, corruption, and terrorism now commands high-level attention because of (1) its endemic nature in many diverse regions of the world, especially in conflict regions; (2) the financial success and extensive influence of nonstate actors on governments, often by means of corruption; (3) the increasing economic role of criminals and terrorists both as employers and participants in the local and global economy; (4) the deleterious impact of crime and terrorism on communities and the political order; and (5) the incapacity of state and multinational organizations to successfully challenge transnational criminals and terrorists at the national, regional, and global levels.

This enveloping threat of crime, corruption, and terrorism (CCT) to economic, political, and social stability is a relatively recent phenomenon – in part a consequence of the end of the Cold War and the decline in support for state-sponsored terrorism. The financial restrictions imposed after September 11 have made crime an important funding source for terrorism. Yet the relationships of crime and terror are not just financial. As this book has shown throughout, they are also operational factors facilitating the development of transnational illicit networks.

Moreover, the relationship of terrorists with crime has a further repercussions – it compounds the harm caused by terrorists. As Gretchen Peters has written, "whether it is drug trafficking, kidnap for ransom, robbery, extortion, smuggling or protection rackets, organized crime not only helps fund anti-state actors across the region, it is also a key element of their asymmetric warfare campaign, spreading instability and fear."[7] As a Taliban leader was quoted as saying in Chapter 6, "whether it is by opium or by shooting, this is our common goal [to harm all infidels as part of jihad]."[8] Harming one's enemies through drug addiction is not exclusive to jihadi terrorism but has also been expressed as a motive of the FARC in Colombia.

The harm caused by this interaction transcends the harm imagined by the Taliban leader or the FARC – it undermines the sustainability of the planet. The entanglement of crime and terrorism has much greater impact than the maiming and killing of hundreds of thousands,[9] or the millions addicted to narcotics, or deprived of property as a result of random acts of criminal activity.

Contemporary illicit trade, a key component of the crime-terror relationship, is different from smuggling in previous millennia. Smuggling has existed since the dawn of history, when states began to raise revenues by imposing taxes on the movement of goods.[10] Yet today's illicit trade carried out by criminals, terrorists, and corrupt officials affects millions, if not billions, of lives by doing irreversible damage to the planet and to existing communities, whether by eliminating species or forests or spreading contagious diseases or components of weapons of mass destruction (WMD).

Destruction, hunger, and disorder can also result from the deadly aftermath of a terrorist and criminal occupation, as is presently the case in Mali. As *New York Times* columnist Nicholas Kristof has written, "stay alert to the risks of Islamists and groups affiliated with Al Qaeda in West Africa and North Africa, but don't overlook the twinned humanitarian challenges. Bombs and machine guns draw television cameras, but the most lethal and immediate threat to children here is now simple, excruciating hunger."[11]

The costs are very visible in Mali. Unfortunately, Mali is only one of the locales where the complex globally linked hybrids have caused great suffering. Syria is another example where crime, corruption, and terrorism coexisted before the conflict and have only been amplified as foreign fighters arrive, arms are smuggled, and the corruption that helped ignite the uprising prevails. Yet there is a contagion effect, as the networks operating in Mali and Syria disperse to other locales. Syria may serve as an incubator or safe haven for terrorists and terrorism, just as Afghanistan did in the 1990s.[12] Therefore, the true long-term costs of the deadly hybrid may only be fully appreciated with the passage of future decades.

Future Trends

In August 2013, the new Egyptian government cracked down on the Muslim Brotherhood and closed the previously discussed smuggling tunnels that linked Egypt and the Gaza Strip. The effort to stamp out illicit trade had an immediate impact on the Palestinian militant group Hamas, which rules Gaza. Hamas suffered a political crisis as a result of this move. "Ministers have met daily. With Gaza's economy facing a $250 million shortfall since Egypt shut down hundreds of smuggling tunnels."[13] The hopes of Hamas for ascendance after the Arab Spring may have been dampened as their financial flows were cut off by ending the illicit but previously tolerated trade.

The Egyptian government has forced change in Gaza, not through the direct military intervention that has had such a bloody outcome in Cairo but through financial mechanisms. The Gaza example illustrates a central theme of this book – illicit financial flows and trade are crucial to the sustenance of a terrorist group, in this case, Hamas, and cutting these funding sources can result in dramatic political crisis and change. The outcome of the shuttered tunnels cannot be determined immediately, but this decisive action by Egypt against the illicit funding sources of Hamas, a named terrorist organization,[14] may have profound consequences in the Middle East and beyond.

The Egyptian and Palestinian future is unpredictable, but certain independent variables identified throughout the book will certainly shape the dirty entanglements of the future: the growth of megacities; rising economic inequality globally and within countries and regions; political forces, poor governance, and retreat of the state; civil wars and conflict; sectarian conflicts; climate change; demographic change, including migration and displacement; food insecurity; evolution of dirty entanglements; and technological change.

Megacities

The first chapter identified the crime and corruption behind the deadly attacks in the megacities of Jakarta, Mumbai, New York, and São Paolo. Extreme violence linked to the deadly triad is ongoing in Pakistan's megacity of Karachi, where approximately half the population lives in slums and numerous criminal groups are deeply entwined into the political structure.[15] According to conservative estimates, there are more than five thousand armed militants from various jihadist groups in Karachi.[16] The same problems may also manifest themselves in India and other South Asian megacities.[17] Mexico City has constructed a monument to the tens of thousands who died in the drug conflict, many victims perishing in criminal attacks that employ the techniques of terrorists.[18] Cairo in the summer of 2013 was wracked by state and nonstate violence.[19]

Megacities that have played a key role in the book's analysis are only going to become more important in human geography in the coming decades. The number of megacities has increased dramatically since the 1970s, at which time there were only New York and Tokyo. "In 2011, 23 urban agglomerations qualified as megacities because they had at least 10 million inhabitants."[20] They represented approximately 10 percent of the world's urban population, a figure that is expected to reach 13.6 percent in 2025. The highest rates of megacity growth are expected in Asia and Africa.[21] Numbers of inhabitants of megacities may become even greater as China has embarked on an ambitious program to move 250 million of its citizens to urban areas.[22] This urbanization should prove traumatic for the peasants who are moved, and destabilizing for the larger society. Therefore, in the future, the link of crime, corruption, and terrorism now primarily seen in western China may not be confined to this region.

Megacities in developed countries, where governability is greater, have the lowest rates of growth. But in many regions of the world, these large urban settlements do not now provide for the basic needs of the majority of their citizens. In the future, employment will not keep up with population growth, and food insecurity may become a serious concern for the majority of urban settlers, who will live in shantytowns without secure rights to reside on the land they inhabit.[23] Daily life will remain highly precarious in these vast unofficial settlements.

In these environments, examined throughout the book, crime and terror groups can step in to provide state services. For example, the urban gangs of Rio and São Paulo, based in the *favelas,* provide ruthless justice along with "diapers, milk, medication and employment, combining terror and public works."[24] Youth crime in Lagos, Nigeria, is attributed to gangs called "area boys," who are involved in a range of crimes, including collecting bribes, engaging in torture, and even arresting innocent citizens without a warrant.[25] Yet because these groups provide employment, they manage to survive. In these vast urban environments, dirty entanglements that ensure urban as well as global insecurity are clearly exposed.

Rising Income Inequality

The megacities are a showcase of rising inequality. Particularly in the developing world, the vast, opulent homes of the very rich stand in sharp contrast to the shantytowns and often illegal settlements of the urban poor. The precariousness of the poor, and their frequent ousters from the land and homes they occupy, compounds the insecurity of their daily existence. Members of the Pakistan-based D-Company gang that engineered the 1993 Mumbai attacks, members of the PCC who attacked the city of São Paolo, and many of the transnational and terrorist organizations discussed throughout this book draw on the urban poor as their foot soldiers. Without access to education, schools, or services, marginalized urban residents often become the employees of crime and terrorist groups, as has been seen in Colombia, Central America, and North Africa. The same problem also exists among recent immigrant communities in some parts of the developed world, whose residents often live in relative deprivation compared to the native inhabitants.[26] Without changes in the urban structure, this trend should continue to provide recruits for both criminal and terrorist organizations, or hybrids of the two.

Economic inequality on a regional and a global level will also prove destabilizing in the future, as it is today. The World Economic Forum, in its 2013 *Global Risks Report*, identified severe income disparity as one of the two most prevalent global risks.[27] Major drug flows move north from Mexico and Central America to the United States, resulting in huge profits for traffickers. Massive flows of money and also arms have moved in the opposite direction from the United States to Mexico. This multi-billion-dollar trade has allowed the Mexican drug organizations to acquire the enormous quantities of arms that have facilitated the "terrorist-like" attacks on their fellow citizens.[28]

Global disparities in income and wealth will remain crucial to the endurance of dirty entanglements. The left-wing extremist group of Naxalites in west Bengal, responsible for significant violence, is also explained by "the unequal distribution of wealth gained from India's burgeoning economy."[29] Money sent to address the problem fails to deliver results because the system to utilize these funds is corrupt. Naxalites raise funds through "extortion or by setting up parallel administrations to collect taxes in rural areas where local governments and the Indian state appear absent."[30] Therefore, wealth disparity combined with crime and corruption contribute to enduring terrorist violence in India.

Many examples in this book have illustrated how kleptocratic leaders, such as in North Africa before the so-called Arab Spring, moved large amounts of their country's resources overseas to financial havens. The draining of the national treasuries contributed to the absence of economic opportunity and social and medical services, and to the radicalization of parts of their population, driving youthful members of these North African societies into criminal and hybrid crime-terror organizations that provide them employment. This problem is not confined to North Africa. The same processes are at work in the Caucasus and Central Asia, several of whose states are ripe for the violence associated with dirty entanglements.[31]

Political Impacts

The decline of state power, the retreat of the state, and the embedding of nonstate actors in the power and governance structures of many regions[32] suggest a different organization of power in the future. Illicit actors, such as criminal and terrorist groups, will continue to gain ground as they substitute for the state and serve as service suppliers, as was discussed in Chapter 3. Citizens in these locales will not cooperate with law enforcement to rid their communities of the criminal and terrorist organizations, because often those meant to enforce the law are corrupt. Furthermore, citizens are indebted to and dependent on the nonstate actors for vital services not provided by weak and corrupted states. Citizen resentment and antagonism toward the insurgent and terrorist groups can be neutralized by the services provided by the nonstate actors. Nonstate actors will continue to gain legitimacy and mobilize for their organizations in the future, based on the perceived benefits they provide – security, mediation, and medical and educational services. States with limited governance capacity as a result of corruption, weak institutions, or the undermining of institutions as a result of conflicts and insurgency will remain breeding grounds and safe havens for malicious nonstate actors.

Civil Wars and Conflict

The end of the Cold War resulted in the demise of superpower hegemony and the emergence of numerous regional conflicts. In the early 1990s, almost 30 percent of the world's countries were experiencing some form of conflict. That figure has dropped since then but still stood at 16 percent of the world's countries in 2011, and the trajectory has been upward since the start of the so-called Arab Spring.[33] Specialists argue whether greed, often satisfied by criminal activity, or grievance is the dominant feature in perpetuating conflicts.[34] But this problem should not demand an either-or answer. Grievance may initiate a conflict, greed may sustain it, but years of suffering imposed by both sides may make resolution unattainable.

The second decade of the twenty-first century started with the hopes of the Arab Spring. But tragically, optimism deteriorated with the serious sectarian conflicts among Sunnis and Shias that resulted in tragic terrorist attacks on communities, markets, and mosques. The loss of life in such diverse countries of the Moslem world as Egypt, Syria, Iraq, and Pakistan suggests that cycles of revenge will ensure continued conflict in subsequent decades, resulting in significant loss of life and the displacement of millions, as seen in the Iraqi and Syrian conflicts. All of this instability will contribute to the strength of dirty entanglements.

Conflicts are by no means confined to the Moslem world. Mexico and Central America have seen serious internal conflict resulting from the international drug trade, with some of the highest homicide rates in the world. The weak states and the corrupt states of Central America are unable to curb the violence of the large and powerful gangs that establish alliances with the drug organizations to the south in Colombia and to the north in Mexico.[35] Predatory and unending conflicts characterize almost half of the African continent's fifty-three countries. Tens of thousands have died in many of these conflicts, and it is estimated by the International Rescue Committee that 5 million have died in the Congo alone since 1998.[36]

Violence results not only from civil conflict but from crime and terrorist acts. Terrorism is, unfortunately, not in retreat. Many parts of Africa, the Middle East, and South Asia continue to experience serious and frequent terrorist acts with numerous fatalities and injuries from groups such as AQIM, Boko Haram, al Shabaab, and many others.[37]

Ethnic and Sectarian Violence

Ethnic and sectarian violence is related to the previously discussed civil conflict but brings some important and distinct dimensions. Much of the uptick in the civil conflict that was seen in the early 1990s was an outgrowth of the end of the superpower conflict and the international realignments as a result of the collapse of the Soviet Union. Yet there is a different dimension to the violence that is proving so destructive in the second decade of the twenty-first century – one that is more tied to sectarian conflicts. As King Abdullah II remarked at an August 2013 conference, in the Jordanian capital, of one hundred religious scholars, Sunni, Shiite, and Christian, from thirty-five countries, "ethnic and sectarian violence sweeping across several Arab countries could lead to the 'destruction' of the Muslim world."[38] Egypt, Bahrain, Iraq, Lebanon, and Pakistan all have had severe outbreaks of sectarian violence between Shia and Sunni, and in Egypt, thirty Coptic churches have been burned in attacks on Christian minority communities.[39] In Myanmar, where conflict has long been suppressed by an authoritarian regime, the process of democratization is being marred by this sectarian violence. Since 2012,

> growing tensions have left more than 250,000 people displaced and more than 200 dead. Most were Muslims living in the western Rakhine state that borders Bangladesh.
>
> Anti-Muslim sentiment has risen, stoked by a radical Buddhist movement whose roots have deepened in the country, leaving many Muslims – 5% of this predominantly Buddhist country – feeling isolated and vulnerable.[40]

Unfortunately, these examples are a few among many that are affecting a broad geographic area ranging from Africa to Asia, far to the east of the conflict in Pakistan. Historically, ethnic and sectarian violence has been among the most destructive of life and property.[41] The Thirty Years War that decimated Central Europe, and was fought between Protestants and Catholics in the first half of the seventeenth century, is illustrative of the ferocity of such conflicts. It remains to see whether this destruction will last as long in the twenty-first century. But as long as this violence persists, it will contribute to and perpetuate the illicit networks of corruption, crime, and terrorism.

Climate Change

Many high-risk regions for conflict and instability are being affected significantly by climate change. This change is exacerbating conditions in which crime, corruption, and terrorism are already significant. Impacts of climate change have been identified in Latin America in both the Amazon and the Andes regions, in which there are already crime and terrorist groups present. But the impacts of climate change are not as profound or disruptive as in North and West Africa, with the spread of the Sahara and increasing desertification. In Egypt, climate change is having a serious impact on the economy and is forcing changes in agricultural practices as well as a serious reduction in available water that must provide for an ever larger population.[42] In the countries affected by the melting of the Himalayas with resultant flooding, such as Pakistan and low-lying Bangladesh, the consequences are even more severe and immediate.[43] These changes are already resulting in population displacement and are discussed in the following section on demography.

Climate change is already having major impacts on some of the most low-lying and desert areas in the world. In Pakistan, poor governance compounds the consequences of climate-related natural disasters. Despite warnings for years that the country and citizens face serious consequences from warming temperatures and flooding of the Sind River and other riverine bodies, the government agencies tasked with planning for the environment and citizen welfare have not responded in a meaningful way to these challenges.[44] Serious flooding occurred again in 2013, displacing 1 million people in the Sindh and Punjab provinces. Refugees were not helped by government officials but instead by an Islamist charity, working with the Pakistani military. This charity was reputedly linked to Lashkar-e-Taiba,[45] a terrorist organization, substituting for the state and offering emergency assistance.

These threats also exist in highly populous Bangladesh, ground zero for climate change, where even more diverse effects are detected: floods and flash floods; cyclones and storm surges; salinity intrusion; and extreme temperature and drought. This is causing death, massive citizen displacement, loss of livelihood, and massive suffering among the poor, especially women.[46] In such a precarious environment without human security and employment, where these conditions will not abate, displaced individuals will be more vulnerable to recruitment by both criminal and terrorist organizations that are already present in the region.

Climate change is contributing to the arc of instability (Nigeria, Niger, Morocco, and Algeria) that spans West and North Africa. For example, in northern Nigeria, as the Sahara has expanded, two hundred villages have been abandoned to desertification, pushing inhabitants toward urban areas in southern Nigeria or toward the Maghreb.[47] Terrorist groups such as Boko Haram are already active in northern Nigeria, and the Maghreb has its deadly entanglement of crime, corruption, and terrorism.

The effects of climate change in the Amazon and the Andes are not as acute as in Pakistan and Bangladesh, or in the Sahel and West Africa, but still promise serious stability challenges for the future. As a group of specialists have argued, in the peripheral regions of the Amazon and the Andes, an effective government presence is absent, rural livelihoods have been undermined, illicit economies have flourished, drug trafficking organizations and nonstate actors have put down deep roots, and the unregulated exploitation of natural resources and vulnerable populations continues apace. New strategies are needed to comprehensively address these sources of instability. We must account for the dislocation caused by climate change and human mobility and facilitate smart and sustainable security strategies.[48]

Demography, Migration, and Displacement of Population

Civil wars, sectarian and ethnic conflict, and climate change have forced large-scale migration and population displacement. The future augurs more refugees and human displacement. Many of the displaced find no permanent homes and reside in refugee camps or shantytowns for decades. Lacking any stability, they are preyed on by criminal networks, insurgencies, and terrorist groups. Women and girls may become victims of human trafficking, thereby enriching the coffers of the illicit actors and compliant officials. Children may be recruited as child soldiers for armed conflicts.[49]

Migration is not only caused by conflict and climate change. The previously analyzed growth of megacities is explained not only by these forces but by the long-term rural to urban migration that has occurred for centuries and has been intensified since the onset of the Industrial Revolution.[50] In many regions, especially China, this urbanization is intensifying. Conflict and crime are destabilizing the communities inhabited by migrants. This is seen in such diverse locales as the cities of Central America or the highly violent Lyari community in Karachi.[51] With continued migration, unstable urban environments will be breeding grounds for diverse forms of dirty entanglements.

Throughout the book, reference has been made to the youth bulge – locales where two-thirds of the population is under thirty. That now includes sub-Saharan Africa, southern Asia, the Middle East, and the Pacific Islands. The frustration and competition for jobs, combined with rapid urbanization and rising expectations, are seen as conducive to civil conflict.[52] The book's analysis also concludes that this phenomenon is highly criminogenic, contributing to the growth of crime, including local crime, gangs, transnational crime, and terrorism. With a youth bulge in the developing world predicted through 2050,[53] there will be ample youths available in the future to join groups of pernicious nonstate actors.

Evolution of the Components of the Dirty Entanglement

Throughout the book, we have seen the ascent and decline of diverse groups of nonstate actors. In the terrorist realm, the Red Brigade that once terrorized Italy is now part of history, and the IRA is no longer a potent terrorist organization. Instead, AQIM in North Africa, Boko Haram in Nigeria and West Africa, and AQAP have emerged as new terrorist groups. Some organized crime groups have declined in significance, such as the American mafia, whereas other groups, such as those from the Balkans, West Africa, Mexico, and Central America, are ascendant. These cycles suggest that the future may not see the same groups dominant as today but that there may be new and powerful nonstate actors that may emerge in conflict regions, locales with key geographic situations and access to potential personnel and markets. Therefore, we may expect new groups to emerge, especially in South Asia, including Pakistan and Afghanistan; Africa; Central America; Central Asia; and the Middle East. These regions have proved such incubators because there are many citizens without access to the basics of life and living in locales conducive to the operation of networks. Other locales may also prove potent suppliers of new groups.

The future will see new kinds of dirty entanglements, and among these groups, such as the recently established relationships between the criminal gangs of Central America and the drug cartels.[54] State-level conflicts do not necessarily deter business relations among nonstate actors. This is seen in the cooperation of Armenian and Azeri criminals in the markets of Russia or in the trafficking of Armenian women to Turkey. Bedouins in Gaza cooperate with criminals in Israel. The desire to make money in the illicit economy transcends long-term hostilities, and in the future, we will continue to see such strange strategic partnerships and new and possibly now unimaginable entanglements.

The involvement of some crime groups in terrorist-like behavior, and the increasing participation of terrorist groups in crime, suggest that in the future, identities may be more blurred.[55] Complicating the conceptualization of the problem is the new reality that some terrorist groups, such as Abu Sayyaf and the IRA, as previously discussed in Chapter 3, are presently more criminal than they are terrorist.[56] Therefore, we may in the future see more terrorist groups getting out of terrorism but staying involved in illicit activity. They cannot be weaned from their addiction to money deriving from crime.

The efforts to target criminal and terrorist kingpins, as discussed more in the section on strategy, are often proved counterproductive, thereby creating a new generation of crime and terror groups. Instead of decapitating a group and leaving it without leadership, it is often having the opposite effect, allowing the criminal organization to operate like the hydra of myth and have two heads replace each that was removed.[57] Therefore, the focus on targeting leaders has the unintended consequence of providing promotion opportunities for the most motivated and violent subordinates.[58] Proliferation of groups in some regions may be anticipated in the future, or hierarchical realignments might make the group even more effective. While each of these groups may not be as potent as the larger group that was targeted, strategic partnerships among groups and corrupt officials may make them leaner, meaner, and more effective. In contrast, in some regions, we may see consolidation or integration of illicit networks to facilitate illicit trade, thereby allowing economies of scale.

Corruption proves an enduring enabler of crime and terrorism. Although the Arab Spring initially began in Tunisia with outrage against corruption, it has not led to a demise of corruption. Rather, conversely, the 2013 Transparency International Corruption Perception index revealed that the problems of corruption in most Arab countries have worsened since their 2011 revolutions.[59] The intractability of corruption is more pervasive. In Colombia, where great strides have been made against both criminal and terrorist groups and the president has made combating corruption a priority, corruption is perceived to have worsened in the country.[60] Therefore, corruption in the future shows no signs of diminishing, even where there is strong popular sentiment against it. It will continue to be a key element of the deadly entanglement.

Technological Change

Criminals, terrorists, and corrupt officials have not only shown the capacity to keep up with technological change but some are at the forefront of its use and acquisition. In 2012, the U.S. federal government concluded a two-year investigation titled Operation Adam Bomb that infiltrated an "on-line narcotics market place – known as 'The Farmer's Market' – which sold a variety of controlled substances to approximately 3,000 customers in 34 countries and 50 states . . . this drug trafficking organization ('DTO') attempted to operate online in secrecy, utilizing the TOR network, IP anonymizers, and covert currency transactions; but investigators were able to infiltrate the DTO and its technology during the course of the investigation."[61]

With TOR, users are able to completely hide the IP addresses of websites and electronic mail communications, thus permitting the spread of information secretly across a range of computers. TOR has been particularly exploited by drug traffickers but can be used for secrecy within a distributed computer network. "The Silk Road," an illicit marketplace that operated using TOR, had grown significantly in recent years, until its shutdown by the FBI in October 2013.[62] "A June 2013 crawl of Silk Road revealed that this black market boasted at least 1,239 active vendors selling at any given moment," double the number counted in August 2012,[63] at which time this network was already conducting $15 million in business annually.[64]

Payments in The Silk Road are made through bitcoin, a highly controversial system of financial payments that is not tied to any national currency. Bitcoin is a virtual currency that provides terrorists and criminals the possibility to launder and transfer funds with anonymity. Within the bitcoin system, tokens are sent electronically between buyers and sellers in exchange for goods or services.[65] Money can be moved rapidly and is not easily traceable, except with penetration of the network, as occurred in Operation Adam Bomb.

Another 2013 case reveals the enormous sums that can be sent virtually through the Internet. The Liberty Reserve case, prosecuted in the United States, disclosed a $6 billion online operation that was "a central hub for criminals trafficking in everything from stolen identities to child pornography."[66] This case involving virtual currency allowed money to be moved only by indicating name, address, and date of birth.[67]

The future will provide even more means of executing financial transfers that are not readily traceable. Apart from the long-established system of underground banking that has been modernized through such innovations as text messaging, the international community will find it more difficult to discover payments made by cell phones and other forms of mobile payments, including e-payments.[68] Bribe payers in Kenya have already been making their payments through mobile phone–based technology, like M-Pesa and Sokotele, for several years.[69] Following the money that is a key tool to counter corruption, crime, and terrorism will increasingly require tech savvy to counter the powerful and financially cunning nonstate actors.

What Can Be Done?

Dirty entanglements will be major determinants of global, regional, and national stability in the future. We need a whole reconceptualization of the international community's response to the problem. The present strategy has contributed to the failures evident in Iraq and Afghanistan. We need to see the combined challenges of crime, corruption, and terrorism not through predefined and stovepiped categories but in terms of the existing reality. We need to see these as interlinked problems. Although corruption can stand alone, neither transnational crime nor terrorism can function without corruption.

Success in countering the influence of potent nonstate actors who corrupt and/or infiltrate state office will be limited, as the previously identified trends will be more powerful determinants than any countermeasures.[70] Despite the investment of billions of dollars worldwide, and the loss of thousands of lives in combating these phenomena, societies around the globe have not been able to eliminate these new nonstate threats. There are no ready technological fixes nor easily identified enemies that can be defeated by military action. The complexity of the "three-body problem" (corruption, crime, and terrorism) suggests that there are no easy or quick strategies to counter their ascendency. Yet the longer one waits to address these entanglements, the more likely it is that they will escalate out of control.

The global community's present successes are inherently limited, as we are addressing a twenty-first-century problem with tools and policies of the nineteenth and twentieth centuries. For example, we continue to adhere to structures of the past, like state-based legal systems, in a world where borders have less meaning. We continue to use institutions, like the prison, even though, thanks to corruption and technology, penal institutions have become the corporate headquarters for many criminals and terrorists in different regions of the world.

The best that has been achieved, as will be discussed, is to reverse the retreat of the state, increase transparency and accountability, and reduce victimization, including lower level of homicides and other forms of violence and diminished civil conflict. Such successes can be achieved only with diverse elements of society working together. Notable progress has been achieved in Colombia by using a *whole-of-society perspective,* bringing together government, civil society, the business community, active investigative journalists, academics, and researchers. Citizens have assumed coresponsibility for the fate of their society along with the state.[71] But these gains have not been without their costs – serious alleged human rights violations and the possible displacement of these problems to the nearby vulnerable states of Central America.[72]

To address deadly entanglement more successfully, the international community needs to (1) develop an accurate conceptualization of the problem evaluated by ongoing serious and independent research; (2) develop a whole-of-society perspective to counter crime, corruption, and terrorism; (3) develop a counterstrategy that employs a more financially based perspective and involves the business community and consumers; (4) develop human capital, especially a greater role for women, in countering these threats; and (5) ensure that countermeasures do not compound harm.

Conceptualizing the Problem

Current security challenges are often described as a list of different forms of criminal activity or a crime-terror nexus. But the problem of crime, corruption, and terrorism-insurgency is not now conceptualized as a three-body problem. At best, most countries and international institutions still see the threat as a two-body problem, solely examining the crime-terror relationship, omitting the crucial corruption component. But even linking the two phenomena of crime and terrorism is recent, and primacy is still given by many to the terrorist part of the equation. Often the stovepiping is more extreme. The UN has its Office on Drugs and Crime and separate branches for corruption, terrorism, and transnational crime.[73] The same can be said for other multilateral bodies, such as the Organization for Security and Co-operation in Europe (OSCE) and the European Union through its Commission and its law enforcement body – Europol.[74] Similar divisions exist at the Organization of American States[75] and other regional bodies. At present, the United States has separate strategies for transnational crime and terrorism, with corruption largely absent from both.[76] These strategies are not consistent – the counterterrorism strategy largely ignores crime, but the counter transnational crime strategy sees an important link with terrorism.

Groups working on anticorruption have chosen to focus more on transparency and accountability rather than the central role of corruption to the operation of organized crime and terrorist groups. Until major international and national bodies develop and implement policies to address dirty entanglements, rather than their component parts, strategy and implementation designed to counter these phenomena are doomed from the inception.

The most egregious consequences of this stovepiping may be seen in Afghanistan. There, the United States and the forty-country coalition for too long treated the elements of crime, corruption, and terrorism as separate phenomena. High-level state corruption was ignored, as was the drug trade, when it was convenient. This tolerance of two legs of the three-body problem was justified in terms of higher policy objectives – the suppression of terrorism and al-Qaeda. The tragic consequences of trying to simplify a three-body problem into its component parts are now evident in Afghanistan, where the drug trade is undiminished, where terrorist violence is a daily reality, and which trails the world in its corruption rating in the Transparency International Corruption Perception Index, standing in last place with Somalia and North Korea.[77] These problems are not confined to Afghanistan; as the book has shown, these entanglements have serious consequences far from their initial point of contact in Afghanistan.

More Profound and Independent Analysis

The Cold War inspired significant investment in education and training, not only in the United States but globally. The Soviet Union, the other side of the superpower conflict, spent significantly funding education for students from the developing world whom it sought to influence. In both the USSR and the United States, academic and government specialists were nurtured through investment in language, regional training, and research centers from the 1950s through the 1980s. Many of these centers established in the Cold War era produced researchers, policy makers, and academicians capable of tackling the diverse problems that this superpower conflict posed. This research was both culturally and historically based, with its specialists possessing in-depth knowledge of language and diverse societies.

Yet no comparable effort exists in the United States or among its allies to understand the rise of nonstate actors who pose a different, but very diverse, challenge to the contemporary order, far different from that of the superpower conflict. Functioning below the state level, they require as great, if not greater, understanding of history, geography, culture, demography, and society than in the past. Yet to counter these potent nonstate actors also requires a knowledge of networks, economics, business, and technology. This approach is far different from merely studying terrorists and insurgents or transnational criminals.

Yet investment in such research has been made on a significant scale in few places in the world. The United States has always been a leader in research and education yet has been derelict in this area. In many of its educational institutions, it continues to focus either on traditional security challenges or on terrorism as a new security challenge, ignoring or isolating the central role of transnational crime and corruption. Moreover, in this era of U.S. government cutbacks, there has been a decline in support for research, and the philanthropic community that sometimes fills the gap has failed to rise to the challenge of support training and research on nontraditional security challenges.

There is one notable exception to this trend – the distinguished Centre for Non-Traditional Security Studies at Nanyang Technological University in Singapore, which began its work in the late 1990s on these new challenges in Asia.[78] Yet this Centre does not focus on corruption, a central new security challenge. But no other university center or think tank of comparable strength and focus exists anywhere in the world to examine nontraditional challenges globally.

Without the absence of needed independent research and teaching, we are neither informing global policy makers on these issues nor training the next generation of leaders capable of addressing a future in which the state will share its role increasingly with potent nonstate actors.

Societal engagement capable of countering illicit actors requires an educated and informed citizenry at all levels. It is no wonder that terrorists have struck at hundreds of schools for girls in Pakistan or that education in rural areas of Colombia has helped reverse the influence of illicit actors in rural communities.[79]

Without citizen education, problems that were once two-body problems (crime and corruption or terrorism and corruption) develop into full-blown three-body problems, in which the possibilities of successful intervention are deeply limited because the problem has become one of greater complexity and unpredictability.

Comprehensive Strategy: Whole-of-Society Perspective

Unlike traditional adversaries of the past, deadly entanglements do not represent a single enemy, nor a conventional war for which Carl von Clausewitz could develop a grand strategy.[80] Instead, the threat to the social, political, and economic order comes from internationally linked networks that traverse the globe and connect states, businesses, and locales of diverse levels of development. Moreover, the global community is now dealing with asymmetric threats on a significant scale.

States must deal with threatening nonstate actors, who are not their symmetric opponents. Much more diverse elements of government are needed to counter these actors than just traditional military forces. But many states' integrity and capacity have been compromised by corruption; they are not capable of opposing illicit actors. Corruption is particularly acute in many states in the developing world, particularly in Africa and the Middle East, that have had their boundaries defined by colonial powers and lack any inherent integrity or citizen loyalty to state institutions that transcend the clan or the tribe.

Yet even stronger states are often not equipped to counter the challenges of nonstate actors and the network structures that facilitate their operations. States may mobilize to counter an insurgency, but they cannot counter the corruption, crime, and terrorism that have penetrated other states.

Rather than a grand strategy, the international community needs a wholistic approach. American officials assert that to address crime and terrorism, we need a whole-of-government approach integrating military, law enforcement, and financial countermeasures with development assistance.[81] But this is too narrow a response for the entanglement problem, which requires much more than a state response.

A whole-of-society approach is needed. But this requires a response from the global community, consisting of the participation of multilateral organizations, international and local business, consumers, religious and secular civil society, journalists and international online communications (which have replaced much print journalism), researchers, and educational institutions. Without the participation and cooperation of different communities outside of government forming strategic partnerships, it will prove impossible to counter the corrosive impact of the deadly entanglements.

As has been shown throughout the book, criminals, terrorists, and insurgents are often deeply embedded within their communities. They are networks that often provide employment and services in the absence of the state. Unless civil society organizes to show communities that there are different ways to have their needs served, rather than depending on illicit actors, there is not a possibility of building coalitions against the criminals and terrorists that exercise political and economic power. Civil society also needs to build resilient communities to counter the attraction of extremism.[82]

The role of civil society and communities have proven crucial in the past in countering the harms caused by corruption and pernicious nonstate actors. Religious organizations in Sicily and Italy's nationwide network of Libera comprising sixteen hundred organizations[83] have worked to combat the pernicious impact of organized crime. Secular groups, such as Transparency International, which has chapters around the world to combat corruption on the national level, have assumed a central role in combating the corruption that facilitates these illicit networks. Moreover, Transparency International develops regional alliances of member chapters to share experiences and develop strategic alliances.[84]

Central to this awareness raising are the courageous investigative journalists, such as those of the Organized Crime and Corruption Reporting Project, the International Consortium of Investigative Journalists, and the Global Investigative Journalism Network.[85] Through print, online media, television, and radio, they communicate to the public around the world the costs of accepting and being complicit in such destructive behavior.

With a whole-of-society approach, the state is more likely to be accountable and provide a functioning legal and justice system. Moreover, efforts to prevent recruitment into diverse illicit networks, including criminal and terrorist groups, and promotion of disengagement from crime and terrorism may have greater chance of success.

As was discussed previously, hostility to corruption is an important recruiting tool for terrorists, and the services provided by criminals and terrorists, in the face of a corrupt state, do much to blunt citizen opposition to non-state actors' deployment of violence and intimidation. With a whole-of-society approach, citizens may not be dependent on criminals and terrorists for services, and citizen mobilization against corruption may reduce antipathy toward the state. Instead, citizen engagement may promote the reassertion of the state and its capacity to serve citizens' needs. It may reverse the retreat of the state.

If a society is engaged in countering the dirty entanglements, the government may engage in policies that might not otherwise be acceptable to the citizenry. For example, it may be possible to promote negotiation with a weakened terrorist organization, such as has been seen with the FARC in Colombia, or to negotiate the release of terrorists from prison, as occurred in Israel.[86] The boundaries of action are expanded in ways that would not otherwise be foreseen.

A Financial Approach to Crime and Terrorism: Involving Business and Consumers

There are other important nonstate actors than illicit ones. As Susan Strange wrote in *The Retreat of the State*, multinational corporations are part of the new global power structures.[87] Global corporations in international trade, production, or finance can serve as either *key facilitators* or *important combatants* of dirty entanglements. Banks, wire transfer businesses, and other financial service companies have been shown to be important facilitators of money laundering by crime and terrorist groups. Local, regional, and multinational businesses engaged in trade, real estate, and production have also facilitated the entry of dirty money into the legitimate economy.[88] Yet international corporations can be victims of illicit trade, diversion of their products, and credit card fraud. But, all too often, credit card companies and banks write off credit card losses as just a cost of doing business rather than investigating the terrorists and criminals who commit these crimes.[89] Therefore, a whole-of-society approach requires a much more financially sophisticated perspective: one that follows the money trails and ensures that multinational and smaller businesses are not facilitators for illicit actors.

A business perspective requires going after the criminal money much more aggressively.[90] Disrupting crime activity is an important, less violent, and less costly way to disrupt terrorism than military strategies but is not sufficiently prioritized in counterterrorism strategies. The Beslan attack may have been less likely if its global financial support network had been curtailed earlier. The In Amenas attack might not have been feasible if large-scale payments had not been made by foreign governments and companies to release kidnapping victims of AQIM, and the Taliban might not have reasserted themselves so forcefully in Afghanistan if they had not benefited from large-scale extortion from foreign aid deliverers, development, and military contractors.

Trade-based money laundering has allowed, and is still facilitating, the transfer of large sums of money to criminal and terrorist groups. The black peso exchange allowed Colombian drug traffickers to launder their money through consumer goods, as they purchased large quantities of household appliances, such as washing machines and refrigerators, from American manufacturers, until stopped by the American government in 2000.[91] A large used car market exists between the United States and West Africa that has helped enrich Hezbollah.[92] Trade in natural resources is also key to sustaining crime and terrorist groups. Illustrative of this is the tungsten mine in Tiger Hill, Colombia, controlled and operated by the FARC, or trade in minerals, timber, and wildlife that keeps armed groups in the Democratic Republic of the Congo, al-Shabaab, and Jundullah in Africa afloat.[93] Following the money flows, particularly linked to commodities, not only limits the profits of crime, terrorism, and corruption but also exposes the supply chains that are crucial to understanding the operation of networks.

Businesses can also be an important part of the solution. It is crucial that they assume a larger role and use their resources and skills to counter the challenges of dirty entanglements. It is not just in society's interest but in their commercial interest, because if they do not help address the dirty entanglements, societies will decay and undermine the businesses' sustainability.

Businesses can work with government to help identify illicit activity and suspicious transactions. Moreover, some businesses have an interest in engaging in strategic partnerships, not only with government, but also with the research community, to understand and counter the illicit trade that undermines their corporate reputations and harms international security.

Many companies have vast insights and comprehensive data to share on the functioning of illicit global networks, as they face counterfeiting of their goods and diversion of their products, as discussed in Chapter 7. Therefore, they are paying increasing attention to the security of their supply chains. Producers must not be the only ones held responsible for the integrity of their products, which travel long distances globally from production to markets. Transporters and distributors must also assume more responsibility for the security of supply chains of goods in transit. Consumers must be much more vigilant in choosing their purchases and understand that perceived bargains may not only harm themselves but help perpetuate the crime and terrorism that kill innocent civilians.

Much more needs to be done to understand negative entrepreneurship, at which criminals and terrorists excel.[94] In conflict and postconflict regions, in the absence of legitimate businesses, there is often extensive criminal and illicit trade in such diverse commodities as natural resources, counterfeit goods, and narcotics. The entrepreneurs who engage in this destructive trade must be identified as entrepreneurs who destroy the ecosystem for honest business.

In Colombia, the government has recently made great efforts to counter the money laundering of the criminal and terrorist organizations from their country and have been able to confiscate more than $1.5 billion in the last three years. The Financial Intelligence Unit of Colombia (UAIF Colombia), by taking a wholistic approach that addresses all three components of the deadly entanglement in a single investigation, has secured large amounts for the state. In one investigation alone, and by receiving international cooperation as well as assistance from the attorney general, the UAIF Colombia was able to freeze $528 million in assets of a total of $790 million identified in many different sectors of the economy. The Colombian success has lessons for others on the need for international cooperation, a focus on key facilitators, and a focus on all the elements of the dirty entanglement simultaneously.[95]

The Colombian anti–money laundering body engages in civil education, to explain that products purchased with laundered money are only initially cheaper. The long-term costs are the decline of healthy competition and the driving out of healthy entrepreneurship.[96] Therefore, consumer strategies and strategies to counter negative entrepreneurship are key in addressing dirty entanglements.

Human Capital and Greater Role for Women

Development of human capital is crucial, whether it is by training the next generation at schools and universities, equipping members of civil society with the capacity to lead, or training writers in the skills to conduct effective investigative journalism. But the greatest impact that can be made on dirty entanglements through enlarging human capital is to educate and mobilize women.

As previously mentioned in discussions of education, the Taliban have particularly targeted schools for girls. This violence has resulted in school closings or the total destruction of schools through bomb attacks. They have made parents reluctant to send their girls to school and girls fearful of obtaining an education.[97] The impact of this violence is more than just the assertion of the Taliban's particular view of Islam. It denies girls a future and undermines their capacity to educate the next generation or be forces to counter the spread of extremism in their society.

The previous analysis of illicit actors reveals that the preponderance of participants in illicit groups – both criminal and terrorist – are men. Women are significantly underrepresented in groups of nonstate actors, and when they do belong, they are rarely decision makers.[98] In the corruption arena, international research reveals that women are not only less likely to participate in bribery but are also less likely to condone such behavior. In some locales, women's lesser power may explain their reduced corruption, but there are striking differences of women in their tolerance of corruption in recorded surveys.[99]

Moreover, women in many parts of the world have been key forces in combating crime, terrorism, and corruption. Not only is the chair of Transparency International, Huguette Labelle, a woman, but many of its most successful chapters in different regions of the world are headed by women.[100] Women have assumed a key role in opposing criminal activity through participation in anti–organized crime nongovernmental organizations, such as Libera in Italy, and through their involvement in fighting human trafficking.[101] Women in many regions are peacemakers and can help counter the force of terrorists. In Nigeria, it has been suggested that women could play a more active role in engaging with Boko Haram.[102] The organization Sisters against Violent Extremism (SAVE), founded in the late 1990s, works in many regions of the world to counter terrorist violence.[103] By facilitating a greater role for women in countering crime, corruption, and terrorism, much more might be done to reduce the harm of dirty entanglements.

Containing the Harm of Countermeasures

One of the fundamental medical principles is the Hippocratic Oath, which states that a doctor should first "do no harm."[104] But when many policies are introduced to counter the problems of crime, corruption, and terrorism, this medical principle is not applied. It comes from a different discipline than the traditional military, law enforcement, and economic policies used to attack these challenges. As the book's analysis has suggested, these great challenges to human, political, and economic security force us to think of and apply principles that are outside the usual tools of government. The concepts of medicine, physics, and many other disciplines can provide us important guidance.

Therefore, as we seek to counter the presently pervasive problems of crime, corruption, and terrorism, strategies must be considered that do not compound existing harm. In thinking through harmful countermeasures, a few, particularly associated with American policy, are given as illustrations.

The U.S. government has relied heavily on drones to attack terrorists who cannot be reached through land-based attacks. Although this may seem to be politically expedient at the moment, such a high-technology military approach may prove countereffective to terrorism in the long term. As Audrey Kurth Cronin has written, "although they can protect the American people from attacks in the short term, they are not helping to defeat al Qaeda, and they may be creating sworn enemies out of a sea of local insurgents. It would be a mistake to embrace killer drones as the centerpiece of U.S. counterterrorism."[105]

The excessive reliance on technology, rather than a whole-of-society approach, has contributed to serious conflicts with the U.S. government's traditional allies. In the name of fighting terrorism and enhancing security, the United States launched an enormous data collection effort to collect telephone records and access the records of millions of users on Yahoo and Google.

This unauthorized invasion of privacy, extending even to the telephone calls of foreign leaders, has caused a major rupture with Brazil and with such traditional allies as France and Germany.[106] The overreliance on technology as a "cure" for the new security challenges has caused serious harm to national and international security.

Another mistaken, but lower-technology, policy has caused significant harm to the southern neighbor of the United States. A federal gun operation run by the Alcohol, Tobacco, and Firearms Administration, called Fast and Furious, moved weapons from the United States to Mexico, allowing the guns to pass into the hands of gun smugglers. The intent of the operation was to trace the weapons to the drug cartels. But the operation resulted in the fatal shooting of a U.S. border patrol agent in December 2010 and the hostility of the Mexican government and people as more deadly weapons wound up in the hands of serious criminals, exacerbating the already violent criminal situation in Mexico.[107]

The United States has developed a kingpin strategy, as mentioned in Chapter 6, to target the heads of transnational criminal organizations and terrorists making their money, often from large-scale drug trade. But much more than a kingpin strategy is needed, because these individuals are embedded in networks, and the networks can often replace the former chief, thereby providing upward movement for subordinates. Or this strategy can provide room for the entry of competitors into this environment. This has been seen in Colombia repeatedly. Therefore, a comprehensive strategy requires targeting not only lead figures but entire organizations, their diversified products, and also their supply chains, financial networks and resources, and facilitators.

Where Do We Go From Here?

Dirty entanglements are unfortunately on a growth trajectory. The forces contributing to their rise – including increased populations without a future, growing income inequality, increased migration and displacement, poor governance, absence of the rule of law, continuing civil unrest and conflict, and climate change – show no signs of abating.

These dirty entanglements are not just problems of fragile states, the less developed world, or the global south. From the very first page, this book has shown that these are mutually shared problems. In the globalized world, we face these problems together, and in our interlinked financial systems, we all share responsibility for their growth. If there were not havens in the developed world for kleptocrats' money, there might be more chances for youth in the developing world. If governments and multinational companies did not pay crime and terrorist groups to release their citizens, these potent nonstate actors would not have working capital.

In our highly interconnected world, diverse communities must work together to counter the scourge of corruption, crime, and terrorism. Unfortunately, until now, without a whole-of-society perspective, we have made little progress globally against the dirty entanglements. Many parts of the world are already deeply victimized by these problems. If we are to bring societies back, transnational networks of diverse communities must work relentlessly to reverse their influence. This will require courage, personal sacrifice, and sustained engagement that transcend a military, technology, and law enforcement response, requiring greater involvement of business and citizens. Any signs of successes should not be met by complacency, as elements of the dirty entanglements quickly reassert themselves. The alternatives to coordinated and sustained action are grim – civil unrest, violence, and human insecurity for many of the planet's inhabitants. Our ineffective action today leaves an unfortunate and deadly legacy for future generations.

Notes

1. "What S.P.E.C.T.R.E. Means!," http://www.youtube.com/watch?v=9BhDeyscOmo.
2. United Nations, "Statement by the President of the Security Council," S/PRST/2013/1, January 15, 2013, http://www.securitycouncilreport.org/atf/cf/%7B65BFCF9B-6D27-4E9C-8CD3-CF6E4FF96FF9%7D/s_prst_2013_1.pdf.
3. "'Nothing Can Justify Terrorism – Ever,' Says Secretary-General, as Security Council Hears from Some 50 Speakers in Day-Long Debate," Security Council SC/10882, January 15, 2013, http://www.un.org/News/Press/docs/2013/sc10882.doc.htm.
4. Michael Miklaucic and Jacqueline Brewer, eds., *Convergence: Illicit Networks and National Security in the Age of Globalization* (Washington, DC: National Defense University Press, 2013), is an attempt to advance the discussion on the convergence of different forms of crime and terrorism.
5. "Strategy to Combat Transnational Organized Crime," July 25, 2011, http://www.whitehouse.gov/administration/eop/nsc/transnational-crime.
6. "How the World Bank Deals with Fraud and Corruption in Its Projects," July 1, 2003, http://www.brettonwoodsproject.org/2003/07/art-16571/.
7. Gretchen Peters, "Crime and Insurgency in the Tribal Areas of Afghanistan and Pakistan," October, 2012, 1, http://www.ctc.usma.edu/posts/crime-and-insurgency-in-the-tribal-areas-of-afghanistan-and-pakistan.
8. U.S. Department of Justice, "Member of Afghan Taliban Sentenced to Life in Prison in Nation's First Conviction on Narco-terror Charges," December 22, 2008, http://www.justice.gov/opa/pr/2008/December/08-crm-1145.html.
9. http://www.state.gov/j/ct/rls/crt/2011/195555.htm.
10. Peter Andreas, *Smuggling Nation: How Illicit Trade Made America* (New York: Oxford University Press, 2013).
11. Nicholas D. Kristof, "Qaeda Rebels Are Gone. Death Isn't," *New York Times*, July 6, 2013, http://www.nytimes.com/2013/07/07/opinion/sunday/kristof-qaeda-rebels-are-gone-death-isnt.html?ref=nicholasdkristof&_r=1&.
12. Liz Sly, "Al-Qaeda's Iraq Affiliate Expands Presence in Syria," *Washington Post*, August 13, 2013, A1, A8.

13. Jodi Rudoren, "Pressure Rises on Hamas as Patrons' Support Fades," *New York Times*, August 24, 2013, A1.

14. The United States has named Hamas as a terrorist organization, "Counterterrorism Calendar 2013: Hamas," http://www.nctc.gov/site/groups/hamas .html; as has the European Union, "Freezing Funds: List of Terrorists and Terrorist Groups," http://europa.eu/legislation_summaries/justice_freedom_security/ fight_against_terrorism/l33208_en.htm; as have other developed countries.

15. Mujtaba Rathore, Masror Hausen, Amir Rana, Safdar Sial, and Abdul Mateen, "Profile: Profiling the Violence in Karachi," *Conflict and Peace Studies* 2, no. 3 (2009): 8–9, http://san-pips.com/download.php?f=161.pdf.

16. Huma Yusuf, "The Karachi Question: Ethnicity or Extremism?," *Daily Dawn*, April 30, 2009, http://archives.dawn.com/archives/66967. The author appreciates Nazia Hussain's insights in this section.

17. Hari Kumar and Ellen Barry, "Leader of Terrorist Group Is Arrested, India Says," *New York Times*, August 29, 2013, http://www.nytimes.com/2013/08/30/world/ asia/leader-of-terrorist-group-is-arrested-india-says.html.

18. Damien Cave, "These Walls Speak, Recalling Victims of Violence," *New York Times*, August 22, 2013, http://www.nytimes.com/2013/08/23/world/americas/ these-walls-speak-recalling-victims-of-violence.html.

19. Steven A. Cook, "Egypt by Egyptians: Is This the End of an Era for the Muslim Brotherhood?," August 22, 2013, http://blogs.cfr.org/cook/2013/08/22/ egypt-by-egyptians-is-this-the-end-of-an-era-for-the-muslim-brotherhood/.

20. United Nations Department of Economic and Social Affairs, Population Division, *World Urbanization Prospects: The 2011 Revision: Highlights* (New York: United Nations, 2012), 5–10, http://esa.un.org/unup/pdf/WUP2011_Highlights.pdf.

21. Ibid.

22. Ian Johnson, "China's Great Uprooting: Moving 250 Million into Cities," *New York Times*, June 15, 2013, http://www.nytimes.com/2013/06/16/world/asia/ chinas-great-uprooting-moving-250-million-into-cities.html.

23. Joel Kotkin, "The Problem with Megacities," *Forbes*, April 4, 2011, http://www .forbes.com/sites/megacities/2011/04/04/the-problem-with-megacities/.

24. James Holston, *Insurgent Citizenship: Disjunctions of Democracy and Modernity in Brazil* (Princeton, NJ: Princeton University Press, 2008), 301.

25. Abeeb Olufemi Salaam, "Motivations for Gang Membership in Lagos, Nigeria: Challenge and Resilience," *Journal of Adolescent Research* 26, no. 6 (2011): 701– 26.

26. William H. Panning, "Inequality, Social Comparison and Relative Deprivation," *American Political Science Review* 77, no. 2 (1983): 323–29.

27. World Economic Forum, "Global Risks," http://www.weforum.org/issues/ global-risks.

28. Marguerite Cawley, "Mexico Gun Trafficking Benefits Nearly 50% US Dealers: Study," March 20, 2013, http://www.insightcrime.org/news-briefs/san-diego- university-study-mexico-gun-trafficking-us.

29. Carin Zissis, "Terror Groups in India," November 27, 2008, http://www.cfr.org/ india/terror-groups-india/p12773.

30. Ibid.

31. Illustrative of this are Dan Wisniewski, "Karimov: World Can Learn from Uzbeks," January 22, 2013, http://www.rferl.org/content/uzbekistan-karimov-fifa-

award/24880406.html; "Video: *Corruption in Azerbaijan*," March 22, 2013, https://reportingproject.net/occrp/index.php/en/ccwatch/52-ccwatch-video/1894-video-corruption-in-azerbaijan-.

32. Camino Kavanagh, "Getting Smart and Scaling Up: Responding to the Impact of Organized Crime on Governance in Developing Countries," June 7, 2013, http://cic.nyu.edu/content/responding-impact-organized-crime-governance-developing-countries.

33. Global Conflict Trends, Figure 4, updated on July 3, 2013, http://www.systemicpeace.org/conflict.htm.

34. Karen Ballentine and Jake Sherman, eds., *The Political Economy of Armed Conflict: Beyond Greed and Grievance* (Boulder, CO: Lynn Rienner, 2003).

35. Steven S. Dudley, "Drug Trafficking Organizations in Central America: Transportistas, Mexican Cartels and Maras," Working Paper Series on U.S.-Mexico Security Collaboration, Woodrow Wilson International Center for Scholars and University of San Diego Trans-Border Institute, 2010, http://www.stevendudley.com/.

36. Jeffrey Gettelman, "Africa's Forever Wars: Why the Continent's Conflicts Never End," March/April 2010, http://www.foreignpolicy.com/articles/2010/02/22/africas_forever_wars.

37. U.S. State Department, *Country Reports on Terrorism 2012*, May 2013, http://www.state.gov/j/ct/.

38. Jamal Halaby, "King of Jordan Abdullah II: Sectarian Violence Could Destroy Muslim World," *Huffington Post*, August 20, 2013, http://www.huffingtonpost.com/2013/08/21/king-jordan-sectarian-violence-destroy-muslim-world_n_3784937.html.

39. Ibid. Haida Saad and Ben Hubbard, "Bombings Strike Lebanon, as Mosques Are Targeted in Growing Violence," *New York Times*, August 23, 2013, http://www.nytimes.com/2013/08/24/world/middleeast/lebanon-bomb-attacks.html; Richard Galpin, "Pakistan Grapples with Rising Tide of Extremist Violence," July 15, 2013, http://www.bbc.co.uk/news/world-asia-23319254; D. Parvaz, "Egypt's Copts Reel from Sectarian Violence: More Than 30 Christian Churches Have Been Burned Recently, Further Stoking Instability in Politically Polarized Egypt," August 20, 2013, http://www.aljazeera.com/indepth/features/2013/08/201382017221869295.html.

40. Shibani Mahtani and Myo Myo, "Myanmar Reports Latest Incident of Sectarian Conflict: No Injuries, Deaths Reported," *Wall Street Journal*, August 25, 2013, http://online.wsj.com/article/SB10001424127887324591204579034934065058304.htm.

41. C. V. Wedgwood, *The Thirty Years War* (London: Methuen, 1981).

42. Louise Sarant, "Climate Change and Water Mismanagement Parch Egypt," *Egypt Independent*, February 26, 2013, http://www.egyptindependent.com/news/climate-change-and-water-mismanagement-parch-egypt; Al-Masry Al-Youm, "Climate Change Forcing Egypt to Change Agricultural Practices," *Egypt Independent*, November 4, 2013, http://www.egyptindependent.com/news/climate-change-forcing-egypt-change-agriculture-practices; "Climate Change Has Devastating Effect on the Egyptian Economy, Says FEMISE Study," October 16, 2013, http://www.enpi-info.eu/medportal/news/latest/34840/Climate-change-has-devastating-effect-on-the-Egyptian-economy,-says-FEMISE-study.

43. Max Hoffman and Ana I. Grigera, "Climate Change, Migration, and Conflict in the Amazon and the Andes: Rising Tensions and Policing Options in South America," February 2013, 1, http://www.scribd.com/doc/127202017/Climate-Change-Migration-and-Conflict-in-the-Amazon-and-the-Andes.

44. "Climate Change Brings Another Flood Onslaught in Pakistan," *Daily Times*, August 19, 2013, http://www.dailytimes.com.pk/?page=2013\08\19\story_19-8-2013_pg7_8.

45. "Pakistani Floods: Nearly One Million Affected," August 24, 2013, http://www.bbc.co.uk/news/world-asia-23829689. The video shows the Islamist organization providing assistance.

46. Anne-Katrien Denissen, "Climate Change and Its Impact on Bangladesh," http://www.ncdo.nl/artikel/climate-change-its-impacts-bangladesh; also see the work of the Bangladesh Institute of Peace and Security Studies and its director, Major General (Ret.) ANM Muniruzzaman, speaking on the impact of climate change, http://www.linktv.org/video/7397/bangladesh-an-uncertain-future.

47. Michael Werz and Laura Cooley, "Climate Change, Migration, and Conflict in Northwest Africa: Rising Dangers and Policy Options across the Arc of Tension," Center for American Progress and Heinich Böll Stiftung, April 2012, 4–5, http://www.scribd.com/doc/88737361/Climate-Change-Migration-and-Conflict-in-Northwest-Africa.

48. Hoffman and Grigera, "Climate Change, Migration, and Conflict in the Amazon and the Andes."

49. "Children and Armed Conflict," http://childrenandarmedconflict.un.org/effects-of-conflict/the-most-grave-violations/child-soldiers/.

50. Louise I. Shelley, *Crime and Modernization: The Impact of Industrialization and Urbanization on Crime* (Carbondale: Southern Illinois University Press, 1981), 16–37.

51. Bailey Cahill, "MQM Party Chief Calls for Military Administration in Karachi," AfPak Daily Brief, August 27, 2013, http://afpak.foreignpolicy.com/posts/2013/08/27/mqm_party_chief_calls_for_military_administration_in_karachi; Cynthia J. Arnson, Eric L. Olson, Steven S. Dudley, James Bosworth, Douglas Farah, and Julie López, "Organized Crime in Central America: The Northern Triangle," Wilson Center Reports on the Americas 29, November 2011, http://www.wilsoncenter.org/node/19779.

52. Lionel Beehner, "The Effects of 'Youth Bulge' on Civil Conflict," April 27, 2007, http://www.cfr.org/world/effects-youth-bulge-civil-conflicts/p13093; Jack A. Goldstone, Eric P. Kaufmann, and Monica Duffy Toft, eds., *Political Demography: How Population Changes Are Reshaping International Security and National Politics* (New York: Oxford University Press, 2012).

53. Justin Yifu Lin, "Youth Bulge: A Demographic Dividend or a Demographic Bomb in Developing Countries?," January 5, 2012, http://blogs.worldbank.org/developmenttalk/youth-bulge-a-demographic-dividend-or-a-demographic-bomb-in-developing-countries.

54. Dudley, "Drug Trafficking Organizations in Central America."

55. Mark S. Hamm, *Terrorism as Crime from Oklahoma City to Al-Qaeda and Beyond* (New York: New York University Press, 2007); Jennifer L. Hesterman, *The Terrorist-Criminal Nexus: An Alliance of International Drug Cartels, Organized Crime, and Terror Groups* (Boca Raton, FL: CRC Press, 2013).

56. Audrey Cronin, *How Terrorism Ends: Understanding the Decline and Demise of Terrorist Campaigns* (Princeton, NJ: Princeton University Press, 2009), 149, 153; Glen Frankel, "Police Pin Bank Heist on IRA," *Washington Post*, January 8, 2005, A1; see John Horgan and Max Taylor, "Playing the 'Green Card': Financing the Provisional IRA: Part I," *Terrorism and Political Violence* 11, no. 2 (1999): 1–38.

57. "Hydra," http://www.theoi.com/Ther/DrakonHydra.html. This should not be confused with the concept used in reference to terrorism by Marvel comicbooks, http://en.wikipedia.org/wiki/HYDRA.

58. Keegan Hamilton, "Why Killing Kingpins Won't Stop Mexico's Drug Cartels," *The Atlantic*, February 27, 2013, http://www.theatlantic.com/international/archive/2013/02/why-killing-kingpins-wont-stop-mexicos-drug-cartels/273558/.

59. "Corruption Worsens in Arab Countries: Poll," July 10, 2013, http://www.hurriyetdailynews.com/corruption-worsens-in-arabic-countries-poll.aspx?pageID=238&nID=50370&NewsCatID=344.

60. 2013 Global Corruption Barometer for Colombia, 2013, in *Briefing Book: Seminar Scenarios for Peace: Transparency and Anticorruption*, Transparencia por Colombia 15th Anniversary, September 5, 2013; Paula Delgado Kling, "Colombia among Countries with Highest Rates of Corruption," July 25, 2013, http://talkingaboutcolombia.com/2013/07/25/transparency-international-colombia-among-countries-with-highest-rate-of-corruption/.

61. U.S. Department of Justice, U.S. Attorney's Office for Central District of California, "Creators and Operators of On-line Narcotics Marketplace on the TOR Network Arrested on First of Its Kind Federal Indictment Charging Drug Trafficking in 34 Countries and 50 States," April 16, 2012, http://www.justice.gov/usao/cac/Pressroom/2012/045.html.

62. Nicholas Christin, "Traveling the Silk Road: A Measurement Analysis of a Large Anonymous Online Marketplace," July 30, 2012, revised November 28, 2012, http://www.cylab.cmu.edu%2Ffiles%2Fpdf; Andy Greenberg, "Lessons from Silk Road: Competing Online Drug Site Shuts Down after Security Breach," *Forbes*, October 18, 2013, http://www.forbes.com/sites/ryanmac/2013/10/17/lessons-from-silk-road-competing-online-drug-site-shuts-down-after-security-breach/.

63. Patrick Howell O'Neill, "How Big Is the Internet's Most Notorious Black Market," July 30, 2013, http://www.dailydot.com/business/silk-road-monthly-sales-black-market-drugs-study/.

64. Ibid.

65. Matt Clinch, "Bitcoin Gets the FBI, Homeland Treatment," August 15, 2013, http://www.cnbc.com/id/100964182; Maria Bustillos, "The Bitcoin Boom," *New Yorker*, April 2, 2013, http://www.newyorker.com/online/blogs/elements/2013/04/the-future-of-bitcoin.html.

66. Marc Santos, William K. Rashbaum, and Nicole Perlroth, "Online Currency Exchange Accused of Laundering $6 Billion," *New York Times*, May 28, 2013, http://www.nytimes.com/2013/05/29/nyregion/liberty-reserve-operators-accused-of-money-laundering.html.

67. Ibid.

68. Josh Meyer, "How Mobile Payments Might Be the Global Money-Laundering Machine Criminals Have Dreamed About," June 17, 2013, http://qz.com/

94570/how-mobile-payments-might-be-the-global-money-laundering-machine-criminals-have-dreamed-about/.

69. "Crooked Police Go Hi-Tech in Hunt for Bribes," August 14, 2008, http://www
.nation.co.ke/News/-/1056/456426/-/tjohqg/-/index.html.

70. Illustrative of this are the high-level political associates of the criminal associations.
See the many different case studies in Luis Jorge Garay Salamanca and Eduardo
Salcedo-Albarán, *Narcotráfico, corrupción y Estados: Cómo las redes ilícitas han
reconfigurado las instituciones en Colombia, Guatemala y México* (Mexico D.F.:
Debate, 2012).

71. Elisabeth Ungar, "Opening Remarks," Seminario Escenarios para la Paz: Transparencia y Anticorrupción, September 5, 2013, http://transparenciacolombia.org
.co/images/eventos/Paz_Transparencia/agenda-seminario-tpc-21082013.pdf.

72. See the website of Human Rights Watch on Colombia, http://www.hrw.org/
americas/colombia; Michael Shifter, *Countering Criminal Violence in Central
America*, Council Special Report 64 (New York: Council on Foreign Relations,
2012).

73. The following links represent the separate offices dedicated by UNODC to these
issues: http://www.unodc.org/unodc/en/corruption/index.html?ref=menuside,
http://www.unodc.org/unodc/en/terrorism/index.html?ref=menuside, http://www
.unodc.org/unodc/en/organized-crime/index.html.

74. http://www.osce.org/what. The author has conferred with these separate offices
and spoken at OSCE conferences concerned with human trafficking and money
laundering. See the organizational structure of Europol, https://www.europol
.europa.eu/content/page/organisational-structure-157. The author also attended
the first European Police Chiefs Convention at Europol in June 2011, and organized crime and terrorism were treated separately.

75. The OAS separates drugs from terrorism. See http://www.oas.org/en/default.asp.

76. "National Strategy for Counterterrorism," June 1, 2011, http://www.whitehouse
.gov/sites/default/files/counterterrorism_strategy.pdf; "Strategy to Address Transnational Organized Crime: Addressing Converging Threats to National Security,"
July 2011, http://www.whitehouse.gov/sites/default/files/Strategy_to_Combat_
Transnational_Organized_Crime_July_2011.pdf.

77. "Corruption Index 2012 from Transparency International: Find Out How Countries Compare," *Guardian,* December 5, 2012, http://www.theguardian.com/
news/datablog/2012/dec/05/corruption-index-2012-transparency-international.

78. See the website of the Centre, which is part of the S. Rajaratnam School of International Studies. The Centre received funding from the MacArthur Foundation.
The author visited the Centre for a regional conference in 2011, http://www.rsis
.edu.sg/nts/system.asp?sid=52.

79. See the Escuela Nueva, http://www.escuelanueva.org/, and its recognition for
rural education. The author has interviewed its founder, Vicky Colbert, on the
challenges she has faced in rural areas. She received the Wise Prize in 2013 for
her work on rural education, http://www.media.wise-qatar.org/2013-wise-prize-
for-education-awarded-to-ms-vicky-colbert/Pakistan and prize; Jennifer Preston, "Malala Yousafzai, Girl Shot by Taliban, Makes Appeal at U.N.,"
July 12, 2013, http://thelede.blogs.nytimes.com/2013/07/12/video-of-malala-
yousafzai-at-u-n-calling-on-world-leaders-to-provide-education-to-every-child/.

80. Carl von Clausewitz, *On War*, ed. and trans. Michael Howard and Peter Paret (Princeton, NJ: Princeton University Press, 1989).

81. Jim Garamone, "New National Strategy Takes 'Whole-of-Government' Approach," May 27, 2010, http://www.defense.gov/news/newsarticle.aspx?id=59377.

82. Naureen Chowdhury Fink, "Countering Violent Extremism Goes Local," October 23, 2013, http://theglobalobservatory.org/analysis/606-countering-violent-extremism-goes-local.html.

83. "Libera," *Global Journal*, January 23, 2012, http://theglobaljournal.net/article/view/484/. The author has interviewed many members of Libera; see Alison Jamieson, *The Antimafia: Italy's Fight against Organized Crime* (New York: St. Martin's Press, 2000).

84. http://www.transparency.org/ discusses the major activities of the organization, but by meeting members of many chapters and discussing with headquarter members, the author has learned much about the way that successful chapters work.

85. Organized Crime and Corruption Reporting Project, https://www.reportingproject.net/; International Consortium of Investigative journalists, http://www.icij.org/; and Global Investigative Journalism Network, http://gijn.org/.

86. Isabel Kershner, "Israel Releases 26 Palestinian Prisoners to Cheers and Anguish," *New York Times*, August 13, 2013, http://www.nytimes.com/2013/08/14/world/middleeast/israel-releases-26-palestinian-prisoners-to-cheers-and-anguish.html; William Neuman, "Colombian Peace Talks Bear Fruit," *New York Times*, May 26, 2013, http://www.nytimes.com/2013/05/27/world/americas/colombian-peace-talks-bear-fruit.html.

87. Susan Strange, *The Retreat of the State: The Diffusion of Power in the World Economy* (New York: Cambridge University Press, 1996).

88. Lowell Bergman, "US Companies Tangled in Web of Drug Dollars," *New York Times*, October 10, 2000, http://www.nytimes.com/2000/10/10/us/us-companies-tangled-in-web-of-drug-dollars.html; Louise Shelley, "Money Laundering into Real Estate," in Miklaucic and Brewer, *Convergence*, 131–46.

89. Author's interviews with individuals in the credit card industry both in the United States and Europe.

90. Juan C. Zarate, *Treasury's War: The Unleashing of a New Era of Financial Warfare* (New York: Public Affairs, 2013).

91. From a Drug War special that revealed the involvement of top appliance manufacturers in laundering drug money, http://www.pbs.org/wgbh/pages/frontline/shows/drugs/special/us.html. See also the related newspaper article by the show's producer, Lowell Bergman.

92. Matthew Levitt, *Hezbollah: The Global Footprint of Lebanon's Party of God* (Washington, DC: Georgetown University Press, 2013), 259.

93. "Tungsten: From the FARC's Mine in Colombia to Global Supply Lines?," *Washington Post*, August 16, 2013, http://articles.washingtonpost.com/2013-08-16/business/41416353_1_amazon-indians-rain-forest-national-police; Monica Medina, "The White Gold of Jihad," *New York Times*, September 30, 2013, http://www.nytimes.com/2013/10/01/opinion/the-white-gold-of-jihad.html; Nir Kairon and Andrea Crosta, "Africa's White Gold of Jihad: Al Shabaab and

Conflict Ivory," Nairobi, 2011–12, http://elephantleague.org/project/africas-white-gold-of-jihad-al-shabaab-and-conflict-ivory/.

94. Zoltan Acs, Sameksha Desai, and Utz Weitzel, "A Theory of Destructive Entrepreneurship: Insights on Conflict, Post-conflict Recovery," *Journal of Conflict Resolution* 57, no. 1 (2013): 20–40.

95. Communication from the Financial Intelligence Unit of Colombia, November 2013. The largest investigation involved a criminal network of 309 people and 88 companies.

96. Interview by Skype with head of Colombian anti–money laundering agency, October 15, 2013.

97. Taha Siddiqui and Declan Walsh, "Siege by Taliban Strains Pakistani Girls' Schools," *New York Times,* July 11, 2013, http://www.nytimes.com/2013/07/12/world/asia/siege-by-taliban-strains-pakistani-girls-schools.html.

98. "Women Terrorists Today Follow Men's Ideologies: Interview with Mia Bloom," August 21, 2013, http://www.theglobalobservatory.org/interviews/563-women-terrorists-today-follow-mens-ideologies-interview-with-mia-bloom.html.

99. Omar Azfar, Stephen Knack, Anand Swamy, and Young Lee, "Gender and Corruption," Working Paper 232, University of Maryland, Center on Institutional Reform and the Informal Sector (IRIS), November 1999, http://papers.ssrn.com/sol3/papers.cfm?abstract_id=260062; Farzana Nawaz, "Gender and Corruption," Anti-corruption Research Network, http://corruptionresearchnetwork.org/resources/frontpage-articles/gender-and-corruption.

100. http://www.transparency.org/whoweare/organisation/board_of_directors/1/, as well as author interviews with several of the most active chapter heads.

101. Author interviews with female leaders of member organizations of Libera as well as extensive meetings with antitrafficking nongovernmental organizations at numerous meetings the author attended.

102. Akinola Olojo, "Engendering Counter-Terrorism in Northern Nigeria," June 24, 2013, http://www.icct.nl/publications/icct-commentaries/engendering-counter-terrorism-in-northern-nigeria.

103. See SAVE's projects, http://www.women-without-borders.org/projects/underway/.

104. http://www.nlm.nih.gov/hmd/greek/greek_oath.html.

105. Audrey Kurth Cronin, "Why Drones Fail When Tactics Drive Strategy," *Foreign Affairs,* July–August 2013, http://home.comcast.net/~lionelingram/562_Why%20Drones%20Fail%20_%20Foreign%20Affairs.pdf; see also a larger project that addresses this at the Kroc Institute at Notre Dame, Ethical, Strategic, and Legal Implications of Drone Warfare, held March 19–21, 2013, http://kroc.nd.edu/news-events/peace-policy/ethical-strategic-legal-implications-drone-warfare-1507.

106. Barton Gellman and Ashkan Soltani, "NSA Taps Yahoo, Google Links," *Washington Post,* October 31, 2013, A1, A6; Karen DeYoung and Michael Birnbaum, "NSA Surveillance Denials Are 'Implausible,' France says," *Washington Post,* October 31, 2013, A7; Anne Edgerton, "NSA Spying Allegations Put Google on Hot Seat in Brazil," October 29, 2013, http://www.bloomberg.com/news/2013-10-29/nsa-spying-allegations-put-google-on-hot-seat-in-brazil.html; Philip Oltermann, "Angela Merkel Warns US Over Surveillance in First Speech of

Third Term 'A Programme in Which the End Justifies All Means... Violates Trust,' German Chancellor Says," *The Guardian,* January 29, 2014, http://www .theguardian.com/world/2014/jan/29/angela-merkel-us-surveillance-speech-germany-chancellor.

107. For a full range of articles on this scandal, see "ATF's Fast and Furious Scandal," *LA Times,* http://www.latimes.com/news/nationworld/nation/atf-fast-furious-sg, 0,3828090.storygallery#.

Index

Abkhazia, 300
accountability, 69, 333–34
Adamov, Yevgeni, 298, 301
Afghan-Tajik border, xii, 243
Afghanistan, 6, 8, 14–15, 31, 37, 40, 46–47,
    67–69, 71, 75, 78, 80, 83–85, 103–04,
    110, 114, 116, 142–43, 146–47, 152,
    167, 174, 182–83, 186, 190, 192, 197,
    218–20, 222, 224–25, 227, 237–46,
    259, 262, 264, 275–76, 280, 284, 288,
    293, 321–22, 324, 331, 333–35,
    339
  Central Bank, 69
  corruption, 68
  Kabul, 6, 238, 241, 276
  Kabul Bank, 241
  Soviet invasion, 238–39
Africa, 4, 65, 73, 84, 100, 104–05, 110,
    114–18, 145, 152, 157, 159, 179–84,
    186–88, 201, 225, 246, 268, 272–73,
    302, 305, 308, 321, 325, 328, 331,
    336
  Central, 17, 40, 47, 75, 85, 142, 218, 225,
    237–39, 243, 245, 304, 308, 326,
    331
  Command, 7
  East, 116–18, 225, 273, 276
  North, xii, 6–7, 36–37, 46, 50–51, 71–75,
    78, 114–16, 118, 139, 143, 152, 173,
    183, 188, 194, 220–21, 234–36, 245,
    273, 295, 308, 323, 326, 329–30
  South, 225
  Sub-Saharan, 182, 330

West, 17, 33, 103, 116, 118, 138, 149, 152,
    196, 225, 230, 231, 234, 236–37,
    244–45, 272, 323
Ahmidan, Jamal, 37–38, 51. See also terrorists
Alec Station, 33
Alexander the Great, 156
al-Qaeda, 190. See also terrorist groups
al-Qaeda inspired terrorism, 37
Algeria, 1–6, 69, 71, 108, 181, 187, 190,
    235–36, 245, 321, 329
Allison, Graham, 295
alternative political power, 43
analysis
  economic, 7
  historical, 7
  political, 7
  sociological, 7
anthrax, 289, 293
antiquities, 31, 51, 259, 261–80, 304
Anwar al Awlaki, 157
A. Q. Khan, 298, 301, 305, 308
A. Q. Khan network, 18, 296–98, 302–03, 308
Arab, 7, 33, 41, 69, 72–74, 111–12, 149
Arab-Israeli conflict, 149
Arab Spring, xii, 2, 3, 6, 67, 69, 71–75, 85,
    155, 308, 324, 326–27, 331
  consequences for crime and terrorism, 73
Arabian Gulf, aka Persian Gulf, 149
Arabian Sea, 147
Arabs, 137
Archeological Institute of America, 263
Argentina, 70, 109, 138, 149–52, 194, 274
Arkan aka Željko Ražnatović, 113–14

arms, 1–4, 41–42, 46–48, 52, 64, 73, 82–84,
    103, 115, 152, 154–56, 178–80,
    193–94, 198, 220, 229, 235, 239, 261,
    270, 290, 304, 306, 323, 328
  smuggling, 52, 84, 155, 269
  trade, 42, 80, 117, 145, 151, 153, 176, 179,
    180, 220, 235, 277
art, 14, 180, 276–77
  smuggling, 14, 18, 180, 259–64, 276
Asia, 2, 8, 34, 46, 64–65, 73, 76, 78, 84, 99,
    100, 114, 116, 132, 146–47, 164, 165,
    180, 192, 205, 222, 227, 238, 239,
    243, 245, 265–66, 268, 275, 286, 290,
    305, 313, 321, 325, 328, 330–31,
    336
  Central, 17, 40, 47, 75, 85, 142, 218, 225,
    237, 238, 243, 245, 304, 308, 326,
    331
  Southeast, 82, 143, 145, 152, 181, 184,
    186, 227, 276, 302, 308, 324
asset forfeiture, 14
asymmetric threat, 11, 291, 323, 336
Atta, Mohammed, 31, 51, 77, 191,
    262
Aum Shinrikyo, 221, 289–90, 293–95
Australia, 8, 34–35, 227, 249, 290
Australian Crime Commission, 194
Austria, 3, 141, 304
authoritarian governments, 73
authoritarian leaderships, 72
authoritarianism, 6
autocracies, 74
Awami National Party, 146

Babylon, 263
Baghdad, 102
Bahrain, 328
Bakiyev, Kurmanbek, 243, 245
Baloch, 243
Balkans, 31, 40, 99, 104, 113–14, 116, 145,
    152–54, 218, 225, 265, 271–72, 302,
    331
Ba'asyir, 36. *See also* terrorists
bank robbery, 43, 109, 112, 116, 132, 175,
    180–81, 183–85, 201
bank secrecy, 13
banks, 69, 111, 133, 190, 196, 221, 229, 267,
    305, 307, 338
  failure to provide oversight, 69
Barakat, Assad Ahmad, 274
Basayev, Shamil, 39, 41, 51, 67, 145, 152,
    321. *See also* terrorists death

Belfer Center for Science and International
    Affairs, 295
Betancourt, Ingrid, 185
Belgium, 137, 190
Belize, 261
Belmokhtar, Mokhtar, 1, 3, 235, 268. *See also*
    terrorists
Benin, 237
Beslan, 39
bitcoin, 332
Black Sea, 136, 147, 302
bioterrorism, 289, 291, 293–94
black markets, 29, 152, 291, 296, 297
Black Muslims, 141
blood diamonds, 33, 181
Bogotá, Colombia, 100, 102, 229
Bollywood, 275
borders, 2
  control, 2–3, 13, 178, 198
  decline, 2, 13, 103, 333
  multiborder, 17, 115, 147–52, 157–58
Borsellino, Paolo, 102
Bosnia, 31, 114, 132, 153–54, 272. *See also*
    Bosnia-Hercegovina
Bouazizi, Mohamed, 71–72
Bout, Victor, 180, 235
Braun, Michael, 221
Brazil, 9, 16, 29, 42–46, 79, 138, 149–52,
    166, 225, 265, 274, 281, 342, 344, 350
  President Lula, 43–44
  police killings, 43
  Rio de Janeiro, 43, 325
  São Paulo, 8, 29, 42, 51, 146, 325
bribery, 68, 70–71, 105, 147, 156, 340
BRIC (Brazil, Russia, Indonesia, China), 29,
    265
Brodie, Neal, 261
Brussels, 259. *See also* Belgium
British Empire, 220
bubonic plague, 295
Bulgaria, 154
Bunn, Matthew, 301
bureaucracy, 64, 79
Burmese rebels, 180
business community, 334, 337–40
Business of Terrorism, 17, 84, 171–202, 244,
    338–39
  capital needs, 178–79
  competitive advantage, 176–77
  cost-benefit analysis, 175
  diversification, 178, 259–61
  entrepreneurship, 178

information technology, 188–89
innovation, 188–89
logic, 14, 156, 259–61, 320
product mix, 179
professional services, 194–97
profit centers, 17, 218
resemble legitimate, 178
strategic alliances, 17, 175, 201, 220, 244,
    337
supply chains, cross-reference supply chains,
    157, 192–93, 201, 219, 245, 266, 276,
    303, 339, 342
targets of opportunity, 201
tax strategies, 202
use of technology, 175, 178, 180, 188–90,
    215
venture capitalists, 200

Cairo, 325
California, 142, 184, 293
Cambodia, 180
Canada, xiii, 2, 31, 133, 137–39, 196–97,
    200, 295
    Montreal, 31, 196
    Toronto, 137, 139
Caribbean, 101, 225
cash couriers, 197
CashU, 189
casinos, 31–32
Castro, Fidel, 231
Caucasus, 42, 64, 78, 99, 104, 134, 136, 147,
    159, 225, 300, 302, 304, 326
    Moslem radicalization, 40
    North, 8, 39, 40, 77, 83, 114, 135, 147,
        152, 186, 272, 296
    South, 8, 114, 135, 296
cell phones, 45, 51–52, 141, 189, 274, 333.
    See communications, cellular
Centre for Non-Traditional Security Studies,
    Singapore, 336
centrifuge, 297
Central America, 10, 76, 103, 105–06, 110,
    146, 182, 230, 234, 245, 261, 274,
    326, 327, 330–31, 334
Chad, 2, 236
charities, 78, 81–82, 135, 177–78, 201
    abuse 136
Chayes, Sarah, 71
Che Guevara, 231
Chechen, 39, 199, 272, 295
    abuse of foreign assistance, 41
    conflict, 4, 103, 333

Gulf financing, 41
Ikeria, 40
    Mosque donations, 41
    Stalinist deportation, 40
Chechnya, 39, 40, 135–37
Chicago, 97, 100
Chicquita, 199
child pornography, 191, 332
child soldiers, 179
Chile, 152, 234
China, 29, 133, 146, 182, 220, 225, 238–39,
    245, 265, 270, 273, 277, 282–83, 286,
    304, 306, 317–18, 325, 330, 344
Christian minorities, 34
CIA, 33
cigarette smuggling, 4, 9, 18, 64, 74, 153, 193,
    235, 260, 264, 267–73, 277, 300
Ciudad Juarez, 105
civil society, 8, 19, 153, 230, 240, 334, 337,
    340
civil wars, 6, 84, 243, 324, 327–28, 330
clans, 158, 336
climate change, 18, 324, 328–30, 342
Clinton, Hilary, 230
Clinton administration, 31
cocaine, 38, 84, 151–52, 219, 222–23, 225,
    227–28, 230–33, 236–37, 260
Cold War, 103, 107–08, 110–11, 118, 133,
    153, 180, 306–08, 323, 327, 335
    post-, 111, 113, 118, 180, 292, 308, 309
Colombia, 8, 14–15, 17, 70–71, 79–82, 84,
    101–02, 144, 152, 181, 185–88, 193,
    194, 199–200, 219, 222, 227–234,
    238, 245, 323, 326–27, 332–33, 336,
    338–40, 342
    President Uribe, 232
colonial era, 2
commodities, 99, 111, 156, 177, 181, 192–93,
    202, 219, 222, 235, 238–39, 245,
    260–61, 266–67, 272, 275–76, 304,
    306, 339
communications, 51, 67, 72, 99, 103, 110,
    115, 157, 177, 188, 190–91, 194, 202,
    332, 337
    cellular, 13, 158
communism, 108
Communist, 100, 108, 140, 220, 231
    era, 140
    Party, 231
communist countries, 12, 100
    former, 12
    post, 66

complicity, 3, 6, 42, 83, 143, 180, 260, 264, 272–73, 297
computers, 36, 115, 141, 174, 180, 191, 267, 332. *See also* technology
  professionals, 189, 194
  terrorist use, 35–36, 45, 51–52, 190–91
conflict regions, 52, 83, 85, 103–04, 110, 113–14, 118, 132–34, 153, 156–57, 186, 272, 321–22, 331
  post-, 339
conflicts, 4, 103, 115, 327–28, 333, 342
Congo, 138, 182, 327
consumers, 334, 337–40
contraband, 41, 48, 71, 103, 194, 259, 271, 296
convergence, 14, 117–18, 152, 158, 262–63, 270, 278, 304
  crime and terrorism, 32, 145
  illiict actors, 268
Cooperative Threat Reduction Program, 300. *See also* Nunn-Lugar Program
corporate world, 194, 199, 202, 264
  complicity, 3, 199–200. *See also* terrorist financing: complicity of the corporate world
corporations, 6, 98, 109, 173, 179, 184, 186, 188, 199–200, 202, 277, 291, 338
corporate security, 7, 9
corruption, 3–4, 14, 16, 30, 32, 37, 41–44, 47, 48, 52, 64–86, 98–99, 101, 103, 104–05, 109–11, 112, 115, 117, 139, 145–46, 149, 154, 158, 174, 197, 201, 228, 235–36, 241–46, 263–80, 290, 296, 298–301, 304, 308–09, 322–23, 333, 335–38, 340
  antipathy toward, 68
  clan-based, 66
  combating, 66
  corrodes society, 79
  costs of, 66
  defining, 12–13, 66
  destabilizing impact, 73
  destroying society, 66
  economic distortion, 76
  enabling environment, 83–85
  grand, 66, 68, 70
  impact, 65
  incubator, 65
  military power, 68
  oligarchical, 66
  one-paty states, 66
  petty, 66, 71

  recruiting tool for terrorists, 68, 71
  revulsion at, 77–78
  risk, 73–76
  terrorists' use, 32, 36, 334
corruption and terrorism, 1, 14, 106–09, 111, 115, 117–18, 273
Corruption Perception Index, 332. *See also* Transparency International
cosmopolitan city, 36
counterfeit money, 32, 264, 267, 269
counterfeiting, 112, 152, 260–61, 264–76, 339
  cigarettes, 74, 260, 264, 269–73, 275
  consumer goods, 260, 264, 269–73, 277
  costs, 271, 273
  DVDs, 14, 18, 192, 260, 267, 269, 271, 272–76
  films, 14, 275–76
  military hardware, 269
  pharmaceuticals, 18, 74, 192, 261, 264, 266, 269, 275, 297
  profits, 265, 268, 71, 275–77
  software, 264, 271–72, 275
  tax policy, 269
counterfeits, 260
counterterrorism, 194, 245, 322, 334, 338
  French, 31, 37
  Los Angeles Police Department (LAPD), 32
  Russian, 40–41
  Spain, 36
  United States, 341
crime
  incubates corruption, 65
crimes
  credit card fraud, 51
  drug trade. *See also* narcotics trafficking
  insurance fraud, 52
crime-terror connection, 117, 136–37, 145
  intersection with legitimate economy, 3, 290
crime-terror groups, 50
  D-company, 48, 145–46, 157, 176, 197, 221, 273, 275–76, 325
  Haqqani network, 183, 174, 197, 221, 244. *See also* terrorist groups
crime-terror nexus, 18, 41–42, 48–49, 309, 334
crime-terror relationship, 111–12, 146, 271–72
criminal capture of the state, 105
criminal financing of terrorism, 171–202
criminal networks, 76, 79
criminal recruitment, 77, 153

criminals
ages, 76
criminal acts, 12
criminal economy, 13
criminal groups, 267, 304
African, 104
Albanian, 102
American, 104
Armenian, 135, 300
Asian, 269
Azeri, 300, 331
Bacrim, 103, 230, 232
Balkan, 105
Black, 141
Cali cartel, 230–32. *See also* Colombia
Camorra, 109–10, 136, 145, 177, 271
Central American, 151, 179
Chechen, 41
Chinese, 151, 267, 274, 290
Colombia, 68, 100, 102, 228, 230–31, 234, 236, 244, 267
Cosa Nostra, 153, 301. *See also* Mafia
Eurasian, 269
Italian, 100, 104, 301
Javanese, 35
Latin American, 269
Lebanese, 269
Mafia, 81, 100–02, 104, 133, 142, 145, 227. *See also* Mafia
Medellín, 230–32
Mexican drug cartels, 234, 236, 267
Middle Eastern, 104
New, 104–06
'ndrangheta, 301
political components, 101
politicized, 15
Post-Soviet, 105, 267
preservation of capital, 104
Primeiro Comando da Capital, or PCC, 42–46, 195, 325
Russian-speaking, 68, 269
service provider, 79–83, 202, 233
Snakeheads, 179
South Asian, 296
triads, 149
yakuza, 80, 101, 104, 149, 151, 290
zetas, 105
criminal kingpins, 18
criminalization of terrorists, 175
Cronin, Audrey Kurth, 341
Crusades, 261

cryptography, 191
cultural patrimony, 277
customs, 31
officials, 13, 48, 145, 198, 259
cyberattacks, 36
cybercrime, 181, 191
cyberterrorism, 191
Cyprus, 152, 265

Daghestan, 77. *See also* Russia; Daghestan
Dawa schools, 81
deadly triad, 6, 32, 321–24
deep state, 108
Della Porta, Donatella, 108
democratization, 72
absence of, 240
demography, 329–30, 335
demographic shifts, 18
destruction of evidence, 36
Deutsche Bank, 69
detection
minimizing risk, 134
Detroit, 137, 195, 270
development, 4
developed countries, 133–34, 325
developing countries, 78–79, 80, 225, 266
developing world, 5–6, 12, 15, 18, 67, 76, 85, 98, 103, 133–34, 138, 144, 260, 262, 265, 321, 325, 342
diamond smuggling, 33, 153, 181
diaspora, 17, 41, 104, 132–33, 135, 138
Armenian, 135
communities, 133, 135–39, 157, 176, 178, 235
Somali, 137, 200
differential association, 140
diffusion economic and political power, 98
diminished living standards, 69
dirty bomb, 292, 295
disengagement from terrorism, 337
Dishman, Chris, 115
displaced people, 103, 149, 153, 157, 328–30
disposable people, 116
dispute resolution, 202
diversion of aid, 66
Africa, 267
Russia, 42
diverted goods, 181, 264–76, 291
document fraud, 32, 51, 64, 140, 176, 193
Dominican Republic, 234
drone, 157, 341

drug abuse, 225, 299
drug addiction, 243–45, 299
drug cartels, 105
drug couriers, 76
Drug Enforcement Agency (DEA), 46, 221
drug trade, 14, 17, 52, 100, 103–04, 106, 109,
    112, 116, 137, 143, 146, 153, 174,
    179, 182, 188, 198, 218–46, 262, 299,
    321, 332, 335, 339, 342. *See also*
    narcotics trafficking; *see also* illicit
    trade; drugs, or drugs: trafficking
  advantages, 242
  business, 219–20
  costs of, 244–45
  eradication, 242
  Global South, 222–27
  political act, 218
  profit, 218–19, 221, 225, 240, 242–43
  regional variations, 222–44
  risk, 218
  routes, 222–25, 227, 243, 245, 299
drugs
  smuggling, 52, 84, 155, 269
  trafficking, 219. *See also* drug trade
dual use crime, 36, 201
dual-use materials, 291, 297, 302–03,
    309
dual use technology, 291
Dubai, 33, 48, 69, 133, 165, 306
Duma, 186
Durand Line, 239

East Germany, 108
Eastern Europe, 105, 180, 265, 271. *See also*
    Europe
ebola, 289
economic growth, 4
economic harm, 29
economic inequality, 18, 43, 65, 73–74, 76,
    78, 144
economic security, 4, 321, 341
economics of terrorism, 113, 173–217
ecosystems, 181
Ecuador, 84, 234
education, 70–71, 76, 336
  lack of, 64
Egypt, 2, 69, 72, 77, 82, 141, 152, 155, 195,
    324, 328
Egold, 189
ElBaradei, Mohamed, 296
El Salvador, 185, 234
elephants, 181–82

employment
  lack of, 64
encryption, 51, 191, 219
enemy combatant, 97
energy
  exports, 4
  gas fields, 1
  infrastructure 181
  oil and gas industry, 2, 4
entanglement, xi, xiii, 5–6, 10, 13, 15–18, 30,
    50, 74, 103–04, 113–15, 118, 152,
    179, 218, 220, 236, 241, 274, 278,
    309, 320, 323–27, 329–34, 327–43
Equatorial Guinea, 69
Escobar, Pablo, 80, 101
ethnic hatred, 52
ethnic conflicts, 244
ethnic rebel, 3
Europe, xii, 2–5, 8–9, 37, 50, 64, 72, 76, 100,
    113, 115–17, 132–34, 138–41, 152,
    155, 176, 183–84, 190, 194, 197, 225,
    227, 230, 234–39, 245, 259, 264–65,
    267–68, 270–72, 290, 292, 301,
    305–06, 322. *See also* Eastern Europe
    and Western Europe
European Customs Union, 271
European Union, 259, 265, 334
Europol, 9, 111, 194, 334
exchange relations, 68
exploitation of loopholes, 13
extortion, 12, 42, 51, 80, 109, 137, 145, 151,
    158, 179–83, 187–88, 201–02, 220,
    246, 274, 320, 326, 339
exclusion from power, 52
extradition, 13, 232
Exxon, 109. *See* oil companies

Facebook, 72
facilitators, 3, 18, 32, 34, 39–40, 42, 49, 65,
    69, 99, 149, 194, 197–99, 213, 219,
    236, 259, 264, 267, 274–75, 277, 291,
    296–97, 303–04, 307–09, 314, 338,
    340, 342
  accountants, 195, 219
  corporate, 199–200
  corrupt officials, 198–99, 218
  lawyers, 194–95, 219
  legitimate world, 158, 177, 194
  money launderers, 194–97, 219
  inner family, 303
"Fa'I", 34
Falcone, Judge Giovanni, 102

false identities, 32, 38, 65, 115, 137–38, 194, 198
fatwa, 78
favelas, 43–44, 51, 79, 144, 325
FBI, 31, 33, 100, 132, 138, 141, 177, 263, 270
Felbab-Brown, Vanda, 229, 233
Filiu, Jean-Pierre, 114
financial abuse of national leaders, 69
Financial Action Task Force (FATF), 184, 270
financial havens, 75, 101, 326
flexians, 115
Florence, 102
flying lessons, 31, 262
food insecurity, 325
Ford, Larry, Dr., 293–94
foreign assistance
    abuse of, 69, 183, 298. *See also* Chechen, abuse of foreign assistance
foreign investment, 1
Foreign Narcotics Kingpin Designation Act, 47, 79, 221
Foreign Terrorist Organization, 196
Foucault, Michel, 52, 143
    Discipline and Punish, 143
Fundación Escuela Nueva, 230
fragile states, xii, 3, 73–75, 97
France, 31, 141, 183, 190, 342
fraud, 188–91, 264
    credit card, 82, 180, 188–91
    food stamp, 82
    internet, 180
fraudulent drivers' licenses. *See* document fraud
free trade zones, 110, 133, 149, 152, 266
Freedom Fighters, 9
front companies, 306
Fujmori, Alberto, President, 220
funding of terrorism, 13, 43, 173–217

G-20 countries, 29, 52, 64, 225
gangs, 103, 141, 325, 327
    Crips, 141
    Mara Salvatrucha, 103
    members, 195
Gastrow, Peter, 273
Gaza, 153, 324, 331
Gaza Strip, 155–56
gender and crime, 76
gender and terrorism, 76
General McCrystal, 78

General Noriega, 219
geopolitical conflict, 73
Georgia, 135–36, 145, 155, 265, 295, 300–02, 305
Germany, 3, 69, 107–08, 137, 179, 189, 200, 262, 305–06, 342
Ghana, 237, 273
Ghani, Ashraf, 238
global economy, 1, 29, 66–67, 189, 321–22
global financial institutions, 66
global financial markets, 99
global governance failure, 73, 74
global health, 15
    eradication of disease, 15
    premature deaths, 15
global instability, 73
Global Islamic state, 99
global security
    threat to, 15, 52, 110, 320
globalization, 1–2, 10, 13–14, 66, 98, 103, 115, 120, 158, 187, 220, 264, 298
    beneficiaries, 14, 66, 115
Godfather, 133
gold, 17, 181, 192
goma explosives, 38
governance, 118, 322, 326, 342
    weak, 139, 236
grand strategy, 336
Great Britain, 3, 75, 109, 132, 137, 139, 141, 175, 190–91, 198
Great Game, 239
greed, 69
greed and grievance, 153
Guatemala, 71, 261
guerillas, 10, 108, 133, 180, 233, 245
Guinea, 157, 237
Guinea-Bissau, 219, 234, 236–37
Gulf of Aden, 193, 200
Gulf Region, 8, 275
Gunaratna, Rohan, 33, 190

Ham, Carter, Commander, 7
Hamas Heights Case, 196
Hanbali, 34
haram, 34
hard targets, 34
hawalas, 47, 266
Hawaladar, 197
Hazardous waste disposal, 301
Headley, David, 46, 49, 51
health. *See also* global health
Hekmatyar, Gulbuddin, 239

heroin, 85, 113, 133, 146, 153, 218, 221–22,
  224, 238, 243, 260, 299
highly enriched uranium (HEU), 291, 299,
  300, 302–03, 305
hijackers, 30–32
  Alhazmi, Nawaf, 31
  Hanjour, Hani, 31
  social status of 9/11, 31
Hindu minorities, 34
historical antecedents to contemporary
  terrorism, 37
historical legacies, 4
Hizb ut-Tahrir, 75
Hobbesian order, 79, 144
Hobsbawm, Eric, 79, 227
Hoffman, Bruce, 14, 220
Hollywood, 67, 135
Holy Land Foundation Case, 195, 269
homicide rates, 70, 105–06, 146, 225, 228,
  327
Honduras, 10, 70, 106, 225, 234
Hong Kong, 84, 306
Horn of Africa, 117, 149, 157, 193, 273
hostages, 1, 2, 39, 49
HSBC bank, 196, 307
human capital, 175, 341
human rights, 9, 42
  activists, 9, 42
  violations, 5, 42, 230, 232, 246, 334
human security, 278, 343
human smuggling, 64, 72, 76, 179–81, 194,
  198, 235
human trafficking, 32, 42, 72, 103, 115,
  179–81, 186, 193–94, 198, 304,
  341
Hussein, Saddam, 67, 154
hybrid identities, 3
hybrid organizations, 14, 116, 237, 244
hybrid threat, 10, 50, 111, 321, 324
hybrids, 134, 219, 235, 323, 326
hydrocarbons, 181, 202

Ibrahim, Dawood, 16, 46–48, 176, 275–76
identity theft, 188, 190
ideology, 99, 106, 116, 141, 174, 178
illicit activity, 4, 7, 9, 33, 41, 81, 103, 114,
  118, 175, 177, 179–80, 192, 198, 200,
  227, 235, 246, 331, 339
illicit actors, 244, 262–63, 266, 268, 276, 278,
  298, 326, 336–37
illicit economy, 153, 174
illicit explosives, 38

illicit financial flows
  failure to repatriate, 70
illicit goods, 75
illicit network, 10–11, 13, 153, 306
illicit political economy, 189
illicit trade, 4, 18, 31, 52, 64–65, 73, 75, 83,
  86, 105, 147, 153, 155, 178, 193–94,
  201, 235, 237, 238, 245, 259–78,
  295–96, 302, 304, 323–24, 339
  drugs. *See also* drug trade; drugs: trafficking
  forestry, 192
  natural resources, 15, 153, 181, 246
  wildlife, 181–82
Illicit whites, 265–66, 282
Illinois, 142
IMF (International Monetary Fund), 69
immigrants
  illegal, 157
  legal, 157
Immigration and Naturalization Service (INS),
  U.S., 32
income inequality, 15, 52, 342
India, 9, 16, 29, 46–49, 73, 108, 115, 144,
  146, 176, 179, 194, 227, 265, 271,
  275–77, 296, 306, 324, 326
  British colonial rule, 46, 112
  Moslems killed by Hindus, 47
Indonesia, 16, 33–36, 108, 157, 193
  Bali, 321. *See also* terrorist attacks: Bali,
    Indonesia
  Denpasar, 33
  Java, 35
insurance companies, 158, 200–01
insurgency, 109, 336
insurgents, 4, 9, 11, 15, 80, 83, 118, 133, 147,
  154–55, 179–80, 186, 218, 229–30,
  232–33, 240, 242–45, 262–64, 272,
  309, 335, 337, 341
insurgent groups, 3, 10, 107, 181, 201, 225,
  231–33, 239, 242, 245, 262, 275, 327
instability, xii, 10, 16, 65, 73, 114, 117–18,
  238, 245, 308, 323, 327–30
  political, 10, 64–65, 106, 115, 238, 245
  social, 16, 245
insurgents, 13, 110, 158, 242
intellectual property crime, 268–69, 277
intelligence failure, 37, 67. *See also* WMD:
    intelligence failure concerning Iraq
  absence of sharing, 37
intelligence services, 108. *See also* secret
    services
  Iraq, 154

Italy, 108
Turkey, 108–09
IAEA (International Atomic Energy Agency),
    296, 303
International Criminal Tribune, 114
International Peace Institute, 198
Internet, 13, 51–52, 117, 139, 141, 157–58,
    181–82, 189, 191, 263–64, 267,
    269–70, 277
Interpol, 114, 261, 267, 273
intifada, 82
investigations of terrorism, 8–9, 35, 41–42, 50,
    135, 137, 146, 149, 151, 269–70, 295
    Beslan, Russia, 41
    India, 48
    Madrid, Spain, 37
    9/11 Commission, 31–33. *See* 9/11
        Commission
    São Paulo, Brazil, 45
investigative journalism, 9, 334, 337
Iran, 64, 65, 110, 151, 153–54, 156, 192–93,
    200, 237–38, 243, 264, 275, 291, 297,
    302, 306–08
Iraq, 8, 15, 64, 67, 104, 111, 143, 153,
    154–55, 159, 173, 186, 189–90, 192,
    195, 201, 261–65, 275, 293, 297–98,
    308, 322, 328, 333
    Commission on Public Integrity, 154
Iraq War, 36
Ireland, 112, 133, 175, 178, 271
Islamic extremism, 46
Islamic insurgents, 191
Islamic law, 34
Israel, 15, 141–42, 151, 154–56, 183–84, 194,
    235, 331, 338
Israeli-Palestinian conflict, 149, 155–56
Istanbul, 225, 245, 306, 308
Italy, 83, 100–01, 107–09, 112, 133, 141,
    184, 191, 267, 271, 301
ivory trade, 181

James, Kevin Lamar, 141
Japan, 80, 144, 200, 222, 225, 289–90
    JGC corporation, 2
    victims, 2
Jenkins, Brian, 108
jihad, 34, 77, 80, 132, 184, 200, 218, 323
jihadi, 1, 3, 4, 107, 140, 178, 225, 290,
    293
    foreign, 40, 154
    guerillas, 118
    movements, 29

rhetoric, 97
terrorists, 4, 6, 15–16
Jordan, 69, 135
journalists, 79
Judge Radhi Hamza al-Radhi, 154

Karachi, 46, 80, 144–45, 276, 324, 330. *See*
    megacities: Karachi, Pakistan
Karzai, President, 68, 85, 241
Karzai, Wali, 241, 245
Kashmir, 115, 146, 194
Kazan, Russia, 105
Kasab, Ajmal, 49
Kazakhstan, 70, 299
Kenya, 79, 157, 197, 273, 333
kidnapping, 33, 41–43, 80, 109, 116, 117,
    173–74, 179–82, 184–87, 188, 200–01,
    220, 246, 290
    functions, 184, 201
kingpin strategy, 342
kinship structures, 220
kleptocracies, 68, 72, 75, 77, 326, 342
Kobe earthquake, 80, 82
Kosovo, 132
Kristof, Nicholas, 323
Kulikov, Anatoly, 41
Kurds, 64, 137, 159, 227, 275
Kyrgyzstan, 75, 142–43, 219, 243, 245
    Maksim, Bakiyev, 75
    President Akiyev, 75
    President Bakiyev, 75

Labelle, Huguette, 341
land grab, 69
land mafias, 146
Laqueur, Walter, 11, 14, 112
Las Vegas, Nevada, 31, 100
Lateran Church, 102
Latin America, 17, 73, 79, 100, 105, 113, 116,
    117–18, 138–39, 145, 152, 158, 180,
    184–85, 187, 193–94, 201, 221–22,
    237, 244, 246, 268, 321
law enforcement, 2, 9, 13, 18, 38–39, 45, 49,
    51, 65, 70, 74, 80, 83–86, 97, 99,
    101–02, 104–05, 109, 111, 115, 134,
    136–38, 141, 144, 149, 155, 158, 174,
    176, 182, 193, 197, 202, 242, 259–60,
    264–66, 272, 275–76, 278, 295, 300,
    303, 305–06, 309, 327, 334, 337, 341,
    343
lawyer, 194–95, 219
    complicity, 141, 177, 194–96, 219

Lebanese Canadian Bank, 138, 196
Lebanon, 82, 108, 138, 149, 151, 178, 196,
   221, 264, 328
Lee, Rensselaer, 233
legacies of colonialism, 118, 147, 159,
   336
legitimate economy, 309
   intersection with crime and terrorism, 196
legitimate and illegitimate economy, 100
Lehder, Carlos, 228
Levitt, Matthew, 142
Libera, 33, 181, 235, 341
Libya, 1, 2, 4, 6, 72, 74, 108, 143, 155–56,
   236, 297, 303, 307–08
   arms, 2, 3
   Colonel Qaddafi. *See also* Qaddafi
   Tripoli, 6, 234
links of criminals and terrorists, 98
London, 50, 104, 132, 139, 261
Los Angeles, California, 41
   Los Angeles Police Department (LAPD), 30,
      135–37, 266, 269

Mafia, 68. *See* criminal groups: Mafia
Maghreb, 57n.62, 236, 329
malaria, 267, 273
Malaysia, 146, 193, 200, 303
Mali, 2, 3, 114, 117, 152, 225, 235–36, 245,
   321, 323
   deals with AQIM, 3
Marcola or Marcos Willians Herbas
      Camacho, 43–44, 51
   self-education in political philosophy, 43
marginalization, 69
marijuana, 219, 231, 299
Marquez, Gabriel Garcia, 231
mass attacks, 9, 29–52, 83, 144, 293, 324
Mauritania, 2, 114, 235–36
Mayor Rudolph Giuliani, 32
Mediterranean, 72, 145, 147, 200, 234, 301
megacity, 49
megacities, 15, 133–34, 144, 157–58, 324–25,
   330
   Karachi. *See also* Pakistan
   Lyari, 80
medreseh or madrrassa, 71, 81–82, 99, 241
Menem, Carlos Saul, President 151
Mengele, Josef, 151
Merah, Mohammed, 37, 97
Mexico, 10, 70, 99, 102–06, 146, 194, 198,
   225, 230, 234, 245, 261, 326–27, 331,
   342

Mexico City, 274, 324
Miami, 271
Middle East, 64, 72, 74, 78, 110, 115, 133,
   149, 152, 157, 173, 180, 184, 192,
   194, 197, 225, 268, 270, 274–76,
   305–06, 308, 330–31, 336
migration, 72, 76, 342
militant groups, 4
militia movements, 294
military siege, 1
mobility, 103
Moldova, 295, 300, 308
money laundering, 13, 31–36, 52, 81, 133,
   140, 179, 229, 338, 340
   trade-based, 13, 111, 182, 268, 339
Mongolia, 304
Montenegro, 267
Montesinos, Vladimiro, 220
Moro, Aldo, President, 184
Morocco, 37, 38, 114, 236
   Casablanca, 46, 114. *See also* terrorist
      attacks: Casablanca, Morocco
   Rabat, 6
Morsi, President, 155
Moscow, 41–42, 51, 108, 199, 295, 298, 302,
   309
mosques, 81–82
MQM Party, 145–46
mujaheddin, 110
Mukhlas, 34
multiborder regions, 133
multinational organizations, 98, 322, 337
   Ecowas, 321
   European Union. *See also* European Union
   NATO, 80. *See also* NATO
   OAS, 334
   OECD, 12, 275
   OSCE, 334. *See also* OSCE
   UN. *See also* United Nations
   World Bank. *See also* World Bank
Mumbai, 29–30, 45–52, 83, 144–46, 176,
   198, 276, 324–25
murder, 109. *See also* homicide rates
Murphy, Martin, 193
Musharaf, Pervez General, 297
Muslim Brotherhood, 155, 195, 324
Myanmar, 307, 328

Naím, Moisés, 89n.36, 123n.58, 270
Naples, 136, 145–46. *See also* ports: Italy
Napoleon, 261
narcocorridos, 80

narco-terrorism, 17, 112–13, 220–21, 246

Nasrallah, Hassan, 269

National Museum in Baghdad, 263

Naxalites, 326

Naylor, Tom, 109

Nepal, 73

Netherlands, 137, 140, 190, 197, 271

nation-state
  decline of, 13, 98

national budget, 4

National Security Agency (NSA), 191

NATO, 6, 108, 259

natural resources, 103. *See* terrorist financing: natural resources

Nemeth, Erik, 262

Nepal
  Maoist insurgents, 179

network structure, 99

networks, 3–4, 10–11, 13–14, 18, 30, 33–38, 41, 66, 74–76, 79, 82, 84, 99, 103–04, 108, 110–11, 114, 116–18, 132–70, 174, 179–80, 183, 187–90, 193–94, 197–98, 219–21, 231, 235, 241–44, 261, 264, 268–71, 273, 296–99, 301–08, 320, 323, 328, 330–32, 335–39, 342–43
  cross-border, 147
  global, 17, 132–33, 175, 336
  illicit, 3, 273, 336
  support networks for crime and terrorism, 134

new terrorism, 2, 14, 16, 29, 99, 106–11, 113, 117, 188, 202

new transnational crime, 99, 102–06, 110–11, 117–18

New York, 29–33, 49, 83, 100, 104, 144, 196, 266, 269–70, 306, 324–25

Nicaragua, 108

Niger, 2, 114, 236

Nigeria, 70, 77, 102, 117, 264, 272, 325, 341

9/11 Commission, 9, 30–31, 33, 37, 198

Noble, Ronald, 273, 275–76

nonstate actor, 1, 13, 65, 68, 71–72, 80, 86, 98, 113, 118, 158, 174, 179, 202, 218, 236, 260–61, 267, 292, 295, 300, 308, 326–27, 333, 335–38, 340, 342

North America, 265, 268–71, 322

North Carolina, 132–33

North Korea, 265, 267, 296–97, 305, 308, 335

Northern Ireland, 114, 175, 268, 272

Norway, 2

nuclear proliferation, 295–98, 308

nuclear terrorism, 18. *See* WMD: nuclear

Nunn-Lugar Program, 300. *See also* Cooperative Threat Reduction Program

NSA (National Security Agency). *See* National Security Agency

Obama administration, 68

obshchak, 75, 143

Ocalan, 108

offshore locale, 104

oil, 6, 153–54, 181, 184, 192

oil for food program, 66

oil companies
  BP (British Petroleum), 2
  Exxon, 109
  Sonatrach, 2
  Statoil, 2

Olson, Mancur, 222

one party state, 103

Operation Pipeline, 193

opium, 240–42

Ordzhonokidze, 112

OSCE (Organization for Security and Cooperation in Europe), 18

organized crime, 73, 75, 83, 103–04, 111, 133, 174, 181, 187, 201, 222, 271, 290, 321, 323, 337
  contracts, 101, 104
  control of territory, 117
  nationalism, 101
  new, 110–11. *See* new transnational crime
  closed nuclear cities, 300
  parasites on the state, 101, 104
  relation to the state, 98, 102, 113
  symbolic targets, 102
  traditional, 100–01, 102
  World War II, 101

organized crime embedded in the state, 70

organized criminal group, 79. *See* criminal groups

Osama Bin Laden, 33–34, 41, 78, 173, 177, 293

Ossetia, 300

Ottoman Empire, 225, 227

Ottoman period, 225

outsourcing, 99

Pacific Rim, 194

Paddy's Bar, 34–35

Pakistan, 8, 17, 30, 37, 40, 46, 48–49, 51, 65,
　　71, 78, 81, 83–84, 97, 99, 111, 114,
　　116, 143, 146–47, 157, 197, 198,
　　237–46, 259, 264, 273, 275–76,
　　296–98, 308, 321, 328, 331,
　　336
　Baluchistan, 244
　Federally Administered Tribal Areas
　　(FATA), 244
　intelligence service (ISI), 46–48, 81, 146,
　　239
　Karachi. *See* megacity: Karachi
　relation to criminals and terrorists, 296
　Waziristan, 244
Palestinians, 149, 324
Palestinian Authority, 155, 275
Panama, 193–94, 219, 271
Paraguay, 138, 149–52, 265, 268, 274
　Ciudad del Este, 274
　President Stroessner, 151
paramilitaries, 103
Paris, 259
Pashtun, 80, 146, 243
passport forgery, 31, 198
Patriot Act, 111
patronage, 69
peacekeeping, 113
Pentagon, 30, 45, 67
perpetuation of conflict, 15
Persia, 245
Peru, 17, 73, 112, 152, 174, 218, 220
Peters, Gretchen, 82–83, 134, 323
petty crime, 31–32, 35, 38, 182
Peyrouse, Sébastien, 242
Philippines, 70, 73, 82, 116, 157, 180, 186,
　　219
Picarelli, John, 14
pickpocketing, 181
pilgrimage routes, 225
pipelines, 17, 134, 136–37, 159
piracy, 16, 116–18, 137, 158, 181, 187, 193,
　　200, 235
Pixote, 43
Plan Colombia, 230
plutonium, 302–03
Podgorecki, Adam, 140
police abuse, 45, 71, 83, 274, 327
police collusion with criminals, 144
police collusion with terrorists, 151
police informant, 38
police "no-go zones", 144
political asylum, 41, 154

political-criminal nexus, 14, 101–02, 228, 324
political economy, 118
political will, 4, 99
Ponzi scheme, 69
population bulge, 76
population growth, 72
ports, 17, 46, 49, 133–34, 145–47, 157–58,
　　266
　criminal organizations, 46
　Naples, 271. *See* Italy
　Rotterdam, 271
poverty, 15, 103, 114, 139
primitive rebels, 227
prison, 38, 42–46, 52, 75, 97–98, 116, 134,
　　139–43, 157–58, 333
　abuse within, 42–45, 52, 75, 139–41
　corruption, 43, 45, 51–52, 75, 98, 134, 141,
　　143, 158, 243, 333
　crime-terror connection, 38
　Europe, 141
　former Soviet Union, 142–43
　mass attacks, 139
　Middle East, 142–43
　radicalization within, 38
　privatization, 69–70
　released inmates, 299
　without transparency, 69
　profit, 218–19, 221, 225, 240, 242–43
prolongation of conflict, 106, 113
prosecution, 9, 14, 17, 156, 184, 194, 277,
　　306–07
prostitution, 105
protection, providing, 80
Putin, Vladimir, President, 40

Qaddafi, Muammar, Col., 2
Qatar, 156
quantum system, 5, 320
Quetta Shura, 241

Rabei Osman Sayed Ahmed, 139
radical Islam, 50–75
radical Islamist, 1–2
radicalization, 141–42
Rafsanjani, Hashemi President, 151
Raleigh, North Carolina. *See* North Carolina
Ramzi ben Yousef, 177
Rand, 33
ransom payment, 5, 110, 116, 199–200
real estate, 111, 178, 196, 229
refugees, 132, 153, 157, 329–30
regional instability, 64, 118

regulation
  absence of, 265–66, 275
repression, 78
research, 335
research method or methodology, 6–9
Ressam, Ahmed, 30–31
revenge, 40
rhinoceros horns, 181
ricin, 294, 295
RICO (Racketeer Influenced and Corrupt
  Organizations Act), 83
Riggs Bank, 33, 69, 196
rising income inequality, 325–26
robbery, 12, 51, 142, 175–76, 181–84
Robin Hood curse, 86
rogue states, 297
Roman era, 264
Romanians, 302
Rome, 102
roving bandits, 222
rule of law, 277, 322, 342
Russia, 16, 29, 42, 70, 78, 83, 99, 105, 108,
  110, 112, 133, 135, 142–44, 186, 218,
  225, 238, 243, 265, 272, 289–90, 295,
  298, 302, 308, 321
  army, 40
  Chelyabinsk, 299
  closed nuclear cities, 298–99
  Daghestan, 77
  Mayak nuclear facility, 299
  Novosibirsk, 298
  Ozersk nuclear facility, 299
  security services, 272

safe haven, 3, 79, 83–84, 133, 138–39, 178,
  230, 321, 327
safe houses, 177
safety nets
  lost, 70
Sageman Marc, 77
Sahara, 225
Sahel, 3, 7, 17, 187, 235–37, 272
Samper, Ernesto, President, 228
Samudra, 34–35, 51, 139, 157
Samurai period, 79
Sari Club, 34–35
sarin, 289, 308
Saudi Arabia, 33, 78, 85, 116, 196
school, 32, 39–40, 45, 68, 70–71, 77–78,
  80–82, 97, 100, 178, 326, 336,
  340
Schrödinger, Erwin, 5

secret service, 108. *See* intelligence
security, 1, 4
  brutality, 45, 51
  collusion, 42, 48
  forces, 40, 45, 49, 80, 136
security threats, 1
Sehgal, Ikhram, 68
Serbia, 114
service providers, 98
  criminals, 16, 79–83, 327, 337–38
  terrorists, 16, 79–83, 228–29, 327, 337–38
sharia, 236
Sheik Omar Abdel Rahman, 141, 195,
  270
Sharjah, 275
Shiia, 146
Shiite militias, 154
Sicily, 79, 101–02, 104, 117, 133, 187, 222,
  337
Sierra Leone, 33, 181, 236
Sikh, 138
Silk Road, 225, 239, 243, 245, 304
Singapore, 146
slave trade, 237, 245
smugglers, 300, 304–05
smuggling, 12, 147, 151, 155, 323
  alien, 193
  art, 14, 180, 276–77
  nuclear materials, 296, 300, 302–05
  oil, 9, 41, 192, 193, 201
smuggling tunnels, 155–56, 193, 324
  Gaza, 155–56, 193, 324
Snowden, Edward, 296
social inequality, 143–44
social service delivery, 79–83
social welfare, 82
societal transitions
  crime and terrorism, 30
soft targets, 34
software piracy, 74
Somalia, 99, 104, 145, 157, 181, 193–94, 200,
  273, 301, 335
South Africa, 194, 273, 293, 303, 307
  Project Coast, 294
South America, 110, 157, 194, 220, 225, 245,
  274
South Sudan, 182
Soviet successor states, 103, 304–05
Soviet Union, 14, 100, 108, 110, 118, 180,
  184, 233, 335
  arms, 323
  closed nuclear cities, 299

Soviet Union (*cont.*)
  collapse, 307
  former, 65
  legacy, 135
Spain, 3, 9, 16, 30, 36–39, 81, 108, 112, 183,
    190–91, 197–98, 222, 271
  Madrid, 36–39, 140, 198
Special Interest Aliens, 193–94
SPECTRE, 320
sports clubs, 82
Stalin, 112, 159, 183
state
  contracts, 100, 142
  decline, 98
  retreat, 79, 98, 118, 158, 229, 244, 326,
    333, 338
state building, 6
state capacity, 65, 98
state failure
  delivery of services, 71, 79–81
state regulatory agencies, 74
state repression, 50
state security, 29
  Germany, 31
  personnel, 83
state-supported terrorism, 65, 108–11, 133,
    156, 323. *See also* terrorism: state
    sponsored
Steganography, 191
sting operation, 142
stock markets, 111
stolen cars, 37, 152
stovepiping, 9, 18, 333–34
Strange, Susan, 338
Sudan, 110, 307
suicide bomber, 34, 40, 72, 97, 102, 179
  Chechen women, 76
suicide bombing, 36, 190
suicide mission, 35, 189
Sunni, 146, 155
superfacilitators, 303
superpower conflict, 110
supplanting the state, 79–83
supply chains, 157, 192–93, 201, 219, 245,
    266, 276, 303, 339, 342
sustainability, 13, 15, 100, 176, 219
sustainability of the planet, 5, 15, 181, 291,
    323
Sutherland, Edwin, 140
Sweden, 114
Switzerland, 141, 303, 305
symbols for terrorists, 34, 36, 39, 49, 67, 135,
    184

synagogue, 184
synthetic drugs, 222
Syria, 64, 74, 108, 110, 152, 156, 159, 275,
    290, 293, 297, 308, 323
  President Bashir al-Assad, 293

Tablighi Jamaat, 75
Taiwan, 102, 306
Tajik–Afghan border, 243
Taj Mahal Palace Hotel, 49
Tajik, 243
Tajikistan, 84, 219, 243, 245
Taliban, 80. *See* terrorist groups: Taliban
Tamil, 127n.97, 137–38, 161n.26, 162n.31,
    227, 249n.48
Tanzania, 181
Taylor, Charles, President, 235
technology, 13, 51, 178, 180, 188, 202, 219,
    244, 290, 332–33, 341
Tepito Market, 274
territorial control, 81, 188, 192–93, 229, 233,
    238, 240, 244
terrorism, 73, 191
  costs of, 178, 244
  definition, 11
  diverse ideologies, 50
  homegrown, 141
  hostility to the state, 111
  old terrorism, 106–12, 202
  relation to the state, 98, 106–10
  state-sponsored, 177. *See also*
    state-supported terrorism
  study of, xii–xiii, 7–10, 13–15
terrorism and corruption, 174–75
terrorist attacks, 11, 29–52
  Air India flight 1985 from Canada, 138
  Bali, Indonesia, 33–36, 45. *See also* mass
    attacks
  cost of attack, 35
  Beslan, Russia, 42, 135, 338. *See also* mass
    attacks
  Boston marathon, 309
  Buenos Aires Jewish Community, 108, 149,
    151
  Burgas, Bulgaria 2012, 154
  Casablanca, Morocco, 46, 114
  duration, 45
  international elements, 50
  São Paulo, Brazil, 42–46. *See also* mass
    attacks
  In Amenas, Algeria, 5, 268, 338
  Ismailovsky Park, Moscow, 1995, 295
  London underground, 2005, 139, 190

London, 2011, 50
Madrid, Spain, 190. *See also* mass attacks
  cost of attacks, 37
millennium bomber Los Angeles airport,
  190
Moscow Domodedovo Airport, 199
multiple locations, 30, 36
Mumbai 1993, 46, 145, 276. *See also* mass
  attacks
Mumbai 2006, 46–49. *See also* mass
  attacks
Mumbai 2008, 46–49, 145, 198. *See also*
  mass attacks
New York and Washington 9/11, 30–33,
  191, 196. *See also* mass attacks
  fraudulent drivers' licenses 32, 50–52
Oklahoma City bombing, 50
Palace of Justice, Colombia, 1985, 228
planned attack Kocaeli, 308
precedents, 46, 51
Timbuktu, Mali, 225
Tokyo sarin attack 1995, 289
Toulouse 2012 (Jewish Day School), 97
World Trade Center 1993, 189, 270
terrorist financing, 4–5, 9, 11, 14, 33, 41,
  52, 82, 109, 111, 116, 135–37, 139,
  149, 152, 158, 171–202, 242, 270,
  276
  al-Qaeda, 35. *See also* al-Qaeda
  charitable organizations
    phony, 51
  cigarette trade, 192–93, 235
  complicity of corporate world, corporations,
    3
  credit card fraud, 36, 179. *See* fraud: credit
    card
  crime, 41, 323
  developed world, 3
  drug trade, 38, 41, 46
  extortion, 41
  gems, 35
  gold, 52
  governments, 3
  human trafficking, 41
  illicit trade, 73, 265. *See* illicit trade
  information technology, 188–89
  kidnapping, 3, 4, 184–87. *See* kidnapping
  natural resources, 339
  ransoms, 3
  robbery, 35
  sources, 52
  start-up, 37
  stolen credit cards, 190

terrorist groups
  Abu Sayyaf, 80, 84, 116, 175, 186–87, 202,
    219
  al-Qaeda, 1, 97, 99, 116, 118, 139, 143,
    146, 149
    and the drug trade, 221–22
    funding, 31
  AQIM, (Al-Qaeda of the Mahgreb), 1, 3–4,
    11, 7, 37, 74, 114, 117, 173, 187–88,
    221, 234–36, 245–46, 328, 330,
    338
  al Shabaab, 117–18, 197, 273, 328,
    339
  Algerian Islamic Salvation Front, 82
  Ansar al-Islam, 180
  Armed Islamic Group (GIA), 235
  Aryan Republic Army, 184
  Chechen, 42, 135, 145. *See* Chechen
  Colombia, 187, 246
  criminal activity, 3
  Croatian Utashe, 112
  Egyptian Islamic Jihad, 293
  ELN, 185, 199, 230–34
  ETA, 36, 81, 107, 109, 145, 154, 183–84,
    222
  extremist groups US, 294–95, 309
  FARC, 8, 68, 81, 107, 112, 116, 149,
    174–75, 181–82, 185–86, 193, 199,
    202, 219–21, 227–34, 236, 244, 323,
    338–39
  Fatah, 275
  FMLN, 185
  Gamaa Islamiya, 80, 82, 152
  Grey Wolves, 109
  Hamas, 68, 82, 118, 141–42, 149, 155–56,
    178, 182, 189, 195, 198, 202, 221,
    275, 324
    Al-Salah Society, 82
  Hezbollah, 66, 68, 80, 108, 117–18, 133,
    138, 149, 151, 154, 178, 182, 189,
    196, 198–99, 202, 221, 235, 264, 267,
    268–70, 274–75, 339
  IRA, 109, 113, 133, 154, 174–76, 183–84,
    189, 191, 202, 222
  Islamic Movement of Uzbekistan, 84
  Jabhat-al-Nusra, 308
  Janjaweed, 182
  Jemaah Islamiah (JI), 34–35
  Jundullah, 221, 339
  Khalistan. *See also* terrorist groups: Sikh
    Khalistan movement
  Kosovo Liberation Army (KLA), 153
  Lashkar-e-Jhangvi, 146

terrorist groups (*cont.*)
  Lashkar-e-Taiba (LeT), 46, 48–49, 77, 81,
    146, 293
    Jamaat-ud-Dawa, 81
    Markaz Dawa Irshad, 81
  legitimacy, 83
  Lord's Resistance Army, 182
  LTTE, 68, 81, 107, 179, 180
  M-19, 228
  Maoist, 179
  Middle East, 189, 193
  Montoneros, 77, 109
  Morrocan, 183
  Mujahidin Indonesia Timur, 183
  North Caucasus, 295
  Palestinian Islamic Jihad, 189
  Phineas Priests, 184
  PKK, 109, 113, 137, 139, 142, 154, 174,
    176, 178, 183, 185, 188–89, 192, 202,
    221, 244, 275
  Provisional IRA, 108–09, 175
  RAF, 109
  Raja Sulayman Movement, 82
  Real IRA, 270
  Red Brigades, 109, 184
  Russian anarchists, 133
  Salafist Group for Prayer and Combat,
    187
  secular, 99
  Sendero Luminoso, 77, 112, 220
  service providers, 68, 202
  Sikh Khalistan movement, 138
  Student Islamic Movement of India, 48
  Taliban, 68, 78, 80–81, 85, 116, 133, 174,
    182–83, 197, 202, 221, 237, 240–41,
    244, 246, 338
  Tamil Tigers, 68, 107, 109, 137–38,
    161n.26, n.31, 162n.37, 186, 206n.48,
    221, 237, 248n.30
  Tehrik-i-Taliban Pakistan aka
    Tehreek-e-Taliban Pakistan (TTP), 83,
    146, 221
  Turkish Hezbollah, 174
  Turkish People's Liberation Front, 183
  Ulster Volunteer Force of Northern Ireland,
    179
  United Self-Defense Forces of Colombia
    (AUC), 199, 232
  Weather Underground, 109
terrorist logistics, 2
terrorist networks, 103
terrorist objectives, 44

terrorist recruitment, 18, 37, 72–78, 81–82,
    97, 110, 114, 139–41, 143, 153, 157
  of criminals, 177, 184
terrorists
  ages, 76
  criminal pasts, 38–39, 50–51, 97, 116, 132
  females, 40
  professions, 77
  social status, 77
  strategy to do harm, 174, 270
  underwear bomber, 77
  weapons, 39, 48
Thachuk, Kim, 112
theft of state assets, 16, 69, 326
think tanks, 14, 115
Thoumi, Francisco, 231
three-body problem, 10, 86, 333–36
Tito, President, 153
TraCCC (Terrorism, Transnational Crime and
    Corruption Center), 8
Togo, 237
Tokyo, 289, 325
Tor network, 332
Tourism
  terrorist impact on, 35
tourists' victimization, 186–87
trade in environmentally protected species, 74.
    See illicit trade: natural resources
trade in natural resources, 74
trade routes, 118, 178, 220, 222, 225, 245,
    265, 268, 271
trade unions, 81
Transdniester, 295–96, 300
transformation of criminals and terrorists,
    98–99, 117
transformation of terrorism, 110–11
transitional states, 103
transnational crime, 11–12, 14–15, 98–100,
    103–06, 115, 225, 276, 278
  defining, 12–13
  relation to the state, 102–103, 104
  relation to corruption, 10, 68, 71, 76,
    102–06, 115
transparency, 333–34
Transparency International, 4, 12, 67, 337,
    341
  Colombia, 8, 230
transport, 103, 307
  hub, 266, 275
trappings of a state, 105
tribal, 2, 46, 154, 178, 238
tribal loyalties, 239, 241

triborder area, 138–39, 149–52, 157, 274
trust, 220
trust in government
  erosion, 71, 76, 78
tsunami, 80
Tuareg, 2, 236
Tunisia, 69, 72–73, 154, 236
  President Ben Ali, 7, 72
Turkey, 8, 9, 64–65, 102, 108–09, 113, 142,
    147, 149, 152, 155, 159, 183, 188,
    192, 218, 221–22, 225, 261, 275, 300,
    302, 303–05, 308
Turkmenistan, 69, 243
two-body problem, 10, 334, 336

Ufizi Museum, 102
Ukraine, 70, 193, 302
undercover operations, 302
underground banking, 13, 111, 197, 266, 268,
    333
underground economy, 71
underpoliced crime, 17, 18, 259–78
unemployment, 76–77, 104, 114, 143
ungoverned spaces, 79
United Arab Emirates (UAE), 47–48, 104,
    146, 157, 240–41, 265, 303, 306
United Kingdom. *See* Great Britain
United Nations, 18, 179
  Convention against Transnational
    Organized Crime, 12
  Global Compact against Corruption, 12
  Office on Drugs and Crime, 218, 238, 334
  response to wmd, 292
  Resolution, 1540, 292
  Security Council, 221, 321
  World Drug Report, 179
United States, 6, 11, 17, 30, 34, 51, 83, 100,
    101, 103, 108, 110–12, 132–33, 135,
    141, 145, 152, 154–55, 182–84, 190,
    193–95, 219, 221, 225, 230, 235, 241,
    259, 263–66, 268–71, 276, 292–94,
    298, 305, 326, 334–35, 341–42
  Alcohol, Tobacco and Firearms, 342
  Department of Defense, 263
  Immigration and Customs Enforcement
    agency (ICE), 193
  Internal Revenue Service, 195
  Justice Department, 199, 306
  State Department, 221
  Transnational Crime Strategy, 9, 111, 309,
    322
  Treasury Department, 82

University of Gottingen, 31
uranium, 303–04
urbanization, 325
urban centers, 144, 158, 160n.9, 292
urban riots, 104
urban violence, 29–30, 43, 50, 79, 146, 225
U.S.–Mexico border, 105
Uzbekistan, 243
Uzbeks, 75, 243

Venezuela, 84, 152, 194, 230, 234, 236
victims, 1
  Australia, 34
  Great Britain, 2
  French, 2
  Indonesia, 34
  Japan, 2
  Norway, 2
  number, 2, 16, 34, 36, 39, 50, 105, 185–86,
    225, 230, 236
  Philippines, 2
  Romania, 2
  Russia, 272
  United States, 2, 34
victimization, 2, 5, 36, 39–40, 45, 49–50, 75,
    83, 152, 154, 185, 188, 200, 230, 236,
    289, 333, 343
violence, 10, 80, 82, 102, 105–06, 113, 139,
    146, 151, 156, 201, 219, 228–30, 232,
    244, 290, 327, 333, 338, 340, 343
  against the state, 102
  monopoly of, 98, 229
violent conflict, 75–76
violent consequences of state repression, 44
violent entrepreneurs, 105, 187, 242
visa fraud, 32
Volkov, Vadim, 105

Wahabi groups, 78
war, 103
warlords, 118, 238, 241–42
Waziristan, 46
weak states, 13, 115–16, 118, 132, 135, 156,
    236
weaponry, 1, 155, 177, 181, 186, 193, 198,
    229, 290, 294, 342
  stolen, 155
WMD (weapons of mass destruction), 14, 17
  biological, 289, 291, 293–95
  chemical, 289, 293–95
  costs, 291
  intelligence failure concerning Iraq, 67

WMD (weapons of mass destruction) (*cont.*)
 nuclear, 289, 295–309
 radiological, 291, 301–02
Wedel, Janine, 115
West Bank, 71, 199, 275
Wesphalian order
 post-, 110
Western Europe, 109, 113, 133, 135, 137,
  141, 178, 188, 190, 218, 221, 234,
  236, 238, 302
Western Union, 199
White Lace case, 32
white supremacism, 294–95
 Aryan Nation, 295
 Minnesota Patriots Council, 295
Williams, Phil, 154, 263
whole of government approach, 337
whole of society approach, 19, 336–38
Wikileaks, 81
Wiretaps, 176

women engagement, 341
World Bank, 6, 12, 69, 269, 322
World Customs Organization, 260
World Economic Forum (WEF), 8, 73
 Global Agenda Councils, i, xiii, 8, 73
 organized crime, 98, 192, 202
 Risk Report, 75, 326
World Health Organization, 272
World Trade Center, 30, 46, 51, 67, 111,
  177

Yemen, 68, 72, 80, 114, 118, 157, 178, 221,
  225
youth bulge, 65, 118
youth without futures, 16, 71–72, 74, 76–77,
  103, 114, 118, 144, 326, 342
Yugoslavia, 103, 114, 153, 271

zakat, 81, 239
Zawahiri, Ayman, 293